lim	limit
ln	natural logarithm
log	common logarithm
max	maximum
min	minimum
$A \equiv B$	A is identically equal to B (equal by definition)
$\displaystyle\sum_i$	summation over i $\left(\text{i.e., } \displaystyle\sum_{i=1}^{n} x_i = x_1 + x_2 + \cdots + x_n\right)$
∞	infinity
$a \Rightarrow b$	a only if b
$a \Leftrightarrow b$	a if and only if (iff) b
A^T	transpose of matrix A
A^{-1}	inverse of square matrix A
$|A|$	determinant of square matrix A
adj A	adjoint of square matrix A
I_n	identity matrix of order n
Δx	discrete change in x
$f: A \to B$	function f maps domain A into range B
$f(x)$	value of function f at x
$f'(x)$	derivative of $f(x)$
$df(x_1, x_2, \ldots x_n)$	total differential of $f(x_1, x_2, \ldots x_n)$
$df(x)/dx$	same as $f'(x)$
$f''(x)$	second derivative of function $f(x)$
$d^2 f(x)/dx^2$	same as $f''(x)$
$\dfrac{d^{(n)} f(x)}{dx^{(n)}}$	nth order derivative of $f(x)$
$\partial f(x_1, x_2, \ldots, x_n)/\partial x_i$	partial derivative of f
$\dfrac{\partial^2 f(x_1, x_2, \ldots, x_n)}{\partial x_i^2}$	second-order partial derivative
H	Hessian matrix of second partial derivatives
H_B	bordered Hessian matrix

A Mathematical
Approach to
Economic Analysis

A Mathematical Approach to Economic Analysis

Peter Toumanoff
Marquette University

Farrokh Nourzad
Marquette University

West Publishing Company

Minneapolis/St. Paul New York Los Angeles San Francisco

Interior Design: Wendy Calmenson
Copyediting: Mary Prescott
Composition: Techset Composition Ltd
Artwork: Lotus Art
Cover Image and Design: Lois Stanfield, Lightsource Images
Production Services: The Book Company
Production, Printing, and Binding by West Publishing Company

West's Commitment to the Environment

In 1906, West Publishing Company began recycling materials left over from the production of books. This began a tradition of efficient and responsible use of resources. Today, up to 95 percent of our legal books and 70 percent of our college texts are printed on recycled, acid-free stock. West also recycles nearly 22 million pounds of scrap paper annually—the equivalent of 181,717 trees. Since the 1960s, West has devised ways to capture and recycle waste inks, solvents, oils, and vapors created in the printing process. We also recycle plastics of all kinds, wood, glass, corrugated cardboard, and batteries, and have eliminated the use of styrofoam book packaging. We at West are proud of longevity and the scope of our commitment to our environment.

COPYRIGHT ©1994   By WEST PUBLISHING COMPANY
610 Opperman Drive
P.O. Box 64526
St. Paul, MN 55164-0526

Printed in the United States of America

01 00 99 98 97 96 95 94   8 7 6 5 4 3 2 1 0

Library of Congress Cataloging-in-Publication Data

Toumanoff, Peter.
    A mathematical approach to economic analyis/Peter Toumanoff, Farrokh Nourzad.
        p.   cm.
    Includes bibliographical references and index.
    ISBN 0-314-02818-8
    1. Economics, Mathematical. I. Nourzad, Farrokh.
    II. Title.
HB135.T68 1994   93-33052
330′.01′51—dc20   CIP

 PRINTED ON 10% POST CONSUMER RECYCLED PAPER

BRIEF CONTENTS

CONTENTS

◆ **CHAPTER 4** **Unconstrained Optimization of Functions with One Independent Variable** 93

◆ CHAPTER 9   **Modeling Consumer Behavior**   259

◆ CHAPTER 10   **A Mathematical Treatment of Production**   297

Mathematical Economics

Mathematical economics can and should become a popular course in the economics curriculum. It has a great deal to offer the typical economics and business student, who needs to learn both math and economics, as well as students from other majors such as engineering and math, who need an exposure to business or economics. We wrote this book with the intention of making mathematical economics accessible and popular with a larger segment of the student population.

What does mathematical economics have to offer these students? First, it has the potential to bind together in a conceptual manner different strands of economic theory that the student ordinarily learns in separate classes. A course in mathematical economics can enable the student to see the common methodological principles that unite the specialized subtopics of economic theory. These include optimization, marginal analysis, comparative statics analysis, equilibrium conditions, *ceteris paribus*, and so on. A student who appreciates how and why economists reason the way they do will see that what otherwise appears to be a bewildering maze of separate theoretical details is actually a road map with methodological principles. Knowing the principles permits one to get to any destination without having to memorize every route in the map. Because of its compactness and precision, mathematical economics makes it easier to learn the method of economic reasoning.

Second, mathematical economics has the potential to motivate students to become literate and competent in mathematical techniques. Quantitative analysis is growing rapidly in importance in many academic disciplines and applications. Economic and financial analysts, marketers, managers, accountants, lawyers, social scientists of all varieties, and others are required at least to understand but also to perform sophisticated quantitative analysis. To do so requires mathematical training that is usually acquired in college courses in algebra, calculus, and statistics. Students who learn the mathematical techniques in an environment separate from their applications often do not see the relevance of their math courses and rapidly forget what they may have learned. A course in mathematical economics can motivate a more profound learning of mathematical techniques by providing immediate valuable and relevant applications of the math. Math can be fun and interesting if it has an immediate payback in the form of a theoretical or practical application.

Third, a course in mathematical economics has the potential to teach a great deal of economics to students who have good math skills but minimal backgrounds in economics and business. There is a population of students who are relatively competent in mathematics because of their backgrounds in engineering, science, or math, but who have little time to take business or economics courses. By taking advantage of their competence in mathematics, mathematical economics can teach them a lot of economic and business analysis with a minimum investment of time. The more "business oriented" engineers and scientists must become, the more a course in mathematical economics makes sense for them.

Rationale

We wrote this text because we found that existing texts did not serve our students well. They do not motivate students well because they are too focused on math and fail to provide immediate applications, or they assume too much prior knowledge of math or economics, or they are too encyclopedic and intimidating. This book is intended not to be intimidating and to be accessible to students who have only a minimal preparation in college-level calculus and economic theory. Even though it is designed to be used by students with relatively little training in math and economics, it teaches techniques and methodologies which can lead to quite sophisticated analysis. Three features of the text are intended to accomplish this.

- First is the careful and complete way that an intuitive understanding of the concepts is provided.
- Second is the thoroughness with which mathematical analysis is integrated with graphical and narrative analyses. Its integrating principle is the comparative statics methodology of economic reasoning.
- Third is the design and sequencing of the material, which presents only the mathematics that is necessary for economic analysis and presents it only when it is needed. There is no "math for math's sake," and all math is given an economic application immediately.

Content and Organization

The content of the text can be divided into three sections, which can be covered in more or less detail depending on the background of the students and the goals of the course. The first section, Chapters 1 through 4, serves as an introduction and review. Chapter 1 introduces the student to the methodological principles of model building and comparative statics that serve to integrate and motivate most of the material that follows. The principles of economic reasoning are illustrated with examples from supply and demand analysis and from national income determination. Chapters 2 and 3 provide a review of mathematical functions and derivatives of functions with one independent variable. Students with a relatively strong mathematics background can skim through them quickly so they can cover more of the later chapters. Chapter 4 reinforces the review of mathematics by concentrating on economics. It introduces optimization by teaching profit-maximization models with one independent variable. Both price-taker and price-searcher behaviors are covered in output and input markets. Students are able to go through the entire modeling process, including comparative statics analysis.

The second section consists of Chapters 5 through 8 and is intended to provide the student with the mathematical tools to handle multivariate functions and models. The math in this section is primarily concentrated in

Chapter 5, with covers partial and total differentiation, and Chapter 8, which covers matrix algebra. This material is integrated with intermediate-level economic theory in Chapter 6, which uses several multivariate profit-maximization models to teach unconstrained optimization, and Chapter 7, which uses several utility-maximization models to teach constrained optimization.

By the time the third section of the book is reached, the student has learned enough math so that Chapters 9 through 14 can teach more sophisticated math and economics in a fully balanced and integrated manner. Chapter 9 combines the economics of consumer behavior with the mathematics of duality and monotonic transformations. Chapter 10 combines the economics of production with the mathematics of homogeneous functions. Chapter 11 teaches the economics of cost minimization while demonstrating the power and versatility of the envelope theorem. Even though Chapter 12 provides little new mathematical technique, it contributes a coherent treatment of intermediate-level macroeconomic theory along with a discussion of the differences between the mathematics of partial and general equilibrium models. Chapter 13 presents some of the specialized mathematical techniques and economic applications associated with linear modeling in its treatment of input–output analysis and linear programming. Finally, Chapter 14 serves as a good synthesizing and concluding chapter for the text by bringing together much of the mathematics and economics of the previous chapters in a discussion of economic efficiency and exchange.

Important mathematical and methodological concepts are introduced early in the text and are repeated in increasingly sophisticated applications in later chapters. In addition to comparative statics analysis, which is introduced in Chapter 1 and serves as an integrating principle throughout, the implicit function theorem first appears in Chapter 3, concave and convex functions in Chapter 4, the envelope theorem in Chapter 7, Cramer's rule in Chapter 8, and so on. These tools are used repeatedly in subsequent chapters, giving the student greater appreciation for their power and greater insight into the roots of economic theory.

We have tried to avoid concentrating too much purely mathematical material in one place. Instead, we provide enough math to enable us to provide immediate economic applications. We have found that doing so motivates the student to learn the math and reinforces what is learned because it is used immediately. This is why we placed matrix algebra in Chapter 8 rather than earlier in the text. The student is able to do quite a lot of economics in Chapters 6 and 7 without using matrices and determinants, but is motivated to learn matrix algebra in order to do more. Instructors who prefer to cover matrix algebra earlier can, of course, do so.

The text is intended to be used primarily at undergraduate levels but will also be appropriate for advanced courses. Senior level courses with students who have stronger backgrounds can spend less time on the first four chapters and cover the higher-level applications in Chapters 9 through 14 in detail. Instructors teaching courses intended for students with more basic backgrounds can spend increased time on the first four chapters to teach algebra and differential calculus and choose whatever higher-level applications they prefer. Chapters 12 and 13 are relatively self-contained, so they can be sequenced according to the instructor's preference. In addition to using the book as the primary text in our undergraduate mathematical economics course, we have used it as a supplementary text in our master's program in applied economics. It enables us to bring students with a wide range of preparatory backgrounds to an even level of math and economics quickly.

Features

Our experience is that students need a considerable amount of help to work through a mathematical economics text. The text has several features intended to help the student. Within the text, we have provided double coverage of most topics by presenting the material in a general and abstract form and with specific numerical examples. Usually, the numerical examples are set apart from the body of the text and labeled. Occasionally, however, the numerical examples are so integral a part of the text that they are not set apart. Important new terms with specialized meanings are identified in the text and defined in the margins. A complete glossary is provided at the end of the text. Every chapter has an introduction providing a perspective for the material that follows, as well as a summary that reminds the student what key concepts were covered.

Problems and exercises the student can use to practice the material are especially important in a mathematical economics text. Where appropriate, subsections of the chapters are followed by exercises so the student can test her understanding of the material. Answers to these exercises are provided at the end of the chapter. Besides these, self-help problems, answered at the back of the text, are included at the end of each chapter. Each chapter also provides supplemental problems, which are not answered in the text.

The supplemental problems are answered in the Instructor's Manual, which also describes each chapter from our point of view. We have found it useful to assign a mixture of end-of-section exercises, self-help problems, and supplemental problems for homework assignments, requiring the students to show all their work.

Acknowledgements

Writing a text on a subject we love to teach is a very rewarding experience for us. Valuable contributions have been made by all of our colleagues at Marquette University, especially Joseph Daniels and Steven Crane. Our students have added tremendous value to the book through their sharp and critical eyes and minds, their tolerance of our very crude early efforts, and their enthusiastic encouragement. The efforts of Marc Von der Ruhr and Chrys Chrysostomou are worthy of particular mention. The book has been improved significantly because of the careful and helpful reviews of:

Burley V. Bechdolt
Northern Illinois University

Brian R. Binger
University of Arizona

Vic Brajer
California State University—
Fullerton

Hugh C. Briggs III
Miami University

John C. Eckalbar
California State University—Chico

E. M. Ekanayake
Florida International University

Richard Fowles
University of Utah

Scott Goldsmith
University of Alaska

Mohamed A. El-Hodiri
University of Kansas

James H. Holcomb
University of Texas—El Paso

Bryce Kanago
Northern Illinois University

Kyoo H. Kim
Bowling Green State University

Fredric R. Kolb
University of Wisconsin—
Eau Claire

Michael A. Lipsman
Drake University

William F. Lott
University of Connecticut

Michael Nelson
Illinois State University

Mark Partridge
University of Montana

Robert C. Scott
Bradley University

Remaining errors are, of course, our fault. Finally, whereas we receive the rewards of the project, our families have borne most of the costs. Thank you, Susanna, Falamak, Nicholas, and Andrew for your patience.

C H A P T E R   1

An Introduction to Economic Reasoning

1.1

INTRODUCTION

Economics is a modest discipline. The object of economic inquiry, the social response to scarcity, is vast and intricate and economic theory enables us to explain only a tiny fraction of the behavior we investigate. You should not be surprised that we are able to explain so little; consider the complexity of the problem. Every individual in society makes hundreds of economic choices daily. Each choice is affected by the individual's tastes and preferences, her talents and skills, past choices she has made, and her expectations regarding the future. Her choices are also affected by other people's tastes and preferences, talents and skills, past decisions, and expectations of the future. In addition, the political and social institutions that govern relationships in society, her physical and natural environment, the state of the art of knowledge and technology, and quite possibly a host of other influences we do not know about or which we have not considered also affect her choices.

Not only is the individual the object of economic inquiry, but so also are all the other members of her society, individually and collectively, and all the individuals comprising all other societies, as well as the interaction of all the societies with each other on the planet. To make matters even more difficult, the factors that influence individuals and societies constantly change. Economic theory itself, as part of the state of art of knowledge, is an accessory to the changes that challenge it. To top it off, we understand very little about human psychology, social and political relations, the formation of expectations, and even the physical environment. It is apparent that students of economics need all the help they can get, and mathematical tools can help a great deal.

The purpose of this text is to show you how mathematical tools can help and to integrate mathematical tools with the graphical and logical tools you may already have been exposed to in classes on microeconomic and macro-economic theory. We hope that learning the mathematical tools will have two effects: (1) economic theory will seem more coherent and organized to you and (2) you will become more adept at using mathematical techniques and you will enjoy mathematics more. When you have finished the text, you will know how to express familiar economic concepts in mathematical language; you will be able to use differential calculus to construct and solve optimization models; you will know how to handle functions and models with many variables using matrix algebra; and you will understand how econometric work is linked to economic theory. You will see applications of this text to much of the economics you have studied in the past or will study in the future.

We have incorporated some features in this text that we hope will help you learn mathematical economics. There is a glossary at the end with definitions of important terms. The first time a term that is defined in the glossary is used in a chapter, it is **boldface** and *italicized*, and its definition appears in the margin of the page. Where appropriate, exercises are given at the end of a section that will help you to recognize if you have mastered the material in that section. Answers to these exercises are provided at the end of the chapter. Each chapter has a summary that briefly describes the important topics covered in the chapter. You should read the summary to give you the big picture; while reading it, try to remember the details of each topic. A list of helpful references for supplementary reading is provided after the summary. These generally provide more advanced coverage of the topics in the chapter. Finally, we provide more problems at the end of the chapter. Some of these, called **Self-Help Problems**, are answered at the end of the textbook. Others we have left unanswered, so that your instructor may choose to assign them to assess your understanding of the material.

Economics in general, and mathematical economics in particular, can be learned only with the active, inquiring participation of the student. As you read the book, be sure you not only follow our logic and reasoning but also can replicate them in your own mind. Understand what we are doing and why we are doing it; we try to explain why we take each step along the way. Don't simply take our word for the accuracy of our reasoning and mathematics, but rather verify it for yourself by going through the same steps. Do the problems and examples that we do, and check your reasoning process and answers against ours. Challenge whatever doesn't make sense to you; the act of challenging will help your understanding. Good luck!

1.2

THE METHODOLOGY OF ECONOMIC REASONING

methodology: a system by which analysis is conducted.

One way to make sense out of economic theory and of mathematical economics is to understand the *methodology* of economic reasoning. You will discover that many seemingly unrelated economic explanations actually follow the same methodological pattern. Once you understand this pattern, filling in the details of one explanation or another is much simpler. The pattern most often employed, and which we will use in this text, is the method of *comparative statics*.

You almost certainly already know the method of comparative statics, even if you do not know that you know it. Consider the simple *model* of a market for a normal good, with a downward-sloping demand curve and an upward-sloping supply curve. If consumer income rises, demand increases, causing price and quantity exchanged to increase. That simple market analysis is an example of comparative statics methodology. Think about what was explained and how it was explained.

First, recognize what was *not* explained. The model does not explain (or predict) the particular values of the initial price and quantity, nor does it explain the exact levels of the new price and quantity. It does not explain the exact position or shape of either the demand or the supply curve. We are asked to assume only that the demand curve is downward sloping (the law of demand), that the supply curve is upward sloping, and that the two intersect at the current *equilibrium* market price and quantity. We are given the information that consumer income has risen (and that all else remains constant), and because we have assumed a normal good we know that an increase in income increases demand.

What *is* explained is that the shift from the initial market equilibrium to the new market equilibrium requires that price and quantity both increase. Comparative statics methodology explains the *changes* required to get from an initial equilibrium to a new one. Another way to say this is that comparative statics compares a new state to an initial state.

We give this example to demonstrate the method of comparative statics, but also to demonstrate just how modest a discipline economics is and how it deals with the complexities and unknowns of its subject matter. The reason we do not predict the initial price and quantity, or the position and shape of demand and supply, is that to do so would require complete knowledge of all the unknowables mentioned above: tastes, technologies, expectations, past choices, the environment, political and social institutions, and so on. To predict the new price and quantity would require the same degree of knowledge. Economists are generally happy just to predict the direction of change correctly, and that is the aim of comparative statics methodology. We assume that all those unknowables that determine the exact positions of the initial and subsequent equilibria remain constant, and we concentrate on the effects of changes in variables that we are capable of observing and analyzing.

The market example we used above to explain comparative statics methodology describes behavior at a relatively aggregated level. That is, the equilibrium of the model meshes the individual decisions of many actors, both consumers and producers. Another example of a model of aggregated behavior is the explanation of national income determination you will see in Section 1.4.2 of this chapter. A class of models that is especially useful in describing the economic behavior of individuals is *optimization models*. When an individual consumer or producer is forced by scarcity to choose among alternatives, he chooses the "best" among his options. Another way of saying this is that his choice brings him closer to whatever his goal is than any other alternative. You may already be familiar with utility maximization as a goal for consumers or profit maximization as a goal for producers. We do not use an optimization model as an example of comparative statics analysis in this

---

comparative statics: a methodology by which behavior is explained as changes in equilibrium positions.

model: an abstract representation of reality.

equilibrium: the logically deduced values of choice variables or endogenous variables for a given set of parameters and exogenous variables.

optimization models: models in which an economic actor makes choices which bring her closer to whatever her goal is than any other alternative.

chapter, because we need to review differential calculus first (which we do in Chapter 3). However, we want to stress that the process of theorizing and the methodology of comparative statics are the same, whether the explanation involves aggregate behavior or individual behavior and optimization models.

1.3

ECONOMIC THEORIZING

Let's summarize our description of economic theorizing using the methodology of comparative statics as a five-step process. The first three steps comprise a model, which is simply an abstract representation of reality. The last two steps of the process utilize the model to generate explanations, or predictions, about economic behavior. The five steps taken together make up a *theory*, whose *hypotheses* can be tested by comparing their predictions to actual behavior. A theory, therefore, is the entire intellectual construct, from the initial abstraction to the behavioral prediction. It requires the building of a model, which is then used to develop hypotheses, or specific predictions about the behavior of economic agents.

theory: a coherent set of propositions, assumptions, and hypotheses that explain a general class of phenomena.

hypothesis: a conditional proposition of how one variable affects another.

choice variables: variables that represent the choices individual economic actors make in their efforts to optimize.

endogenous variables: those variables which are explained by a simultaneous equations model.

exogenous variables: those variables which represent information that is external to a simultaneous equations model, used to explain the endogenous variables.

parameters: necessary information considered as "given" to a model. Parameters can be interpreted to include the exogenous variables.

1. *Choose a problem to investigate.* What is the question to be answered? This step determines the *choice variables* of optimization models, or the *endogenous variables* of models that involve systems of equations. Choice variables are so named because they represent the choices individuals make in their efforts to optimize. Endogenous variables are those whose values we seek to determine by solving systems of equations.

   Examples: *Market behavior*: the endogenous variables are market price and quantity.

   National income determination: the endogenous variables are income and consumption.

   Consumer behavior: the choice variables are the quantities of goods and services chosen.

   Producer behavior: the choice variables are the quantities of output produced and the quantities of inputs used.

2. *Determine what is and is not relevant to the problem.* This is what modeling does. Models purposely abstract from reality in order to classify information as either important or unimportant in answering a particular problem. This step identifies the *exogenous variables* and *parameters* of the model. Exogenous variables represent information that is external to a simultaneous equations model, used to explain the endogenous variables. Parameters also represent given information necessary to a model, and they often appear in equations as coefficients or multipliers.

   Examples: *Market behavior*: the model of demand and supply. Exogenous variables are "other variables" in the demand and supply functions, e.g., income, prices of complements and substitutes, and prices of inputs.

National income determination: the model of aggregate income and consumption. Exogenous variables include autonomous investment and government spending.

Consumer behavior: the model of constrained utility maximization. Parameters include relative prices and income.

Producer behavior: the model of profit maximization. For a competitive firm, parameters include prices of inputs and price of output.

equilibrium condition:
the behavioral rule that
determines the equilibrium
of a model.

3. *Determine the **equilibrium condition** for the model.* This step describes the observed behavior of the choice (or endogenous) variables in the context of the model chosen in step 2. It assumes the model is an accurate representation of reality. Although we are not saying that economic agents must obey the equilibrium conditions of the model, the equilibrium conditions must be consistent with observed behavior. Another way of saying this is that the equilibrium conditions are *descriptive* rather than *prescriptive*. In order to use the model to develop explanations of behavior, it is very important to recognize that *imposing the equilibrium conditions allows the endogenous (or choice) variables to be described as functions of the exogenous variables and parameters.* We demonstrate this important point in the applications of Section 1.4.

Examples: *Market behavior*: quantity demanded equals quantity supplied.

National income determination: income equals planned expenditures.

Consumer behavior: marginal utility per dollar spent is the same for all goods.

Producer behavior: marginal revenue equals marginal cost.

4. *Change an exogenous variable or a parameter.* This is the step that permits a prediction, or economic explanation, to be made. Although we do not have sufficient information to predict an initial equilibrium, we can often predict *changes* in behavior due to isolated changes in exogenous variables or parameters.

Examples: *Market behavior*: change consumer income, or labor's wage rate, or any other factor that shifts demand or supply.

National income determination: change autonomous investment.

Consumer behavior: change a relative price or income.

Producer behavior: change output price or the price of an input.

5. *Compare the new equilibrium to the initial equilibrium.* This step gives us the name "comparative statics." We are comparing the initial state to the subsequent state after changing an exogenous variable or a parameter. This step also gives us a hypothesis, or prediction, that can be used to judge the usefulness of the model. The hypothesis is a conditional statement about how the change in a parameter or exogenous variable leads to a

change in the equilibrium position of the choice (or endogenous) variables; and has the form "if A then B."

Examples: *Market behavior*: If consumer income rises, market price and quantity increase (assume the good is normal).

National income determination: If autonomous investment increases, then income and consumption increase.

Consumer behavior: If the relative price of a good rises, quantity consumed decreases.

Producer behavior: If the relative price of an input rises, less of that input is employed.

Any economic explanation can be expressed in narrative, as we did in the market example above, or it can be expressed using graphs or mathematical methods such as algebra and calculus. Narrative explanations can be understood by anyone who can read and follow logical reasoning, but they tend to be lengthy, cumbersome (especially as models become more complex), and imprecise. Graphical models have the advantage of being relatively compact and easily understood. However, they lack the precision and power of explanations utilizing mathematics. Furthermore, graphs are limited to two or at most three dimensions and, therefore, variables. The focus of this text is on mathematical explanations, but we are careful to integrate the mathematics with more familiar graphical and narrative explanations throughout.

1.4

APPLICATIONS

Let's examine two of the most basic theories in economics from the point of view of the comparative statics methodology discussed in the previous section. Our purpose is twofold: (1) to demonstrate the modeling process in contexts that are probably already familiar to you and (2) to show that comparative statics is an analytical method that can be carried out in any of the languages of economics. That is, the analysis can be expressed in words, with graphs, or using mathematics.

1.4.1   The Market Model

Consider again the example of a market model, this time expressed graphically and mathematically. We are describing market exchanges of some good or service. Let Q_d = quantity demanded per unit time, Q_s = quantity supplied per unit time, P = price, Y = consumer income, and w = wage. The endogenous variables are Q_d, Q_s, and P. The exogenous variables are Y and w. The equilibrium condition of the model is that quantity demanded equals quantity supplied, or $Q_d = Q_s$.

Figure 1.1 pictures an initial equilibrium where the demand curve (DD) intersects the supply curve (SS) at (P^*, Q^*). The demand curve DD is drawn assuming that consumer income remains constant at some level Y, and the

Figure 1.1

The Market Model

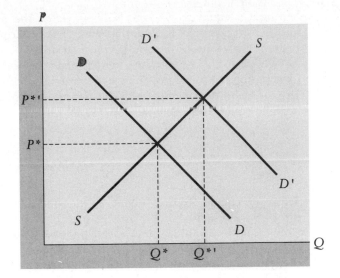

supply curve SS assumes that the wage rate remains constant at some level w. We can obtain comparative statics results by changing an exogenous variable and observing the resulting change in equilibrium. In Figure 1.1, consumer income is increased, which has the effect of shifting the demand curve to $D'D'$ and the equilibrium to $(P^{*\prime}, Q^{*\prime})$. Notice that, in Figure 1.4a, we place price on the vertical axis and quantity on the horizontal, even though, as you can see in the numerical example that follows, we typically model market quantities as functions of market price. This practice is a convention of economic theory that is often attributed to Alfred Marshall, although several classical economists before Marshall also placed price on the vertical axis.

NUMERICAL EXAMPLE

We can use mathematics to examine this model by expressing Q_d and Q_s in algebraic form. Suppose that quantity demanded and quantity supplied have the form

$$Q_d = 50 - 0.2P + 0.1Y \tag{1-1}$$

$$Q_s = 0.8P - 4w \tag{1-2}$$

If we assign numerical values to Y and w, we can find numerical values for equilibrium price and quantity. Let $Y = \$4400$ and $w = \$5.00$. The numerical constants and coefficients of the demand and supply equations are the parameters of the model, and $Q_d = Q_s$ is the equilibrium condition. Substituting in $Y = 4400$ and $w = 5.00$ into equations (1-1) and (1-2) gives us

$$Q_d = 490 - 0.2P \tag{1-3}$$

$$Q_s = -20 + 0.8P \tag{1-4}$$

Setting Q_d equal to Q_s and solving yields the solutions that $P^* = 510$ and $Q_d^* = Q_s^* = 388$. Note that we use superscript asterisks (*) to denote equilibrium values of the endogenous variables.

To perform comparative statics analysis and generate an economic explanation we need to change a parameter or an exogenous variable. Suppose that Y increases to $5500. On the graph, DD shifts to $D'D'$. Our demand equation reflects the increase in Y.

$$Q_d = 600 - 0.2P \tag{1-3a}$$

$$Q_s = -20 + 0.8P \tag{1-4}$$

Setting Q_d equal to Q_s and solving for the equilibrium values P^* and Q^* yields the new solutions that $P^{*\prime} = 620$ and $Q^{*\prime} = 476$. Comparing the new equilibrium to the initial gives us our prediction or explanation: that equilibrium price and quantity both rise in response to an increase in income.

Recognize that if you accept the model as true, equilibrium price and quantity (P^* and Q^*) depend on the values of the parameters and exogenous variables Y and w. To see this, set the original expression for quantity demanded, equation (1-1), equal to the original expression for quantity supplied, equation (1-2).

$$Q_d = 50 + 0.1Y - 0.2P^* = -4w + 0.8P^* = Q_s \tag{1-5}$$

We attached the asterisk (*) on price in (1-5) because, having set Q_d equal to Q_s, this price is the one which satisfies the equilibrium condition. Solving (1-5) for P^* gives us

$$P^* = 50 + 0.1Y + 4w \tag{1-6}$$

In equation (1-6) P^* is equal to an expression involving the exogenous variables Y and w. Substituting the expression for P^* into either equation for Q, (1-1) or (1-2), yields

$$Q^* = 40 + 0.08Y - 0.8w \tag{1-7}$$

Similarly, in equation (1-7) Q^* is equal to an expression involving the exogenous variables. Notice that we have dropped the subscript on Q^* because, at equilibrium, Q_d always equals Q_s and they both equal Q^*.

When we examine equations (1-6) and (1-7), in which P^* and Q^* are expressed in terms of w and Y, we can see that, in general, for any change in Y, P^* changes by a factor of 0.1 times the change in Y. The value of Q^* changes by a factor of 0.08 times any change in Y. Similarly, if w changes, P^* changes by a factor of 4 times the change in w, and Q^* changes by a factor of -0.8 times the change in w.

A More General Model

The numerical example above is too specific and detailed to be useful in making economic explanations. Although numerical examples are very concrete and effective for teaching purposes, they assume that we know much more about the nature and exact position of demand and supply than we actually do know. Suppose we specify the model in more general terms. In the following specification we do not pretend to know the numerical values of the constants associated with demand or supply. Instead, we express them as parameters of the model by using the symbols a, b, c, d, and e to represent them. All that is assumed in this more generalized model is that the demand is linear and downward sloping with respect to price, the good is normal, the supply is linear and upward sloping with respect to price, and that higher wages decrease supply.

$$Q_d = a - bP + cY \qquad (1\text{-}8)$$

$$Q_s = dP - ew \qquad (1\text{-}9)$$

assume a, b, c, d, and $e > 0$

We assume that all the parameters are positive, so you can easily see how P, Y, and w affect Q_d and Q_s simply by looking at the signs of the terms in the equations. You can see, for example, that price decreases quantity demanded but increases quantity supplied. The equilibrium is obtained by setting quantity demanded equal to quantity supplied.

$$Q_d = a - bP^* + cY = dP^* - ew = Q_s \qquad (1\text{-}10)$$

This equation can be solved for the equilibrium value of price (P^*) in terms of the exogenous Y and w. An equation in which one of the endogenous variables is expressed solely in terms of the parameters and exogenous variables of the model is called a ***reduced-form equation***. We solve this equation by collecting all the terms containing P^* on one side and all other terms on the other and solving for P^*, the equilibrium value of price.

reduced-form equation: an equation in which an endogenous variable is expressed as a function solely of exogenous variables and parameters.

$$P^* = \frac{a}{b+d} + \frac{c}{b+d}Y + \frac{e}{b+d}w \qquad (1\text{-}11)$$

Substituting this expression for P^* into either quantity equation yields the reduced-form equation for Q^*, the equilibrium value of quantity.

$$Q^* = \frac{ad}{b+d} + \frac{cd}{b+d}Y - \frac{be}{b+d}w \qquad (1\text{-}12)$$

Without more specific information regarding the exact values of the parameters a, b, c, d, and e, as well as the values taken by the exogenous variables Y and w, we are unable to determine the exact values of P^* and Q^*.[1]

econometrics: the branch of economics that uses statistical methods to estimate the unknown parameters of theoretical relationships, test hypotheses about these parameters, and use the estimates to make quantitative predictions.

---

[1]This is true of almost all analytical economic models; they cannot be solved for specific equilibrium values of endogeneous variables. But this is not the purpose for which they are designed. Comparative statics methodology uses theoretical models to make qualitative predictions about the direction in which endogeneous variables respond to changes in exogeneous variables and parameters. The branch of economics called ***econometrics*** provides methods to test these predictions against observed behavior. Econometrics uses statistical methods to estimate the unknown parameters of theoretical relationships, test hypotheses about these parameters, and use the estimates to make quantitative predictions.

We can, however, inspect the reduced-form equations to ascertain the effects that changes in Y or w would have on the equilibrium values of price and quantity. For example, suppose Y were to increase. The equilibrium price, P^*, would change by an amount equal to $c/(b + d)$ times the change in Y. Since c, b, and d are all greater than zero, we know that an increase in income increases equilibrium price. Similarly, Q^* would change by an amount equal to $cd/(b + d)$ times the change in Y. Again, an increase in income increases equilibrium quantity.

Consider the procedure we have followed in this extended example of demand and supply analysis. In each version (the narrative, the graphical, and both mathematical versions) we utilized a model that describes what we can observe regarding our subject (an initial equilibrium). In this case we use demand and supply to describe market price and quantity. We assume that our model is true. In this case we assume the truth of our model by setting demand equal to supply in order to obtain the reduced-form equations. If our model is true, it is legitimate to suggest that equilibrium price and quantity are functions of income and wage. We then introduce a change in an exogenous variable, compare the new equilibrium to the old, and predict the changes in behavior due to the change in the exogenous variable.

The more generalized version of the market theory, in which the parameters appear as the symbols a, b, c, d, and e, permits us to illustrate how information can be incorporated into a theoretical model. We stated that the only assumptions we made about demand were that the demand curve was linear and downward sloping and that the good was normal. The downward slope of the demand curve was built into the model when we assumed that the coefficient b was greater than zero and gave the term bP a negative sign. Normality was built in by assuming that c was positive and that the term cY had a positive sign. Suppose we wanted to assume that the good was inferior. We could have done so by assuming that c was negative and the term cY still positive. Examining the reduced-form equations (1-11) and (1-12) tells you that, if the good were inferior and c were less than zero, an increase in income would decrease equilibrium price and quantity.

EXERCISES
Section 1.4.1
The Market Model

For the following exercises, suppose that, for the widget market, quantity demanded equals $Q_d = 10 - P + 0.1Y$, and quantity supplied equals $Q_s = 2P - 4w$, where P is price, Y is income, and w is the wage rate.

1. Let $w = 5$. Find the equilibrium market price and quantity, first mathematically and then graphically, if
   a. $Y = 1000$ b. $Y = 500$ c. $Y = 250$

2. Let $Y = 1000$. Find the equilibrium market price and quantity, first mathematically and then graphically, if
   a. $w = 2.5$ b. $w = 7.50$ c. $w = 10.00$

3. Find the reduced-form equations for P^* and Q^*. Describe in narrative the comparative statics effects of changes in income and wage. Are widgets normal or inferior in this market?

1.4.2   A Simple Model of National Income Determination

Let's consider another application of comparative statics methodology. Suppose that we are interested in investigating aggregate income and consumption. We will use a simple theory of national income determination to illustrate the narrative, graphic, and mathematical presentations of the same economic theory.

Narrative Explanations

Income, Y, must, by definition, equal expenditures, E. In the simplest case where we assume there is no government or foreign trade, expenditures are either for consumption, C, or investment, I. To further simplify the exposition, we assume investment is exogenous while consumption depends on income. When investment is determined by forces entirely external to the model, it can be called ***autonomous investment***. The equilibrium condition requires that income equal planned or intended expenditures, when the level of income elicits exactly that much consumption which, when added to planned investment, equals income. From this description, you can see that the choice variables, income and consumption, are explained by the theory, while investment is the exogenous variable. An increase in investment increases income, which increases consumption, which itself increases income, and a new equilibrium is achieved only when a new level of income is reached that simultaneously equals planned expenditures and elicits the appropriate amount of consumption. The effect of the increased investment is multiplied because of the interaction of income and consumption.

autonomous investment: that component of investment that is exogenous, that is, investment determined by forces entirely external to the model.

Graphical Explanation

Figure 1.2 illustrates the theory of national income determination graphically. The ray coming out of the origin at a 45° angle represents the notion that income must equal planned expenditures. The lines EE and $E'E'$ represent levels of intended expenditure, or consumption plus investment, recognizing

Figure 1.2

National Income Determination

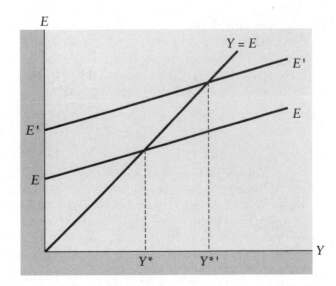

that consumption rises with income. Line EE incorporates an initial level of investment, while $E'E'$ assumes a higher level of investment. The initial equilibrium is at Y^*, where income generates just enough consumption that consumption plus investment equals income. To perform comparative statics analysis, we change the exogenous variable by increasing investment. Consumption plus the increased level of investment is represented by line $E'E'$. The new equilibrium is at $Y^{*'}$, where $E'E'$ intersects the 45° line.

Mathematical Explanations

We need algebraic expressions for the notions that in equilibrium income equals planned expenditures and that consumption depends on income. The equilibrium condition is represented by equation (1-13) and the relation between consumption spending and income is the consumption function in equation (1-14).

$$Y = E = C + I \tag{1-13}$$

$$C = C_0 + \beta Y \quad \text{where } C_0 > 0 \text{ and } 0 < \beta < 1 \tag{1-14}$$

autonomous consumption: that component of consumption that is exogenous, that is, consumption determined by forces entirely external to the model.

The exogenous variable, C_0, represents ***autonomous consumption***, and β is a parameter of the consumption function. Substituting (1-14) into (1-13) yields an equation that simultaneously satisfies (1-13) and (1-14). Because equation (1-13) is the equilibrium condition and equation (1-14) states the relationship between income and consumption, both are satisfied and we have described an equilibrium level of income at Y^*.

$$Y^* = (C_0 + \beta Y^*) + I \tag{1-15}$$

Solving (1-15) for Y^*, the equilibrium value of income, yields

$$Y^* = Y^*(I, C_0) = \frac{C_0}{1 - \beta} + \frac{1}{1 - \beta} I \tag{1-16}$$

Note that we have written the equilibrium level of income as $Y^*(I, C_0)$. This notation emphasizes that equilibrium income depends on the exogenous variables I and C_0, or that Y^* is a function of I and C_0. We review the mathematical concept of the function in detail in Chapter 2.

Substituting (1-16), the expression for Y^*, into (1-14) yields an equation for the equilibrium value of consumption, C^*.

$$C^* = C_0 + \beta Y^* = \frac{C_0}{1 - \beta} + \frac{\beta}{1 - \beta} I \tag{1-17}$$

Equations (1-16) and (1-17) are the reduced-form equations, in which the endogenous variables are expressed in terms of the parameter β and the exogenous variables, C_0 and I. The parameter β can be interpreted as the marginal propensity to consume, that is, the fraction of an additional dollar of income that is spent rather than saved. Examination of equation (1-16) shows the multiplier effect of an increase in investment. Income rises by a factor of $1/(1 - \beta)$ times the increased investment. If the marginal propensity to consume is, say, 75%, then the multiplier is 4; income rises by a factor of 4 times any increase in investment.

Consider again the procedure we have followed in this example of a theory of national income determination. In each explanation (the narrative, the graphical, and mathematical versions) we specified a model that describes what we can observe regarding our subject (an initial equilibrium of income and consumption). In this case we describe income and consumption using the exogenous variables, investment and autonomous consumption, and a relationship between consumption and income. We assume that our model is true. In this case we assume the truth of our model by finding the value of income that satisfies both the equilibrium condition that planned expenditures equal income and the consumption relationship. Doing so gives us the reduced-form equations. If our model is true, it is legitimate to suggest that equilibrium income and consumption depend on investment, autonomous consumption, and the parameter β. We then introduce a change in investment, compare the new equilibrium to the old, and predict the changes in behavior. Any predictions regarding the responses of the equilibrium values to changes in the parameters of the model assume the model is true.

Notice again a notational convention we have followed consistently. When we assume the model is true and solve the system for equilibrium values of the endogenous variables, we mark them with the superscript asterisk. The asterisk means that these are values of the choice variables that satisfy the equilibrium conditions associated with the model. Next we illustrate this simple model of national income determination with a numerical example.

NUMERICAL EXAMPLE

Suppose we are given the following details on consumption and investment. Consumption equals $C = C_0 + \beta Y = 400 + 0.9Y$, while investment equals $I = 600$. Our equilibrium condition states that income, Y, equals planned expenditures, or $Y = E = C + I$. We substitute in the numerical values for C and I, obtaining

$$Y^* = 400 + 0.9Y^* + 600 \tag{1-18}$$

Note that we mark the fact that we have imposed the equilibrium condition by attaching a superscript asterisk to income. Equation (1-18) can be solved for Y^* by combining $400 + 600$ and subtracting $0.9Y^*$ from both sides, giving us

$$Y^* - 0.9Y^* = Y^*(1 - 0.9) = 1000 \tag{1-19}$$

If we divide both sides by $(1 - 0.9)$ we find a solution for Y^*,

$$Y^* = \frac{1000}{1 - 0.9} = \frac{1000}{0.1} = 10,000 \tag{1-20}$$

We can substitute the equilibrium value for income into the consumption function in order to find equilibrium consumption, C^*,

$$C^* = 400 + 0.9Y^* = 400 + 0.9(10,000) = 9400 \tag{1-21}$$

We can perform comparative statics analysis on this numerical example by changing the numerical value for investment and observing what happens to our equilibrium values for income and consumption. Suppose investment falls to $I' = 500$. Then equations (1-19) and (1-20) become

$$Y^{*'} - 0.9Y^{*'} = Y^{*'}(1 - 0.9) = 900 \qquad \text{(1-19a)}$$

$$Y^{*'} = \frac{900}{1 - 0.9} = \frac{900}{0.1} = 9,000 \qquad \text{(1-20a)}$$

Substituting $Y^{*'} = 9,000$ into the consumption function gives us the new equilibrium level of consumption, $C^{*'}$:

$$C^{*'} = 400 + 0.9Y^{*'} = 400 + 0.9(9,000) = 8500 \qquad \text{(1-21a)}$$

Check for yourself to see that a decrease in investment decreases income by a factor of $1/(1 - \beta) = 10$ times the decrease in investment. Similarly, consumption is decreased by a factor of $\beta/(1 - \beta) = 9$ times the decrease in investment. Investment decreased by 100, while income decreased by 1000 and consumption decreased by 900.

EXERCISES
Section 1.4.2
A Simple Model Of National Income Determination

For the following exercises, let consumption equal $C = 100 + 0.75Y$. The equilibrium condition is that income (Y) equals planned expenditures, or $Y = C + I$, where I is investment.

1. Solve mathematically and graphically for equilibrium levels of income and consumption if

   a. $I = 500$;   **b.** $I = 750$;   **c.** $I = 1000$

2. Find reduced-form equations (RFE) for Y^* and C^* in terms of the exogenous variable, I.

3. Describe the comparative statics results of this system with respect to changes in I.

1.5

SUMMARY

Milton Friedman, the 1976 Nobel laureate in economics, has suggested that a theory consists of two components: a language whose purpose it is to organize the reasoning process and a body of substantive hypotheses regarding the relationships among relevant variables.[2] The language of a theory is

---

[2]Milton Friedman, *Essays in Positive Economics* (Chicago: The University of Chicago Press, 1953), pp. 3–43.

tautological; that is, it is true by definition. The substantive hypotheses are purposely abstract and unreal; they must simplify an impossibly complex reality in order to be useful.

Look at the simple market theory presented in Section 1.4.1 from the point of view expressed by Friedman. The language of our market theory is the language of supply and demand. Supply organizes the reasoning process by suggesting that the variables relevant to our explanation of sellers' behavior include price and wages. Demand organizes the reasoning process by suggesting that the variables relevant to our explanation of buyers' behavior are price and income. Price and quantity exchanged are determined by the interaction of buyers' and sellers' behavior; where demand equals supply. *Whatever price and quantity we observe, they must be where demand equals supply.* That is, demand equals supply by definition. The language of the theory is tautological. In the mathematical expressions of our theories, the tautology is evident in the reduced-form equations, when we have solved for the equilibrium values of the dependent variables in terms of the exogenous variables and parameters. The equilibrium quantity Q^* can be considered to depend on Y and w only if the model we constructed is assumed to be true.

The substantive hypotheses in our theory come from changing a parameter or an exogenous variable. What happens to quantity when income changes or when wages change? If our theory is a useful abstraction from reality, and if it has done a good job of separating the relevant information from the irrelevant, then the predictions it makes will be good ones. If our theory has left important variables out, or if it has organized the variables in a substantially incorrect way, then its predictions will not be accurate.[3]

The most important concept introduced in this chapter is the methodology of economic theorizing called comparative statics analysis. It is not only a mathematical methodology; we showed that it can take a purely narrative form. Nor is mathematical economics some separate branch of the social science. It is just another way to express economic analysis, along with narrative and graphical modes of expression. The method of economic reasoning, along with the subject matter, is what is really distinctive about economics. Knowing the method of economic reasoning will make all forms of economic analysis seem easier, because it is the thread that binds all the different topics and techniques together.

We demonstrated the method of economic reasoning by examining two theories that are familiar to any student who has completed microeconomic and macroeconomic principles courses: a theory of market price and quantity and a theory of national income determination. Our purpose is not really that you master demand and supply or consumption functions and multipliers. Rather, we want you to see how the same explanation can be presented using words or graphs or equations. We also want you to see that the reasoning process is the same in both theories. Analysis is much easier if you can use the same methodology to answer all your questions.

The models presented in this chapter are very simple and too specific to be very useful. They are principles-level theories best suited for teaching. As

---

[3]Testing theories against facts is one of the major tasks of econometrics. Our confidence in a given theory increases when that theory is repeatedly supported by empirical evidence. On the other hand, repeated refutation of a theory on empirical grounds by econometric tests using different samples and methodologies suggests that the theory should be revised or reformulated.

the questions we want to answer become more complex, our theories become simultaneously more complicated (with more variables) and more general (we presume to know less and less regarding the functional forms which describe the relationships among variables). To handle more complicated questions we need more powerful mathematical techniques. In the next two chapters we will review some necessary math, and then we will return to economic applications. Recognize that the comparative statics methodology that we have introduced in this chapter will not change. We will follow the same procedure to generate substantive hypotheses throughout the text.

◆ REFERENCES

Friedman, Milton, *Essays in Positive Economics* (Chicago: The University of Chicago Press, 1953).

Robbins, Lionel, *An Essay on the Nature and Significance of Economic Science* (London: Macmillan and Co. Ltd., 1932).

Samuelson, Paul, *Foundations of Economic Analysis* (Cambridge, MA: Harvard University Press, 1947).

◆ ANSWERS TO END-OF-SECTION EXERCISES

Section 1.4.1: The Market Model

1. **a.** $P^* = 43.33$; $Q^* = 66.67$; **b.** $P^* = 26.67$; $Q^* = 33.33$; **c.** $P^* = 18.33$; $Q^* = 16.67$

2. **a.** $P^* = 40$; $Q^* = 70$; **b.** $P^* = 46.67$; $Q^* = 63.33$; **c.** $P^* = 50$; $Q^* = 60$

3. RFE: $P^* = 3.33 + 0.033Y + 1.33w$;
   $Q^* = 6.67 + 0.067Y - 1.33w$

   Equilibrium price changes in the same direction as income changes, by a factor of 0.033 times the change in income, holding the wage rate constant. Equilibrium price also changes in the same direction as changes in wage, by a factor of 1.33 times the change in the wage rate, holding income constant.

   Equilibrium quantity changes in the same direction as changes in income, by a factor of 0.067, holding the wage rate constant. Equilibrium quantity changes in the opposite direction as changes in the wage rate, by a factor of 1.33, holding income constant.

   Widgets are normal goods in this market, because Q_d increases with increases in income, and decreases with decreases in income.

Section 1.4.2: A Simple Model of National Income Determination

1. **a.** $Y^* = 2400$; $C^* = 1900$; **b.** $Y^* = 3400$; $C^* = 2650$; **c.** $Y^* = 4400$; $C^* = 3400$

2. RFE: $Y^* = 400 + 4I$; $C^* = 400 + 3I$

3. A change in investment changes income in the same direction by a multiplier of 4 times the change in investment. A change in investment changes consumption in the same direction by a multiplier of 3.

◆ SELF-HELP PROBLEMS

Answers to these problems are given at the end of the text.

1. Consider the following model of national income determination, where G is government spending, which is assumed to be exogenous, and T is taxes, which is also assumed to be exogenous. Note that with taxes in the model consumption is a function of disposable or after-tax income, $Y_d = Y - T$.

$$C = 300 + 0.75(Y - T)$$
$$T = 100$$
$$I = 475$$
$$G = 150$$
$$Y = E = C + I + G$$

   a. Find the equilibrium value of the endogenous variables.

   b. Suppose government expenditures increase by 50. Find the new equilibrium value of the endogenous variables.

   c. Draw a graph comparing your answers to parts a and b.

2. Suppose that quantity of widgets demanded is a linear function of price of widgets, income, and the price of twidgets. Suppose that quantity supplied is a linear function of price of widgets, wages, and the price of energy. Specify a model to describe equilibrium price and quantity of widgets, assume it is true, and discuss how price and quantity are affected by changes income, the price of twidgets, wages, and the price of energy. Perform the analysis in narrative, graphically, and mathematically. Describe the procedures you followed in your analysis. *Bonus*: Are twidgets and widgets substitutes or complements in your model? Explain. $\quad Q_d = P_w + I + P_t \qquad Q_s = P_w + w + P_e$

3. Consider the following market model $\quad Q_d = P_w + I + P_t = P_w + w + P_e = Q_s$

$$Q_d = a + bP$$
$$Q_s = \alpha + \beta(P - t)$$
$$Q_d = Q_s$$

   where Q_d and Q_s represent quantities demanded and supplied, P is price, and t is a tax per unit of output paid by suppliers.

   a. Assume the model is true and find reduced-form equations for quantity and price.

   b. Using the mathematical and graphical approaches, perform comparative statics analysis of the effect of a change in the tax rate on equilibrium levels of quantity and price. Is the tax shifted (passed on) to consumers completely? Explain and defend your answer.

   c. Replace the above model with the following,

$$Q_d = a + b(P + t)$$
$$Q_s = \alpha + \beta P$$
$$Q_d = Q_s$$

where t is a per-unit tax paid by consumers. Assuming the model to be true, derive reduced-form equations for quantity and price and use them to perform comparative statics analysis of the effect of a change in the tax rate, t.

d. Write a narrative describing your comparative statics results of a change in the tax rate in parts b and c.

◆ SUPPLEMENTAL PROBLEMS

1. Consider the following model of national income determination where Y is national income, C denotes consumption expenditures, β is marginal propensity to consume, Y_d is disposable (after-tax) income, t represents the income tax rate, I denotes investment expenditures, and G is government expenditures:

$$Y = C + I + G$$
$$C = C_0 + \beta Y_d$$
$$Y_d = (1 - t)Y$$

a. Which variables are endogenous and which are exogenous? How do you know? Explain. What is(are) the parameter(s) of this model?

b. Suppose $C_0 = 50$, $\beta = 0.8$, $t = 0.25$, $I = 150$, and $G = 100$. Assuming the model to be true, find the equilibrium values of all endogenous variables. Draw a picture showing the determination of equilibrium national income.

c. Using the mathematical and graphical approaches, conduct comparative statics analysis of the effect of a change in investment expenditures on equilibrium level of income. As far as your comparative statics results are concerned, what difference, if any, would it make if instead of investment, government expenditures had changed? Explain.

2. Consider the market for compact discs (CDs). Suppose quantity of CDs demanded is a linear function of price of CDs, price of cassette tapes, and consumers' income (assume CDs are a normal good). Suppose quantity of CDs supplied is a linear function of price of CDs and wages.

a. Specify a model of the CD market that would allow you to analyze equilibrium price and quantity of CDs. Identify the behavioral equations of your model and the model's equilibrium condition. Also, identify endogenous and exogenous variables of your model and its parameters. Finally, explain why each parameter in your model has the sign you assigned to it.

b. Assume the model you specified in part a is true and derive reduced-form equations for quantity and price of CDs. Draw a picture showing the initial equilibrium of this market.

c. Perform, both mathematically and graphically, comparative statics analysis of the effect of a change in income on equilibrium price and quantity of CDs. How would your results change if CDs were an inferior good? Explain.

d. Perform, both mathematically and graphically, comparative statics analysis of the effect of a change in price of cassette tapes on equilibrium price and quantity of CDs.

3. Suppose that, in Problem 2, in addition to being a linear function of price of CDs, price of cassette tapes, and consumers' income, quantity of CDs demanded is also a linear function of price of CD players. Conduct a complete comparative statics analysis of the effect of a change in price of CD players on equilibrium price and quantity of CDs.

4. Suppose that aggregate income equals planned expenditures, which equals consumption plus investment plus government spending, G. Suppose that consumption depends on disposable income, Y_d, and that Y_d equals one minus the tax rate, t, times aggregate income, $Y_d = (1 - t)Y$. Specify a model to describe equilibrium levels of consumption, income, and disposable income in terms of the exogenous variables I and G and the parameter t. Assume your model is true, and explain how the equilibrium values of C, Y, and Y_d are affected by changes in the exogenous variables of the model. Perform the analysis in narrative, graphically, and mathematically. Describe the steps you follow in your analytic methodology.

5. For Problems 2 and 4, discuss which part of each theory is its language and which part contains its substantive hypotheses. Explain why the language is tautological and how the substantive hypotheses can be used to test the theories.

6. Suppose quantity demanded equals $Q_d = 10 - P - t + 0.1Y$ and quantity supplied equals $Q_s = 2P - 4w$, where P is price, t is a per-unit sales tax, Y is income, and w is the wage rate. Find the reduced-form equations for P^* and Q^*. Describe the narrative the comparative statics effects of changes in the tax rate.

$Y = E$

$$Y = C_0 + b\big((1-t)Y\big) + I + G$$

$$Y = 50 + .8(.75Y) + 150 + 100$$

$$(Y - .6Y) = 300 \qquad Y = 750$$

$$Y(1 - .6) = 300$$

$$Y = \frac{300}{.4}$$

C H A P T E R   2

Relations and Functions

2.1

INTRODUCTION

Theories of the type discussed in Chapter 1 require us to describe relationships among variables. That is how we create the language of a theory and separate relevant information from irrelevant. Demand describes the relationship between the quantities of a good consumers are willing and able to purchase and variables such as price, income, prices of other goods, and tastes. Supply describes the relationship between the quantities of a good producers are willing and able to supply and variables such as price (again), price of inputs, and technology. The consumption function from the model of national income determination describes the relationship between consumption and income. The way we describe the relationships embodies what we know about them.

The first numerical example of demand and supply assumed we knew everything that determined quantity demanded and quantity supplied, including the exact relationships among the variables. The more generalized model of demand and supply (with the coefficients expressed symbolically instead of numerically), as well as the consumption function, assumed that we knew the general nature of the relationships but not the quantitative details.

The mathematical concepts for describing relationships among variables are *relations* and *functions*. In this chapter we review what is meant by these terms, and then we examine some particular types of functions that turn out to be quite useful in economics. These include polynomial, rational, exponential, and logarithmic functions.

2.2

RELATIONS

relation: an association between one entity and another, or a set of ordered pairs.

A **_relation_** is a mathematical concept that is intended to represent the most general form of connection between variables. It simply says that there exists an association between one thing and another. The nature of the association is not specified. For example, we might say that there exists a relation between bees and flowers. The exact nature of the relationship is not specified. At this level of generality, we cannot say whether each bee is connected with one or many flowers or whether each flower is connected with one or many bees. We cannot say whether all flowers are associated with a bee or bees, or whether all bees are associated with a flower or flowers. No dependence is implied by a relation; that is, we cannot say either that bees depend on flowers or that flowers depend on bees.

set: any definable collection of entities.

elements: the name for the entities that comprise a set.

Relations are best defined mathematically with the help of set theory. A **_set_** is any definable collection of **_elements_**, which can represent anything. Sets are expressed by placing the elements between braces. For example, we could represent the set of all flowers as {all flowers}, or $\{a_1, a_2, a_3, \ldots, a_n\}$ where a_i, $i = 1, 2, \ldots, n$, represents an individual flower and n represents the number of all flowers. We could represent the set of all bees as {all bees}, or $\{b_1, b_2, b_3, \ldots, b_m\}$ where b_j, $j = 1, 2, \ldots, m$, represents an individual bee and m represents the number of all bees. To say that a relation exists between flowers and bees is to say that we can pair off elements of the set of all flowers and the set of all bees. We denote a pair of elements with parentheses; for example, (a_1, b_3) is a pair of elements from the set of all flowers and the set of all bees. When we consistently pair off elements from one set (flowers) with another (bees), we have a set of **_ordered pairs_**, which defines a relation in the terms of set theory. An example of a set of ordered pairs from these two sets is

ordered pair: a pair of elements (x_i, y_j) such that the first element is from one set {X} and the second element is from another set {Y}. A set of ordered pairs expresses a relation.

$$\{(a_1, b_3), (a_1, b_2), (a_2, b_2), (a_3, b_1), (a_3, b_4)\}$$

We consider the pairs in this set to be ordered because in each case the first element of a pair is from the set of flowers and the second element is from the set of bees. This set of ordered pairs, or relation between flowers and bees, is pictured in Figure 2.3*a*. In it, the uppercase letter A is used to denote the set of elements a_i and the uppercase letter B is used to denote the set of elements b_j. Notice that some flowers (a_1 and a_3) are associated with more than one bee and that one bee (b_2) is associated with more than one flower. We cannot say, from this relation, that a single flower can be determined by a bee, or vice versa. The flower of a pair cannot be said to depend on a particular bee, and the bee of a pair cannot be said to depend on a particular flower.

NUMERICAL EXAMPLES

1. Find five ordered pairs belonging to the relation $\{(x, y); y = 5x\}$. We can find the ordered pairs by substituting values of x into the equation that describes the relation and computing the corresponding value of y. For example, substitute in $x = -4, -2, 0, 2, 4$. We find the ordered pairs

Figure 2.1

$\{(x, y); y = 5x\}$

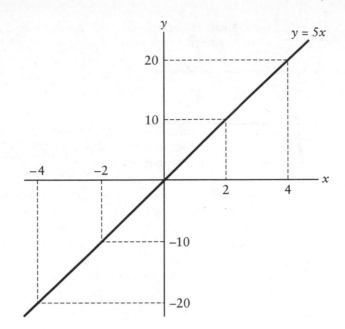

$(-4, -20)$, $(-2, -10)$, $(0, 0)$, $(2, 10)$, and $(4, 20)$. This relation can be described graphically by plotting the ordered pairs on a pair of axes, as we do in Figure 2.1. The relation is described as the line labeled $y = 5x$.

2. Find five ordered pairs belonging to the relation $\{(x, y); y \le x\}$. Following a procedure similar to the one we used in the first example, we find $(-4, -5)$, $(-2, -2)$, $(2, 0)$, $(2, 2)$, $(4, 3.5)$. Note that, in this example, more than one value of y can be associated with any particular value of x. Because of this, when we graph this relation (Figure 2.2), we describe it as

Figure 2.2

$\{(x, y); y \le x\}$

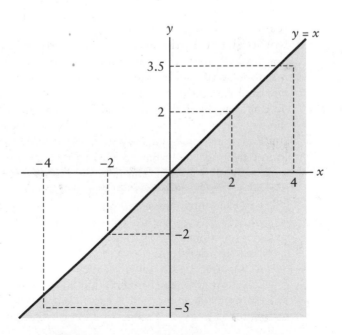

the shaded area below and including the line labeled $y = x$. Note that some of our ordered pairs fall on the line $y = x$, and some fall below it.

Specifying a relation helps us to choose a theory when we are engaged in the process of economic modeling. Remember from Chapter 1 that economic modeling requires us first to choose a problem to investigate and second to determine what information is and is not relevant to the investigation by choosing a theory. The first step determines the choice of endogenous variable(s). If the problem we want to investigate is market behavior, the endogenous variables are market price and quantity. In order to choose a theory to explain market price and quantity, we need to know what other variables are somehow *related* to them. You could list the things you believe might have some association to prices and quantities: weather, tastes, wealth, inputs, etc. At this stage you are indicating that relations exist among these variables without specifying any details regarding the nature of the relation. In order to have a theory it is necessary to be more detailed about the nature of relationships. *Functions*, which are a subset of relations, provide more detail.

2.3

FUNCTIONS

function: a set of ordered pairs $\{X_i, Y_j\}$, $i = 1, 2, \ldots n$ and $j = 1, 2, \ldots m$, with the property that any X value determines a unique Y value.

A *function* is a particular type of relation that does suggest dependence of one variable on another. Consider a relation between the set of workers, $\{w_1, w_2, w_3, \ldots, w_n\}$, and the set of occupations, $\{o_1, o_2, o_3, \ldots, o_m\}$, in which each worker has one and only one occupation but many workers have the same occupation. Knowing the worker gives us enough information to know the occupation. In a sense, we can say the occupation depends on the worker. Recognize that the converse is not true. Knowing the occupation does not provide us with enough information to determine the worker. This relation describes occupations as a function of workers, because knowing the worker tells us the occupation. Conversely, workers are not a function of occupations, because knowing the occupation is not sufficient to determine the worker.

Functions come in many forms and are capable of embodying any level of information we might have regarding relationships among variables. In their most general form, functions describe a situation in which we know only that some dependence exists but nothing else. In more specific forms, functions can describe every qualitative and quantitative detail about a relation among sets of elements. We now turn to a more formal discussion of functions and specific functional forms that will prove useful in describing important economic relationships.

A function is a set of ordered pairs $\{(x_i, y_j)\}$, $i = 1, 2, \ldots n$ and $j = 1, 2, \ldots m$, with the property that any x value determines a unique y value. For example, the set $\{(x_1, y_3), (x_2, y_2), (x_3, y_1), (x_4, y_3)\}$ associates one and only one value of y for each value of x. This function is pictured in Figure 2.3*b*.

Figure 2.3

(*a*) A Relation Between
A and *B*; (*b*) A Function
$y = f(x)$

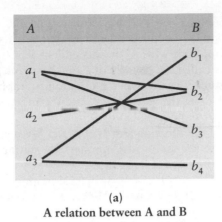
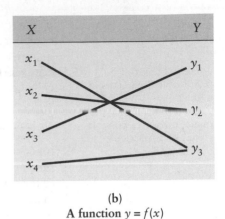

(a)
A relation between A and B

(b)
A function $y = f(x)$

Recognize that the relation pictured in Figure 2.3*a* is not a function because both a_1 and a_3 have more than one value of *b* associated with them. Therefore *b* cannot be considered a function of *a*. Likewise, b_2 has more than one value of *a* associated with it, so *a* cannot be considered a function of *b*. Knowing a value of *a* is not always sufficient to determine a value for *b*, and knowing a value of *b* is not always sufficient to determine a value for *a*.

Functions are written as $y = f(x)$. A function can also be called a mapping or a transformation. All these terms convey the same notion, namely that the value of *y* depends on the value of *x*. That is to say, all the information that we need to know to determine the value of *y* is the value of *x* and the function. In the statement $y = f(x)$, the functional notation (*f*) may be interpreted as a rule according to which the set of all values of *x* is mapped or transformed to the set of all values of *y*. Thus we may write

$$f : X \to Y$$

where, once again, the uppercase letter denotes the set of all elements symbolized by lowercase letters, and the symbol → connotes a mapping.

Note that, according to the above definition, every function is a relation, but not every relation is a function. A relation is a function only if *x* determines *y* *uniquely*. The converse is not required; i.e., more than one *x* value may be associated with the same *y* value. The function pictured in Figure 2.3*b* is an example of this. Each *x* has only one *y* associated with it, while y_3 has both x_1 and x_4 associated with it. Another example is the function $y = f(x) = x^2$, which yields $y = 1$ for both $x = 1$ and $x = -1$. In this example, *y* is a function of *x*, or $y = f(x)$, because every value of *x* has one and only one value of *y* associated with it. However, *x* is not a function of *y*, because values of *y* have more than one value of *x* associated with them.

In order to use functions to describe and analyze economic behavior, we should review the vocabulary associated with them. We are using the symbols *x* and *y* to represent, in general form, the individual elements of the sets $\{x_i\}$, $i = 1, 2, \ldots, n$, and $\{y_j\}, j = 1, 2, \ldots, m$. In the vocabulary of functions, *x* and *y* are called *variables*, because the value of what they represent can vary. The variable that is described uniquely by a functional relationship is called the *dependent variable*, and the variable (or variables) that provides the information is called the *independent variable*. Functions have *arguments* and *values*.

variable: mathematical symbol representing something that can vary in its value.

dependent variable: the variable that is described uniquely by a functional relationship.

independent variable: the variable (or variables) that provides the information that uniquely determines the dependent variable.

argument: if the function is $Y = f(X)$, then its arguments are the particular quantities taken by *X*, the independent variable.

values: if the function is $Y = f(X)$, its values are the quantities taken by *Y*, the dependent variable.

argument - ind. variable
value - dep. variable

domain: the set of permissible arguments of a function.

range: the set of possible values of a function.

monotonic function: a function whose values either increase or decrease consistently as its argument increases.

inverse function: a monotonic function has an inverse function, in which the dependent and independent variables reverse roles. The value of the original function is the argument of the inverse, and the argument of the original is the value of the inverse.

If the function is $y = f(x)$, then its argument is the particular quantity associated with x, the independent variable, and its value is the corresponding quantity associated with y, the dependent variable. The set of permissible arguments is called the *domain* of a function, and the set of possible values is called the *range*. Usually, when a function is graphed, the dependent variable is measured along the vertical axis and the independent variable is measured along the horizontal axis.

Consider the function $y = f(x) = 5x$. We may define the domain of the function to be the set of real numbers by stating $-\infty < x < +\infty$.[1] Then the range is also the set of real numbers, or $-\infty < y < +\infty$. If $x = 5$, then the value of the function is $y = f(x) = 5(5) = 25$. For another example, consider the demand function, $Q_d = f(P) = a - bP, a, b > 0$. If we restrict the domain of this function to $0 \le P \le a/b$, then the range equals $0 \le Q_d \le a$. We do so in order to confine the demand function to positive values for both quantity and price.

A function is *monotonic* if its value either increases or decreases consistently as its argument increases. For example, a downward-sloping demand curve is a consistently decreasing function, whereas an upward-sloping supply curve is consistently increasing. A function whose values increase for some increases in the arguments but decrease for others is not monotonic. Compare the total cost function to the average cost function pictured in Figure 2.4. Total cost increases consistently as output increases, whereas average cost decreases at first and then increases. To know that a function is monotonic is to have some specific knowledge about the nature of the functional relationship between an independent and dependent variable.

An important property of monotonic functions is that not only does the independent variable determine the dependent variable uniquely but also, for these functions, the converse is true. That is, if $y = f(x)$ is monotonic, y is determined uniquely by x, and x is determined uniquely by y. Looking at Figure 2.4 shows you why. If a function is monotonic, as the total cost function is, then no value of y can be associated with more than one level of x. If a function is not monotonic, such as the average cost function, then some values of y are associated with more than one value of x.

This is an important property because a monotonic function has an *inverse function* which is itself monotonic. If $y = f(x)$ is monotonic, its inverse can be described as $x = f^{-1}(y)$. The argument of the original function is the value of the inverse, and the value of the original is the argument of the inverse. Functions that are not monotonic do not have inverse functions, because y does not determine x uniquely. The roles of dependent and independent variables can be reversed only if a function is monotonic. As you can see in Figure 2.4, when the independent and dependent variables of the average cost function are reversed, the resulting relation is not a function. You should note that when the graph of a relation has a vertical segment to it, or when it bends over backward or forward on itself in the vertical direction, it is not a function.

---

[1] The set of real numbers includes all rational and irrational numbers. Rational numbers can all be expressed as the ratio of two integers and, of course, include integers and fractional numbers. Irrational numbers cannot be expressed as the ratio of two integers. Examples of irrational numbers include the square root of 2, the number $\pi = 3.141589\ldots$, and the base of the natural logarithm $e = 2.71828\ldots$. The only numbers not included in the set of real numbers are *imaginary* numbers, which are the square roots of negative numbers.

Figure 2.4

Functions and Inverses

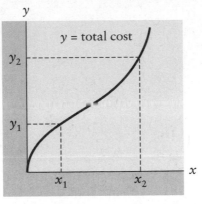

Total cost = $y = f(x)$

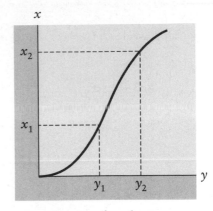

Inverse of total cost
$x = f^{-1}(y)$

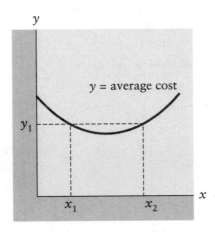

Average cost = $y = g(x)$

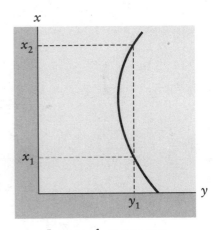

Inverse of average cost

NUMERICAL EXAMPLES

1. Consider the function $y = f(x) = 2x + 6$, $-\infty < x < +\infty$. The range is also the set of real numbers, or $-\infty < y < +\infty$. It is a monotonically increasing function, and it has an inverse. We find the inverse function by solving the original function for x in terms of y. In this case, we find that $x = f^{-1}(y) = y/2 - 3$. The range of the inverse is the domain of the original, and vice versa. We graph the function and its inverse in Figure 2.5. Note that the inverse function is the reflection of the original, reflected about the 45° line where $y = x$.

2. Next, consider the function $y = f(x) = -x^2 + 1$, $-\infty < x < +\infty$. The range is $-\infty < y \leq 1$. It is an increasing function for $-\infty < x \leq 0$ and decreasing thereafter, so it is not monotonic. It is graphed in Figure 2.6, along with its inverse relation, $x = \pm\sqrt{1 - y}$. As you can see, the original function is not monotonic, and the inverse relation bends over itself backward so it is not a function.

Figure 2.5

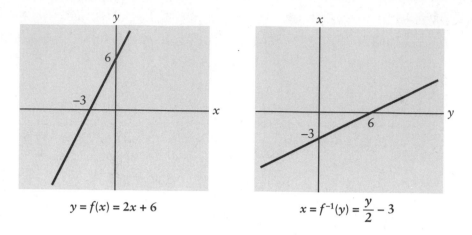

$$y = f(x) = 2x + 6$$

$$x = f^{-1}(y) = \frac{y}{2} - 3$$

Figure 2.6

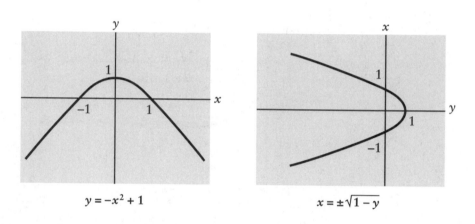

$$y = -x^2 + 1$$

$$x = \pm\sqrt{1 - y}$$

composite function: a function whose argument is itself a function. It is the function of a function.

explicit function: a function in which the dependent variable is isolated on one side of the equation, as in $Y = f(x)$.

implicit function: a function in which the dependent variable is not isolated on one side of the equation, but rather some expression containing the function is expressed as equal to zero, as in $F(Y, X) = 0$.

identity: an equation that is true for all values of the variables. It is signified by the symbol $\equiv$.

Composite functions are functions of functions. If $y = f(x)$ and $x = g(z)$ then the composite function of these is $y = f[g(z)] = h(z)$. Consider, for example, the total revenue of a firm, y, which can be expressed as a function of output, x, or $y = f(x) = 10x$. Output is itself a function of the labor, z, used to produce it, $x = g(z) = 5z$. Total revenue can be expressed as a composite function of labor, $y = f[g(z)] = 10(5z) = 50z = h(z)$.

Functions may be expressed in *explicit* form, as $y = f(x)$, or in *implicit* form, as in $y - f(x) \equiv F(x, y) = 0$. Note that we use the symbol $\equiv$ to indicate an *identity*; that is, an equation that is true for all values of the variables. Any explicit function can easily be made into an implicit function simply by subtracting whatever is on the right-hand side from both sides of the equation, as we did above. However, sometimes the relationship between two variables can only be expressed implicitly. For example, try to solve the implicit relationship $x^2 + 3xy - 2y^2 = 0$ explicitly for y! At this point, we do not know for certain whether or not y is a function of x. If you can graph the relation, you can determine that a function exists if it has no vertical segment, or it doesn't bend over backward or forward in the vertical direction. It will be important to remember this point when we discuss the differentiation of implicit functions in Chapter 3 and again in Chapter 5.

EXERCISES
Section 2.3
Functions

For the following equations,

a. Determine whether it is a relation or a function.

b. Determine whether it is an implicit or an explicit function. If an implicit function, try to express it explicitly, and if an explicit function, express it implicitly.

c. Determine if it is monotonic and if so find its inverse function.

d. Determine if it is a composite function and if so, through proper substitutions, write it as a simple function.

1. $Y = 5$
2. $Y = 5X$, if $X \geq 0$
3. $X = 5Z^2$, if $-\infty < Z < +\infty$
4. $Z = (1/5)\sqrt{W}$, $W \geq 0$
5. $XY = 5$, if $X \neq 0$
6. $Y/X = 5$, if $X \neq 0$
7. $Y = (X + 1)^2$
8. $Y^2 - X^2 = 0$
9. $Y - X^2 = 0$
10. $Y^2 = X$
11. $Y = 2X^2 + 1$
12. $Y = \sqrt{X}$, if $X \geq 0$
13. $\sqrt{Y} = X$, if $Y \geq 0$
14. $Y = 4X^2 - 2X^4$, if $X = \sqrt{Z}$, $Z \geq 0$

2.4

ALTERNATIVE FUNCTIONAL FORMS

polynomial function: a function that has the following general form:

$$Y = f(X) = a_0 X^0 + a_1 X^1 + a_2 X^2 + \cdots + a_n X^n$$

nonpolynomial functions: functions that cannot be expressed as a polynomial or rational function.

Now that we have defined and discussed functions, we shall consider some of the specific forms that functions might take which have applications in economic analysis. In the following discussion we shall consider only functions with one dependent variable (Y) and one independent variable (X), i.e., $Y = f(X)$. In general, functional forms may be classified into two broad categories: *polynomial functions*, also known as algebraic functions, and *nonpolynomial functions*, which are also known as nonalgebraic or transcendental functions. Before proceeding, however, we should define what we mean by a polynomial.

polynomial — multiterm

2.4.1   Polynomial Functions

The word polynomial means *multiterm*. A polynomial function of a real-valued variable is a function of that variable that has the following general form:

$$Y = f(X) = a_0 X^0 + a_1 X^1 + a_2 X^2 + \cdots + a_n X^n \qquad (2\text{-}1)$$
$$= a_0 + a_1 X + a_2 X^2 + \cdots + a_n X^n$$
$$= \sum_{i=0}^{n} a_i X^i$$

polynomial functions
constant   rational
linear
quadratic
cubic

degree of a polynomial:
the highest power in a
polynomial.

where the coefficients $a_0, a_1, \ldots, a_n$ are all real numbers. Note that all powers, including (n), are nonnegative integers. The ***degree of a polynomial*** refers to the highest power of that polynomial, n in the above case. The most frequently used polynomial functions in economic analysis are *constant functions*, *linear functions*, *quadratic functions*, *cubic functions*, and *rational functions*.

Constant Functions

constant function: a
polynomial of degree zero.

A function whose range consists of only one element is called a ***constant function***, e.g., $Y = f(X) = 10$. Here the value of Y or $f(X)$ stays the same regardless of the value of X. Note that a constant function is nothing but a polynomial of degree zero, i.e.,

$$Y = f(X) = a_0 X^0 = a_0 \qquad (2\text{-}2)$$

The graph of a constant function is a horizontal straight line. An example of this in economics is the supply of a fixed resource such as land. Suppose we graph the functional relation between the quantity of land (T) and the price of land (P), $T = f(P) = T_0$. When we place T on the vertical axis and P on the horizontal, as in Figure 2.7*a*, the graph is a horizontal line at a quantity of T_0.

As we mentioned in Chapter 1, Section 1.4, demand and supply curves are typically graphed with price on the vertical axis and quantity on the horizontal. This means reversing the roles of the dependent and independent

Figure 2.7

**A Constant Function
and Its Inverse**

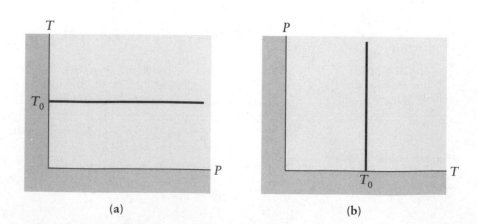

(a)   (b)

variables in the graph, or graphing the inverse of the supply function, which we do in Figure 2.7*b*. As you can see, the inverse of a constant function is not itself a function, because its graph is a vertical line.

Linear Functions

linear function: a polynomial of degree 1.

A polynomial of degree one is called a *linear function*

$$Y = f(X) = a_0 + a_1 X^1 = a_0 + a_1 X \tag{2-3}$$

The graph of a linear function is a straight line. When $X = 0$, the linear function yields $Y = a_0$, which is called the Y intercept or the vertical intercept of the function. The vertical intercept of the line represents the ordered pair $(0, a_0)$. When $Y = 0$, the linear function yields $X = -a_0/a_1$, which is called the X intercept or the horizontal intercept of the function. The horizontal intercept represents the ordered pair $(-a_0/a_1, 0)$.

The coefficient a_1 of X measures the slope or steepness of the line, which is a measure of the response of Y to a change in X. That is,

$$a_1 = \frac{\Delta Y}{\Delta X} = \frac{Y_2 - Y_1}{X_2 - X_1} = \frac{Y_1 - Y_2}{X_1 - X_2} = \frac{\text{rise}}{\text{run}} \tag{2-4}$$

If a_1 is positive, the line has a positive slope; it rises from left to right. For example, suppose $Y = f(X) = -5 + 5X$. The Y intercept equals -5, the X intercept equals 1, and the slope equals 5. The slope is positive, as graphed in Figure 2.8*a*.

Figure 2.8

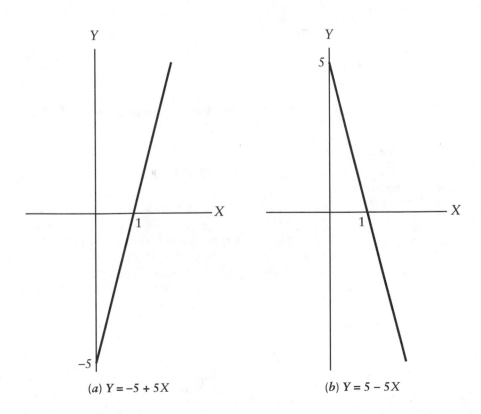

(*a*) $Y = -5 + 5X$ (*b*) $Y = 5 - 5X$

horizontal - o slope
vertical - undefined

If a_1 is negative, the line has a negative slope; it falls from left to right. Suppose $Y = f(X) = 5 - 5X$. The Y intercept equals 5, the X intercept equals 1, and the slope equals -5. The slope is negative, as graphed in Figure 2.8*b*. If a_1 is zero, we are back to a constant function, a horizontal line with a slope of zero. A vertical line, on the other hand, has an undefined slope, which we customarily refer to as an infinitely sloped line. Examples of linear functions in economics are the consumption function from the model of income determination and the simple linear demand and supply curves discussed in Chapter 1.

linear functions monotonic ∴ inverses

Linear functions are monotonic, so they have inverse functions. Sometimes the inverse function has an important role in economic theory. Consider the linear demand curve[2]

$$Q = f(P) = a_0 + a_1 P, \qquad a_1 < 0 < a_0 \qquad (2\text{-}5)$$

The inverse function exists and is equal to

$$P = f^{-1}(Q) = AR = \frac{-a_0}{a_1} + \frac{1}{a_1} Q \qquad (2\text{-}6)$$

average revenue: total revenue, PQ, divided by quantity Q. It equals price, P. The graph of average revenue is the inverse of the demand curve.

The graph of this function can be interpreted as the *average revenue (AR)* curve. Average revenue equals total revenue (PQ) divided by Q and so is equal to price. Note that when we graph a demand curve with price on the vertical axis and quantity on the horizontal, we are actually graphing average revenue versus quantity. See Figure 2.9 for graphs of both the demand function and its inverse, the average revenue function.

Quadratic Functions

In introductory and intermediate economics courses, linear functions are often used because of their simplicity. However, economic relationships are generally nonlinear. One group of nonlinear functions is polynomials of degree greater than 1. One of the most often used nonlinear functions is the *quadratic function*, or a polynomial of degree 2, such as

quadratic function: a polynomial of degree 2. When equal to zero, a quadratic function becomes a quadratic equation.

$$Y = f(X) = a_0 + a_1 X + a_2 X^2 \quad \text{or} \quad Y = f(X) = aX^2 + bX + c \quad (2\text{-}7)$$

The graph of a quadratic function is called a *parabola*, a curve with a single peak or trough. The coefficient a_0 represents the vertical intercept of a parabola. If the coefficient a_2 is negative, the resulting parabola will be an inverted U shape and it will reach a maximum value. If a_2 is positive, it will have a U shape with a minimum value.

parabola: the graph of a second-degree polynomial. It is a U-shaped or inverted U-shaped curve.

a_2 coeff ⊖
max
min
a_2 coeff ⊕

A distinction should be made between a quadratic *function* and a quadratic *equation*. A quadratic function is what we have been discussing to this point. It specifies a rule of mapping from X to Y. Examples of quadratic functions in economics are numerous; total revenue, total profits, average

---

[2]Note that, because we are discussing only a demand function and no supply function, we can denote quantity demanded with Q rather than Q_d. Also note that there, in contrast to Chapter 1, we have expressed the demand curve in the general form of a first-degree polynomial, with coefficients a_0 and a_1. We have restricted the values of the coefficients so that the demand curve has a positive vertical intercept and a negative slope.

Figure 2.9

A Demand Function and Its Inverse, Average Revenue

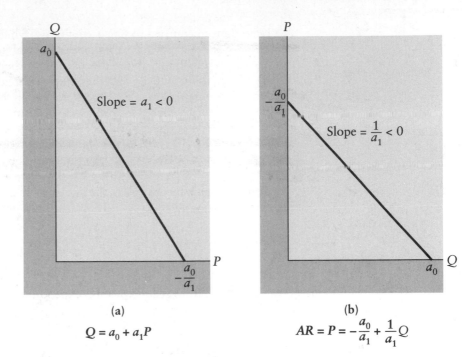

(a)

$$Q = a_0 + a_1 P$$

(b)

$$AR = P = -\frac{a_0}{a_1} + \frac{1}{a_1} Q$$

quadratic-functions
- TR
- TP
- AC
- MC
- Prod. func.
- Utility fun.

$\Downarrow$

$= 0$ - quad. equation

cost, marginal cost, production functions, and utility functions can all be represented by quadratic functions. Once a quadratic function is set equal to zero, the result is a quadratic equation

$$f(X) = a_0 + a_1 X + a_2 X^2 = 0 \tag{2-8}$$

With $f(X)$ restricted to a zero value, only a select number of X values can satisfy the quadratic equation and qualify as its solution values, which are also called critical roots. Graphically, the critical roots of a quadratic equation are those X values at which the parabola intersects the horizontal axis, which is where Y equals zero. This distinction between quadratic functions and quadratic equations also applies to higher-degree polynomials. A polynomial function can be turned into a polynomial equation by setting it equal to zero.

Critical roots = X int. horizontal Y = zero

quadratic formula: a formula for solving a quadratic equation.

A general approach to solving a quadratic equation is to use the *quadratic formula*

$$X = \frac{-a_1 \pm \sqrt{a_1^2 - 4a_2 a_0}}{2a_2} \tag{2-9}$$

or, if the quadratic equation is written in the form

$$aX^2 + bX + c = 0 \tag{2-10}$$

then the solution is

$$X = \frac{-b \pm \sqrt{b^2 - 4ac}}{2a} \tag{2-11}$$

quadratic eq.
2, 1, no solutions

discriminant ⊕
2 ≠ roots

0
1 real

⊖
2 ≠ i

Note that, in contrast to linear equations, which have only one solution, quadratic equations may have two, one, or no solutions. We can use a simple rule to learn something about the nature of the critical roots of a given quadratic equation, namely whether they are real or imaginary, equal or unequal. This rule makes use of the term under the square-root sign in the quadratic formula, which is known as the discriminant of the equation. If the discriminant is positive, then the corresponding quadratic equation has two unequal real roots. If it is zero, the quadratic equation has one real root. If the discriminant is negative, then the function has two unequal imaginary roots.

Consider again the inverse of the demand function, or the average revenue function, equation (2-6),

$$P = AR = \frac{-a_0}{a_1} + \frac{1}{a_1} Q \qquad (2\text{-}6)$$

Total revenue, TR, to sellers (or total expenditures by buyers) equals average revenue times quantity.

$$TR = AR \cdot Q = \left[\frac{-a_0}{a_1} + \frac{1}{a_1} Q \right] Q = \frac{-a_0}{a_1} Q + \frac{1}{a_1} Q^2 \qquad (2\text{-}12)$$

Recall that, according to the law of demand, $a_1 < 0$. That means that, given a linear demand curve, total revenue is a quadratic function with an inverted U shape. There are a few things worth noting about this total revenue function, which is pictured graphically in Figure 2.10. Because the parabola is an inverted U shape, it reaches a maximum value.

The graph is **symmetric** around the vertical line that cuts through the maximum; that is, the behavior of the graph on the right side of the line is the mirror image of the behavior of the graph on the left side of the line. This means that the parabola intersects the Q axis equal distances on either side of

symmetric: the property by which the graph of a function on one side of a straight line is the mirror image of the graph on the other side.

Figure 2.10

Total Revenue =
$(-a_0/a_1)Q + Q^2/a_1$

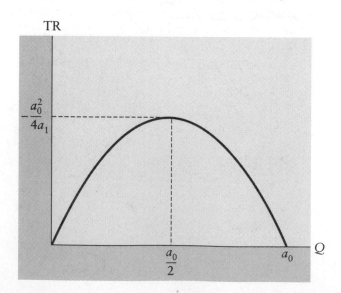

the point where it reaches its maximum value. If we could find the points where the graph touches the Q axis, we could find the maximum point by looking midway between them. Those points are the solutions of the quadratic equation you obtain by setting total revenue equal to zero.

Let's use the quadratic formula to find the solutions of the quadratic equation

$$\text{TR} = 0 = \frac{-a_0}{a_1} Q + \frac{1}{a_1} Q^2 \tag{2-13}$$

Substituting the coefficients of (2-13) into the quadratic formula, equation (2-11), gives us

$$Q = \frac{-(-a_0/a_1) \pm \sqrt{(-a_0/a_1)^2 - 4(1/a_1)0}}{2(1/a_1)} \tag{2-14}$$

$$Q = 0 \quad \text{or} \quad Q = a_0$$

We find that total revenue equals zero when $Q = 0$ and when $Q = a_0$. The maximum value taken by total revenue is midway between these two points, where $Q = a_0/2$. We find the value of total revenue at that point by substituting $Q = a_0/2$ into the total revenue function, finding that $\text{TR} = -a_0^2/4a_1$ (remember that a_1 is a negative number). You should compare Figure 2.10 to Figure 2.9b, the graph of the average revenue curve we used to generate total revenue. The horizontal intercept of the average revenue curve is the quantity at which price is zero, and is equal to a_0. It should not surprise you that total revenue equals zero when either price or quantity equals zero.

NUMERICAL EXAMPLE

Suppose we are given the demand function $Q = f(P) = 10 - 4P$. Average revenue is the inverse function to demand. Solving for P, we find that $\text{AR} = P = 2.5 - 0.25Q$. We can obtain the expression for total revenue by multiplying average revenue by quantity, or $\text{TR} = PQ = 2.5Q - 0.25Q^2$. This is, of course, a quadratic function that, when graphed, is described by an inverted U-shaped parabola, as we show in Figure 2.11. We can find the horizontal intercepts of the parabola by setting TR equal to zero and using the quadratic formula to solve the quadratic equation, $0 = 2.5Q - 0.25Q^2$. We find that total revenue equals zero if $Q = 0$ and if $Q = 10$.

Cubic Functions

Another nonlinear function that is used frequently in economic analysis is the *cubic function*. A cubic function is a third-degree polynomial

cubic function: a polynomial of degree 3.

$$f(X) = a_0 + a_1 X + a_2 X^2 + a_3 X^3 \tag{2-15}$$

Figure 2.11

$$TR = 2.5Q - 0.25Q^2$$

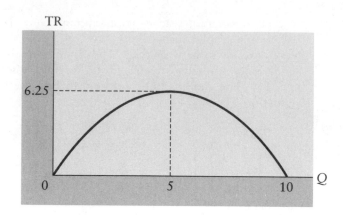

The graph of a cubic function may be a curve with a positive and continuously increasing slope, or, as is the case in most economic applications, it may be a curve with two wiggles. Examples of this type of function in economics include the **short-run** total cost function (for $a_0 \neq 0$), and the **long-run** total cost function (for $a_0 = 0$).

We can generate a cubic total cost function by multiplying a quadratic average cost function by output. Suppose average cost (AC) is the quadratic function

short-run: a situation in which some variable is arbitrarily held constant.

long-run: a situation in which nothing is arbitrarily held constant.

$$AC = c_0 + c_1 Q + c_2 Q^2, \quad \text{where } c_0 > 0,\ c_1 < 0,\ \text{and } c_2 > 0 \quad \text{(2-16)}$$

Total cost equals average cost times quantity, or

$$TC = (AC)Q = (c_0 + c_1 Q + c_2 Q^2)Q = c_0 Q + c_1 Q^2 + c_2 Q^3 \quad \text{(2-17)}$$

This is a cubic function that passes through the origin. Because it passes through the origin, total cost equals zero when quantity equals zero. The economic interpretation of a total cost curve that passes through the origin is that there is no fixed cost. Fixed costs are associated with fixed inputs and are incurred even if no output is produced. Therefore, the total cost function of (2-17) must represent long-run total cost.

[handwritten note: fixed cost associated w/ fixed inputs]

NUMERICAL EXAMPLE

Suppose a firm faces the average cost function $AC = 100 - 15Q + Q^2$. Total cost is average cost multiplied by quantity, or $TC = 100Q - 15Q^2 + Q^3$. The graph of this function is presented in Figure 2.12 (see page 37).

Rational Functions

rational function: a function that is the ratio of two polynomials.

A function in which Y is expressed as a ratio of two polynomials is known as a **rational** (RATIO-nal) **function**. According to this definition, any polynomial function must itself be a rational function, since it can always be written as

Figure 2.12

Total Cost =
$100Q - 15Q^2 + Q^3$

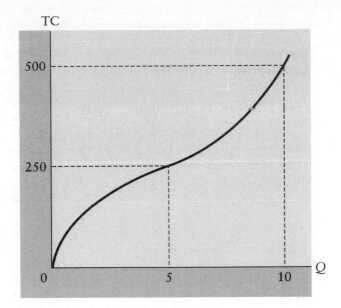

a ratio to 1, which is a constant polynomial function. An example of a rational function is

$$Y = f(X) = \frac{X + 1}{X^2 - 2X + 5} \tag{2-18}$$

A special rational function that has many applications in economics is the function

$$Y = \frac{a}{X} \quad \text{or} \quad XY = a, \tag{2-19}$$

a = constant, $x \neq 0$, both X and Y real numbers

rectangular hyperbola: the graph of functions that have the form $Y = k/X$.

The graph of this function is a ***rectangular hyperbola,*** which has the property that it never touches the axes. Rather, it approaches the axes asymptotically, which means that it gets closer and closer to the axes without ever touching them.

Examples of this type of rational function include unit elastic demand functions and average fixed cost. Consider the following demand function:

$$Q = f(P) \quad \text{or} \quad PQ = a_0 \tag{2-20}$$

Recognize that PQ also equals total revenue, TR, which is constant for this demand curve. Elasticity of demand, which we treat in more detail in Chapter 3, measures the responsiveness of quantity demanded to changes in price, or

$$\varepsilon_{QP} = \frac{\text{percentage change in quantity demanded}}{\text{percentage change in price}} \tag{2-21}$$

Equation (2-20) describes a demand curve for which elasticity of demand must be equal to -1, no matter what the price. This is true because, for total revenue to remain constant, any percentage change in price must be accompanied by an equal but opposite percentage change in quantity. Therefore, the numerator in (2-21) will always be equal but opposite in sign to the denominator, and elasticity equals -1. The average revenue curve corresponding to this demand function is graphed in Figure 2.13.

Let's look at a second example of a rational function, the average fixed cost curve. Given that fixed cost, FC, equals a constant, then average fixed cost, AFC, equals the constant divided by quantity.

$$\text{FC} = a_0 \underset{\text{implies}}{\Rightarrow} \text{AFC} = \frac{\text{FC}}{Q} = \frac{a_0}{Q} \tag{2-22}$$

Note that we use the symbol $\Rightarrow$ in (2-22). This symbol can be interpreted to mean "implies." Formally, $A \Rightarrow B$ means that A is true only if B is true. The graph of AFC will always be a rectangular hyperbola. Recall our earlier example of an average cost function which, when multiplied by quantity, gave us a long-run total cost curve. The reason it had to be a long-run total cost was that it passed through the origin; there was no fixed cost. If we want short-run cost curves, we need to incorporate fixed costs into our functional forms.

Consider the following short-run average total cost (SRATC) function.

$$\text{SRATC} = \underbrace{\frac{a_0}{Q}}_{\text{AFC}} + \underbrace{a_1 + a_2 Q + a_3 Q^2}_{\text{AVC}} \tag{2-23}$$

Figure 2.13

$P = a_0/Q$

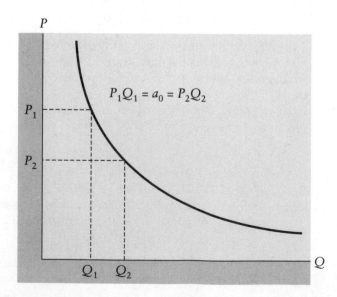

$P_1 Q_1 = a_0 = P_2 Q_2$

Recognize that this average cost function is the sum of a rational function (AFC) and a quadratic function, which is average variable cost (AVC). If we multiply SRATC by quantity Q, we find short-run total cost (SRTC).

$$\text{SRTC} = (\text{SRATC})Q = \left(\frac{a_0}{Q} + a_1 + a_2 Q + a_3 Q^2\right)Q \qquad (2\text{-}24)$$

$$\text{SRTC} = a_0 + a_1 Q + a_2 Q^2 + a_3 Q^3 \qquad (2\text{-}25)$$

As you can see, this total cost function is a cubic function with a positive vertical intercept, a_0, which we can interpret as equal to fixed cost.

There are, of course, many more rational and polynomial functions. However, we do not often see polynomials of degree greater than 3 in economic applications, so now we turn to another class of functions, the nonpolynomials. Nonpolynomial functions, also known as nonalgebraic or transcendental functions, include *exponential functions* and *logarithmic functions*. These are used widely in economic analysis.

EXERCISES
Section 2.4.1
Polynomial
Functions

1. Determine whether each of the following equations is a polynomial and, if so, indicate its degree.
   a. $Y = 0$ b. $Y = 1/\sqrt{X}$
   c. $Y = 1 + X^{1/2} + X^2$ d. $Y = (24X - 1)/(X^2 - 8)$
   e. $Y = \sqrt{(X + 1)}, \ X \geq -1$ f. $Y = 2 + X^4$

2. Use the quadratic formula to solve the following equations.
   a. $3X^2 - 4X + 1 = 0$ b. $X^2 - 4X + 4 = 0$

2.4.2   Exponential Functions

exponential function: a function whose independent variable appears as the exponent of a parameter.

A function whose independent variable appears as the exponent of a parameter is called an *exponential function*. We distinguish between two types of exponential functions: simple exponential functions and generalized exponential functions.

Simple exponential functions take the form

$$Y = f(X) = b^X \qquad (2\text{-}26)$$

where $b > 1$ is a parameter and x is a real-valued variable, so that the domain of the function is the set of all real numbers. Thus, unlike the exponents of a polynomial, the variable exponent, X, is not limited to positive integers.

Although the base (b) can be any real number greater than one, only the numbers 10 and e ($e = 2.7182818\ldots$), the irrational number that is the base of natural logarithms, are commonly used as bases. A base of 10 is used primarily for numerical computational purposes; a base of e has some very nice properties that we will take advantage of using differential calculus.

Because we are not primarily concerned with purely numerical computations, we will restrict ourselves to exponential functions of base e in this text. In this case the resulting function is referred to as a natural exponential function

$$Y = f(X) = e^X \quad \text{or} \quad Y = f(X) = \exp(X) \tag{2-27}$$

This simple exponential function can be generalized to the form

$$Y = f(X) = ae^{cX} \tag{2-28}$$

where a and c are shift and slope parameters. When assigned various values, they will alter the position of the graph of the function, thus generating a whole family of exponential functions.

If both a and c are positive, the graph of the exponential function is generally upward sloping and shaped as in Figure 2.14. The parameter a represents the vertical intercept of the exponential curve and thus may be considered the shift parameter of the curve. As a becomes larger, the entire curve shifts up while keeping its slope, and as a becomes smaller, the curve shifts down. The parameter c may be considered the slope parameter of the exponential function. As the value of c increases, the curve becomes steeper, and as c becomes smaller, the curve becomes flatter.

We frequently see exponential functions in economic applications that require some value to grow over time. For example, population growth may be modeled with the following exponential function.

$$POP_t = f(t) = POP_0 e^{rt} \tag{2-29}$$

In this growth function, POP_t represents the population at some time period t, POP_0 is the population at the starting time period, r is the rate at which

Figure 2.14

Natural Exponential
Functions $Y = ae^{cX}$

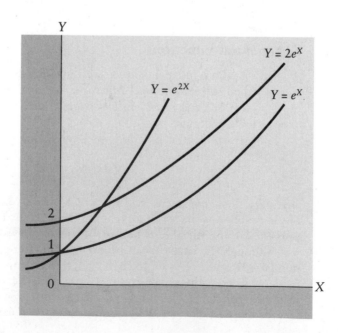

population grows per unit of time (r is assumed constant in this case), and t represents time.

Another useful example of an exponential function is the formula by which the future values, FV_t, at time t of some principal, P, can be calculated. If the principal is invested at a rate of interest, r, expressed as a percentage per year, and compounded continuously for t years, then

$$FV_t = Pe^{rt} \tag{2-30}$$

In order to work with exponential functions, we review the rules that govern the arithmetic manipulation of exponents next.

Rules of Exponents

Recall the following laws concerning the use of exponents.

1. $X^m \cdot X^n = X^{m+n}$
2. $X^{-n} = 1/X^n$
3. $X^m/X^n = X^{m-n}$
4. $X^0 = 1$
5. $(X^m)^n = X^{mn}$
6. $X^n \cdot Y^n = (XY)^n$
7. $X^n/Y^n = (X/Y)^n$

Remember that if exponents appear in fractional form, they can be expressed in root notation

$$X^{a/b} = \sqrt[b]{X^a} \tag{2-31}$$

These rules of exponents are related to one another, and in fact many can be rather easily derived from the rest. For example, let's derive rule 3 from rules 1 and 2. We know that

$$\frac{X^m}{X^n} = X^m\left(\frac{1}{X^n}\right) \tag{2-32}$$

According to rule 2, we can substitute $1/X^n = X^{-n}$ into (2-32), obtaining

$$\frac{X^m}{X^n} = X^m X^{-n} \tag{2-33}$$

Applying rule 1 to (2-32) gives us rule 3,

$$\frac{X^m}{X^n} = X^{m-n} \tag{2-34}$$

EXERCISES
Section 2.4.2
Exponential
Functions

Using the rules of exponents,

1. Simplify the following expressions.

   a. $x^3 x^5$ b. $x^2 y^{-1} x^{-3}$ c. $(x^{12} x^{-5} y^{21})^{1/7}$ d. $(x^3/x^{-3})^{1/2} y^3$

2. Derive rule 4 using rules 2 and 3.

3. Derive rule 5 using rule 1.

2.4.3   Logarithmic Functions

logarithmic function: the
inverse of an exponential
function. The dependent
variable is expressed as
the logarithm of the
independent variable.

Logarithmic functions are very closely related to exponential functions. The logarithm of a number is the exponent or power to which a base must be raised in order to obtain the original number. More formally, the logarithm of a variable Y to the base b, $b > 1$, is the power to which we must raise the base b in order to obtain the value Y

$$Y = b^x \Leftrightarrow \log_b Y = X \qquad (2\text{-}35)$$

The symbol $\Leftrightarrow$ is used to signify that the implication between two expressions works in both directions. When we write $A \Leftrightarrow B$, we mean that, if A is true, so is B, and if B is true, so is A. It can be read "A is true *if and only if (iff)* B is true." As you can see in (2-35), the logarithmic function is the inverse of the exponential function. If $Y = f(X) = b^X$, then $X = f^{-1}(Y) = \log_b Y$. As we saw in the graph of the exponential function, it is monotonic, and so its inverse exists and is also monotonic.

Note that, because the range of the exponential function $Y = b^x$ is the set of all positive real numbers, it follows that the domain of $\log_b Y$ is also the set of all positive real numbers. Logarithms are not defined for negative numbers. On the other hand, because the domain of exponential functions is the set of all real numbers, the range of a logarithmic function is also the set of all real numbers. Therefore, the logarithm of a positive number can be any real number, including negative numbers and the number zero. Any real number b that satisfies the restriction that $b > 1$ can be chosen as the base of logarithms. However, there are two popular choices for the base b, the number 10 and the number e. As in the case of the exponential function, we will restrict ourselves to using e as the base. When e is the base, the logarithm is known as the natural logarithm and is denoted $\log_e$ or, simply, ln.

Rules of Logarithms

1. $\ln e = \log_e e = 1$ 2. $\ln 1 = 0$
3. $\ln XY = \ln X + \ln Y$ 4. $\ln X/Y = \ln X - \ln Y$
5. $\ln X^m = m \ln X$

We have seen that logarithmic functions are the inverse functions of exponential functions. Thus rules of logarithms can be derived from the rules of exponents, keeping in mind that they are inverse functions. For example, recognize that

$$Y = e^{\ln Y} \quad \text{and} \quad X = e^{\ln X} \tag{2-36}$$

If we multiply X times Y and use rule 1 from the rules of exponents, we obtain

$$XY = e^{\ln X} e^{\ln Y} = e^{\ln X + \ln Y} \tag{2-37}$$

Taking the natural log of both sides gives us

$$\ln XY = \ln X + \ln Y \tag{2-38}$$

which you should recognize as rule 3 of the rules of logarithms. Although the examples all use natural logs, the rules apply to logarithms to any base.

The graph of a logarithmic function is the mirror image of (or is symmetrical to) the graph of its associated exponential function with respect to the 45° line drawn through the origin, as the graph of any pair of inverse functions must be. In other words, given the graph of an exponential function, we can obtain the graph of the corresponding logarithmic function by replotting the original graph with the two axes transposed.

This mirror-image relationship has the following implications. First, in both cases the base, b, determines the curvatures of the graphs. Second, both functions are monotonically increasing. However, whereas the exponential function increases at an increasing rate, the corresponding logarithmic function increases at a decreasing rate. Third, while the exponential function has a positive range, the logarithmic function has a positive domain. On the other hand, while the domain of an exponential function is the set of all real numbers, the range of the logarithmic function is the set of all real numbers. Fourth, the horizontal intercept of a logarithmic function is the same as the vertical intercept of its corresponding exponential function. We picture the graphical relationship between exponential and logarithmic functions in Figure 2.15.

Finally, for any base b satisfying the restriction $b > 1$, we have the following relationships:

$$0 < Y < 1 \Leftrightarrow \log(Y) < 0$$
$$Y = 1 \Leftrightarrow \log(Y) = 0$$
$$Y > 1 \Leftrightarrow \log(Y) > 0$$
$$Y \to \infty \Leftrightarrow \log(Y) \to +\infty$$
$$Y \to 0 \Leftrightarrow \log(Y) \to -\infty$$

EXERCISES
Section 2.4.3
Lorgarithmic
Functions

1. Take logarithms of both sides of the following expressions and simplify, using the rules of logarithms.

   a. $z = (a/b)[x^\beta y^{1-\beta}]^\gamma$ **b.** $Y = (X/Z)^{100}$

2. Prove the rules of logarithms, using the rules of exponents.

Figure 2.15

Graphs of Exponential
and Logarithmic
Functions Compared

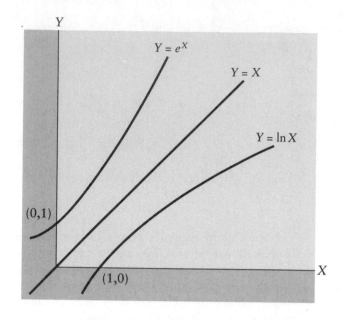

2.5

FUNCTIONS WITH MORE THAN ONE INDEPENDENT VARIABLE

Most economic relationships are multivariate; that is, the dependent variable depends on more than one independent variable. Consider again the very simple models presented in Chapter 1. Quantity demanded was expressed as a function of price and income and quantity supplied was expressed as a function of price and wages.

$$Q_d = Q_d(P, Y) = a - bP + cY \qquad (1\text{-}8)$$

and

$$Q_s = Q_s(P, w) = dP - ew \qquad (1\text{-}9)$$

We solved for equilibrium price and equilibrium quantity and found the reduced-form equations, in which the endogenous variables were expressed as functions of the exogenous variables and parameters.

$$P^* = P^*(Y, w) = \frac{a}{b+d} + \frac{c}{b+d}Y + \frac{e}{b+d}w \qquad (1\text{-}11)$$

and

$$Q^* = Q^*(Y, w) = \frac{ad}{b+d} + \frac{cd}{b+d} Y - \frac{be}{b+d} w \qquad (1\text{-}12)$$

These are examples of functions with two independent variables. They happen to be linear in both independent variables. Of course, functions with multiple independent variables do not have to be linear. For example,

$$Q = f(K, L) = AK^\alpha L^\beta \qquad (2\text{-}39)$$

Cobb-Douglas production function: a general class of production functions that take the form $Y = AX_1^\alpha X_2^\beta$, where Y represents rate of output, X_1 and X_2 represent inputs, and A, α, and β are parameters.

in which Q is output and K and L represent capital and labor, is the well-known *Cobb-Douglas production function*, which we will see again in the next chapter, as well as in Chapters 5 and 10.

Algebraically, functions with multiple independent variables do not present any particular difficulties. Instead of representing a unique mapping from a single argument to a value, they represent a unique mapping from a pair, or triplet, or quadruplet, etc., to a value. When they are expressed in a very general form, a notation in which the independent variables are distinguished by subscripts is employed, as in the following utility function.

$$U = U(X_1, X_2, X_3, \ldots, X_n) \qquad (2\text{-}40)$$

The variable U represents utility and X_i represents the quantity of the ith good consumed. This notation can be read as "utility depends on the quantities consumed of n different goods."

Functions with multiple independent variables do present difficulties when we attempt to graph them. There are three strategies for handling multiple dimensions in a graph. First, three-dimensional space can be pictured graphically, but it is cumbersome and beyond the chalkboard technique of most economics professors, ourselves included. Dimensions greater than three are, of course, completely infeasible to graph. A second strategy is to hold all but one independent variable constant, to isolate the relationship between the single independent variable and the dependent variable of the function. Students of economics will recognize this strategy in the practice of graphing quantity demanded versus price, holding constant income, prices of complements and substitutes, tastes, expectations, and any other demand factors. A change in one of the other factors shifts the demand curve. A third strategy is to use *level curves*, or *contour curves*, to picture a relationship between two independent variables and a dependent variable. This strategy is to graph the behavior of the two independent variables when the dependent variable is held constant at some level. Indifference curves and isoquants are prominent examples of this strategy. The last two graphing strategies are illustrated in Figure 2.16.

level curves: the graph of the relationship between two independent variables when the dependent variable is held constant at some level. Also called a contour curve.

contour curve: same as a level curve.

The graph of the demand curve follows convention, showing price plotted on the vertical axis versus quantity on the horizontal axis, holding constant all other independent variables, such as the price of substitutes, price of complements, and income (P_s, P_c, Y). If Y changes to Y', the entire demand curve shifts (to the right for a normal good). The graph of the indifference curves shows the two independent variables, X_1 and X_2, plotted on the axes, while utility is held constant along the level curve.

Figure 2.16

(*a*) Demand Curves;
(*b*) Indifference Curves

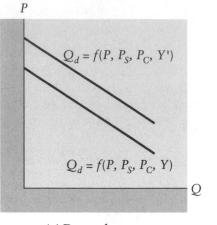

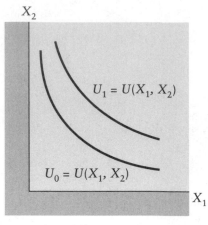

(a) Demand curves

(b) Indifference curves

2.6

SUMMARY

This chapter introduces the mathematical concepts of relations and functions and examines the properties of some specific functions that are especially useful in economic applications. We need to be comfortable with functional notation and specific functional forms so that we can express economic explanations in mathematical language. Functions permit us to do this and at almost any level of generality. Relations are the most general; they say only that there exists some connection between one thing and another. Functions, which assign a unique value to one variable for any value or set of values of the other variable(s), permit us to express dependence in a relation. We can be even more specific about the nature of a relation by suggesting a particular functional form, such as a polynomial or logarithmic function. The most specific (and least general) information is incorporated in functions that assume not only a functional form but also the numerical values of the coefficients and constants in the function.

The important thing to remember about generality and specificity in economic modeling is this: specificity and detail are wonderful and yield very exact predictions and explanations *if the specifics and details are entirely accurate.* Generality in a model is a virtue when you are unsure about all the details of a relationship. It permits a model to apply to situations in which the details differ. As you are already aware, we actually know very little about the social relationships that affect economic behavior. This fact suggests that we need to be careful when we incorporate detail in our functional forms, and that we strive for just enough detail to allow us to generate useful substantive hypotheses without losing generality.

Functional notation and functional forms are what we need to express a problem and choose a theory in our method of economic reasoning. The next step is to determine equilibrium conditions; that is to use our theory to describe economic behavior. It turns out that differential calculus provides us with some extremely useful techniques for determining equilibrium conditions in a wide range of economic models. For this reason, we turn to a review of basic differential calculus in the next chapter.

◆ REFERENCES

Allen, R. G. D., *Mathematical Analysis for Economists* (New York: St. Martin's Press, Inc., 1938), Chapters 1, 2, and 3.

Barnett, Raymond A. and Ziegler, Michael R., *College Mathematics for Business, Economics, Life Sciences, and Social Sciences*, 5th edition (San Francisco: Dellen Publishing Company, 1990), Chapters 1, 2, and 3.

Chiang, Alpha C., *Fundamental Methods of Mathematical Economics*, 3rd edition (New York: McGraw-Hill Book Company, 1984), Chapter 2.

◆ ANSWERS TO END-OF-SECTION EXERCISES

Section 2.3: Functions

a. All are functions except 4, 8, and 10.

b. Equations 2, 5, and 6 represent monotonic functions whose inverse functions are $X = Y/5$, $X = 5/Y$, and $X = Y/5$, respectively.

c. All are explicit except 8 and 9. Equation 8 is a relation. Equation 9 can be written explicitly as $Y = X^2$.

d. Equation 14 represents a composite function; it can be written $Y = 4Z - 2Z^2$.

Section 2.4.1: Polynomial Functions

1. Only equations a and f are polynomials. Equation a is a polynomial of degree zero, a constant function. Equation f is a fourth-degree polynomial. Note that equation d is a rational function, a ratio of a first-degree polynomial to a second-degree polynomial.

2. **a.** $X = 1, 1/3$ **b.** $X = 2$.

Section 2.4.2: Exponential Functions

1. **a.** x^8 **b.** $(xy)^{-1}$ **c.** xy^3 **d.** $(xy)^3$.

2. From rule 2 and rule 3, we write $X^n/X^n = X^n X^{-n} = 1$. Applying rule 1 gives us $X^n/X^n = X^{n-n} = X^0 = 1$, which is rule 4.

3. Given the meaning of an exponent along with rule 1, we write

$$(X^m)^n = \underbrace{X^m X^m X^m X^m \cdots}_{n \text{ times}} = \underbrace{X^{m+m+m+m+\cdots}}_{n \text{ times}}$$

Factoring the m in the exponent gives us rule 5, $(X^m)^n = X^{mn}$.

Section 2.4.3: Logarithmic Functions

1. **a.** $\ln z = \ln a - \ln b + \gamma\beta \ln x + \gamma(1 - \beta) \ln y$

   b. $\ln Y = 100(\ln X - \ln Z)$.

2. Rule 1. Let $e = e^1$. Take the natural log of both sides, yielding $\ln e = 1$, which is rule 1 of logarithms.

   Rule 2. From rule 4 of exponents we write $e^0 = 1$. Take the natural log of both sides, yielding $0 = \ln 1$, which is rule 2 of logarithms.

   Rule 3. This question was answered in the chapter in Section 2.4.3.

   Rule 4. Let $Y = e^{\ln Y}$ and $X = e^{\ln X}$. If we divide X by Y and use rule 3 from the rules of exponents, we obtain $X/Y = e^{\ln X}/e^{\ln Y} = e^{\ln X - \ln Y}$. Taking the natural log of both sides gives us $\ln X/Y = \ln X - \ln Y$, which is rule 4 of logarithms.

   Rule 5. Let $X = e^{\ln X}$. Then $X^m = (e^{\ln X})^m$. According to rule 5 of exponents, we can write $X^m = e^{m\ln X}$. Taking the natural log of both sides gives us $\ln X^m = m \ln X$, which is rule 5 of logarithms.

◆ SELF-HELP PROBLEMS

Answers to these problems are given at the end of the text.

1. Determine the domain and range of each of the following relations and indicate which of them are functions:

   a. $Y = e^{(2X)}$ **b.** $Y = \log(X)$

   c. $Y = |X|$ **d.** $Y = c$, where c is a constant.

2. You are given the following information.

$$\text{Quantity demanded} = Q = f(P) = 100 - 2P$$
$$\text{AR} = f^{-1}(Q), \text{TR} = (\text{AR})Q$$
$$\text{Average cost} = \text{AC} = 20$$
$$\text{TC} = (\text{AC})Q, \pi = \text{TR} - \text{TC}$$

   a. Find expressions for average revenue (AR) and total revenue (TR) as functions of quantity, and sketch the graphs of both (in different graphs). Find the quantity where total revenue is at a maximum.

   b. Find an expression for total cost (TC) as a function of quantity. Sketch the total cost function on the same set of axes as total revenue.

   c. Find an expression for profit (π) as a function of quantity. What is its functional form? Sketch the profit function on the same set of axes as total revenue and total cost. Be sure to show where it crosses the horizontal axis and where it is at a maximum.

3. Suppose that quantity demanded is a linear function of price, and it has a negative slope. Average cost is a constant function. Profit equals total revenue minus total cost.

   a. Give algebraic expressions for quantity demanded and for average cost.

   b. Find expressions for average revenue and total revenue as functions of quantity, and sketch the graphs of both (in different graphs). Find the quantity where total revenue is at a maximum.

   c. Find an expression for total cost as a function of quantity. Sketch the total cost function on the same set of axes as total revenue.

    d. Find an expression for profit as a function of quantity. What is its functional form? Sketch the profit function on the same set of axes as total revenue and total cost. Be sure to show where it crosses the horizontal axis and where its turning point is.

4. Consider the following special forms of demand functions, where Q is quantity demanded, P is price, and Y is income. These are called semilog functional forms because only one side of the equation is expressed in logs. For each of these functions determine the original function whose logarithmic transformation yields the semilog function. In each case draw a picture of the original function holding income constant.

    a. $Q = \alpha + \gamma \ln Y - \beta \ln P$ **b.** $\ln Q = \alpha + \gamma Y - \beta P$

◆ SUPPLEMENTAL PROBLEMS

1. Find five ordered pairs from the following relations, and picture them graphically. For each, determine whether or not x can be considered a function of y, and y can be considered a function of x.

    a. $\{(x, y); y = x \text{ and } x \geq 0\}$ **b.** $\{(x, y); -x \leq y \leq x\}$

2. Demand functions can be specified in two ways: quantity as a function of price, $Q = f(P)$, or price as a function of quantity, $P = g(Q)$. What mathematical properties of demand functions allow us to do this?

3. For each of the following relations, find five ordered pairs, graph the relation, and determine whether or not the relation is a function.

    a. $\{(x, y); y = x\}$ **b.** $\{(x, y); y = x \text{ and } x \geq 0\}$ **c.** $\{(x, y); y \leq x\}$

4. For the following demand functions, (i) find and graph the average revenue function, (ii) find and graph the total revenue function, and (iii) find the quantity at which total revenue is at a maximum.

    a. $Q = 50 - 2P$ **b.** $Q = 125/P$ **c.** $Q = 10 - \ln P, 1 \leq P \leq 725$

5. Graph each of the following functions and determine whether or not it is monotonic. If it is monotonic, find and graph its inverse. If it is not monotonic, restrict the domain so that it is.

    a. $y = x$ **b.** $y = x^2 + 1$ **c.** $Y = 1/X$ **d.** $Y = -2X^2 + 5$

6. Graph each of the following quadratic functions. Use the quadratic formula to find the X intercepts, if there are any.

    a. $Y = -X^2 + 4X - 3$ **b.** $Y = -39X + 6X^2$

    c. $Y = -25 + 10X - X^2$

7. Consider the following functions:

    (i) $Y = f(X) = a_0 + a_1 X$

    (ii) $Y = f(X) = a_0 + a_1 X + a_2 X^2$

    (iii) $Y = f(X) = a_0 + a_1 X + a_2 X^2 + a_3 X^3$

    (iv) $Y = f(X) = a/X$

For each of the following pairs of variables, indicate which of the above functional forms you would choose to represent the relationship and why:

    a. average fixed cost (Y) and output (X)

    b. total fixed cost (Y) and output (X)

    c. short-run total cost (Y) and output (X)

    d. marginal cost (Y) and output (X)

    e. quantity (Y) and price (X) for a unit-elastic-demand curve.

8. Consider a unit-elastic-demand function and a standard U-shaped average cost function that is symmetrical about its minimum point.

    a. Give algebraic expressions for quantity demanded (Q) as a function of price (P) and for average cost (AC) as a function of output (Q). Be sure to specify the signs of the parameters that enter these functions. Identify the functional form of each of these and sketch their graphs in two different pictures.

    b. Find expressions for average revenue (AR) and total revenue (TR) and sketch their graphs in two different pictures. Comment on the results.

    c. Find an expression for total cost (TC) as a function of quantity and sketch its graph on the same axes as total revenue. Interpret the graph.

    d. Find an expression for profit (π) as a function of quantity. What is its functional form? Sketch the graph of this profit function and comment on its shape.

9. Recall the Cobb–Douglas production function of Section 2.5,

$$Q = f(K, L) = AK^\alpha L^\beta$$

where Q is output, K is input of capital (machine hour), L is input of labor (worker hour), and A is a positive constant.

    a. Using rules of logarithms, take the natural log of both sides of this function.

    b. What functional form best represents this function? Why?

    c. Using all three of the strategies for handling multiple dimensions in a graph (see Section 2.5), graph the logarithmic transformation of the function that you found in part b. Be sure to label the axes and the curves properly in each case.

C H A P T E R   3

Derivatives with Economic Applications

3.1

INTRODUCTION

This chapter reviews the fundamentals of differential calculus using economic applications as examples. Its purpose is to provide enough familiarity with differential calculus so that we can proceed to economic modeling in subsequent chapters. There are two reasons why one cannot overstate the usefulness of differential calculus to economic analysis. Both reasons are related to the comparative statics methodology of economic reasoning.

The first reason has to do with formulating equilibrium conditions when creating a model. Frequently, equilibrium occurs where something has been maximized or minimized. For example, equilibrium in consumer models occurs where the consumer maximizes utility for a given budget. Equilibrium in producer models occurs where the producer maximizes profit, or where the producer minimizes the cost of producing a given rate of output. There exist some useful techniques for maximizing or minimizing (generically, we say optimizing for both) that require us to find the derivative of (that is, to differentiate) some objective function. We elaborate on this notion in Chapters 4, 6 and 7.

The second reason for the usefulness of differential calculus to economic analysis has to do with the substantive hypotheses generated by the comparative statics methodology. Recall our discussion of the method of economic reasoning in Chapter 1. In describing the methodology of comparative statics, we suggested that the substantive hypotheses generated by economic models explained how dependent, or endogenous, variables respond to changes in parameters or exogenous variables. In our examples, we saw how equilibrium price and quantity changed when income changed and how national income and aggregate consumption changed when investment changed. Mathematically, we express responses of one variable to changes in another as a rate of

51

change of one variable with respect to changes in another. For a linear function, this rate of change is constant and is equal to the slope of the function. For example, in equations (1-11) and (1-12) we found the following reduced-form equations for equilibrium price and quantity:

$$P^* = \frac{a}{b+d} + \frac{c}{b+d}Y + \frac{e}{b+d}w \tag{1-11}$$

and

$$Q^* = \frac{ad}{b+d} + \frac{cd}{b+d}Y - \frac{be}{b+d}w \tag{1-12}$$

These are linear functions in Y and w. The rate of change of P^* with respect to changes in Y, holding w constant, equals

$$\frac{\Delta P^*}{\Delta Y} = \frac{c}{b+d} > 0 \tag{3-1}$$

The rate of change of Q^* with respect to changes in w, holding Y constant, equals

$$\frac{\Delta Q^*}{\Delta w} = \frac{-be}{b+d} < 0 \tag{3-2}$$

Unfortunately, most economic relationships cannot be described as linear functions, so the rate of change of one variable with respect to changes in another is not constant and is not so easily determined. When a slope is not constant, we must refer either to the slope over an interval or to the slope at a point. Intervals are cumbersome and imprecise, so we need to develop a technique for finding the slope at a point, or the *instantaneous* rate of change of one variable with respect to changes in another. As you may already know, the slope of a function at a point is its **derivative** at that point, and the technique for finding the instantaneous rate of change of one variable with respect to changes in another is known as **differentiation**. If $Y = f(X)$, then the derivative equals

derivative: the instantaneous rate of change of a dependent variable with respect to a change in an independent variable, or the slope of the line tangent to a function at a point.

differentiation: the act of determining the derivative of a function.

limit: the value of a function as the argument approaches some value.

$$\frac{dY}{dX} \equiv f'(X) \equiv \lim_{\Delta X \to 0} \frac{\Delta Y}{\Delta X} \tag{3-3}$$

In order to understand the applications of differentiation to economics, it is helpful to review what a derivative is. To do that we must review *limits* first.

3.2

LIMITS

Limits tell us how the value of a function behaves as the argument approaches some number. For example, if Y is some function of X,

$$\lim_{X \to n} Y = C \tag{3-4}$$

reads "as X approaches n, Y approaches C," or "the limit of Y as X approaches n equals C." The limit is a useful concept because there are times (when a function is discontinuous) when the value of a function *at* a particular value of its argument is very different from its value as the argument *approaches* that point. Moreover, there are times when the value of a function is undefined at a point but we need to know its behavior as it approaches that point. Recall equation (3-3), our definition of a derivative as an instantaneous rate of change of Y with respect to a change in X. In this case, the expression $\Delta Y/\Delta X$ is undefined if $\Delta X = 0$, so to discover the behavior of $\Delta Y/\Delta X$ we must find the limit of the ratio as ΔX approaches 0.

3.2.1 Evaluating ("Taking") Limits

The general approach to evaluating limits is to let X approach a certain number n and observe the value to which Y approaches. In other words, we take limits by inspection. Note that, when possible (that is, when X is not approaching either $+\infty$ or $-\infty$), the limit must be the same whether X approaches from the right (numbers greater than n) or from the left (numbers less than n). If this is the case, the limit is said to exist. If not, the limit does not exist. In what follows, we first illustrate the general process of evaluating limits by way of some examples and then look at some general rules for evaluating limits.

NUMERICAL EXAMPLES

1. Given $Y = 2 + X^2$, find the limit of Y as $X \to 0$. To find the left-side limit, substitute a series of negative values $(-1, -0.10, -0.0010, -0.00010, \dots)$ for X, and observe that Y decreases steadily and approaches 2 (since X^2 gets smaller and smaller and eventually approaches zero). To find the right-side limit, substitute a series of positive values $(1, 0.10, 0.0010, 0.00010, \dots)$, and observe that the same limit is obtained. Since both limits are equal, we consider the limit of $f(X)$ as X approaches 0 to be 2 and write

$$\lim_{X \to 0} (2 + X^2) = 2 \tag{3-5}$$

Note that in this example it appears that to obtain the limit of Y as X approaches 0 all we have to do is set $X = 0$ and solve for Y. However, this is a special case; the general rule is that $X \to n$ does not mean $X = n$. In general, we should avoid substituting in $X = n$ as it can get us in trouble. For example, if n is not in the domain of the function and if we try to substitute n for X in the function, obviously Y will not be defined. The following example illustrates this point.

2. Given $Y = (1 - X^2)/(1 - X)$, find the limit of Y as $X \to 1$. Note that here $X = 1$ is not in the domain of f, so if we simply substitute 1 for X the resulting ratio will be of the form 0/0, which is undefined. Furthermore, in this case the approach we used in example 1 will not work either, because as $X \to 1$ both the numerator and the denominator approach 0 and division is impossible.

One way out of this difficulty is to transform the ratio so that X is not in the denominator. Since $X \to 1$ implies $X \neq 1$, we can divide the numerator and denominator by $(1 - X)$ to get $Y = 1 + X$, $X \neq 1$. Now the limit of Y as $X \to 1$ equals 2 from either side. Thus we conclude that

$$\lim_{X \to 1} \left(\frac{1 - X^2}{1 - X} \right) = 2 \qquad (3\text{-}6)$$

3. Given

$$Y = \frac{2X + 5}{X + 1} \qquad (3\text{-}7)$$

find the limit of Y as $X \to +\infty$. Again, X appears in both the numerator and denominator. This means that simply substituting ∞ for X will result in a ratio of the form ∞/∞, which is undefined. To solve this problem, we should try to get X out of the numerator (compare this with example 2, where we took X out of the denominator). This can be accomplished simply by carrying out the division to get

$$Y = 2 + \frac{3}{X + 1} \qquad (3\text{-}8)$$

Now, since the denominator approaches (∞) as (X) approaches $(+\infty)$, it follows that

$$\lim_{X \to +\infty} \left(\frac{2X + 5}{X + 1} \right) = 2 \qquad (3\text{-}9)$$

In the numerical examples we illustrate some approaches to taking limits that depend on manipulating particular expressions. The process of taking limits can be simplified somewhat by making use of general rules that can apply to more general classes of functions. We now present some useful rules for evaluating limits.

Rules for Evaluating Limits

Single Function Rules $Y = f(X)$ as $X \to n$	Examples
1. If $Y = aX + b$, then $\lim\limits_{X \to n} Y = an + b$	$\lim\limits_{X \to 2} (2X + 6) = 10$
2. If $Y = C$, then $\lim\limits_{X \to n} Y = C$	$\lim\limits_{X \to 2} 5 = 5$
3. If $Y = X$, then $\lim\limits_{X \to n} Y = n$	$\lim\limits_{X \to 8} X = 8$
4. If $Y = X^k$, then $\lim\limits_{X \to n} Y = n^k$	$\lim\limits_{X \to 2} X^{10} = 1024$
5. If $Y = f(X)$, then $\lim\limits_{X \to n} kY = k \lim\limits_{X \to n} Y$	$Y = 2X + 6$ $\lim\limits_{X \to 2} 3Y = 30$

Note that in the first three rules we simply substituted n for X in $f(X)$ to obtain the limit of Y as X approaches n. But these are special cases. In general, $X \to n$ does not necessarily mean that $X = n$.

Suppose we have two functions of the same independent variable, $Y = f(X)$ and $Z = g(X)$, and they both have finite limits as $X \to n$. Then the following rules apply:

Rules Involving Two Functions	Examples
6. $\lim\limits_{X \to n}(Y \pm Z) = \lim\limits_{X \to n} Y \pm \lim\limits_{X \to n} Z$	$\lim\limits_{X \to 1}(X^2 + 4X) = \lim\limits_{X \to 1} X^2 + \lim\limits_{X \to 1} 4X = 5$
7. $\lim\limits_{X \to n}(YZ) = \lim\limits_{X \to n} Y \cdot \lim\limits_{X \to n} Z$	$\lim\limits_{X \to 1}[(X^2)(4X)] = \lim\limits_{X \to 1} X^2 \cdot \lim\limits_{X \to 1} 4X = 4$
8. $\lim\limits_{X \to n}\left(\dfrac{Y}{Z}\right) = \dfrac{\lim\limits_{X \to n} Y}{\lim\limits_{X \to n} Z}, \lim\limits_{X \to n} Z \neq 0$	$\lim\limits_{X \to 1} \dfrac{X^2}{4X} = \dfrac{\lim\limits_{X \to 1} X^2}{\lim\limits_{X \to 1} 4X} = \dfrac{1}{4}$

We are now prepared to review derivatives. For simplicity, we consider functions of one independent variable, i.e., $Y = f(X)$. We extend the review of calculus to include functions of several variables in Chapter 5.

**EXERCISES
Section 3.2.1
Evaluating
("Taking") Limits**

Find the following limits, if they exist.

1. $\lim\limits_{X \to 2}(X^3 + 1)$

2. $\lim\limits_{X \to 1}(5X^2 - 2X + 1)$

3. $\lim\limits_{X \to -1} \dfrac{(X^2 - 1)}{X + 1}$

4. $\lim\limits_{X \to 0} \dfrac{(X^2 + X)}{X}$

5. $\lim\limits_{X \to 1} \dfrac{(\sqrt{X} - 1)}{X - 1}, X > 0$

6. $\lim\limits_{X \to \infty} \dfrac{(X + 1)}{X}$

3.3

DERIVATIVES

A derivative measures the instantaneous rate of change of a dependent variable with respect to a change in an independent variable. It measures the slope of the line tangent to the graph of a function. Consider the function graphed in Figure 3.1. The ratio of finite changes $\Delta Y/\Delta X$ (called a **difference quotient**) represents the slope of the graph between the points A and C; it is the slope over an interval. As we make ΔX smaller, the interval gets closer to a point. The limit of $\Delta Y/\Delta X$ as ΔX approaches 0 measures the slope of the function at a point, or the slope of the line tangent to the graph at the point. In Figure 3.1, line NN is tangent to the graph at point B, and the slope of the graph of the function at B is the same as the slope of line NN.

difference quotient: a ratio of finite changes, e.g., $\Delta Y/\Delta X$.

$\Delta X \to 0$ pt. tangency

Figure 3.1

The Slope of a
Curvilinear Function
$Y = f(X)$

$$\frac{dY}{dX} \equiv f'(X) \equiv \lim_{\Delta X \to 0} \frac{\Delta Y}{\Delta X}$$

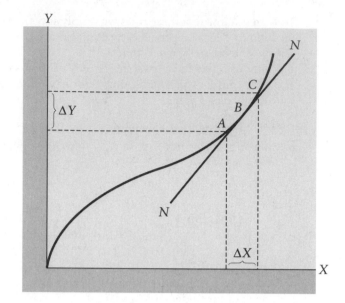

smooth: a function is
smooth if it does not have
sharp corners.

continuous: a function is
continuous at a point if
the function and its limit
exist at that point and are
equal to one another.

A function must be **smooth** and **continuous** at the point where we wish
to find the derivative. Mathematically, a function $Y = f(X)$ is continuous at
the point $x = c$ if

1. $\lim_{X \to c} f(X)$ exists.   2. $f(c)$ exists.

3. $\lim_{X \to c} f(X) = f(c)$.

These conditions mean that the function has values for all points in the
domain and that the value at any point is not radically different from the value
at neighboring points. An example of a function that is not continuous is
$Y = f(X) = 1/X^2$. At the point $X = 0$ the value is undefined; that is, $f(0)$ does
not exist. When a function is **discontinuous**, its graph has an interruption.
Either the value does not exist at a point or it makes a jump so that the limit
does not exist at that point or the limit does not equal the value. Look at the
behavior of the graph of $Y = 1/X^2$, shown in Figure 3.2a, around the Y axis.
The graph of the function jumps over the Y axis where $X = 0$ and Y
approaches $+\infty$.

discontinuous: a function
is discontinuous at a point
if the three conditions for
continuity are not satisfied
at that point.

Continuity does not rule out a sharp corner in a function, so we must also
ensure that it is smooth at the point where we wish to find the derivative.
Smoothness ensures that the limit of the difference quotient converges to a
single value. The slope of a function at a sharp corner does not; the limit of
the difference quotient has one value when approaching from the right and
another when approaching from the left. Consider the absolute value function
$Y = f(X) = |X|$, graphed in Figure 3.2b. This function transforms X into
$Y = X$ if $X \geq 0$ and $Y = -X$ if $X < 0$. Therefore, it has a sharp corner at
$X = 0$. The limit of the difference quotient as ΔX approaches zero *from the
left*, denoted $\Delta X \to 0^-$, equals

$$\lim_{\Delta X \to 0^-} \frac{\Delta Y}{\Delta X} = \lim_{\Delta X \to 0^-} \frac{-(0 - X)}{0 - X} = -1 \qquad (3\text{-}10)$$

Figure 3.2

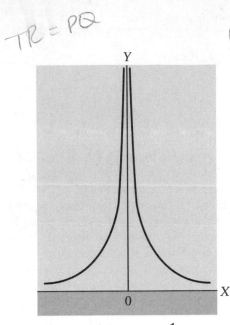

(a) Graph of $Y = \dfrac{1}{X^2}$

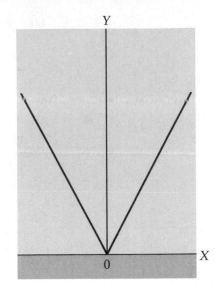

(b) Graph of $Y = |X|$

If we approach $X = 0$ from the right, denoted $\Delta X \to 0^+$, we obtain

$$\lim_{\Delta X \to 0^+} \frac{\Delta Y}{\Delta X} = \lim_{\Delta X \to 0^+} \frac{X - 0}{X - 0} = +1 \qquad (3\text{-}11)$$

Because the limit as ΔX approaches 0 from the left differs from the limit as ΔX approaches 0 from the right, the limit does not exist, and the function is not smooth at the point $X = 0$. There is no single line tangent to the graph of the function at that point, so we cannot find a unique value for the derivative there. A function that is smooth and continuous is said to be ***differentiable***.[1]

differentiable: a function is differentiable if it is both smooth and continuous.

Let's use the definition of a derivative to find the derivative of a familiar function, the linear demand function from Chapter 1.

$$Q = f(P) = a - bP$$

We find the change in Q by subtracting Q_1 from Q_2.

$$\Delta Q = Q_2 - Q_1$$
$$\Delta Q = (a - bP_2) - (a - bP_1)$$
$$\Delta Q = a - a - b(P_2 - P_1)$$
$$\Delta Q = -b(\Delta P)$$

$$\frac{\Delta Q}{\Delta P} = -b$$

[1]All polynomial, exponential, and logarithmic functions are smooth and continuous, and therefore differentiable, over their entire domain.

Take the limit as $\Delta P \to 0$:

$$\lim_{\Delta P \to 0} \left(\frac{\Delta Q}{\Delta P} \right) \equiv \frac{dQ}{dP} = -b$$

We have followed the convention of graphing the inverse of the demand curve, $AR = P = a/b - (1/b)Q$ in Figure 3.3. You should try to find the derivative of the inverse function, dP/dQ, as an exercise, by taking the limit of the difference quotient as ΔQ approaches 0.

The derivative of a linear demand curve is a particularly easy example. The slope is a constant, so it is the same no matter what the value of Q and no matter what the size of the interval. Let's choose a slightly more difficult example to illustrate what a derivative is. As we showed in Chapter 2, Section 2.4, if demand is linear, total revenue, TR, is a second-degree polynomial. Let $TR = f(Q) = a_1 Q + a_2 Q^2$, where $a_2 < 0 < a_1$. We know that $\Delta TR = f(Q_2) - f(Q_1)$, and $\Delta Q = Q_2 - Q_1$. Therefore $\Delta TR / \Delta Q$ equals

$$\frac{\Delta TR}{\Delta Q} = \frac{f(Q_2) - f(Q_1)}{Q_2 - Q_1} = \frac{(a_1 Q_2 + a_2 Q_2^2) - (a_1 Q_1 + a_2 Q_1^2)}{Q_2 - Q_1} \qquad (3\text{-}12)$$

Rearranging the terms gives us

$$\frac{\Delta TR}{\Delta Q} = \frac{a_1(Q_2 - Q_1) + a_2(Q_2^2 - Q_1^2)}{Q_2 - Q_1} \qquad (3\text{-}13)$$

Note that, if $\Delta Q = Q_2 - Q_1$, then $Q_2 = Q_1 + \Delta Q$. Substitute these expressions into (3-13) to obtain

$$\frac{\Delta TR}{\Delta Q} = \frac{a_1 \Delta Q + a_2[(Q_1 + \Delta Q)^2 - Q_1^2]}{\Delta Q} \qquad (3\text{-}14)$$

$\longrightarrow$ con't

Figure 3.3

The Graph of
$AR = P = a/b - (1/b)Q$

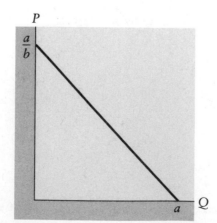

Multiply out the squared expression to get

$$\frac{\Delta TR}{\Delta Q} = \frac{a_1\,\Delta Q + a_2[Q_1^2 + 2Q_1\,\Delta Q + \Delta Q^2 - Q_1^2]}{\Delta Q}$$

$$\frac{a_1\,\Delta Q + 2a_2Q_1\,\Delta Q + a_2\Delta Q^2}{\Delta Q} \tag{3-15}$$

Canceling ΔQ leaves us with

$$\frac{\Delta TR}{\Delta Q} = a_1 + 2a_2Q_1 + a_2\,\Delta Q \tag{3-16}$$

Take the limit as ΔQ approaches 0.

$$\lim_{\Delta Q \to 0} \frac{\Delta TR}{\Delta Q} = \lim_{\Delta Q \to 0}(a_1 + 2a_2Q_1 + a_2\,\Delta Q) = a_1 + 2a_2Q_1 = \frac{dTR}{dQ} \equiv f'(Q) \tag{3-17}$$

Both the total revenue function and its derivative are pictured in Figure 3.4. Note that whereas the total revenue function is a polynomial of degree 2, its derivative is a polynomial of degree 1. Note also that, while TR is rising, its derivative (or slope) is positive, and that while TR is falling, its derivative is negative. Remember that in Chapter 2, Section 2.4, we found the maximum

Figure 3.4

Graph of
$TR = f(Q) = a_1Q + a_2Q^2$
and Its Derivative,
$TR' = a_1 + 2a_2Q$

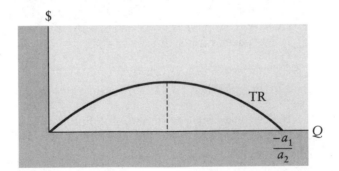

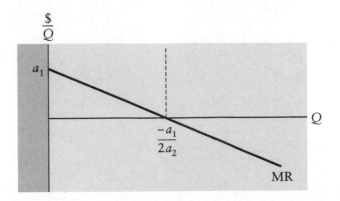

marginal revenue (MR): the incremental revenue for an increase in quantity.

of an inverted U-shaped parabola to be midway between its X intercepts. The derivative or slope of the parabola equals zero at that point. The derivative of total revenue with respect to quantity has an economic interpretation; it is the incremental revenue for a change in quantity and is called *marginal revenue*, or *MR*.

EXERCISES
Section 3.3
Derivatives

1. Determine whether each of the following functions is continuous and, if not, indicate the point(s) at which it is not continuous.

    a. $Y = f(x) = 5X^2 + 4X - 2$ b. $Y = f(X) = 1/X$

    c. $Y = f(X) = (2X^2 - 4X + 1)^3$ d. $Y = f(X) = \sqrt{(X^2 + 1)}$

    e. $Y = f(X) = (X^2 + X - 2)/(X - 1)$

2. Given that total cost equals $TC = a_0 + a_1 Q^2$, find marginal cost (the derivative of TC with respect to Q) by taking the limit of $\Delta TC/\Delta Q$ as ΔQ approaches zero.

3.4

RULES OF DIFFERENTIATION

We need not go through the process of limit taking each time we wish to take the derivative of a differentiable function. This is because there are several rules of differentiation that allow us to take the derivative of a given function directly. Let's review these rules using the simple case of functions of one independent variable, i.e., $Y = f(X)$.

3.4.1   Differentiation of Polynomial or Algebraic Functions

Rules for a Single Differentiable Function

Rule 1: Power Function Rule

$$Y = f(X) = X^n$$

$$\frac{dY}{dX} \equiv f'(X) = nX^{n-1}$$

Examples

Production function with one input;

$$Q = f(L) = L^\alpha$$

$$\frac{dQ}{dL} \equiv f'(L) = \alpha L^{\alpha-1}$$

Rule 2: Constant Function Rule

$$Y = f(X) = k$$

$$\frac{dY}{dX} \equiv f'(X) = 0$$

This can be derived from rule 1.

$$Y = k = kX^0$$

$$\frac{dY}{dX} = 0kX^{-1} = 0$$

$$y = x^4$$
$$\frac{dy}{dx} = 4x^3$$

Rule 3: Inverse Function Rule

If $f(X)$ is monotonic, and

The inverse of the demand curve is average revenue.

$$Y = f(X), \text{ so that } X = f^{-1}(Y),$$

If $Q_d = a - bP$, then $\dfrac{dQ}{dP} = -b$

then $\dfrac{dX}{dY} \equiv f^{-1\prime}(Y) = \dfrac{1}{dY/dX} \equiv \dfrac{1}{f'(X)}$

$P = \dfrac{a}{b} - \dfrac{1}{b}Q$, and $\dfrac{dP}{dQ} = -\dfrac{1}{b}$

Two or More Functions of the Same Independent Variable

In the previous rules, we were concerned with a single function. Now suppose our dependent variable is some combination of two differentiable functions of the same independent variable, X, say $f(X)$ and $g(X)$, and we want to differentiate the sum, difference, product, or ratio of these two functions. For these we have the following rules:

Rule 4: Sum-Difference Rule

Examples

$$Y = f(X) \pm g(X)$$

Total cost $\equiv$ TC $= a + bQ + cQ^2$

$$\dfrac{dY}{dX} = f'(X) \pm g'(X)$$

Marginal cost $\equiv$ MC $= \dfrac{d\text{TC}}{dQ} = b + 2cQ$

The sum-difference rule is applicable to any finite number of functions added or subtracted together. This rule, together with rules 1 and 2 allows us to differentiate any polynomial function, because polynomials are nothing but sums of power functions. Note also that in the case of polynomials the constant term has no effect on the derivative of the function because the derivative of a constant term is zero. That is, in contrast to a multiplicative constant, which is retained during differentiation, an additive constant drops out. This provides the mathematical explanation of the well-known economic principle that fixed cost of a firm does not affect its marginal cost. In the preceding example, a is the constant term of the polynomial and can be interpreted as the fixed component of total cost.

Rule 5: Product Rule

Total cost = (average cost)(quantity)

$$Y = f(X)g(X)$$

TC(Q) = AC$(Q) \cdot Q$

$$\dfrac{dY}{dX} = f(X)g'(X) + g(X)f'(X)$$

$\dfrac{d\text{TC}}{dQ} = \text{TC}'(Q)$

$= \text{AC}(Q)(1) + Q\,\text{AC}'(Q)$

Be aware that this rule is applicable to any finite number of functions. Note also that if $Y = cf(X)$, where c is a constant, the product rule plus the constant-function rule (rule 2) imply that

$$dY/dX = 0f(X) + cf'(x) = cf'(X).$$

Rule 6: Quotient Rule

Average cost = (total cost) ÷ Q

$$Y = \frac{f(X)}{g(X)}$$

$$AC(Q) = \frac{TC(Q)}{Q}$$

$$\frac{dY}{dX} = \frac{g(X)f'(X) - f(X)g'(X)}{[g(X)]^2}$$

$$\frac{dAC(Q)}{dQ} \equiv AC'(Q)$$

$$= \frac{QTC'(Q) - TC(Q)}{Q^2}$$

Close inspection reveals that the examples for the product rule and the quotient role yield exactly the same expression for the relationship between marginal cost and average cost. To see this, take the expression for $TC'(Q)$ that we found in the example for rule 5 and solve for $AC'(Q)$.

Rule 7: Chain Rule or Composite Function Rule

$$Y = f[g(X)]$$

$$C(L) = TC(Q) = TC(f(L))$$

$$\frac{dY}{dX} = \frac{dY}{dg(X)}\frac{dg(X)}{dX} \equiv f'(g)g'(X)$$

$$\frac{dC(L)}{dL} \equiv C'(L) \equiv MFC = TC'(Q)f'(L)$$

$$= \frac{dTC}{dQ}\frac{dQ}{dL} = MC \times MP_L$$

In the example of the chain rule we have recognized that cost, $C(L)$, can be written as a composite function of labor, because total cost, $TC(Q)$, is a function of quantity and quantity is a function of labor, or $Q = f(L)$. When we apply the chain rule we discover that the derivative of cost with respect to labor equals the marginal cost of production times the marginal product of labor.

3.4.2   Differentiation of Nonpolynomial Functions

Recall from Chapter 2, Section 2.4.2, that nonpolynomial functions, also known as nonalgebraic or transcendental functions, include exponential functions and logarithmic functions. Let's look at the differentiation of these functions.

Rule 8: Exponential Function Rule

$$Y = b^{f(X)}, b > 1$$

$$Y = f(X) = e^X$$

$$\frac{dY}{dX} = [f'(X)b^{f(X)}] \ln b$$

$$\frac{dY}{dX} \equiv f'(X) = 1e^X \ln e = e^X$$

The natural exponential function has the interesting property that its derivative is equal to itself. That is, the slope of the function equals the value of the function for all values of X.

Rule 9: Logarithmic Function Rule

We provide this rule as it applies to natural logarithms.

$$Y = f(X) = \ln(g(X))$$
$$\frac{dY}{dX} \equiv f'(X) = \frac{g'(X)}{g(X)}$$

Suppose $Y = \ln(g(X)) = \ln X$. Because $g(X) = X$, $g'(X) = 1$. Therefore, we find

$$\frac{dY}{dX} = f'(X) = \frac{g'(X)}{g(X)} = \frac{1}{X}$$

This rule is easily demonstrated using the inverse function, the chain, and the exponential function rules, numbers 3, 7, and 8. If $Y = \ln(g(X))$, then, according to the chain rule,

$$\frac{dY}{dX} = \frac{d[\ln(g(X))]}{d[g(X)]} \frac{d[g(X)]}{dX} = \frac{d[\ln(g(X))]}{dg(X)} g'(X) \tag{3-18}$$

To find $d[\ln(g(X))]/d[g(X)]$, recognize that the function $Y = f(g(X)) = \ln(g(X))$ has an inverse, $g(X) = f^{-1}(Y) = e^Y$. We can use the exponential function rule to find $d[g(X)]/d[\ln(gX)] = e^Y = e^{\ln(g(X))} = g(X)$. According to the inverse function rule, the derivative $d[\ln(g(X))]/d[g(X)]$ equals the inverse of $d[g(X)]/d[\ln(gX)]$, or $1/g(X)$. Substituting this result into (3-18) gives us

$$\frac{dY}{dX} = \frac{d[\ln(g(X))]}{dg(X)} g'(X) = \frac{g'(X)}{g(X)} \tag{3-19}$$

EXERCISES
Section 3.4.2
Differentiation of Nonpolynomial Functions

Find derivatives for the following functions.

1. $Y = \sqrt{X}$ 2. $Y = 100$
3. $Y = 1/X^2$ 4. $Y = (X^2 + 1)^3 + (X^2 + 1)^2 - 1$
5. $Y = 4e^{-X/4}$ 6. $Y = \ln(5X^2 + 2X + 1)$

If $f(X) = X^3$ and $g(X) = 1/X$, find the following derivatives.

7. $Y = f(X) + g(X)$ 8. $Y = f(X)g(X)$ 9. $Y = f(X)/g(X)$

3.5

SECOND- AND HIGHER-ORDER DERIVATIVES

We have seen that the derivative dY/dX of a function $Y = f(X)$ is itself a function of X, as indicated by the notation $f'(X)$. If $f'(X)$ is continuous and smooth, it will be differentiable with respect to X. The result of this

second-order derivative: the derivative of the derivative of a function.

differentiation is known as the ***second-order derivative*** (or simply second derivative) and is denoted $f''(X)$ or $f^{(2)}(X)$ or d^2Y/dX^2. In other words,

$$\frac{d[f'(X)]}{dX} \equiv \frac{d(dY/dX)}{dX} \equiv \frac{d^2Y}{dX^2} \equiv f''(X) \equiv f^{(2)}(X) \tag{3-20}$$

Second- and higher-order derivatives obey the definition of the derivative. That is,

$$f''(X) = \lim_{\Delta X \to 0} \frac{\Delta f'(X)}{\Delta X} = \lim_{\Delta X \to 0} \frac{f'(X + \Delta X) - f'(X)}{\Delta X} \tag{3-21}$$

If this second derivative exists for all X in the domain, the original (primitive) function, $f(X)$, is said to be twice differentiable. Furthermore, if f'' is continuous, then $f(X)$ is said to be twice continuously differentiable.

Since $f''(X)$ is itself a function of X, it too can be differentiated with respect to X if it is differentiable. The result will be the third-order (or simply the third) derivative of $f(X)$ with respect to X and is denoted $f'''(X)$ or $f^{(3)}(X)$ or d^3Y/dX^3. We can write third-order derivatives as

$$\frac{d[f''(X)]}{dX} \equiv \frac{d(d^2Y/dX^2)}{dX} \equiv \frac{d^3Y}{dX^3} \equiv f'''(X) \equiv f^{(3)}(X) \tag{3-22}$$

This process of obtaining higher-order derivatives can be repeated indefinitely as long as the differentiability conditions are met. Thus, the nth-order derivative of $f(X)$ is

$$\frac{d[f^{(n-1)}(X)]}{dX} \equiv \frac{d(d^{n-1}Y/dX^{n-1})}{dX} \equiv \frac{d^nY}{dX^n} \equiv f^{(n)}(X) \tag{3-23}$$

3.5.1   Interpretation of the Second-Order Derivative

Recall that the first derivative $f'(X)$ of the function $f(X)$ measures the (instantaneous) rate of change or the slope of that function. Similarly, the second derivative f'' measures the rate of change of the first derivative f', that is, the *rate of change of the slope of $f(x)$*. Thus the second derivative measures the *rate of change of the rate of change* of the original function, which we call the ***primitive function***. Knowing the values of the first and second derivatives can give us useful information about the primitive function, such as

primitive function: the original function from which first-, second-, and higher-order derivatives may be taken.

$$f' > 0 \Leftrightarrow Y = f(X) \text{ increases for an infinitesimal increase in } X$$
$$\Leftrightarrow f(X) \text{ is positively sloped}$$

$$f' < 0 \Leftrightarrow Y = f(X) \text{ decreases for an infinitesimal increase in } X$$
$$\Leftrightarrow f(X) \text{ is negatively sloped}$$

$$f'' > \Leftrightarrow f'(X) \text{ increases for an infinitesimal increase in } X$$
$$\Leftrightarrow \text{ slope of } f(X) \text{ increases}$$

$$f'' < 0 \Leftrightarrow f'(X) \text{ decreases for an infinitesimal increase in } X$$
$$\Leftrightarrow \text{ slope of } f(X) \text{ decreases}$$

Therefore, if the first and second derivatives are positive at a point on the curve, the slope of the curve is positive and increasing at that point; the value of the function is increasing at an increasing rate. An example of such a function is illustrated by Figure 3.5, where three graphs showing the primitive function $Y = f(X) = X^2$, its first derivative $f'(X) = 2X$, and its second derivative $f''(X) = 2$ are displayed.

Notice that we have stacked the three graphs vertically. Doing so lets you compare the behavior of the primitive function to that of its derivatives. We

Figure 3.5

Graphs of $Y = X^2$ and Its First and Second Derivatives

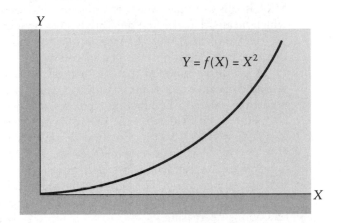

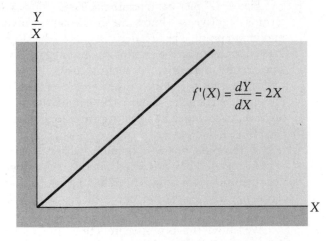

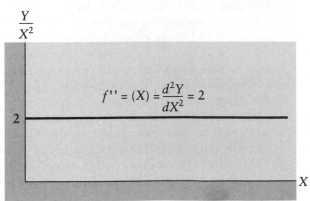

are able to stack them because they are all functions of X, so they all have the same units of X measured along the horizontal axis. Note, however, that they have different units along the vertical axis. The dependent variable of the primitive function is, simply, Y. If it were total cost, for example, Y would be measured in dollar units. The first derivative is the slope of the primitive function, so it is measured in units of Y/X. If it were the derivative of total cost with respect to output, it would be marginal cost and its units would be \$/X. The second derivative is the slope of the slope, so it is measured in units of $(Y/X)/X$, or Y/X^2. The units of the second derivative of total cost would be \$/X^2$. In this example, we see that the first and second derivatives are positive, which means that the first derivative must be increasing (because its slope is positive) and the primitive function must be increasing at an increasing rate (because its slope is positive and increasing).

A primitive function that has a positive first derivative and a negative second derivative at a point has a slope that is positive but decreasing at that point; the value of the function increases at a decreasing rate. This situation is pictured in Figure 3.6, where we graph the primitive function $Y = f(X) = 10X^{1/2}$ and its first and second derivatives. The first derivative, $f'(X) = 5X^{-1/2}$, is positive, while the second derivative, $f''(X) = -(5/2)X^{-3/2}$, is negative. The fact that the first derivative is positive tells us that the primitive function is increasing. The fact that the second derivative is negative tells us that the first derivative has a negative slope, so the slope of the primitive function is decreasing.

Figure 3.7 pictures a parabola, $Y = f(X) = 5X - X^2$. Because the squared term is negative, we know the graph has an inverted U-shaped curve with a maximum point. The first derivative (i.e., the slope) is positive to the left of the maximum, zero at the maximum, and negative to the right of the maximum. The second derivative of such a curve, however, is everywhere negative, indicating that the slope of the curve decreases continuously as X increases. Note, in particular, that to the left of the maximum, where the slope is positive, it becomes less positive (the slope decreases and the curve becomes flatter) as X increases.

To the right of the maximum, where the first derivative is negative, the negative second derivative indicates that the slope of the primitive function is negative and decreasing. This refers to a slope that is negative and is becoming more negative; i.e., the curve is becoming *more negatively steep* as X increases.

We show the primitive function, the first derivative, and the second derivative of a U-shaped parabola, $Y = f(X) = 10 - 5X + X^2$ in Figure 3.8. The first derivative is negative to the left of the minimum, zero at the minimum, and positive to the right of the minimum. The second derivative of this curve, however, is everywhere positive, indicating that the slope of the curve increases as X increases. In particular, to the left of the minimum, where the slope is negative, the slope becomes less negative (it increases and the curve becomes flatter) as X increases.

A positive first derivative coupled with a positive second derivative indicates that the slope of the primitive function is positive and increasing. This refers to a slope that is positive and is becoming steeper. This is the case to the right of the minimum point of the parabola in Figure 3.8.

Finally, note that the second derivative can actually be zero or it can change sign. For example, for the cubic function pictured in Figure 3.9,

Figure 3.6

Graphs of $Y = 10X^{1/2}$ and Its First and Second Derivatives

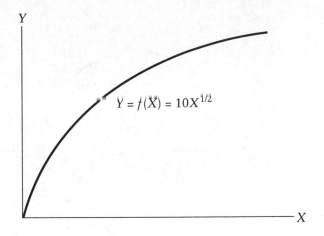

$Y = f(X) = 10X^{1/2}$

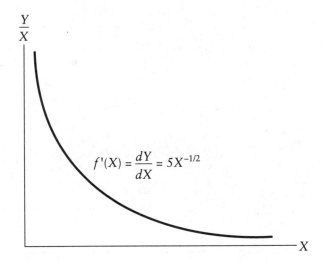

$f'(X) = \dfrac{dY}{dX} = 5X^{-1/2}$

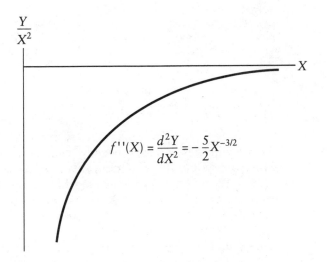

$f''(X) = \dfrac{d^2Y}{dX^2} = -\dfrac{5}{2}X^{-3/2}$

Figure 3.7

Graphs of $Y = 5X - X^2$ and Its First and Second Derivatives

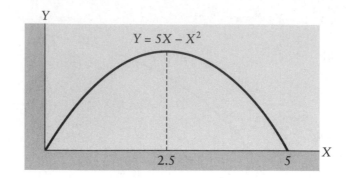

$Y = 5X - X^2$

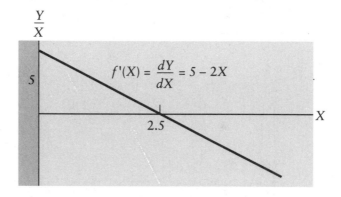

$f'(X) = \dfrac{dY}{dX} = 5 - 2X$

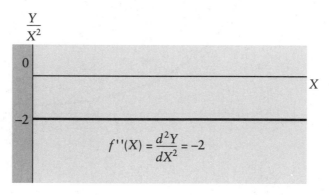

$f''(X) = \dfrac{d^2Y}{dX^2} = -2$

point of inflection: a point on the graph of a primitive function where its slope changes from increasing to decreasing, or vice versa.

$Y = f(X) = 12X - 6X^2 + X^3$ the second derivative equals $f''(X) = -12 + 6X$. It changes sign from negative to positive at $X = 2$, which is a ***point of inflection***. While the first derivative, or the slope of the cubic function, $f'(X) = 12 - 12X + 3X^2$, is greater than or equal to 0 everywhere, it changes from decreasing to increasing at $X = 2$. This point is the point of inflection. Therefore we see a first derivative that is nonnegative throughout, but changes from decreasing to increasing at $X = 2$, and a second derivative that is negative to the left of $X = 2$ and positive to the right. The value of the second derivative equals zero at the point of inflection. In short, whereas the first derivative reflects the *slope* of the graph of a function, the second derivative reflects the *curvature* of the graph of that function.

Figure 3.8

Graphs of
$Y = 10 - 5X + X^2$ and
Its First and Second
Serivatives

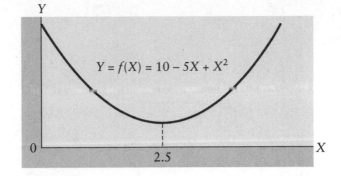

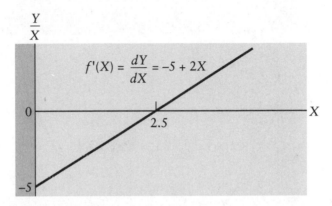

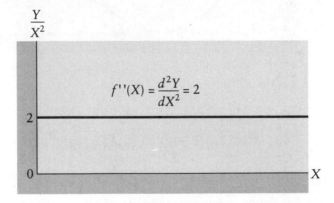

strictly concave function: a function whose graph looks like a concave curve to a viewer looking up from the horizontal axis.

strictly convex function: a function whose graph looks like a convex curve to a viewer looking up from the horizontal axis.

A function whose graph has a decreasing slope, as in Figures 3.6 and 3.7, is considered to be a ***strictly concave function***, because a viewer looking up from the horizontal axis sees a concave curve. Similarly, a function whose graph has an increasing slope, as in Figures 3.5 and 3.8, is a ***strictly convex function***.[2] The function whose graph is pictured in Figure 3.9 is concave from

_____

[2]A function can be concave or convex even though it has a straight line segment in it. *Strict* concavity or convexity rules out straight line segments in the graph of the function. Obviously, strict concavity or convexity is a stronger statement about curvature than concavity or convexity. A strictly concave or convex function is necessarily also concave or convex, but the converse is not true.

Figure 3.9

Graphs of
$Y = 12X - 6X^2 + X^3$
and Its First and Second
Derivatives

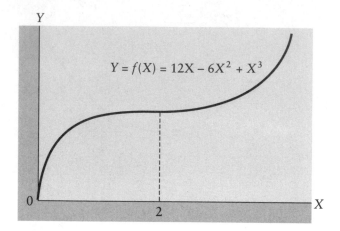

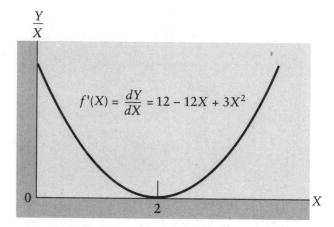

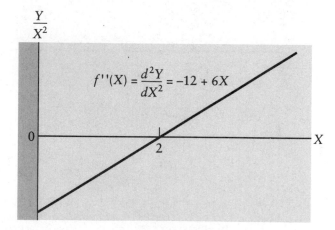

$X = 0$ to $X = 2$ and convex where $X > 2$. Because the second derivative of a function reflects the curvature of its graph, we can use it to express the concepts of strict concavity and convexity. The function $Y = f(X)$ is strictly concave if $f''(X) < 0$ and strictly convex if $f''(X) < 0$.[3]

---

[3] We can remove the qualifier *strictly* is we replace the strong inequalities, $<$ and $>$, with the weak inequalities $\leq$ and $\geq$.

3.6

IMPLICIT DIFFERENTIATION

Recall from Chapter 2 that a function that is specified in the form $Y = f(X)$ is called an explicit function because Y is explicitly expressed as a function of X. The function could be written in implicit form

$$F(Y, X) \equiv Y - f(X) = 0 \tag{3-24}$$

How do we take the derivative of an implicit function? Of course, we could try to express the function in an explicit form, so that we could take the derivative normally. We know, however, that we may or may not be able to write an implicit function in an explicit form. As an example, consider the function

$$F(X, Y) \equiv Y^2 + X^2 + XY = 0 \tag{3-25}$$

This cannot be solved explicitly for Y in terms of X. However, we can find the derivative dY/dX by recognizing that, if Y is a function of X, we can substitute the function $Y = Y(X)$ for Y in (3-25), obtaining

$$F(X, Y) \equiv (Y(X))^2 + X^2 + X(Y(X)) = 0 \tag{3-26}$$

Take the derivative of $F(X, Y)$ with respect to X. Remember to use the chain rule and the product rule where appropriate. You should obtain

$$\frac{d(F(X, Y))}{dX} = 2Y \frac{dY}{dX} + 2X + Y + X \frac{dY}{dX} = 0 \tag{3-27}$$

Equation (3-27) can be solved for dY/dX. We find

$$\frac{dY}{dX} = -\frac{2X + Y}{2Y + X} \tag{3-28}$$

This example suggests that we can take derivatives of implicit functions even when they cannot be written in an explicit form.

3.6.1 Implicit Function Rule

In fact, there is a rule for the differentiation of implicit functions.

Rule 10: Implicit Function Rule

Given the implicit function $F(Y, X) = 0$, if the corresponding explicit function $Y = f(X)$ exists, then the derivative of Y with respect to X equals

$$\frac{dY}{dX} = \frac{-F_X}{F_Y} \quad \text{provided that } F_Y \neq 0 \tag{3-29}$$

where

$$F_X \equiv \frac{dF}{dX}\bigg|_{\text{treating } Y \text{ as a constant}} \quad \text{and} \quad F_Y \equiv \frac{dF}{dY}\bigg|_{\text{treating } X \text{ as a constant}} \tag{3-30}$$

An alternative notation that tells us we are treating the "other" variables of a multivariable function as constants is to use d's with backward-bending tails on them (∂) when we write the derivative. Therefore, we can write

$$F_X \equiv \frac{dF}{dX}\bigg|_{\text{treating } Y \text{ as a constant}} \equiv \frac{\partial F}{\partial X} \quad \text{and} \quad F_Y \equiv \frac{dF}{dY}\bigg|_{\text{treating } X \text{ as a constant}} \equiv \frac{\partial F}{\partial Y}$$

$$\tag{3-31}$$

The expression $\partial F/\partial X$ is called the partial derivative of F with respect to X, and $\partial F/\partial Y$ is called the partial derivative of F with respect to Y. We cover partial derivatives in detail and define them formally in Chapter 5.

The implicit function rule is useful because it does not require that we know the exact form of the explicit function $Y = f(X)$. All we need to know in order to use the implicit function rule is that a functional relationship between Y and X exists and it is smooth and continuous. The value of the implicit function rule is that it permits us to find a derivative even though we are unable to express a functional relationship explicitly. We will discover that many important functional relations in economics can be expressed only implicitly.

NUMERICAL EXAMPLE

Recall the implicit function $F(Y, X) = Y^2 + X^2 + XY = 0$. To find the derivative of Y with respect to X using the implicit function rule you need to find the partial derivatives of the implicit function. They are

$$F_X \equiv \frac{dF}{dX}\bigg|_{\text{treating } Y \text{ as a constant}} = 2X + Y \tag{3-32}$$

and

$$F_Y \equiv \frac{dF}{dY}\bigg|_{\text{treating } X \text{ as a constant}} = 2Y + X \tag{3-33}$$

In order to find the derivative of X with respect to Y we apply the implicit function rule using the partial derivatives.

$$\frac{dY}{dX} \equiv -\frac{F_X}{F_Y} = -\frac{2X + Y}{2Y + X} \tag{3-34}$$

As you can see, this is the same result as we obtained in equation (3-28).

3.6.2 Implicit Function Theorem

The rule for differentiating an implicit function is closely connected to an important theorem regarding the existence of implicit functions. Remember from Chapter 2, Section 2.3, that you can determine that a function exists if its graph has no vertical segment or it doesn't bend over backward or forward in the vertical direction. Any vertical segment to a graph, or any point at which the graph does double over on itself backward or forward, would have a slope equal to infinity. Remembering that the derivative of a function is equal to the slope of its graph at a point tells you that, as long as the derivative is not infinite, the function must exist. Recall the implicit function rule, equation (3-29)

$$\frac{dY}{dX} = \frac{-F_X}{F_Y} \quad \text{provided that } F_Y \neq 0 \qquad (3\text{-}29)$$

As long as F_X and F_Y exist at a point and $F_Y \neq 0$ at that point, we are assured that the derivative dY/dX is not infinite, and the functional relationship $Y = f(X)$ exists in the neighborhood of that point. This notion results in the important *implicit function theorem*, and it provides us with a way to ensure that an implicit relationship is an implicit function. The implicit function theorem states that

> Given the implicit relation $F(X, Y) = 0$, if F_X and F_Y are continuous at a point and $F_Y \neq 0$ at that point, then the explicit function $Y = f(X)$ exists in the neighborhood of that point. Furthermore, the function $f(X)$ is continuous and so is its derivative, dY/dX.[4]

We extend the implicit function theorem to apply to implicitly defined functions with many independent variables in Chapter 5, where we discuss differentiation of functions with many independent variables.

implicit function theorem: theorem describing the conditions under which the function $Y = f(X)$ exists, given the relationship $F(X, Y) = 0$.

EXERCISES
Section 3.6.2
Implicit Function
Theorem

Find the first derivative for each of the following functions.

1. $Y = f(X) = 3X^3 + 2X^2 + X - 1$ 2. $Y = f(X) = (2X + X^3)^4$
3. $Y = f(X) = (X^4)^{1/5}$ 4. $Y = f(X) = 1/\sqrt{X}$
5. $F(X, Y) = X^2 + Y^2 + (XY)^{1/2} = 0$ 6. $Y = f(X) = X^2(X - 1)^8$
7. $Y = f(X) = \ln X/\ln(2X + 1)$ 8. $Y = f(X) = X^{1/2} + X^2$, if $X = g(Z) = Z^4/(Z + 1)$
9. $Y = f(X) = X(\ln X)^2$ 10. $F(X, Y) = XY^2e^Y = 0$
11. $Y = f(X) = 15/(6X^{2/3})$ 12. $F(X, Y) = X^2Y + Y^2X + Y = 0$
13. $Y = f(X) = X^4 - 3X^3$, if $X = g(Z) = Z^2 - 2Z + 1$

---

[4]Note that, although the conditions of the implicit function theorem assure us that an explicit function exists, its converse is not true. That is, it is not safe to say that, if $F_Y = 0$, a function $Y = f(X)$ does not exist. It might still exist, if the slope of the graph of the function is vertical at only one point and the graph does not double over on itself either backward or forward. Because of this possibility, we say that the implicit function theorem gives us *sufficient* but not *necessary* conditions for the existence of the function.

3.7

APPLICATIONS OF DIFFERENTIAL CALCULUS TO ECONOMIC THEORY

At the beginning of this chapter we suggested that differential calculus is extremely useful for the study of economics because it provides useful techniques for optimizing objective functions and because substantive hypotheses are often expressed as derivatives. Even before we develop optimization techniques in Chapter 4 and even without performing comparative statics analysis, we can see that some familiar economic concepts are easily expressed using derivatives. In this section we look at how derivatives help us to describe aspects of cost theory, demand and revenue, elasticity of demand, short-run production, and indifference curves and isoquants.

3.7.1 Cost Theory

We can describe total cost, TC, as the sum of fixed cost, FC, and variable cost, VC,

$$TC = FC + VC \tag{3-35}$$

The conceptual difference between fixed cost and variable cost is that fixed cost does not depend on quantity, Q, and variable cost varies with quantity. In mathematical terms, this means that FC is a constant function and VC is a function of Q. Therefore, we can write

$$FC = k \quad \text{and} \quad VC = VC(Q) \tag{3-36}$$

and

$$TC(Q) = k + VC(Q) \tag{3-37}$$

In general, whenever you see the word "marginal" used in economic terminology, the concept being expressed is a derivative in mathematical terms. For example, marginal cost of production, MC, is the derivative of total cost with respect to quantity, or

$$MC = TC'(Q) = \frac{dTC}{dQ} = \frac{dVC}{dQ} = VC'(Q) \tag{3-38}$$

Note that, because fixed cost is a constant whose derivative with respect to Q is zero, the derivative of total cost with respect to Q equals the derivative of variable cost with respect to Q and both equal marginal cost.

We can describe the slope of the marginal cost curve by taking the derivative of MC with respect to Q, which is equivalent to the second derivative of the total cost function.

$$MC' = \frac{dMC}{dQ} = VC''(Q) = \frac{d^2TC}{dQ^2} = TC''(Q) \tag{3-39}$$

When we speak of average costs, we divide cost by quantity. Therefore average total cost, ATC, equals

$$\text{ATC} = \frac{\text{TC}(Q)}{Q} \qquad\qquad (3\text{-}40)$$

and average variable cost, AVC, equals

$$\text{AVC} = \frac{\text{VC}(Q)}{Q} \qquad\qquad (3\text{-}41)$$

Both average total cost and average variable cost are quotients involving functions of Q. Therefore, we use the quotient rule to take the derivative of average cost. In fact, our example of the quotient rule in Section 3.4 was to find the derivative of average cost. Taking the derivative of ATC gives us an expression for the slope of the average total cost curve.

$$\text{ATC}' = \frac{Q\text{TC}' - \text{TC}}{Q^2} \qquad\qquad (3\text{-}42)$$

Remember that $\text{TC}' = \text{MC}$, $\text{ATC} = \text{TC}/Q$, and recognize that you can factor out $1/Q$. Then

$$\text{ATC}' = \frac{1}{Q}(\text{MC} - \text{ATC}) \qquad\qquad (3\text{-}43)$$

Similarly, we can find the slope of the average variable cost curve by taking the derivative of AVC with respect to Q.

$$\text{AVC}' = \frac{d\text{AVC}}{dQ} = \frac{Q\text{VC}' - \text{VC}}{Q^2} = \frac{1}{Q}(\text{MC} - \text{AVC}) \qquad (3\text{-}44)$$

These expressions tell us that the slopes of the average cost curves are related to the difference between marginal cost and average cost. For positive rates of output, $Q > 0$, we are able to say that

$$\text{ATC}' \gtreqqless 0 \Leftrightarrow \text{MC} \gtreqqless \text{ATC} \qquad\qquad (3\text{-}45)$$

and

$$\text{AVC}' \gtreqqless 0 \Leftrightarrow \text{MC} \gtreqqless \text{AVC} \qquad\qquad (3\text{-}46)$$

These relationships are illustrated in the familiar cost curve diagram pictured in Figure 3.10. They tell us that, when marginal cost is less than average cost, the average cost curve has a negative slope. When marginal cost is greater than average cost, the average cost curve has a positive slope. When marginal cost equals average cost, the slope of the average cost curve equals zero and the average cost curve is at a minimum. These relationships are true for both average total cost and average variable cost.

Figure 3.10

Graphs of Average
Total Cost, Average
Variable Cost, and
Marginal Cost

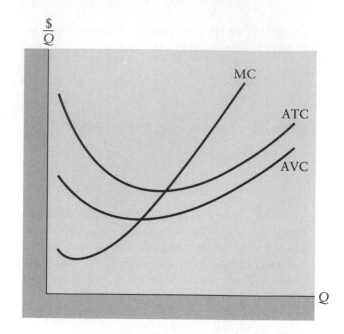

NUMERICAL EXAMPLE

Suppose variable cost equals $VC = 100Q - 15Q^2 + Q^3$ and fixed cost equals $FC = 50$. Then total cost equals $TC = FC + VC = 50 + 100Q - 15Q^2 + Q^3$. Marginal cost equals $MC = dTC/dQ = 100 - 30Q + 3Q^2$. Note that you obtain the same expression for marginal cost if you take the derivative of VC rather than TC. Average total cost is $ATC = TC/Q = 50/Q + 100 - 15Q + Q^2$, and average variable cost is $AVC = VC/Q = 100 - 15Q + Q^2$. We find the slope of ATC by taking its derivative, obtaining $ATC' = -50/Q^2 - 15 + 2Q$. You should verify that this expression satisfies equation (3-43). Similarly, we find the slope of AVC to be $AVC' = -15 + 2Q$, and you should verify that this satisfies equation (3-44). We can find the points where MC crosses AVC by setting them equal,

$$MC = 100 - 30Q + 3Q^2 = 100 - 15Q + Q^2 = AVC \qquad \textbf{(3-47)}$$

Subtracting the right-hand side from both sides of (3-47) gives us

$$-15Q + 2Q^2 = Q(2Q - 15) = 0 \qquad \textbf{(3-48)}$$

Therefore,

$$Q = 0 \quad \text{or} \quad Q = 7.5 \qquad \textbf{(3-49)}$$

We can also find where MC crosses ATC by setting them equal and solving for Q. Doing so gives us $Q = 7.9$.

3.7.2   Demand and Revenue

We typically think of demand as a function in which quantity demanded, Q, is the dependent variable and price, P, is the independent variable. In Chapter 2, Section 2.4.1, we noted that we usually graph the demand curve with P on the vertical axis and Q on the horizontal and that this graph actually represents the inverse of the demand function. For a firm selling a product, price expressed as a function of quantity is its average revenue, $P = \mathrm{AR}(Q)$. We know this to be the case because total revenue equals price multiplied by quantity. Recognizing that average revenue equals total revenue divided by quantity and that marginal revenue equals the derivative of total revenue with respect to quantity gives us the following mathematical expressions for average revenue, AR, and total revenue, TR.

$$\mathrm{AR} = P = \mathrm{AR}(Q) \tag{3-50}$$

$$\mathrm{TR} = PQ = \mathrm{AR}(Q) \cdot Q \tag{3-51}$$

Differentiate TR using the product rule to find marginal revenue, MR.

$$\mathrm{MR} = \frac{d\mathrm{TR}}{dQ} = \mathrm{AR} + Q \cdot \mathrm{AR}' \tag{3-52}$$

If we subtract AR from both sides of the expression we generate an important relationship between marginal revenue and average revenue.

$$\mathrm{MR} - \mathrm{AR} = Q \cdot \mathrm{AR}' \tag{3-53}$$

Remember that AR' is the slope of the average revenue curve facing the firm. Under perfect competition, price is constant to the firm so average revenue is a constant function. That is, it is a horizontal straight line equal to price and $\mathrm{AR}' = 0$. It follows from equation (3-48) that in this situation $\mathrm{AR} = \mathrm{MR} = P$. Under imperfect competition, however, the firm faces a downward-sloping AR curve, so AR' is negative. In this case, $\mathrm{AR} > \mathrm{MR}$; that is, $P > \mathrm{MR}$. You might remember from microeconomic theory that, since profit maximization requires the firm to produce the level of output at which $\mathrm{MC} = \mathrm{MR}$, it follows that under perfect competition $P = \mathrm{MC}$, whereas under imperfect competition $P > \mathrm{MC}$. We demonstrate that profit maximization requires that $\mathrm{MC} = \mathrm{MR}$ formally and in more detail in Chapter 4.

NUMERICAL EXAMPLES

1. A Linear Demand Function

Let average revenue be $\mathrm{AR} = P = 20 - 12Q$. Its slope equals $\mathrm{AR}' = -12$. Total revenue is $\mathrm{TR} = \mathrm{AR} \cdot Q = 20Q - 12Q^2$. The slope of TR, marginal revenue, is $\mathrm{MR} = 20 - 24Q$. The slope of MR is $\mathrm{MR}' = -24 = 2\mathrm{AR}'$. In this example we see that linear average revenue curves have linear marginal revenue curves which are *twice* as steep as the corresponding demand curves while having the same vertical intercept. This is true only of *linear* demand curves. These AR and MR curves are graphed in Figure 3.11*a*.

2. A Nonlinear Demand Function

Let average revenue be $AR = P = 20 - 12Q - 2Q^2$. Its slope is $AR' = -12 - 4Q$. Total revenue is $TR = 20Q - 12Q^2 - 2Q^3$, and its slope, marginal revenue, is $MR = 20 - 24Q - 6Q^2$. The slope of MR is $MR' = -24 - 12Q$. Note in Figure 3.11*b*, that although MR is steeper than AR, it is not always twice as steep, as it was in example 1. Also note that AR and MR do have the same vertical intercept.

Figure 3.11

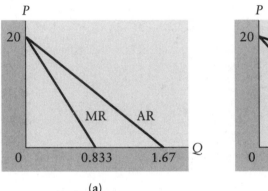

(a)
$AR = 20 - 12Q,$
$MR = 20 - 24Q$

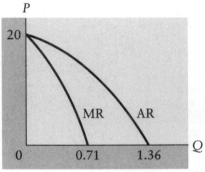

(b)
$AR = 20 - 12Q - 2Q^2$
$MR = 20 - 24Q - 6Q^2$

These examples suggest that there is a relationship between the slopes of the marginal revenue and average revenue curves. A general expression for that relationship can be generated by taking the second derivative of the total revenue function. Because the first derivative of total revenue is marginal revenue, the second derivative is the slope of the marginal revenue curve.

$$TR = AR \cdot Q \tag{3-54}$$

$$TR' = MR = Q \cdot AR' + AR \tag{3-55}$$

$$TR'' = MR' = Q \cdot AR'' + AR' + AR' = Q \cdot AR'' + 2AR' \tag{3-56}$$

If the average revenue function is linear, then AR″ equals zero and the slope of the marginal revenue curve is twice the slope of average revenue. If the average revenue function is not linear, then AR″ does not equal zero, and we cannot say that the slope of MR is twice the slope of AR.

3.7.3 Price Elasticity of Demand

elasticity: a unitless measure of the response of a dependent variable to a change in an independent variable.

arc elasticity: a unitless measure of the discrete response of a dependent variable to a discrete change in an independent variable.

point elasticity: a unitless measure of the instantaneous response of a dependent variable to an infinitesimal change in an independent variable.

price elasticity of demand: the responsiveness of quantity demanded to changes in price.

Elasticity is a unitless measure used to describe the responsiveness of a dependent variable to changes in an independent variable. The fact that it is a unitless measure means that we can compare directly elasticities of different goods without having to account for the different units in which prices or quantities might be measured. We described elasticity of demand in Chapter 2 as

$$\varepsilon_{QP} = \frac{\text{percentage change in quantity demanded}}{\text{percentage change in price}} \tag{2-21}$$

If we measure the changes called for in (2-21) over finite intervals, we call the elasticity an *arc elasticity*. It can be imprecise because its value depends on the interval that is chosen. If we measure infinitesimal changes we call the elasticity a *point elasticity*. Point elasticities are best defined using derivatives. In particular, *price elasticity of demand* is defined as

$$\varepsilon_{QP} = \frac{dQ}{dP}\frac{P}{Q} \tag{3-57}$$

Remember that the units of dQ/dP are the units of Q divided by the units of P. When we multiply dQ/dP by P over Q the units cancel each other and we have a measure of elasticity that is unitless.

$4\% > 1\%$

NUMERICAL EXAMPLES

1. A Variable-Elasticity Demand Function

Consider the demand function $Q = 100 - 12P - 2P^2$. To find the price elasticity of demand, multiply the derivative of the demand function by P/Q.

$$\varepsilon_{QP} = \frac{dQ}{dP}\frac{P}{Q} = (-12 - 4P)\frac{P}{Q} = \frac{-12P - 4P^2}{Q} \tag{3-58}$$

In this case the elasticity changes when price and quantity change. It must be evaluated at a point on the demand curve. For example, at $P = 2$, $Q = 68$ and $\varepsilon_{QP} = -10/17$. This means that consumers would respond to a 1.7% increase (decrease) in price by demanding 1% less (more) of the good or service. Because the percentage change in quantity demanded is  less than the percentage change in price, total revenue to suppliers increases with increases in the price and decreases with decreases in the price.

2. A Constant-Elasticity Demand Function

Suppose the demand function is $Q = 5P^{-2}$. The price elasticity of demand is

$$\varepsilon_{QP} = \frac{dQ}{dP}\frac{P}{Q} = -10P^{-3}\frac{P}{Q} = -\frac{10}{P^2 Q} \tag{3-59}$$

If we substitute in $Q = 5P^{-2}$ and simplify, we obtain

$$\varepsilon_{QP} = -\frac{10}{P^2 5P^{-2}} = -\frac{10}{5} = -2 \tag{3-60}$$

A constant elasticity of demand equal to -2 means that, no matter what the price and quantity, consumers respond to a 1% change in price with an opposite 2% change in quantity demanded. In this situation, total revenue to the suppliers decreases with increases in the price and increases with decreases in the price. In general, demand functions of the form $Q = aP^{-c}$ where $a,c > 0$ are constant generate constant elasticities equal to $-c$. Thus $Q = kP^{-1}$ results in an elasticity equal to -1.

Relationship Between Marginal Revenue and Price Elasticity of Demand

inelastic demand: a situation in which the price elasticity of demand, ε_{QP}, is between 0 and -1 and quantity demanded changes by a smaller percentage than the change in price.

elastic demand: a situation in which the price elasticity of demand, ε_{QP}, is less than -1 and quantity demanded changes by a larger percentage than the change in price.

In each of the numerical examples, we see that knowing the elasticity of demand can tell us how total revenue changes when price and quantity demanded change. When ε_{QP} is between 0 and -1, quantity demanded changes by a smaller percentage than the change in price, and demand is considered to be *inelastic*. When ε_{QP} is less than -1, quantity demanded changes by a larger percentage than the change in price, and demand is considered to be *elastic*. When ε_{QP} is equal to -1, demand is considered to be unitary elastic.

To better understand the relationship between changes in price and quantity and changes in total revenue, remember that the inverse of a demand function is average revenue. We can write

$$P = \mathrm{AR}(Q) \tag{3-61}$$

The law of demand allows us to assert that $dP/dQ = \mathrm{AR}' < 0$. Total revenue, TR, equals $\mathrm{AR}(Q) \times Q$. We use the product rule to differentiate TR in order to obtain an expression for marginal revenue, MR,

$$\mathrm{MR} = \mathrm{TR}' = \mathrm{AR} + Q\mathrm{AR}' = P + Q\mathrm{AR}' \tag{3-62}$$

If we factor out P we obtain

$$\mathrm{MR} = P\left(1 + \mathrm{AR}'\frac{Q}{P}\right) = P\left(1 + \frac{dP}{dQ}\frac{Q}{P}\right) \tag{3-63}$$

The inverse function rule allows us to write

$$\frac{dP}{dQ} = \frac{1}{dQ/dP} \tag{3-64}$$

Substituting (3-64) into (3-63) and inverting the fraction Q/P and placing it in the denominator gives us

$$\text{MR} = P\left(1 + \frac{1}{\dfrac{dQ}{dP}\dfrac{P}{Q}}\right) = P\left(1 + \frac{1}{\varepsilon_{QP}}\right) \tag{3-65}$$

Mathematically, equation (3-65) describes the following relationship between marginal revenue and the price elasticity of demand.

$$\varepsilon_{QP} < -1 \Leftrightarrow \text{demand is elastic} \quad\;\; \Leftrightarrow \text{MR} > 0$$

$$\varepsilon_{QP} = -1 \Leftrightarrow \text{demand is unit elastic} \Leftrightarrow \text{MR} = 0$$

$$\varepsilon_{QP} > -1 \Leftrightarrow \text{demand is inelastic} \quad\; \Leftrightarrow \text{MR} < 0$$

Under conditions of perfect competition, firms face a constant price. Therefore, $dP/dQ = 0$ and $\varepsilon_{QP} \to -\infty$, and $\text{MR} = P$. Since profit maximization requires the firm to produce that level of output where $\text{MR} = \text{MC}$, for a perfect competitor $\text{MC} = P$. Under monopoly conditions, firms face a downward-sloping average revenue curve, ε_{QP} is finite (and of course negative), so $\text{MR} < P$. Again, profit maximization implies that $\text{MC} = \text{MR}$, so $\text{MC} < P$. We examine profit maximization under conditions of monopoly and perfect competition in more detail in Chapter 4.

3.7.4 Short-Run Production

Consider the production function

$$Q = f(K, L) \tag{3-66}$$

In Chapter 2 we define short-run as a situation in which some variable is arbitrarily held constant. In the context of production, at least one factor of production is fixed. In this case we fix K at K_0 so that $Q = f(K_0, L) = \text{TP}(L)$. The function TP$(L)$ is the short-run production function and can be considered the total product of labor. We find the average product of labor, AP_L, by dividing total product by output.

marginal product: the rate of change of output per unit change in the quantity of one input, holding all other inputs constant.

$$\text{AP}_L = \frac{Q}{L} = \frac{\text{TP}(L)}{Q} \tag{3-67}$$

We find the *marginal product* of labor, MP_L, by taking the derivative of total product.

diminishing marginal returns to a variable input: the incremental output from additional units of a variable input decreases as more of the variable input is added, holding other inputs constant.

$$\text{MP}_L = \frac{dQ}{dL} = \text{TP}'(L) \tag{3-68}$$

The law of *diminishing marginal returns to a variable input* asserts that the incremental output from additional units of a variable input decreases as more of the variable input is added, holding other inputs constant. This simply means that the slope of marginal product is negative. Mathematically, the slope of marginal product is its first derivative and the second derivative of total product. Therefore, the law of diminishing marginal returns is expressed mathematically as

$$\frac{d\text{MP}_L}{dL} = \frac{d^2Q}{dL^2} = \text{TP}''(L) < 0 \qquad (3\text{-}69)$$

The slope of the total product curve is decreasing, and the slope of the marginal product curve is negative.

We can illustrate the law of diminishing marginal returns with the Cobb-Douglas production function, which we saw first in Chapter 2, Section, 2.5. It is popular for both its theoretical and its econometric properties. It can be written as

$$Q = f(K, L) = AK^\alpha L^{1-\alpha}, \qquad 0 < \alpha < 1, A > 0 \qquad (3\text{-}70)$$

If we fix capital, K, at K_0 we define a short-run situation in which one input is held constant. This gives us a production function with one independent variable, labor, L. We find the average product of labor by dividing Q by L.

$$\text{AP}_L = \frac{AK_0^\alpha L^{1-\alpha}}{L} = AK_0^\alpha L^{-\alpha} \qquad (3\text{-}71)$$

We find the marginal product of labor by taking the derivative of the production function with respect to labor.

$$\text{MP}_L = \frac{dQ}{dL} = (1 - \alpha)AK_0^\alpha L^{-\alpha} \qquad (3\text{-}72)$$

The second derivative with respect to labor equals

$$\frac{d\text{MP}_L}{dL} = \frac{d^2Q}{dL^2} = -\alpha(1 - \alpha)AK_0^\alpha L^{-(1+\alpha)} \qquad (3\text{-}73)$$

Because $0 < \alpha < 1$, the second derivative is negative, so the Cobb-Douglas production function exhibits diminishing returns to labor.

NUMERICAL EXAMPLE

Suppose $Q = 100K^{0.25}L^{0.75}$. If we fix capital at $K = 16$, then the total product of labor can be expressed as $\text{TP}(L) = 100(16)^{0.25}L^{0.75} = 200L^{0.75}$. The average product of labor equals $\text{AP}_L = \text{TP}(L)/L = 200L^{-0.25}$. The marginal product of labor is the first derivative of the total product function, $\text{MP}_L = 150L^{-0.25}$. We can determine the slope of the marginal product curve by taking its derivative, which is the second derivative of the total product function, obtaining $\text{TP}''(L) = \text{MP}'(L) = -37.5L^{-1.25}$. The slope of the marginal product curve is negative, so this production function exhibits diminishing marginal returns to labor. The total product, average product, and marginal product curves are displayed in Figure 3.12.

Figure 3.12

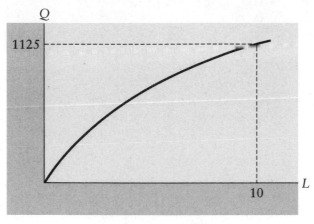

(a) $TP(L) = 200L^{0.75}$

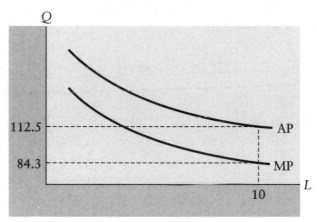

(b) $AP(L) = 200L^{-0.25}$, $MP(L) = 150L^{-0.25}$

3.7.5 Indifference Curves and Isoquants

An Indifference Curve

Suppose a particular level of utility, U_0, is determined by the utility function

$$U_0 = U(S, F) \qquad (3\text{-}74)$$

This expression describes a relationship between the quantities of two goods, shelter, S, and food, F, given a utility function, $U(S, F)$, and a constant level of utility, U_0. The relationship is pictured in Figure 3.13.

The relationship can be expressed implicitly as

$$H(S, F) \equiv U_0 - U(S, F) = 0 \qquad (3\text{-}75)$$

Figure 3.13

Graph of Indifference Curve: $U_0 = U(S, F)$

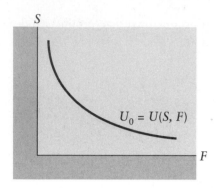

The implicit function theorem tells us that, if H_S and H_F are continuous and $H_S \neq 0$, a functional relationship exists between S and F, $S = S(F)$. Even though we are unable to find this explicit relationship between S and F, we can find the derivative of S with respect to F through implicit differentiation. When you apply the implicit differentiation rule, remember that U_0 is a constant. The two partial derivatives of the implicit function are

$$H_S = \left.\frac{dH}{dS}\right|_{\text{treating } F \text{ as a constant}} = -\left.\frac{dU}{dS}\right|_{\text{treating } F \text{ as a constant}} = -\frac{\partial U}{\partial S} \quad (3\text{-}76)$$

and

$$H_F = \left.\frac{dH}{dF}\right|_{\text{treating } S \text{ as a constant}} = -\left.\frac{dU}{dF}\right|_{\text{treating } S \text{ as a constant}} = -\frac{\partial U}{\partial F} \quad (3\text{-}77)$$

indifference curve: a graphical representation of the consumption rates of two goods that achieve a given rate of utility.

The derivative of S with respect to F equals

$$\frac{dS}{dF} = -\frac{dU/dF|_{\text{treating } S \text{ as a constant}}}{dU/dS|_{\text{treating } F \text{ as a constant}}} = -\frac{\partial U/\partial F}{\partial U/\partial S} = -\frac{MU_F}{MU_S} = -MRS_{F,S} \quad (3\text{-}78)$$

marginal rate of substitution (MRS): the rate at which one good can be substituted for another, holding utility constant.

Remember that the implicit function describes values of S and F that achieve the particular level of utility U_0. That is how we define an ***indifference curve*** mathematically. The derivative of the implicit function represents the slope of the indifference curve, or the ***marginal rate of substitution***, $MRS_{F,S}$, between the two goods. The $MRS_{F,S}$ represents the rate at which food can be substituted for shelter, holding utility constant. The numerator of our expression is the rate of change of utility with respect to a change in F, holding S constant, otherwise known as the ***marginal utility*** of good F. The denominator of our expression is the rate of change of utility with respect to a change in S, holding F constant, or the marginal utility of good S.

marginal utility: the rate of change of utility for a change in the quantity of one good, holding all other goods constant.

NUMERICAL EXAMPLE

Suppose an individual's utility can be described by the function $U = 10S^{0.2}F^{0.8}$. We identify an indifference curve by setting utility equal to some constant level, $U = U_0 = 10S^{0.2}F^{0.8}$. The indifference curve describes a relationship between S and F that can be expressed as the implicit function $H(S, F) \equiv U_0 - 10S^{0.2}F^{0.8} = 0$. We use implicit differentiation to find the slope of the indifference curve, dS/dF. The derivative of H with respect to S, holding F constant, equals

$$H_S = \frac{dH}{dS}\bigg|_{\text{treating } F \text{ as a constant}} = -2S^{-0.8}F^{0.8} \tag{3-79}$$

The derivative of H with respect to F, holding S constant, equals

$$H_F = \frac{dH}{dF}\bigg|_{\text{treating } S \text{ as a constant}} = -8S^{0.2}F^{-0.2} \tag{3-80}$$

The derivative of S with respect to F equals

$$\frac{dS}{dF} = -\frac{dU/dF|_{\text{treating } S \text{ as a constant}}}{dU/dS|_{\text{treating } F \text{ as a constant}}} = -\frac{-8S^{0.2}F^{-0.2}}{-2S^{-0.8}F^{0.8}} = -4\frac{S}{F} \tag{3-81}$$

Therefore, the indifference curve associated with this utility function is downward sloping, with a slope equal to $-4(S/F)$. The marginal rate of substitution between food and shelter equals $\text{MRS}_{F,S} = 4S/F$.

An Isoquant

Suppose a particular level of output is determined by the production function

$$Q_0 = f(K, L) \tag{3-82}$$

This expression describes a relationship between the quantities of two inputs, capital K and labor L, given a production function, $f(K, L)$, and a constant level of output, Q_0. The relationship is pictured in Figure 3.14.

The relationship can be expressed implicitly as

$$G(K, L) \equiv Q_0 - f(K, L) = 0 \tag{3-83}$$

Just as in the case of the indifference curve, we are unable to find the explicit relationship between the variables K and L. However, given the

Figure 3.14

Graph of Isoquant:
$Q_0 = f(K, L)$

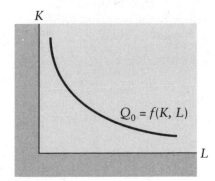

conditions of the implicit function theorem, we can find the derivative of K with respect to L through implicit differentiation. The two partial derivatives of the implicit function are

$$G_K = \frac{dG}{dK}\bigg|_{\text{treating } L \text{ as a constant}} = -\frac{df}{dK}\bigg|_{\text{treating } L \text{ as a constant}} = -\frac{\partial f}{\partial K} \quad (3\text{-}84)$$

and

$$G_L = \frac{dG}{dL}\bigg|_{\text{treating } K \text{ as a constant}} = -\frac{df}{dL}\bigg|_{\text{treating } K \text{ as a constant}} = -\frac{\partial f}{\partial L} \quad (3\text{-}85)$$

The derivative of K with respect to L equals

$$\frac{dK}{dL} = -\frac{df/dL|_{\text{treating } K \text{ as a constant}}}{df/dK|_{\text{treating } L \text{ as a constant}}} = -\frac{\partial f/\partial L}{\partial f/\partial K} = -\frac{\text{MP}_L}{\text{MP}_K} = -\text{MRTS}_{L,K} \quad (3\text{-}86)$$

isoquant: a graphical representation of the rates of usage of two inputs that achieve a given rate of output.

marginal rate of technical substitution (MRTS): the rate at which one input can be substituted for another, holding output constant.

Remember that the implicit function describes values of K and L that produce the particular level of output Q_0. This is how we define an **isoquant** mathematically. The derivative of the implicit function represents the slope of the isoquant, or the ***marginal rate of technical substitution, MRTS$_{L,K}$***, between the two factors of production. The MRTS$_{L,K}$ represents the rate at which labor can be substituted for capital, holding output constant. The numerator of our expression is the rate of change of output with respect to a change in labor, holding capital constant, or the marginal product of labor. The denominator of our expression is the rate of change of output with respect to a change in capital, holding labor constant, or the marginal product of capital.

NUMERICAL EXAMPLE

Suppose a firm's production function is $Q = K^{0.3}L^{0.4}$. We identify an isoquant by setting output equal to some constant level, $Q = 200 = K^{0.3}L^{0.4}$. The isoquant describes a relationship between K and L that can be expressed as the implicit function $G(K, L) \equiv 200 - K^{0.3}L^{0.4} = 0$. We use implicit differentiation to find the slope of the isoquant, dK/dL. The derivative of G with respect to K, holding L constant, equals

$$G_K = \frac{dG}{dK}\bigg|_{\text{treating } L \text{ as a constant}} = -0.3K^{-0.7}L^{0.4} \quad (3\text{-}87)$$

The derivative of G with respect to L, holding K constant, equals

$$G_L = \frac{dG}{dL}\bigg|_{\text{treating } K \text{ as a constant}} = -0.4K^{0.3}L^{-0.6} \quad (3\text{-}88)$$

The derivative of K with respect to L equals

$$\frac{dK}{dL} = -\frac{dQ/dL\,|_{\text{treating } K \text{ as a constant}}}{dQ/dK\,|_{\text{treating } L \text{ as a constant}}} = -\frac{-0.4K^{0.3}L^{-0.6}}{-0.3K^{-0.7}L^{0.4}} = -\frac{4}{3}\frac{K}{L} \qquad (3\text{-}89)$$

Therefore, the isoquant associated with this production function is downward sloping, with a slope equal to $-(4/3)(K/L)$. The marginal rate of technical substitution between labor and capital equals $\text{MRTS}_{L,K} = (4/3)(K/L)$.

EXERCISES
Section 3.7.5
Indifference curves
and Isoquants

1. For each of the following demand functions, find the slope and the price elasticity. Also, find the average revenue (AR), total revenue (TR), and marginal revenue (MR) functions associated with each of the following demand functions.

   a. $Q = P^{-1/2}$ b. $Q = 18 - 2P$ c. $Q = 18 - 2P^2$

2. For each of the following total cost (TC) functions, identify the fixed cost (FC) and variable cost (VC). Also, find the average fixed cost (AFC), average variable cost (AVC), average total cost (ATC), and marginal cost (MC) functions associated with each of the following cost functions and sketch their graphs on the same set of axes.

   a. $\text{TC} = 5Q - 10Q^2 + 2Q^3$ b. $\text{TC} = 25 + Q$
   c. $\text{TC} = 25 + Q^2$

3. For each of the following short-run production functions, find the average and marginal products of the input L and sketch their graphs on the same set of axes. In each case, indicate whether the input of labor is subject to the law of diminishing marginal return.

   a. $Q = 100L^{1/2}$ b. $Q = 100L$ c. $Q = 100L^2$

4. For each of the following production functions, find the slope of an isoquant.

   a. $Q = 5(KL)^{1/2}$ b. $Q = 100K^{0.2}L^{0.8}$ c. $Q = 100/(KL)$

5. For each of the following utility functions, find the slope of an indifference curve.

   a. $U = 0.75 \ln X + 0.25 \ln Y$ b. $U = 10(0.8X^{-2} + 0.2Y^{-2})^{-1/2}$
   c. $U = X + Y + XY$

3.8

SUMMARY

In this chapter we review the concept of derivatives of functions with one independent variable. In order to understand what a derivative is, we discuss limits. After developing a good understanding of how a derivative measures the slope of a function at a point, we review various rules of differentiation, which relieve us of the need to take limits every time we wish to evaluate a derivative. Recognizing that the derivative of a function is itself a function of the same independent variable allows us to take the derivative of the derivative, so we introduce second- and higher-order derivatives. These give us useful information about the nature of the original function, its slope and curvature.

Implicit functions play an important role in economic theory, because frequently we do not have enough information to be able to specify a function explicitly. The implicit function theorem specifies conditions under which we can be assured that an implicitly defined relation describes an explicit function. We show that we can take the derivative of an implicit function, and we apply it to examine indifference curves and isoquants and their slopes. Implicit differentiation and partial derivatives are topics we will return to in Chapter 5. Finally, we begin the process of using derivatives to explore other topics in economic theory. We use derivatives to look at the relationships among total, average, and marginal costs; to examine topics in demand and revenue, including the price elasticity of demand; to look at production functions with one variable input; and to explore the mathematical description of indifference curves and isoquants. In Chapter 4 we continue to apply differential calculus to economic theory by looking at some simple optimization models.

◆ REFERENCES

Allen, R. G. D., *Mathematical Analysis for Economists* (New York: St. Martin's Press, Inc., 1938), Chapters 4–7 and 9–10.

Thomas, George B. Jr., *Calculus and Analytic Geometry*, 3rd Edition (Reading, MA: Addison-Wesley Publishing Co., 1960), Chapters 1, 2, and 3.

◆ ANSWERS TO END-OF-SECTION EXERCISES

Section 3.2.1: Evaluating ("Taking") Limits

1. 9   2. 4   3. −2   4. 1

5. 1/2   6. 1

Section 3.3: Derivatives

1. **a.** This is a polynomial; thus it is continuous over entire domain.

   b. Continuous everywhere except at $X = 0$, where the limit does not exist.

   c. This is a polynomial; thus it is continuous over entire domain.

   d. Continuous for all real valued X.

   e. Continuous everywhere except at $X = 1$, where the limit does not exist.

2.

$$MC = \frac{dTC}{dQ} = \lim_{\Delta Q \to 0} \frac{\Delta TC}{\Delta Q} = \lim_{\Delta Q \to 0} \left(\frac{2a_1 Q \, \Delta Q + a_1 (\Delta Q)^2}{\Delta Q} \right)$$

$$= \lim_{\Delta Q \to 0} (2a_1 Q + a_1 \Delta Q) = 2a_1 Q$$

Section 3.4.2: Differentiation of Nonpolynomial Functions

1. $dY/dX = 1/(2\sqrt{X})$ 2. $dY/dX = 0$

3. $dY/dX = -2/X^3$ 4. $dY/dX = 6X^5 + 16X^3 + 10X - 1$

5. $dY/dX = -e^{-X/4}$ 6. $dY/dX = (10X + 2)/(5X^2 + 2X + 1)$

7. $dY/dX = 3X^2 - 1/X^2$ 8. $dY/dX = 2X$

9. $dY/dX = 4X^3$

Section 3.6.2: Implicit Function Theorem

1. $9X^2 + 4X + 1$ 2. $4(2 + 3X^2)(2X + X^3)^3$

3. $(4/5)X^{-1/5}$ 4. $(-1/2)X^{-3/2}$

5. $-[2X + (1/2)(Y/X)^{1/2}]/[2Y + (1/2)(X/Y)^{1/2}]$

6. $3X^2(X - 1)^5(3X - 1)$

7. $[(1/X)\ln(2X + 1) - (1/(2X + 1))\ln X]/[\ln(2X + 1)]^2$

8. $[(1/2)X^{-1/2} + 2X][(4Z^3(Z + 1) - Z^4)/(Z + 1)^2]$

9. $(\ln X)^2 + 2\ln X$

10. $-Y/[X(2 + Y)]$

11. $5/(3X^{5/3})$

12. $-(2XY + Y^2)/(X^2 + 2XY + 1)$

13. $(4X^3 - 9X^2)(2Z - 2)$

Section 3.7.5: Indifference Curves and Isoquants

1. **a.** $dQ/dP = (-1/2)P^{-3/2}$; $\varepsilon = -1/2$; $AR = 1/Q^2$; $TR = 1/Q$; $MR = -1/Q^2$

   b. $dQ/dP = -2$; $\varepsilon = -P/(9 - P)$; $AR = 9 - Q/2$; $TR = 9Q - Q^2/2$;
   $MR = 9 - Q$

   c. $dQ/dP = -4P$; $\varepsilon = -2P^2/(9 - P^2)$; $AR = (9 - Q/2)^{1/2}$;
   $TR = Q(9 - Q/2)^{1/2}$; $MR = (-Q/4)/[(9 - Q/2)^{1/2}] + (9 - Q/2)^{1/2}$

2. **a.** $FC = 0$; $VC = 5Q - 10Q^2 + 2Q^3$; $AFC = 0$;
   $AVC = ATC = 5 - 10Q + 2Q^2$; $MC = 5 - 20Q + 6Q^2$

   b. $FC = 25$; $VC = Q$; $AFC = 25/Q$; $AVC = 1$; $ATC = 25/Q + 1$; $MC = 1$

   c. $FC = 25$; $VC = Q^2$; $AFC = 25/Q$; $AVC = Q$; $ATC = 25/Q + Q$;
   $MC = 2Q$

3. **a.** $AP = 100/\sqrt{L}$; $MP = 50/\sqrt{L}$; $MP' = -25L^{-3/2}$, Diminishing MP
   b. $AP = MP = 100$; $MP' = 0$, Constant MP
   c. $AP = 100L$; $MP = 200L$; $MP' = 200$, Increasing MP

4. **a.** $dK/dL = -K/L$ **b.** $dK/dL = -4(K/L)$ **c.** $dK/dL = -K/L$

5. **a.** $dY/dX = -3Y/X$ **b.** $dY/dX = -4(Y/X)^3$
   c. $dY/dX = -(1 + Y)/(1 + X)$

◆ SELF-HELP PROBLEMS

Answers to these problems are given at the end of the text.

1. Do you believe that the world of economic behavior is smooth and continuous? That is, is it reasonable to assume that functions describing economic behavior are differentiable?

2. Prove that the derivative of a polynomial of degree n is itself a polynomial of degree $n - 1$.

3. **a.** Show that the quotient rule can be derived from the product rule, the chain rule, and the power function rule.

   b. Show that the logarithmic function rule can be derived from the exponential function rule and the inverse function rule.

4. Consider a firm whose average revenue, AR, and total cost, TC, which are functions of the level of output, Q, are as follows:

$$AR = 20 - 5Q - Q^2, \qquad TC = 4 + 14Q - 5Q^2 + Q^3$$

   a. Find this firm's marginal revenue, MR, and marginal cost, MC, functions.

   b. If firms maximize profit where MR = MC, find this firm's profit-maximizing levels of output, Q, and price, P.

   c. Find the value of price elasticity of demand at the levels of output and price that you found in part b.

   d. Is this firm operating under perfect or imperfect competition? Why?

5. A firm uses inputs of capital, K, and labor, L, to produce output, Q, according to the following production function:

$$Q = K^{0.5}L^{0.5}$$

   Capital is fixed at a level $K = 25$.

   a. Express this production function in logarithmic form (take the natural log of both sides of the equation).

   b. What does the graph of Q vs. L look like?

   c. What is the marginal product of labor?

   d. What is the slope of the marginal product of labor? Does the marginal product of labor increase or decrease as L increases?

◆ SUPPLEMENTAL PROBLEMS

1. Find first- and second-order derivatives for

a. $y = 10^{\sqrt{x}}$ b. $Y = 2^{X^2}$ c. $Y = \ln[(X + 1)/(X + 2)]$, $X \neq -2$
d. $Y = (\ln X)/X$

2. Find second-order derivatives for the following functions.
    a. $Y = \sqrt{X}$ b. $Y = 100$ c. $Y = 1/X2$
    d. $Y = (X^2 + 1)^3 + (X^2 + 1) - 1$ e. $Y = 4e^{-X/4}$ f. $Y = \ln(5X^2 + 2X + 1)$

3. If $f(X) = X^3$ and $g(X) = 1/X$, find second-order derivatives for
    a. $Y = f(X) + g(X)$ b. $Y = f(X)g(X)$ c. $Y = f(X)/g(X)$

4. Consider the demand function $Q = f(P)$, where $f'(P) < 0$.
    a. Show that MR $= d\text{TR}/dQ = P(1 + 1/\varepsilon_{QP})$, where TR is total revenue and ε_{QP} is price elasticity of demand.
    b. According to this result, what is the relationship between price elasticity of demand, total revenue, and changes in quantity?
    c. Show that $d\text{TR}/dP = Q(1 + \varepsilon_{QP})$
    d. According to this result, what is the relationship between price elasticity of demand, total revenue, and changes in price?

5. Consider that TC $=$ FC $+$ VC $= c + g(Q)$, where TC $\equiv$ total cost, FC $\equiv$ fixed cost, VC $\equiv$ variable cost, $c \equiv$ constant, and $Q \equiv$ output. Assume that $g(Q)$ is twice differentiable.
    a. Show that slope of ATC $= -c/Q^2 + (1/Q)(\text{MC} - \text{AVC})$, where MC is marginal cost, ATC is average total cost, and AVC is average variable cost.
    b. Using this result, discuss the relation between MC, AVC, and ATC curves.

6. You are given the following: quantity demanded $= Q_d = f(P)$; $f'(P) < 0$; average revenue $=$ AR $= P = f^{-1}(Q_d)$
    a. Find expressions for total revenue (TR), marginal revenue (MR), and the slope of MR.
    b. Use your answers to a to show that MR $<$ AR. Use your answers to a to show that, if AR is a <u>linear function</u> of Q_d, the slope of MR equals two times the slope of AR.
    c. If $Q_d = f(P) = 100 - 2P$, find expressions for and sketch the graphs of TR, MR, and AR.

7. You are given the following total cost function: TC $= 30Q - 8Q^2 + Q^3$.
    a. Find expressions for marginal cost and average total cost (MC and ATC. Sketch the graphs of TC, MC, and ATC (put MC and ATC on the same set of axes).
    b. Identify turning points and points of inflection.
    c. Verify that, *for this cost function,*

$$\text{ATC}' \gtreqless 0 \Leftrightarrow \text{MC} \gtreqless \text{AC}$$

8. A farm produces wheat according to the production function $W = TL^{0.3}F^{0.5}$, in which W equals wheat, T equals land, L equals labor, and F equals fertilizer. Land is fixed at $T = 100$.
    a. Find this farm's short-run production function and the marginal products of labor and fertilizer.
    b. Find an expression for the labor-fertilizer isoquant if $W = 5000$.
    c. What is the slope of the isoquant?

9. A consumer derives utility from the consumption of food, *F*, clothing, *C*, and shelter, *S*. Shelter is fixed at 20 units.

a. Find this consumer's marginal utility of food and clothing, if her utility function is $U = FCS$.

b. Find her marginal rate of substitution between clothing and food.

C H A P T E R   4

Unconstrained Optimization of Functions with One Independent Variable

4.1

INTRODUCTION

In this chapter we get our first opportunity actually to "do" some mathematical economics. We present some economic models, complete with comparative statics analysis, in narrative, graphical, and, most important, mathematical form. What makes it possible to concentrate on economics is that you have all the mathematical tools you need in order to use the technique of *mathematical optimization* of functions with one independent variable. We show you how to use this technique and then immediately apply it to economics in the form of the theory of the profit-maximizing firm. You will see in this chapter that a wide range of behavior of firms can be explained by relatively small variations of the general model of profit maximization.

Recall from Chapter 1 the general pattern of the methodology of comparative statics. In order to examine economic behavior, we must create a model that permits us to identify factors which are important and relevant and to ignore irrelevant information. In addition, our model must specify an equilibrium—that is, some relationship between the choice or endogenous variables and the given set of parameters or exogenous variables that the system tends to achieve. This relationship is specified so that we may change a parameter or exogenous variable to compare two equilibria. The equilibrium for our market model was described by making quantity demanded equal to quantity supplied, and the equilibrium in our income determination model was described by making income satisfy the equality of income and planned expenditures. These are both highly aggregated models expressed as systems of equations, and the equilibrium conditions are simply the values of the endogenous variables that solve the systems of equations.

mathematical optimization: the mathematical technique of finding the maximum or minimum value of some objective function.

93

Frequently, our models describe optimizing behavior of one sort or another. As we suggested in Chapter 1, this is due to the nature of economics. Scarcity forces us, as consumers or producers, to choose among alternatives. The nature of making a choice is optimization; we choose the alternative that helps us to attain our goal. Any goal-oriented behavior can be expressed in terms of optimizing some objective, that is, maximizing or minimizing some *objective function*. Consumers are modeled as maximizing utility for a given income; producers are modeled as maximizing profit or minimizing the cost of producing a given rate of output. Equilibrium in such models is described as the values of the choice variables that maximize or minimize an objective function. Differential calculus gives us some extremely powerful tools for describing mathematically the maxima or minima of objective functions.

objective function: the mathematical function whose dependent variable is to be optimized, that is, maximized or minimized.

4.2

MATHEMATICAL OPTIMIZATION

critical point: a point at which a function is neither increasing nor decreasing, where the first derivative equals zero. Also known as **stationary point**.

necessary condition for optimization: same as first-order condition.

sufficient condition for optimization: same as second-order condition.

first-order condition for optimization: condition that must necessarily hold for a function to have a critical point.

second-order condition: condition which, given the necessary condition, is sufficient to guarantee the existence of a maximum or a minimum.

In Chapter 3, we pointed out some important relationships between a primitive function and its derivatives. Specifically, we saw that when a function is increasing, its first derivative is positive, and when a function is decreasing, its first derivative is negative. We found that when a function is neither increasing nor decreasing, its first derivative equals zero. We call the point at which a function is neither increasing nor decreasing a *critical point*, or a *stationary point*.

A critical point may be either a maximum or a minimum value or a point of inflection, and it must be true that at the critical point the slope of the objective function (its first derivative) equals zero. If the slope of the function is decreasing in the neighborhood of the critical point, the critical point must be a maximum. In this case, the slope of the slope of the function (its second derivative) is negative. If the slope of the function is increasing in the neighborhood of that point, the critical point must be a minimum. In this case the slope of the slope of the function (its second derivative) is positive. These simple relationships are all we need to develop our mathematical tools for optimizing objective functions. In the language of mathematical optimization, the behavior of the first and second derivatives at a critical point is referred to as the *necessary and sufficient conditions*, or *first- and second-order conditions* of optimization.

4.2.1   First- and Second-Order Conditions

Unconstrained optimization refers to situations in which the objective function itself has a maximum or minimum. The economic agent simply chooses the value of the choice variable that maximizes or minimizes the objective function and has no external constraints on his or her behavior. A good example is the economic model of the profit-maximizing firm. If profit, π, is a function of quantity, Q, and we want to postulate that the firm chooses the quantity that maximizes profit, then our model can be expressed as follows,

> Objective function to be maximized: Total profit $= \pi(Q)$
> First-order (necessary) condition: $\pi'(Q) = 0$
> Second-order (sufficient) condition: $\pi''(Q) < 0$

The choice variable in this model is Q. The first-order condition tells us that the quantity chosen by the profit-maximizing firm is a quantity for which $\pi'(Q)$ is equal to zero. If $\pi'(Q) = 0$, the second-order condition tells us that, if $\pi''(Q)$ is negative, the firm is *maximizing* profit. If, however, $\pi''(Q)$ is positive, then the firm is *minimizing* profit where $\pi'(Q) = 0$. If $\pi''(Q)$ equals 0, there may be neither a maximum nor a minimum, but rather a point of inflection in the profit function.[1]

NUMERICAL EXAMPLE

Suppose a firm faces the following profit function.

$$\pi(Q) = -5Q + 3Q^2 - \tfrac{1}{3}Q^3 \qquad (4\text{-}1)$$

The graph of this third-degree polynomial and graphs of its first and second derivatives appear in Figure 4.1*a–c*. They must be graphed separately because, as we indicated in Chapter 3, they are all measured in different units. If the primitive function is measured in units of profit, the first derivative is measured in units of profit/quantity and the second derivative is measured in units of profit/(quantity)^2, as indicated on the vertical axes of the graphs.

The first-order condition stipulates that, if a critical point exists, the first derivative equals zero at that point. We take the first derivative of the profit function to see if and where it equals zero.

$$\frac{d\pi}{dQ} \equiv \pi'(Q) = -5 + 6Q - Q^2 = 0 \qquad (4\text{-}2)$$

$$(1 - Q)(Q - 5) = 0 \qquad (4\text{-}3)$$

$$Q = 1 \quad \text{or} \quad Q = 5 \qquad (4\text{-}4)$$

The first-order condition, graphed in Figure 4.1*b*, is a quadratic equation with two solutions. This is not too surprising, because we know that the profit

nth-order derivative test: a general test by which one may determine whether a critical point is a maximum, a minimum, or a point of inflection.

---

[1] To find out, continue taking higher-order derivatives until one is reached that is nonzero. Suppose it is $\pi^{(n)}(Q)$. If the order of the derivative, n, is an even number, then a negative nth-order derivative indicates a maximum and a positive nth-order derivative indicates a minimum. If n is an odd number, then a point of inflection is indicated. This procedure is called the **nth-order derivative test**.

Figure 4.1

(*a*) The Objective
Function
$\pi(Q) = -5Q + 3Q^2 - (1/3)Q^3$
(*b*) The First-Order
Condition
$\pi'(Q) = -5 + 6Q - Q^2 = 0$
(*c*) The Second-Order
Condition
$\pi''(Q) = 6 - 2Q < 0$

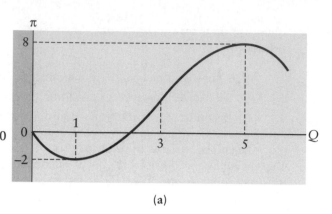

(a)

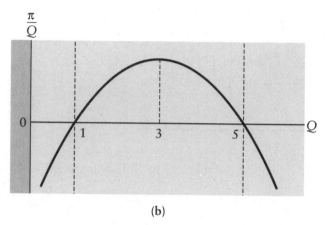

(b)

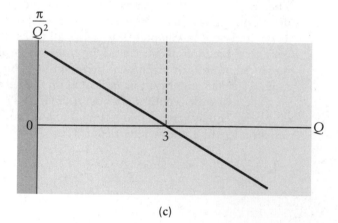

(c)

**local maximum or
minimum:** a point that is
a maximum or minimum
value relative to its
immediate neighbors.

function is cubic and we see that it has two critical points.[2] Note that, in
equation (4-3), we factor the quadratic equation in order to solve it. There is
a *local minimum* at $Q = 1$ where $\pi = -2.33$, and there is a *local maximum*
at $Q = 5$ where $\pi = 8.33$. We call the critical points *local* minima or maxima

---

[2] Because the profit function is cubic, its first derivative is quadratic. Remember that we asked you
to demonstrate that the derivative of a polynomial of degree *n* was itself a polynomial of degree
n − 1 in question 2 of the self-help problems in Chapter 3.

because there may be other points in the range of the function that have values less than − 2.33 or greater than 8.33. The local maximum at (5, 8.33) is only the maximum value relative to its immediate neighbors. If a function has a *global maximum or minimum*, then its value must be a maximum or minimum relative to every other point in its entire range. Note that any global optimum is also a local optimum, but a local optimum is not necessarily a global optimum.

global maximum or minimum: a point that is the maximum or minimum value relative to every other point in the entire range of the function.

The existence of the minimum at $Q = 1$ and the maximum at $Q = 5$ can be verified by examining the second-order condition. We take the second derivative of the profit function to see whether its slope is increasing or decreasing at the critical points.

$$\frac{d^2\pi}{dQ^2} \equiv \pi'' = 6 - 2Q \tag{4-5}$$

At $Q = 1$, $\pi'' = 4 > 0$; $\pi(Q)$ is at a minimum at $\pi = -2.33$
At $Q = 5$, $\pi'' = -4 < 0$; $\pi(Q)$ is at a maximum at $\pi = 8.33$

The second derivative is graphed in Figure 4.1*c*. At $Q = 1$ the second derivative is positive, and the profit function has a local minimum. At $Q = 5$ the second derivative is negative, and the profit function has a local maximum. Note that at $Q = 3$, where the profit function has a point of inflection, the second derivative equals zero.[3]

Notice how important both the first- and second-order conditions are in optimization models. The first-order condition is called *necessary* because it *must* be satisfied at any critical point. But although the first-order condition is necessary, it does not guarantee the existence of an optimum value, nor does it tell us the type of optimum if one does exist. The second-order condition is *sufficient* to guarantee the type of optimum, if the first-order condition is also satisfied. To underscore the significance of the necessary and sufficient conditions, recall Figure 3.9 from Chapter 3, reproduced here.

The function that is graphed is $Y = f(Q) = 12Q - 6Q^2 + Q^3$. The first derivative, $f'(Q) = 12 - 12Q + 3Q^2$, equals zero at the critical point $Q = 2$. But at the critical point the second derivative, $f''(Q) = -12 + 6Q$, is neither positive nor negative; it also equals zero. The third derivative, $f^{(3)}(Q) = -6$, is the first nonzero higher-order derivative, telling us that, at the critical point, the primitive function has a point of inflection with a slope equal to zero. Both the first- and second-order conditions must be satisfied in order to be certain that the objective function achieves a maximum or a minimum.

---

[3] We know that the function pictured in Figure 4.1 has a point of inflection because the second derivative changes sign when it passes through 0 at the point $Q = 3$; it goes from positive to negative. A second derivative that only touches the horizontal axis but does not cut through it does not indicate a point of inflection in the primitive function. Consider the function $Y = f(X) = X^4$ as an example. At the critical value $X = 0$, the first through third derivatives are all equal to zero. The fourth-order derivative equals 24, so the *n*th-order derivative test tells us that the critical point is a minimum.

Figure 3.9, repeated

Graphs of
$Y = 12X - 6X^2 + X^3$
and Its First and Second
Derivatives

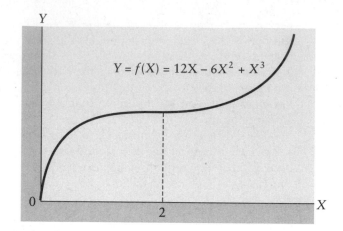

$$Y = f(X) = 12X - 6X^2 + X^3$$

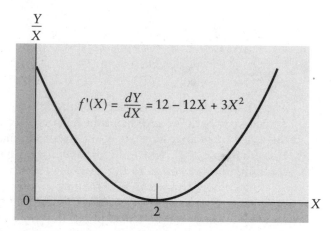

$$f'(X) = \frac{dY}{dX} = 12 - 12X + 3X^2$$

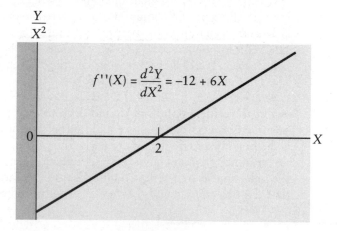

$$f''(X) = \frac{d^2Y}{dX^2} = -12 + 6X$$

EXERCISES
Section 4.2.1
First- and Second-
Order Conditions

1. A firm has a total cost function $TC(Q) = 100 + 100Q + Q^3/100$, where Q is rate of output, $Q > 0$.

   a. Find an expression for the average cost of output.

   b. What rate of output minimizes this firm's average cost of production?

2. A firm has a total product function $TP(L) = Q = 24L + 100L^2 - 2L^3$, in which L is employment of labor, $L > 0$.

   a. Find an expression for the average product of labor.

   b. What employment of labor maximizes this firm's average product of labor?

4.3

APPLICATIONS IN ECONOMIC THEORY

How can we use the technique of mathematical optimization to build economic models and find comparative statics results? Recall the five-step description of economic theorizing in Section 1.3 of Chapter 1. The first two steps of the process (step 1: choosing a problem and identifying choice variables and step 2: choosing a model) can describe an objective function in an optimization problem. For example, suppose we are interested in investigating the problem: what explains the rate of output produced by firms? Rate of output is our choice variable. Step 2 requires us to choose a model. This means we must postulate a behavioral rule: how do firms choose a rate of output? For the following applications of mathematical optimization, we postulate that firms choose a rate of output that maximizes profit.[4] All that we have to do to use mathematical optimization for economic theorizing is to specify our objective function—in this case, a profit function with the rate of output as its argument. Then the first- and second-order conditions for profit maximization become the equilibrium conditions of our economic model. Let's explore the theory of profit maximization in a general form.

4.3.1 Profit Maximization: The General Case

We are not ever likely to know a specific functional form for profit (as we used in the numerical example above) when we attempt to model the behavior of the firm. We do know some things about profit functions, however, and by incorporating different information into our specification we can develop a surprisingly rich theory of the profit-maximizing firm. Consider the following general specification of the profit-maximization problem.

Maximize $\pi = TR(Q) - TC(Q)$, where $TR(Q)$ is the revenue function, $TC(Q)$ is the cost function, and Q is the rate of output. To save space, we refer

---

[4] We do not have to postulate that firms maximize profits. Other models about behavior of firms might have them maximizing sales or market share or minimizing average cost.

to the first-order condition as FOC and the second-order condition as SOC.

Objective function: $\pi(Q) = TR(Q) - TC(Q)$ (4-6)

FOC: $\pi'(Q) \equiv \dfrac{d\pi}{dQ} = TR'(Q) - TC'(Q) = 0$ (4-7)

SOC: $\pi''(Q) \equiv \dfrac{d^2\pi}{dQ^2} = TR''(Q) - TC''(Q) < 0$ (4-8)

Rewrite the FOC, equation (4-7), as

$TR'(Q) = TC'(Q)$ (4-9)

Recognize that $TR'(Q)$ is marginal revenue and $TC'(Q)$ is marginal cost. The first-order condition gives us the familiar rule that, to maximize profit, firms produce the quantity at which marginal revenue equals marginal cost. Now rewrite the SOC as

$TR''(Q) < TC''(Q)$ (4-10)

You should be able to recognize that $TR''(Q)$ is the slope of the marginal revenue function and that $TC''(Q)$ is the slope of the marginal cost function. The SOC requires that the slope of marginal revenue be less than the slope of marginal cost. This means that the firm's profit-maximizing rate of output occurs at the point where marginal revenue equals marginal cost, provided the marginal cost curve cuts through the marginal revenue curve from below.

To become adept at using economic models, it is important to be able to make intuitive and graphical sense out of necessary and sufficient conditions. Take the FOC of the general profit-maximization model as an example. The FOC means that it is necessary that marginal revenue equal marginal cost if profit is maximized. To make sense of this condition, consider the situation if it did *not* hold. If marginal revenue were greater than marginal cost, then producing at an incrementally higher rate of output would bring in more revenue than it would cost, and profit would increase. On the other hand, if marginal revenue were less than marginal cost, then producing at an incrementally lower rate of output would save more in costs than it would lose in revenue, and once again profit would increase. It follows that profit cannot be at a maximum unless marginal revenue equals marginal cost.

The second-order condition also makes good intuitive sense. It states that at the profit-maximizing rate of output the slope of the marginal revenue curve must be less than the slope of the marginal cost curve, or that marginal cost must approach marginal revenue from below. This means that, as the firm's rate of output approaches the profit-maximizing rate from below, marginal cost is less than marginal revenue. Any incremental increase in the rate of output adds more to revenue than to cost, and it increases profit until profit is maximized where marginal revenue equals marginal cost. If, contrary to the second-order condition, marginal cost approached marginal revenue from above, any increase in the rate of output would add more to cost than to revenue and would decrease profit. If this were the case, profit would be minimized, not maximized, where marginal revenue equals marginal cost.

To make graphical sense out of the first- and second-order conditions, look at Figure 4.2. In Figure 4.2*a*, revenue, TR, and cost, TC, are both graphed as increasing functions of Q, the rate of output. Profit, π, equals revenue minus cost, or the vertical difference between the two functions. Where cost is greater than revenue, profit is negative. Maximum profit occurs at Q^*, where the vertical distance between revenue and cost is greatest. As the rate of output approaches Q^*, the revenue and cost functions are diverging because the slope of the revenue function is greater than the slope of the cost function. This can be seen in Figure 4.2*b*, where the first derivatives (or slopes) of the revenue, cost, and profit functions are graphed. At Q^* the slopes of the revenue and cost functions are equal to one another, and after Q^* the functions converge because the slope of the cost function is greater than the slope of the revenue function. Because the slope of a function is its first derivative, profits are maximized where $TR'(Q)$ equals $TC'(Q)$, provided that TC' approaches TR' from below.

Figure 4.2

(*a*) **Total Revenue, Total Cost, and Profit: The General Case**
(*b*) **Marginal Revenue, Marginal Cost, and Marginal Profit**

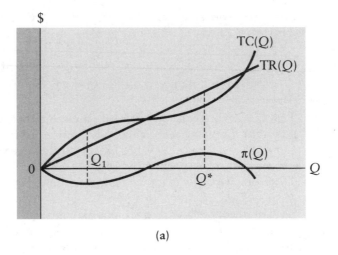

(a)

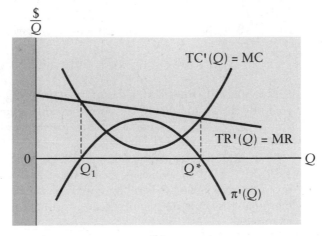

(b)

The slopes of the revenue and cost functions are also equal at Q_1 in Figure 4.2. At Q_1, cost exceeds revenue and profit is minimized. The SOC for maximization is not satisfied at this point, because the slope of the marginal cost curve is less (more negative) than the slope of the marginal revenue curve. This is a point at which profit is minimized, not maximized. These relationships can also be seen in the graphs of the profit function in Figure 4.2a and its first derivative in Figure 4.2b. At Q_1 the profit function achieves a local minimum, and its derivative is equal to zero but rising. At Q^* the profit function achieves a local maximum, and its derivative is equal to zero but decreasing.

NUMERICAL EXAMPLE

Let revenue equal $TR = 20Q - Q^2$ and cost equal $TC = 40Q - 15Q^2 + 2Q^3$. Profit equals revenue minus cost, or $\pi = 20Q - Q^2 - (40Q - 15Q^2 + 2Q^3) = -20Q + 14Q^2 - 2Q^3$. Working directly with the simplified version of the profit function, we can find the first- and second-order conditions for profit maximization by taking the first and second derivatives of π.

$$\text{FOC:} \qquad \pi' = -20 + 28Q - 6Q^2 = 0 \qquad \text{(4-11)}$$

$$\text{SOC:} \qquad \pi'' = 28 - 12Q < 0 \qquad \text{(4-12)}$$

The FOC represents a quadratic equation that can be solved using the quadratic formula (see Chapter 2, Section 2.4.1). The two solutions are $Q = 0.88$ and $Q = 3.79$. When we substitute these values for Q into the SOC, we see that π'' is positive when $Q = 0.88$ and negative when $Q = 3.79$. Therefore, we know that profit is at a minimum at $Q = 0.88$ and a maximum at $Q = 3.79$.

Our theory tells us that profit is maximized when marginal revenue equals marginal cost, and the slope of marginal revenue is less than the slope of marginal cost. These theoretical propositions ought to hold for our numerical example. Marginal revenue is the derivative of revenue, or, in this case, $MR = 20 - 2Q$. Similarly, marginal cost is the derivative of cost, or $MC = 40 - 30Q + 6Q^2$. Setting them equal gives us

$$MR = 20 - 2Q = 40 - 30Q + 6Q^2 = MC \qquad \text{(4-13)}$$

Subtracting MC from both sides of the equation gives us the same quadratic equation as we found for π', with the same solutions for Q. We take the second derivatives of TR and TC to find the slopes of the marginal revenue and marginal cost curves, finding $TR'' = MR' = -2$ and $TC'' = MC' = -30 + 12Q$. At $Q = 0.88$, $MC' = -19.44$, which is less than MR'. At $Q = 3.79$, $MC' = 15.48$, which is greater than MR'. Therefore, the theory that profit is maximized where marginal revenue equals marginal cost and marginal cost cuts marginal revenue from below holds for this numerical example.

4.4

PROFIT MAXIMIZATION IN THE OUTPUT MARKET

The profit-maximization model that has been presented is extremely general. That is, it incorporates the least amount of information possible in the profit function. All that is assumed is that profit is revenue minus cost. The model applies equally well to all profit-maximizing behavior and makes no distinctions among monopolists, oligopolists, monopsonists, and perfect competitors. Although generality is a virtue in behavioral models, it is usually achieved by sacrificing detail. Often, we want a model to include more information in order to answer more specific questions. One way to incorporate more information in this model is to be more specific regarding the nature of the revenue function. Suppose, for example, that we want to model the behavior of *price-taking* profit-maximizing firms. A **price-taker** treats price as a constant, or a parameter, determined by the market. Price is unaffected by the firm's rate of output. **Perfect competition** is described by models which assume price-taking firms. We examine the economic model of the price-taking firm as an extension of profit-maximizing behavior in the following section.

price-taker: a firm whose output or input decisions have no effect on output or input price.

perfect competition: a market condition in which there are sufficient numbers of buyers and sellers that no single buyer or seller can influence price.

4.4.1 Price Taking in the Output Market

We incorporate the information that price is a parameter by writing the revenue function as

$$\text{TR}(Q) = PQ \tag{4-14}$$

in which P equals price and is treated as a constant. As before, Q represents the rate of output. Our aim is to maximize the objective function

$$\pi(Q) = PQ - \text{TC}(Q) \tag{4-15}$$

The first- and second-order conditions are

$$\text{FOC:} \quad \pi'(Q) = P - \text{TC}'(Q) = 0 \Leftrightarrow P = \text{TC}'(Q) = \text{MC} \tag{4-16}$$

$$\text{SOC:} \quad \pi''(Q) = -\text{TC}''(Q) < 0 \Leftrightarrow \text{TC}''(Q) = \text{MC}' > 0 \tag{4-17}$$

These conditions give us the rules that price-takers produce where price equals marginal cost and that marginal cost must be upward sloping. Demonstrating these conditions graphically requires only slight modification of Figure 4.2. The revenue function becomes a straight upward-sloping line with a slope of P, while the marginal revenue function becomes a horizontal line equal to P. The profit-maximizing rate of output, Q^*, occurs where $P = \text{MR} = \text{MC}$. These changes are made in Figure 4.3.

Figure 4.3

Price Taking in the
Output Market
(*a*) Total Revenue, Total
Cost, and Profit
(*b*) Price, Marginal
Cost, and Marginal
Profit

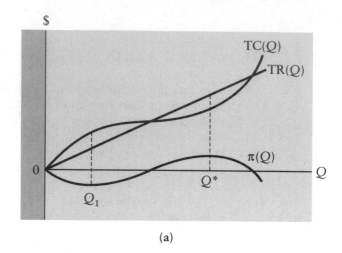

(a)

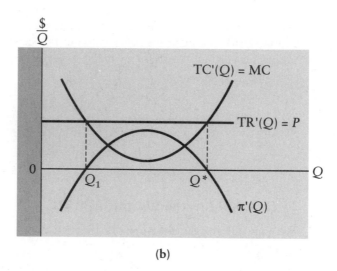

(b)

NUMERICAL EXAMPLE

Let $P = 16$, where P is output price. If the firm is a price-taker, revenue equals $TR = 16Q$. Let the cost function equal $TC = 40Q - 15Q^2 + 2Q^3$, as in our earlier numerical example. Profit equals

$$\pi = TR - TC = 16Q - (40Q - 15Q^2 + 2Q^3) = -24Q + 15Q^2 - 2Q^3$$
$$(4\text{-}18)$$

We take the first and second derivatives of the profit function to state the first- and second-order conditions for profit maximization.

FOC: $\pi' = TR' - TC' = -24 + 30Q - 6Q^2 = 0$ (4-19)

SOC: $\pi'' = TR'' - TC'' = 30 - 12Q < 0$ (4-20)

The FOC is a quadratic equation that can be factored.

$$\pi' - 6(-4 + 5Q - Q^2) = 6[(4 - Q)(Q - 1)] = 0 \qquad (4\text{-}21)$$

We find that $Q = 1$ or $Q = 4$. Substituting these values into the SOC reveals that profit is maximized when $Q = 4$.

The theory of profit maximization can be adapted to focus on a wide range of behavior of firms in addition to the price-taker model. Two more useful extensions are to (1) price-searching behavior and (2) input utilization decisions. First let's consider price-searching behavior.

4.4.2 Price Searching in the Output Market

price-searcher: a firm whose output or input decisions have an effect on output or input price.

monopoly: a market in which there is a single seller of a commodity or input, modeled as a price-searcher.

The *price-searcher* firm influences the price of its product when it varies the rate of output. This means that its price, or average revenue, is not a parameter of the model to be treated as a constant but rather is a function of quantity. *Monopoly* is described by models that assume price-searcher behavior on the part of the firm. The firm's profit function becomes

$$\pi(Q) = P(Q)Q - \text{TC}(Q) \qquad (4\text{-}22)$$

Differentiating equation (4-22) requires that we invoke the product rule to find the derivative of the revenue function. The first- and second-order conditions are

$$\text{FOC:} \qquad \pi'(Q) = P(Q) + \frac{dP}{dQ}Q - \text{TC}'(Q) = 0 \qquad (4\text{-}23)$$

$$\text{SOC:} \qquad \pi''(Q) = Q\frac{d^2P}{dQ^2} + 2\frac{dP}{dQ} - \text{TC}''(Q) < 0 \qquad (4\text{-}24)$$

Remember from Chapter 3, Section 3.7.2, that marginal revenue, MR, equals $P(Q) + QP'(Q)$, and you can see that the first-order condition states that profit is maximized when MR equals MC. Marginal revenue is, of course, less than price because $P'(Q)$ is negative. Recognize also that $QP''(Q) + 2P'(Q)$ equals MR', or the slope of the marginal revenue function. The second-order condition stipulates that marginal revenue have a more negative slope than marginal cost. Note that the price-searcher model does not require upward-sloping marginal cost.[5] This model is illustrated in Figure 4.4, in which we depict the demand curve as linear and the marginal cost curve as

---

[5] Remember that, in the price-taker model, MR equals price, which is a horizontal line with a slope equal to zero. In order to have a greater slope than MR, MC must be positively sloped. In the price-searcher model, MR has a negative slope. Therefore MC could be negatively sloped and still have a slope greater than MR. This is an important point in the theory of natural monopoly.

Figure 4.4

Output Market
Equilibrium for the
Price-Searcher Firm

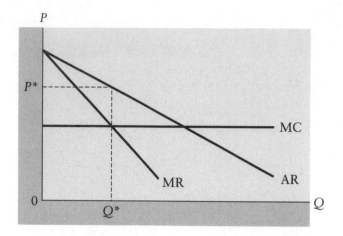

constant for convenience. In fact, there is nothing in the mathematics of the model that requires these functions to be linear or constant.

NUMERICAL EXAMPLE

Suppose a firm is a price-searcher, facing an average revenue function equal to $AR = P = 6 - Q/2$ and total cost equal to $TC = 20Q - 5Q^2 + \frac{1}{3}Q^3$, where Q is the rate of output. We find total revenue by multiplying AR by output, obtaining $TR = 6Q - Q^2/2$. Profit, therefore, is total revenue minus total cost, or $\pi = -14Q + 4.5Q^2 - \frac{1}{3}Q^3$. We can find the profit-maximizing rate of output by taking the first and second derivatives of the profit function, finding the FOC and SOC.

$$\text{FOC:} \quad \pi' = -14 + 9Q - Q^2 = 0 \qquad \text{(4-25)}$$

$$\text{SOC:} \quad \pi'' = 9 - 2Q < 0 \qquad \text{(4-26)}$$

The FOC is a quadratic equation that can be solved by factoring.

$$\pi' = (7 - Q)(Q - 2) = 0 \Leftrightarrow Q = 7 \text{ and } Q = 2 \qquad \text{(4-27)}$$

Substituting these values into the SOC, we find that π'' is negative when $Q = 7$ and positive when $Q = 2$; therefore $Q = 7$ is the profit-maximizing rate of output. We can find the price and the amount of profit by substituting $Q = 7$ into the average revenue function and the profit function. We discover that $P = 2.5$ and $\pi = 8.17$.

We have described the equilibrium in the output market of both price-taking and price-searching firms mathematically, graphically, and in narrative. To illustrate further optimization models with one independent variable, we turn now to input market behavior, in which the firm's choice of inputs is the focus of our interest.

EXERCISES
Section 4.4.2
Price-Searching in
the Output Market

For Exercises 1 through 4, consider a firm whose average revenue, AR, and total cost, TC, are the following functions of the rate of output, Q.

$$AR = P = 20 - 5Q - Q^2, \qquad TC = 4 + 14Q - 5Q^2 + Q^3$$

1. Find this firm's marginal revenue and marginal cost functions.

2. Assume that the firm maximizes profit. What are its objective function, its first-order condition for maximization, and its second-order condition for maximization?

3. What rates of output satisfy the first-order condition? What rate of output satisfies the second-order condition? What price is associated with the profit-maximizing level of output? |4

4. Find the value of price elasticity of demand at the profit-maximizing levels of output and price. Is this firm a price-taker or a price-searcher?

5. Model the profit-maximizing behavior of a price-taker firm facing the cost function $TC = 10 + Q + Q^2/2$. Provide

    a. the objective function and the first- and second-order conditions for optimization.

    b. the profit-maximizing rate of output and the optimum level of profit if price equals $P = 10$.

4.5

PROFIT MAXIMIZATION IN INPUT MARKETS

In this section we extend the profit-maximization model to focus on the firm's behavior in input markets. To do this, it is necessary to recognize that the firm's production function relates rate of output to the quantity of inputs employed. Because we are dealing with models with only one independent variable, we restrict ourselves to production functions with only one input, labor, L. Focusing on input markets directs our attention to the cost side of the profit function. Costs, in general, equal the prices of inputs times the quantity of inputs employed. We can treat the price of the input, w, for the wage rate, either as a parameter or as a function of the amount of labor employed. The former instance is one of price-taking or perfect competition in input markets; the latter is one of price-searching or *monopsony* in input markets.[6] Let's consider price-taking behavior in input markets first.

monopsony: a market in which there is a single buyer of a commodity or input, modeled as a price-searcher.

4.5.1 Price Taking in Input Markets

Our model requires us to maximize the objective function

$$\pi(L) = TR(Q(L)) - wL \tag{4-28}$$

---

[6] The word *monopoly* is derived from the Greek for "one seller," and *monopsony* is derived from the Greek for "one buyer."

where Q equals the rate of output. Total revenue is represented by the composite function, $TR(Q(L))$. Revenue is, of course, a function of output, $TR = TR(Q)$, and output is a function of the quantity of the input L, $Q = Q(L)$. The choice variable in this model is L, the amount of labor, and the wage rate, w, is a parameter. Remember the *chain rule* (Chapter 3, Section 3.4) when differentiating the objective function. The first- and second-order conditions for profit maximization are

$$\text{FOC:} \qquad \pi'(L) = TR'(Q)\frac{dQ}{dL} - w = 0 \Leftrightarrow TR'(Q)\frac{dQ}{dL} \equiv MRP = w \qquad \textbf{(4-29)}$$

$$\text{SOC:} \qquad \pi''(L) = TR''(Q)\left(\frac{dQ}{dL}\right)^2 + TR'(Q)\frac{d^2Q}{dL^2} = MRP' < 0 \qquad \textbf{(4-30)}$$

The first-order condition states that the profit-maximizing firm will utilize an input in such quantity that marginal revenue, $TR'(Q)$, times marginal product, $Q'(L)$, equals its price. Marginal revenue times marginal product is more commonly known as *marginal revenue product, MRP*, so we can express the FOC as $MRP = w$. This result can be interpreted intuitively by recognizing that MRP represents the incremental increase in revenue due to employing another unit of labor, while the wage represents the incremental increase in cost. Profit is maximized when, for the marginal unit of labor, the increment to revenue equals the increment to costs.

Be sure that you understand how we found the second-order condition and what it means. The SOC simply requires that the second derivative of the profit function be negative. We find the second derivative of the profit function by differentiating the first derivative, which we found in the FOC. To carry out this differentiation we must use both the chain rule, because Q is a function of L, and the product rule, because TR' is multiplied by dQ/dL in the first derivative. Because the cost side of the profit function is represented only by the parameter w in the first derivative, it drops out in the second derivative. The second derivative of the profit function is simply the second derivative of the revenue function with respect to labor, or the slope of MRP. The SOC simply requires that the MRP be downward sloping. This ensures that, when

marginal revenue product (MRP): the incremental change in revenue due to an incremental change in the employment of some input.

Figure 4.5

Equilibrium for the Price-Taker Firm in the Input Market

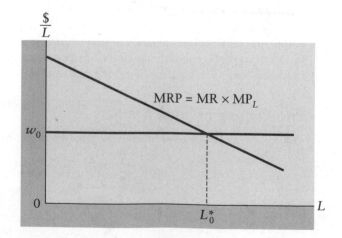

MRP is equal to wage, profit is maximized and not minimized. All the incremental units of labor which add more to revenue than cost are employed, and none which add more to cost than to revenue are employed. These equilibrium conditions are illustrated graphically in Figure 4.5. At a wage of w_0, profit is maximized at L_0^*.

NUMERICAL EXAMPLE

Suppose that a firm is a price-taker in the output market, facing a price equal to 16. Total revenue equals price times output, or TR $= 16Q$, where Q is the rate of output. The firm produces according to the production function $Q = 2L^{1/2}$, where L is the amount of labor employed. The wage rate equals 4. Profit equals

$$\pi(L) = \text{TR}(Q(L)) - wL = 16(2L^{1/2}) - 4L \qquad (4\text{-}31)$$

Note that we substituted the production function for output in the total revenue function. The first- and second-order conditions for profit maximization are

$$\text{FOC:} \qquad \pi'(L) = \text{TR}'(Q)Q'(L) - w = 16L^{-1/2} - 4 = 0 \qquad (4\text{-}32)$$

$$\text{SOC:} \qquad \pi''(L) = \text{TR}''(Q')^2 + \text{TR}'Q'' = -8L^{-3/2} < 0 \qquad (4\text{-}33)$$

Solving the FOC for L^*, we find that $L^{-1/2} = 4/16$ or $L^* = 16$. Substituting $L^* = 16$ into the SOC, we discover that the second derivative is negative, and 16 is a profit-maximizing value of L^*. Maximum profit equals $\pi^* = 32(16^{1/2}) - 64 = 64$.

Note that our model of a firm's input choice is general enough to accommodate both possibilities regarding the output market. As we showed in Section 4.4, firms can be either price-takers or price-searchers in the output market. The difference between these two types of behavior is modeled in the revenue function, which in our analysis of input markets we have left in its most general form. If we want to model the input choices of firms which are price-takers in the output market (as in the numerical example), then total revenue is output price, P, times the rate of output, and the FOC becomes

$$\pi'(L) = \text{TR}'(Q)\frac{dQ}{dL} - w = P\frac{dQ}{dL} - w = 0 \Leftrightarrow P\frac{dQ}{dL} = w \qquad (4\text{-}34)$$

value of marginal product (VMP): output price multiplied by the marginal product of the input. It is the same thing as marginal revenue product when a firm is a price-taker in the output market.

Price times dQ/dL is the marginal revenue product for firms that are price-takers in their output markets, and it is often referred to as *value of marginal product* (VMP). Because P is a parameter in this model and $\text{TR}'(Q)$ equals P and $\text{TR}''(Q)$ equals zero, the second-order condition is

$$P\frac{d^2Q}{dL^2} < 0 \qquad (4\text{-}35)$$

We know that d^2Q/dL^2 is the slope of the marginal product; therefore this second-order condition is equivalent to assuming downward-sloping, or diminishing, marginal product.

If firms are price-searchers in the output market, then output price is a function of quantity. Recall from Chapter 3, Section 3.7.3, the relationship between marginal revenue and elasticity of demand. Remembering this relationship allows us to express the FOC in this instance as

$$\pi'(L) = \text{TR}'(Q)\frac{dQ}{dL} - w = P\left(1 + \frac{1}{\varepsilon_{QP}}\right)\frac{dQ}{dL} - w = 0 \qquad (4\text{-}36)$$

Equation (4-36) shows how the input market equilibrium is affected by conditions in the output market. The less elastic the demand curve facing the firm in the output market, the less labor will be demanded at any wage rate in the input market. Next, we turn to the case where the firm is a price-searcher in the input model.

4.5.2   Price Searching in Input Markets

In general, we distinguish price-searching models from price-taking models through our treatment of the relevant price. Price-taking behavior is modeled mathematically by treating price as a parameter, or a constant, in the objective function. Price-searching behavior is modeled by treating price as a function of some quantity. As you have seen, price-searching in the output market requires that we consider price of output to be a function of the rate of output. Price-searching in an input market requires us to consider price of the input as a function of the amount of the input employed. Just as monopoly firms are modeled as price-searchers in an output market, monopsony firms are modeled as price-searchers in an input market. In our simple, one-input model we express price-searching behavior by making wage rate a function of the labor utilized or

$$w = w(L) \qquad (4\text{-}37)$$

A firm that is the only buyer of some input affects the price of the input by the amount it employs because, being the only buyer, it faces the market supply of the input. We usually think of market supply curves as upward sloping; that is, the quantity of labor supplied increases with the wage rate. The function $w(L)$ describes the inverse of the labor supply curve, so it is also an increasing function. Therefore

$$w'(L) \equiv \frac{dw}{dL} > 0 \qquad (4\text{-}38)$$

The firm maximizes profit, so the objective function in this model is

$$\pi(L) = \text{TR}(Q(L)) - w(L)L \qquad (4\text{-}39)$$

Remember to use both the chain rule (because total revenue is a composite function) and the product rule [because $w(L)$ is multiplied by L] when differentiating the profit function. The first-order condition for profit maximization is

$$\text{FOC:} \qquad \pi'(L) = \text{TR}'(Q)\frac{dQ}{dL} - \left[w(L) + L\frac{dw}{dL}\right] = 0 \qquad (4\text{-}40)$$

which can be rewritten as

$$\text{FOC:} \qquad \text{TR}'(Q)\frac{dQ}{dL} = w(L) + L\frac{dw}{dL} \qquad (4\text{-}41)$$

To interpret the first-order condition, recall that

$$\text{TR}'(Q)\frac{dQ}{dL} \qquad (4\text{-}42)$$

is the firm's MRP and that it is the derivative of revenue with respect to labor. The expression

$$w(L) + L\frac{dw}{dL} \qquad (4\text{-}43)$$

marginal factor cost (MFC): the incremental change in total cost due to an incremental change in the employment of some input.

is the derivative of cost with respect to labor and is known as ***marginal factor cost (MFC)***. It measures the effect of an incremental change in the employment of labor on the total cost of the firm. Because $w'(L)$ is positive, MFC is greater than the wage rate, or MFC lies above the inverse labor supply curve $w(L)$. Profit is maximized when, for the marginal unit of labor, the contribution to cost just equals the contribution to revenue, or MFC equals MRP. In Figure 4.6 MRP is downward sloping and MFC is upward sloping and lies above the inverse supply curve. Profit is maximized when the firm employs L^* amount of labor, at a wage equal to w^*.

The second-order condition is

$$\text{SOC:} \qquad \pi''(L) = \text{TR}''(Q)\left(\frac{dQ}{dL}\right)^2 + \text{TR}'(Q)\frac{d^2Q}{dL^2} - \left(L\frac{d^2w}{dL^2} + 2\frac{dw}{dL}\right) < 0$$
$$(4\text{-}44)$$

To interpret the second-order condition, recognize that the expression

$$\text{TR}''(Q)\left(\frac{dQ}{dL}\right)^2 + \text{TR}'(Q)\frac{d^2Q}{dL^2} \qquad (4\text{-}45)$$

is MRP′, or the slope of MRP, and that the expression

$$L\frac{d^2w}{dL^2} + 2\frac{dw}{dL} \qquad (4\text{-}46)$$

is MFC′, or the slope of MFC. The second-order condition requires that the slope of MFC be greater than the slope of MRP. In Figure 4.6 we have drawn

Figure 4.6

Input Market
Equilibrium for the
Price-Searcher Firm

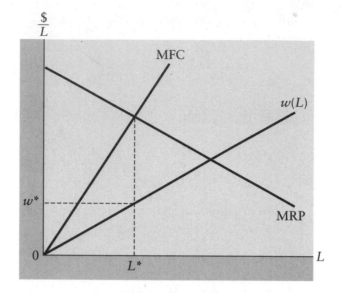

MRP as downward sloping and MFC as upward sloping (as, in general, we expect them to be), so the second-order condition is satisfied.

NUMERICAL EXAMPLE

Suppose, as in the previous numerical example, that a firm is a price-taker in the output market, facing a price equal to 16. Total revenue equals price times output, or TR = 16Q, where Q is the rate of output. The firm produces according to the production function $Q = 2L^{1/2}$, where L is the amount of labor employed. The firm is a price-searcher in the input market, so the wage rate is a function of the amount of labor employed, $w(L) = 4L^{1/2}$. Profit equals

$$\pi(L) = \text{TR}(Q(L)) - wL = 16(2L^{1/2}) - 4L^{3/2} \qquad (4\text{-}47)$$

The first- and second-order conditions for profit maximization are

FOC: $\pi'(L) = \text{TR}'(Q)Q'(L) - w'L - w(L) = 16L^{-1/2} - 6L^{1/2} = 0$

$$\qquad (4\text{-}48)$$

SOC: $\pi''(L) = \text{TR}''Q'^2 + \text{TR}'Q'' - Lw'' - 2w' = -8L^{-3/2} - 3L^{-1/2} < 0$

$$\qquad (4\text{-}49)$$

Solving the FOC for L^*, we find that

$$L^{*\,-1/2} = (6/16)L^{*\,1/2} \qquad (4\text{-}50)$$

Dividing through by $L^{*\,1/2}$ and inverting both sides gives us

$$L^* = 16/6 = 2.67 \qquad (4\text{-}51)$$

Substituting $L^* = 2.67$ into the SOC, we discover that the second derivative is negative, and 2.67 is a profit-maximizing value of L^*. At $L^* = 2.67$, profit equals 34.84.

Reexamine the FOC. You should be able to recognize that the first term of the expression, $16L^{1/2}$, represents the derivative of the composite revenue function with respect to L, or MRP, and the second term, $-6L^{1/2}$, represents the derivative of the cost function with respect to L, or MFC. The FOC simply sets MFC equal to MRP, and the SOC ensures that the MFC cuts through MRP from below.

So far, we have investigated only the equilibrium conditions of profit-maximizing firms. We have demonstrated how different assumptions regarding output and input markets can be incorporated in the objective functions and the first- and second-order conditions of profit-maximization models. As you know from Chapter 1, Section 1.3, having a problem to investigate, choosing a model, and finding equilibrium conditions constitute only the first three steps of economic reasoning. We haven't really explained any behavior; we have only abstract descriptions of firms' output and input choices which we hope to use to do comparative statics analysis. Now we turn to the comparative statics analysis of profit-maximizing firms.

EXERCISES
Section 4.5.2
Price Searching in
Input Markets

Consider a firm which is a price-searcher in both its output and its input markets and which faces the inverse labor supply function $w = 2 + 2L$, where w is the wage rate and L is quantity of labor. Suppose the firm's production function is $Q = 2L$, where Q is the rate of output. Suppose the average revenue function for the firm's product is given by $AR = P = 25 - 0.5Q$.

1. Derive the firm's marginal revenue product (MRP) and marginal factor cost (MFC) as functions of labor utilization, L.

2. Find the equilibrium labor utilization, L^*, and the equilibrium wage rate, w^*.

4.6

COMPARATIVE STATICS ANALYSIS OF THE PROFIT-MAXIMIZING FIRM

In order to do comparative statics, we have to assume that our descriptions of equilibrium are true, change a parameter or exogenous variable, and compare the new equilibrium with the original. Among the models we have presented in this chapter, only the price-taker models have a parameter that can be changed to generate comparative statics results. As you know, the fact that price is a parameter is the detail that distinguishes price-taker from price-searcher behavior. For this reason, we will use the price-taker models to illustrate comparative statics analysis of profit-maximizing firms.

4.6.1 Comparative Statics Analysis of a Change in Output Price

To perform comparative statics analysis, we must *assume the model is true*. We did this in Chapter 1 by solving the equilibrium conditions for the endogenous variables, obtaining reduced-form equations in which the endogenous variables were expressed as functions of the parameters and exogenous variables. We follow a similar procedure in this analysis. As we have indicated, the equilibrium conditions for an optimization model are its first-and second-order conditions, and we repeat the FOC and SOC we found earlier in Section 4.4.1.

$$\text{FOC:} \quad \pi'(Q) = P - \text{TC}'(Q) = 0 \Leftrightarrow P = \text{TC}'(Q) = \text{MC} \quad \textbf{(4-16)}$$

$$\text{SOC:} \quad \pi''(Q) = -\text{TC}''(Q) < 0 \Leftrightarrow \text{TC}''(Q) = \text{MC}' > 0 \quad \textbf{(4-17)}$$

The FOC describes implicitly a relation between Q^* and P, which we can write as[7]

$$F(P, Q^*) \equiv P - \text{TC}'(Q^*) = 0 \quad \textbf{(4-52)}$$

The implicit function theorem (see Chapter 3, Section 3.6.2) tells us that the explicit function $Q^* = Q^*(P)$ exists if

$$F_{Q^*} \equiv \frac{dF}{dQ^*}\bigg|_{\text{treating } P \text{ as a constant}} \quad \text{and} \quad F_P \equiv \frac{dF}{dP}\bigg|_{\text{treating } Q^* \text{ as a constant}} \quad \textbf{(4-53)}$$

are continuous and if $F_Q \neq 0$. Differentiating equation (4-52) tells us that $F_P = 1$ and that $F_Q = -\text{TC}''(Q)$. The constant function, $F_P = 1$, is clearly continuous; we can assume that the cost function $\text{TC}(Q)$ is twice differentiable; and the SOC, equation (4-17), assures us that $F_Q = -\text{TC}''(Q) \neq 0$. Therefore, we conclude that the explicit function $Q^* = Q^*(P)$ exists and is continuous, as is its derivative, dQ^*/dP.

In recognizing the functional relationship between the equilibrium value of the choice variable, Q^*, and the parameter, P, we assume that the model is true; that is, we assume that the FOC and SOC hold. If we substitute $Q^*(P)$ back into the FOC we create the identity

$$P - \text{TC}'(Q^*(P)) \equiv 0 \equiv F(P, Q^*) \quad \textbf{(4-54)}$$

This identity is an implicit function, and the derivative dQ^*/dP can be found by *implicit differentiation* of $F(Q^*, P)$. Recall implicit differentiation from Chapter 3.

$$\frac{dQ^*}{dP} = -\frac{F_P}{F_{Q^*}} = \frac{1}{\text{TC}''} > 0 \quad \textbf{(4-55)}$$

---

[7] Remember that we use the superscript asterisk to denote an equilibrium value of a choice variable. Only the equilibrium or profit-maximizing rate of output can be considered a function of price.

Figure 4.7

Effect of a Change in
Price on a Price-Taker's
Output

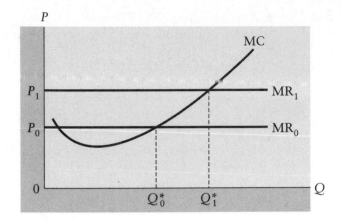

The second-order condition tells us that $TC''(Q)$ is greater than zero, and, therefore, so is dQ^*/dP. The profit-maximizing rate of output increases when price increases and decreases when price decreases. The comparative statics analysis is illustrated graphically in Figure 4.7. At the higher price, P_1, the producer chooses a greater rate of output, Q_1^*. The graph indicates clearly the importance of the second-order condition in determining the response of the choice variable to a change in the parameter. It is because marginal cost is upward sloping at the optimum rate of output that the profit-maximizing rate of output increases with an increase in price.

Note how we have conformed to the methodology of economic reasoning. We create a model to explain the price-taking firm's choice of output rate, identifying price as an important parameter. The equilibrium conditions are simply the first- and second-order conditions of the optimization model. We assume the model is true by assuming the first- and second-order conditions hold. Doing so defines for us (implicitly) an equation in which the equilibrium value of the choice variable is expressed as a function of the parameter. To discover how the equilibrium value of the choice variable responds to changes in the parameter, we implicitly differentiate the identity created by substituting the equilibrium value of the choice variable back into the first-order condition whence it came. The second-order condition made it possible for us to sign the derivative of the choice variable with respect to the parameter. We will follow the same method to perform comparative statics analyses with all the optimization models discussed throughout this text.

NUMERICAL EXAMPLE

Recall the numerical example of Section 4.4.1, in which $P = 16$, revenue equals $TR = 16Q$, and cost is $TC = 40Q - 15Q^2 + 2Q^3$. The objective function and equilibrium conditions are

$$\pi = TR - TC = 16Q - (40Q - 15Q^2 + 2Q^3) = -24Q + 15Q^2 - 2Q^3$$

(4-18)

$$\text{FOC:} \quad \pi' = TR' - TC' = -24 + 30Q - 6Q^2 = 0 \quad \text{(4-19)}$$

$$\text{SOC:} \quad \pi'' = TR'' - TC'' = 30 - 12Q < 0 \quad \text{(4-20)}$$

We find maximum profit at $Q^* = 4$.

In order to illustrate the effects of a rise in price, suppose price were equal to 20 instead of 16. Then $TR = 20Q$ and profit equals $\pi = -20Q + 15Q^2 - 2Q^3$. The FOC and SOC become

$$\text{FOC:} \qquad \pi' = -20 + 30Q - 6Q^2 = 0 \qquad \text{(4-56)}$$

$$\text{SOC:} \qquad \pi'' = 30 - 12Q < 0 \qquad \text{(4-57)}$$

We need to use the quadratic formula to solve the FOC for Q^*. We find that $Q = 0.79$ or $Q = 4.21$. The SOC tells us that profit is maximized when $Q^* = 4.21$. As you can see, at a higher price, profit-maximizing quantity is greater.

In this section, we have discussed the comparative statics of the output market price-taker model. Next, we use exactly the same procedure to examine the comparative statics of the input market price-taker model.

4.6.2   Comparative Statics Analysis of a Change in the Wage Rate

The employment of labor is the choice variable, and the wage rate is the parameter in the model of a price-taker in the input market model, so we can perform comparative statics analysis by observing how the employment of labor responds to changes in the wage rate. To accomplish this mathematically, we repeat the FOC and SOC we found earlier in Section 4.5.1.

$$\text{FOC:} \qquad \pi'(L) = TR'(Q)\frac{dQ}{dL} - w = 0 \Leftrightarrow TR'(Q)\frac{dQ}{dL} \equiv MRP = w \qquad \text{(4-29)}$$

$$\text{SOC:} \qquad \pi''(L) = TR''(Q)\left(\frac{dQ}{dL}\right)^2 + TR'(Q)\frac{d^2Q}{dL^2} = MRP' < 0 \qquad \text{(4-30)}$$

Recognize that implicit in the FOC is a relation between the equilibrium value of labor, L^*, and the parameter w, or

$$F(w, L^*) \equiv TR'(Q)\frac{dQ}{dL} - w = 0 \qquad \text{(4-58)}$$

You should verify that the conditions of the implicit function theorem hold, assuring us that the explicit function $L^* = L^*(w)$ exists. Substituting L^* back into the first-order condition (and remembering that Q is a function of L) yields the identity

$$F(w, L^*) \equiv TR'(Q)\frac{dQ}{dL^*} - w \equiv 0 \qquad \text{(4-59)}$$

Figure 4.8

Comparative Statics of
a Change in the Wage
Rate

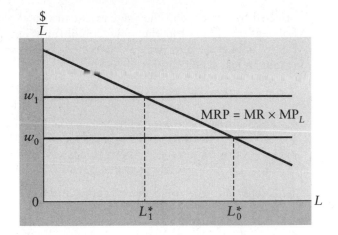

We find the derivative dL^*/dw by implicit differentiation of the identity, just as we did in Section 4.6.1.

$$\frac{dL^*}{dw} = \frac{1}{\text{TR}''(Q)(dQ/dL)^2 + \text{TR}'(Q)(d^2Q/dL^2)} < 0 \qquad \text{(4-60)}$$

You should recognize the denominator of this expression from equation (4-30), the second-order condition for profit maximization. The SOC tells us that the denominator is negative, and so is the derivative dL^*/dw. We find that the profit-maximizing firm responds to an increase in the wage rate by reducing the quantity of labor employed. In other words, the firm's demand curve for labor is downward sloping.

The comparative statics results of a change in the wage rate are unaffected by our assumptions regarding the output market. We derived those results from a model which is general enough to apply to either case. Figure 4.8 is a graphical representation of the comparative statics analysis of a wage rate change. At a wage rate of w_0 the firm chooses L_0^* units of labor, and at a wage rate of w_1 the firm chooses L_1^*.

NUMERICAL EXAMPLE

Recall the numerical example from Section 4.5.1 in which $\text{TR} = 16Q$, $Q = 2L^{1/2}$, and the wage rate equals 4. The objective function and FOC and SOC are

$$\pi(L) = \text{TR}(Q(L)) - wL = 16(2L^{1/2}) - 4L \qquad \text{(4-31)}$$

$$\text{FOC:} \quad \pi'(L) = \text{TR}'(Q)Q'(L) - w = 16L^{-1/2} - 4 = 0 \qquad \text{(4-32)}$$

$$\text{SOC:} \quad \pi''(L) = \text{TR}''(Q')^2 + \text{TR}'Q'' = -8L^{-3/2} < 0 \qquad \text{(4-33)}$$

We find that $L^{-1/2} = 4/16$ or $L^* = 16$. Maximum profit equals $\pi^* = 32(16^{1/2}) - 64 = 64$.

Suppose the wage rate rises to $w = 5$. In this case, the profit function is $\pi(L) = 16(2L^{1/2}) - 5L$, and the FOC is $\pi' = 16L^{-1/2} - 5 = 0$. The SOC is not affected by a change in the wage rate (can you explain why this is the case?). Solving the FOC for the new equilibrium employment of labor yields $L^* = 10.24$ and a new profit of $\pi = 51.2$. As we expect, a rise in the wage rate results in less labor employed.

Consider a profit-maximizing firm which uses labor, L, as an input to produce its output, Q, according to the production function $Q = Q(L) = L^{1/2}$. Labor is paid an hourly wage rate, w, which is independent of the level of employment of labor. The firm's total revenue is given by $TR = TR(Q) = 2Q$.

1. Identify the firm's objective function, choice variable, and the parameter it faces.

2. What are the first- and second-order conditions for the firm's optimization problem?

3. Solve the first-order condition to obtain an expression for the equilibrium level of the choice variable as an explicit function of the parameter of the model. Using this expression, find the derivative of the equilibrium value of the choice variable with respect to the parameter and determine its sign. What is the economic interpretation of this result?

4.7

SUMMARY

In this chapter we use our understanding of the meaning of derivatives to investigate the optimum values of functions with one independent variable. We find that, to have a critical point, a function's first derivative must equal zero. This is the *first-order condition* (abbreviated as *FOC* and also known as the *necessary condition*) for optimization. We find that the critical point is a maximum value if the second derivative is negative and a minimum if the second derivative is positive. This is the *second-order condition* (abbreviated as *SOC* and also known as the *sufficient condition*). We use this knowledge to investigate profit-maximizing behavior of firms in output markets and in input markets.

Our models of profit-maximizing behavior conformed to the comparative statics methodology we discussed in Chapter 1. First, we define the problem we wish to examine. This step tells us what our choice variable is. In the case of output market behavior, the choice variable is the firm's rate of output. In the case of input market behavior, the choice variable is the firm's employment of the input. The next step is to choose a model. This gives us an objective function (answering the question, "What is to be optimized?"). In the models we discussed in this chapter the objective function is some form of profit function. Our next step is to define an equilibrium. In optimization models the first- and second-order conditions for optimization define the equilibrium.

In order to perform comparative statics analysis it is necessary that our model include a parameter or explanatory variable that can be changed exogenously. Our price-taker models in this chapter treat output price and input price as parameters. In those cases, the equilibrium conditions of the model implicitly define a functional relationship between the choice variable and the parameter. By assuming the equilibrium conditions hold (substituting the equilibrium value of the choice variable back into the first-order condition) we are able to find the derivative of the choice variable with respect to the parameter by implicit differentiation. The sign of the derivative tells us how the choice variable changes in response to changes in the parameter. In our examples we find that the rate of output and price are positively related for price-takers in the output market and that the employment of an input is negatively related to the input price for price-takers in the input market. In each case, it was the second-order condition for optimization that enabled us to sign the derivative.

The purpose of this chapter is to give you an opportunity to perform some useful economic analysis using the mathematical tools of differentiation presented in Chapter 3. You should recognize the common methodology we followed in each of the models we examined. You should also notice the common elements of these profit-maximization models. (1) Profit is always total revenue minus total cost. (2) Output market conditions affect the firm's revenue function. (3) Input market conditions affect the firm's cost function. (4) Price-taking behavior means that price is a parameter of the model. (5) Price-searching behavior means that price is a function of quantity. These are characteristics of profit-maximization models which you can use to model other variations of behavior of firms in addition to the ones we discussed in this chapter.

As you have seen, much economic behavior can be analyzed using models that have only one independent variable. However, much more can be accomplished if we can extend our understanding of differential calculus to functions with two or more independent variables. In Chapter 5, we show you how to differentiate multivariate functions, so that we can return to a richer spectrum of economic analysis in Chapters 6 and 7.

◆ REFERENCES

Allen, R. G. D., *Mathematical Analysis for Economists* (New York: St. Martin's Press, 1938), Chapter 8.

Chiang, Alpha C., *Fundamental Methods of Mathematical Economics*, 3rd edition (New York: McGraw-Hill Book Company, 1984), Chapter 9.

◆ ANSWERS TO END-OF-SECTION EXERCISES

Section 4.2.1: First- and Second-Order Conditions

1. **a.** $AC = TC/Q = 100/Q + 100 + Q^2/100$; **b.** $Q^* = 5000^{1/3} = 17.1$

2. **a.** $AP = TP/L = 24 + 100L - 2L^2$; **b.** $L^* = 25$

Section 4.4.2: Price Searching in the Output Market

1. $MR = 20 - 10Q - 3Q^2$; $MC = 14 - 10Q + 3Q^2$

2. Objective function: $\pi = -4 + 6Q - 2Q^3$
   FOC: $\pi' = +6 - 6Q^2 = 0$
   SOC: $\pi'' = -12Q < 0$

3. $\pi' = +6 - 6Q^2 = 0 \Rightarrow Q = \pm 1$;
   $\pi'' = -12Q < 0 \Rightarrow \pi$ is a maximum at $Q^* = 1$
   $P = AR = 14$

4. $\varepsilon_{QP} = -2$; firm is a price-searcher, because $MR < P$.

5. **a.** Objective function: $\pi = PQ - (10 + Q + Q^2/2)$
   FOC: $\pi' = P - 1 - Q = 0$
   SOC: $\pi'' = -1 < 0$
   b. $Q^* = 9$; $\pi^* = 38.5$

Section 4.5.2: Price Searching in Input Markets

1. $MRP = 50 - 4L$; $MFC = 2 + 4L$

2. $L^* = 6$; $w^* = 14$

Section 4.6.2: Comparative Statics Analysis of a Change in the Wage Rate

1. Objective function: $\pi = 2L^{1/2} - wL$; choice variable: L; parameter: w

2. FOC: $\pi' = L^{-1/2} - w = 0$; SOC: $\pi'' = -0.5L^{-3/2} < 0$

3. $L^* = w^{-2}$; $dL^*/dw = -2w^{-3}$

   The profit-maximizing employment of labor is negatively related to the wage rate. As wages increase (decrease), equilibrium quantity of labor employed decreases (increases). The demand by the firm for labor is downward sloping.

◆ SELF-HELP PROBLEMS

Answers to these problems are given at the end of the text.

1. Compare and contrast the first- and second-order conditions of two profit-maximizing models: a firm which is a price-taker in both its input and output markets and a firm which is a price-searcher in both its input and output markets. Be sure to explain the comparison algebraically, graphically, and in narrative.

2. Suppose a firm is a price-taker in its output market and a price-searcher in its input market.

   a. Give expressions for the firms's revenue function, its cost function, and its profit function. What is the choice variable and what is the parameter in your model?

   b. What are the first- and second-order conditions for maximization of profit for this firm? Provide a graphical interpretation of the first- and second-order conditions.

   c. Perform comparative statics analysis for this problem. How does the firm's profit-maximizing employment L respond to changes in its output price?

d. How is your answer to part c affected if the firm is a price-taker in its input market?

3. Consider a firm which is a price-searcher in both its output and input markets and which faces the inverse labor supply function $w = 2 + 2L$, where w is the wage rate and L is quantity of labor. Suppose the monopolist's production function is $Q = 2L$, where Q is the rate of output. Suppose the inverse demand function for the monopolist's product is given by $P = 25 - 0.5Q$.

    a. If the labor market is completely unionized and the union is able to enforce a minimum wage below which no labor is supplied, what minimum wage would guarantee L^* amount of labor (L^* comes from your answer to question 2 of the exercises at the end of Section 4.5.2) a maximum of total wage income? *Hint*: A graph will help you with the analysis.

    b. What minimum wage would yield maximum employment? Explain.

4. A firm's total cost equals $TC = TC(Q) = 3Q^3 - 7.5Q^2 + 2Q + 5$.

    a. Find this firm's marginal cost, MC, function.

    b. Find the rate of output at which this firm's MC is minimum.

5. As we noted earlier in this chapter (in footnote 4), profit maximization is one of several possible theories of behavior of firms. In this exercise you will be asked to apply the principles of unconstrained optimization you learned in this chapter to some alternative postulates about the behavior of firms. Consider a firm with a production function $Q = Q(L)$, a total revenue function $TR = TR(Q)$, and a total cost function $TC = TC(Q)$.

    a. Suppose the firm's goal is to maximize sales (total revenue). Find and interpret the first- and second-order conditions for the firm's problem. Draw a picture of the result in terms of the marginal conditions that are implied by the first- and second-order conditions.

    b. Suppose the firm's goal is to maximize output. Find and interpret the first- and second-order conditions for the firm's problem. Draw a picture of the result in terms of the marginal conditions that are implied by the first- and second-order conditions.

    c. Based on your answers to parts a and b, under what condition(s) is output maximization equivalent to revenue maximization? Explain carefully and defend your answer mathematically. Draw pictures if they help you make your point.

◆ SUPPLEMENTAL PROBLEMS

1. Suppose a firm is a price-taker in its output market.

    a. Identify the firm's objective function, the choice variable, and the parameter if the firm maximizes profits.

    b. Present the first- and second-order conditions for profit maximization.

    c. Assume the equilibrium conditions are satisfied, and derive the identity obtained when the equilibrium value of the choice variable is substituted into the first-order conditions.

    d. Use implicit differentiation to find the derivative of the choice variable with respect to the parameter, and interpret your result.

    e. Does the second-order condition allow you to sign this derivative?

2. Suppose a firm is a price-taker in its input market.

    a. Identify the firm's objective function, choice variable, and parameter if the firm maximizes profits.

    b. Present the first- and second-order conditions for profit maximization. Assume the equilibrium conditions are satisfied, and derive the identity obtained when the equilibrium value of the choice variable is substituted into the first-order conditions.

    c. Use implicit differentiation to find the derivative of the choice variable with respect to the parameter. Does the second-order condition allow you to sign this derivative? Does it matter whether the firm is a perfect competitor or a monopolist in its output market?

3. Consider a profit-maximizing firm which uses labor, L, as an input to produce its output, Q, according to the production function $Q(L) = 4L^{0.25}$. Labor is paid an hourly wage rate, w, which is independent of the level of employment of labor. The firm's total revenue is given by TR = $TR(Q) = 0.5Q$.

    a. Identify the firm's objective function, choice variable, and the parameter it faces.

    b. Derive the first- and second-order conditions for the firm's optimization problem.

    c. Solve the first-order condition you found in part b to obtain an expression for the equilibrium level of the choice variable as an explicit function of the parameter of the model. Using this expression, find the derivative of the equilibrium value of the choice variable with respect to the parameter and determine its sign. What is the economic interpretation of this result? Draw a picture showing your answer.

Consider a price-taker firm with cost function TC = $10 + Q + Q^2/2$ *and price that equals* P = 10 *to answer questions 4 through 6.*

4. The firm is subject to a per unit tax, t, on output. Therefore, its total cost is increased by an amount tQ.

    a. Find the objective function, the first- and second-order conditions for profit maximization, and the profit-maximizing quantity and profit as functions of the per unit tax.

    b. Find the derivative dQ^*/dt. This is the mathematical expression of the comparative statics results of a change in t. Illustrate the effects of an increase in the per unit tax graphically.

5. The firm is subject to a proportional profit tax, τ. Therefore, its profits are reduced by an amount $\tau\pi$.

    a. Find the objective function, the first- and second-order conditions for profit maximization, and the profit-maximizing quantity and profit as functions of the proportional profit tax.

    b. Find the derivative $dQ^*/d\tau$. This is the mathematical expression of the comparative statics results of a change in τ. Illustrate the effects of an increase in the proportional profits tax graphically.

6. The firm is subject to a lump sum tax, λ. Therefore, its total costs are increased by an amount λ.

    a. Find the objective function, the first- and second-order conditions for profit maximization, and the profit-maximizing quantity and profit as functions of the lump sum tax.

   b. Find the derivative $dQ^*/d\lambda$. This is the mathematical expression of the comparative statics results of a change in λ. Illustrate the effects of an increase in the lump sum tax graphically.

For questions 7 through 9, consider a price-searcher firm with the same cost function as the firm in questions 4 through 6, but with an average revenue function equal to $\text{AR} = P = 10 - Q$

7. The firm is subject to a per unit tax, t, on output. Therefore, its total cost is increased by an amount tQ.

   a. Find the objective function, the first- and second-order conditions for profit maximization, and the profit-maximizing quantity and profit as functions of the per unit tax.

   b. Find the derivative dQ^*/dt. Illustrate the effects of an increase in the per unit tax graphically. Compare your results in this question to the result you obtained in Problem 4.

8. The firm is subject to a proportional profit tax, τ. Therefore, its profits are reduced by an amount $\tau\pi$.

   a. Find the objective function, the first- and second-order conditions for profit maximization, and the profit-maximizing quantity and profit as functions of the proportional profit tax.

   b. Find the derivative $dQ^*/d\tau$. Illustrate the effects of an increase in the proportional profits tax graphically. Compare your results in this question to the result you obtained in Problem 5.

9. The firm is subject to a lump sum tax, λ. Therefore, its total costs are increased by an amount λ.

   a. Find the objective function, the first- and second-order conditions for profit maximization, and the profit-maximizing quantity and profit as functions of the lump sum tax.

   b. Find the derivative $dQ^*/d\lambda$. Illustrate the effects of an increase in the lump sum tax graphically. Compare your results in this question to the result you obtained in Problem 6.

10. A firm has total revenue equal to $\text{TR} = \text{TR}(Q)$ and total cost equal to $\text{TC} = \text{TC}(Q)$. The firm is taxed at a per unit rate equal to t, which has the effect of increasing the total costs by an amount tQ.

   a. Find the objective function and the first- and second-order conditions for profit maximization.

   b. Find the derivative dQ^*/dt. This is the mathematical expression of the comparative statics results of a change in t. Do the results depend on whether or not the firm is a price-taker or a price-searcher in the output market?

   c. How are your answers to parts a and b affected if the per unit tax is charged to the firm's customers? In this case, the effect of the tax is to decrease total revenue by an amount tQ.

11. Consider a firm which is a price-searcher in both its output and input markets and which faces the inverse labor supply function $w = 2 + 2L$, where w is the wage rate and L is quantity of labor. Suppose the firm's production function is $Q = 2L$, where Q is the rate of output. Suppose the average revenue function for the firm's product is given by $\text{AR} = P = 25 - 0.5Q$. The firm has

to pay social security tax equal to a proportion σ of its total wage bill. Therefore, its costs are increased by an amount $\sigma w L$.

a. Find the objective function and the first- and second-order conditions for profit maximization. Also find the profit-maximizing employment of labor as a function of the social security tax and the equilibrium wage rate as a function of the social security tax.

b. Find the derivatives $dL^*/d\sigma$ and $dw^*/d\sigma$. Illustrate the effects of an increase in the social security tax graphically.

c. Suppose $\sigma = 20\%$. What is the profit-maximizing level of employment? What is the profit-maximizing wage rate?

12. A "natural monopoly" is a firm whose average and marginal cost curves may be declining throughout its relevant output range. Use the profit-maximization models for price-takers and for price-searchers to demonstrate that this situation is inconsistent with the perfect competition (price-taking) model but that it can be consistent with the monopoly (price-searching) model. Illustrate your explanation graphically wherever possible.

13. Consider the total cost function, $TC = TC(Q)$, where Q is output. Show that average total cost, ATC, reaches its minimum point where $MC = ATC$. Would this result still hold if the production function $Q(L)$ replaced Q in the total cost function?

C H A P T E R   5

Partial Derivatives and Total Differentials with Economic Applications

5.1

INTRODUCTION

So far in our discussion of derivatives, we have considered functions of only one independent variable, $Y = f(X)$. In economic applications, as well as in comparative statics analysis, we often deal with functions in which a dependent variable is related to two or more independent variables. For example, in demand analysis we specify quantity demanded as a function not only of the price of the good in question but also of prices of related goods and consumer income. For another example, in our profit-maximization models we would like to be able to analyze firms that use more than one input or that produce more than one output. We must learn how to differentiate functions of more than one independent variable. In this chapter we introduce the concepts of partial derivatives and total differentials and provide some insights into how they can be used in economic analysis.

5.2

PARTIAL DERIVATIVES

Consider the function

$$Y = f(X_1, X_2, \ldots, X_n) \tag{5-1}$$

which has n independent variables X_i, $i = 1, 2, \ldots, n$. They are assumed to be independent of one another in the sense that each can vary by itself without affecting the others. If the variable X_1 changes by ΔX_1 while $X_2, X_3, \ldots, X_n$

125

remain fixed, the dependent variable will change by some amount which we denote ΔY. Dividing ΔY by ΔX_1 gives us

$$\frac{\Delta Y}{\Delta X_1} = \frac{f(X_1 + \Delta X_1, X_2, \ldots, X_n) - f(X_1, X_2, \ldots, X_n)}{\Delta X_1} \quad (5\text{-}2)$$

If we take the limit of this quotient as $\Delta X_1 \to 0$, it will constitute a derivative, which is called the **partial derivative** of Y with respect to X_1. That is,

$$\lim_{\Delta X_1 \to 0} \frac{\Delta Y}{\Delta X_1} \equiv \frac{dY}{dX_1}\bigg|_{\text{holding } X_2, \ldots, X_n \text{ constant}} \equiv \frac{\partial Y}{\partial X_1} \quad (5\text{-}3)$$

partial derivative: if $Y = f(X_1, X_2, \ldots, X_n)$ a partial derivative represents the instantaneous rate of change of Y with respect to one of the independent variables, holding all the others constant.

partial differentiation: the process of finding partial derivatives.

The term *partial* indicates that in the process of finding the derivative with respect to X_1, all other independent variables in the function are held constant. Obviously, similar partial derivatives can be defined for the other independent variables. This process is called **partial differentiation**. The symbol used to identify partial derivatives is ∂. We also sometimes find it convenient to symbolize a partial derivative by using the symbol of the function (in this case, f) with a subscript identifying the independent variable involved in the partial differentiation. Therefore, we write our partial derivatives as

$$\frac{\partial Y}{\partial X_i} \equiv f_i \equiv \lim_{\Delta X_i \to 0} \frac{\Delta Y}{\Delta X_i}, \qquad i = 1, 2, \ldots, n \quad (5\text{-}4)$$

higher-order total derivative: the partial derivative of a partial derivative.

The function must be smooth and continuous, in other words, differentiable, in any dimension a partial derivative is taken. It is important to note that each partial derivative, f_i, is itself a function of all of the independent variables, $X_1, X_2, \ldots, X_n$. You will need to remember this when we examine **higher-order partial derivatives** in Section 5.9.

As was the case with functions of one independent variable, we need not take limits in order to take a partial derivative. Next, we show how to find partial derivatives using the rules of differentiation from chapter 3, Section 3.4.

For a differentiable multivariate function, $Y = f(X_1, X_2, \ldots, X_n)$, a total of n partial derivatives are defined. In taking the partial derivative of Y with respect to X_i, we treat the remaining $n - 1$ independent variables as constants and apply the rules of differentiation that we learned for functions of only one independent variable. Therefore, when taking the partial derivative with respect to X_i, the variables $X_j, j \neq i$, will be dropped out in the process if X_j are additive in the function, but will be retained if they are multiplicative.

NUMERICAL EXAMPLES

1. Let $Y = f(X_1, X_2) = 5X_1^3 - X_2^2 + 3X_1^2X_2^3$. Because there are two independent variables in the function, there are two first-order partial derivatives. They are

$$\frac{\partial Y}{\partial X_1} \equiv f_1 = 15X_1^2 + 6X_2^3X_1, \qquad \frac{\partial Y}{\partial X_2} \equiv f_2 = -2X_2 + 9X_1^2X_2^2 \quad (5\text{-}5)$$

In this example X_1 appears additively in the first term of the function, X_2 appears additively in the second term, and they both appear multiplicatively in the last term. Therefore, when we take the partial derivative of Y with respect to X_1 the second term drops out but the third term retains X_2^3. When we take the partial derivative of Y with respect to X_2 the first term drops out but the third term retains X_1^2.

2. Let $Y = f(X_1, X_2, X_3) = X_1^{1/2}X_2X_3^{3/2}$. There are three independent variables in this function, so we have three first-order partial derivatives to find. They are

$$\frac{\partial Y}{\partial X_1} \equiv f_1 = \tfrac{1}{2}X_1^{-1/2}X_2X_3^{3/2}, \qquad \frac{\partial Y}{\partial X_2} \equiv f_2 = X_1^{1/2}X_3^{3/2},$$

$$\frac{\partial Y}{\partial X_3} \equiv f_3 = \tfrac{3}{2}X_1^{1/2}X_2X_3^{1/2} \tag{5-6}$$

In this example all three independent variables are multiplicative. Therefore, the "other" two independent variables remain as multiplicative constants when we find the partial derivative with respect to one.

3. Let $Y = f(X_1, X_2) = 4X_2^2$. The first-order partial derivatives are

$$\frac{\partial Y}{\partial X_1} \equiv f_1 = 0, \qquad \frac{\partial Y}{\partial X_2} \equiv f_2 = 8X_2 \tag{5-7}$$

In this example X_1 does not appear on the right-hand side of the equation, so Y does not vary when X_1 changes. Therefore, the partial derivative of Y with respect to X_1 is zero.

EXERCISES
Section 5.2
Partial Derivatives

Find the partial derivatives for each of the following functions.

1. $Y = f(X_1, X_2) = 5X_1 + 3X_1X_2 + X_2^2$
2. $Y = f(X_1, X_2) = X_1^{1/2} + X_1 \ln X_2$
3. $Y = f(X_1, X_2, X_3, X_4) = X_1X_2X_3X_4$
4. $Y = f(X_1, X_2) = \dfrac{(X_1 - 2X_1X_2^{1.5})}{(3 + (X_1X_2)^2)}$
5. $Y = f(X, Z) = e^X \ln Z$
6. $Q = f(K, L, M) = 25K^{1/5}L^{1/5}M^{3/5}$
7. $Q_d = D(P, P_r, Y) = YP_r/P^2$
8. $U = U(X_1, X_2) = 10X_1X_2^2 - 3(X_1X_2)^{1/2}$

5.3

GRAPHICAL INTERPRETATION OF PARTIAL DERIVATIVES

We have seen that, for a function of one independent variable, $Y = f(X)$, the derivative dY/dX represents the instantaneous rate of change of Y for an infinitesimally small change in X, that is, the slope of the graph of the function at a point. What is the meaning of $\partial Y/\partial X_1$ and $\partial Y/\partial X_2$ for the function $Y = f(X_1, X_2)$? Like all derivatives, partial derivatives measure the instantaneous rate of change of Y, that is, the slope of the graph of the underlying function. However, each partial derivative measures the rate of change of the dependent variable with respect to a small change in one independent variable, holding all other independent variables constant. That is, the partial derivative measures the slope of the graph with respect to one independent variable, holding all of the others constant. Let us illustrate this in terms of a production function,

$$Q = f(K, L) \tag{5-8}$$

which we assume to be everywhere differentiable so that $\partial Q/\partial K$ and $\partial Q/\partial L$ exist. Graphically, this represents a *production surface* in three-dimensional space. The domain of the function is the set of all ordered pairs of nonnegative real numbers. The partial derivative f_K is the slope in the Q direction of the production surface sliced at a constant distance out along the L axis parallel to the K axis. The partial derivative f_L is the slope in the Q direction of the production surface sliced at a constant distance out along the K axis parallel to the L axis. Figure 5.1 illustrates this type of three-dimensional production surface.

Figure 5.1

Production Function in Two Inputs

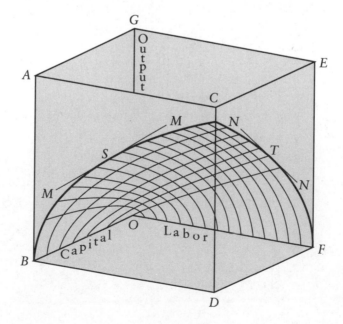

In this diagram, output is measured as height in the vertical dimension along line segment OG, BA, DC, or FE. The labor input is measured as width, in the direction of line segment OF, BD, AC, or GE. The capital input is measured as depth, in the direction of line segment OB, FD, GA, or EC. The plane $ABDC$ represents a slice through the production surface parallel to the labor axis a constant distance OB out on the capital axis. The slope of MM in that plane represents the instantaneous rate of change of output with respect to labor at point S, holding capital constant at OB, or the partial derivative of output with respect to labor. The plane $CDFE$ represents a slice through the production surface parallel to the capital axis a constant distance OF out on the labor axis. The slope of NN in that plane represents the instantaneous rate of change of output with respect to capital at point T, holding labor constant at OF, or the partial derivative of output with respect to labor.

5.4

COMPARATIVE STATICS ANALYSIS OF NATIONAL INCOME MODEL

Recall the national income model presented in Chapter 1. We described a model in which income Y and consumption C were endogenous variables and investment I was an exogenous variable. Now that we can handle functions with more than one independent variable, let us enrich this model slightly by adding a government sector. Government expenditures G are added to planned expenditures E, which equal income at equilibrium. Consumption depends on disposable income Y_d, which is equal to one minus the tax rate τ times national income Y. The endogenous variables of the model are now Y, Y_d, and C, and the exogenous variables are I, G, and C_0. Our model becomes

$$Y = E = C + I + G, \qquad I > 0, G > 0 \tag{5-9}$$

$$C = C_0 + \beta Y_d, \qquad C_0 > 0, 0 < \beta < 1 \tag{5-10}$$

$$Y_d = (1 - \tau)Y, \qquad 0 < \tau < 1 \tag{5-11}$$

The parameters of the model are β (the marginal propensity to consume) and τ (the tax rate). All exogenous variables and parameters are assumed to be independent of each other, so any one of them can change without the others changing. The system can be solved for the reduced-form equations, which give us equilibrium values of the endogenous variables Y^*, C^*, and Y_d^*. Consider the reduced-form equation for Y^*,

$$Y^* = \frac{1}{1 - \beta + \beta\tau} C_0 + \frac{1}{1 - \beta + \beta\tau} I + \frac{1}{1 - \beta + \beta\tau} G = \frac{C_0 + I + G}{1 - \beta(1 - \tau)} \tag{5-12}$$

Because five parameters and exogenous variables enter this reduced-form equation for income, five partial derivatives can be taken to obtain comparative statics results. Two of these have special policy significance. They are

$$\frac{\partial Y^*}{\partial G} = \frac{1}{1 - \beta(1 - \tau)} > 0, \qquad \frac{\partial Y^*}{\partial \tau} = \frac{-\beta(C_0 + I + G)}{[1 - \beta(1 - \tau)]^2} < 0 \qquad (5\text{-}13)$$

The first of these results suggests that an increase in government spending increases national income by a factor of $1/[1 - \beta(1 - \tau)]$, which is probably familiar to you as the *expenditures multiplier*. The second result suggests that an increase in income tax rates changes (reduces) equilibrium national income by a factor of $[-\beta(C_0 + I + G)]/[1 - \beta(1 - \tau)]^2$.

Substituting (5-12) into (5-11) yields the reduced-form equation for Y_d^*, and substituting the resulting expression for Y_d^* into (5-10) yields the reduced-form equation for C^*,

$$Y_d^* = \frac{1 - \tau}{1 - \beta + \beta\tau} C_0 + \frac{1 - \tau}{1 - \beta + \beta\tau} I + \frac{1 - \tau}{1 - \beta + \beta\tau} G$$

$$= \frac{(1 - \tau)(C_0 + I + G)}{1 - \beta(1 - \tau)} \qquad (5\text{-}14)$$

$$C^* = \frac{C_0}{1 - \beta + \beta\tau} + \frac{\beta(1 - \tau)}{1 - \beta + \beta\tau} I + \frac{\beta(1 - \tau)}{1 - \beta + \beta\tau} G$$

$$= \frac{C_0 + \beta(1 - \tau)(I + G)}{1 - \beta(1 - \tau)} \qquad (5\text{-}15)$$

These reduced-form equations can be differentiated with respect to G and τ to yield some more comparative statics results.

$$\frac{\partial Y_d^*}{\partial G} = \frac{1 - \tau}{1 - \beta(1 - \tau)} > 0, \qquad \frac{\partial Y_d^*}{\partial \tau} = \frac{-(C_0 + I + G)}{(1 - \beta(1 - \tau))^2} < 0 \qquad (5\text{-}16)$$

$$\frac{\partial C^*}{\partial G} = \frac{\beta(1 - \tau)}{1 - \beta(1 - \tau)} > 0, \qquad \frac{\partial C^*}{\partial \tau} = \frac{-\beta(C_0 + I + G)}{(1 - \beta(1 - \tau))^2} < 0 \qquad (5\text{-}17)$$

These results suggest that an increase in government spending increases the equilibrium levels of disposable income and consumption, whereas an increase in the income tax rate decreases equilibrium levels of both disposable income and consumption. The reduced-form equations could also be differentiated with respect to I, C_0, or β in order to obtain even more comparative statics results. A property of reduced-form equations that are linear in variables, as these are, is that the coefficients of exogenous variables represent their marginal impact on the dependent variable.

EXERCISES
Section 5.4
Comparative Statics
Analysis of National
Income Model

Given equations (5-12), (5-14), and (5-15), the reduced-form equations for Y^*, Y_d^*, and C^*, find the comparative statics results expressing how equilibrium income, disposable income, and consumption are affected by changes in the following exogenous variables and parameters.

1. I **2.** C_0 **3.** β

5.5

DIFFERENTIALS OF FUNCTIONS WITH ONE INDEPENDENT VARIABLE

As you know, derivatives and partial derivatives are instantaneous rates of change of a dependent variable with respect to changes in some independent variable. Sometimes it is more convenient to focus attention on actual changes in the variables than on rates of change. You are already aware that large, or discrete, changes in variables are usually denoted by the Δ symbol. A knowledge of derivatives and partial derivatives enables us to describe infinitesimal changes in variables, or *differentials.*

differential: an infinitesimal change in a variable, denoted by the symbol d in front of the variable.

In our discussion of derivatives we defined the derivative of $Y = f(X)$ as the limit of the ratio $\Delta Y/\Delta X$ as ΔX approaches zero, which we have denoted as dY/dX or $f'(X)$. Let us now reinterpret dY/dX as the ratio of two quantities, dY and dX, which are called the differentials of Y and X, respectively. The differential represents an infinitesimally small (but nonzero) change in a variable. According to this interpretation, any derivative can be considered as ratio of two differentials. This gives us the following identities:

$$dY \equiv \frac{dY}{dX}\, dX \equiv f'(X)\, dX \tag{5-18}$$

where, as noted above, dY and dX are the differentials of Y and X, respectively. Based on (5-18), we can interpret the derivative $f'(X)$ as a rate of change that converts an infinitesimal change in X, dX, into a corresponding change in Y, dY. It should be clear that, given a differentiable function $Y = f(X)$, we can always transform a given differential, dY, into the derivative dY/dX by dividing it by dX; and we can transform a given derivative, dY/dX, into the differential dY by multiplying it by dX.

Recall that we used the term differentiation to describe the process of taking a derivative. We also call the process of finding a differential differentiation. The only distinction that may be made is that when we take the derivative dY/dX, we may call the process differentiation with respect to X, whereas when taking differentials, we call the process simply differentiation.

NUMERICAL EXAMPLES

1. Given $Y = f(X) = 5X^2 - 3X$, find the differential of Y. First find the derivative of the function

$$\frac{dY}{dX} = 10X - 3 \tag{5-19}$$

Next, multiply both sides by dX to obtain the differential.

$$dY = (10X - 3)\,dX \tag{5-20}$$

Recall that the notion of differentials (e.g., dY and dX) applies only to infinitesimal changes. In other words, if X changes by a large magnitude, say ΔX, and if we substitute this in (5-20), the resulting dY only approximates the exact change in Y, ΔY.

2. Recall that for the demand function $Q = f(P)$, the (point) price elasticity is given by

$$\varepsilon_{QP} = \frac{dQ}{dP}\frac{P}{Q} \tag{5-21}$$

The notion of a differential allows us to write this in the equivalent form

$$\varepsilon_{QP} = \frac{dQ/Q}{dP/P} = \frac{\text{proportional change in } Q}{\text{proportional change in } P} \tag{5-22}$$

Remember the logarithmic-function rule of differentiation from Chapter 3. It tells us that

$$\frac{d(\ln Q)}{dQ} = \frac{1}{Q} \quad \text{and} \quad \frac{d(\ln P)}{dP} = \frac{1}{P} \tag{5-23}$$

Multiplying both sides of each equation in (5-23) by dQ and dP, respectively, gives us

$$d(\ln Q) = \frac{dQ}{Q} \quad \text{and} \quad d(\ln P) = \frac{dP}{P} \tag{5-24}$$

Substituting these expressions into equation (5-22) gives us the useful result that

$$\varepsilon_{QP} = \frac{d(\ln Q)}{d(\ln P)} \tag{5-25}$$

The usefulness of this result becomes evident when you consider demand functions of the form $Q = kP^{-\alpha}$. Taking the natural logarithm of both sides gives us

$$\ln Q = \ln k - \alpha \ln P \tag{5-26}$$

Remember the expression we found for price elasticity of demand, and take the derivative of ln Q with respect to ln P. We obtain

$$\varepsilon_{QP} = \frac{d(\ln Q)}{d(\ln P)} = -\alpha \qquad (5\text{-}27)$$

The exponent on the price variable in demand functions of the form $Q = kP^{-\alpha}$ represents the price elasticity of demand, which is constant for all price-quantity combinations.

5.6

TOTAL DIFFERENTIALS OF MULTIVARIATE FUNCTIONS

We have discussed the concept of differentials in the context of a function of a single independent variable. However, the notion of differentials can be extended to functions of two or more independent variables. For example, consider the demand function $Q = f(P, Y)$ where Q is quantity demanded, P is the price of the good in question, and Y is consumer income. Assuming f to be differentiable everywhere, we know that there are two partial derivatives, $\partial Q/\partial P$ and $\partial Q/\partial Y$, which have the usual interpretation. Given these, the change in Q due to an infinitesimal change in P, holding Y constant, can be specified as

$$dQ|_{\text{holding } Y \text{ constant}} = \frac{\partial Q}{\partial P}\, dP = f_P\, dP \qquad (5\text{-}28)$$

Similarly, the change in Q resulting from a small change in Y, holding P constant, can be specified as

$$dQ|_{\text{holding } P \text{ constant}} = \frac{\partial Q}{\partial Y}\, dY \equiv f_Y\, dY \qquad (5\text{-}29)$$

The *total* change in Q from both sources is then given by

$$dQ = \frac{\partial Q}{\partial P}\, dP + \frac{\partial Q}{\partial Y}\, dY \equiv f_P\, dP + f_Y\, dY \qquad (5\text{-}30)$$

total differential: The differential of a function with more than one independent variable.

total differentiation: the process of finding the total differential.

The expression dQ, which is the sum of the changes from all sources, is called the ***total differential*** of Q and the process of obtaining it is called ***total differentiation***.

Note an important implication of total differentials: If P changes while Y remains constant, then $dY = 0$ and we obtain[1]

$$dQ = \frac{\partial Q}{\partial P} dP \equiv f_P \, dP \tag{5-31}$$

Dividing both sides by dP, we obtain the familiar partial derivative

$$\left. \frac{dQ}{dP} \right|_{dY=0} \equiv \frac{\partial Q}{\partial P} \equiv f_P \tag{5-32}$$

Partial derivatives, therefore, may be considered as the ratio of two differentials, with the qualification that all other independent variables are held constant in the process.

To generalize the concept of total differentials, consider the following function of n independent variables:

$$Y = f(X_1, X_2, \ldots, X_n) \tag{5-33}$$

The total differential of this function can be written as

$$dY = \frac{\partial Y}{\partial X_1} dX_1 + \frac{\partial Y}{\partial X_2} dX_2 + \cdots + \frac{\partial Y}{\partial X_n} dX_n \tag{5-34}$$

This expression is, of course, equivalent to

$$dY = f_1 \, dX_1 + f_2 \, dX_2 + \cdots + f_n \, dX_n = \sum_{i=1}^{n} f_i \, dX_i \tag{5-35}$$

An intuitively appealing interpretation of the total differential is the following. The total differential captures changes in the dependent variable from all possible sources, i.e., from all of the independent variables. It is the sum of the changes caused by the individual independent variables. The partial derivative f_i is the rate at which X_i changes Y. Multiply the rate by a particular infinitesimal change in X_i, denoted by dX_i, and you obtain the effect on Y of the change in X_i. Each term in the total differential measures the effect on Y of an infinitesimal change in one independent variable. Sum them all, and all possible changes are accounted for. Note that, no matter what the functional form of the primitive function, the total differential is always a linear function of the partial derivatives. This property allows us to solve for partial derivatives of functions that we can express only in general form.

Understanding the relationship between derivatives and differentials, and between partial derivatives and total differentials, gives us a much more complete notion of what differentiation of functions means. This more complete comprehension enables us to clarify one issue, implicit differentiation, which we first discussed in Chapter 3. More important, it provides some powerful tools with which we can manipulate mathematical functions

---

[1] A variable that is constant does not change, so its differential equals zero.

to perform economic analysis. First let's take a new look at implicit differentiation.

Find the total differentials for each of the following functions.

1. $Y = f(X_1, X_2) = 5X_1 + 3X_1X_2 + X_2^2$
2. $Y = f(X_1, X_2) = X_1^{1/2} + X_1 \ln X_2$
3. $Y = f(X_1, X_2, X_3, X_4) = X_1X_2X_3X_4$
4. $Y = f(X_1, X_2) = \dfrac{(X_1 - 2X_1X_2^{1.5})}{(3 + (X_1X_2)^2)}$
5. $Y = f(X, Z) = e^X \ln Z$
6. $Q = f(K, L, M) = 25K^{1/5}L^{1/5}M^{3/5}$
7. $Q_d = D(P, P_r, Y) = YP_r/P^2$
8. $U = U(X_1, X_2) = 10X_1X_2^2 - 3(X_1X_2)^{1/2}$

5.7

IMPLICIT FUNCTIONS REVISITED

Recall that in our discussion of rules of differentiation of functions of one independent variable, the implicit function rule in Chapter 3 asserted that for the implicit function $F(X, Y) = 0$, the derivative of Y with respect to X is given by

$$\frac{dY}{dX} = \frac{-F_X}{F_Y}, \quad \text{provided that } F_Y \neq 0 \tag{5-36}$$

where

$$F_X \equiv \frac{dF}{dX}\bigg|_{\text{treating } Y \text{ as a constant}} \tag{5-37}$$

and

$$F_Y \equiv \frac{dF}{dY}\bigg|_{\text{treating } X \text{ as a constant}} \tag{5-38}$$

Recall that the implicit function theorem assures us of the existence of the explicit function $Y = f(X)$ if F_X and F_Y are continuous and $F_Y \neq 0$ at the point where the derivative is taken.

Obviously, F_X and F_Y are nothing but the partial derivatives of $F(X, Y)$ with respect to X and Y, respectively. Now we can see where the formula came from. Take the total differential of the implicit function, $F(X, Y) = 0$,

$$d[F(X, Y)] = F_X \, dX + F_Y \, dY = 0 \tag{5-39}$$

Solve for dY/dX:

$$\frac{dY}{dX} = -\frac{F_X}{F_Y}, \qquad F_Y \neq 0 \tag{5-40}$$

Note that by the same reasoning

$$\frac{dX}{dY} = -\frac{F_Y}{F_X}, \qquad F_X \neq 0 \tag{5-41}$$

The condition that $F_X \neq 0$ assures us that the functional relationship between X and Y exists and is monotonic in the neighborhood of the point at which we find the derivative of the inverse function.

The total differential approach can be extended to implicit functions of more than two variables. Thus for $F(X_1, X_2, \ldots, X_n) = 0$ we have

$$dF(X_1, X_2, \ldots, X_n) = 0 \tag{5-42}$$

$$\frac{\partial F}{\partial X_1} dX_1 + \frac{\partial F}{\partial X_2} dX_2 + \cdots + \frac{\partial F}{\partial X_n} dX_n = 0 \tag{5-43}$$

$$F_1 \, dX_1 + F_2 \, dX_2 + \cdots + F_n \, dX_n = \sum_{i=1}^{n} F_i \, dX_i = 0 \tag{5-44}$$

from which we can find the partial derivative of any variable with respect to any other variable. Thus to find $\partial X_k / \partial X_j$, $k \neq j$, we set the differentials of all other variables equal to zero to obtain

$$F_k \, dX_k + F_j \, dX_j = 0 \tag{5-45}$$

or

$$\left. \frac{dX_k}{dX_j} \right|_{dX_i = 0, \, i \neq k, j} \equiv \frac{\partial X_k}{\partial X_j} = -\frac{F_j}{F_k}, \qquad F_k \neq 0 \tag{5-46}$$

Notice that here we have found a partial derivative, because we held all the other variables constant.

To find the partial derivatives $\partial X_k / \partial X_j$, $k \neq j$, we must be assured that the appropriate explicit functions exist; that is, we need to state the implicit function theorem for multivariate functions.

Given the implicit relation $F(X_1, X_2, \ldots, X_n) = 0$, if the partial derivatives $F_i, i = 1, 2, \ldots, n$, are continuous at a point and $F_k \neq 0$ at that point, then the explicit function $X_k = f(X_j)$, $j = 1, 2, \ldots, k - 1, k + 1, \ldots, n$ exists in the neighborhood of that point. Furthermore, the function $f(X_j)$ is continuous and so are its partial derivatives, f_j.[2]

---

[2] Just as in the case of the bivariate implicit function, the implicit function theorem as stated here gives us *sufficient* but not *necessary* conditions for the existence of the function.

Therefore, as long as the implicit function is twice differentiable in all dimensions, the partial derivatives of any variable X_k with respect to all the other variables X_j, $j \neq k$, can be found if $F_k \neq 0$.

We have seen that understanding partial derivatives and total differentials permits us to make sense out of the formula for implicit differentiation. Next let's apply the concepts to economic theory.

5.8

ECONOMIC APPLICATIONS OF PARTIAL DERIVATIVES AND TOTAL DIFFERENTIALS

In this section we show that, even without much specific information regarding particular functional forms, we can glean many useful insights into economic behavior by examining the total differentials of functions and carefully interpreting the results. First we take another look at isoquants and indifference curves, and then we reexamine the theory of market behavior from Chapter 1.

5.8.1   Slopes of Isoquants and Indifference Curves

Since we revisited implicit differentiation in Section 5.7, let's also revisit the economic applications of implicit differentiation from Chapter 3. There, we set the production function $Q = f(K, L)$ equal to a particular level of output and implicitly defined a functional relationship between the two inputs K and L, $F(K, L) = 0$. Using implicit differentiation, we find that

$$\frac{dK}{dL} = -\frac{dF/dL|_{\text{treating } K \text{ as a constant}}}{dF/dK|_{\text{treating } L \text{ as a constant}}} = -\frac{f_L}{f_K} = -\frac{\text{MP}_L}{\text{MP}_K} = -\text{MRTS}_{LK} \quad (5\text{-}47)$$

where f_K and f_L are the partial derivatives of Q with respect to capital and labor, respectively. These partial derivatives are the marginal products of capital and labor, and their ratio is the marginal rate of technical substitution (MRTS) between the two inputs.

The same result can be found by taking the total differential of the production function.

$$dQ = f_K \, dK + f_L \, dL \qquad (5\text{-}48)$$

If we hold output constant, then $dQ = 0$ and we can solve for dK/dL,

$$\left. \frac{dK}{dL} \right|_{dQ=0} = -\frac{f_L}{f_K} \qquad (5\text{-}49)$$

Because we have held output constant, the implicit functional relationship between K and L is that defined by an isoquant, which we know as combinations of two inputs that generate the same level of output. The MRTS is -1 times the slope of the isoquant, a positive value because isoquants have a negative slope.

NUMERICAL EXAMPLE

Suppose $Q = f(K, L) = LK^2$. The total differential of this production function is

$$dQ = f_L \, dL + f_K \, dK = K^2 \, dL + 2LK \, dK \qquad (5\text{-}50)$$

If we hold output constant, then $dQ = 0$ and we can solve for dK/dL,

$$\left. \frac{dK}{dL} \right|_{dQ=0} = -\frac{f_L}{f_K} = -\frac{K}{2L} = -\text{MRTS}_{LK} \qquad (5\text{-}51)$$

Note that, when we are given a specific production function, we can find the equation of the isoquant directly by setting $Q = Q_0$ and solving for K in terms of L. In this case we obtain

$$K = Q_0^{1/2} L^{-1/2} \qquad (5\text{-}52)$$

Recognize that, if we differentiate (5-52) with respect to L directly, we obtain the same result for dK/dL as in equation (5-51). Try it yourself, remembering to substitute $Q_0 = LK^2$ into your expression for dK/dL.

Similar reasoning can be applied to the utility function $U = U(X_1, X_2)$. Taking the total differential gives us

$$dU = U_1 \, dX_1 + U_2 \, dX_2 \qquad (5\text{-}53)$$

In this case we hold utility constant to define an indifference curve. If utility is constant, then $dU = 0$ and we can solve for the slope of the indifference curve

$$\frac{dX_2}{dX_1}\bigg|_{dU=0} = -\frac{U_1}{U_2} \qquad (5\text{-}54)$$

In equation (5-54), U_1 and U_2 are the partial derivatives of the utility function with respect to goods X_1 and X_2 and can be interpreted as marginal utilities. Their ratio is the marginal rate of substitution between the goods X_1 and X_2 (MRS_{12}), or

$$\text{MRS}_{12} = -\frac{dX_2}{dX_1}\bigg|_{dU=0} = \frac{U_1}{U_2} \qquad (5\text{-}55)$$

Total differentiation provides information about how a function changes, even when little is known about the specifics of the function itself. As you can see, even if we assume nothing about the specific functional forms of production functions or utility functions, we can describe some important components of producer and consumer theory by taking total differentials. In the next section, we use the technique of total differentiation to perform comparative statics analysis of a market model. In this case it also permits us to gain much by way of results with few assumptions.

EXERCISES
Section 5.8.1
Slopes of Isoquants
and Indifference
Curves

1. Find the marginal rate of technical substitution for the following production functions.

   a. $Q = f(L, K) = 10(0.2L^{-0.5} + 0.8K^{-0.5})^{-2}$

   b. $Q = f(L, K) = (1/3)\ln L + (2/3)\ln K$

2. Find the marginal rate of substitution for the following utility functions.

   a. $U(X_1, X_2) = 10 + 0.2\ln X_1 + 0.8\ln X_2$

   b. $U(X_1, X_2) = X_1 X_2$

5.8.2 Analysis of a Competitive Market

Recall the extended example of demand and supply analysis in Chapter 1, Section 1.4.1. We began the extended example with a specific numerical model of demand and supply. Then we generalized the example by replacing the numerical coefficients in the model with symbols. This more generalized model still assumed that we knew the explicit functional form of demand and supply, that they were both linear. Now that we have introduced implicit functions and differentiation of functions with more than one independent variable, we can specify the demand and supply functions even more generally. Let

$$Q_d = D(P, Y); \qquad Q_s = S(P, w); \qquad Q_s = Q_d \qquad (5\text{-}56)$$

where Q_d is quantity demanded, Q_s is quantity supplied, P is price, Y is consumer income, and w is the wage rate. We assume the equilibrium condition holds.

$$D(P, Y) = Q_d = Q_s = S(P, w) \tag{5-57}$$

This can be rewritten as the implicit function

$$F(P, Y, w) = D(P, Y) - S(P, w) = 0 \tag{5-58}$$

According to the implicit function theorem, if F_P, F_Y, and F_w are continuous and $F_P \neq 0$, then the equilibrium value of the endogenous variable P^* can be expressed as an explicit function of the exogenous variables Y and w. It is reasonable to assume that these conditions do, in fact, hold. As long as the demand curve is downward sloping and the supply curve is horizontal or upward sloping, the partial derivative $F_P = D_P - S_P < 0$. The partial derivative F_Y equals D_Y, which represents the marginal effect of a change in income on quantity demanded. The partial derivative F_w equals $-S_w$, which represents the marginal effect of a change in wages on quantity supplied. Therefore, we assume that the requirements of the implicit function theorem are met and write $P^* = P^*(Y, w)$.

If we substitute $P^*(Y, w)$ into either the demand or the supply equation we obtain an expression for equilibrium quantity, Q^*, in terms of Y and w, or $Q^* = Q^*(Y, w)$. Our comparative statics methodology requires us to substitute the equilibrium value, P^*, back into the equilibrium condition, generating the identity

$$D(P^*, Y) \equiv S(P^*, w) \tag{5-59}$$

We differentiate both sides of the identity, remembering that P^* is a function of Y and w. This means that we must use the chain rule when we perform the differentiation.

$$D_{P^*} \frac{\partial P^*}{\partial w} dw + \left(D_{P^*} \frac{\partial P^*}{\partial Y} + D_Y \right) dY \equiv \left(S_{P^*} \frac{\partial P^*}{\partial w} + S_w \right) dw + S_{P^*} \frac{\partial P^*}{\partial Y} dY \tag{5-60}$$

This total differential can be used to find comparative statics results for the behavior of equilibrium price when the exogenous variables, Y or w, change. For example, if we hold w constant by setting dw equal to zero and divide both sides by dY, we can solve for $\partial P^*/\partial Y$. If we hold Y constant by setting dY equal to zero and divide both sides by dw, we can solve for $\partial P^*/\partial w$.

$$\frac{\partial P^*}{\partial Y} = -\frac{D_Y}{D_{P^*} - S_{P^*}} \quad \text{and} \quad \frac{\partial P^*}{\partial w} = \frac{S_w}{D_{P^*} - S_{P^*}} \tag{5-61}$$

We have assumed that the denominator in these expressions is negative. The sign of $\partial P^*/\partial Y$ depends on whether the good is normal or inferior. The partial derivative D_Y is the rate of change of quantity demanded with respect to income; it is positive for a normal good and negative for an inferior good. The sign of $\partial P^*/\partial w$ is positive as long as S_w is negative. Remember that S_w is the partial derivative of quantity supplied with respect to the wage rate, and it is negative because higher wages reduce the quantity supplied. Graphically, the fact that S_w is negative means that an increase in an input price shifts the supply curve (graphed with price on the vertical axis and quantity on the horizontal) to the left.

To find comparative statics results for Q^*, substitute P^* into either the demand or the supply equation.

$$Q^* = D(P^*, Y) \tag{5-62}$$

Totally differentiating (5-62) yields

$$dQ^* = D_{P^*} \frac{\partial P^*}{\partial w} \, dw + \left(D_{P^*} \frac{\partial P^*}{\partial Y} + D_Y \right) dY \tag{5-63}$$

To solve (5-63) for $\partial Q^*/\partial Y$, set dw equal to zero and divide both sides by dY,

$$\frac{\partial Q^*}{\partial Y} = D_{P^*} \frac{\partial P^*}{\partial Y} + D_Y \quad . \tag{5-64}$$

Substituting the results obtained for $\partial P^*/\partial Y$ in (5-61) allows us to write

$$\frac{\partial Q^*}{\partial Y} = \frac{-D_{P^*} D_Y}{D_{P^*} - S_{P^*}} + D_Y = D_Y \left(1 - \frac{D_{P^*}}{D_{P^*} - S_{P^*}} \right) \cdot \tag{5-65}$$

As long as the supply curve is upward sloping, $S_{P^*} > 0$, we can say that $0 < D_{P^*}/(D_{P^*} - S_{P^*}) < 1$, and the sign of $\partial Q^*/\partial Y$ depends on the normality or inferiority of the good. To solve equation (5-63) for $\partial Q^*/\partial w$, set dY equal to zero and divide both sides by dw,

$$\frac{\partial Q^*}{\partial w} = D_{P^*} \frac{\partial P^*}{\partial w} \tag{5-66}$$

Recalling the results we obtained for $\partial P^*/\partial w$ in equation (6-61), we see that $\partial Q^*/\partial w$ is unambiguously negative.

These results allow us to come to the same conclusions we reached in Chapter 1 when we assumed linear relationships in the demand and supply functions. Here, however, we have assumed nothing about the functional forms of demand and supply except the law of demand, $D_P < 0$; upward-sloping or horizontal supply, $S_{P^*} \geq 0$; and that an increase in an input price reduces quantity supplied, $S_w < 0$. Being able to get results with fewer assumptions is good; it makes our models more generally applicable and more consistent with our actual lack of detailed information about economic relationships.

When we introduced the concept of partial derivatives in Section 5.2, we emphasized that a partial derivative is itself a function of the same independent variables that appeared in the primitive function. This means that partial derivatives can themselves be differentiated with respect to each of the independent variables. We turn to this procedure next.

5.9

SECOND- AND HIGHER-ORDER PARTIAL DERIVATIVES

first-order partial derivative: same as partial derivative.

second-order partial derivatives: the partial derivative of a first-order partial derivative.

second partial: an abbreviated name for second-order partial derivative.

Consider the function $Z = f(X, Y)$. If this function is differentiable, two *first-order partial derivatives* can be defined, $f_X = \partial Z/\partial X$ and $f_Y = \partial Z/\partial Y$. Remember that both of these first-order partial derivatives are themselves functions of X and Y. We can differentiate them further to find their rates of change (the rate of change of the rate of change of Z). We have the following four *second-order partial derivatives* (or *second partials* for short):

$$f_{XX} \equiv \frac{\partial^2 Z}{\partial X^2} = \text{partial derivative of } f_X \text{ with respect to } X$$

$$f_{XY} \equiv \frac{\partial^2 Z}{\partial X \, \partial Y} = \text{partial derivative of } f_X \text{ with respect to } Y$$

$$f_{YY} \equiv \frac{\partial^2 Z}{\partial Y^2} = \text{partial derivative of } f_Y \text{ with respect to } Y$$

$$f_{YX} \equiv \frac{\partial^2 Z}{\partial Y \, \partial X} = \text{partial derivative of } f_Y \text{ with respect to } X$$

cross-partial derivative: a higher-order partial derivative for which you first differentiate with respect to one independent variable and subsequently differentiate infinitesimal change in a variable.

The two second partial derivatives f_{XY} and f_{YX} are called *cross-partial derivatives*. To take a cross-partial derivative, you first differentiate with respect to one independent variable, holding all others constant, and then differentiate with respect to a second independent variable, again holding all others (including the first) constant. Note that the second-order partial derivatives are themselves functions of X and Y, so they can be differentiated further to obtain third- and higher-order partial derivatives.

NUMERICAL EXAMPLE

Let $Z = f(X, Y) = X^3 + 5XY - Y^2$
First-order partials: $f_X = 3X^2 + 5Y$; $f_Y = 5X - 2Y$
Second-order partials: $f_{XX} = 6X$; $f_{XY} = 5$; $f_{YY} = -2$; $f_{YX} = 5$
Third-order partials: $f_{XXX} = 6$; all others in this example equal 0.

Young's theorem: the mathematical theorem that cross-partial derivatives are invariant to the order of differentiation, provided that the primitive function is twice differentiable.

It is not merely a coincidence that, in our example, $f_{XY} = f_{YX} = 5$; that is, that the cross-partials equal one another. In fact, cross-partial derivatives are *invariant* to the order of differentiation. It does not matter whether you first differentiate with respect to X and then differentiate with respect to Y, or vice versa. This extremely useful property of cross-partials is known as *Young's theorem*, which states that, if f_X and f_Y are differentiable, then $f_{XY} = f_{YX}$.

As another example of higher-order partial derivatives and of Young's theorem, consider the production function $Q = f(K, L) = K^{1/3}L^{2/3}$. There exist 2 first-order partial derivatives. They are

$$f_K = \frac{\partial Q}{\partial K} = \frac{1}{3}K^{-2/3}L^{2/3}; \qquad f_L = \frac{\partial Q}{\partial L} = \frac{2}{3}K^{1/3}L^{-1/3} \qquad (5\text{-}67)$$

These first-order partials represent the instantaneous rate of change of output with respect to changes in each input in turn, holding the other constant. They are the marginal products of capital and labor, respectively. The first-order partials of any production function are the marginal products of its inputs. As you can see, they are themselves functions of K and L.

There exist 4 second-order partial derivatives of this production function

$$f_{KK} \equiv \frac{\partial^2 Q}{\partial K^2} = -\frac{2}{9}K^{-5/3}L^{2/3}; \qquad f_{LL} \equiv \frac{\partial^2 Q}{\partial L^2} = -\frac{2}{9}K^{1/3}L^{-4/3} \qquad (5\text{-}68)$$

$$f_{KL} \equiv \frac{\partial^2 Q}{\partial K\, \partial L} = \frac{\partial^2 Q}{\partial L\, \partial K} \equiv f_{LK} = \frac{2}{9}K^{-2/3}L^{-1/3} \qquad (5\text{-}69)$$

The second-order partials of a production function also have a useful economic interpretation. They measure the instantaneous rate of change of the marginal products with respect to changes in the inputs. In the preceding example, the second partial f_{KK} is the slope of the marginal product of capital and f_{LL} is the slope of the marginal product of labor. The fact that these marginal products have negative slopes reflects the *law of diminishing marginal returns*.

The cross-partials tell how the marginal product of one input is affected by a change in the other input. In this case, the cross-partials are positive, indicating that the marginal product of capital is increased when labor increases, and vice versa. In general, however, the cross-partials of a production function can be either positive or negative. Let's turn now to a more general treatment of the production function as an example of how higher-order partial derivatives can help us to understand economic behavior.

law of diminishing marginal returns: the empirical observation that, the more something is utilized, the smaller is its incremental contribution, holding everything else constant.

EXERCISES
Section 5.9
Second- and Higher-Order Partial Derivatives

Find all of the second-order partial derivatives for each of the following functions, and verify that Young's theorem holds for the cross-partials.

1. $Y = f(X_1, X_2) = 5X_1 + 3X_1X_2 + X_2^2$
2. $Y = f(X_1, X_2) = X_1^{1/2} + X_1 \ln X_2$
3. $Y = f(X_1, X_2, X_3, X_4) = X_1X_2X_3X_4$
4. $U = U(X_1, X_2) = 10X_1X_2^2 - 3(X_1X_2)^{1/2}$
5. $Y = f(X, Z) = e^X \ln Z$
6. $Q = f(K, L, M) = 25K^{1/5}L^{1/5}M^{3/5}$
7. $Q_d = D(P, P_r, Y) = YP_r/P^2$

5.10

APPLICATIONS OF HIGHER-ORDER PARTIAL DERIVATIVES TO PRODUCTION AND COST

Consider the production function $Y = f(X_1, X_2)$, where Y represents the rate of output and X_1 and X_2 are the utilization rates of two inputs.[3] As we suggested with the preceding example of the production function, the marginal products of the two inputs are represented by the partial derivatives f_1 and f_2, respectively. The second-order partials tell us about the behavior of the marginal products. If f_{11} and f_{22} are negative, we have diminishing marginal product for both inputs. The cross-partials tell us how changes in one input affect the marginal productivity of the other. If two inputs work together, more of one increases the productivity of the other and the cross-partial, f_{12}, is positive. If the inputs accomplish similar tasks, that means one is used instead of the other and the cross-partial is negative.

Because production functions are multivariate functions, we frequently use level curves to describe them graphically. Remember from Chapter 2 that a level curve is the graph of the relationship between two independent variables when the dependent variable is held constant. In the case of the production function, the level curve is the isoquant, which we always draw as convex to the origin. Convexity is an important property of both isoquants and indifference curves, and it is a property that can be usefully described mathematically. We explain the mathematical description of convex isoquants next.

5.10.1   Convexity of Isoquants

We showed in Section 5.8.1 that, to obtain the slope of an isoquant, you take the total differential of the production function and hold output constant by setting its differential, dY, equal to zero.

$$dY = f_1 \, dX_1 + f_2 \, dX_2 = 0 \tag{5-70}$$

$$\left. \frac{dX_2}{dX_1} \right|_{dY=0} = -\frac{f_1}{f_2} \tag{5-71}$$

As long as the marginal products of the two factors of production are positive, the slope of the isoquant is negative. We recall that the negative of this ratio is the MRTS. Looking at the graph of the isoquant in Figure 5.2 we see that not only does the isoquant have a negative slope but also it is convex, or it bows downward and inward. Recall from Chapter 3, Section 3.5 that a function is strictly convex if its second derivative is positive. What makes an isoquant convex is that, as X_1 increases, its slope becomes flatter or less negative.

---

[3] Notice that we are using different symbols for output and inputs than in our examples of the production function. We do this for two reasons: first, to accustom you to the use of different symbols; second, because when we express the inputs as $X_1, X_2, \ldots$ we can easily generalize our production function to include any number of inputs.

Figure 5.2

Isoquant

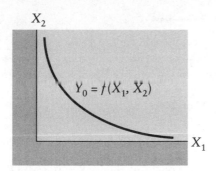

In order to find the second derivative, we use the quotient rule to differentiate the first derivative, dX_2/dX_1, with respect to X_1 again.

$$\left.\frac{d^2X_2}{dX_1^2}\right|_{dY=0} = -\frac{1}{f_2^2}\left[f_2\left(f_{11}+f_{12}\frac{dX_2}{dX_1}\right)-f_1\left(f_{21}+f_{22}\frac{dX_2}{dX_1}\right)\right] \quad (5\text{-}72)$$

In taking this derivative we are careful to keep in mind that X_2 is a function of X_1 because we are holding output constant. Multiply through the expression in brackets and remember that $dX_2/dX_1 = -f_1/f_2$ and that $f_{12} = f_{21}$,

$$\left.\frac{d^2X_2}{dX_1^2}\right|_{dY=0} = -\frac{1}{f_2^2}\left(f_2 f_{11}-2f_1 f_{12}+\frac{f_1^2 f_{22}}{f_2}\right) \quad (5\text{-}73)$$

Multiply and divide the first two terms in the brackets by f_2 and factor out $1/f_2$.

$$\left.\frac{d^2X_2}{dX_1^2}\right|_{dY=0} = -\frac{1}{f_2^3}\left(f_2^2 f_{11}-2f_1 f_2 f_{12}+f_1^2 f_{22}\right) > 0 \quad (5\text{-}74)$$

Remember that the isoquant is strictly convex if this expression for the second derivative of X_2 with respect to X_1 is positive. Equation (5-74) describes convexity of the production isoquants in mathematical terms. Look at it carefully, because you will see that this expression or expressions very similar to it play important roles in models of consumer and producer behavior in Chapters 7, 9, 10, 11 and 14. If (5-74) were negative, the isoquant would be strictly concave; if it were equal to zero, the isoquant would be a straight line.

One feature of this expression to note is that the convexity of isoquants is distinct from diminishing marginal productivity of the inputs. We mention this because students of economics frequently explain convexity to themselves by remarking that, "as one input, X_1, is increased its marginal product decreases, while as the other input, X_2, is decreased its marginal product increases." This would cause the ratio f_1/f_2 to decrease as one "moved down" an isoquant. Reexamine equation (5-74), and remember that diminishing marginal productivity means that f_{11} and f_{22} are negative. Because of the middle term in the brackets, which includes the cross-partial f_{12}, isoquants can be convex even if the inputs do not experience diminishing productivity, and vice versa.

NUMERICAL EXAMPLE

Recall the production function $Y = f(X_1, X_2) = X_1 X_2^2$. This is the same production function as we used in the example in Section 5.8.1, except that we are employing the notation in which Y is output, with inputs X_1 and X_2. The total differential is

$$dY = f_1\, dX_1 + f_2\, dX_2 = X_2^2\, dX_1 + 2X_1 X_2\, dX_2 \qquad (5\text{-}75)$$

If we hold output constant, then $dY = 0$ and we can solve for dX_2/dX_1,

$$\left.\frac{dX_2}{dX_1}\right|_{dY=0} = -\frac{f_1}{f_2} = -\frac{X_2}{2X_1} = -\text{MRTS}_{12} \qquad (5\text{-}76)$$

Differentiating once more with respect to X_1, using the quotient rule and remembering that X_2 is a function of X_1, we obtain

$$\frac{d^2X_2}{dX_1^2} = -\frac{2X_1\, dX_2/dX_1 - 2X_2}{4X_1^2} \qquad (5\text{-}77)$$

Substituting in equation (5-76) for dX_2/dX_1 gives us

$$\frac{d^2X_2}{dX_1^2} = -\frac{-2X_1(X_2/2X_1) - 2X_2}{4X_1^2} = \frac{3X_2}{4X_1^2} > 0 \qquad (5\text{-}78)$$

As you can see, (5-78) is positive, so the isoquants for this production function are strictly convex. This is the case even though neither input experiences diminishing marginal productivity. We know this because neither of the second-order partial derivatives is negative. We see that $f_{11} = 0$ and $f_{22} = 2X_1$.

EXERCISES
Section 5.10.1
Convexity of
Isoquants

Show that the isoquants for the following production function are convex by finding

$$\left.\frac{d^2X_2}{dX_1^2}\right|_{dY=0} > 0$$

1. $Y = f(X_1, X_2) = 10(0.2X_1^{-0.5} + 0.8X_2^{-0.5})^{-2}$
2. $Y = f(X_1, X_2) = \alpha \ln X_1 + \beta \ln X_2$
3. $Y = f(X_1, X_2) = X_1 X_2$

5.10.2   Minimum-Cost Choice of Inputs

isocost line: a graph of the combinations of two inputs that cost the same.

We superimpose an *isocost line* on the graph of the isoquant in Figure 5.3. The isocost line is a graph of the combinations of two inputs that cost the same. Given that we have two inputs, X_1 and X_2, the cost function can be expressed as

$$C = w_1 X_1 + w_2 X_2 \tag{5-79}$$

where w_1 is the price of input 1 and w_2 is the price of input 2. We treat the input prices as constants, or parameters, in the cost function. It is a linear function that can be solved explicitly for X_2 in terms of C, X_1, and the parameters.

$$X_2 = \frac{C}{w_2} - \frac{w_1}{w_2} X_1 \tag{5-80}$$

Equation (5-80) represents the equation of an isocost line for any given level of C. As you can see in Figure 5.3, the vertical intercept of the isocost line is equal to C/w_2.

The isocost line and the isoquant are tangent at (X_1^*, X_2^*), the input combination that produces a rate of output Y_0 at minimum cost. At the point of tangency, the slope of the isocost line is equal to the slope of the isoquant. We can find the slope of the isocost line by taking the total differential of the cost function. Recall that an isocost line consists of input combinations that cost the same; that is, cost is constant along the isocost line. To express this concept mathematically, find the total differential of equation (5-79), the cost function, and set $dC = 0$,

$$dC = \frac{\partial C}{\partial X_1} dX_1 + \frac{\partial C}{\partial X_2} dX_2 = w_1 \, dX_1 + w_2 \, dX_2 = 0 \tag{5-81}$$

Figure 5.3

Isoquant with Isocost Line Superimposed

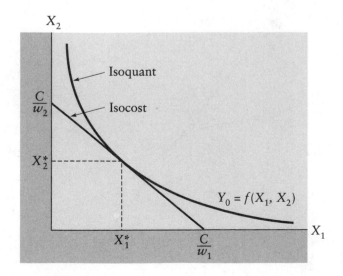

Solving for the slope of the isocost line gives us

$$\frac{dX_2}{dX_1}\bigg|_{dC=0} = -\frac{w_1}{w_2} \tag{5-82}$$

At the point of tangency the slope of the isoquant equals the slope of the isocost line,

$$\frac{dX_2}{dX_1}\bigg|_{dY=0} = \frac{dX_2}{dX_1}\bigg|_{dC=0} \tag{5-83}$$

or

$$-\frac{f_1}{f_2} = -\frac{w_1}{w_2} \tag{5-84}$$

Equation (5-84) tells us that the cost-minimizing combination of inputs is that at which the ratio of input prices is equal to the ratio of their marginal products, or the MRTS. We examine the model of cost minimization and the theory of cost in more detail in Chapter 11.

Another place in economic theory where you will see a graph similar to the isoquant/isocost diagram is in consumer theory. The indifference curve, pictured in Figure 5.4, represents the combinations of goods and services that yield a constant level of utility. We examined the indifference curve in Section 5.8.1 of this chapter. Note that everything we have just demonstrated

Figure 5.4

Indifference Curve and Budget Constraint

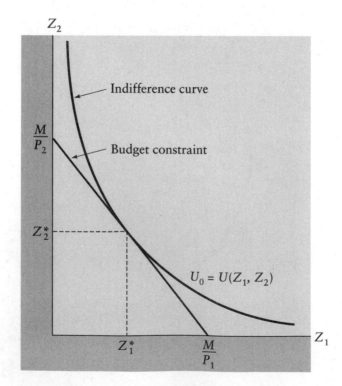

regarding the slope and convexity of the isoquant, we can easily duplicate to discuss the slope and convexity of the indifference curve. In place of the production function $Y = f(X_1, X_2)$ substitute a utility function $U = U(Z_1, Z_2)$, where Z_1 and Z_2 represent amounts of goods or services that an individual consumes and U represents utility.

Everything we demonstrated regarding the slope of the isocost line and its point of tangency with the isoquant could as easily have referred to the slope of the ***budget constraint*** and its point of tangency with the indifference curve. In place of the cost function $C = w_1 X_1 + w_2 X_2$ substitute the budget constraint, $M = P_1 Z_1 + P_2 Z_2$, where M is money income and P_1 and P_2 are the prices of the goods. The budget constraint represents the combinations of goods and services that a consumer can purchase with a given money income. In Figure 5.4 the point of tangency (Z_1^*, Z_2^*) represents the maximum utility obtainable from a given money income and prices.

In Sections 5.9 and 5.10 we use the fact that partial derivatives are themselves functions of the independent variables of the primitive function to discuss higher-order partial derivatives. Because partial derivatives are prominent in total differentials, the fact that they are functions also means that ***higher-order total differentials*** exist, and we turn next to them. They will prove especially useful when we examine optimization of multivariate functions in Chapters 6 and 7.

budget constraint: the combinations of goods and services that a consumer can purchase with a given money income and prices.

higher-order total differentials: the total differential of a total differential.

5.11

SECOND- AND HIGHER-ORDER TOTAL DIFFERENTIALS

With the aid of second- and higher-order partial derivatives we can take second- and higher-order total differentials. Suppose you are given the function

$$Y = f(X_1, X_2) \tag{5-85}$$

When we totally differentiate this function we obtain

$$dY = f_1(X_1, X_2)\, dX_1 + f_2(X_1, X_2)\, dX_2 \tag{5-86}$$

Remember, the first-order total differential captures changes in the dependent variable from all possible sources. If the dependent variable, Y, is constant, dY is zero; if Y is increasing, dY is positive; if Y is decreasing, dY is negative. The ***second-order total differential*** captures changes in dY from all possible sources. We find it by taking the total differential of the first-order total differential, obtaining

second-order total differential: see higher-order total differential.

$$d^2Y = (f_{11}\, dX_1 + f_{12}\, dX_2)\, dX_1 + (f_{22}\, dX_2 + f_{21}\, dX_1)\, dX_2 \tag{5-87}$$

We use d^2 to denote a second-order total differential. Multiplying through and combining terms gives us

$$d^2Y = f_{11}\, dX_1^2 + 2f_{12}\, dX_1\, dX_2 + f_{22}\, dX_2^2 \qquad (5\text{-}88)$$

The same reasoning we use to interpret the first-order total differential applies when we interpret the second-order total differential. The change in Y, or dY, is a function. If dY is constant, then its total differential, $d(dY)$ or d^2Y is zero; if dY is increasing, d^2Y is positive; if dY is decreasing, d^2Y is negative.

This understanding of the first- and second-order total differentials enables us to develop an optimization technique for functions of several variables, which is discussed in Chapter 6. For Y to achieve a critical point, it must be neither increasing nor decreasing in any direction. That is, dY must be zero. If dY is decreasing in the neighborhood of the critical point, then d^2Y is negative, the function is strictly concave, and the critical point must be a local maximum. If dY is increasing in the neighborhood of the critical point, then d^2Y is positive, the function is strictly convex, and the critical point must be a local minimum. We discuss the implications of this more fully in the next chapter.

As long as the functions and their differentials are differentiable, we can continue to find higher-order total differentials. The third-order total differential of Y is denoted d^3Y and can be found by differentiating d^2Y. We will not investigate higher-order total differentials here, however, because we have no immediate economic applications of third- or higher-order total differentiation.

Find the second-order total differential for each of the following functions.

1. $Y = f(X_1, X_2) = 5X_1 + 3X_1X_2 + X_2^2$

2. $Y = f(X_1, X_2) = X_1^{1/2} + X_1 \ln X_2$

3. $Y = f(X_1, X_2) = X_1 X_2$

4. $U = U(X_1, X_2) = 10X_1X_2^2 - 3(X_1X_2)^{1/2}$

5. $Y = f(X, Z) = e^X \ln Z$

6. $Q = f(K, L) = 25K^{1/5}L^{1/5}$

7. $Q_d = D(P, Y) = Y/P^2$

5.12

SUMMARY

This chapter is devoted primarily to developing mathematical techniques for differentiating functions with more than one independent variable. We introduce the notion of partial derivatives. The only difference between partial derivatives of multivariate functions and simple derivatives of functions of one independent variable is that we treat the other independent variables as though they are constant when we differentiate with respect to one particular independent variable. We apply the concept of partial derivatives to perform comparative statics analysis of a model of national income determination.

The concepts of the differential and the total differential are introduced to provide a more complete notion of what differentiation of functions means. The discussion of the total differential allows us to revisit the concept of implicit differentiation. It also permits us to examine a very generally applicable market model, in which we make only the minimum possible assumptions regarding demand and supply functions.

It turns out that knowledge of partial and total differentiation can be immediately applied to describe some important properties of production functions and their isoquants. We show what is meant by diminishing marginal productivity, convexity of isoquants, and the cost-minimizing choice of inputs. The same reasoning can be applied to utility functions and consumer theory.

Finally, we briefly discuss higher-order total differentials, which become important in the next chapter when we show how to optimize functions of many independent variables. Now that we can differentiate functions with many independent variables, we can turn to some more interesting and detailed optimization models.

◆ **REFERENCES**

Allen, R. G. D., *Mathematical Analysis for Economists* (New York: St. Martin's Press, 1938), Chapters 11, 12, and 13.

Barnett, Raymond A. and Ziegler, Michael R., *College Mathematics for Business, Economics, Life Sciences, and Social Sciences*, 5th edition (San Francisco: Dellen Publishing Company, 1990), Chapter 15.

Thomas, George B., Jr., *Calculus and Analytic Geometry*, Third Edition (Reading, Massachussetts: Addison-Wesley Publishing Company, 1960), Chapter 14.

◆ **ANSWERS TO END-OF-SECTION EXERCISES**

Section 5.2: Partial Derivatives

1. $\partial Y/\partial X_1 \equiv f_1 = 5 + 3X_2$; $\partial Y/\partial X_2 \equiv f_2 = 3X_1 + 2X_2$

2. $\partial Y/\partial X_1 \equiv f_1 = X_1^{-1/2}/2 + \ln X_2$; $\partial Y/\partial X_2 \equiv f_2 = X_1/X_2$

3. $\partial Y/\partial X_1 \equiv f_1 = X_2 X_3 X_4$; $\partial Y/\partial X_2 \equiv f_2 = X_1 X_3 X_4$;
   $\partial Y/\partial X_3 \equiv f_3 = X_1 X_2 X_4$; $\partial Y/\partial X_4 \equiv f_4 = X_1 X_2 X_3$

4. $\dfrac{\partial Y}{\partial X_1} \equiv f_1 = \dfrac{(3 + X_1^2 X_2^2)(1 - 2X_2^{1.5}) - 2X_1 X_2^2(X_1 - 2X_1 X_2^{1.5})}{[3 + (X_1 X_2)^2]^2}$

   $\dfrac{\partial Y}{\partial X_2} \equiv f_2 = \dfrac{(3 + X_1^2 X_2^2)(-3X_1 X_2^{0.5}) - 2X_1^2 X_2(X_1 - 2X_1 X_2^{1.5})}{[3 + (X_1 X_2)^2]^2}$

5. $\partial Y/\partial X \equiv f_X = e^X \ln Z$; $\partial Y/\partial Z \equiv f_Z = e^X/Z$

6. $\partial Q/\partial K \equiv f_K = 5K^{-4/5}L^{1/5}M^{3/5} = Q/(5K)$;
$\partial Q/\partial L \equiv f_L = 5K^{1/5}L^{-4/5}M^{3/5} = Q/(5L)$;
$\partial Q/\partial M \equiv f_M = 5K^{1/5}L^{1/5}M^{-2/5} = 3Q/(5M)$

7. $\partial Q/\partial P = D_P = -2YP_r/P^3$; $\partial Q/\partial P_r \equiv D_{P_r} = Y/P^2$; $\partial Q/\partial Y \equiv D_Y = P_r/P^2$

8. $\partial U/\partial X_1 \equiv U_1 = 10X_2^2 - (3/2)(X_1^{-1/2}X_2^{1/2})$;
$\partial U/\partial X_2 \equiv U_2 = 20X_1X_2 - (3/2)(X_1^{1/2}X_2^{-1/2})$

Section 5.4: Comparative Statics Analysis of National Income Model

1. $\partial Y^*/\partial I = 1/[1 - \beta(1 - \tau)]$; $\partial Y_d^*/\partial I = (1 - \tau)/[1 - \beta(1 - \tau)]$;
$\partial C^*/\partial I = \beta(1 - \tau)/[1 - \beta(1 - \tau)]$

2. $\partial Y^*/\partial C_0 = 1/[1 - \beta(1 - \tau)]$; $\partial Y_d^*/\partial C_0 = (1 - \tau)/[1 - \beta(1 - \tau)]$;
$\partial C^*/\partial C_0 = 1/[1 - \beta(1 - \tau)]$

3. $\partial Y^*/\partial \beta = Y^*(1 - \tau)/[1 - \beta(1 - \tau)]$; $\partial Y_d^*/\partial \beta = Y_d^*(1 - \tau)/[1 - \beta(1 - \tau)]$;
$\partial C^*/\partial \beta = (1 - \tau)(C_0 + I + G)/[1 - \beta(1 - \tau)]^2$

Section 5.6: Total Differentials of Multivariate Functions

1. $dY = (5 + 3X_2)dX_1 + (3X_1 + 2X_2)dX_2$

2. $dY = (X_1^{-1/2}/2 + \ln X_2)dX_1 + (X_1/X_2)dX_2$

3. $dY = (X_2X_3X_4)dX_1 + (X_1X_3X_4)dX_2 + (X_1X_2X_4)dX_3 + (X_1X_2X_3)dX_4$

4. $dY = \dfrac{(3 + X_1^2X_2^2)(1 - 2X_2^{1.5}) - 2X_1X_2^2(X_1 - 2X_1X_2^{1.5})}{[3 + (X_1X_2)^2]^2} dX_1$

$+ \dfrac{(3 + X_1^2X_2^2)(-3X_1^2X_2^{0.5}) - 2X_1^2X_2(X_1 - 2X_1X_2^{1.5})}{[3 + (X_1X_2)^2]^2} dX_2$

5. $dY = e^X \ln Z \, dX + (e^X/Z) \, dZ$

6. $dQ = 5K^{-4/5}L^{1/5}M^{3/5} \, dK + 5K^{1/5}L^{-4/5}M^{3/5} \, dL + 15K^{1/5}L^{1/5}M^{-2/5} \, dM$

7. $dQ = (-2YP_r/P^3)dP + (Y/P^2)dP_r + (P_r/P^2)dY$

8. $dU = [10X_2^2 - (3/2)(X_1^{-1/2}X_2^{1/2})]dX_1 + [20X_1X_2 - (3/2)(X_1^{1/2}X_2^{-1/2})]dX_2$

Section 5.7: Implicit Functions Revisited

1. $F_1 = 2X_1 + X_2 + X_3$; $F_2 = 2X_2 + X_1 + X_3$; $F_3 = 2X_3 + X_1 + X_2$. Therefore, $dF(X_1, X_2, X_3) = F_1 \, dX_1 + F_2 \, dX_2 + F_3 \, dX_3$. $X_1 = f(X_2, X_3)$ if $F_1 \neq 0$. Then, $f_2 = -F_2/F_1$, and $f_3 = -F_3/F_1$.

2. $F_1 = 1/(X_1 + X_2) + (\ln X_2)/X_1$, $F_2 = 1/(X_1 + X_2) + (\ln X_1)/X_2$. Therefore, $dF(X_1, X_2) = F_1 \, dX_1 + F_2 \, dX_2$. $X_1 = f(X_2)$ if $F_1 \neq 0$. Then, $f' = -F_2/F_1$.

3. $F_1 = 2(X_1 + X_2) - X_2e^{X_1X_2}$; $F_2 = 2(X_1 + X_2) - X_1e^{X_1X_2}$. Therefore, $dF(X_1, X_2) = F_1 \, dX_1 + F_2 \, dX_2$. $X_1 = f(X_2)$ if $F_1 \neq 0$. Then, $f' = -F_2/F_1$.

4. $F_1 = -2X_1 + (1/2)(X_1X_2)^{-1/2}X_2$; $F_2 = -2X_2 + (1/2)(X_1X_2)^{-1/2}X_1$. Therefore, $dF(X_1, X_2) = F_1 \, dX_1 + F_2 \, dX_2$. $X_1 = f(X_2)$ if $F_1 \neq 0$. Then, $f' = -F_2/F_1$.

Section 5.8.1: Slopes of Isoquants and Indifference Curves

1. **a.** $\text{MRTS}_{LK} = (1/4)(K/L)^{1/2}$;   **b.** $\text{MRTS}_{LK} = (1/2)(K/L)$

2. **a.** $\text{MRS}_{12} = (1/4)(X_2/X_1)$;   **b.** $\text{MRS}_{12} = X_2/X_1$

Section 5.9: Second- and Higher-Order Partial Derivatives

1. $f_{11} = 0$; $f_{22} = 2$; $f_{12} = 3 = f_{21}$

2. $f_{11} = -X_1^{-3/2}/4$; $f_{22} = -X_1/X_2^2$; $f_{12} = 1/X_2 = f_{21}$

3. $f_{11} = f_{22} = f_{33} = f_{44} = 0$; $f_{12} = X_3 X_4 = f_{21}$; $f_{13} = X_2 X_4 = f_{31}$;
   $f_{14} = X_3 X_2 = f_{41}$; $f_{23} = X_1 X_4 = f_{32}$; $f_{24} = X_1 X_3 = f_{42}$; $f_{34} = X_1 X_2 = f_{43}$

4. $U_{11} = (3/4)X_2^{1/2}X_1^{-3/2}$; $U_{22} = 20X_1 + (3/4)X_1^{1/2}X_2^{-3/2}$;
   $U_{12} = 20X_2 - (3/4)(X_1 X_2)^{-1/2}$

5. $f_{XX} = e^X \ln Z$; $f_{ZZ} = -e^X/Z^2$; $f_{XZ} = e^X/Z = f_{ZX}$

6. $f_{KK} = -4K^{-9/5}L^{1/5}M^{3/5}$; $f_{LL} = -4K^{1/5}L^{-9/5}M^{3/5}$; $f_{MM} = -6K^{1/5}L^{1/5}M^{-7/5}$;
   $f_{KL} = K^{-4/5}L^{-4/5}M^{3/5} = f_{LK}$; $f_{KM} = 3K^{-4/5}L^{1/5}M^{-2/5} = f_{MK}$;
   $f_{LM} = 3K^{1/5}L^{-4/5}M^{-2/5} = f_{ML}$

7. $D_{PP} = 6YP_r/P^4$; $D_{P_r P_r} = 0$; $D_{rr} = 0$; $D_{PP_r} = -2Y/P^3 = D_{P_r P}$;
   $D_{PY} = -2P_r/P^3 = D_{YP}$; $D_{YP_r} = 1/P^2 = D_{P_r Y}$.

Section 5.10.1: Convexity of Isoquants

1. $d^2X_2/dX_1^2 = (3/8)X_2^{-2.5}X_2^{1.5} > 0$

2. $d^2X_2/dX_1^2 = [\alpha(\beta + \alpha) \neq \beta^2](X_2 \neq X_1^2) > 0$

3. $d^2X_2/dX_1^2 = 2X_2 \neq X_1^2 > 0$

Section 5.11: Second- and Higher-Order Total Differentials

1. $d^2Y = 6dX_1 dX_2 + 2dX_2^2$

2. $d^2Y = (-X_1^{-3/2}/4)dX_1^2 + (2/X_2)dX_1 dX_2 - (X_1/X_2^2)dX_2^2$

3. $d^2Y = 2dX_1 dX_2$

4. $d^2U = [(3/4)X_2^{1/2}X_1^{-3/2}]dX_1^2 + [40X_2 - (3/2)X_1^{-1/2}X_2^{-1/2}]dX_1 dX_2 + [20X_1 + (3/4)X_1^{1/2}X_2^{-3/2}]dX_2^2$

5. $d^2Y = e^X \ln Z dX^2 + (2e^X/Z)dX dZ + (-e^X/Z^2)dZ^2$

6. $d^2Q = -4K^{-9/5}L^{1/5}dK^2 + 2K^{-4/5}L^{-4/5}dK dL - 4K^{1/5}L^{-9/5}dL^2$

7. $d^2Q_d = (6Y/P^4)dP^2 - (4/P^3)dP dY - (2/P^3)dY^2$

◆ SELF-HELP PROBLEMS

Answers to these problems are given at the end of the text.

For Problems 1 through 4 use the following standard model of national income determination where Y is income, C is consumption expenditures, Y_d is disposable income, T is income taxes, I is investment expenditures, which is assumed to be exogenous, and G is government expenditures, also exogenous.

$$Y = C + I + G$$
$$C = C(Y_d),\ 0 < C' < 1$$
$$Y_d = Y - T$$
$$T = T(Y),\ 0 < T' < 1$$

1. Perform comparative statics analysis of the effect of a change in government expenditures on equilibrium level of income.

2. Some favor a constitutional amendment requiring the federal government to limit its spending level to total tax revenue. Incorporate this into the given standard model and determine whether such a policy would increase or decrease the size of the spending multiplier.

3. A former chairman of the Federal Reserve once told Congress he favors legislation to curb federal spending by limiting it to a fixed share of GNP. Incorporate this proposal into the given standard model and determine whether such a policy would increase or decrease the size of the spending multiplier.

4. Some favor changing the base of federal taxes from income to consumption. Incorporate this into the given standard model and determine whether such a change would increase or decrease the size of the spending multiplier.

Hint: Replace $T = T(Y)$ with $T = T(C)$. Substitute this into $Y_d = Y - T$ and substitute the result into $C = C(Y_d)$. Totally differentiate the resulting consumption function using the chain rule and solve for the total differential of C. Substitute the result into the total differential of the equilibrium condition and solve for dY. Now either set $dI = 0$ and solve for $\partial Y/\partial G$, or set $dG = 0$ and solve for $\partial Y/\partial I$.

For questions 5 through 7 you are given a market model in which $Q_d = D(P, Y, P_c, P_s)$, where Q_d is quantity demanded, P is the price of the product, Y is income, P_c is the price of a complementary good, and P_s is the price of a substitute good. Suppose also $Q_s = S(P, w, r)$, where Q_s is quantity supplied, w is the wage paid to labor, and r is the rental rate (price) of capital.

5. What signs do you expect for $\partial Q_d/\partial Y$, $\partial Q_d/\partial P_c$, $\partial Q_d/\partial P_s$, $\partial Q_s/\partial w$, and $\partial Q_s/\partial r$? Explain your reasoning.

6. What is the equilibrium condition for this model and what are its endogenous and exogenous variables? What implicit relationships exist between the endogenous and exogenous variables if the equilibrium condition is assumed to hold?

7. Find and interpret the comparative statics results $\partial Q^*/\partial Y$, $\partial P^*/\partial Y$, $\partial Q^*/\partial P_c$, $\partial P^*/\partial P_c$, $\partial Q^*/\partial P_s$, $\partial P^*/\partial P_s$, $\partial Q^*/\partial w$, $\partial P^*/\partial w$, $\partial Q^*/\partial r$, and $\partial P^*/\partial r$.

◆ SUPPLEMENTAL PROBLEMS

1. Consider the following revised model of national income determination where Y is income, C is consumption expenditures, Y_d is disposable income, T is income taxes, I is investment expenditures, G is government expenditures, and r is the rate of interest.

$$Y = C + I + G$$
$$C = C(Y_d, r), \quad 0 < \delta C/\delta Y_d < 1$$
$$Y_d = Y - T$$
$$T = T(Y), \quad 0 < T' < 1$$

a. Explain what it means to include the rate of interest, r, in the consumption function. What sign do you expect $\partial C/\partial r$ to have? Why? Explain.

  b. Derive an expression for the effect of a change in the rate of interest on the equilibrium level of income and determine its sign.

2. For the following production functions, (i) find the marginal products of each input; (ii) show algebraically whether the marginal products are diminishing; (iii) find the cross-partial derivatives and interpret their signs; and (iv) find the slope of the isoquant.

   a. $Q = 100K^{0.5}L^{0.7}$ **b.** $Q = 10K + 25L$
   c. $Q = AK^{\alpha}L^{1-\alpha}$ **d.** $Q = 10K + 25L - 3L^2 - 5KL - K^2$

3. For each production function in Problem 2, find the total differential and determine whether or not the isoquants are strictly convex.

4. Consider the following production function: $Y = f(X_1, X_2, X_3)$.

   a. Define marginal product in words and express them mathematically for all three inputs.

   b. Explain diminishing marginal product in words and mathematically.

   c. What is the total differential of the production function? Explain what it means in words.

   d. When there are three inputs, there are three different isoquants: the X_1-X_2 isoquant, the X_1-X_3 isoquant, and the X_2-X_3 isoquant. The isoquant between any two inputs holds the third input constant. Find expressions for the slopes of all three isoquants associated with this production function.

You are given the following production function for questions 5 through 8:

$$Y = f(X_1, X_2) = AX_1^{1/2}X_2^{2/3}$$

5. Find expressions for marginal product of X_1 and marginal product of X_2. Does this production function demonstrate diminishing marginal productivity?

6. Show that $f_{12} = f_{21}$. What is a reasonable economic interpretation of the cross-partial derivative?

7. Write the equation of an isoquant for this production function and picture it graphically. What is the slope of the isoquant? What is an economic interpretation of the slope of the isoquant?

8. Is the isoquant strictly convex?

9. Suppose the production function is $Y = f(X_1, X_2) = AX_1^{1.5}X_2^2$. Does it demonstrate diminishing marginal productivity in both inputs? Is the isoquant strictly convex?

Unconstrained Optimization of Functions of Two or More Choice Variables

6.1

INTRODUCTION

In Chapter 4, we introduced the concept of unconstrained optimization of functions with one independent variable. We used models with one independent variable to generate some familiar and useful results concerning economic behavior. We found, for example, that profit-maximizing firms produce at a rate of output such that marginal revenue equals marginal cost and that they employ an input at a rate such that marginal revenue product equals marginal factor cost. We found that we could adapt our basic profit-maximization model to accommodate price-taking and price-searching behavior in either output or input markets. In models where prices serve as parameters, we found comparative statics results in which the choice variables could be expressed as functions of the parameters and responses to changes in the parameters could be predicted.

Now that we have discussed differentiation of functions with two or more independent variables in Chapter 5, we are ready to introduce optimization in more complete models. You will find that much of the theory of consumer and producer behavior that is typically learned in an intermediate theory course is easily derived from models with two choice variables. This is because the major analytical tool used in intermediate courses is the graph, which restricts analysis to a maximum of three dimensions. This chapter discusses unconstrained optimization of models with two independent variables using several examples from economics, the most important of which is profit maximization by a firm with two inputs. Then we demonstrate how to generalize the optimization technique to functions with any number of independent variables.

6.2

FIRST- AND SECOND-ORDER CONDITIONS REVISITED

In models with one independent variable, we identified critical points in the dependent variable by examining the behavior of the first and second derivatives. To be at a critical point it must be true that the dependent variable is neither increasing nor decreasing; that is, the first derivative must be equal to zero. If the second derivative is negative when evaluated at the critical point, then the function is strictly concave in the neighborhood. This means that it is increasing before the critical point and decreasing after; therefore the critical point is a maximum. If the second derivative is positive when evaluated at the critical point, then the function is strictly convex in the neighborhood. This means that it is decreasing before its critical point and increasing after; therefore the critical point is a minimum. If the second derivative is zero, the critical point may be a point of inflection.

We remind you of these results from the problem with one independent variable because the same principles hold with functions of two or more independent variables. The only difference is that there is more than one source of change in a multivariate model, and we must account for all possible movements in the dependent variable. To do this we will examine the behavior of the first and second total differentials of an objective function with two independent variables.

Consider the function

$$Y = f(X_1, X_2) \tag{6-1}$$

For a particular value of Y to be a maximum or a minimum, the function must be neither increasing nor decreasing at that point. That is, it must be stationary, or its total differential must be equal to zero. This means that at a critical point it is necessary that

$$dY = f_1\, dX_1 + f_2\, dX_2 = 0 \tag{6-2}$$

As long as dX_1 and dX_2 are not simultaneously zero, the total differential can equal zero only if both the partial derivatives equal zero, or

$$f_1 = 0 \quad \text{and} \quad f_2 = 0 \tag{6-3}$$

Therefore, we have two first-order (necessary) conditions for optimization: both first-order partial derivatives must equal zero. To understand this result, recall the meaning of the partial derivative. It is the instantaneous rate of change of the dependent variable with respect to one independent variable holding all other independent variables constant. A mountaineering analogy to the first-order conditions is this: at the top of the mountain, when you look in the north-south direction, you must see no points higher than where you stand, and when you look in the east-west direction, you must see no points higher than where you stand. Where you stand is level in both directions.

When the necessary conditions are satisfied, all we know is that the

saddle point: a point on a surface that is flat in every direction but is neither a local minimum or maximum because it increases in one direction but decreases in another.

dependent variable is stationary: it may be a maximum, a minimum, a point of inflection, or a *saddle point.* A critical point in functions of two or more independent variables that is a maximum in one direction but a minimum in another is called a saddle point because the seat of a saddle is a surface that is flat in every direction but is not a local minimum or maximum. For example, Figure 6.1 is a graph of the function $Y = X_2^2 - X_1^2$. At the origin, where the axes cross, there is a saddle point. Moving forward or backward along the X_1 axis causes Y to decrease, and moving forward or backward along the X_2 axis causes Y to increase, so the function has neither a maximum nor a minimum at the saddle point.

To assure ourselves that we have reached the optimum value of the dependent variable, we must examine how the dependent variable behaves in the vicinity of the stationary point. If the second total differential is negative, then the function is changing from increasing to decreasing in the vicinity of the stationary point and we have identified a local maximum. If the second total differential is positive, then the function is changing from decreasing to increasing in the vicinity of the stationary point and we have identified a local minimum. If the second total differential is zero, we may have identified a saddle point or a point of inflection. Therefore, our second-order (sufficient) condition for optimization can be expressed as

$$d^2Y = (f_{11}\, dX_1 + f_{12}\, dX_2)\, dX_1 + (f_{21}\, dX_1 + f_{22}\, dX_2)\, dX_2 \quad \begin{matrix} < 0 \text{ for a maximum} \\ > 0 \text{ for a minimum} \end{matrix} \quad \text{(6-4)}$$

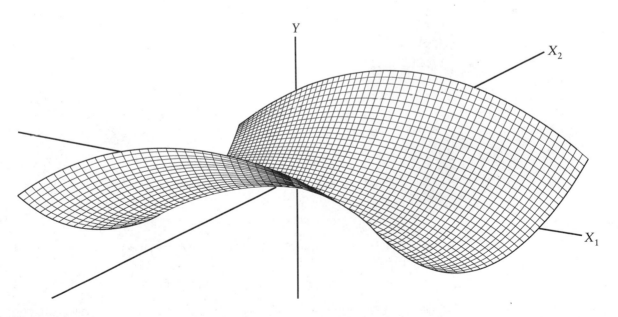

Figure 6.1

Saddle Point

or, if we multiply through and combine like terms,

$$d^2Y = f_{11}\, dX_1^2 + 2f_{21}\, dX_2\, dX_1 + f_{22}\, dX_2^2 \quad \begin{matrix} < 0 \text{ for a maximum} \\ > 0 \text{ for a minimum} \end{matrix} \quad (6\text{-}5)$$

To interpret the sufficient condition, consider all the ways Y can change: X_1 can change while X_2 is constant, X_2 can change while X_1 is constant, and both X_1 and X_2 can change. In the first case, dX_2 equals zero, in the second dX_1 equals zero, and in the third dX_1 and dX_2 are both nonzero. No matter what the source of change, d^2Y must be negative for a maximum and positive for a minimum. Recognizing all this gives us the following second-order conditions for optimization of functions with two independent variables.

I. $dX_2 = 0$: $d^2Y = f_{11}\, dX_1^2 \begin{matrix}<\\>\end{matrix} 0 \text{ if } f_{11} \begin{matrix}<\\>\end{matrix} 0 \begin{matrix} \text{for a maximum} \\ \text{for a minimum} \end{matrix}$ (6-6)

II. $dX_1 = 0$: $d^2Y = f_{22}\, dX_2^2 \begin{matrix}<\\>\end{matrix} 0 \text{ if } f_{22} \begin{matrix}<\\>\end{matrix} 0 \begin{matrix} \text{for a maximum} \\ \text{for a minimum} \end{matrix}$ (6-7)

III. $dX_2, dX_1 > 0$: $f_{11} f_{22} - f_{12}^2 > 0$ for a maximum and a minimum[1]

(6-8)

NUMERICAL EXAMPLES

Find critical points for the following function. Determine for each whether it is a maximum or a minimum.

$$Y = f(X_1, X_2) = 8X_1^3 + 2X_1 X_2 - 3X_1^2 + X_2^2 + 1 \qquad (6\text{-}9)$$

---

[1] To see this last result, recognize that

$$d^2Y = f_{11}\, dX_1^2 + 2f_{21}\, dX_2\, dX_1 + f_{22}\, dX_2^2$$

Factor out f_{11}, leaving

$$d^2Y = f_{11}[dX_1^2 + 2f_{21}\, dX_2\, dX_1/f_{11} + f_{22}\, dX_2^2/f_{11}]$$

Add and subtract the expression $(f_{21}\, dX_2/f_{11})^2$ inside the brackets, leaving the value unchanged.

$$d^2Y = f_{11}[dX_1^2 + 2f_{21}\, dX_2\, dX_1/f_{11} + (f_{21}\, dX_2/f_{11})^2 - (f_{21}\, dX_2/f_{11})^2 + f_{22}\, dX_2/f_{11}]$$

Recognize that the first three terms in the brackets can be expressed as the square of a sum and the last two terms can be factored.

$$d^2Y = f_{11}[\{dX_1 + (f_{21}\, dX_2/f_{11})\}^2 + (dX_2/f_{11})^2\{f_{11} f_{22} - f_{21}^2\}]$$

Examination of this last expression reveals that the expression inside the brackets must be positive as long as $f_{11} f_{22} - f_{21}^2 > 0$. When this is the case, the sign of d^2Y is determined by f_{11}. For a maximum, $f_{11} < 0$, as is d^2Y. For a minimum, $f_{11} > 0$ and so is d^2Y. Therefore a second-order condition for both a minimum and a maximum is that $f_{11} f_{22} - f_{21}^2 > 0$.

The first-order conditions for optimization are

$$f_1 = 24X_1^2 + 2X_2 - 6X_1 = 0 \tag{6-10}$$

$$f_2 = 2X_1 + 2X_2 = 0 \tag{6-11}$$

The first-order conditions provide two equations in two unknowns. We solve them by subtracting f_2 from f_1, obtaining solutions of $(X_1, X_2) = (1/3, -1/3)$ and $(X_1, X_2) = (0, 0)$. These are critical points for the function. To determine whether the solutions are maxima or minima (or neither) we examine the second-order conditions.

$$\text{SOC;} \quad f_{11} = 48X_1 - 6 > 0 \quad \text{if } (X_1, X_2) = (1/3, -1/3) \tag{6-12}$$
$$< 0 \quad \text{if } (X_1, X_2) = (0, 0)$$

$$f_{22} = 2 > 0 \tag{6-13}$$

$$f_{11}f_{22} - f_{12}^2 = (48X_1 - 6)(2) - 2^2 > 0 \quad \text{if } (X_1, X_2) = (1/3, -1/3) \tag{6-14}$$
$$< 0 \quad \text{if } (X_1, X_2) = (0, 0)$$

Evaluating the SOC at the critical points, we find that the solution $(X_1, X_2) = (1/3, -1/3)$ is a local minimum, at which $Y = 23/27$. The solution $(X_1, X_2) = (0, 0)$ does not satisfy the second-order conditions for optimization, and it is neither a maximum nor a minimum, but a saddle point. Both the local minimum, M, and the saddle point, N, are labeled in Figure 6.2, the graph of the objective function.

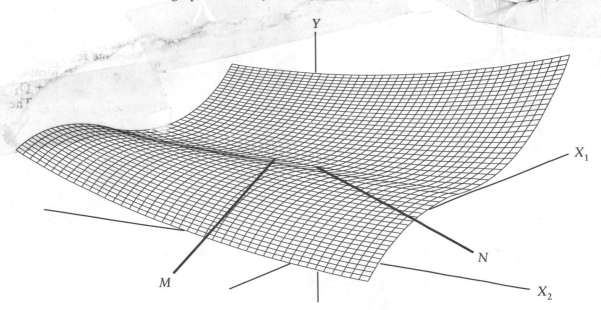

Figure 6.2

$Y = f(X_1, X_2) = 8X_1^3 + 2X_1X_2 - 3X_1^2 + X_2^2 + 1$

Use the first- and second-order conditions for maximization to find local maxima and/or minima for the following functions.

1. $Y = f(X_1, X_2) = 10 + 20X_1 - 2X_1^2 + 16X_2 - X_2^2 - 2X_1X_2$

2. $Y = f(X_1, X_2) = 100 - 5X_1 + 4X_1^2 - 9X_2 + 5X_2^2 + 8X_1X_2$

3. $Y = f(X_1, X_2) = 20X_1 - X_1^2/2 + 2X_2^2 - 5X_2$

6.3

APPLICATIONS TO ECONOMIC THEORY

In Chapter 4 we stressed the importance of optimization models for economic theorizing: all choices imply some goal-oriented behavior. All goal-oriented behavior can be expressed as some optimization model. In this section we illustrate the mathematics of optimization with some economic models. We develop these models briefly to indicate the usefulness of the approach and to convince you of the ease with which many economic problems can be solved.

6.3.1   Profit Maximization by a Price-Discriminating Monopolist

price discrimination: the practice of selling the same product at different prices, unjustified by different costs.

Suppose a price-searching firm can sell its product in two separable markets (1 and 2). By separable we mean that there is no resale between the two markets and that the markets have different average revenue functions. Under these conditions, the possibility exists for the firm to practice *price discrimination*, which is to sell the same product at different prices in the two markets, unjustified by different costs. We denote the different average revenue functions as $P_1(Q_1)$ and $P_2(Q_2)$. The product sold in the two markets is identical and is produced according to the cost function $C(Q_T)$, where $Q_T \equiv Q_1 +$ What values of Q_1 and Q_2 does this firm choose to maximize profits, π? objective function for the firm is

$$\pi = P_1(Q_1)Q_1 + P_2(Q_2)Q_2 - C(Q_T) \tag{6-15}$$

Note that

$$\partial C/\partial Q_1 = C'(Q_T)\,\partial Q_T/\partial Q_1 = C'(Q_T) = \partial C/\partial Q_2 = C'(Q_T)\,\partial Q_T/\partial Q_2$$

because $\partial Q_T/\partial Q_2 = 1 = \partial Q_T/\partial Q_1$. This simply means that the marginal cost of production is the same whether the output is sold in market 1 or market 2. The first-order conditions for this maximization problem are

$$\pi_1 = P_1 + Q_1 \frac{dP_1}{dQ_1} - C' = \mathrm{MR}_1 - C' = 0 \tag{6-16}$$

$$\pi_2 = P_2 + Q_2 \frac{dP_2}{dQ_2} - C' = \mathrm{MR}_2 - C' = 0 \tag{6-17}$$

You should recognize $P_1 + Q_1(dP_1/dQ_1)$ as the marginal revenue in market 1 (MR_1) and $P_2 + Q_2(dP_2/dQ_2)$ as the marginal revenue in market 2 (MR_2). The derivative of the cost function (C') is, of course, marginal cost (MC).

The first-order conditions tell us that, in order to maximize profits, it is necessary that the firm choose Q_1 and Q_2 such that $MR_1 = MC = MR_2$. In order to make some sense out of this finding, imagine the situation if MR_1 exceeded MR_2. If the firm were to sell one unit more in market 1 and one unit less in market 2, more revenue would be gained than lost, and total revenue would increase for the same level of production. Profits could not be maximized if the marginal revenue in one market were greater than that in the other, so a necessary condition for profit maximization is that marginal revenues be equal in the two markets. We also see from these FOC what we already know from the general profit-maximization model in Chapter 4, that marginal revenue must equal marginal cost.

The second-order conditions for this problem are:

$$\pi_{11} = 2\frac{dP_1}{dQ_1} + Q_1\frac{d^2P_1}{dQ_1^2} - C'' = MR_1' - C'' < 0 \qquad (6\text{-}18)$$

$$\pi_{22} = 2\frac{dP_2}{dQ_2} + Q_2\frac{d^2P_2}{dQ_2^2} - C'' = MR_2' - C'' < 0 \qquad (6\text{-}19)$$

$$\pi_{11}\pi_{22} - \pi_{12}^2 = (MR_1' - C'')(MR_2' - C'') - C''^2 > 0 \qquad (6\text{-}20)$$

The second-order conditions are easy to interpret when you recall from Chapter 4, Section 4.4.2, that $2(dP_1/dQ_1) + Q_1(d^2P_1/dQ_1^2)$ equals MR_1', or the slope of the marginal revenue curve in market 1, and that $2(dP_2/dQ_2) + Q_2(d^2P_2/dQ_2^2)$ equals MR_2', or the slope of the marginal revenue curve in market 2. Then the first two of these conditions can be interpreted as the requirement that the slope of MC must be greater than the slope of both MR curves, or that MC must cut through the two MR curves from below. This will be the case as long as MR is downward sloping and MC is horizontal or upward sloping. The third condition is also satisfied under these circumstances. The equilibrium implied by the first- and second-order conditions of this model is pictured in Figure 6.3.

In Figure 6.3c the curve labeled MC represents the marginal cost of production and the curve labeled MR_T represents the horizontal summation of MR_1 and MR_2 in Figures 6.3a and b, respectively. As you can see, the marginal cost of production, determined in panel (c), is set equal to marginal revenue in each separate market, as required by the first-order conditions. The price in each market is determined by the separate market demands, or AR_1 and AR_2. You can also see that the slopes of the marginal revenue curves are less than the slope of marginal cost, as required by the second-order conditions.

We showed in Chapter 3, Section 3.7.3, the following relationship between marginal revenue and price elasticity of demand.

$$MR = P\left(1 + \frac{1}{\dfrac{dQ}{dP}\dfrac{P}{Q}}\right) = P\left(1 + \frac{1}{\varepsilon_{QP}}\right) \qquad (3\text{-}60)$$

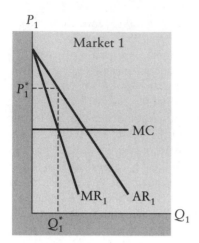
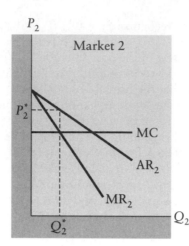
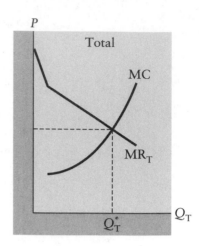

Figure 6.3

Simple Price Discrimination

Using this relationship and the first-order conditions that $MR_1 = MR_2 = MC$ gives us

$$MR_1 = P_1\left(1 + \frac{1}{\varepsilon_1}\right) = P_2\left(1 + \frac{1}{\varepsilon_2}\right) = MR_2 \qquad (6\text{-}21)$$

Divide both sides of equation (6-21) by P_2 and $(1 + 1/\varepsilon_1)$ to obtain

$$\frac{P_1}{P_2} = \frac{1 + 1/\varepsilon_2}{1 + 1/\varepsilon_1} \qquad (6\text{-}22)$$

where ε_1 and ε_2 are the price elasticities of demand in markets 1 and 2. Remembering that price elasticities of demand are negative, it is easy to see that a higher price will be charged in the market with the less elastic demand.

NUMERICAL EXAMPLE

Suppose that average revenue in market 1 equals $P_1 = 20 - 2Q_1$ and average revenue in market 2 equals $P_2 = 15 - 1.5Q_2$. Total cost equals $TC = 5(Q_1 + Q_2)$. To find total revenue for the firm, we sum total revenue in each market. In market 1, total revenue equals $P_1 Q_1 = 20Q_1 - 2Q_1^2$, and in market 2, total revenue equals $P_2 Q_2 = 15Q_2 - 1.5Q_2^2$. Profit, which is the objective function for the firm, equals the sum of the total revenues minus total cost, or

$$\pi = P_1 Q_1 + P_2 Q_2 - TC = 20Q_1 - 2Q_1^2 + 15Q_2 - 1.5Q_2^2 - 5(Q_1 + Q_2)$$
$$(6\text{-}23)$$

Profit is a function of the two choice variables, Q_1 and Q_2. The first-order conditions require us to set the partial derivatives of the objective function equal to zero. They are

$$\pi_1 = 20 - 4Q_1 - 5 = 0 \tag{6-24}$$

$$\pi_2 = 15 - 3Q_2 - 5 = 0 \tag{6-25}$$

Recognize that marginal cost in this numerical example equals 5, so the first-order conditions set marginal revenue in each market equal to marginal cost. The FOC can be solved for optimizing values of Q_1 and Q_2, which we denote with superscript asterisks.

$$Q_1^* = 15/4 \quad \text{and} \quad Q_2^* = 10/3 \tag{6-26}$$

Price in each market can be found by substituting Q_1^* and Q_2^* into their respective average revenue functions. We find

$$P_1^* = 12.5 \quad \text{and} \quad P_2^* = 10 \tag{6-27}$$

We need to verify that these are profit-maximizing choices by checking the second-order conditions. They are

$$\pi_{11} = -4 < 0 \tag{6-28}$$

$$\pi_{22} = -3 < 0 \tag{6-29}$$

$$\pi_{11}\pi_{22} - \pi_{12}^2 = (-4)(-3) - 0 = 12 > 0 \tag{6-30}$$

The SOC are satisfied, and we conclude that $Q_1^* = 15/4$, $Q_2^* = 10/3$, $P_1^* = 12.5$, and $P_2^* = 10$ are profit-maximizing values. When looking at the FOC, recognize that π_{11} is the slope of MR_1, which equals -4, minus the slope of MC, which equals 0. Similarly, π_{22} is the slope of MR_2, which equals -3, minus zero.

These results indicate that the optimum price in market 1 is higher than the optimum price in market 2. We suggested in equation (6-22) that the lower price is charged where the price elasticity of demand is more elastic. Let's compute the price elasticities to see if this relationship holds. In market 1, price elasticity of demand equals

$$\varepsilon_1 = \frac{dQ_1}{dP_1}\frac{P_1}{Q_1} = -\frac{1}{2}\frac{(12.5)(4)}{15} = -\frac{5}{3} \tag{6-31}$$

In market 2, price elasticity of demand equals

$$\varepsilon_2 = \frac{dQ_2}{dP_2}\frac{P_2}{Q_2} = -\frac{2}{3}\frac{(10)(3)}{10} = -2 \tag{6-32}$$

As you can see, demand in market 2 is more elastic than demand in market 1, and the optimum price in market 2 is lower. Finally, let's verify that the ratio of prices is as predicted by equation (6-22). We substitute our optimum values of prices and elasticities into (6-22) to obtain the expected result.

$$\frac{12.5}{10} = 1.25 = \frac{1 - 1/2}{1 - \frac{1}{5/3}} = \frac{1/2}{2/5} = \frac{5}{4} = 1.25 \tag{6-33}$$

Suppose a firm is a monopolist domestically, where it faces an average revenue function $AR_D = P_D = 50 - 4Q_D$, and a price-taker in the world market, where it faces a world price of $P_W = 20$. It produces output at a cost of $C = 6 - Q_T + 2Q_T^2$. The total quantity is the sum of what the firm sells domestically and in the world market, or $Q_T \equiv Q_D + Q_W$.

1. Find the firm's objective function, if its goal is to maximize profit.

2. What are the first- and second-order conditions for maximization? What total quantity maximizes profit? What quantity does the firm sell domestically, and what quantity does it sell in the world market?

3. What is the domestic price of the product? What is the elasticity of domestic demand? What is the elasticity of world demand?

6.3.2   Profit Maximization by a Firm with Two Plants

In the model of a price-discriminating monopolist the firm faced different average revenue functions but production costs were the same. In this section we examine the output decision of a firm with a single average revenue function but two different cost functions. Suppose a firm produces the same product in two different plants, each with its own cost function, $C_1(Q_1)$ and $C_2(Q_2)$. The product is sold in one market, earning the firm a revenue equal to $R(Q_T)$, where $Q_T = Q_1 + Q_2$. The firm maximizes profit, which in this case is

$$\pi = R(Q_T) - C_1(Q_1) - C_2(Q_2) \tag{6-34}$$

The first-order conditions for this maximization problem are

$$\pi_1 = R'(Q_T) - C_1'(Q_1) = 0 \tag{6-35}$$
$$\pi_2 = R'(Q_T) - C_2'(Q_2) = 0 \tag{6-36}$$

Note that the derivative of the revenue function with respect to Q_1 is $\partial R/\partial Q_1 = R'(Q_T)(\partial Q_T/\partial Q_1) = R'(Q_T)$. This equals the derivative of the revenue function with respect to Q_2, $\partial R/\partial Q_2 = R' \partial(Q_T)(\partial Q_T/\partial Q_2) = R'(Q_T)$, because revenue is a composite function of Q_1 and Q_2, and $\partial Q_T/\partial Q_1 = \partial Q_T/\partial Q_2 = 1$. The first-order conditions tell us that there is a critical point in the profit function at the rates of output at which marginal cost in each plant is equal to marginal revenue in the output market.

The intuition behind these conditions is easy to comprehend if you imagine that they are not satisfied. If, for example, the marginal cost of production in plant 1 is higher than marginal cost in plant 2, then by producing fewer units in plant 1 and more in plant 2 the same output could be produced at a lower cost. Clearly, profits cannot be maximized unless the output is produced at the lowest possible cost. Therefore, marginal costs must be the same in both plants. As we saw in Chapter 4, Section 4.3.1, no matter how we specify revenues and costs, profits are maximized where marginal revenue equals marginal cost. These first-order conditions are consistent with that general principle.

The second-order conditions for this problem are

$$\pi_{11} = R''(Q_T) - C_1''(Q_1) < 0 \tag{6-37}$$

$$\pi_{22} = R''(Q_T) - C_2''(Q_2) < 0 \tag{6-38}$$

$$\pi_{11}\pi_{22} - \pi_{12}^2 = (R'' - C_1'')(R'' - C_2'') - R''^2 > 0 \tag{6-39}$$

The second-order conditions are satisfied if the slope of the marginal revenue curve is less than the slopes of both plants' marginal cost curves. These equilibrium conditions are pictured in Figure 6.4.

In the case that we have pictured in Figure 6.4, the firm is a price-searcher in its output market. The mathematics of the objective function and the first- and second-order conditions are general enough to accommodate either price-searching or price-taking behavior in the output market. Simply specifying the revenue function as $R = PQ_T$ and treating P as a constant would adapt this

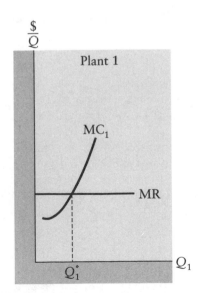
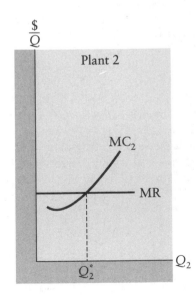
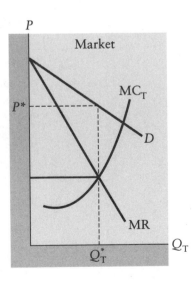

Figure 6.4

Producer with Two Plants

model to price-taking behavior. In the graphs, MR would equal price and would be a horizontal line.

NUMERICAL EXAMPLE

Suppose that a firm which produces an identical product in two plants is a price-searcher in its output market, facing an average revenue function equal to $AR = 40 - Q_T$, where the total quantity produced in both plants is $Q_T = Q_1 + Q_2$. The output from plant 1, Q_1, is produced at a total cost of $C_1 = Q_1 + Q_1^2$. The output from plant 2, Q_2, is produced at a total cost of $C_2 = 4Q_2 + 0.5Q_2^2$. What levels of output in the two plants maximize profit, π?

Profit equals total revenue minus total cost. We find total revenue by multiplying average revenue by total quantity, or $R = 40Q_T - Q_T^2$. We substitute in for Q_T, obtaining $R = 40(Q_1 + Q_2) - (Q_1 + Q_2)^2$. Total cost is the sum of costs from both plants. Therefore, profit, our objective function, can be written

$$\pi = 40(Q_1 + Q_2) - (Q_1 + Q_2)^2 - (Q_1 + Q_1^2) - (4Q_2 + 0.5Q_2^2) \quad (6\text{-}40)$$

We set the first-order partial derivatives equal to zero to establish the FOC.

$$\pi_1 = 40 - 2(Q_1 + Q_2) - (1 + 2Q_1) = 0 \qquad (6\text{-}41)$$

$$\pi_2 = 40 - 2(Q_1 + Q_2) - (4 + Q_2) = 0 \qquad (6\text{-}42)$$

We have two equations, (6-41) and (6-42), and two unknowns. We can solve for the values of Q_1 and Q_2 that satisfy the FOC by doubling (6-42) and subtracting it from (6-41), obtaining

$$-40 + 4Q_2 + 7 = 0 \qquad (6\text{-}43)$$

Equation (6-43) can be solved, giving us $Q_2 = 8.25$. This value for Q_2 can be substituted into either (6-41) or (6-42) and the equation can be solved for the other unknown, yielding $Q_1 = 5.625$.

While these values satisfy the necessary conditions, the FOC, for optimization, we must also check the sufficient conditions, or the SOC. To do so, we need to find the second-order partial derivatives of the objective function.

$$\pi_{11} = -4 < 0 \qquad (6\text{-}44)$$

$$\pi_{22} = -3 < 0 \qquad (6\text{-}45)$$

$$\pi_{11}\pi_{22} - \pi_{12}^2 = (-4)(-3) - (-2)^2 = 8 > 0 \qquad (6\text{-}46)$$

As you can see, the SOC are satisfied, so $Q_1^* = 5.625$ and $Q_2^* = 8.25$ represent profit-maximizing values. We indicate that these values satisfy the necessary and sufficient conditions for optimization by using superscript asterisks.

EXERCISES
Section 6.3.2
Profit-Maximization
by a Firm with
Two Plants

One firm with two plants selling in the same market is, for analytical purposes, the same as a two-firm cartel sharing a market between them. Their goal is to maximize combined profits. Suppose average revenue in the market equals $AR(Q_T) = 10 - Q_T/2$. Total quantity sold by the cartel equals $Q_T \equiv Q_1 + Q_2$, where Q_1 and Q_2 are the quantities produced and sold by the two firms in the cartel. Firm 1 faces costs equal to $C_1(Q_1) = 4Q_1$, while firm 2 faces costs equal to $C_2(Q_2) = 10Q_2 - 9Q_2^2/2 + 5Q_2^3/8$.

1. What is the profit function for the cartel? What is the profit function for each firm in the cartel?

2. What are the first- and second-order conditions for profit maximization? What values of Q_1 and Q_2 maximize profits for the cartel?

3. What are the combined and individual levels of profit for the firms?

6.3.3 Profit Maximization by a Firm with Two Inputs

This is one of the more important models in microeconomic theory, and we will see it again in later chapters. In this illustration we look at the objective function and the first- and second-order conditions. Assume that the firm is a price-taker in both its input and output markets. It produces at a rate of output $Q = f(K, L)$, where K is the rate at which capital is employed and L is the rate at which labor is employed. Output price is P, and the input prices are r and w, respectively. The objective function is

$$\pi = Pf(K, L) - rK - wL \qquad (6\text{-}47)$$

The choice variables are K and L and the parameters are P, r, and w. The necessary conditions for maximization require us to set the first-order partial derivatives with respect to the choice variables equal to zero.

$$\pi_K = Pf_K - r = 0 \Leftrightarrow Pf_K = r \qquad (6\text{-}48)$$
$$\pi_L = Pf_L - w = 0 \Leftrightarrow Pf_L = w \qquad (6\text{-}49)$$

These first-order conditions give us some sensible and familiar principles regarding the behavior of the profit-maximizing firm. The partial derivative of output with respect to an input (f_K or f_L) is the marginal product of the input. The FOC imply that output price times the marginal product of each input must be equal to the price of that input. Recall the model of the firm that is a price-taker in the input market from Chapter 4, Section 4.5.1. There, we stated that the marginal revenue product of the price-taker firm is called the value of the marginal product (VMP), and it equals the output price times the marginal product of the input. Therefore, we can write

$$Pf_K = \text{VMP}_K = r \quad \text{and} \quad Pf_L = \text{VMP}_L = w \qquad (6\text{-}50)$$

Profit is maximized when the VMP of each input equals its price. If the VMP of an input exceeds its price, profit could be increased by employing more of the input until its VMP equals its price. Conversely, if the price of an input exceeds its VMP, profit could be increased by employing less of the input until its price equals its VMP. The FOC of the two-input model require that this principle hold for both inputs.

It is possible to manipulate the FOC further in order to gain more insight into the equilibrium of the two input profit-maximizing firm. If you divide equation (6-48) by (6-49) you can obtain

$$\frac{Pf_K}{Pf_L} = \frac{r}{w} \quad \text{or} \quad \frac{f_K}{f_L} = \frac{r}{w} \tag{6-51}$$

This result tells us that the ratio of marginal products equals the ratio of input prices. We saw in Chapter 5, Section 5.10.2, that the ratio of marginal products equals the negative of the slope of an isoquant, while the ratio of factor prices equals the negative of the slope of an isocost line. This implication of the FOC tells us that the equilibrium values of K and L occur where an isoquant is tangent to an isocost line, or where cost is minimized for the profit-maximizing rate of output.

A final implication we can draw from the FOC requires us to solve both equations (6-48) and (6-49) for P. We find that $P = r/f_K = w/f_L$. The price of capital, r, is the rate at which cost increases per unit of K. The marginal product of capital, f_K, is the rate at which output increases per unit of K. Dividing these two rates gives us the rate at which cost increases per unit of output, or marginal cost. Similarly, w/f_L also equals marginal cost. This tells us that, when the firm has chosen profit-maximizing quantities of inputs, a small increase in output will contribute the same incremental cost whether it is obtained from labor or capital. Finally, at equilibrium, price equals marginal cost, or $P = \text{MC} = r/f_K = w/f_L$.

We illustrate the implications of the first-order conditions for this important two-input model in the graphs of Figure 6.5. Panel (a) pictures the equilibrium level of capital, K^*, where the rental rate of capital is equal to the value of the marginal product of capital. Similarly, panel (b) illustrates that the equilibrium level of labor, L^*, occurs where the wage rate is equal to the value of the marginal product of labor. Panel (c) shows the profit-maximizing output, where price equals marginal cost, and panel (d) illustrates that K^* and L^* are at a point of tangency between an isocost line C^* and the isoquant representing the optimum quantity, Q^*.

The second-order conditions for maximization are

$$\pi_{KK} = Pf_{KK} < 0 \tag{6-52}$$

$$\pi_{LL} = Pf_{LL} < 0 \tag{6-53}$$

$$\pi_{KK}\pi_{LL} - \pi_{KL}^2 = P^2(f_{KK}f_{LL} - f_{KL}^2) > 0 \tag{6-54}$$

They indicate that the marginal products (and the VMPs) are declining. We obtain this result by noting that price must be greater than zero ($P > 0$) and dividing (6-52) and (6-53) by P. This tells us that f_{KK} and f_{LL} must both be negative. Recall from Chapter 5, Section 5.9, that these second partials represent the slopes of the marginal products, and when they are negative we have diminishing marginal product.[2] In Figure 6.5, we have pictured the VMP curves as declining and the MC curve as upward sloping.

Figure 6.5

**Equilibrium Conditions
of the Two-Input Model**

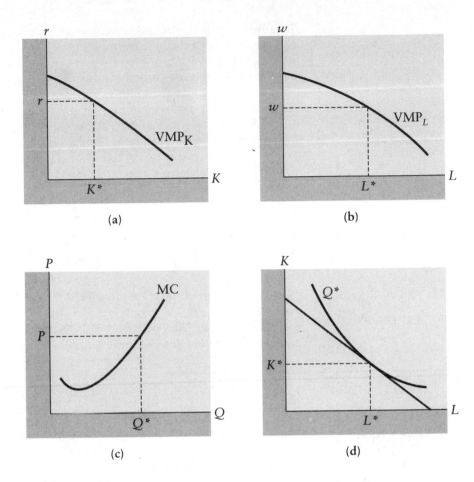

(a)   (b)

(c)   (d)

NUMERICAL EXAMPLE

Suppose a firm uses inputs of labor, L, and capital, K, to produce its output, Q, according to the production function $Q = f(K, L) = 10L^{1/4}K^{1/4}$. Labor is paid an hourly wage rate of $w = 25$ and the rental price of capital is $r = 6.25$. The firm sells its output at a price of $P = 10$ per unit. The firm's optimum levels of employment of the two inputs are determined by maximizing the profit function,

$$\pi(K, L) = Pf(K, L) - wL - rK = 100L^{1/4}K^{1/4} - 25L - 6.25K \quad \text{(6-55)}$$

The first-order conditions for profit maximization are

$$\pi_K = 25L^{1/4}K^{-3/4} - 6.25 = 0 \quad \text{(6-56)}$$
$$\pi_L = 25L^{-3/4}K^{1/4} - 25 = 0 \quad \text{(6-57)}$$

---

[2] We will see in Chapter 11 that if $f_{KK}f_{LL} - f_{KL}^2 > 0$, marginal cost is upward sloping.

To solve the FOC for K and L we first use either equation to find L in terms of K, and then we substitute the resulting expression into the other FOC. Thus we find that $L = K^3/256$ from equation (6-56). Substituting this value of L into (6-57) gives us the solution values $L^* = 2$ and $K^* = 8$.

We have denoted the solution values with asterisks because these values satisfy the necessary conditions for profit maximization. Before we can conclude that these are, in fact, the optimal values for K and L, we must examine the sufficient conditions. To do this, we partially differentiate (6-56) and (6-57) with respect to the two choice variables to find the second-order partials of the objective function. These give us the sufficient conditions for profit maximization.

$$\pi_{KK} = (25)(-0.75)K^{-7/4}L^{1/4} < 0 \tag{6-58}$$

$$\pi_{LL} = (25)(-0.75)K^{1/4}L^{-7/4} < 0 \tag{6-59}$$

$$\pi_{KK}\pi_{LL} - \pi_{KL}^2 = 351.5625(KL)^{-3/2} - 39.0625(KL)^{-3/2} > 0 \tag{6-60}$$

When we evaluate the SOC at the values of K and L that satisfy the FOC, we find that $\pi_{KK} = -0.586$, $\pi_{LL} = -9.375$, and $\pi_{KK}\pi_{LL} - \pi_{KL}^2 = 4.885$. Therefore, we conclude that when $L^* = 2$ and $K^* = 8$ both the necessary and sufficient conditions for profit maximization are met.

EXERCISES
Section 6.3.3
Profit-Maximization
by a Firm with
Two Inputs

Find the objective function, the FOC and SOC, and the optimum values for labor (L) and capital (K) for profit-maximizing firms with the following production functions and prices.

1. $Q = f(K, L) = 100K^{2/5}L^{2/5}$ $P = 0.5; w = 10; r = 5$

2. $Q = f(K, L) = 100 + 20 \ln K + 30 \ln L$ $P = 4; w = 6; r = 10$

6.4

COMPARATIVE STATICS ANALYSIS OF THE FIRM WITH TWO INPUTS

This model has two choice variables (K and L) and three parameters (r, w, and P). When we examined optimization models in Chapter 4, whenever we had parameters in a model we were able to perform comparative statics analysis. This is true in optimization models with two independent variables as well. It is possible to find comparative statics results for each choice variable with respect to all three parameters. We will follow the same procedure we used in Chapter 4 to perform the comparative statics analysis. Remember that, for optimization models, the first- and second-order conditions are the equilibrium conditions. First, assume that the equilibrium conditions are met; that is, assume that the FOC and SOC are true. In this case, the FOC are equations (6-48) and (6-49), and the two choice variables are K and L. Look at equations

(6-48) and (6-49) and remember that f_K and f_L are both functions of K and L. If we assume that the conditions of the implicit function theorem are satisfied, then implicit in the simultaneous solution of these equations are functional relationships between the equilibrium values of the choice variables and the parameters.

$$K^* = K^*(r, w, P) \quad \text{and} \quad L^* = L^*(r, w, P) \tag{6-61}$$

These functions represent the profit-maximizing firm's equilibrium choices of capital and labor. Employment of labor and capital are functions of the price of output and the input prices. They are the firm's input demand functions.

The next step in our comparative statics procedure is to substitute the equilibrium values of the choice variables back into the first-order conditions whence they came, creating the identities

$$\pi_K = Pf_K(K^*(r, w, P), L^*(r, w, P)) - r \equiv 0 \tag{6-62}$$
$$\pi_L = Pf_L(K^*(r, w, P), L^*(r, w, P)) - w \equiv 0 \tag{6-63}$$

These implicit functions can be differentiated with respect to any of the parameters. To illustrate, let's differentiate equations (6-62) and (6-63) with respect to r. Remember that f_K and f_L are functions of K^* and L^* and that K^* and L^* are both functions of P, w, and r. Differentiating them with respect to r gives us

$$Pf_{KK}\frac{\partial K^*}{\partial r} + Pf_{KL}\frac{\partial L^*}{\partial r} - 1 \equiv 0 \tag{6-64}$$

$$Pf_{LK}\frac{\partial K^*}{\partial r} + Pf_{LL}\frac{\partial L^*}{\partial r} \equiv 0 \tag{6-65}$$

These are two equations that can be solved for the two unknowns $\partial K^*/\partial r$ and $\partial L^*/\partial r$. To solve them, add one to both sides of (6-64) and multiply both sides by Pf_{LL}. Multiply both sides of (6-65) by Pf_{KL}. These operations give us

$$P^2 f_{KK} f_{LL}\frac{\partial K^*}{\partial r} + P^2 f_{KL} f_{LL}\frac{\partial L^*}{\partial r} \equiv Pf_{LL} \tag{6-66}$$

$$P^2 f_{LK}^2 \frac{\partial K^*}{\partial r} + P^2 f_{LL} f_{KL}\frac{\partial L^*}{\partial r} \equiv 0 \tag{6-67}$$

Subtracting (6-67) from (6-66) allows us to eliminate the terms with $\partial L^*/\partial r$, giving us an expression that can be solved for $\partial K^*/\partial r$.

$$P^2 (f_{KK} f_{LL} - f_{KL}^2)\frac{\partial K^*}{\partial r} \equiv Pf_{LL} \tag{6-68}$$

$$\frac{\partial K^*}{\partial r} \equiv \frac{Pf_{LL}}{P^2(f_{KK} f_{LL} - f_{KL}^2)} \tag{6-69}$$

The second-order conditions for maximization allow us to determine the sign of $\partial K^*/\partial r$.[3] They tell us that Pf_{LL} is negative and $P^2(f_{KK}f_{LL} - f_{KL}^2)$ is positive; therefore, $\partial K^*/\partial r$ is negative. That is, profit-maximizing firms that are price-takers in both input and output markets will reduce the amount of capital they use when the price of capital increases. That simply means that the demand for capital is negatively related to its price.

Recognize that this comparative statics result is a partial derivative. Remember that assuming the equilibrium conditions to be true enables us to express the choice variables K^* and L^* as functions of P, w, and r. The partial derivative, $\partial K^*/\partial r$, tells us the effect on the equilibrium value of K of a change in r, holding P and w constant. Expressing comparative statics results as partial derivatives is the mathematical way of holding all other variables constant. Our model tells us the other variables that must be held constant.[4]

We can also solve equations (6-64) and (6-65) for $\partial L^*/\partial r$. Either substitute the solution for $\partial K^*/\partial r$ into either (6-64) or (6-65) and simplify; or add one to both sides of (6-64), multiply both sides by Pf_{LK}, and then multiply both sides of (6-65) by Pf_{KK}. Following the second strategy, we subtract the resulting identities to eliminate the terms with $\partial K^*/\partial r$, allowing us to find

$$\frac{\partial L^*}{\partial r} \equiv - \frac{Pf_{KL}}{P^2(f_{KK}f_{LL} - f_{KL}^2)} \tag{6-70}$$

competitive factors of production: factors of production that compete to perform similar tasks. When more of a competitive factor is employed, the marginal product of the other factor is decreased.

cooperative factors of production: factors of production that perform complementary tasks. When more of a cooperative factor is employed, the marginal product of the other factor is increased.

The denominator of this expression is positive, but the numerator cannot be given a sign because we do not know the sign of f_{KL}. Recall from Chapter 5, Section 5.9, that the cross-partial derivative could be either positive or negative. The SOC do not tell us the sign of f_{KL} either. The relationship between the price of capital and the equilibrium employment of labor can be either positive (if they are *competitive factors of production*) or negative (if they are *cooperative factors of production*). Performing comparative statics analysis does not always provide unambiguous results.

We could have differentiated the first-order identities, equations (6-62) and (6-63), with respect to either w or P in order to obtain other comparative statics results. No matter what parameter we choose to investigate, we follow the same procedure to obtain comparative statics results as we followed above and in Chapter 4. First we invoke the implicit function theorem to find implicit relationships between the choice variables and the parameters by assuming that our equilibrium conditions are true. Then we create identities by substituting the implicit relationships between the choice variables and the parameters back into the FOC whence they came. Next we differentiate with

---

[3] When you examine equation (6-69), you notice that there is no solution for $\partial K^*/\partial r$ unless the denominator, $P^2(f_{KK}f_{LL} - f_{KL}^2)$ is not equal to zero. This is the condition that the implicit function theorem requires for K^* and L^* to exist as explicit functions of the parameters P, w, and r. As you can see, the SOC of the optimization model assure us that the implicit function theorem is satisfied. This fact, that the SOC of optimization models satisfy the implicit function theorem for choice variables as functions of parameters, is true in general for all optimization models.

[4] This is an important point for econometric modeling. When attempting to measure an economic relationship, one must know what variables to include in the model. The theory guides the investigator in determining the appropriate variables to include. In this case, an econometrician attempting to measure firm demand for an input is guided to include output price and all input prices in the econometric model.

respect to a parameter, and our SOC may allow us to sign the partial derivative that is our comparative statics result.

NUMERICAL EXAMPLE

Recall the previous numerical example. A profit-maximizing firm faces a production function of $Q = f(K, L) = 10L^{1/4}K^{1/4}$. Labor is paid an hourly wage rate of $w = 25$ and the rental price of capital is $r = 6.25$. The firm sells its output at a price of $P = 10$ per unit. To illustrate our comparative statics analysis, suppose that r increases to $r = 10$. Then our objective function becomes

$$\pi(K, L) = Pf(K, L) - wL - rK = 100L^{1/4}K^{1/4} - 25L - 10K \quad \textbf{(6-71)}$$

The FOC are

$$\pi_K = 25L^{1/4}K^{-3/4} - 10 = 0 \tag{6-72}$$

$$\pi_L = 25L^{-3/4}K^{1/4} - 25 = 0 \tag{6-73}$$

Solving for K and L gives us $K^* = 3.953$ and $L^* = 1.58$. We leave it to you to demonstrate that the SOC are satisfied in this example. As you can see, the optimum value for capital decreased from 8 to less than 4 when the rental rate increased. Notice that, when you are provided with a specific function for profit, you can find the effect of a change in the rental rate of capital on the profit-maximizing level of labor. For this production function, capital and labor are cooperative factors of production, and an increase in the price of one decreases the employment of the other.

A more general way to approach comparative statics in a model that provides a specific functional form is to leave the parameters expressed in symbolic form. Then the FOC can be solved for the explicit input demand functions, which can then be used to find comparative statics results. In this example, we express the profit function as

$$\pi = P(10K^{1/4}L^{1/4}) - rK - wL \tag{6-74}$$

Then the FOC are

$$\pi_K = (10/4)PK^{-3/4}L^{1/4} - r = 0 \tag{6-75}$$

$$\pi_L = (10/4)PK^{1/4}L^{-3/4} - w = 0 \tag{6-76}$$

Equations (6-75) and (6-76) can be solved to obtain explicit functions of equilibrium values of the choice variables in terms of the parameters P, w, and r:

$$K^* = 6.25P^2r^{-3/2}w^{-1/2} \tag{6-77}$$

$$L^* = 6.25P^2r^{-1/2}w^{-3/2} \tag{6-78}$$

We can substitute in $P = 10$, $r = 10$, and $w = 25$ to obtain the same result as we obtained above. Alternatively, equations (6-77) and (6-78) can be differentiated directly with respect to the parameters to obtain comparative statics results. For example, the partial derivatives of (6-77) tell us how the demand for capital is affected by changes in P, r, and w:

$$\frac{\partial K^*}{\partial P} = 12.5 P r^{-3/2} w^{-1/2}; \qquad \frac{\partial K^*}{\partial r} = -9.375 P^2 r^{-5/2} w^{-1/2};$$

$$\frac{\partial K^*}{\partial w} = -3.125 P^2 r^{-3/2} w^{-3/2} \tag{6-79}$$

We leave it to you to differentiate (6-78) to obtain similar comparative statics results for labor.

Solving simultaneous equations is tedious work. For that reason, we defer further comparative statics analysis until after Chapter 8, where we will review enough matrix algebra to make such simultaneous solutions simpler. So far in this chapter, we have discussed optimization of functions with two independent variables. In the next section we show how to extend the optimization technique introduced in this chapter to functions with any number of independent variables.

EXERCISES
Section 6.4
Comparative Statics
Analysis of the Firm
with Two Inputs

Find the objective function, the FOC and SOC, and the optimum values for labor (L) and capital (K) for profit-maximizing firms with the following production functions. Leave output price, P, the price of capital, r, and the price of labor, w, in symbolic form. Then substitute in the values indicated to find optimum values for L and K. Compare your answers with those you obtained in the exercises following Section 6.3.3.

1. $Q = f(K, L) = 100 K^{2/5} L^{2/5}$ $P = 0.5; w = 10; r = 7.5$

2. $Q = f(K, L) = 100 + 20 \ln K + 30 \ln L$ $P = 6; w = 6; r = 10$

6.5

GENERALIZATION OF UNCONSTRAINED OPTIMIZATION TO ANY NUMBER OF INDEPENDENT VARIABLES

In Section 6.2, we used the first-order total differential to generate first-order conditions for optimization of functions with two independent variables. We used the second-order total differential to generate second-order conditions. We can do the same for any number of independent variables. Consider, for example, the function

$$Y = f(X_1, X_2, \ldots, X_n) \tag{6-80}$$

For a particular value of Y to be a maximum or a minimum, it must be neither increasing nor decreasing at that point. That is, it must be stationary, or its total differential must be equal to zero. This means that, at a critical point, it is necessary that

$$dY = f_1 \, dX_1 + f_2 \, dX_2 + \cdots + f_n \, dX_n = 0 \qquad (6\text{-}81)$$

No matter what the changes in X_1 through X_n, as long as they are not all zero, the total differential will equal zero if all of the partial derivatives equal zero, or

$$f_i = 0, \qquad i = 1, 2, \ldots, n \qquad (6\text{-}82)$$

Therefore, we have n first-order (necessary) conditions for optimization: all n first-order partial derivatives must equal zero. To understand this result, recall the meaning of the partial derivative. It is the instantaneous rate of change of the dependent variable with respect to one independent variable holding all other independent variables constant. If any one of the partial derivatives, f_i, is not equal to zero, then a change in X_i will change the value of Y. If an infinitesimal change in X_i can either increase or decrease Y, then Y cannot be at a local maximum or minimum. Therefore, for Y to attain either a local maximum or minimum it is necessary that all first-order partial derivatives equal zero.

The first-order conditions for optimization do not tell us whether a critical point in the dependent variable is a maximum or a minimum, and in fact they cannot ensure that there is either (there may be a saddle point). As you have probably suspected, we need to investigate second-order (sufficient) conditions to ensure that either a maximum or a minimum has been reached. As in the two-variable case, we need to look at the behavior of the second total differential, d^2Y. Remember that each partial derivative f_i is a function of all of the independent variables X_j, $j = 1, 2, 3, \ldots, n$, when you evaluate the second total differential.

$$
\begin{aligned}
d^2Y = d(dY) = {} & (f_{11} \, dX_1 + f_{12} \, dX_2 + f_{13} \, dX_3 + \cdots + f_{1n} \, dX_n) \, dX_1 \\
& + (f_{21} \, dX_1 + f_{22} \, dX_2 + f_{23} \, dX_3 + \cdots + f_{2n} \, dX_n) \, dX_2 \\
& + (f_{31} \, dX_1 + f_{32} \, dX_2 + f_{33} \, dX_3 + \cdots + f_{3n} \, dX_n) \, dX_3 \\
& \quad \vdots \qquad\quad \vdots \qquad\quad \vdots \qquad\quad \vdots \qquad\quad\quad \vdots \qquad\quad \vdots \\
& + (f_{n1} \, dX_1 + f_{n2} \, dX_2 + f_{n3} \, dX_3 + \cdots + f_{nn} \, dX_n) \, dX_n \\
= {} & \sum_{j=1}^{n} \sum_{i=1}^{n} f_{ij} \, dX_i \, dX_j \qquad (6\text{-}83)
\end{aligned}
$$

If this expression is negative, then dY is decreasing as it approaches the point where it equals zero. In other words, the function is strictly concave, and Y goes from increasing to decreasing as it passes the critical point. Therefore, when d^2Y is negative, the critical point is a maximum. The critical point is a minimum when d^2Y is positive. In that situation, the function is strictly convex, and Y goes from decreasing to increasing as it passes the critical point. Expressions like d^2Y are most easily evaluated with the help of matrix algebra.

For that reason, we wait until Chapter 8 to demonstrate how to find the second-order conditions of optimization problems with n independent variables.

6.6

SUMMARY

In this chapter we extend our understanding of optimization theory, first introduced in Chapter 4, to functions with two or more independent variables. We derive the first- and second-order conditions for optimization from the first- and second-order total differentials of the objective function. We illustrate unconstrained optimization with three different profit-maximization models: a price-discriminating monopolist, a two plant firm, and a perfectly competitive firm with two inputs. We show how to perform comparative statics analysis with the last model.

We extend our understanding of optimization to functions with any number of independent variables. The first-order conditions are that each partial derivative of the objective function equal zero. The second-order conditions require that the second total differential be negative for a local maximum and positive for a local minimum. We defer further discussion of the second-order conditions until Chapter 8, where we review matrix algebra, which allows us to evaluate the second-order conditions more easily. Before we get to matrix algebra, we want to introduce one more optimization technique: optimization subject to constraints. We turn to this topic in Chapter 7.

◆ REFERENCES

Chiang, Alpha C., *Fundamental Methods of Mathematical Economics*, 3rd edition (New York: McGraw-Hill Book Company, 1984), Chapter 11.

Silberberg, Eugene, *The Structure of Economics*, 2nd Edition (New York: McGraw-Hill Book Company, 1990), Chapter 4.

◆ ANSWERS TO END-OF-SECTION EXERCISES

Section 6.2: First- and Second-Order Conditions Revisited

1. FOC: $f_1 = 20 - 4X_1 - 2X_2 = 0$, $f_2 = 16 - 2X_1 - 2X_2 = 0$
   SOC: $f_{11} = -4 < 0$, $f_{22} = -2 < 0$, $f_{11}f_{22} - f_{12}^2 = 4 > 0$
   $\therefore (X_1^*, X_2^*) = (2, 6)$ is a maximum.

2. FOC: $f_1 = -5 + 8X_1 + 8X_2 = 0$, $f_2 = -9 + 8X_1 + 10X_2 = 0$
   SOC: $f_{11} = 8 > 0$, $f_{22} = 10 > 0$, $f_{11}f_{22} - f_{12}^2 = 16 > 0$
   $\therefore (X_1^*, X_2^*) = (-11/8, 2)$ is a minimum.

3. FOC: $f_1 = 20 - X_1 = 0$, $f_2 = -5 + 4X_2 = 0$
   SOC: $f_{11} = -1 < 0$, $f_{22} = 4 > 0$, $f_{11}f_{22} - f_{12}^2 = -4 < 0$
   $\therefore (X_1^*, X_2^*) = (20, 1.25)$ may be a saddle point.

Section 6.3.1: Profit Maximization by a Price-Discriminating Monopolist

1. Maximize $\pi = -6 + 51Q_D - 6Q_D^2 + 21Q_W - 2Q_W^2 - 4Q_DQ_W$

2. FOC: $\pi_{Q_D} = 51 - 12Q_D - 4Q_W = 0$, $\pi_{Q_w} = 21 - 4Q_W - 4Q_D$
   SOC: $\pi_{Q_wQ_w} = -4 < 0$, $\pi_{Q_DQ_D} = -12 < 0$,
   $\quad \pi_{Q_wQ_w}\pi_{Q_DQ_D} - \pi_{QWQD}^2 = 32 > 0$
   $\therefore (Q_D^*, (Q_W^*) = (3.75, 1.5)$ is a maximum.

3. $P_D = 35$, $\varepsilon_{DD} = -2.33$, $\varepsilon_{DW} = -\infty$

Section 6.3.2: Profit Maximization by a Firm with Two Plants

1. Cartel's profit $= 6Q_1 - Q_1^2/2 - Q_1Q_2 + 4Q_2^2 - 5Q_2^3/8$
   First firm's profit $= 6Q_1 - Q_1^2/2 - Q_1Q_2/2$
   Second firm's profit $= 4Q_2^2 - 5Q_2^3/8 - Q_1Q_2/2$

2. FOC: $\pi_1 = 6 - Q_1 - Q_2 = 0$
   $\quad \pi_2 = -Q_1 + 8Q_2 - 15Q_2^2/8 = 0$
   SOC: $\pi_{11} = -1 < 0$, $\pi_{22} = 8 - 30Q_2^*/8 < 0$,
   $\quad \pi_{11}\pi_{22} - (\pi_{12})^2 = -9 + 30Q_2^*/8 > 0$
   Critical values: $Q_1 = 5.2, 2$ $Q_2 = 0.8, 4$
   Optimum values: The solution values $Q_1 = 2$ and $Q_2 = 4$ satisfy the SOC for a maximum $[\pi_{22} = -7 < 0$ and $\pi_{11}\pi_{22} - (\pi_{12})^2 = 7 > 0]$ but $Q_1 = 5.2$ and $Q_2 = 0.8$ do not satisfy the SOC $[\pi_{22} = 5 > 0$ and $\pi_{11}\pi_{22} - (\pi_{12})^2 = -4 < 0]$. Thus the optimum values are $Q_1^* = 2$ and $Q_2^* = 4$.

3. First firm's profit $= 6$, second firm's profit $= 20$, cartel profit $= 26$.

Section 6.3.3: Profit Maximization by a Firm with Two Inputs

1. Objective function: $\pi = 50K^{2/5}L^{2/5} - 10L - 5K$
   FOC: $\pi_K = 20K^{-3/5}L^{2/5} - 5 = 0$, $\pi_L = 20K^{2/5}L^{-3/5} - 10 = 0$
   SOC: $\pi_{KK} = -12K^{-8/5}L^{2/5} < 0$, $\pi_{LL} = -12K^{2/5}L^{-8/5} < 0$,
   $\quad \pi_{KK}\pi_{LL} - \pi_{KL}^2 = 80K^{-6/5}L^{-6/5} > 0$
   $\therefore (K^*, L^*) = (256, 128)$ is a maximum.

2. Objective function: $\pi = 400 + 80\ln K + 120\ln L - 10K - 6L$
   FOC: $\pi_K = 80/K - 10 = 0$, $\pi_L = 120/L - 6 = 0$
   SOC: $\pi_{KK} = -80/K^2 < 0$, $\pi_{LL} = -120/L^2 < 0$,
   $\pi_{KK}\pi_{LL} - \pi_{KL}^2 = 9600/K^2L^2 > 0$
   $\therefore (K^*, L^*) = (8, 20)$ is a maximum.

Section 6.4: Comparative Statics Analysis of the Firm with Two Inputs

1. Objective function: $\pi = P100K^{2/5}L^{2/5} - wL - rK$
   FOC: $\pi_K = 40PK^{-3/5}L^{2/5} - r = 0$, $\pi_L = 40PK^{2/5}L^{-3/5} - w = 0$
   SOC: $\pi_{KK} = -24PK^{-8/5}L^{2/5} < 0$, $\pi_{LL} = -24PK^{2/5}L^{-8/5} < 0$,
   $\quad \pi_{KK}\pi_{LL} - \pi_{KL}^2 = 320P^2K^{-6/5}L^{-6/5} > 0$
   $\therefore K^* = (40P)^5/(w^2r^3) = 75.85$, $L^* = (40P)^5/(w^3r^2) = 56.86$ is a maximum.

2. Objective function: $\pi = P(100 + 20\ln K + 30\ln L) - rK - wL$
   FOC: $\pi_K = 20P/K - r = 0$, $\pi_L = 30P/L - w = 0$
   SOC: $\pi_{KK} = -20P/K^2 < 0$, $\pi_{LL} = -30P/L^2 < 0$,
   $\quad \pi_{KK}\pi_{LL} - \pi_{KL}^2 = 600P^2/(K^2L^2) > 0$
   $\therefore K^* = 20P/r = 12$, $L^* = 30P/w = 30$ is a maximum.

◆ SELF-HELP PROBLEMS

Answers to these problems are given at the end of the text.

1. Find the critical point of each of the following functions and in each case determine if the critical point is a maximum or a minimum.
   a. $Y = X_1^3 - aX_1 - X_2^2$, where $a =$ constant
   b. $Y = X_1^{-1} + X_2^{-1} + X_1 X_2$

2. Suppose a profit-maximizing monopolist can sell its only product in two separate markets (1 and 2), where it faces the average revenue functions $P_1 = 6 + 7/Q_1$ and $P_2 = 12 - 8Q_2^2$, respectively. Assume that the product purchased in one market cannot be resold in the other. Suppose total cost of production is $TC = 10 + 3Q^2$, where $Q = Q_1 + Q_2$.
   a. Determine the first- and second-order conditions for profit maximization and find optimum levels of Q_1 and Q_2 and the price set in each market.
   b. Find the price elasticities of this monopolist's demand functions at the optimum levels of Q_1 and Q_2.

3. Suppose a firm produces two products. Let the demand functions for the two products be $Q_1 = 40 - 2P_1 + P_2$ and $Q_2 = 15 + P_1 - P_2$, where Q_1 and P_1 are the quantity and price of one product and Q_2 and P_2 are the quantity and price of the other product. The products are jointly produced at a total cost of $TC = Q_1^2 + Q_1 Q_2 + Q_2^2$. If the firm's objective is to maximize profits, find optimizing levels of Q_1, Q_2, P_1, P_2, and π.

4. Consider a profit-maximizing competitive firm producing two products, Q_1 and Q_2, which are sold at $P_1 = 12$ and $P_2 = 18$. Thus, the firm's total revenue is $R = P_1 Q_1 + P_2 Q_2 = 12Q_1 + 18Q_2$. Assume that the firm's total cost function is $TC = 2Q_1^2 + Q_1 Q_2 + 2Q_2^2$. Find the profit-maximizing levels of outputs of the two products.

5. Consider a competitive firm with the production function $Q = K^{0.5} + L^{0.5}$, where Q is the rate of output, K is the amount of capital, and L is the employment level of labor. Suppose output price is $P = 40$, the rental rate of capital is $r = 10$, the wage rate is $w = 20$, and the firm faces fixed costs of $FC = 60$.
   a. Find the profit-maximizing levels of employment of K and L.
   b. Show that these inputs are paid their VMP.

6. Review Section 6.4 and then differentiate the identities (6-62) and (6-63) with respect to w. Solve the resulting equations first for $\partial L^*/\partial w$ and then for $\partial K^*/\partial w$. Show whether or not the second-order conditions permit you to determine the signs of the partial derivatives. Interpret the economic meaning of your results.

◆ SUPPLEMENTAL PROBLEMS

1. A profit-maximizing monopolist sells its only product in two separate markets. In market 1 the monopolist faces the average revenue function $P_1 = 104 - 5Q_1$ and in market 2 the average revenue function is $P_2 = 27 - 10Q_2 - Q_2^2$. Assume that the product purchased in one market cannot be resold in the other. Suppose total cost of production is $TC = 10 + 4Q$, where $Q = Q_1 + Q_2$.

    a. Identify the first- and second-order conditions for profit maximization and determine optimum levels of Q_1 and Q_2 and the price set in each market.

    b. Draw a three-panel picture showing the determination of total output, Q, its allocation between the two markets, Q_1 and Q_2, and the determination of price in each market, P_1 and P_2.

2. Consider a profit-maximizing firm that is a price-taker in both its input and output markets. It produces its output, Q, according to the production function $Q = Q(K, L)$, where K is the input of capital and L is the input of labor. Output price is P, and prices of K and L are r and w, respectively.

    a. Identify the objective function, choice variables, and parameters of this optimization problem.

    b. Determine the first-order conditions for profit maximization by this firm. Demonstrate that, at equilibrium output, price equals marginal cost, $P = MC$.

    c. Determine the second-order conditions for profit maximization by this firm and interpret the result.

    d. Perform comparative statics analysis of the effect of a change in price of capital, r, on the equilibrium value of capital. Determine the sign of the resulting partial derivative and interpret the result.

3. A profit-maximizing monopolist produces a single product at a total rate of output Q_T, using two different plants. The cost functions associated with plants 1 and 2 are as follows

$$C_1(Q_1) = (4/3)Q_1^3 - 8Q_1^2 + 16Q_1$$
$$C_2(Q_2) = 4Q_2$$

The firm's total revenue is $R = 16Q_T - 2Q_T^2$.

    a. Determine the monopolist's profit-maximizing rate of output and the price level and indicate how much is produced in each plant.

    b. Draw a three-panel picture of your solution, with graphs of the equilibrium quantities of Q_T^*, Q_1^*, and Q_2^*.

4. Identify the objective function, the choice variables, the parameters, the first-order (necessary) conditions, and the second-order (sufficient) conditions for optimization for the following problems.

    a. A firm that is a monopolist in its output market wishes to maximize profits. It produces output according to the production function $Y = f(K, L)$. It purchases its inputs (K and L) in competitive markets at prices r and w.

    b. The firm in part a is a price-taker in its output market but a monopsonistic buyer of labor. That is, w is a function of L.

5. Suppose an automobile manufacturer produces its output in two plants, one in the U.S. and the other in Canada. The costs of producing in the two plants are identical, except that the output produced in the U.S. is subject to a per unit tax, t. Therefore the two cost functions are $C_{US} = Q_{US}^2/2 + Q_{US} + 1 + tQ_{US}$ and $C_{CAN} = Q_{CAN}^2/2 + Q_{CAN} + 1$. The firm is a price-searcher, with an average revenue function equal to $AR = 26 - Q_T$.

    a. Find the first- and second-order conditions for profit maximization.

    b. Solve the first-order conditions for equilibrium values of Q_{US}^* and Q_{CAN}^*. Your solutions will express the equilibrium values as functions of the parameter t.

    c. Find the derivatives dQ^*_{US}/dt and dQ^*_{CAN}/dt. Describe in words and in graphs the effect of the tax on output in the U.S. and Canada.

6. Consider the same situation as in Problem 5, but from the point of view of the taxing authority. Total tax revenue equals $T = tQ^*_{US}$.

    a. Find the tax rate that maximizes tax revenue.

    b. Find the values of total tax revenue, T^*, Q^*_{US}, and Q^*_{CAN}, if the tax rate is the one that maximizes tax revenue.

7. Consider again the same situation as in Problem 5. This time, however, instead of a tax on output, the firm is taxed on its total profit, from operations in the U.S. and in Canada.

    a. Find the first- and second-order conditions for profit maximization if the tax is a proportion of total profit, τ, where $0 < \tau < 1$. Solve the first-order conditions for equilibrium values of Q^*_{US} and Q^*_{CAN} . Find the derivatives $dQ^*_{US}/d\tau$ and $dQ^*_{CAN}/d\tau$.

    b. Find the first- and second-order conditions for profit maximization if the tax is a lump sum, T, deducted from the total profit. Solve the first-order conditions for equilibrium values of Q^*_{US} and Q^*_{CAN}. Find the derivatives dQ^*_{US}/dT and dQ^*_{CAN}/dT.

8. A firm is a price-taker in both its output and input markets, with production function $Q = 10L^{1/4}K^{1/2}$, facing output price equal to $P = 10$, wage rate $w = 25$, and rental rate for capital $r = 50$.

    a. Find profit-maximizing levels of labor, L, and capital, K.

    b. Now suppose that the firm is subject to a tax on its payroll equal to t, where $0 < t < 1$. This means that total cost increases by an amount twL. Find profit-maximizing values of capital and labor as functions of the parameter t.

    c. Find dK^*/dt and dL^*/dt.

9. Suppose a firm produces output Y with three inputs, capital (K), labor (L), and materials (M). It faces the production function $Y = F(K, L, M)$. It buys K, L, and M in competitive input markets at prices r, w, and v, respectively. The firm is a price-taker in its output market, where it faces a price equal to P. The firm's objective is to maximize profits.

    a. Find the objective function and identify the choice variables and the parameters of the optimization problem.

    b. Find the first- and second-order conditions for maximization. Provide an economic interpretation of the FOC.

10. A firm jointly produces two products, Q_1 and Q_2, using the input of labor, L, according to the implicit production function $F(Q_1, Q_2) - L = 0$, where $\partial F/\partial Q_1$ and $\partial F/\partial Q_2$ are positive. Assume the firm is a price-taker in both the output and input markets, where P_1 and P_2 are prices of the two goods, respectively, and w is labor's wage rate.

    a. Determine the FOC for profit maximization by this firm and provide an economic interpretation of the result.

    b. Determine the SOC for profit maximization by this firm and interpret the result.

    c. Perform comparative statics analysis of the effect of a change in P_1 on the equilibrium values of Q_1 and Q_2. Determine the signs of the partial derivatives and interpret the results.

    d. Perform comparative statics analysis of the effect of a change in w on the equilibrium values of Q_1 and Q_2. Determine the signs of the partial derivatives and interpret the results.

11. Suppose that the average revenue functions for two products are represented by $AR_1 = P_1 = f(Q_1, Q_2)$ and $AR_2 = P_2 = g(Q_1, Q_2)$ and that the cost functions of the two products are $C_1 = C_1(Q_1)$ and $C_2 = C_2(Q_2)$, respectively.

    a. If the two goods are unrelated in consumption, then $f_2 = 0$ and $g_1 = 0$. Show that it does not matter whether the two products are produced by separate monopolists or a single monopolist.

    b. Now suppose that f_2 and g_1 are either both positive or both negative. In which situation would consumers prefer the products are produced by separate monopolists? By a single monopolist? [Assume the second-order conditions for profit maximization hold].

Dialogue

steel

Circ Cogn Int erp premium
when

C H A P T E R 7

Constrained Optimization

7.1

INTRODUCTION

In Chapter 6, we discuss optimization of unconstrained objective functions with two or more choice variables. We consider an objective function to be unconstrained when no conditions are placed on the values that the choice variables might take. The problem is simply to find the values of the choice variables that optimize the objective function. As we showed in our examples, an important group of topics that can be addressed using the technique of unconstrained optimization is profit-maximization problems.

Another large class of economic behavior can best be described as optimization subject to constraints, or **constrained optimization**. In these models, economic agents have objectives but are not free to choose any values of the choice variables. In other words, there are conditions or constraints on the permissible values of the choice variables. For example, limited income constrains the consumption choices of consumers seeking to maximize utility. Limited resources constrain the production choices of firms. Limited time constrains the labor-leisure choice of the household. In each case, the economic agent is not free to choose any values of the choice variables. The constraint specifies which combinations of choice variables are feasible and which are not.

The fact that so much economic behavior falls in the category of optimization subject to constraints should not surprise you when you remember the basic definition of economic behavior. Economics is usually defined as the study of human behavior resulting from the problem of scarcity. Scarcity means that there are insufficient resources for all possible uses of those resources. The fact of scarcity means that people must choose how to allocate resources. That is, they must decide what (and how much) to produce because resources are insufficient to produce an abundance of everything. They must decide how to produce because the insufficiency of resources requires that

constrained optimization: behavioral model in which the choice variables of the objective function are constrained by some other functional relationship.

185

production techniques economize on inputs. They must decide what (and how much) to consume, because resources are insufficient to permit them to consume as much as they would like of everything. Scarcity imposes constraints on human behavior. People are not free to choose any combinations of inputs or products in their production and consumption decisions because scarcity constrains the combinations that are available to them. To illustrate the mathematical technique of constrained optimization, let's look at how limited income constrains consumer choices.

7.2

CONSTRAINED UTILITY MAXIMIZATION

What is the effect of a constraint on the optimal choices made? To answer this, consider the example of a utility-maximizing consumer who consumes two goods in amounts X_1 and X_2 and who has the following utility function:

$$U = U(X_1, X_2) \tag{7-1}$$

Without constraints on the consumer's choice, the maximum for this problem would be found where $U_1 = U_2 = 0$; that is, all goods and services would be consumed up to the rate at which marginal utility equals zero. Scarcity, in the form of a budget constraint, limits the choices available to the consumer to those that her income permits her to purchase.

$$M = P_1 X_1 + P_2 X_2 \tag{7-2}$$

M represents the consumer's money income and P_1 and P_2 are the prices of the two goods. The constraint reduces the domain of the objective function. More constraints could be added, which would decrease the domain of the objective function more. Too many constraints would eliminate all but one alternative, trivializing the problem. In general, to obtain nontrivial results the number of constraints should be smaller than the number of choice variables. Let's look at the problem of consumer choice with just the constraint imposed by a limited budget. The problem is to incorporate the information contained in the constraint into the objective function. Next, we discuss two ways to accomplish this: the substitution method and the Lagrange method.

7.2.1 The Substitution Method

The method of incorporating constraints that makes the most intuitive sense is substitution. Note that the constraint implies a relationship between the two choice variables. If we recognize that a functional relationship between choice variables is implicit in the constraint and substitute this function into the objective function, we incorporate the constraint in the objective. Consider again the utility maximization problem: maximize $U = U(X_1, X_2)$ subject to the constraint that $M = P_1X_1 + P_2X_2$. The constraint can be solved for X_2 in terms of X_1 and the parameters M, P_1, and P_2, giving us

$$X_2 = X_2(X_1) = \frac{M}{P_2} - \frac{P_1}{P_2} X_1 \tag{7-3}$$

The derivative of X_2 with respect to X_1 equals

$$\frac{dX_2}{dX_1} = -\frac{P_1}{P_2} \tag{7-4}$$

If we substitute $X_2 = X_2(X_1)$ into the utility function, we incorporate the constraint into the consumer's objective function. The consumer wishes to maximize utility, which she derives by consuming goods 1 and 2, but the choices she can make are limited by her budget constraint. Choosing X_1 determines the amount she can spend on X_2. Therefore, her problem is to maximize

$$U = U(X_1, X_2(X_1)) \tag{7-5}$$

Because X_2 is a function of X_1, there is only one independent choice variable, X_1. We treat the maximization problem as an unconstrained optimization with one choice variable, always remembering to treat X_2 as a function of X_1.[1] Differentiate equation (7-5), the utility function that incorporates the budget constraint, remembering to use the chain rule because X_2 is a function of X_1, in order to obtain the first-order condition.

$$\text{FOC:} \quad \frac{dU}{dX_1} = U_1 + U_2\frac{dX_2}{dX_1} = 0 \tag{7-6}$$

Substituting equation (7-4) gives us

$$\frac{dU}{dX_1} = U_1 - U_2\frac{P_1}{P_2} = 0 \Leftrightarrow \frac{U_1}{U_2} = \frac{P_1}{P_2} \tag{7-7}$$

Remember that U_1/U_2 is the marginal rate of substitution between good 2 and good 1, or the negative of the slope of an indifference curve, and that P_1/P_2 is the negative of the slope of the budget constraint. The graphical interpretation of the FOC is that consumer equilibrium is attained where the budget constraint is tangent to an indifference curve. This equilibrium is pictured graphically at point E in Figure 7.1.

In order to explore the equilibrium of this constrained optimization further, we must examine the second-order condition. We must remember that U_1 and U_2 are both functions of X_1 and X_2 and that X_2 is a function of X_1 when we find the second-order condition. We must again use the chain rule when we differentiate equation (7-6) in order to find the second derivative of

---

[1] You might wish to review Chapter 4, Section 4.2, where we introduced unconstrained optimization of functions with one choice variable.

Figure 7.1

Equilibrium of
Constrained Utility
Maximization

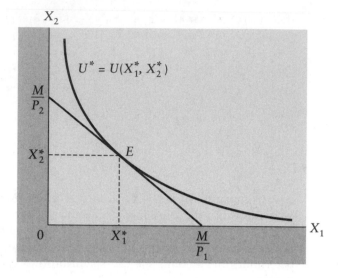

the constrained utility function.

$$\frac{d^2U}{dX_1^2} = U_{11} + U_2 \frac{d^2X_2}{dX_1^2} + 2U_{12} \frac{dX_2}{dX_1} + U_{22}\left(\frac{dX_2}{dX_1}\right)^2 < 0 \qquad \textbf{(7-8)}$$

Substitute in equation (7-4), recognizing that $-P_1/P_2 = -U_1/U_2$. Also note that, because P_1 and P_2 are constants,

$$\frac{d^2X_2}{dX_1^2} = 0 \qquad \textbf{(7-9)}$$

Therefore,

$$\frac{d^2U}{dX_1^2} = U_{11} - 2U_{21}\frac{U_1}{U_2} + U_{22}\left(-\frac{U_1}{U_2}\right)^2 < 0 \qquad \textbf{(7-10)}$$

If we factor out $1/U_2^2$ we obtain

$$\frac{d^2U}{dX_1^2} = \frac{1}{U_2^2}\left(U_2^2 U_{11} - 2U_1 U_2 U_{21} + U_1^2 U_{22}\right) < 0 \qquad \textbf{(7-11)}$$

　　The SOC is satisfied when the expression in the brackets is negative. Compare this expression with equation (5-71) in Chapter 5, Section 5.10.1, where we examined convexity of isoquants. The SOC of the constrained utility maximization model corresponds to the requirement that indifference curves be convex. Another look at Figure 7.1 tells you why indifference curves must be convex in order to maximize utility subject to a linear budget constraint. The point of tangency at (X_1^*, X_2^*) maximizes utility because it is on the highest indifference curve attainable by combinations of X_1 and X_2 that satisfy the budget constraint.

　　If the indifference curve were not convex, there would be no guarantee of a maximization. A linear indifference curve would have no single point of

Figure 7.2

(*a*) Concave Indifference curve
(*b*) Wavy Indifference Curve

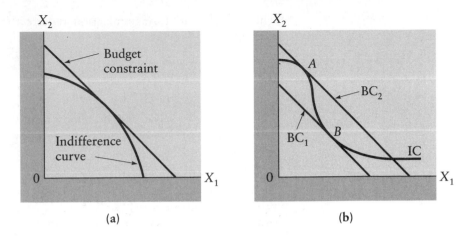

(a)   (b)

tangency. A concave indifference curve would *minimize*, not maximize, utility at a point of tangency, as in Figure 7.2*a*. A wavy indifference curve could have several points of tangency, some of which might be local minima, as at point *A* in Figure 7.2*b*, and others of which might be local maxima, as at point *B* in the same figure. Near point *A* the indifference curve IC is concave, and point *A*, where IC is tangent to budget constraint BC_2, provides the lowest attainable utility of the neighboring points on the budget constraint. Near point *B* the indifference curve is convex, and point *B* provides the highest attainable utility of the neighboring points on budget constraint BC_1.

TWO NUMERICAL EXAMPLES

1. A consumer gains satisfaction from the consumption of two goods according to the utility function $U = U(X_1, X_2) = X_1 X_2$. She earns an income of $M = 100$ and faces prices of $P_1 = 10$ and $P_2 = 5$. Her problem is to maximize utility subject to the budget constraint $100 = 10X_1 + 5X_2$. Solving the budget constraint for X_2 in terms of X_1 provides an explicit expression of the functional relationship between the two goods.

$$X_2 = 20 - 2X_1 \tag{7-12}$$

We substitute this function into the utility function in order to impose the budget constraint on the consumer's choices. The constrained utility function is

$$U = X_1 X_2(X_1) = X_1(20 - 2X_1) = 20X_1 - 2X_1^2 \tag{7-13}$$

We set the first derivative equal to zero to find the FOC:

$$\text{FOC:} \quad \frac{dU}{dX_1} = 20 - 4X_1 = 0 \tag{7-14}$$

The SOC for utility maximization require the second derivative to be negative.

$$\frac{d^2U}{dX_1^2} = -4 < 0 \tag{7-15}$$

The FOC can be solved for the maximizing value of X_1, giving $X_1^* = 5$. This value can be substituted into the expression for X_2, giving $X_2^* = 10$.

2. A firm wishes to minimize the cost of production, $C = 20L + 5K$, subject to the constraint that it produces 4 units of output according to the production function $4 = Q = K^{0.25}L^{0.25}$. We solve the constraint for K in order to find the functional relationship between K and L, obtaining

$$K = K(L) = \frac{256}{L} \tag{7-16}$$

We substitute (7-16) into the cost function to obtain the constrained cost function,

$$C = 20L + 5\left(\frac{256}{L}\right) \tag{7-17}$$

We find the FOC by setting the derivative of (7-17) with respect to L equal to zero, obtaining

$$\text{FOC:} \quad \frac{dC}{dL} = 20 - \left(\frac{12280}{L^2}\right) = 0 \tag{7-18}$$

We solve (7-18) for L, obtaining $L^* = 8$. We substitute this result into equation (7-16) to obtain the critical value for capital, $K^* = 32$. To determine whether these critical values are cost-minimizing values of capital and labor, we examine the SOC. The SOC requires that the second derivative of (7-17) with respect to L is positive. We find

$$\text{SOC:} \quad \frac{d^2C}{dL^2} = \frac{2560}{L^3} = \frac{2560}{(8)^3} = 5 > 0 \tag{7-19}$$

Therefore, we conclude that 8 units of labor and 32 units of capital minimize the cost of producing 4 units of output, given this firm's cost and production functions.

Lagrange method of constrained optimization: a method of constrained optimization in which the constraint is incorporated in the objective function.

The method of substitution becomes too tedious, if not impossible, for solving constrained optimization problems if the constraint is a complicated function or if there are several constraints. For this and other reasons, it is desirable to devise a more generally useful method for handling constrained optimization problems. Fortunately, the *Lagrange method of constrained optimization* is available. We turn to a discussion of the Lagrange method next.

EXERCISES
Section 7.2.1
The Substitution
Method

Use the substitution method to find the first-order conditions and the optimum values of the choice variables for each of the following constrained optimization problems. Also find the second-order conditions and check to see whether they are satisfied.

1. Maximize $U = X_1 + 2X_1X_2$ subject to $M = 100 = 2X_1 + 4X_2$
2. Minimize $Y = X_1 + X_2^2$ subject to $Z = 1 = X_1 + X_2$
3. Minimize $Y = 3X_1^2 + X_2^2 - 2X_1X_2$ subject to $Z = 6 = X_1 + X_2$
4. Maximize $Y = -\ln(X_1 + X_2)$ subject to $Z = 1 = X_1X_2$

7.2.2 The Lagrange Method

The idea behind the Lagrange method of constrained optimization is to incorporate the constraint into the objective function in such a way that the first-order conditions themselves ensure that the constraint is satisfied. In order to accomplish this, we assume that the constraint is satisfied. Now we are able to manipulate the constraint so that the right-hand side is equal to zero. In the utility maximization problem this can be done by subtracting $P_1X_1 + P_2X_2$ from both sides of the budget constraint, obtaining

$$M - P_1X_1 - P_2X_2 = 0 \qquad (7\text{-}20)$$

Lagrangian objective function: a constraint-augmented objective function.

Define a *Lagrangian objective function* as follows

$$\mathscr{L}(X_1, X_2, \mu) = U(X_1, X_2) + \mu(M - P_1X_1 - P_2X_2) \qquad (7\text{-}21)$$

Lagrange multiplier: a contrived variable used in the Lagrange method of constrained optimization. See Lagrangian objective function.

in which μ is a constant known as the *Lagrange multiplier*. Note that the Lagrange objective function, or simply, the Lagrangian, is nothing but a constraint-augmented objective function. We contrive an arbitrary multiplier μ, multiply it by an expression that is equal to zero if the constraint is satisfied, and add the product to our objective function.

A key to the Lagrange method is to treat μ as a choice variable, along with X_1 and X_2. This means that you must differentiate the Lagrangian objective function with respect to three choice variables, X_1, X_2, and μ, in order to find the first-order conditions[2]

$$\mathscr{L}_1 = U_1 - \mu P_1 = 0 \qquad (7\text{-}22)$$

$$\mathscr{L}_2 = U_2 - \mu P_2 = 0 \qquad (7\text{-}23)$$

$$\mathscr{L}_\mu = M - P_1X_1 - P_2X_2 = 0 \qquad (7\text{-}24)$$

---

[2] You might wish to review Chapter 6, Section 6.2, where we introduced optimization of functions with multiple choice variables.

Look at equation (7-24) and note that, by treating the Lagrange multiplier as a choice variable and requiring $\mathcal{L}_\mu = 0$, we guarantee that the constraint is satisfied. Note also that, *because we wrote the constraint so that it is equal to zero, when the first-order conditions are satisfied, the value of $\mathcal{L}$ equals the value of the original objective function,* U. Finally, note that we can add the second term in equations (7-22) and (7-23) to both sides and then divide equation (7-22) by (7-23). When we do so, we obtain the same implication that we obtained by the substitution method, that

$$\frac{U_1}{U_2} = \frac{P_1}{P_2} \tag{7-25}$$

Recalling the discussion of the optimization of functions with any number of independent variables from Chapter 6, Section 6.5, you might expect that we need to look at the second total differential of the Lagrangian objective function to find the SOC. Unfortunately, this procedure will not work when we use the Lagrange method. This is because of the contrived variable, the Lagrange multiplier. The consumer chooses values of X_1 and X_2 that maximize utility, but not values of μ. The role of the Lagrange multiplier is only to impose the constraint on the permissible values of X_1 and X_2. For this reason, for now we refer you to the substitution method for the second-order condition for this constrained optimization problem (Section 7.2.1). We revisit the second-order conditions of both unconstrained and constrained optimization problems in Chapter 8, because second-order conditions in models with three or more choice variables are much more easily expressed in terms of the determinants of matrices. Comparative statics results are also much easier to obtain using matrix algebra, so an exploration of the comparative statics of the constrained utility maximization model is deferred until Chapter 10.

The Lagrange multiplier, which seems up to this point only to have complicated the solution of optimization problems, turns out to have an interesting and useful interpretation. We turn to a discussion of interpreting the Lagrange multiplier next.

7.2.3   Interpretation of the Lagrange Multiplier

One bonus of the Lagrange method is that the Lagrange multiplier has an extremely useful interpretation. Remember that the Lagrange multiplier is simply the coefficient associated with the constraint in the Lagrangian objective function. This fact might enable you to guess intuitively that the Lagrange multiplier measures the effect of relaxing the constraint on the optimum value of the objective function. In the example we presented in the preceding section, this means that μ measures the effect on maximum obtainable utility of increasing the budget M. That is, μ is the partial derivative of U^* with respect to M, where U^* is obtained by substituting X_1^* and X_2^*, the equilibrium values of X_1 and X_2, into the utility function. Let's demonstrate mathematically our intuition about the interpretation of the Lagrange multiplier.

The three FOC [equations (7-22), (7-23), and (7-24)] implicitly define for us a functional relationship between the equilibrium values of the three choice variables $(X_1^*, X_2^*,$ and $\mu^*)$ and the parameters $(P_1, P_2,$ and $M)$.[3] We can write

$$X_1^* = X_1^*(P_1, P_2, M); \qquad X_2^* = X_2^*(P_1, P_2, M); \qquad \mu^* = \mu^*(P_1, P_2, M)$$
$$(7\text{-}26)$$

These represent values of the choice variables that optimize the Lagrangian objective function. When subject to a budget constraint, the utility-maximizing values of goods and services depend on money income and the prices of the goods and services.

indirect utility function: the optimum level of utility obtainable in a model of constrained utility maximization, expressed as a function of the parameters of the model.

We define the ***indirect utility function***, U^*, as the optimum level of utility obtainable given the constraint. Its arguments are the parameters of the original maximization model, which determine maximum obtainable utility. This is because we obtain the indirect utility function by replacing X_1 and X_2 by their equilibrium values, X_1^* and X_2^*. Because X_1^* and X_2^* are functions of the parameters P_1, P_2, and M, the indirect utility function is itself a function of the parameters.

$$U^* \equiv U^*(X_1^*(P_1, P_2, M), X_2^*(P_1, P_2, M)) \equiv U^*(P_1, P_2, M) \quad (7\text{-}27)$$

The indirect utility function can be differentiated with respect to any of the parameters. Because we are trying to show that μ^* is the partial derivative of U^* with respect to M, let's differentiate with respect to M. Remember to use the chain rule, because U^* is a function of X_1^* and X_2^*, but X_1^* and X_2^* are functions of P_1, P_2, and M.

$$\frac{\partial U^*}{\partial M} = U_1 \frac{\partial X_1^*}{\partial M} + U_2 \frac{\partial X_2^*}{\partial M} \tag{7-28}$$

Recall from the FOC, equations (7-22) and (7-23), that $U_1 \equiv \mu^* P_1$ and $U_2 \equiv \mu^* P_2$. Note that here we are using the identities created by substituting the equilibrium values of the choice variables back into the first-order conditions. We substitute for U_1 and U_2, obtaining

$$\frac{\partial U^*}{\partial M} = \mu^* P_1 \frac{\partial X_1^*}{\partial M} + \mu^* P_2 \frac{\partial X_2^*}{\partial M} = \mu^* \left(P_1 \frac{\partial X_1^*}{\partial M} + P_2 \frac{\partial X_2^*}{\partial M} \right) \tag{7-29}$$

In order to evaluate the expression inside the parentheses, look at the third first-order condition, equation (7-24). If we replace X_1 and X_2 by their equilibrium values, X_1^* and X_2^*, we obtain the identity

$$M - P_1 X_1^* - P_2 X_2^* \equiv 0 \tag{7-30}$$

Differentiating this identity with respect to M, we find

$$1 - P_1 \frac{\partial X_1^*}{\partial M} - P_2 \frac{\partial X_2^*}{\partial M} \equiv 0 \quad \text{or} \quad 1 \equiv P_1 \frac{\partial X_1^*}{\partial M} + P_2 \frac{\partial X_2^*}{\partial M} \tag{7-31}$$

---

[3] As we suggested in footnote 3 of Chapter 6, the SOC of optimization models satisfy the implicit function theorem for choice variables as functions of parameters. This is true for constrained optimization models as well.

When we utilize this result in the expression for $\partial U^*/\partial M$, equation (7-29), we obtain the desired result

marginal utility of money income: the rate of change of utility with respect to money income, *ceteris paribus.*

$$\frac{\partial U^*}{\partial M} = \mu^* \tag{7-32}$$

indirect objective function: a function created by substituting the optimum values of the choice variables, which are themselves functions of the parameters, into the original objective of an optimization model.

This tells us that the Lagrange multiplier measures the effect on the maximum attainable level of utility of increasing the budget M, or the **marginal utility of money income.** The exercise we went through to derive this result is an illustration of an important proposition. Whenever we use the Lagrange technique to solve constrained optimization problems, the Lagrange multiplier can be interpreted as the partial derivative of the **indirect objective function** with respect to the constraint.[4] We will use the Lagrange technique for many interesting economic models. In each case, the Lagrange multiplier will have a useful economic interpretation.

NUMERICAL EXAMPLE

We can use the first numerical example that we used for the substitution method to illustrate the Lagrange method of constrained optimization. Recall that the consumer maximizes the utility function $U = U(X_1, X_2) = X_1 X_2$ subject to the budget constraint $M = P_1 X_1 + P_2 X_2$, where $M = 100$, $P_1 = 10$, and $P_2 = 5$. In order to construct the Lagrangian objective function, we first write the constraint so that its right-hand side is equal to zero: $M - (P_1 X_1 + P_2 X_2) = 0$. We multiply this expression by the Lagrange multiplier and add the product to the utility function in order to obtain the Lagrangian

$$\mathcal{L} = X_1 X_2 + \mu[M - (P_1 X_1 + P_2 X_2)] \tag{7-33}$$

The FOC are

$$\mathcal{L}_1 = X_2 - \mu P_1 = 0 \tag{7-34}$$

$$\mathcal{L}_2 = X_1 - \mu P_2 = 0 \tag{7-35}$$

$$\mathcal{L}\mu = M - (P_1 X_1 + P_2 X_2) = 0 \tag{7-36}$$

From (7-34) and (7-35) we find that $X_2 = (P_2/P_1)X_1$, which we substitute into (7-36) to find $X_1^* = M/(2P_1)$. From this result we find $X_2^* = M/(2P_2)$. From the first two FOC we can solve for μ^* by substituting X_1^* or X_2^*, obtaining $\mu^* = M/(2P_1 P_2)$. Substituting in values for P_1, P_2, and M gives us $X_1^* = 5$ and $X_2^* = 10$, which are the same as the results we obtained by the substitution method. We also find that $\mu^* = 1$.

direct objective function: the function to be optimized in an optimization model, in which the choice variables appear as independent variables and the parameters appear as constants.

We can use this numerical example to demonstrate the interpretation of the Lagrange multiplier. We said that the Lagrange multiplier was equal to the

---

[4] We can define the **direct objective function** as the objective function of the optimization problem in which the choice variables appear as independent variables and the parameters appear as constants. The indirect objective function is a function of the optimum values of the choice variables, which are themselves functions of the parameters. Therefore, the parameters enter the indirect objective function *indirectly* through the optimum values of the choice variables.

partial derivative of the indirect objective function with respect to the constraining parameter. The indirect objective function is found by substituting the optimum values of the choice variables into the direct objective function. In this case,

$$U^* = X_1^* X_2^* = \frac{M^2}{4P_1 P_2} \qquad (7\text{-}37)$$

As you can see, the indirect utility function is a function of the parameters M, P_1, and P_2. The partial derivative of U^* with respect to M is, as expected,

$$\frac{\partial U^*}{\partial M} = \frac{M}{2P_1 P_2} = \mu^* = 1 \qquad (7\text{-}38)$$

EXERCISES
Section 7.2.3
Interpretation of the
Lagrange Multiplier

Use the Lagrange method to find the first-order conditions and the optimum values of the choice variables for each of the following constrained optimization problems. In each case, show that, at the optimum, the Lagrange multiplier equals the partial derivative of the indirect objective function with respect to the constraining parameter. Also provide an economic interpretation for the Lagrange multiplier where applicable.

1. Maximize $U = X_1 + 2X_1 X_2$ subject to $M = 100 = 2X_1 + 4X_2$

2. Minimize $Y = X_1 + X_2^2$ subject to $Z = 1 = X_1 + X_2$

3. Minimize $C = 20L + 5K$ subject to $Q = 4 = K^{0.25} L^{0.25}$

4. Minimize $Y = 3X_1^2 + X_2^2 - 2X_1 X_2$ subject to $Z = 6 = X_1 + X_2$

5. Maximize $Y = -\ln(X_1 + X_2)$ subject to $Z = 1 = X_1 X_2$

7.3

AN APPLICATION TO ECONOMICS: LABOR-LEISURE CHOICE

One choice problem that an individual faces is how to allocate time between work and leisure. Supplying labor services in the labor market earns her an income which can be used to buy goods and services, but leisure is also a good, and it can be consumed only by not working. A simple model of this choice problem treats money income, M, and leisure, R, as choice variables in a constrained utility maximization framework. The constraint on the individual's choice is that there are only T hours to allocate between work, L, and leisure. Money income equals the wage rate, w, times the number of hours worked. The model can be described mathematically as a constrained optimization problem. Maximize

$$U(M, R) \qquad (7\text{-}39)$$

subject to the constraint that

$$T = L + R \qquad (7\text{-}40)$$

where

$$M = wL \quad \text{or} \quad L = \frac{M}{w} \qquad (7\text{-}41)$$

We can incorporate the constraint into the objective function using either the substitution method or the Lagrange method.[5] First, we utilize the substitution method so that we can obtain the second-order condition.

7.3.1   Labor-Leisure Choice Using the Substitution Method

In order to use the substitution method, we must find the functional relationship between the two choice variables, M and R, that is implied by the constraint. If we substitute the expression for L, equation (7-41), into the constraint, (7-40), we find that

$$T = \frac{M}{w} + R \qquad (7\text{-}42)$$

Solving (7-42) for M provides us with a functional relationship between M and R, such that

$$M = M(R) = w(T - R) \qquad (7\text{-}43)$$

and

$$\frac{dM}{dR} = -w \qquad (7\text{-}44)$$

We substitute (7-43), the functional relationship between the choice variables implied by the constraint, into the objective function. Our objective now is to maximize

$$U(M(R), R) \qquad (7\text{-}45)$$

We can find the first-order condition by taking the derivative of U with respect to R, remembering to use the chain rule when differentiating by M.

$$\frac{dU}{dR} = U_M \frac{dM}{dR} + U_R = 0 \qquad (7\text{-}46)$$

---

[5] This very simple variant of the labor-leisure choice model assumes that the only source of income is wage earnings. Nonwage income can easily be incorporated into the model by recognizing that money income $M = wL + E$, where E represents some endowment of nonwage income. In this case we find that $L = (1/w)(M - E)$ and our constraint is $T = (1/w)(M - E) + R$.

Figure 7.3

Equilibrium of the Labor-Leisure Choice

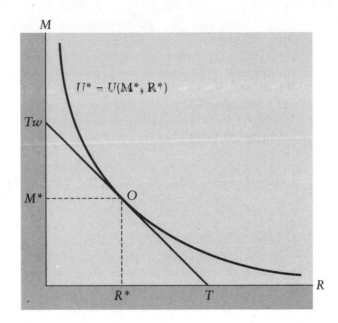

We find from (7-44) that the derivative of M with respect to R equals $-w$. Substituting that finding into (7-46) and solving for w gives us

$$w = \frac{U_R}{U_M} \qquad (7\text{-}47)$$

You should recognize that U_R/U_M is the individual's marginal rate of substitution between money income and leisure, or the slope of an indifference curve. The wage rate w is the slope of the income-leisure trade-off implied by the constraint. The FOC describes the point of tangency between the constraint and the individual's indifference curves that is pictured in Figure 7.3.

We can find the second-order condition of this optimization problem by examining the second derivative of the objective function, again remembering that, because of the constraint, M is a function of R.

$$\frac{d^2U}{dR^2} = U_{MR}\frac{dM}{dR} + U_M\frac{d^2M}{dR^2} + U_{RR} + U_{MM}\frac{dM}{dR}\frac{dM}{dR} + U_{RM}\frac{dM}{dR} < 0 \quad (7\text{-}48)$$

Substitute equation (7-44) into (7-48) and recognize that, because w is constant, we know that $d^2M/dR^2 = 0$. Collecting terms (remember that $U_{MR} = U_{RM}$) gives us

$$\frac{d^2U}{dR^2} = U_{RR} - 2wU_{MR} + w^2 U_{MM} < 0 \qquad (7\text{-}49)$$

The FOC tells us that $w = U_R/U_M$. If we substitute this expression into (7-49) and factor out $1/U_M^2$, we obtain

$$\frac{d^2U}{dR^2} = \left(\frac{1}{U_M}\right)^2 (U_{RR}U_M^2 - 2U_{MR}U_M U_R + U_{MM}U_R^2) < 0 \qquad (7\text{-}50)$$

We hope that you are beginning to recognize the expression in parentheses. You saw similar expressions in Chapter 5 [equation (5-74)] and in equation (7-11) in this chapter. When this expression is negative, the contour curves of the original function—in this case, $U(M, R)$ are convex to the origin. The contour curves of a utility function are indifference curves. Now that we have used the substitution method to explore the first- and second-order conditions of the labor-leisure model, let's use the same model to demonstrate the Lagrange method again.

7.3.2   Labor-Leisure Choice Using the Lagrange Method

The first step in using the Lagrange method to examine a constrained optimization problem is to write the constraint so that the right-hand side is equal to zero. The fact that time is scarce imposes the constraint on the individual's labor-leisure choice. There is insufficient time in which to earn all the money income and consume all the leisure the individual might desire. Mathematically,

$$T = L + R \quad \text{or} \quad T - (L + R) = 0 \tag{7-51}$$

Remember that $L = M/w$ and substitute into (7-51)

$$T - \left(\frac{M}{w} + R\right) = 0 \tag{7-52}$$

Next we write our Lagrangian objective function by adding the product of the constraint and our contrived Lagrange multiplier to the utility function. We use the symbol τ for our Lagrange multiplier to distinguish it from the multiplier we used in the previous example.

$$\mathcal{L} = U(M, R) + \tau\left[T - \left(\frac{M}{w} + R\right)\right] \tag{7-53}$$

We find the first-order conditions for optimization by taking the partial derivatives of the Lagrangian with respect to M, R, and τ and setting them equal to zero

$$\mathcal{L}_M = U_M - \frac{\tau}{w} = 0 \tag{7-54}$$

$$\mathcal{L}_R = U_R - \tau = 0 \tag{7-55}$$

$$\mathcal{L}_\mu = T - \left(\frac{M}{w} + R\right) = 0 \tag{7-56}$$

From (7-55) we find that $\tau = U_R$. Substituting this into (7-54) and solving for w gives us the same result that we obtained from the first-order condition using the substitution method, namely that

$$w = \frac{U_R}{U_M} \tag{7-57}$$

As in Figure 7.3, equilibrium occurs where the constraint is tangent to an indifference curve. Again, we refer you to the substitution method for the second-order condition of this constrained optimization problem.

When we introduced the Lagrange method in Section 7.2.2, we claimed that the Lagrange multiplier measures the effect of relaxing the constraint on the optimum value of the objective function. We interpreted it as the partial derivative of the indirect objective function with respect to the constraint. In this instance, this means that τ can be interpreted as the partial derivative of utility with respect to time, or the marginal utility of time. We can prove this by following the same procedure that we used in the original example to show that μ can be interpreted as the marginal utility of money in the constrained utility maximization model.

First, we recognize that functional relationships between the equilibrium values of the choice variables and the parameters of the model are implicit in the first-order conditions. In this case we denote equilibrium values of M and R with superscript asterisks in the usual way and recognize that they are functions of the parameters T and w.

$$M^* = M^*(T, w) \quad \text{and} \quad R^* = R^*(T, w) \tag{7-58}$$

Then we define the indirect objective function as the individual's direct objective function with equilibrium values of the choice variables substituted in. In this case the indirect utility function is

$$U^* = U^*(M^*(T, w), R^*(T, w)) \tag{7-59}$$

We differentiate the indirect utility function with respect to the constraining parameter, T.

$$\frac{\partial U^*}{\partial T} = U_M \frac{\partial M^*}{\partial T} + U_R \frac{\partial R^*}{\partial T} \tag{7-60}$$

From the first-order conditions [equations (7-54) and (7-55)] we know that $U_M \equiv \tau^*/w$ and $U_R \equiv \tau^*$. Note again that we are using the identities created by substituting the equilibrium values of the choice variables back into the first-order conditions. Substituting these values gives us

$$\frac{\partial U^*}{\partial T} = \tau^* \frac{1}{w} \frac{\partial M^*}{\partial T} + \tau^* \frac{\partial R^*}{\partial T} = \tau^* \left(\frac{1}{w} \frac{\partial M^*}{\partial T} + \frac{\partial R^*}{\partial T} \right) \tag{7-61}$$

In order to find the value of the expression in parentheses, we differentiate the constraint [equation (7-56)] with respect to the constraining parameter, T. We can do this only if we have first replaced M and R by their optimum values, M^* and R^*, which are functions of T and w.

$$1 - \frac{1}{w} \frac{\partial M^*}{\partial T} - \frac{\partial R^*}{\partial T} \equiv 0 \Leftrightarrow 1 \equiv \frac{1}{w} \frac{\partial M^*}{\partial T} + \frac{\partial R^*}{\partial T} \tag{7-62}$$

Substituting (7-62) into (7-61) gives us our desired result, that

$$\frac{\partial U^*}{\partial T} = \tau^* \tag{7-63}$$

At the optimum, the Lagrange multiplier, τ^*, equals the partial derivative of the indirect utility function with respect to T, or the marginal utility of time.

We call this the labor-leisure choice model, yet we find equilibrium values of leisure and money income, not labor. Recall from equations (7-40) and (7-41) that labor equals $L = T - R = M/w$. We can find the equilibrium value for labor, L^*, by substituting R^* into (7-40) or M^* into (7-41). In each case, we obtain an expression for the equilibrium value of labor,

$$L^*(T, w) = T - R^* = \frac{M^*}{w} \tag{7-64}$$

Recognize that, because R^* and M^* are functions of the parameters T and w, L^* is also. In fact, equation (7-64) can be interpreted as the consumer's supply function of labor.

NUMERICAL EXAMPLE

Suppose an individual has the utility function $U = 10MR^2$. There are 24 hours in the day, so her time constraint is $T = 24$. She can spend her time working, earning money income (M) at a wage rate of $w = \$5/\text{hour}$. Any time not spent working is leisure (R). Therefore, she wishes to maximize

$$U = 10MR^2 \tag{7-65}$$

subject to

$$T - \frac{M}{w} - R = 0 \tag{7-66}$$

The Lagrangian objective function is

$$\mathcal{L} = 10MR^2 + \tau\left(T - \frac{M}{w} - R\right) \tag{7-67}$$

The first-order conditions are

$$\mathcal{L}_M = 10R^2 - \frac{\tau}{w} = 0 \tag{7-68}$$

$$\mathcal{L}_T = 20MR - \tau = 0 \tag{7-69}$$

$$\mathcal{L}_\tau = T - \frac{M}{w} - R = 0 \tag{7-70}$$

Solve (7-68) for τ in terms of R and substitute into (7-69). Doing so enables you to find $M = (w/2)R$. Substitute this result into (7-70) to find $R^* = (2/3)T$. Substitute R^* into the expression for M to find $M^* = (w/3)T$. We can find the amount of labor supplied by subtracting R^* from T, or dividing M^* by w, obtaining $L^* = (1/3)T$. We can solve for τ^* by substituting R^* into (7-68), obtaining $\tau^* = (40/9)wT^2$. If we replace the parameters by their numerical values, we find that the optimum leisure time is 16 hours per day and that the individual earns a daily money income of \$40 by working 8 hours at \$5/hour. We leave it to you to demonstrate that this utility function satisfies the SOC [see equation (7-50)].

We can illustrate our interpretation of the Lagrange multiplier using this example. We have shown that τ^* represents the partial derivative of the indirect objective function with respect to the constraining parameter, T. To find the indirect objective function, substitute R^* and M^* into the utility function. We find

$$U^* = 10M^*R^{*2} = 10\left(\frac{wT}{3}\right)\left(\frac{2T}{3}\right)^2 = \frac{40}{27}wT^3 \qquad (7\text{-}71)$$

Taking the derivative of U^* with respect to T gives us

$$\frac{\partial U^*}{\partial T} = \frac{40}{9}wT^2 = \tau^* \qquad (7\text{-}72)$$

Therefore, we see in this example that τ^* is the marginal utility of time.

Solve the following problems of labor-leisure choice using (a) the substitution method and (b) the Lagrange method. Make certain the second-order conditions are satisfied when using the substitution method, and ascertain that the Lagrange multiplier equals the marginal utility of time when using the Lagrange method.

1. Maximize $U(M, R) = MR$, subject to $T = M/w + R$, where $w = \$5.00$/hour and $T = 24$ hours.

2. Maximize $U(M, R) = 10 + (MR)^{0.5}$, subject to $T = (M - E)/w + R$, where $w = \$7.50$/hour, $E = \$50$, and $T = 24$ hours.

7.4

THE ENVELOPE THEOREM

We have twice gone through the exercise of demonstrating that, at the optimum, the Lagrange multiplier can be interpreted as the effect on the indirect objective function of relaxing the constraint. Our demonstrations involved differentiating the indirect objective function with respect to the constraining parameter and substituting relationships from the FOC in order to achieve the desired result. The ***envelope theorem*** provides a much more direct method for finding the effects of changes in parameters on the indirect objective function, and it adds considerable power to our ability to analyze optimization models.

Note that, with the model of constrained utility maximization, if we simply differentiate the Lagrangian objective function,

$$\mathcal{L}^M = U(X_1, X_2) + \mu(M - P_1 X_1 - P_2 X_2) \tag{7-21}$$

with respect to M and evaluate it at its optimum, we obtain μ^*. Similarly, if we simply differentiate the Lagrangian objective function from the model of labor-leisure choice,

$$\mathcal{L}^T = U(M, R) + \tau\left[T - \left(\frac{M}{w} + R\right)\right] \tag{7-53}$$

with respect to T and evaluate it at its optimum, we obtain τ^*. Note that we have denoted the Lagrangian for the constrained utility maximization problem with a superscript M and the Lagrangian for the labor-leisure choice problem with a superscript T.

What we have found are not purely coincidences. Rather, these results are examples of the envelope theorem. The envelope theorem states that *the partial derivative of the indirect objective function with respect to a parameter equals the partial derivative of the direct objective function with respect to the same parameter, evaluated at the optimum*. As we have seen,

$$\frac{\partial U^*(X_1^*, X_2^*)}{\partial M} = \mu^* = \frac{\partial \mathcal{L}^M}{\partial M} \tag{7-73}$$

and

$$\frac{\partial U^*(M^*, R^*)}{\partial T} = \tau^* = \frac{\partial \mathcal{L}^T}{\partial T} \tag{7-74}$$

To understand the envelope theorem, make sure you understand the distinction between the indirect objective function and the direct objective function. The direct objective function has only the unoptimized values of the choice variables as its independent variables. In the case of constrained utility maximization, that means X_1 and X_2. The parameters M, P_1, and P_2 enter the direct objective function as constants. When we take the partial derivative of the direct objective function with respect to a parameter, the other parameters and the choice variables remain constant. The indirect objective function is a function of the *equilibrium values* of the choice variables, which are themselves functions of the parameters. In this case the equilibrium values of the choice variables are X_1^* and X_2^*. The parameters enter the indirect objective function *indirectly*, through X_1^* and X_2^*. When we take the partial derivative of the indirect objective function with respect to a parameter, the choice variables adjust to their new optimum values.

The direct and indirect objective functions are conceptually different. In fact, because the indirect utility function is by definition always the maximum utility, it will, in general, be greater than the value of the Lagrangian. Recall that, in the case of constrained optimization, *because we wrote the constraint so that it is equal to zero, at the optimum the value of $\mathcal{L}$ equals the value of the direct objective function, U.* At other points, the indirect utility function is greater than the Lagrangian; therefore the two functions are tangent at the optimum. For infinitesimally small changes about the optimum the slopes of the two functions are the same. Therefore, the responses of the direct objective function and the indirect objective function to infinitesimal changes in the parameters are the same.

Figure 7.4 illustrates the envelope theorem in the context of the constrained utility maximization problem. We compare the value of the Lagrangian objective function, labeled $\mathcal{L}$, with the indirect utility function, labeled U^*, for different values of money income, M, holding all other parameters constant. Because the values of X_1^* and X_2^* in U^* automatically adjust to the optimum values as M changes, while X_1 and X_2 in $\mathcal{L}$ do not, U^* lies above $\mathcal{L}$. Only if $\mathcal{L}$ is evaluated at the optimum are the values of the two functions equal, as at point E in the graph. Because the two functions are tangent at that point, their slopes, or partial derivatives, are equal.

The envelope theorem is so called because the indirect objective function can be viewed as the envelope of all points where the direct objective function is evaluated at optimum values of the choice variables. If M changes, so do X_1^* and X_2^*; the indirect utility function incorporates these new values but the direct objective function does not. In Figure 7.5, we see three separate Lagrangian objective functions, each tangent to U^* at a separate point (points D, E, and F). Each Lagrangian function is drawn assuming values of X_1 and X_2 that are optimal at one level of money income but not, of course, at any other.

The envelope theorem is valid for both constrained and unconstrained optimization problems. To illustrate, consider the unconstrained profit maxi-

Figure 7.4

Graphical Representation of the Envelope Theorem

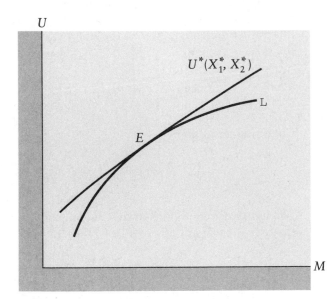

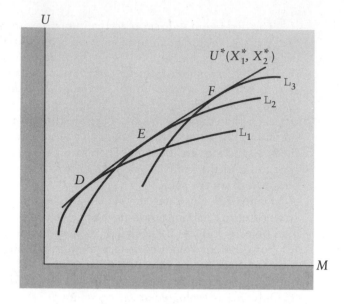

mization problem from Chapter 6, Section 6.3.3. The objective function of the perfectly competitive firm with two inputs is

$$\pi = Pf(K, L) - rK - wL \tag{6-47}$$

The indirect objective function is the profit function with the optimum values of the choice variables, K^* and L^*, substituted in. Remember that K^* and L^* are functions of the parameters P, w, and r.

$$\pi^* = Pf(K^*(P, w, r), L^*(P, w, r)) - rK^*(P, w, r) - wL^*(P, w, r) \tag{7-75}$$

The envelope theorem states that the partial derivative of π^* with respect to any of the parameters is equal to the partial derivative of the direct profit function with respect to that parameter, evaluated at the optimum. To illustrate, differentiate (7-75), the indirect profit function, with respect to r, the price of capital.

$$\frac{\partial \pi^*}{\partial r} = Pf_K \frac{\partial K^*}{\partial r} + Pf_L \frac{\partial L^*}{\partial r} - \left(r \frac{\partial K^*}{\partial r} + K^* \right) - w \frac{\partial L^*}{\partial r} \tag{7-76}$$

Collecting terms gives us

$$\frac{\partial \pi^*}{\partial r} = (Pf_K - r) \frac{\partial K^*}{\partial r} + (Pf_L - w) \frac{\partial L^*}{\partial r} - K^* \tag{7-77}$$

The first-order conditions of this model (see Chapter 6, Section 6.3.3) tell us that $Pf_K - r = 0$ and $Pf_L - w = 0$; therefore

$$\frac{\partial \pi^*}{\partial r} = -K^* \tag{7-79}$$

This is, of course, the result that we obtain by differentiating the direct objective function with respect to r and evaluating it at the optimum.

Combining the envelope theorem with Young's theorem provides considerable power in economic analysis. Consider, for example, the result we obtained by differentiating the indirect profit function, (7-75), with respect to the parameter r,

$$\pi_r^* = -K^* \tag{7-79}$$

Differentiate again, this time with respect to the parameter w:

$$\pi_{rw}^* = -\frac{\partial K^*}{\partial w} \tag{7-80}$$

Now differentiate the indirect objective function with respect to w. The envelope theorem tells us that it equals the derivative of the direct profit function with respect to w, evaluated at the optimum, or

$$\pi_w^* = -L^* \tag{7-81}$$

Differentiating π_w^* with respect to r gives us the cross-partial π_{wr}^*, which, by Young's theorem, is equal to π_{wr}^*

$$\pi_{wr}^* = -\frac{\partial L^*}{\partial r} = -\frac{\partial K^*}{\partial w} = \pi_{wr}^* \tag{7-82}$$

or

$$\frac{\partial L^*}{\partial r} = \frac{\partial K^*}{\partial w} \tag{7-83}$$

This result means that inputs' prices have reciprocal effects on each other's optimum quantities. The effect on the optimum utilization of capital of a change in the price of labor is equal to the effect on the optimum utilization of labor of a change in the price of capital. You can verify this result by comparing the comparative statics result we obtained for $\partial L^*/\partial r$ in Chapter 6, Section 6.4 with the answer you obtained for $\partial K^*/\partial w$ when you answered self-help problem 6 at the end of Chapter 6.

The value of the envelope theorem is that, in many instances, it permits us to find the effects of changes in parameters rather simply. Often, it provides a shortcut to comparative statics results, as we have shown in the profit-maximization example. At other times, because of its simplicity, it leads us to results we might not otherwise have detected. The reasoning behind the envelope theorem is that, at only one point, the indirect objective function and the direct objective function are equal to one another and, in fact, tangent. That point is where the choice variables are at their optimum values. Because they are tangent at that point, their slopes, or partial derivatives, are equal.

7.5

A MODEL OF INTERTEMPORAL CHOICE

Let's look at another interesting constrained optimization model in order to see the usefulness of the envelope theorem. This model examines the timing of consumption decisions by allowing for borrowing or saving between two periods of time. A consumer maximizes the utility, $U(N, F)$, she can gain by consuming quantities of a good in the present, N, and in the future, F. For generality, consider that the good is a composite of all goods and services, represented by their dollar value. The consumer has an endowment of present and future earnings equal to (N_0, F_0). She can consume more than she earns in the present by borrowing from her future earnings at an interest rate of r, or she can save by consuming less than she earns in the present and saving the difference at the same rate of interest. Either way, we can characterize her consumption possibilities as being constrained by her earnings endowments in the following way.

$$N_0 - N = \frac{F - F_0}{1 + r}, \qquad 0 < r < 1 \tag{7-84}$$

The left-hand side of (7-84) represents savings in the present if it is positive and borrowing in the present if it is negative. If the consumer does borrow, the right-hand side of (7-84) tells us that she must consume less in the future than she earns, by an amount that is discounted by $(1 + r)$. We can also write (7-84) as

$$(N_0 - N)(1 + r) = F - F_0 \tag{7-85}$$

Equation (7-85) indicates that any savings in the present are augmented by $(1 + r)$ to increase future consumption over future earnings.

Our constrained optimization problem can be characterized as maximizing $U(N, F)$ subject to the constraint imposed by either (7-84) or (7-85). Here, we subtract the terms on the right-hand side of (7-84) from both sides to obtain an expression that is equal to zero, and we formulate a Lagrangian objective function by multiplying the constraint by the Lagrange multiplier, λ, and adding the product to utility,

$$\mathscr{L} = U(N, F) + \lambda \left[(N_0 - N) + \frac{F_0 - F}{1 + r} \right] \tag{7-86}$$

We differentiate with respect to N, F, and λ in order to find the first-order conditions,

$$\mathscr{L}_N = U_N - \lambda = 0 \tag{7-87}$$

$$\mathscr{L}_F = U_F - \frac{\lambda}{1 + r} = 0 \tag{7-88}$$

$$\mathscr{L}_\lambda = (N_0 - N) + \frac{F_0 - F}{1 + r} = 0 \tag{7-89}$$

For now, we assume that the second-order conditions are satisfied. (Supplemental problem 1 at the end of the chapter asks you to find the second-order conditions to this problem using the substitution method.)

As you might expect, the first-order conditions describe an equilibrium that can be pictured graphically as the point of tangency between an indifference curve and a budget constraint, as in Figure 7.6. The constraint is represented by equation (7-89), which we can solve for N to obtain

$$N = \left(N_0 + \frac{F_0}{1 + r} \right) - \frac{1}{1 + r} F \qquad (7\text{-}90)$$

Equation (7-90) is linear, with a vertical intercept equal to $N_0 + [F_0/(1 + r)]$ and a slope equal to $-1/(1 + r)$, as pictured in Figure 7.6. The consumer's endowment of earnings is the point (F_0, N_0), and the equilibrium is at point A.

If we subtract the terms containing λ from both sides of equations (7-87) and (7-88) and divide the resulting expressions, we describe the equilibrium mathematically as

$$\frac{U_F}{U_N} = \frac{1}{1 + r} \qquad (7\text{-}91)$$

The left-hand side of (7-91), U_N/U_F, is the negative of the slope of the indifference curve, or the consumer's marginal rate of substitution between consumption in the present and consumption in the future. The right-hand side, $1/(1 + r)$, is the negative of the slope of the budget constraint, so (7-91) describes the point of tangency pictured at point A, where the slope of the indifference curve equals the slope of the budget constraint. At the equilibrium, $N_0 - N^* > 0$, so we have pictured a situation in which the consumer chooses to save in the present and consume more than she earns in the future. Had the initial endowment of earnings been different, with higher future earnings and lower present earnings, the same consumer (with the same set of preferences) might have chosen to borrow in the present.

Figure 7.6

Equilibrium in the Intertemporal Choice Model

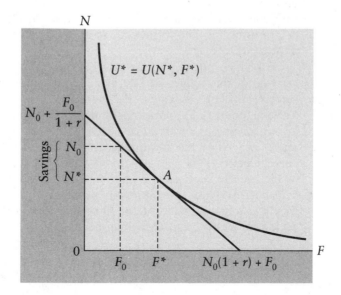

How can the envelope theorem give us insight into intertemporal consumption behavior? The envelope theorem permits us to find the partial derivatives of the indirect objective function with respect to the parameters simply by differentiating the Lagrangian objective function with respect to the parameters and evaluating them at the optimum. In this model, the indirect utility function is $U^* = U(N^*, F^*)$; the parameters are N_0, F_0, and r; and equation (7-86) is the Lagrangian objective function. Differentiating (7-86) by each parameter in turn and invoking the envelope theorem gives us

$$\frac{\partial U^*}{\partial N_0} = \frac{\partial \mathscr{L}}{\partial N_0} = \lambda^* \tag{7-92}$$

$$\frac{\partial U^*}{\partial F_0} = \frac{\partial \mathscr{L}}{\partial F_0} = \frac{\lambda^*}{1 + r} \tag{7-93}$$

$$\frac{\partial U^*}{\partial r} = \frac{\partial \mathscr{L}}{\partial r} = -\lambda \frac{F_0 - F^*}{(1 + r)^2} = \lambda \frac{N_0 - N^*}{1 + r} \tag{7-94}$$

We learn from (7-92) that the Lagrange multiplier can be interpreted as the marginal utility of present earnings. Comparing (7-92) and (7-93) permits us to conclude that a consumer benefits more from an increase in present earnings than from an increase in future earnings, because the marginal utility of future earnings is discounted by the factor $1/(1 + r)$. This finding reflects the fact that a positive rate of interest represents a premium for earlier availability of purchasing power. Forgoing earnings until the future means forgoing consumption opportunities in the present, and those opportunities are valuable.

Finally, equation (7-94) provides some insight into the effects of changes in the rate of interest. Note that we used the constraint, equation (7-89), evaluated at the optimum, to obtain the final expression in (7-94). It tells us that the effect on a consumer's utility of a change in the interest rate depends on whether the consumer is a saver or a borrower. If the consumer is a saver, $N_0 - N^* > 0$, so an increase in the interest rate increases utility. If the consumer is a borrower, $N_0 - N^* < 0$, so an increase in the interest rate decreases utility. The former situation, in which the consumer is a saver, is illustrated in Figure 7.7.

A change in the interest rate, holding N_0 and F_0 constant, implies a rotation of the budget constraint about the endowment point, because the slope, $-1/(1 + r)$, changes. An increase in the interest rate increases the denominator of the slope, making the slope less negative, or flatter, as illustrated in the Figure. The new equilibrium is at point B, the point of tangency between the new budget constraint and the new, higher indifference curve, labeled $U^{*\prime}$.

Recognize the intuitive logic behind the result in equation (7-94). If a consumer is saving present income in order to increase future consumption, then an increase in the rate of interest increases those future consumption opportunities even more, making her better off.[6] Had the consumer been a

---

[6] She is better off whether the increased interest causes her to increase, decrease, or maintain her level of savings. Although we have pictured an increase in savings in Figure 7.7, she could have

borrower, the future consumption she must forgo in order to increase present consumption is discounted by the factor $1 + r$. A higher interest rate means she must give up more future consumption to increase present consumption by some given amount. Therefore, an increase in r makes her worse off. If she neither saves nor borrows, she consumes exactly her earnings in both the present and the future, and an infinitesimal change in the interest rate has no effect on her utility at all.

Figure 7.7

Effect of an Increase in Interest on a Saver

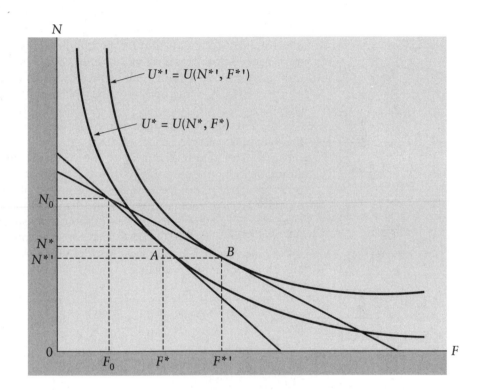

EXERCISES
Section 7.5
A Model of
Intertemporal
Choice

Suppose a consumer has an intertemporal utility function equal to $U = U(N, F) = N^{0.2}F^{0.8}$, in which N is present consumption and F is future consumption. The consumer has an earnings endowment of 10 in both the present and the future. The rate of interest equals 10%.

1. Using the Lagrange method, find the objective function and the first-order conditions for utility maximization.

2. Solve the first-order conditions for equilibrium values of N^* and F^*.

3. Find the marginal utility of present earnings, the marginal utility of future earnings, and the effect on the consumer's utility of an increase in the interest rate.

7.6

SUMMARY

In this chapter we suggest that, in many economic models, constraints on choices are important in explaining optimizing behavior. Using the model of constrained utility maximization, we show two techniques for incorporating constraints into objective functions: the substitution method and the Lagrange method. The substitution method converts the constrained problem with two independent variables into an unconstrained problem with one independent variable, and it permits us to find first- and second-order conditions for optimization by applying familiar optimization techniques. The disadvantage of the substitution method becomes evident when we consider more general problems with more choice variables or constraints, and for this reason we introduce the Lagrange method to analyze constrained optimization problems. Both methods are used to examine the problem of labor-leisure choice.

We find that the Lagrange method leads us to two important discoveries: the economic interpretation of the Lagrange multiplier and the envelope theorem. The Lagrange multiplier measures the effect of relaxing the constraint on the optimum value of the objective function. The envelope theorem provides a useful tool for examining the effects of changes in the parameters on the objective function, which we demonstrate using a model of intertemporal consumer choice. At several points we suggest that, to exploit fully the optimization techniques developed in this chapter, we ought to know some matrix algebra. In Chapter 8 we turn to some useful applications of matrix algebra to economic modeling.

◆ REFERENCES

Allen, R. G. D., *Mathematical Analysis for Economists* (New York: St. Martin's Press, 1938), Chapter 14.

Chiang, Alpha C., *Fundamental Methods of Mathematical Economics*, 3rd edition (New York: McGraw-Hill Book Company, 1984), Chapter 12.

Dixit, Avinash K., *Optimization in Economic Theory*, 2nd edition (Oxford: Oxford University Press, 1990), Chapter 2.

Intriligator, Michael, D., *Mathematical Optimization and Economic Theory* (Englewood Cliffs: Prentice-Hall, 1971), Chapter 3.

Silberberg, Eugene, *The Structure of Economics*, 2nd edition (New York: McGraw-Hill Book Company, 1990), Chapters 6, 7, and 12.

◆ ANSWERS TO END-OF-SECTION EXERCISES

Section 7.2.1: The Substitution Method

1. FOC: $dU/dX_1 = 51 - 2X_1 = 0$
    Optimum values: $X_1^* = 25.5$; $X_2^* = 12.25$
    SOC: $d^2U/dX_1^2 = -2 < 0$, which is sufficient for a maximum

2. FOC: $dY/dX_1 = 2X_1 - 1 = 0$
   Optimum values: $X_1^* = 0.5$; $X_2^* = 0.5$
   SOC: $d^2Y/dX_1^2 = 2 > 0$, which is sufficient for a minimum

3. FOC: $dY/dX_1 = 12X_1 - 24 = 0$
   Optimum values: $X_1^* = 2$; $X_2^* = 4$
   SOC: $d^2Y/dX_1^2 = 12 > 0$, which is sufficient for a minimum

4. FOC: $dY/dX_1 = -2X_1/(X_1^2 + 1) + (1/X_1) = 0$
   Optimum values: $X_1^* = 1$; $X_2^* = 1$
   SOC: $d^2Y/dX_1^2 = [-2(X_1^2 + 1) + 4X_1^2]/(X_1^2 + 1)^2] - (1/X_1^2)$
   $= [-2(1 + 1) + 4(1)]/(1 + 1)^2 - (1/1) = 0 - 1$
   $= -1 < 0$, which is sufficient for a maximum

Section 7.2.3: Interpretation of the Lagrange Multiplier

1. FOC: $\mathcal{L}_1 = 1 + 2X_2 - 2\mu = 0$
   $\mathcal{L}_2 = 2X_1 - 4\mu = 0$
   $\mathcal{L}_\mu = M - 2X_1 - 4X_2 = 0$
   Optimum values: $X_1^* = (M + 2)/4 = 25.5$; $X_2^* = (M - 2)/8 = 12.25$;
   $\mu^* = (M + 2)/8 = 12.75$

To find the indirect objective function, substitute the optimum values of the choice variables into the original expression for U:

$$U^* = X_1^* + 2X_1^* X_2^* = (M + 2)^2/16$$

Now differentiate U^* with respect to M

$$\frac{dU^*}{dM} = (M + 2)/8 = \mu^*$$

In this case μ^* measures the marginal utility of money income.

2. FOC: $\mathcal{L}_1 = 1 - \mu = 0$
   $\mathcal{L}_2 = 2X_2 - \mu = 0$
   $\mathcal{L}_\mu = Z - X_1 - X_2 = 0$
   Optimum values: $X_1^* = Z - 1/2 = 0.5$; $X_2^* = 0.5$; $\mu^* = 1$

To find the indirect objective function, substitute the optimum values of the choice variables into the original expression for Y:

$$Y^* = X_1^* + X_2^{*2} = (Z - 0.5) + 0.5^2$$

Now find the derivative of Y^* with respect to Z:

$$\frac{dY^*}{dZ} = 1 = \mu^*$$

3. FOC: $\mathcal{L}_L = 20 - 0.25K^{0.25}L^{-0.75}\mu = 0$
   $\mathcal{L}_K = 5 - 0.25L^{0.25}K^{-0.75}\mu = 0$
   $\mathcal{L}_\mu = Q - K^{0.25}L^{0.25} = 0$
   Optimum values: $L^* = Q^2/2 = 8$; $K^* = 2Q^2 = 32$; $\mu^* = 40Q = 160$

To find the indirect objective function, substitute the optimum values of the choice variables into C.

$$C^* = 10Q^2 + 10Q^2 = 20Q^2$$

Differentiate C^* with respect to Q.

$$\frac{dC^*}{dQ} = 40Q = \mu^*$$

In this case μ^* measures the marginal cost of output.

4. FOC:

$$\mathcal{L}_1 = 6X_1 - 2X_2 - \mu = 0$$
$$\mathcal{L}_2 = 2X_2 - 2X_1 - \mu = 0$$
$$\mathcal{L}_\mu = Z - X_1 - X_2 = 0$$

Optimum values: $X_1^* = Z/3 = 2$; $X_2^* = 2Z/3 = 4$; $\mu^* = 2Z/3 = 4$

Find the indirect objective function by substituting the optimum values of the choice variables into the original expression for Y.

$$Y^* = (X_1^*)^2 + (X_2^*)^2 - 2X_1^* X_2^* = Z^2/3$$

The derivative of Y^* with respect to Z is

$$\frac{dY^*}{dZ} = \frac{2Z}{3} = \mu^*$$

5. FOC:

$$\mathcal{L}_1 = -1/(X_1 + X_2) - \mu X_2 = 0$$
$$\mathcal{L}_2 = -1/(X_1 + X_2) - \mu X_1 = 0$$
$$\mathcal{L}_\mu = Z - X_1 X_2 = 0$$

Optimum values: $X_1^* = Z^{0.5} = 1$; $X_2^* = Z^{0.5} = 1$; $\mu^* = -1/2Z = -1/2$

Find the indirect objective function by substituting the optimum values of the choice variables into the original objective.

$$Y^* = -\ln(2Z^{0.5})$$

The derivative of Y^* with respect to Z is

$$\frac{dY^*}{dZ} = \frac{-1}{2Z} = \mu^*$$

Section 7.3.2: Labor-Leisure Choice Using the Lagrange Method

1. $\mathcal{L} = MR + \tau(T - M/w - R)$

FOC: $\mathcal{L}_M = R - \tau/w = 0$
$$\mathcal{L}_R = M - \tau = 0$$
$$\mathcal{L}_\tau = T - M/w - R = 0$$

Optimum values: $M^* = wT/2 = 60$; $R^* = T/2 = 12$; $\tau^* = wT/2 = 60$
SOC: $d^2U/dR^2 = -10 < 0$, sufficient for a maximum

Find the indirect objective function by substituting the optimum values of the choice variables into the original objective.

$$U^* = wT^2/4$$

The derivative of U^* with respect to T is

$$\frac{dU^*}{dT} = \frac{wT}{2} = 60 = \tau^*$$

2. $\mathcal{L} = 10 + (MR)^{0.5} + \tau(T - (M - E)/w - R)$

FOC: $\mathcal{L}_K = 0.5(R/M)^{0.5} - \tau/w = 0$
$$\mathcal{L}_R = 0.5(M/R)^{0.5} - \tau = 0$$
$$\mathcal{L}_\tau = T - (M - E)/w - R = 0$$

Optimum values: $M^* = (w/2)[T + (E/w)] = \$115;$
$R^* = (T + E/w)/2 = 15.33$ hours;
$\tau^* = 0.5w^{0.5} = 1.37$

SOC: $d^2U/dR^2 = -0.138 < 0,$ sufficient for a maximum

Find the indirect objective function by substituting the optimum values of the choice variables into the original objective.

$$U^* = 10 + \left(\frac{w^{0.5}}{2}\right)\left(T + \frac{E}{w}\right)$$

The derivative of U^* with respect to T is

$$\frac{dU^*}{dT} = 0.5w^{0.5} = 1.37 = \tau^*$$

Section 7.5: A Model of Intertemporal Choice

1. $\mathcal{L} = N^{0.2}F^{0.8} + \lambda[10 - N + (10 - F)/1.1]$
$\mathcal{L}_N = 0.2N^{-0.8}F^{0.8} - \lambda = 0$
$\mathcal{L}_F = 0.8N^{0.2}F^{-0.2} - \lambda/1.1 = 0$
$\mathcal{L}_\lambda = 10 - N + (10 - F)/1.1 = 0$

2. $N^* = 3.82, F^* = 16.81$

3. Marginal utility of present earnings $= \lambda^* = 0.654$
Marginal utility of future earnings $= \partial U^*/\partial F_0 = 0.595$
Effect on utility of change in interest $= \partial U^*/\partial r = 0.562$

◆ SELF-HELP PROBLEMS

Answers to these problems are given at the end of the text.

Answer questions 1 through 3 using the following objective functions and constraints.

   a. Maximize $U = 5X_1^{0.5}X_2^{0.5}$, subject to $M = 100 = 10X_1 + 5X_2$
   b. Maximize $U = 30X_1^2X_2$, subject to $M = 500 = X_1 + 25X_2$
   c. Minimize $E = 10X_1 + 5X_2$, subject to $U_0 = 50 = X_1X_2$
   d. Maximize $U = M^{0.25}L^{0.25}$, subject to $T = 24 = M/10 + L$
   e. Maximize $U = M^2L^3$, subject to $T = 168 = M/25 + L$

1. Use the substitution method to find the first-order conditions, the second-order conditions, and the optimum values of the choice variables for each of the constrained optimization problems.

2. Use the Lagrange method to find the first-order conditions and the optimum values of the choice variables as well as the Lagrange multiplier for each of the constrained optimization problems.

3. Show that the optimum value of the Lagrange multiplier equals the partial derivative of the indirect objective function for each of the constrained optimization problems. Provide an economic interpretation of your result in each case.

For questions 4 through 6, use the Lagrangian technique for constrained maximization. Identify the objective function, the choice variables, the parameters, and the first-order (necessary) conditions for optimization for the following problems. In each case, give an economic interpretation of the Lagrange multiplier.

4. A consumer with utility function $U(X_1, X_2)$ wishes to maximize utility, but is subject to a budget constraint $M = P_1 X_1 + P_2 X_2$.

5. The consumer in Problem 4 wishes to minimize expenditures but must attain a level of satisfaction equal to U_0.

6. An individual maximizes a utility function $U(M, R)$ in which M equals money income and R equals leisure time. Money income equals $wL + E$, where E represents some endowment of nonwage income, w equals the wage rate, and L equals time spent working. He has T hours available each week in which he can either earn money by working or consume leisure.

◆ SUPPLEMENTAL PROBLEMS

1. A consumer maximizes the utility, $U(N, F)$, she can gain by consuming quantities of a good in the present, N, and in the future, F. She earns an endowment of present and future quantities equal to (N_0, F_0). She can consume more than she earns in the present by borrowing from her future earnings at an interest rate of r on her borrowings, so $N = N_0 + (F_0 - F)/(1 + r)$. Using the substitution method, find the first- and second-order conditions for maximization.

2. Consider the following objective function $f(X_1, X_2) = X_1^2 + X_2^2 - X_1 X_2$, subject to the constraint $1 = X_1 + X_2$.

   a. Using the substitution method, find the first-order condition for optimization and use it to determine the optimum values of the two choice variables.

   b. Using the Lagrange method, find the first-order conditions for optimization and use them to determine the optimum values of the two choice variables.

   c. Do the optimum values of the choice variables you found in parts a and b represent a constrained maximum or minimum? Show your work and defend your answer.

3. Suppose a firm has a cost function $C = rK + wL$ and a production function $Q = f(K, L)$, where K and L represent capital and labor and r and w represent the prices of capital and labor, respectively. The firm is perfectly competitive in both its input markets and in its output market, where it faces output price P.

   a. Set up the Lagrangian for the assumption that the firm maximizes output subject to the constraint that profit $= \pi = 0$.

   b. What are the first-order conditions for maximization?

   c. What is an economic interpretation of the Lagrange multiplier?

4. Continue with the output maximization problem in Problem 3 but assume the firm's production function is $Q = f(K, L) = KL$. What is your answer to parts a and b of problem 3 now? Also, use the substitution method to find and interpret the second-order condition for the firm's maximization problem.

5. A firm wishes to minimize cost, $C = rK + wL$, subject to the constraint that it produces a particular rate of output, Q_0, with production function $f(K, L)$. That is, its input choices are limited by the fact that $Q_0 = f(K, L)$. Use the Lagrangian technique for constrained maximization to
   a. identify the objective function, the choice variables, and the parameters of the constrained optimization problem.
   b. identify the first-order (necessary) conditions for optimization. Give an economic interpretation of the first-order conditions.

6. For the firm in Problem 5, show that the Lagrange multiplier can be interpreted as the effect of increasing output on the minimum cost of production. Show this first by differentiating the indirect objective function by the parameter Q_0 and second by using the envelope theorem.

For questions 7 through 12, suppose that an individual has the utility function

$$U = U(X_1, X_2) = aX_1 + bX_1X_2, \quad a, b > 0$$

7. Determine whether the indifference curves associated with this utility function are negatively sloped, assuming X_1 and X_2 are positive.

8. Determine whether the indifference curves associated with this utility function are convex, assuming X_1 and X_2 are positive.

9. Suppose the individual maximizes the given utility function subject to the budget constraint

$$P_1X_1 + P_2X_2 = M$$

where P_1 is the price of good 1, P_2 is the price of good 2 and M is the individual's money income. Using the Lagrange method, find the first-order conditions for this constrained optimization problem and use them to find expressions for the optimum quantities of goods 1 and 2 as functions of the parameters of the model. What economic concept best describes these expressions? Explain.

10. Demonstrate that, at the optimum, the Lagrange multiplier represents the effect on the *indirect objective function* of relaxing the constraint. What is the economic interpretation of this result in the present case?

11. Demonstrate that, at the optimum, the Lagrange multiplier equals the partial derivative of the *Lagrangian objective function* with respect to the constraining parameter.

12. Refer to questions 10 and 11. What mathematical concept best describes these results? Explain.

13. A firm which is a price-taker in input markets has the production function

$$Q = f(K, L) = 0.25(\ln K) + 0.25(\ln L)$$

where Q is the rate of output, K is input of capital, and L is input of labor. Suppose the rental price of capital is r and the hourly wage rate is w. The firm's objective is to minimize cost, $C = rK + wL$, subject to the constraint that it must produce a rate of output equal to Q_0.
   a. Use the Lagrangian technique for constrained maximization to identify the first-order conditions for optimization and use them to find expressions for the optimum values of the choice variables. What is the economic interpretation of these expressions? Explain.

b. Show by differentiating the indirect objective function with respect to Q_0 that, for this case, the Lagrange multiplier can be interpreted as the effect of increasing output on the minimum cost of production.

c. Using the envelope theorem, show that, for this case, the Lagrange multiplier can be interpreted as the effect of increasing output on the minimum cost of production.

Matrix Algebra

8.1

INTRODUCTION

As we look at more and more complicated models of economic behavior, we find ourselves having frequently to solve multiple equations for multiple unknowns. The most obvious example arises when we attempt to obtain comparative statics results for optimization models with two or more choice variables. Review, for example, the procedure we followed to obtain comparative statics results for the perfectly competitive profit-maximizing firm with two inputs in Chapter 6, Section 6.4. Imagine the difficulty of trying to generalize those results to models with 3, 4, or n inputs. What we need is a technique that simplifies the solution of systems of simultaneous equations.

Matrix algebra provides just such a technique, with the important qualification that *the systems of equations must be linear.* Fortunately, the process of differentiation ensures that our comparative statics results are found in systems of linear equations. There are many other instances as well in which systems of linear equations must be solved. Therefore, in this chapter we review enough matrix algebra to be able to apply it to simplify our economic modeling. We would like to accomplish three tasks with the help of matrix algebra. First, we want to be able to express a system of linear equations in a compact form. Second, we want to be able to determine when a solution to the system exists and what that solution is. Third, we want to be able to use matrix algebra to express the second-order conditions of constrained and unconstrained optimization models.

8.2

LINEAR MODELS AND MATRICES

Consider the following system of m linear equations in n variables X_1, $X_2, \ldots, X_n$.

$$a_{11}X_1 + a_{12}X_2 + \cdots + a_{1n}X_n = C_1 \qquad \text{(8-1)}$$
$$a_{21}X_1 + a_{22}X_2 + \cdots + a_{2n}X_n = C_2$$
$$\vdots \qquad\qquad \vdots \qquad\qquad\qquad \vdots$$
$$a_{m1}X_1 + a_{m2}X_2 + \cdots + a_{mn}X_n = C_m$$

We write our system of equations in a systematic fashion. We have lined up vertically all the terms in which X_1 appears, all the terms in which X_2 appears, and all the terms in which X_n appears. In general, X_j appears only in the jth column, $j = 1, 2, \ldots, n$, on the left side of the equality sign. The parameters a_{ij} represent the coefficients of the j_{th} variable appearing in the ith equation, for all i and j. Thus a_{21} is the coefficient of X_1 in the second equation. The parameter C_i, which is not the coefficient of any variable, represents the constant term in the ith equation. Therefore, while i is the **index** of equations or *rows*, $i = 1, 2, \ldots, m$, the letter j is the index of variables or *columns*, $j = 1, 2, \ldots, n$. Hence the ith equation or row of the preceding system may be written

index: the subscripts that indicate the row and column of an element in a matrix.

$$\sum_{j=1}^{n} a_{ij}X_j = C_i, \qquad i = 1, 2, \ldots, m \qquad \text{(8-2)}$$

matrix: a systematic arrangement of elements in rows and columns.

A **matrix** is simply a systematic arrangement of **elements**. In our case, the elements that are systematically arranged are the coefficients a_{ij}, the variables X_j, and the constants C_i. These elements are expressed in matrix form by

elements: placeholders in a matrix. Each element is associated with a row and a column in a matrix.

$$A = \begin{bmatrix} a_{11} & a_{12} & \cdots & a_{1n} \\ a_{21} & a_{22} & \cdots & a_{2n} \\ \vdots & \vdots & & \vdots \\ a_{m1} & a_{m2} & \cdots & a_{mn} \end{bmatrix}, \quad X = \begin{bmatrix} X_1 \\ X_2 \\ \vdots \\ X_n \end{bmatrix}, \quad C = \begin{bmatrix} C_1 \\ C_2 \\ \vdots \\ C_m \end{bmatrix} \qquad \text{(8-3)}$$

vector: a matrix with only one row or one column.

row vector: a vector with one row.

column vector: a vector with one column.

The matrix A is a rectangular matrix with m rows and n columns, while X and C are both **vectors** (with n and m rows, respectively). A vector is a matrix with only one row or one column. We call X and C **column vectors**, because they each have only one column. A **row vector** is a horizontally arrayed matrix with only one row.

The order in which the elements appear in a matrix is critically important and is denoted by the indices, which are displayed in the subscript(s) of the elements. The elements of a matrix are usually enclosed in square brackets. A matrix can also be written in a more compact form as

$$A = [a_{ij}], \qquad i = 1, 2, \ldots, m \quad \text{and} \quad j = 1, 2, \ldots, n \qquad \text{(8-4)}$$

dimension: the number of rows and columns of a matrix.

square matrix: a matrix with the same number of rows as columns.

order: the dimension of a square matrix.

We refer to the number of rows and columns of a matrix as its **dimension**. Thus matrix A is an "m by n" ($m \times n$) matrix. Note that the first number in the dimension of a matrix is the number of rows and the second number is the number of columns of the matrix. Similarly, when we refer to an element, a_{ij}, of a matrix, the first index, i, refers to the row the element appears in, and the second index, j, refers to the column the element appears in. Elements of vectors, of course, need only one subscript, which refers to the row of an element in a column vector or the column of an element in a row vector. If the number of rows in a matrix equals the number of columns (i.e., $m = n$), that matrix is called a **square matrix** of **order** equal to its dimension.

NUMERICAL EXAMPLE

Consider the following set of three linear equations:

$$5X_1 - 3X_2 + X_3 = 14 \qquad (8\text{-}5)$$

$$2X_2 - 3X_3 = 1 \qquad (8\text{-}6)$$

$$6X_1 + 9X_3 = -1 \qquad (8\text{-}7)$$

We can express the components of this system of equations in matrix and vector form. The coefficients of the linear equation form the 3×3 square matrix

$$A = \begin{bmatrix} 5 & -3 & 1 \\ 0 & 2 & 3 \\ 6 & 0 & 9 \end{bmatrix} \qquad (8\text{-}8)$$

Note that, when a variable does not appear in an equation, its coefficient is considered to be equal to zero. The variables and the right-hand side constants both form 3×1 column vectors,

$$X = \begin{bmatrix} X_1 \\ X_2 \\ X_3 \end{bmatrix}, \qquad C = \begin{bmatrix} 14 \\ 1 \\ -1 \end{bmatrix} \qquad (8\text{-}9)$$

8.3

MATRIX AND VECTOR OPERATIONS

Let's see how matrices enable us to write a system of linear equations in a compact form. The system of linear equations (8-1) may be written as $AX = C$. It is often helpful to identify the dimensions of the matrix and vectors involved in matrix equations by writing them in parentheses and placing them under the corresponding matrix and vectors. In the case of the preceding $(m \times n)$ system, we write

$$
\begin{array}{ccc}
A & X & = & C \\
(m \times n) & (n \times 1) & & (m \times 1)
\end{array}
\tag{8-10}
$$

In order to understand this matrix equation, we need to review how to multiply matrices and what it means for two matrices to be equal.

Two matrices $A = [a_{ij}]$ and $B = [b_{ij}]$ are equal if and only if they have the same dimension and have identical elements in the corresponding locations. According to this understanding of matrix equality, the product AX in equation (8-10) must be an $m \times 1$ column vector and must imply that the m elements in AX are equal to the corresponding m elements in C. How do we multiply two matrices so that this can be the case?

8.3.1   Matrix Multiplication

Suppose we want to multiply two matrices A and B, where

$$
\underset{(3 \times 3)}{A} =
\begin{bmatrix}
a_{11} & a_{12} & a_{13} \\
a_{21} & a_{22} & a_{23} \\
a_{31} & a_{32} & a_{33}
\end{bmatrix}
\quad \text{and} \quad
\underset{(3 \times 2)}{B} =
\begin{bmatrix}
b_{11} & b_{12} \\
b_{21} & b_{22} \\
b_{31} & b_{32}
\end{bmatrix}
\tag{8-11}
$$

premultiply: find the product of two matrices such that the lead matrix is placed before the lag matrix.

lead matrix: the first matrix in the product of two matrices.

lag matrix: the second matrix in the product of two matrices.

Let's **premultiply** matrix B by matrix A to obtain the product matrix AB. Matrix A can be called the **lead matrix** and B the **lag matrix**. Matrix multiplication is an operation in which the ijth element in the product matrix is equal to the sum of the products of the elements of row i in the lead matrix and the elements of column j in the lag matrix. The product AB of the preceding matrices is

$$
C =
\begin{bmatrix}
a_{11}b_{11} + a_{12}b_{21} + a_{13}b_{31} & a_{11}b_{12} + a_{12}b_{22} + a_{13}b_{32} \\
a_{21}b_{11} + a_{22}b_{21} + a_{23}b_{31} & a_{21}b_{12} + a_{22}b_{22} + a_{23}b_{32} \\
a_{31}b_{11} + a_{32}b_{21} + a_{33}b_{31} & a_{31}b_{12} + a_{32}b_{22} + a_{33}b_{32}
\end{bmatrix}
$$

$$
=
\begin{bmatrix}
\sum\limits_{j=1}^{3} a_{1j}b_{j1} & \sum\limits_{j=1}^{3} a_{1j}b_{j2} \\
\sum\limits_{j=1}^{3} a_{2j}b_{j1} & \sum\limits_{j=1}^{3} a_{2j}b_{j2} \\
\sum\limits_{j=1}^{3} a_{3j}b_{j1} & \sum\limits_{j=1}^{3} a_{3j}b_{j2}
\end{bmatrix}
\tag{8-12}
$$

In each element of C we are summing the index j over the number of columns in A, which equals the number of rows in B, which equals 3 in this case. From this description of matrix multiplication, it should be clear that there must be the same number of elements in each row of A as there are in each column of B. That is, the lead matrix, A, must have the same number of columns as the lag matrix, B, has rows. In our example A has 3 columns and B has 3 rows. Our description of matrix multiplication also ensures that the product matrix C has the same number of rows as the lead matrix and the same number of columns as the lag matrix. Because A is a 3×3 matrix and B is a 3×2 matrix, C is a 3×2 matrix. More generally, if $A = [a_{ik}]$ is $(m \times n)$ and $B = [b_{kj}]$ is $(n \times p)$, the elements of the product matrix $AB = C = [c_{ij}]$ can be written as

$$c_{ij} = \sum_{k=1}^{n} a_{ik} b_{kj}, \qquad i = 1, 2, \ldots, m \quad \text{and} \quad j = 1, 2, \ldots, p \quad (8\text{-}13)$$

conformable: of the appropriate dimension for some matrix operation.

To check whether two matrices can be multiplied, we compare the number of columns of the lead matrix with the number of rows of the lag matrix. If they are the same, the two matrices are **conformable** for multiplication. If not, they cannot be multiplied. If the condition is in fact satisfied, the product matrix AB will have the same number of rows as the lead matrix A and the same number of columns as the lag matrix B. Thus if A is $(m \times n)$ and B is $(n \times p)$, the product matrix will be defined and will be of dimension $(m \times p)$. Always look at the dimensions of matrices you wish to multiply.

identity matrix: an $n \times n$ matrix with ones as elements on its principal diagonal and zeros elsewhere.

principal diagonal: the elements in a square matrix that lie in the same-numbered row as column.

A special matrix associated with multiplication of matrices is the **identity matrix**. An identity matrix is a square matrix that has ones as the elements in the positions with the same-numbered row as column and has zeros elsewhere. The elements that are equal to one lie on the diagonal running from the upper left-hand corner to the lower right-hand corner of the square matrix, and they make up the **principal diagonal**. The identity matrix plays a role similar to the number one in scalar algebra; that is, the product of any matrix and the identity matrix of conformable dimensions equals the original matrix, or $I_n X = X$. For example, if we premultiply B in (8-11) by the three-dimensional identity matrix, I_3, we obtain

commutative property: the arithmetic property that the result of the operation is unaffected by the order in which the components appear in the operation.

associative property: the arithmetic property that the result of the operation is unaffected by the groupings of the components in the operation.

$$\begin{bmatrix} 1 & 0 & 0 \\ 0 & 1 & 0 \\ 0 & 0 & 1 \end{bmatrix} \begin{bmatrix} b_{11} & b_{12} \\ b_{21} & b_{22} \\ b_{31} & b_{32} \end{bmatrix} = \begin{bmatrix} b_{11} & b_{12} \\ b_{21} & b_{22} \\ b_{31} & b_{32} \end{bmatrix} \qquad (8\text{-}14)$$

Unlike regular multiplication, matrix multiplication is not, in general, **commutative**. Whereas A and B in (8-11) are conformable as long as A is the lead matrix and B is the lag matrix, they are not conformable if their positions are reversed. In fact, even if two matrices are conformable regardless of the order in which they appear, matrix multiplication is still not commutative. We ask you to demonstrate this in Exercise 4 at the end of Section 8.3.3. Matrix multiplication does, however, have the **associative** property as long as conformability conditions are satisfied, so $A(BC) = (AB)C$.

NUMERICAL EXAMPLE

Let's use the following matrices to demonstrate matrix multiplication and the associative property:

$$A = \begin{bmatrix} 3 & 1 & 2 & 4 \\ 1 & -1 & 0 & 2 \\ 2 & 3 & 1 & -2 \end{bmatrix}, \quad B = \begin{bmatrix} 8 & 3 \\ 2 & -1 \\ 1 & 0 \\ 9 & 2 \end{bmatrix}, \quad C = \begin{bmatrix} 1 & -1 \\ 0 & 3 \end{bmatrix} \quad (8\text{-}15)$$

A is a 3×4 matrix and B is 4×2, so they are conformable for the multiplication AB, and the product is a 3×2 matrix. Carrying out the multiplication, we find

$$AB = \begin{bmatrix} 3 & 1 & 2 & 4 \\ 1 & -1 & 0 & 2 \\ 2 & 3 & 1 & -2 \end{bmatrix} \begin{bmatrix} 8 & 3 \\ 2 & -1 \\ 1 & 0 \\ 9 & 2 \end{bmatrix}$$

$$= \begin{bmatrix} (3 \times 8) + (1 \times 2) + (2 \times 1) + (4 \times 9) & (3 \times 3) + (1 \times -1) + (2 \times 0) + (4 \times 2) \\ (1 \times 8) + (-1 \times 2) + (0 \times 1) + (2 \times 9) & (1 \times 3) + (-1 \times -1) + (0 \times 0) + (2 \times 2) \\ (2 \times 8) + (3 \times 2) + (1 \times 1) + (-2 \times 9) & (2 \times 3) + (3 \times -1) + (1 \times 0) + (-2 \times 2) \end{bmatrix}$$

$$= \begin{bmatrix} 64 & 16 \\ 24 & 8 \\ 5 & -1 \end{bmatrix} \tag{8-16}$$

Because C is a 2×2 matrix, it is conformable for the multiplication $(AB)C$. We find

$$(AB)C = \begin{bmatrix} 64 & 16 \\ 24 & 8 \\ 5 & -1 \end{bmatrix} \begin{bmatrix} 1 & -1 \\ 0 & 3 \end{bmatrix}$$

$$= \begin{bmatrix} (64 \times 1) + (16 \times 0) & (64 \times -1) + (16 \times 3) \\ (24 \times 1) + (8 \times 0) & (24 \times -1) + (8 \times 3) \\ (5 \times 1) + (-1 \times 0) & (5 \times -1) + (-1 \times 3) \end{bmatrix} = \begin{bmatrix} 64 & -16 \\ 24 & 0 \\ 5 & -8 \end{bmatrix} \tag{8-17}$$

In order to demonstrate the associative property, we must next find the product BC and premultiply it by A. B is a 4×2 matrix and C is 2×2, so they are conformable, and the product BC is 4×2,

$$BC = \begin{bmatrix} 8 & 3 \\ 2 & -1 \\ 1 & 0 \\ 9 & 2 \end{bmatrix} \begin{bmatrix} 1 & -1 \\ 0 & 3 \end{bmatrix}$$

$$= \begin{bmatrix} (8 \times 1) + (3 \times 0) & (8 \times -1) + (3 \times 3) \\ (2 \times 1) + (-1 \times 0) & (2 \times -1) + (-1 \times 3) \\ (1 \times 1) + (0 \times 0) & (1 \times -1) + (0 \times 3) \\ (9 \times 1) + (2 \times 0) & (9 \times -1) + (2 \times 3) \end{bmatrix} = \begin{bmatrix} 8 & 1 \\ 2 & -5 \\ 1 & -1 \\ 9 & -3 \end{bmatrix} \quad \text{(8-18)}$$

We are able to premultiply BC by A, because A has dimensions 3×4, making it conformable for the multiplication $A(BC)$, which equals

$$A(BC) = \begin{bmatrix} 3 & 1 & 2 & 4 \\ 1 & -1 & 0 & 2 \\ 2 & 3 & 1 & -2 \end{bmatrix} \begin{bmatrix} 8 & 1 \\ 2 & -5 \\ 1 & -1 \\ 9 & -3 \end{bmatrix}$$

$$= \begin{bmatrix} (3 \times 8) + (1 \times 2) + (2 \times 1) + (4 \times 9) & (3 \times 1) + (1 \times -5) + (2 \times -1) + (4 \times -3) \\ (1 \times 8) + (-1 \times 2) + (0 \times 1) + (2 \times 9) & (1 \times 1) + (-1 \times -5) + (0 \times -1) + (2 \times -3) \\ (2 \times 8) + (3 \times 2) + (1 \times 1) + (-2 \times 9) & (2 \times 1) + (3 \times -5) + (1 \times -1) + (-2 \times -3) \end{bmatrix}$$

$$= \begin{bmatrix} 64 & -16 \\ 24 & 0 \\ 5 & -8 \end{bmatrix} \quad \text{(8-19)}$$

Comparing (8-17) with (8-19), you see that $(AB)C = A(BC)$, so the associative property is demonstrated for these matrices.

8.3.2 Matrix Addition and Subtraction

distributive property: the arithmetic property that one operation can be distributed over another operation, leaving the result unchanged.

Matrix multiplication also has the ***distributive*** property of multiplication over addition, so that $A(B + C) = AB + AC$. The distributive property requires that you know what is meant by matrix addition. Two matrices can be added and subtracted if and only if they have the same dimensions. When this dimensional requirement is met, the two matrices are said to be *conformable for addition and subtraction*. When this is the case, the two matrices are added or subtracted by adding or subtracting each pair of corresponding elements, and the resulting sum or difference matrix has a dimension equal to that of the original matrices. For example,

$$\begin{bmatrix} a_{11} & a_{12} \\ a_{21} & a_{22} \end{bmatrix} \pm \begin{bmatrix} b_{11} & b_{12} \\ b_{21} & b_{22} \end{bmatrix} = \begin{bmatrix} a_{11} \pm b_{11} & a_{12} \pm b_{12} \\ a_{21} \pm b_{21} & a_{22} \pm b_{22} \end{bmatrix} \quad (8\text{-}20)$$

More generally, $[a_{ij}] \pm [b_{ij}] = [c_{ij}]$ where $c_{ij} = a_{ij} \pm b_{ij}$.

NUMERICAL EXAMPLE

Let's use the following matrices to demonstrate matrix addition and the distributive property of matrix multiplication over addition.

$$A = \begin{bmatrix} 1 & -1 & 0 \\ 3 & 0 & 4 \\ 0 & 1 & 1 \end{bmatrix}, \quad B = \begin{bmatrix} 3 & 1 & -3 \\ 2 & 1 & 0 \\ -1 & -2 & 1 \end{bmatrix}, \quad C = \begin{bmatrix} 1 & 1 & -1 \\ -1 & 1 & 0 \\ 0 & 1 & 0 \end{bmatrix} \quad (8\text{-}21)$$

Note that all three matrices have the same dimension, 3×3, so they are conformable for both multiplication and addition. The distributive property states that $A(B + C) = AB + AC$. In order to demonstrate this property for the matrices in (8-21), first we add B and C, obtaining

$$B + C = \begin{bmatrix} 3 & 1 & -3 \\ 2 & 1 & 0 \\ -1 & -2 & 1 \end{bmatrix} + \begin{bmatrix} 1 & 1 & -1 \\ -1 & 1 & 0 \\ 0 & 1 & 0 \end{bmatrix} = \begin{bmatrix} 3+1 & 1+1 & -3-1 \\ 2-1 & 1+1 & 0+0 \\ -1+0 & -2+1 & 1+0 \end{bmatrix}$$

$$= \begin{bmatrix} 4 & 2 & -4 \\ 1 & 2 & 0 \\ -1 & -1 & 1 \end{bmatrix} \quad (8\text{-}22)$$

Premultiplying $B + C$ by A gives us

$$A(B + C) = \begin{bmatrix} 1 & -1 & 0 \\ 3 & 0 & 4 \\ 0 & 1 & 1 \end{bmatrix} \begin{bmatrix} 4 & 2 & -4 \\ 1 & 2 & 0 \\ -1 & -1 & 1 \end{bmatrix} = \begin{bmatrix} 3 & 0 & -4 \\ 8 & 2 & -8 \\ 0 & 1 & 1 \end{bmatrix} \quad (8\text{-}23)$$

Now we want to find AB and AC, so that we can see if their sum equals (8-23). Premultiplying both B and C by A gives us

$$AB = \begin{bmatrix} 1 & -1 & 0 \\ 3 & 0 & 4 \\ 0 & 1 & 1 \end{bmatrix} \begin{bmatrix} 3 & 1 & -3 \\ 2 & 1 & 0 \\ -1 & -2 & 1 \end{bmatrix} = \begin{bmatrix} 1 & 0 & -3 \\ 5 & -5 & -5 \\ 1 & -1 & 1 \end{bmatrix};$$

$$AC = \begin{bmatrix} 1 & -1 & 0 \\ 3 & 0 & 4 \\ 0 & 1 & 1 \end{bmatrix} \begin{bmatrix} 1 & 1 & -1 \\ -1 & 1 & 0 \\ 0 & 1 & 0 \end{bmatrix} = \begin{bmatrix} 2 & 0 & -1 \\ 3 & 7 & -3 \\ -1 & 2 & 0 \end{bmatrix} \qquad \text{(8-24)}$$

The sum of AB and AC equals

$$AB + AC = \begin{bmatrix} 1 & 0 & -3 \\ 5 & -5 & -5 \\ 1 & -1 & 1 \end{bmatrix} + \begin{bmatrix} 2 & 0 & -1 \\ 3 & 7 & -3 \\ -1 & 2 & 0 \end{bmatrix} = \begin{bmatrix} 3 & 0 & -4 \\ 8 & 2 & -8 \\ 0 & 1 & 1 \end{bmatrix} \qquad \text{(8-25)}$$

As you can see, (8-25) equals (8-23), so the distributive property is demonstrated for these matrices.

Because addition and subtraction of matrices involve addition and subtraction of elements in the same row and column of matrices with identical dimensions, matrix addition and subtraction have the same properties as regular arithmetic addition and subtraction. Therefore, both the commutative and distributive properties hold for matrix addition and subtraction. That is, $A + B = B + A$, $A - B = -B + A$, and $A \pm (B \pm C) = (A \pm B) \pm C$. We ask you to demonstrate these properties in Exercises 1, 2, and 3 at the end of Section 8.3.3.

8.3.3 Scalar Multiplication

scalar: a number, as opposed to a matrix.

scalar multiplication: the operation of multiplying a matrix by a number.

The subtraction operation $A - B$ may be considered as an addition operation involving matrices A and $-B$. This raises the question of what is meant by multiplying a matrix B by a single number such as -1. A single number is called a *scalar* in the terminology of matrix algebra, and the operation in which a matrix is multiplied by a number is called *scalar multiplication*.

In order to multiply a matrix by a scalar, we multiply every element of the matrix by that scalar. Thus

$$k \begin{bmatrix} a_{11} & a_{12} \\ a_{21} & a_{22} \end{bmatrix} = \begin{bmatrix} ka_{11} & ka_{12} \\ ka_{21} & ka_{22} \end{bmatrix} \qquad \text{(8-26)}$$

where k is any real number (i.e., it may be positive, negative, or zero). From this, the rationale for the name scalar should be clear; it scales the matrix up or down. Therefore, subtraction of B from A is the same as multiplying B by the scalar -1 and adding the result to A.

EXERCISES
Section 8.3.3
Scalar 2106
Multiplication

Use the following matrices to answer questions 1 through 7

$$A = \begin{bmatrix} 2 & 3 & 1 \\ -1 & 0 & 1 \\ 0 & -2 & 1 \end{bmatrix}, \quad B = \begin{bmatrix} 2 & 10 & 6 \\ 5 & 6 & -4 \\ 0 & 2 & 8 \end{bmatrix}, \quad C = \begin{bmatrix} 1 & 0 & 0 \\ 0 & 2 & 1 \\ 0 & 0 & 1 \end{bmatrix}$$

1. Show that $A + B = B + A$.
2. Show that $(A + B) + C = A + (B + C)$.
3. Show that $A - B = -B + A$.
4. Using matrices A and B, demonstrate that matrix multiplication is not commutative.
5. Show that $A(BC) = (AB)C$.
6. Show that $A(B + C) = AB + AC$.
7. Show that $4A = 2A + 2A$

8.4

MATRIX REPRESENTATION OF SYSTEMS OF LINEAR EQUATIONS

Let's reexamine the system of linear equations with which we began ou discussion of matrices. We claimed that our system could be represented by the matrix equation

$$\begin{array}{ccc} A & X & = & C \\ (m \times n) & (n \times 1) & (m \times 1) \end{array} \tag{8-10}$$

where

$$A = \begin{bmatrix} a_{11} & a_{12} & \cdots & a_{1n} \\ a_{21} & a_{22} & \cdots & a_{2n} \\ \vdots & \vdots & \vdots & \vdots \\ a_{m1} & a_{m2} & \cdots & a_{mn} \end{bmatrix}, \quad X = \begin{bmatrix} X_1 \\ X_2 \\ \vdots \\ X_n \end{bmatrix}, \quad C = \begin{bmatrix} C_1 \\ C_2 \\ \vdots \\ C_m \end{bmatrix} \tag{8-3}$$

The lead matrix is A, and it does have the same number of columns, n, as the lag matrix X has rows, so they are conformable for matrix multiplication.

The product matrix has the same number of rows as A, m, and the same number of columns as X, 1. The element in the intersection of row 1 and column 1 of C, C_1, is equal to the sum of the products of the elements in the first row of A and the first (and only) column of X. The element in row 2, column 1 of C, C_2, is equal to the sum of the products of the elements in the second row of A and the first column of X, and so on. That is,

$$a_{11}X_1 + a_{12}X_2 + \cdots + a_{1n}X_n = C_1$$
$$a_{21}X_1 + a_{22}X_2 + \cdots + a_{2n}X_n = C_2$$
$$\vdots \qquad \vdots \qquad \qquad \vdots$$
$$a_{m1}X_1 + a_{m2}X_2 + \cdots + a_{mn}X_n = C_m \qquad (8\text{-}1)$$

This is, of course, the original system of linear equations that we set out to express in matrix notation.

8.4.1 Linear Independence

The next task we want matrix algebra to help us accomplish is to determine whether a system of linear equations has a solution and, if so, what that solution might be. In general, there must be as many *linearly independent* equations as there are unknowns for a system of linear equations to have a unique solution. When there are only two equations in a system, they are linearly independent if one equation cannot be multiplied by a constant to get the other. For example, $X + 2Y = 5$ and $3X + 6Y = 15$ are not linearly independent. The second equation is just the first equation multiplied by 3. They cannot be solved for X and Y (try if you do not believe us). On the other hand $X + 2Y = 5$ and $3X + Y = 7.5$ are linearly independent and can be solved for X and Y ($X = 2$, $Y = 1.5$). Expressing these two systems in matrix notation gives us

linearly independent: the property that it is impossible to express any one equation in a linear system as some linear combination of the other equations.

$$\begin{bmatrix} 1 & 2 \\ 3 & 6 \end{bmatrix} \begin{bmatrix} X \\ Y \end{bmatrix} = \begin{bmatrix} 5 \\ 15 \end{bmatrix} \quad \text{and} \quad \begin{bmatrix} 1 & 2 \\ 3 & 1 \end{bmatrix} \begin{bmatrix} X \\ Y \end{bmatrix} = \begin{bmatrix} 5 \\ 7.5 \end{bmatrix} \quad (8\text{-}27)$$

In the matrix equation on the left, the rows and columns of the square matrix of coefficients are multiples of one another; they are linearly dependent. This is not the case with the matrix equation on the right. A matrix with linearly dependent rows or columns is said to be a *singular matrix*. A matrix with linearly independent rows or columns is *nonsingular.*

singular matrix: a matrix in which one row (column) is a linear combination of the other rows (columns).

The reason that two equations that are not linearly independent cannot be solved for two unknowns is that the second equation brings no *new* information regarding the relationship between the variables. When there are many equations in a linear system, they are independent if it is impossible to express any one equation as some linear combination of the other equations.

nonsingular matrix: a matrix in which all the rows (columns) are linearly independent.

We began the chapter with a system of m linear equations which we have expressed as the matrix equation $AX = C$. This system can be solved for the variables $X_1, X_2, \ldots, X_n$ provided there are as many linearly independent equations as there are unknowns. That means that m, the number of rows in matrix A, must equal n, the number of columns, and the equations must be linearly independent. Therefore, in order to have a unique solution to our system of linear equations, A must be a square matrix and it must be nonsingular. Now we need a method for determining whether the rows (columns) of a matrix are linearly independent. It turns out that one of the simplest tests of linear independence (and hence of nonsingularity) is based on the concept of **determinants**, to which we turn next.

determinant: a number associated with a square matrix.

8.5

DETERMINANTS AND THEIR PROPERTIES

Any square matrix has a determinant, which is nothing more than a number associated with that matrix. We use straight vertical lines to denote the determinant of a matrix; it is a notation that looks like the symbol for absolute value, but it is not and you must not confuse determinants and absolute values. The order of a determinant, like the order of a square matrix, is equal to the number of rows or columns it has. We find the determinant of a 2×2, or second-order matrix, by the following method. If

$$A = \begin{bmatrix} a_{11} & a_{12} \\ a_{21} & a_{22} \end{bmatrix}, \quad \text{then} \quad |A| = \begin{vmatrix} a_{11} & a_{12} \\ a_{21} & a_{22} \end{vmatrix} = a_{11}a_{22} - a_{12}a_{21} \quad \text{(8-28)}$$

which is a number. The determinant of a 2×2 matrix is obtained by multiplying the upper left and lower right elements and then subtracting the product of the upper right and lower left elements. The upper left and lower right elements, a_{11} and a_{22}, comprise the principal diagonal of the determinant. The process by which the determinant of a matrix is found is called **expansion** or **evaluation** of that determinant.

expansion of a determinant: same as evaluation of a determinant.

evaluation of a determinant: the process of computing the number that is the determinant. Also called expansion of a determinant.

Even at this early stage of discussion, we can see how the concept of determinants can be used to decide whether the rows (columns) of a given matrix are linearly independent. To see this, recall the matrix equations we used in our numerical example of linear dependence,

$$\begin{bmatrix} 1 & 2 \\ 3 & 6 \end{bmatrix} \begin{bmatrix} X \\ Y \end{bmatrix} = \begin{bmatrix} 5 \\ 15 \end{bmatrix} \quad \text{and} \quad \begin{bmatrix} 1 & 2 \\ 3 & 1 \end{bmatrix} \begin{bmatrix} X \\ Y \end{bmatrix} = \begin{bmatrix} 5 \\ 7.5 \end{bmatrix} \quad \text{(8-27)}$$

If we let A and B represent the coefficient matrices, we obtain

$$A = \begin{bmatrix} 1 & 2 \\ 3 & 6 \end{bmatrix} \quad \text{and} \quad B = \begin{bmatrix} 1 & 2 \\ 3 & 1 \end{bmatrix} \quad \text{(8-29)}$$

Their determinants are

$$|A| = \begin{vmatrix} 1 & 2 \\ 3 & 6 \end{vmatrix} \quad \text{and} \quad |B| = \begin{vmatrix} 1 & 2 \\ 3 & 1 \end{vmatrix} \quad \text{(8-30)}$$

Note that in the determinant $|A|$ the second column equals twice the first column and the second row equals three times the first row. In $|B|$ the rows and columns are linearly independent. Let us evaluate the determinants of these two matrices:

$$|A| = (1)(6) - (2)(3) = 6 - 6 = 0 \tag{8-31}$$

$$|B| = (1)(1) - (2)(3) = 1 - 6 = -5 \tag{8-32}$$

These examples suggest that when a matrix is singular (remember that means that there is linear dependence in the matrix), the determinant of that matrix is zero. This result can be generalized to give us a simple test of linear independence for any square matrix. Although we are able to expand or evaluate a second-order determinant, we have not yet reviewed how to evaluate higher-order determinants, which we need to do in order to handle linear systems with more than two equations.

8.5.1 Evaluating Third- and Higher-Order Determinants

Laplace method: a method of expanding a determinant by which the result equals the sum of the products of the elements of a row or column with their cofactors.

cofactor: a minor that has a sign equal to $(-1)^{i+j}$ associated with it.

minor: the subdeterminant associated with an element a_{ij} of some determinant, $|A|$, obtained by deleting the ith row and jth column $|A|$ and denoted $|A_{ij}|$.

principal minors: the minors associated with the diagonal elements.

We use a technique called the *Laplace method* to evaluate third- and higher-order determinants. The Laplace method involves two concepts: *minors* and *cofactors*. A minor, denoted by $|A_{ij}|$, associated with an element, a_{ij}, of a determinant, $|A|$, is a subdeterminant of $|A|$ obtained by deleting the ith row and jth column of $|A|$. Note that the element a_{ij} will be at the intersection of the deleted row and column. Note also that since a minor is itself a determinant, it is a number. To illustrate how to determine the minors of a determinant, consider the following third-order determinant:

$$|A| = \begin{vmatrix} a_{11} & a_{12} & a_{13} \\ a_{21} & a_{22} & a_{23} \\ a_{31} & a_{32} & a_{33} \end{vmatrix} \tag{8-33}$$

The minors associated with the diagonal elements, called *principal minors*, are

$$|A_{11}| = \begin{vmatrix} a_{22} & a_{23} \\ a_{32} & a_{33} \end{vmatrix}, \quad |A_{22}| = \begin{vmatrix} a_{11} & a_{13} \\ a_{31} & a_{33} \end{vmatrix}, \quad |A_{33}| = \begin{vmatrix} a_{11} & a_{12} \\ a_{21} & a_{22} \end{vmatrix} \tag{8-34}$$

A *cofactor* is a minor that has a sign (+ or −) associated with it. Cofactors are denoted by $|C_{ij}|$. The rule for obtaining the cofactor of minor $|A_{ij}|$ is to assign to the cofactor the same sign as that of $|A_{ij}|$ if $(i + j)$ is an even number and assign a sign opposite that of the minor if $(i + j)$ is an odd number. That is,

$$|C_{ij}| \equiv (-1)^{i+j} |A_{ij}| \tag{8-35}$$

Note that, like minors, cofactors are determinants, and thus each is a number.

With the aid of cofactors, we can expand determinants of any order by following these steps.

Step 1. Choose a row or a column of the determinant. Any row or column will do. Choose an "easy" row, one with lots of zeros and/or ones or integers. If a row is chosen, then we refer to the corresponding expansion as *expansion by row*. Otherwise, we call it *expansion by column*.

Step 2. Determine all cofactors of the elements of that row or column. Remember, an element and its cofactor may have the same signs or opposite signs, depending on where the element is located in the underlying determinant.

Step 3. Find the sum of products of each element and its associated cofactor. Again, be careful with signs.

Step 4. Reduce the order of cofactors by repeating this process until the second-order cofactors are reached. Now apply the rule for expansion of second-order determinants.

These steps can be written in a compact form for an *n*th-order determinant as follows:

$$|A| = \sum a_{ij}|C_{ij}| \qquad \text{(8-36)}$$

Make the summation from $j = 1$ to n and you are expanding by the *i*th row. Make the summation from $i = 1$ to n and you are expanding by the *j*th column.

alien cofactor: the cofactor of some other element.

When using the Laplace method, be sure to use the correct cofactors. If you expand a determinant by cofactors of a wrong row or column, called *alien cofactors*, the result will be zero. For example, if you choose to expand a determinant by the first-row elements while using second-row cofactors, you will end up with a zero value.

Let's apply the Laplace method to a third-order determinant and expand it by the first row,

$$|A| = \begin{vmatrix} a_{11} & a_{12} & a_{13} \\ a_{21} & a_{22} & a_{23} \\ a_{31} & a_{32} & a_{33} \end{vmatrix} = a_{11}\begin{vmatrix} a_{22} & a_{23} \\ a_{32} & a_{33} \end{vmatrix} - a_{12}\begin{vmatrix} a_{21} & a_{23} \\ a_{31} & a_{33} \end{vmatrix} + a_{13}\begin{vmatrix} a_{21} & a_{22} \\ a_{31} & a_{32} \end{vmatrix}$$

$$\text{(8-37)}$$

Evaluate the second-order determinants and you find

$$|A| = a_{11}(a_{22}a_{33} - a_{23}a_{32}) - a_{12}(a_{21}a_{33} - a_{23}a_{31}) + a_{13}(a_{21}a_{32} - a_{22}a_{31})$$

$$\text{(8-38)}$$

Suppose that, in expanding the determinant, instead of using cofactors of the first-row elements we use alien cofactors: the cofactors of the second row. We have

$$a_{11}\begin{vmatrix} a_{12} & a_{13} \\ a_{32} & a_{33} \end{vmatrix} - a_{12}\begin{vmatrix} a_{11} & a_{13} \\ a_{31} & a_{33} \end{vmatrix} + a_{13}\begin{vmatrix} a_{11} & a_{12} \\ a_{31} & a_{32} \end{vmatrix} \qquad \text{(8-39)}$$

Upon evaluating the second-order determinants we obtain

$$a_{11}(a_{12}a_{33} - a_{13}a_{32}) - a_{12}(a_{11}a_{33} - a_{13}a_{31}) + a_{13}(a_{11}a_{32} - a_{12}a_{31}) = 0 \quad \text{(8-40)}$$

This confirms our earlier assertion that expansion by alien cofactors yields a zero determinant.

NUMERICAL EXAMPLE

Evaluate the following determinant by the Laplace method.

$$|A| = \begin{vmatrix} 5 & 3 & 11 \\ 4 & 15 & 7 \\ 9 & 12 & 1 \end{vmatrix} \quad \text{(8-41)}$$

Let's expand by the third row.

$$|A| = +9 \begin{vmatrix} 3 & 11 \\ 15 & 7 \end{vmatrix} - 12 \begin{vmatrix} 5 & 11 \\ 4 & 7 \end{vmatrix} + 1 \begin{vmatrix} 5 & 3 \\ 4 & 15 \end{vmatrix} \quad \text{(8-42)}$$

This can be evaluated as

$$|A| = 9(-144) - 12(-9) + 1(63) = -1125 \quad \text{(8-43)}$$

We can also use this numerical example to illustrate expansion by alien cofactors. The cofactors of the third row will be alien if we multiply them by the elements of the second row. Thus we have

$$4(-144) - 15(-9) + 7(63) = 0 \quad \text{(8-44)}$$

8.5.2   Properties of Determinants

Determinants have many useful arithmetic properties, four of which are presented below.

1. Interchanging any two rows or any two columns will alter the sign, but not the numerical value of the determinant.

$$\begin{vmatrix} a & b \\ c & d \end{vmatrix} = ad - bc; \quad \begin{vmatrix} c & d \\ a & b \end{vmatrix} = bc - ad = -(ad - bc) \quad \text{(8-45)}$$

2. Multiplying any one row or one column of $|A|$ by a scalar (k) changes the value of the determinant k-fold.

$$\begin{vmatrix} ka & kb \\ c & d \end{vmatrix} = kad - kbc = k(ad - bc) = k\begin{vmatrix} a & b \\ c & d \end{vmatrix} \quad (8\text{-}46)$$

Note an important fact about this property. Unlike the case of matrices, when multiplying a determinant by a scalar only one row or column will be multiplied by that scalar.

$$k\begin{vmatrix} a & b \\ c & d \end{vmatrix} = \begin{vmatrix} ka & kb \\ c & d \end{vmatrix} \quad (8\text{-}47)$$

Note, however, that if we multiply *all* elements of an nth-order determinant by a scalar the value of the determinant will be changed k^n-fold. That is,

$$|kA| = k^n|A| \quad (8\text{-}48)$$

This property allows us to factor a determinant. Whenever a single row or column of a determinant has a common divisor, it may be factored out of the determinant. This can be done for as many rows and columns as there may be.

$$\begin{vmatrix} 12 & 4 \\ 6 & 5 \end{vmatrix} = 4\begin{vmatrix} 3 & 1 \\ 6 & 5 \end{vmatrix} = 4(3)\begin{vmatrix} 1 & 1 \\ 2 & 5 \end{vmatrix} = 12(5 - 2) = 36 \quad (8\text{-}49)$$

Directly evaluating the original determinant, without factoring, produces the same result ($12 \times 5 - 4 \times 6 = 36$).

3. Adding or subtracting a multiple of any row or column to or from another row or column will leave the value of the determinant unchanged.

$$\begin{vmatrix} a & b \\ c + ka & d + kb \end{vmatrix} = a(d + kb) - b(c + ka) = ad - bc = \begin{vmatrix} a & b \\ c & d \end{vmatrix}$$

$$(8\text{-}50)$$

4. If one row (column) is a multiple of another row (column), then the determinant will have a value of zero. We have already discussed this property of determinants. We assure ourselves that the rows and columns are linearly independent if the determinant is not equal to zero.

The properties of determinants can be used to facilitate expansion of higher-ordered determinants using the Laplace method. When we explained the first step of this method we suggested that, if possible, you should choose an "easy" row or column, one with zeros and ones as elements, to expand the determinant. However, determinants frequently do not have easy rows to choose. Sometimes the properties of determinants can be used to simplify them.

NUMERICAL EXAMPLE

Suppose we want to expand the following 3×3 determinant,

$$\begin{vmatrix} 18 & 54 & 9 \\ -4 & 12 & 24 \\ 3 & 5 & 1 \end{vmatrix} \qquad (8\text{-}51)$$

Our goal is to simplify the determinant before expanding it. Noting that 9 is a common divisor of the first row, we can use property 2 to factor it out of the determinant,

$$9 \begin{vmatrix} 2 & 6 & 1 \\ -4 & 12 & 24 \\ 3 & 5 & 1 \end{vmatrix} \qquad (8\text{-}52)$$

Similarly, we can factor 4 out of the second row,

$$36 \begin{vmatrix} 2 & 6 & 1 \\ -1 & 3 & 6 \\ 3 & 5 & 1 \end{vmatrix} \qquad (8\text{-}53)$$

Having factored out all possible divisors, we now try to create a simple row by which to expand the determinant. Using property 3, we add -1 times the last row to the first,

$$36 \begin{vmatrix} -1 & 1 & 0 \\ -1 & 3 & 6 \\ 3 & 5 & 1 \end{vmatrix} \qquad (8\text{-}54)$$

Now add the second column to the first,

$$36 \begin{vmatrix} 0 & 1 & 0 \\ 2 & 3 & 6 \\ 8 & 5 & 1 \end{vmatrix} \qquad (8\text{-}55)$$

The first row has the simplest form and can be used for expansion,

$$36\left(0\begin{vmatrix}3 & 6\\5 & 1\end{vmatrix} - 1\begin{vmatrix}2 & 6\\8 & 1\end{vmatrix} + 0\begin{vmatrix}2 & 3\\8 & 5\end{vmatrix}\right) = -36\begin{vmatrix}2 & 6\\8 & 1\end{vmatrix}$$

$$= -36(2 - 48) = 1656$$

$$(8\text{-}56)$$

By now it should be obvious that, although related, matrices and determinants are not the same thing. Among some of the major differences are the following:

1. A matrix is not a number; it is an ordered array of elements. On the other hand, a determinant is a number associated with a square matrix.

2. Matrices may be of any dimension. Determinants, on the other hand, can only be square.

3. Recall property 2 of determinants: In multiplying a determinant by a scalar, only one row or column will be multiplied by that scalar. On the other hand, in multiplying a matrix by a scalar all elements of the matrix are multiplied by the scalar, not just one row or one column. Thus, if A is a square matrix, kA and $k|A|$ are two different things.

EXERCISES
Section 8.5.2
Properties of
Determinants

1. Evaluate the following determinants

a. $|A| = \begin{vmatrix} 2 & 3 & 1 & 3 \\ -1 & 0 & 1 & 6 \\ 5 & -2 & 1 & 3 \\ 1 & 4 & -2 & 3 \end{vmatrix}$

b. $|B| = \begin{vmatrix} 2 & 10 & 6 \\ 5 & 6 & -4 \\ 0 & 2 & 8 \end{vmatrix}$

c. $|C| = \begin{vmatrix} 1 & 2 & 3 \\ 3 & 2 & 1 \\ 4 & 4 & 4 \end{vmatrix}$

2. a. Express the following system of four linear equations in four unknowns as a matrix equation,

$$2X_1 + X_2 - X_4 = 1$$
$$X_1 + X_2 = X_3 + X_4$$
$$X_1 = (2X_2 + 3X_3 + 4X_4 + 6)/2$$
$$X_2 - X_4 = 2X_1$$

b. Determine whether or not this system of equations is linearly independent by examining the determinant of the matrix of coefficients.

8.6

SOLVING SYSTEMS OF SIMULTANEOUS LINEAR EQUATIONS

matrix inversion: the process of finding the inverse of a matrix.

We have introduced the concept of determinants in order to discover the conditions under which a system of linear equations can be solved. We discovered that, given the matrix equation,

$$AX = C \qquad (8\text{-}57)$$

Cramer's rule: a method of solving for individual elements of the vector X in the matrix equation $AX = C$.

a unique solution for the vector X exists if and only if the matrix A is square and its determinant is not equal to zero. Now we want to find out what that solution is. The two methods we will use to solve systems of linear equations are **matrix inversion** and **Cramer's rule**.

8.6.1 The Inverse-Matrix Approach

Recall from basic algebra that we solve the scalar equation $ax = c$ by multiplying both sides of the equation by the inverse of a to get $x = c/a, a \neq 0$. The inverse-matrix approach to solving matrix equations is essentially the same except that instead of $1/a$ we use what is known as a **multiplicative inverse matrix** denoted A^{-1}.[1] If we premultiply both sides of the matrix equation $AX = C$ by such a matrix we get

multiplicative inverse matrix: a matrix which, when multiplied by another matrix, yields a product equal to the identity matrix.

$$A^{-1}AX = I_n X = X = A^{-1}C \qquad (8\text{-}58)$$

where I_n is the *n-dimensional* identity matrix. The result in (8-58), that $X = A^{-1}C$, uses the properties that the product of a matrix and its inverse equals an identity matrix, $A^{-1}A = I_n$ and that the product of any matrix and an identity matrix equals the original matrix, $I_n X = X$. The inverse-matrix approach solves for the vector of unknowns, X, by premultiplying the vector of the constant terms of the equation by the inverse of the coefficient matrix. But how do we find the inverse of the coefficient matrix? To answer this question we must first define the notions of the **transpose** and the **adjoint** of a matrix.

transpose: a matrix that is obtained by interchanging the rows and columns of another matrix. If A is a matrix, its transpose is denoted A'.

The transpose of a matrix A, denoted A', is a matrix that is obtained from A by interchanging its rows and columns. Therefore, if

adjoint: the transpose of a matrix obtained from an original matrix A by replacing its elements a_{ij} with their corresponding cofactors $|C_{ij}|$. Denoted by adj(A).

$$A = \begin{bmatrix} a_{11} & a_{12} & a_{13} \\ a_{21} & a_{22} & a_{23} \\ a_{31} & a_{32} & a_{33} \end{bmatrix}, \quad \text{then} \quad A' = \begin{bmatrix} a_{11} & a_{21} & a_{31} \\ a_{12} & a_{22} & a_{32} \\ a_{13} & a_{23} & a_{33} \end{bmatrix} \qquad (8\text{-}59)$$

If you were to interchange the rows and columns of a matrix twice, you would end up with the same matrix; therefore, the transpose of a transpose is the

---

[1]Note that, unlike scalar algebra where a^{-1} equals $1/a$, in matrix algebra A^{-1} is *not* equal to $1/A$.

original matrix, $(A')' = A$. The transpose operation can also be distributed over addition and multiplication; therefore, $(A + B)' = A' + B'$ and $(AB)' = B'A'$. Note that when we distribute the transpose operation over multiplication, the order of multiplication is reversed. This is because the number of rows of the original matrix becomes the number of columns in the transpose, and vice versa. Reversing the order of multiplication of transposed matrices ensures that they will be conformable.

The second concept we need to define is the adjoint of a matrix A, denoted $\text{adj}(A)$. This is defined only for square matrices and is the transpose of a matrix obtained from the original matrix by replacing its elements a_{ij} by their corresponding cofactors $|C_{ij}|$. For example, given the 3×3 matrix

$$A = \begin{bmatrix} a_{11} & a_{12} & a_{13} \\ a_{21} & a_{22} & a_{23} \\ a_{31} & a_{32} & a_{33} \end{bmatrix} \tag{8-60}$$

the adjoint matrix is

$$\text{adj}(A) \equiv C' = \begin{bmatrix} |C_{11}| & |C_{21}| & |C_{31}| \\ |C_{12}| & |C_{22}| & |C_{32}| \\ |C_{13}| & |C_{23}| & |C_{33}| \end{bmatrix} \tag{8-61}$$

where the elements of the adjoint are the cofactors of A. For example,

$$|C_{23}| = - \begin{vmatrix} a_{11} & a_{12} \\ a_{31} & a_{32} \end{vmatrix} = -(a_{11}a_{32} - a_{12}a_{31}) \tag{8-62}$$

Note that the adjoint of a square matrix is itself a square matrix and has the same dimensions as the original matrix. This means that a matrix and its adjoint are conformable for multiplication.

We are now prepared to derive a procedure for finding the inverse of a nonsingular matrix. We will do this using the 3×3 matrix we introduced above, but the method can easily be generalized for application to matrices of larger dimensions. First, we find the product of A and its adjoint,

$$AC' = \begin{bmatrix} a_{11} & a_{12} & a_{13} \\ a_{21} & a_{22} & a_{23} \\ a_{31} & a_{32} & a_{33} \end{bmatrix} \begin{bmatrix} |C_{11}| & |C_{21}| & |C_{31}| \\ |C_{12}| & |C_{22}| & |C_{32}| \\ |C_{13}| & |C_{23}| & |C_{33}| \end{bmatrix} = \begin{bmatrix} |A| & 0 & 0 \\ 0 & |A| & 0 \\ 0 & 0 & |A| \end{bmatrix} = |A|I_3$$

$$\tag{8-63}$$

Notice how we obtained this result. The diagonal elements of the product matrix all represent Laplace expansions of the determinant of A, by the first, second, and third columns, respectively. All of the off-diagonal elements represent expansions by alien cofactors, resulting in zeros. Therefore, the product of matrix A and its adjoint matrix equals the product of the determinant of A and a third-order identity matrix, as in (8-63).

If A is a nonsingular matrix, its determinant is nonzero and we can divide both sides of equation (8-63) by $|A|$, obtaining

$$\frac{AC'}{|A|} = I, \tag{8-64}$$

Premultiply both sides by the inverse of A or A^{-1} in order to obtain the result that

$$A^{-1}\frac{AC'}{|A|} = A^{-1}I_3 = A^{-1} \tag{8-65}$$

or

$$\frac{C'}{|A|} = A^{-1} \tag{8-66}$$

This result tells us that the inverse of a nonsingular matrix equals its adjoint matrix divided by its determinant.

We can summarize the matrix inversion procedure in five steps. Given the matrix A:

Step 1. Find the determinant $|A|$. Proceed only if $|A| \neq 0$.

Step 2. Find cofactors of all elements of A and arrange them as a matrix of cofactors, C.

Step 3. Transpose C to get the adjoint of A.

Step 4. Multiply adj(A) by the reciprocal of the determinant of A to get A^{-1}.

Step 5. Check your answer by examining whether $AA^{-1} = I_n$.

NUMERICAL EXAMPLE

Let's use matrix inversion to solve the following system of linear equations.

$$
\begin{aligned}
X_1 - X_2 \quad\quad &= 2 \\
3X_1 + 2X_2 + X_3 &= 4 \\
2X_1 + X_2 + X_3 &= 6
\end{aligned}
\tag{8-67}
$$

which may be written in matrix form

$$
\begin{bmatrix} 1 & -1 & 0 \\ 3 & 2 & 1 \\ 2 & 1 & 1 \end{bmatrix}
\begin{bmatrix} X_1 \\ X_2 \\ X_3 \end{bmatrix} =
\begin{bmatrix} 2 \\ 4 \\ 6 \end{bmatrix}.
\tag{8-68}
$$

First we must ascertain that the coefficient matrix is nonsingular so that the inverse matrix A^{-1} exists. It is easy to verify that $|A| = 2$, so A is nonsingular and the system has a unique solution. The next step is to invert the coefficient matrix. The cofactors of matrix A are

$$
\begin{aligned}
&|C_{11}| = 1, \qquad |C_{12}| = -1, \qquad |C_{13}| = -1 \\
&|C_{21}| = 1, \qquad |C_{22}| = 1, \qquad |C_{23}| = -3 \\
&|C_{31}| = -1, \qquad |C_{32}| = -1, \qquad |C_{33}| = 5
\end{aligned}
$$

Therefore, the matrix of cofactors C and its transpose C' [which is adj(A)] are

$$
C = \begin{bmatrix} 1 & -1 & -1 \\ 1 & 1 & -3 \\ -1 & -1 & 5 \end{bmatrix} \quad \text{and} \quad C' = \text{adj}(A) = \begin{bmatrix} 1 & 1 & -1 \\ -1 & 1 & -1 \\ -1 & -3 & 5 \end{bmatrix} \tag{8-69}
$$

Multiplying the adjoint of A by $1/|A|$ produces the inverse of A, A^{-1}:

$$
A^{-1} = \frac{C'}{|A|} = \begin{bmatrix} \frac{1}{2} & \frac{1}{2} & -\frac{1}{2} \\ -\frac{1}{2} & \frac{1}{2} & -\frac{1}{2} \\ -\frac{1}{2} & -\frac{3}{2} & \frac{5}{2} \end{bmatrix} \tag{8-70}
$$

Let us check our inverse matrix to make sure we did it correctly. The product of a matrix and its inverse equals an identity matrix.

$$
A^{-1}A = \begin{bmatrix} \frac{1}{2} & \frac{1}{2} & -\frac{1}{2} \\ -\frac{1}{2} & \frac{1}{2} & -\frac{1}{2} \\ -\frac{1}{2} & -\frac{3}{2} & \frac{5}{2} \end{bmatrix} \begin{bmatrix} 1 & -1 & 0 \\ 3 & 2 & 1 \\ 2 & 1 & 1 \end{bmatrix} = \begin{bmatrix} 1 & 0 & 0 \\ 0 & 1 & 0 \\ 0 & 0 & 1 \end{bmatrix} = I_3 \tag{8-71}
$$

The solution vector of the system of linear equations equals $X = A^{-1}C$. Therefore, to find the solution we must premultiply the vector of constants by the inverse matrix of coefficients.

$$
\begin{bmatrix} X_1 \\ X_2 \\ X_3 \end{bmatrix} = \begin{bmatrix} \frac{1}{2} & \frac{1}{2} & -\frac{1}{2} \\ -\frac{1}{2} & \frac{1}{2} & -\frac{1}{2} \\ -\frac{1}{2} & -\frac{3}{2} & \frac{5}{2} \end{bmatrix} \begin{bmatrix} 2 \\ 4 \\ 6 \end{bmatrix} = \begin{bmatrix} 0 \\ -2 \\ 8 \end{bmatrix} \tag{8-72}
$$

Consider the same system of four linear equations in four unknowns that we used in the exercises at the end of Section 8.5.2.

$$2X_1 + X_2 - X_4 = 1$$
$$X_1 + X_2 = X_3 + X_4$$
$$X_1 = (2X_2 + 3X_3 + 4X_4 + 6)/2$$
$$X_2 - X_4 - 2X_1$$

Use the inverse-matrix approach to find the solution values of X_1, X_2, X_3, and X_4, if they exist.

8.6.2   Cramer's Rule

An alternative approach to solving systems of linear equations is to use Cramer's rule. This rule is derived from the method of matrix inversion, but, unlike that method, Cramer's rule yields the solution value of only one endogenous variable at a time. An advantage of using Cramer's rule is that, although it is derived from the matrix inversion method, in practice it bypasses the process of matrix inversion.

Cramer's rule allows us to solve for individual elements of the vector X in the matrix equation $AX = C$, where A is an $n \times n$ matrix of coefficients, X is an $n \times 1$ vector of unknowns, and C is an $n \times 1$ vector of constant terms. Cramer's rule gives us the following solution:

$$x_j = \frac{|A_j|}{|A|}, \qquad j = 1, 2, \ldots, n \tag{8-73}$$

where $|A_j|$ is a determinant obtained from the original determinant $|A|$ by replacing its jth column with the column vector of the constants. Note that the condition $|A| \neq 0$ is required for the application of Cramer's rule. Here is how Cramer's rule works in words. To solve for the element in the kth *row* of X, create a determinant by replacing the kth *column* of the matrix A with the vector C. Divide the determinant you have created by the determinant of the unaltered matrix A.

Let's use Cramer's rule in a number of familiar contexts. First, we will use it to solve the numerical example of a system of linear equations we looked at when introducing determinants. We said in Section 8.4.1 that the two equations

$$X + 2Y = 5 \tag{8-74}$$
$$3X + Y = 7.5 \tag{8-75}$$

were linearly independent and so could be solved for X and Y. They can be expressed as a matrix equation as follows:

$$\begin{bmatrix} 1 & 2 \\ 3 & 1 \end{bmatrix} \begin{bmatrix} X \\ Y \end{bmatrix} = \begin{bmatrix} 5 \\ 7.5 \end{bmatrix} \tag{8-76}$$

Cramer's rule tells us that, to solve for X, we create a determinant by replacing the first column of the matrix of coefficients with the vector of constants and divide it by the unaltered determinant of the matrix of coefficients. To solve for Y, create the numerator by replacing the second column of the matrix of coefficients with the vector of constants.

$$X = \frac{\begin{vmatrix} 5 & 2 \\ 7.5 & 1 \end{vmatrix}}{\begin{vmatrix} 1 & 2 \\ 3 & 1 \end{vmatrix}} = \frac{-10}{-5} = 2 \quad \text{and} \quad Y = \frac{\begin{vmatrix} 1 & 5 \\ 3 & 7.5 \end{vmatrix}}{\begin{vmatrix} 1 & 2 \\ 3 & 1 \end{vmatrix}} = \frac{-7.5}{-5} = 1.5 \quad (8\text{-}77)$$

You may verify for yourself that Cramer's rule has given us the correct answers.

Next, let's use Cramer's rule to solve the system of simultaneous equations that gave us comparative statics results for the model of the perfectly competitive profit-maximizing firm with two inputs that we examined in Chapter 6, Section 6.4. Remember the objective function, equation (6-47), the FOC, equations (6-48) and (6-49), and the SOC, equations (6-52) through (6-54) from this model. We reproduce them for your convenience.

$$\pi = Pf(K, L) - rK - wL \qquad (6\text{-}47)$$

$$\pi_K = Pf_K - r = 0 \Leftrightarrow Pf_K = \text{VMP}_K = r \qquad (6\text{-}48)$$

$$\pi_L = Pf_L - w = 0 \Leftrightarrow Pf_L = \text{VMP}_L = w \qquad (6\text{-}49)$$

$$\pi_{KK} = Pf_{KK} < 0 \qquad (6\text{-}52)$$

$$\pi_{LL} = Pf_{LL} < 0 \qquad (6\text{-}53)$$

$$\pi_{KK}\pi_{LL} - \pi_{KL}^2 = P^2(f_{KK}f_{LL} - f_{KL}^2) > 0 \qquad (6\text{-}54)$$

In order to perform comparative statics analysis we substituted into the FOC equilibrium values for K and L to generate identities which we could differentiate with respect to the parameters. Differentiating with respect to the parameter r gave us equations (6-64) and (6-65),

$$Pf_{KK}\frac{\partial K^*}{\partial r} + Pf_{KL}\frac{\partial L^*}{\partial r} - 1 \equiv 0 \qquad (6\text{-}64)$$

$$Pf_{LK}\frac{\partial K^*}{\partial r} + Pf_{LL}\frac{\partial L^*}{\partial r} \equiv 0 \qquad (6\text{-}65)$$

As you can see, these make up a system of two linear equations in two unknowns: $\partial K^*/\partial r$ and $\partial L^*/\partial r$. Add 1 to both sides of equation (6-64) and express this system as the matrix equation

$$\begin{bmatrix} Pf_{KK} & Pf_{KL} \\ Pf_{LK} & Pf_{LL} \end{bmatrix} \begin{bmatrix} \dfrac{\partial K^*}{\partial r} \\[2mm] \dfrac{\partial L^*}{\partial r} \end{bmatrix} = \begin{bmatrix} 1 \\ 0 \end{bmatrix} \qquad (8\text{-}78)$$

We can use Cramer's rule to solve this matrix equation, obtaining

$$\frac{\partial K^*}{\partial r} = \frac{\begin{vmatrix} 1 & Pf_{KL} \\ 0 & Pf_{LL} \end{vmatrix}}{\begin{vmatrix} Pf_{KK} & Pf_{KL} \\ Pf_{LK} & Pf_{LL} \end{vmatrix}} = \frac{Pf_{LL}}{P^2(f_{KK}\, f_{LL} - f_{LK}^2)} \tag{8-79}$$

and

$$\frac{\partial L^*}{\partial r} = \frac{\begin{vmatrix} Pf_{KK} & 1 \\ Pf_{LK} & 0 \end{vmatrix}}{\begin{vmatrix} Pf_{KK} & Pf_{KL} \\ Pf_{LK} & Pf_{LL} \end{vmatrix}} = -\frac{Pf_{LK}}{P^2(f_{KK}\, f_{LL} - f_{LK}^2)} \tag{8-80}$$

Notice the denominators in these comparative statics results obtained by applying Cramer's rule to the profit-maximization model. They are equal to the determinant of the matrix of coefficients, which also appears in the second-order conditions of the model. This is no accident. It turns out that it is convenient and easy to express second-order conditions of optimization models in determinant form. This ease and convenience become evident when models with more than two independent variables are discussed. We turn to this topic next.

EXERCISE
Section 8.6.2
Cramer's Rule

Consider the same system of four linear equations in four unknowns that we need in the exercises at the end of Section 8.6.1,

$$2X_1 + X_2 - X_4 = 1$$
$$X_1 + X_2 = X_3 + X_4$$
$$X_1 = (2X_2 + 3X_3 + 4X_4 + 6)/2$$
$$X_2 - X_4 = 2X_1$$

Use Cramer's rule to find the solutions for X_1, X_2, X_3, and X_4.

8.7

MATRIX REPRESENTATION OF SECOND-ORDER CONDITIONS

Compare the objective function and the matrix of coefficients in the preceding profit-maximizing example.

$$\pi = Pf(K, L) - rK - wK \tag{6-47}$$

$$H = \begin{bmatrix} Pf_{KK} & Pf_{KL} \\ Pf_{LK} & Pf_{LL} \end{bmatrix} \qquad (8\text{-}81)$$

Notice that the matrix of coefficients, which we have labeled as the matrix H, can be generated by taking the second-order partials of the objective function and ordering them as follows.

$$H = \begin{bmatrix} \pi_{KK} & \pi_{KL} \\ \pi_{LK} & \pi_{LL} \end{bmatrix} \qquad (8\text{-}82)$$

Hessian matrix: the matrix of second-order partial derivatives of an objective function.

naturally ordered principal minors: principal minors of ascending order k that start with the upper left diagonal element and include k contiguous rows and columns. Alternatively, they may start with the lower right diagonal element.

diagonal elements: the elements whose row and column indices are the same, i.e., $a_{11}, a_{22}, \ldots, a_{nn}$.

We call the matrix of second-order partials of an objective function the **Hessian matrix**. Because $\pi_{KL} = \pi_{LK}$, the matrix H is symmetrical about the principal diagonal. We can express the second-order conditions of an optimization problem in terms of the determinant of the Hessian matrix and its **naturally ordered principal minors**.

Recall what a minor of a determinant is. It is the subdeterminant obtained when rows and columns associated with a given element are deleted from the original determinant. *Principal minors* are the minors associated with **diagonal elements**, that is, the elements whose row and column indices are the same: $a_{11}, a_{22}, \ldots, a_{nn}$. The order of a principal minor is its dimension. Note that an $n \times n$ determinant has many principal minors. The first-order principal minors are those obtained by eliminating $n - 1$ identically numbered rows and columns from the original determinant. There will be n of them, and they will be simply the diagonal elements themselves.

The second-order principal minors are obtained by eliminating $n - 2$ identically numbered rows and columns from the original determinant, the third-order principal minors are obtained by eliminating $n - 3$ identically numbered row and columns, and so forth. The naturally ordered principal minors of order k are those that start with the upper left diagonal element and include k contiguous rows and columns.[2] The $n \times n$ determinant $|A|$ has the following naturally ordered principal minors. Note that the last of the naturally ordered principal minors is the original determinant itself, $|A|$.

$$|a_{11}|, \begin{vmatrix} a_{11} & a_{12} \\ a_{21} & a_{22} \end{vmatrix}, \begin{vmatrix} a_{11} & a_{12} & a_{13} \\ a_{21} & a_{22} & a_{23} \\ a_{31} & a_{32} & a_{33} \end{vmatrix}, \ldots, \begin{vmatrix} a_{11} & a_{12} & \cdots & a_{1n} \\ a_{21} & a_{22} & \cdots & a_{2n} \\ \vdots & \vdots & \vdots & \vdots \\ a_{n1} & a_{n2} & \cdots & a_{nn} \end{vmatrix} \qquad (8\text{-}83)$$

Recall that we signify minors of a determinant, $|A|$, with the notation $|A_{ij}|$, where i and j represent the element associated with the minor or, alternatively, the indices of the crossed-out row and column from $|A|$. Minors of lower order, that eliminate more than one row and column, are denoted with subscripts that indicate all the eliminated rows and columns. Therefore,

---

[2]It does not matter whether you start at the upper left corner and work your way down to the lower right, or start at the lower right corner and work your way up to the upper left, when determining the naturally ordered principal minors.

$|A_{34,34}|$ indicates the minor created by eliminating rows 3 and 4 and columns 3 and 4 from $|A|$.

Now that you know what the Hessian matrix is and what its naturally ordered principal minors are, it is easy to describe second-order conditions of optimization models with any number of choice variables. First we look at unconstrained optimization models.

8.7.1   Unconstrained Optimization

Recall from Chapter 6, Section 6.2, the unconstrained optimization of models with two choice variables. Our objective function was

$$Y = f(X_1, X_2) \tag{6-1}$$

and our second-order conditions were demonstrated to be

I. $dX_2 = 0$: $d^2Y = f_{11}dX_1^2 \begin{smallmatrix} < \\ > \end{smallmatrix} 0$ if $f_{11} \begin{smallmatrix} < \\ > \end{smallmatrix} 0$ $\begin{smallmatrix} \text{for a maximum} \\ \text{for a minimum} \end{smallmatrix}$ $\tag{6-6}$

II. $dX_1 = 0$: $d^2Y = f_{22}dX_2^2 \begin{smallmatrix} < \\ > \end{smallmatrix} 0$ if $f_{22} \begin{smallmatrix} < \\ > \end{smallmatrix} 0$ $\begin{smallmatrix} \text{for a maximum} \\ \text{for a minimum} \end{smallmatrix}$ $\tag{6-7}$

III. $dX_2, dX_1 > 0$: $f_{11}f_{22} - f_{12}^2 > 0$ for a maximum and a minimum $\tag{6-8}$

We can express the second-order conditions of this model, as well as all unconstrained optimization models generally, in terms of the determinant of the Hessian matrix and its principal minors.

> For an unconstrained optimization model, the second-order conditions for *maximization* require that the naturally ordered principal minors of dimension *m* of the determinant of the Hessian matrix of second partial derivatives have the sign $(-1)^m$. The second-order conditions for *minimization* require that the naturally ordered principal minors of the determinant of the Hessian matrix all be positive.

For maximization, this implies that starting with the first diagonal element, which must be negative, as the dimension of a principal minor increases by 1, the principal minors alternate in sign. For a minimization, all principal minors of any dimension are positive. The Hessian matrix for the objective function, equation (6-1), is

$$H = \begin{bmatrix} f_{11} & f_{12} \\ f_{21} & f_{22} \end{bmatrix} \tag{8-84}$$

Its naturally ordered principal minors are

$$|f_{11}| \quad \text{and} \quad \begin{vmatrix} f_{11} & f_{12} \\ f_{21} & f_{22} \end{vmatrix} \tag{8-85}$$

The first-order principal minor is $|f_{11}| = f_{11}$, and the second-order principal minor is $f_{11}f_{22} - f_{12}^2$. For a maximum, the first-order principal minor must have the sign $(-1)^1$; that is, it must be negative. The second-order principal minor must have the sign $(-1)^2$; that is, it must be positive. For a minimum, both naturally ordered principal minors must be positive.

Note that if $f_{11} < 0$ and $f_{11}f_{22} - f_{12}^2 > 0$, then f_{22} must be negative. Similarly, if $f_{11} > 0$ and $f_{11}f_{22} - f_{12}^2 > 0$, then f_{22} must be positive. In this case, as well as in the case of the constrained optimization discussed in Section 8.7.2, if the naturally ordered principal minors have the appropriate signs for optimization, then *all* principal minors of the same order have the same sign as the naturally ordered principal minor. As you can see, f_{22} is the other first-order principal minor of the preceding two-variable model, and it has the same sign as f_{11}, the naturally ordered principal minor of order 1. Our determinant-based rules for second-order conditions are the same as those we found in Chapter 6.

We suggested that the Hessian matrix for the two-input profit maximization model is

$$H = \begin{bmatrix} Pf_{KK} & Pf_{KL} \\ Pf_{LK} & Pf_{LL} \end{bmatrix} \tag{8-86}$$

Its naturally ordered principal minors are $|Pf_{KK}|$ and the determinant of the Hessian matrix itself. Our second-order conditions suggest that $Pf_{KK} < 0$ and $P^2[f_{KK}f_{LL} - f_{KL}^2] > 0$. Taken together, these imply that $Pf_{LL} < 0$.

NUMERICAL EXAMPLE

Suppose a firm is a price-taker in both its input markets and its output market, facing the profit function,

$$\pi(K, L) = Pf(K, L) - wL - rK = PL^{1/4}K^{1/4} - wL - rK \tag{8-87}$$

The first-order conditions are

$$\pi_K = (P/4)L^{1/4}K^{-3/4} - r = 0 \tag{8-88}$$

$$\pi_L = (P/4)L^{-3/4}K^{1/4} - w = 0 \tag{8-89}$$

The Hessian matrix of second partial derivatives of the profit function, (8-87), is

$$H = \begin{bmatrix} -\frac{3}{16}PL^{1/4}K^{-7/4} & \frac{1}{16}PL^{-3/4}K^{-3/4} \\ \frac{1}{16}PL^{-3/4}K^{-3/4} & -\frac{3}{16}PL^{-7/4}K^{1/4} \end{bmatrix} \tag{8-90}$$

The naturally ordered principal minors of the determinant of the Hessian matrix are

$$\left| -\frac{3}{16}PL^{1/4}K^{-7/4} \right| \quad \text{and} \quad \begin{bmatrix} -\frac{3}{16}PL^{1/4}K^{-7/4} & \frac{1}{16}PL^{-3/4}K^{-3/4} \\ \frac{1}{16}PL^{-3/4}K^{-3/4} & -\frac{3}{16}PL^{-7/4}K^{1/4} \end{bmatrix} \tag{8-91}$$

When we evaluate the determinants we find that, for positive values of P, K, and L, $Pf_{KK} = -(3/16)PL^{1/4}K^{-7/4} < 0$ and $P^2[f_{KK}f_{LL} - f_{KL}^2] = (1/32)P^2L^{-3/2}K^{-3/2} > 0$. We also see by inspection that the other first-order principal minor is negative, $Pf_{LL} = -(3/16)PL^{-7/4}K^{1/4} < 0$.

We stated in Section 6.5 at the end of Chapter 6 that the second-order conditions of unconstrained optimization models with many independent variables are most easily expressed with the help of matrix algebra. Now, we see how to do it. Suppose we want to optimize the function

$$Y = f(X_1, X_2, \ldots, X_n) \tag{8-92}$$

We know that the first-order conditions require us to set all first partials equal to zero.

$$f_1 = 0 \tag{8-93}$$
$$f_2 = 0$$
$$\vdots$$
$$f_n = 0$$

We find the elements of each row of the Hessian matrix by differentiating each FOC by each independent variable in turn, generating

$$\begin{bmatrix} f_{11} & f_{12} & f_{13} & \cdots & f_{1n} \\ f_{21} & f_{22} & f_{23} & \cdots & f_{2n} \\ f_{31} & f_{32} & f_{33} & \cdots & f_{3n} \\ \vdots & \vdots & \vdots & \vdots & \vdots \\ f_{n1} & f_{n2} & f_{n3} & \cdots & f_{nn} \end{bmatrix} \tag{8-94}$$

The second-order conditions of this generalized, n-dimensional unconstrained optimization problem can be expressed in terms of the naturally ordered principal minors of the determinant of the Hessian matrix. For a maximization, all naturally ordered principal minors of dimension m must have the sign $(-1)^m$. Therefore,

$$|f_{11}| < 0, \quad \begin{vmatrix} f_{11} & f_{12} \\ f_{21} & f_{22} \end{vmatrix} > 0, \quad \begin{vmatrix} f_{11} & f_{12} & f_{13} \\ f_{21} & f_{22} & f_{23} \\ f_{31} & f_{32} & f_{33} \end{vmatrix} < 0, \ldots,$$

$$\begin{vmatrix} f_{11} & f_{12} & f_{13} & \cdots & f_{1n} \\ f_{21} & f_{22} & f_{23} & \cdots & f_{2n} \\ f_{31} & f_{32} & f_{33} & \cdots & f_{3n} \\ \vdots & \vdots & \vdots & \vdots & \vdots \\ f_{n1} & f_{n2} & f_{n3} & \cdots & f_{nn} \end{vmatrix} \text{ has sign } (-1)^n \tag{8-95}$$

For a minimization, all the naturally ordered principal minors must be positive. Once again, all principal minors of dimension m are assured to have the same sign as the naturally ordered principal minor of the same dimension.

We have illustrated that you can express the second-order conditions for optimization of unconstrained optimization in determinant form. Our next task is to express the second-order conditions for constrained optimization problems in a similar manner.

**EXERCISES
Section 8.7.1
Unconstrained
Optimization**

For each of the following unconstrained optimization problems, find the Hessian matrix of second partial derivatives. Express the second-order conditions for optimization in terms of the principal minors of the determinant of the Hessian matrix, and determine whether the SOC indicate a maximum, a minimum, or neither.

1. $Y = f(X_1, X_2) = 10 + 20X_1 - 2X_1^2 + 16X_2 - X_2^2 - 2X_1X_2$
2. $Y = f(X_1, X_2, X_3) = -100X_3 - 5X_1X_3 + 4X_1^2 - 9X_2 + 4X_3^2 + 5X_2^2 + 8X_1X_2$
3. $\pi = \pi(K, L, M) = 25K^{1/5}L^{1/5}M^{2/5} - 10L - 5K - 20M$

8.7.2   Constrained Optimization

Consider the example of constrained optimization from Chapter 7, Section 7.2.2, utility maximization subject to a budget constraint. The problem is to maximize a utility function, $U(X_1, X_2)$, subject to a budget constraint, $M - P_1X_1 - P_2X_2 = 0$. We express our objective function as the Lagrangian

$$\mathcal{L}(X_1, X_2, \mu) = U(X_1, X_2) + \mu[M - P_1X_1 - P_2X_2] \qquad \text{(7-21)}$$

The FOC for maximization are

$$\mathcal{L}_1 = U_1 - \mu P_1 = 0 \qquad \text{(7-22)}$$

$$\mathcal{L}_2 = U_2 - \mu P_2 = 0 \qquad \text{(7-23)}$$

$$\mathcal{L}_\mu = M - P_1X_1 - P_2X_2 = 0 \qquad \text{(7-24)}$$

Remember that the Hessian matrix is the matrix of second-order partial derivatives of the objective function. In this case, the Lagrangian is our objective function. Remember also that we treat the Lagrange multiplier as a choice variable along with X_1 and X_2, so we must find the second partial derivatives with respect to X_1, X_2, and μ in order to generate the Hessian matrix. One easy way to find the second partials is to differentiate each first-order condition with respect to each choice variable in turn. The elements in the first row of the Hessian matrix are the derivatives of equation (7-22) with respect to X_1, X_2, and μ, respectively. The elements of the second row of the Hessian are the derivatives of equation (7-23) with respect to X_1, X_2, and μ, respectively. The elements of the third row of the Hessian are the derivatives of the constraint, equation (7-24), with respect to X_1, X_2, and μ, respectively.

$$H_B = \begin{bmatrix} \mathscr{L}_{11} & \mathscr{L}_{12} & \mathscr{L}_{1\mu} \\ \mathscr{L}_{21} & \mathscr{L}_{22} & \mathscr{L}_{2\mu} \\ \mathscr{L}_{\mu 1} & \mathscr{L}_{\mu 2} & \mathscr{L}_{\mu\mu} \end{bmatrix} = \begin{bmatrix} U_{11} & U_{12} & -P_1 \\ U_{21} & U_{22} & -P_2 \\ -P_1 & -P_2 & 0 \end{bmatrix} \quad (8\text{-}96)$$

bordered Hessian matrix: the Hessian matrix for a constrained optimization, in which the second partials involving the Lagrange multiplier make up the borders.

The Hessian matrix for a constrained optimization is called a *bordered Hessian matrix*, where the second partials involving the Lagrange multiplier make up the borders, and is denoted with a subscript B. Although we have written the bordered Hessian matrix in such a way that the borders are the last column and row, it need not be that way. Had we differentiated our Lagrangian objective function first with respect to μ and then with respect to X_1 and X_2, the border of the bordered Hessian would be the first column and row. Our second-order conditions can be expressed in terms of the naturally ordered principal minors of the bordered Hessian.

> For a constrained optimization model in which the number of constraints equals *r*, the second-order conditions for *maximization* require that the naturally ordered *border-preserving* principal minors of dimension *m* of the determinant of the bordered Hessian matrix have the sign $(-1)^{m-r}$. The second-order conditions for *minimization* require that the naturally ordered *border-preserving* principal minors of dimension *m* of the determinant of the bordered Hessian matrix have the sign $(-1)^r$. For both maximization and minimization, consider only principal minors of dimension $1 + 2r$ and greater.

border-preserving principal minor: a principal minor not associated with an element that belongs to the border of a bordered Hessian.

This description of the second-order conditions for constrained optimization models is sufficiently novel and complicated to need further explanation. Let's consider the concept of a *border-preserving principal minor*. It means exactly what it sounds like, a principal minor that preserves the border. The second-order conditions for constrained optimization do not impose signs on principal minors which are obtained by eliminating the border rows and columns; that is, they refer only to border-preserving principal minors.[3] For example, the determinant

$$\begin{vmatrix} U_{11} & U_{12} \\ U_{21} & U_{22} \end{vmatrix} \quad (8\text{-}97)$$

is a principal minor of the determinant of the bordered Hessian we obtained from the constrained utility maximization model. It is not, however, a border-

---

[3]Remember from Chapter 7, Section 7.2.2, that, although we treat the Lagrange multiplier as a choice variable when we find the first-order conditions, the economic agent (in this case, the consumer) does not choose optimizing values of the Lagrange multiplier. The second-order conditions for optimization do not impose signs on the border-eliminating principal minor, $|H_{33}|$, because that is the minor involving the second-order partial derivatives of the Lagrangian with respect to the Lagrange multiplier.

preserving principal minor, and the second-order conditions tell us nothing about its sign.

Our constrained utility maximization model has only one constraint, the budget constraint, and one Lagrange multiplier. Given that r equals 1, what is the rule about second-order conditions in this model? The determinant of the bordered Hessian is

$$|H_B| = \begin{vmatrix} U_{11} & U_{12} & -P_1 \\ U_{21} & U_{22} & -P_2 \\ -P_1 & -P_2 & 0 \end{vmatrix} > 0 \qquad (8\text{-}98)$$

It must be positive because our rule says it should have the same sign as $(-1)^{3-1} = 1$. Evaluating the determinant and remembering that $U_1 = \mu P_1$ and $U_2 = \mu P_2$ gives us

$$\begin{vmatrix} U_{11} & U_{22} & -P_1 \\ U_{21} & U_{22} & -P_2 \\ -P_1 & -P_2 & 0 \end{vmatrix} = -P_1(-P_2 U_{21} + P_1 U_{22}) + P_2(-U_{11}P_2 + P_1 U_{12})$$

$$= \frac{1}{\mu^2} [-U_1^2 U_{22} + 2U_1 U_2 U_{21} - U_2^2 U_{11}] > 0 \qquad (8\text{-}99)$$

Compare this result with the second-order condition we found in equation (7-11) in Chapter 7, Section 7.2.1, and you will see that the same condition is imposed on the utility function. This is the familiar requirement that indifference curves be convex. There are no other second-order conditions for this model because there are no more border-preserving principal minors of dimension 3 or greater.

We summarize the determinantal representation of the second-order conditions of both unconstrained and constrained optimization models in Table 8.1. Note that the rule for unconstrained optimization corresponds to the column in which the number of constraints equals zero.

Table 8.1 Second-Order Conditions in Terms of Signs of Principal Minors of Dimension m of the Hessian Matrix

	Number of Constraints		
	0	1	r
Maximization	$(-1)^m$	$(-1)^{m-1}, m \geq 3$	$(-1)^{m-r}, m \geq 1 + 2r$
Minimization	$(-1)^0 > 0$	$(-1)^1 < 0, m \geq 3$	$(-1)^r, m \geq 1 + 2r$

TWO NUMERICAL EXAMPLES

1. Cost Minimization Subject to a Given Level of Output

A firm is a price-taker in both its output and input markets. Its production function is

$$Q = L^{0.75}K^{0.25} \tag{8-100}$$

The firm wishes to produce 100 units of output using a combination of inputs of labor, L, and capital, K, that minimize total production cost, $TC = wL + rK$. Labor's wage is $w = 15$ and the price of capital is $r = 5$.

The Lagrangian for this constrained cost-minimization problem is

$$\mathscr{L} = 15L + 5K + \mu(100 - L^{0.75}K^{0.25}) \tag{8-101}$$

The first-order conditions for minimization are

$$\mathscr{L}_L = 15 - 0.75\mu L^{-0.25}K^{0.25} = 0 \tag{8-102}$$

$$\mathscr{L}_K = 5 - 0.25\mu L^{0.75}K^{-0.75} = 0 \tag{8-103}$$

$$\mathscr{L}_\mu = 100 - L^{0.75}K^{0.25} = 0 \tag{8-104}$$

The solution values are $L^* = K^* = 100$ and $\mu^* = 20$.

You should verify that the bordered Hessian matrix associated with this problem is

$$|H_B| = \begin{bmatrix} 0.0375 & -0.0375 & -0.750 \\ -0.0375 & 0.0375 & -0.250 \\ -0.750 & -0.250 & 0 \end{bmatrix} \tag{8-105}$$

Given that our example involves one constraint, all the second-order condition for minimization requires is that the determinant of the bordered Hessian matrix be negative. If you use the Laplace method to expand this determinant, you will find $|H_B| = -0.0375$, ensuring that we have actually located a local minimum of the objective function.

2. Constrained Utility Maximization with Three Goods

A consumer maximizes the utility function $U = \ln X_1 + 2(\ln X_2) + 3(\ln X_3)$, subject to the budget constraint $X_1 + 2X_2 + 3X_3 = 6$. The Lagrangian objective function is

$$\mathscr{L} = \ln X_1 + 2(\ln X_2) + 3(\ln X_3) + \mu(6 - X_1 - 2X_2 - 3X_3) \tag{8-106}$$

The first-order necessary conditions are

$$\mathscr{L}_1 = 1/X_1 - \mu = 0 \tag{8-107}$$

$$\mathscr{L}_2 = 2/X_2 - 2\mu = 0 \tag{8-108}$$

$$\mathscr{L}_3 = 3/X_3 - 3\mu = 0 \tag{8-109}$$

$$\mathscr{L}_\mu = 6 - X_1 - 2X_2 - 3X_3 = 0 \tag{8-110}$$

The solution values are $X_1^* = X_2^* = X_3^* = \mu^* = 1$. The bordered Hessian matrix of second partial derivatives of $\mathscr{L}$ is

$$H_B = \begin{bmatrix} -1 & 0 & 0 & -1 \\ 0 & -2 & 0 & -2 \\ 0 & 0 & -3 & -3 \\ -1 & -2 & -3 & 0 \end{bmatrix} \qquad (8\text{-}111)$$

With four choice variables, two naturally ordered border-preserving principal minors of dimension 3 or greater are defined. The 3×3 naturally ordered principal minor is

$$|H_{11}| = \begin{vmatrix} -2 & 0 & -2 \\ 0 & -3 & -3 \\ -2 & -3 & 0 \end{vmatrix} = 30 \qquad (8\text{-}112)$$

and the 4×4 determinant of the bordered Hessian matrix itself equals -36. These satisfy the second-order conditions for a maximum; the third-order principal minor determinant has the required $(-1)^{3-1} > 0$ sign and the principal minor of dimension four has the required $(-1)^{4-1} < 0$ sign.

EXERCISES
Section 8.7.2
Constrained
Optimization

For each of the following constrained optimization problems, find the bordered Hessian matrix of second partial derivatives. Express the second-order conditions for optimization in terms of the principal minors of the determinant of the bordered Hessian matrix, and determine whether the SOC indicate a maximum, a minimum, or neither.

1. $U = X_1 + 2X_1 X_2$ subject to $M = 100 = 2X_1 + 4X_2$

2. $Y = -\ln(X_1 + X_2)$ subject to $Z = 1 = X_1 X_2$

3. $C = 20L + 5K + 10M$ subject to $Q = 4 = K^{0.25} L^{0.25} M^{0.25}$

8.8

SUMMARY

Our purpose in this chapter is to review enough of the principles of matrix algebra to enable you to express a system of linear equations as a matrix equation, to determine when a solution exists and what that solution is, and to express the second-order conditions of optimization problems in determinant form. In order to accomplish this, we introduce the concepts of matrices and vectors and review the notational conventions of matrix algebra. We discuss the meaning of matrix multiplication and its properties. This leads us to brief discussions of other arithmetic operations in the context of matrices, namely addition and subtraction, and multiplication by a scalar.

We see that systems of linear equations require as many linearly independent equations as unknowns in order to have solutions, and we introduce the concept of a determinant to test for linear independence. Familiarity with determinants enables us to present Cramer's rule as a method for solving systems of linear equations. We illustrate the use of Cramer's rule with the profit-maximization model from Chapter 6 and notice a similarity between the determinant of the Hessian matrix and the second-order conditions. We show how to express second-order conditions in terms of principal minors of the Hessian matrix for both unconstrained and constrained optimization problems.

The combination of matrix algebra and optimization theory enables us to handle economic models of great generality and power relatively easily. We turn now to the use of these tools to develop the neo-classical model of consumer behavior in Chapter 9.

◆ REFERENCES

Chiang, Alpha C., *Fundamental Methods of Mathematical Economics*, 3rd edition (New York: McGraw-Hill Book Company, 1984), Chapters 4 and 5.

Hadley, G., *Linear Algebra* (Reading, MA: Addison-Wesley Publishing Company, 1961).

Silberberg, Eugene, *The Structure of Economics*, 2nd Edition (New York: McGraw-Hill Book Company, 1990), Chapter 5 and 6.

◆ ANSWERS TO END-OF-SECTION EXERCISES

Section 8.3.3 Scalar Multiplication

1. $A + B = \begin{bmatrix} 4 & 13 & 7 \\ 4 & 6 & -3 \\ 0 & 0 & 9 \end{bmatrix} = B + A$

2. $(A + B) + C = \begin{bmatrix} 5 & 13 & 7 \\ 3 & 8 & -2 \\ 0 & 0 & 10 \end{bmatrix} = A + (B + C)$

3. $A - B = \begin{bmatrix} 0 & -7 & -5 \\ -6 & -6 & 5 \\ 0 & -4 & -7 \end{bmatrix} = -B + A$

4. $AB = \begin{bmatrix} 19 & 40 & 8 \\ -2 & -8 & 2 \\ -10 & -10 & 16 \end{bmatrix} \neq \begin{bmatrix} -6 & -6 & 18 \\ 4 & 23 & 7 \\ -2 & -16 & 10 \end{bmatrix} = BA$

5. $(AB)C = \begin{bmatrix} 19 & 80 & 48 \\ -2 & -16 & -6 \\ -10 & -20 & 6 \end{bmatrix} = A(BC)$

6. $A(B + C) = \begin{bmatrix} 21 & 46 & 12 \\ -3 & -8 & 3 \\ -10 & -14 & 15 \end{bmatrix} = AB + AC$

7. $4A = \begin{bmatrix} 8 & 12 & 4 \\ -4 & 0 & 4 \\ 0 & -8 & 4 \end{bmatrix} = 2A + 2A$

Section 8.5.2 Properties of Determinants

1. **a.** 381   **b.** −228   **c.** 0

2. **a.** $AX = C = \begin{bmatrix} 2 & 1 & 0 & -1 \\ 1 & 1 & -1 & -1 \\ 1 & -1 & -1.5 & -2 \\ -2 & 1 & 0 & -1 \end{bmatrix} \begin{bmatrix} X_1 \\ X_2 \\ X_3 \\ X_4 \end{bmatrix} = \begin{bmatrix} 1 \\ 0 \\ 3 \\ 0 \end{bmatrix}$

   b. $|A| = \begin{vmatrix} 2 & 1 & 0 & -1 \\ 1 & 1 & -1 & -1 \\ 1 & -1 & -1.5 & -2 \\ -2 & 1 & 0 & -1 \end{vmatrix} = 12$

   Because $|A| \neq 0$, the system is linearly independent.

Section 8.6.1 The Inverse-Matrix Approach

$$X = \begin{bmatrix} X_1 \\ X_2 \\ X_3 \\ X_4 \end{bmatrix} = A^{-1}C = \begin{bmatrix} 0.250 & 0.000 & 0.000 & -0.250 \\ 0.042 & 0.500 & -0.333 & 0.125 \\ 0.750 & -1.000 & 0.000 & 0.250 \\ -0.485 & 0.500 & -0.333 & -0.375 \end{bmatrix} \begin{bmatrix} 1 \\ 0 \\ 3 \\ 0 \end{bmatrix}$$

$$= \begin{bmatrix} 0.250 \\ -0.958 \\ 0.750 \\ -1.458 \end{bmatrix}$$

Section 8.6.2 Cramer's Rule

$$X_1 = \frac{\begin{vmatrix} 1 & 1 & 0 & -1 \\ 0 & 1 & -1 & -1 \\ 3 & -1 & -1.5 & -2 \\ 0 & 1 & 0 & -1 \end{vmatrix}}{|A|} = \frac{3}{12} = 0.250$$

$$X_2 = \frac{\begin{vmatrix} 2 & 1 & 0 & -1 \\ 1 & 0 & -1 & -1 \\ 1 & 3 & -1.5 & -2 \\ -2 & 0 & 0 & -1 \end{vmatrix}}{|A|} = -\frac{11.5}{12} = -0.958$$

$$X_3 = \frac{\begin{vmatrix} 2 & 1 & 1 & -1 \\ 1 & 1 & 0 & -1 \\ 1 & -1 & 3 & -2 \\ -2 & 1 & 0 & -1 \end{vmatrix}}{|A|} = \frac{9}{12} = 0.750$$

$$X_4 = \frac{\begin{vmatrix} 2 & 1 & 0 & 1 \\ 1 & 1 & -1 & 0 \\ 1 & -1 & -1.5 & 3 \\ -2 & 1 & 0 & 0 \end{vmatrix}}{|A|} = -\frac{17.5}{12} = -1.458$$

Section 8.7.1 Unconstrained Optimization

1. $$H = \begin{bmatrix} -4 & -2 \\ -2 & -2 \end{bmatrix}; |H_{11}| = -4 < 0, |H| = 4 > 0$$

indicates a maximum.

2. $$H = \begin{bmatrix} 8 & 8 & -5 \\ 8 & 10 & 0 \\ -5 & 0 & 8 \end{bmatrix}; |H_{23,23}| = 8 > 0, |H_{33}| = 16 > 0, |H| = -122 > 0$$

indicates neither a maximum nor a minimum.

3.

$$H = \begin{bmatrix} -4K^{-9/5}L^{1/5}M^{2/5} & K^{-4/5}L^{-4/5}M^{2/5} & 2K^{-4/5}L^{1/5}M^{-3/5} \\ K^{-4/5}L^{-4/5}M^{2/5} & -4K^{1/5}L^{-9/5}M^{2/5} & 2K^{1/5}L^{-4/5}M^{-3/5} \\ 2K^{-4/5}L^{1/5}M^{-3/5} & 2K^{1/5}L^{-4/5}M^{-3/5} & -6K^{1/5}L^{1/5}M^{-8/5} \end{bmatrix}$$

$$|H_{23,23}| = -4K^{-9/5}L^{1/5}M^{2/5} < 0, \quad |H_{33}| = 15K^{-8/5}L^{-8/5}M^{4/5} > 0,$$
$$|H| = -50K^{-7/5}L^{-7/5}M^{-4/5} < 0$$

indicates a maximum

Section 8.7.2 Constrained Optimization

1.

$$H_B = \begin{bmatrix} 0 & 2 & -2 \\ 2 & 0 & -4 \\ -2 & -4 & 0 \end{bmatrix}; \quad |H_B| = 32 > 0$$

indicates a maximum.

2.

$$H_B = \begin{bmatrix} \dfrac{1}{(X_1 + X_2)^2} & \dfrac{1}{(X_1 + X_2)^2} - \mu^* & -X_2 \\ \dfrac{1}{(X_1 + X_2)^2} - \mu^* & \dfrac{1}{(X_1 + X_2)^2} & -X_1 \\ -X_2 & -X_1 & 0 \end{bmatrix}; \quad |H_B| = -2 \text{ because } X_1^* = X_2^* = \mu^* = 1$$

indicates neither a maximum nor a minimum.

3.

$$H = \begin{bmatrix} .1875\mu K^{.25}L^{-1.75}M^{.25} & -.0625\mu K^{-.75}L^{-.75}M^{.25} & -.0625\mu K^{.25}L^{-.75}M^{-.75} & -.25K^{.25}L^{-.75}M^{.25} \\ -.0625\mu K^{-.75}L^{-.75}K^{.25} & .1875\mu K^{-1.75}L^{.25}M^{.25} & -.0625\mu K^{-.75}L^{.25}M^{-.75} & -.25K^{-.75}L^{.25}M^{.25} \\ -.0625\mu K^{.25}L^{-.75}M^{-.75} & -.0625\mu K^{-.75}L^{.25}M^{-.75} & .1875\mu K^{.25}L^{.25}M^{-1.75} & -.25K^{.25}L^{.25}M^{-.75} \\ -.25K^{.25}L^{-.75}M^{.25} & -.25K^{-.75}L^{.25}M^{.25} & -.25K^{.25}L^{.25}M^{-.75} & 0 \end{bmatrix}$$

$$|H_{11}| < 0, \quad |H| < 0$$

indicates a minimum.

◆ SELF-HELP PROBLEMS

Answers to these problems are given at the end of the text.

1. Consider a profit-maximizing firm with the following production function:
$$Q = f(X_1, X_2) = AX_1^\alpha X_2^B$$
The firm is a price-taker in both input markets and its output market. It faces an output price P and input prices w_1 and w_2.

a. Find the objective function for this firm, the first-order conditions, and the Hessian matrix of second partial derivatives.

b. Express the second-order conditions for profit maximization in terms of the principal minors of the determinant of the Hessian matrix.

c. Derive a system of linear equations (expressed as a matrix equation) which will permit you to solve for

$$\frac{\partial X_1^*}{\partial w_1} \quad \text{and} \quad \frac{\partial X_2^*}{\partial w_1}$$

d. Use Cramer's rule to solve your system of equations. Interpret your results.

2. Consider a consumer who wishes to maximize $U = U(X_1, X_2, X_3)$ subject to the budget constraint $M - P_1X_1 - P_2X_2 - P_3X_3$.

a. Set up the Lagrangian objective function and find the FOC for maximization.

b. Find the bordered Hessian matrix for this constrained optimization problem and express the SOC in terms of the border-preserving principal minors of the determinant of the bordered Hessian.

3. A consumer chooses the quantities of two goods, X_1 and X_2, so as to maximize $U = (0.5X_1^{-2} + 0.5X_2^{-2})^{-0.5}$ subject to $48X_1 + 6X_2 = 810$.

a. Set up the Lagrangian objective function and find the first-order conditions for maximization.

b. Find the optimum quantities of goods X_1 and X_2.

c. Find the bordered Hessian matrix for this constrained optimization problem and check the second-order conditions in terms of the border-preserving, principal minors of the determinant of the bordered Hessian.

4. Consider the following simple model of national income determination,

$$Y = C + I + G$$
$$C = 108 + 0.8Y_d$$
$$Y_d = Y - T$$
$$T = 10 + 0.25Y$$
$$I = 100 + 0.2Y$$
$$G = 400$$

a. Express this system of linear equations in the form of a matrix equation.

b. Show that the matrix equation in part a has a unique solution.

c. Use Cramer's rule to solve the matrix equation in part a for the equilibrium values of the endogenous variables.

d. Use the inverse-matrix approach to solve the matrix equation in part a for the equilibrium values of the endogenous variables.

5. Consider the following system of linear equations,

$$2X - Y - Z = 0$$
$$-X + 4Y - Z = 0$$
$$X + Y = 0$$

Equations of this type, in which all elements of the vector of constants are zero, are called *homogeneous* equations.

a. Show that the system has a unique solution.

b. Solve the system using matrix inversion.

c. Replace the matrix of coefficients associated with the system with *any* 3×3 nonsingular matrix but retain the vector of constants and solve the resulting system.

d. What conclusion do you draw from this exercise? Explain.

◆ SUPPLEMENTAL PROBLEMS

1. Consider the following linear model of a two-commodity market

$$Q_{d1}^* = a_0 + a_1 P_1^* + a_2 P_2^* = Q_{s1}^* = b_0 + b_1 P_1^* + b_2 P_2^*$$
$$Q_{d2}^* = \alpha_0 + \alpha_1 P_1^* + \alpha_2 P_2^* = Q_{s2}^* = \beta_0 + \beta_1 P_1^* + \beta_2 P_2^*$$

These equilibrium conditions can be rewritten as

$$a_0 + a_1 P_1^* + a_2 P_2^* - b_0 - b_1 P_1^* - b_2 P_2^* = 0$$
$$\alpha_0 + \alpha_1 P_1^* + \alpha_2 P_2^* - \beta_0 - \beta_1 P_1^* - \beta_2 P_2^* = 0$$

or

$$(a_0 - b_0) + (a_1 - b_1)P_1^* + (a_2 - b_2)P_2^* = 0$$
$$(\alpha_0 - \beta_0) + (\alpha_1 + \beta_1)P_1^* + (\alpha_2 - \beta_2)P_2^* = 0$$

a. Express the last pair of linear equations as a matrix equation in which P_1^* and P_2^* are the unknowns.

b. Assuming the two goods to be substitutes, use Cramer's rule to solve for P_1^* and P_2^*. Also solve for Q_1^* and Q_2^*.

c. Assuming the two goods to be complements, use Cramer's rule to solve for P_1^* and P_2^*. Also solve for Q_1^* and Q_2^*.

2. Consider the simple national income model:

$$Y = C + I + G$$
$$C = C_0 + cY, \qquad C_0 > 0, 0 < c < 1$$
$$I = I_0$$
$$G = G_0$$

This represents a system of two linear equations in two unknown endogenous variables, Y and C. The solution values will be the equilibrium values of the endogenous variables expressed in terms of exogenous variables and parameters.

$$Y^* - C^* = I_0 + G_0$$
$$-cY^* + C^* = C_0$$

a. Express this system of linear equations as a matrix equation.

b. Solve for Y^* and C^*.

3. Consider the following model of the market for a product:

$$Q_d = a - bP$$
$$Q_s = \alpha + \beta(P - T)$$
$$Q_d = Q_s$$

where a, b, α, and β are positive constants, Q_d and Q_s represent quantities demanded and supplied, respectively, P is output price, and T is a tax per unit of output.

a. Express this system in the form of a matrix equation.

b. Use Cramer's rule to find the equilibrium values of P and Q.

c. Solve this system for the equilibrium values of P using the inverse-matrix method.

For Problems 4-6 use the following model of a firm which is a price-taker in all markets and which uses inputs of labor, L, capital, K, and energy, E, to produce its output, Q, according to the following production function:

$$Q = 4K^{0.25}(L^{0.5} + E^{0.5})$$

The hourly wage rate for labor is $w = 20$, the rental price of capital is $r = 10$, the price of energy is $u = 20$, and the output price is $P = 10$.

4. Suppose the firm's objective is to maximize profit.

   a. Determine the first-order conditions and solve them for the values of the choice variables, employment of labor, capital, and energy.

   b. Check the second-order conditions to determine if the solutions in part a do constitute a maximum of the objective function.

5. Assume that owners of the firm ask the firm's manager to maximize output subject to the constraint that a total of $120 is spent on the three inputs.

   a. Determine the first-order conditions and solve them for the values of the choice variables, employment of labor, capital, and energy.

   b. Check the second-order condition to determine if the solutions in part a do constitute a maximum of the objective function.

6. Assume that owners of the firm ask the firm's manager to maximize output subject to the constraints that a total of $120 is spent on the three inputs and that $30 of profits is generated.

   a. Determine the first-order conditions and solve them for the values of the choice variables, employment of labor, capital, and energy.

   b. Check the second-order condition to determine if the solutions in part a do constitute a maximum of the objective function.

Hint: Set up the Lagrangian using *two* Lagrange multipliers, one for each constraint, and proceed as usual. Differentiate the Lagrangian with respect to *both* Lagrange multipliers.

C H A P T E R   9

Modeling Consumer Behavior

9.1

INTRODUCTION

In this chapter we develop in more detail the model of constrained utility maximization that was used as an example of constrained optimization in Chapters 7 and 8. This model serves as an excellent example of how much we can do with very little knowledge; we actually know next to nothing regarding consumers' tastes and preferences. Even so, our model enables us to identify important parameters influencing consumer behavior and equilibrium conditions for utility maximization. The comparative statics results derivable from the model are consistent with what we know to be a rich variety of consumer behavior, and they provide us with insights into that behavior. You will find that virtually all the staples of the intermediate-level microeconomic theory of the consumer can be easily and concisely expressed mathematically. Among the more interesting concepts to examine are the income and substitution effects of a price change. Examining this issue gives us a good platform for introducing the principle of duality in constrained optimization problems using the Lagrangian technique.

9.2

THE BEHAVIORAL POSTULATES OF UTILITY THEORY

Conventional microeconomic theory treats the consumer as a kind of mysterious machine that converts goods and services into something called utility, which is usually interpreted to mean well-being or satisfaction. This process of converting goods and services into utility is denoted by the utility function

$$U = U(X_1, X_2, X_3, \ldots, X_n) \tag{9-1}$$

where X_i indicates the rate per unit of time of consumption of the ith good or service. A given combination of rates of consumption of goods 1 through n is referred to as a "bundle" of goods and services. The utility function is a mathematical representation of consumer tastes and preferences. Because we know so little about consumer tastes, we want to develop our notion of utility with as few assumptions about the nature of preferences as possible. The minimum assumptions that we need are these:

1. *Completeness.* Consumers can rank any bundle of goods and services with regard to any other bundle. That is, a consumer can determine that any bundle A is preferred or not preferred to any other bundle. Note that not preferring bundle A to another can mean being indifferent between the two or finding bundle A less satisfactory than the other bundle.

2. *Transitivity.* Consumer rankings are transitive, or logically consistent. That is, if bundle A is preferred to bundle B, and B is preferred or equivalent to bundle C, then A is preferred to C.

3. *Nonsatiation.* Higher rates of consumption are preferred to lower rates of consumption. In other words, the partial derivatives $U_i \equiv \partial U/\partial X_i > 0$.

4. *Convexity.* If a consumer is indifferent between two commodity bundles, A and B, any bundle, C, which is a weighted average of A and B is preferred to either A or B.

To discuss the utility function that results from these behavioral postulates regarding consumer preferences, let us restrict the range of goods and services from which the consumer chooses to two. In this case, the utility function becomes

$$U = U(X_1, X_2) \tag{9-2}$$

We picture the utility function with the use of contour lines, or level curves which you know as indifference curves. As you know, an indifference curve joins consumption bundles which the consumer ranks as equivalent. The four behavioral postulates result in a map of indifference curves which are downward sloping (from nonsatiation), which do not intersect (from transitivity and nonsatiation), which rank every bundle in X_1-X_2 space (from completeness), and which are convex to the origin (from convexity). Three such indifference curves are pictured in Figure 9.1.

It is worth noting a few important points about the map of indifference curves. First, every point in X_1-X_2 space is associated with an indifference curve. For clarity, we choose to highlight only three curves, which we have labeled U_0, U_1, and U_2, with the subscript denoting a particular level of utility. Second, a map of indifference curves represents a particular utility function; a change in tastes or another consumer's utility function must be represented

Figure 9.1

Map of Indifference
Curves

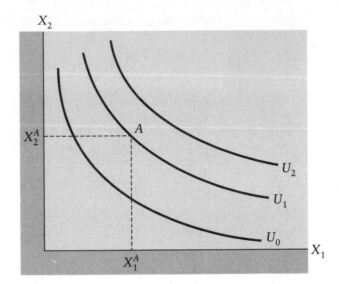

by another map of indifference curves. Third, an indifference curve pictures a consumer's ranking of a bundle. Consider, for example, bundle A on indifference curve U_1. The indifference curve distinguishes A from (1) all bundles that are preferred to it (those lying to the "northeast" of U_1 in the map), (2) all bundles it is preferred to (those lying to the "southwest" of U_1 in the map), and (3) all bundles considered of equal utility to A (those lying on U_1). Finally, the labels U_0, U_1, and U_2 are just that, labels. Any labeling system that preserves the rankings of the bundles will do as well. It is not important what units we assign to indifference curves; only the rank ordering that they represent is important. This final point is the crux of *ordinal utility*. We demonstrate that any labeling system will do in Section 9.7, when we discuss monotonic transformations of the utility function.

ordinal utility: a concept of utility according to which the individual is capable only of rank ordering consumption bundles.

9.3

THE MATHEMATICS OF INDIFFERENCE CURVES

We have already discussed briefly some of the mathematics pertinent to indifference curves in Chapters 3 and 7. In this section we review briefly what has already been discussed and extend our understanding of the mathematical properties of indifference curves.

An indifference curve joins bundles of goods and services which the consumer considers equivalent in terms of utility. By this we mean that the bundles on an indifference curve are all equally ranked and represent the same level of utility; that is, utility is constant along an indifference curve. The equation of a particular indifference curve is implicit in the expression

$$U_0 = U(X_1, X_2) \Leftrightarrow F(X_1, X_2) = U_0 - U(X_1, X_2) = 0 \qquad (9\text{-}3)$$

where U_0 represents a constant level of utility. As long as the conditions of the implicit function theorem, that the utility function is twice differentiable and

$U_2 \neq 0$, are satisfied, there is a functional relationship between X_2 and X_1 that can be written

$$X_2 = X_2(X_1) \tag{9-4}$$

It makes sense to talk of X_2 as a function of X_1 only if utility is constant.

If we knew the particular functional form of the utility function, $U(X_1, X_2)$, we could solve explicitly for X_2 in terms of X_1 with U_0 as a parameter. For example, suppose that

$$U_0 = U(X_1, X_2) = X_1^{\alpha} X_2^{\beta} \tag{9-5}$$

We can solve equation (9-5) for X_2 in terms of X_1 and the parameters α, β, and U_0:

$$X_2^{\beta} = U_0 X_1^{-\alpha} \tag{9-6}$$

or

$$X_2 = U_0^{1/\beta} X_1^{-\alpha/\beta} = \left(\frac{U_0}{X_1^{\alpha}}\right)^{1/\beta} \tag{9-7}$$

Equation (9-7) represents the equation of the indifference curve labeled U_0. We can differentiate this expression to find the derivative of X_2 with respect to X_1, which represents the slope of the indifference curve.

$$\frac{dX_2}{dX_1} = -\frac{\alpha}{\beta} U_0^{1/\beta} X_1^{-(\alpha + \beta)/\beta} \tag{9-8}$$

We can simplify (9-8) by substituting $U_0 = X_1^{\alpha} X_2^{\beta}$.

$$\frac{dX_2}{dX_1} = -\frac{\alpha}{\beta}(X_1^{\alpha} X_2^{\beta})^{1/\beta} X_1^{-(\alpha + \beta)/\beta} = -\frac{\alpha}{\beta}\frac{X_2}{X_1} \tag{9-9}$$

Usually we do not know the specific form of the utility function, and we must satisfy ourselves with an explicit expression only for the derivative dX_2/dX_1, which we can find either through implicit differentiation, as in Chapter 3, or by taking the total differential of the utility function, as in Chapter 5. If utility is constant, then $dU = 0$. Therefore, along an indifference curve we have

$$dU = 0 = \frac{\partial U}{\partial X_1} dX_1 + \frac{\partial U}{\partial X_2} dX_2 = U_1\, dX_1 + U_2\, dX_2 \tag{9-10}$$

or

$$\left.\frac{dX_2}{dX_1}\right|_{dU=0} = -\frac{\partial U/\partial X_1}{\partial U/\partial X_2} = -\frac{U_1}{U_2} = -\mathrm{MRS}_{1,2} \tag{9-11}$$

Equation (9-11) represents the slope of an indifference curve. We already defined (in Chapter 3) the marginal rate of substitution (MRS) as the rate at which a consumer is just willing to substitute one good for another and retain the same level of satisfaction. It is equal to −1 times the slope of the indifference curve, which we have shown to be the negative of the ratio of marginal utilities of the goods.

Consumer postulate 4 (convexity) states that a weighted average of any two equally ranked consumption bundles is preferred to either of the bundles. Graphically, we represent weighted averages of two bundles by the straight line that runs between them, as shown in Figure 9.2. The convexity postulate means that the indifference curve that joins points A and B must bow away from (to the southwest of) the line segment between A and B. This means that any bundles on the line segment between points A and B are preferred to bundles on the indifference curve. For this to be the case, the slope of the indifference curve must become flatter, or less negative from left to right, as shown in the figure. It follows from this that the indifference curve is strictly convex, so the second derivative of X_2 with respect to X_1 is positive.

We take the second derivative of X_2 with respect to X_1 in order to express convexity mathematically. When taking this second derivative, remember to treat X_2 as a function of X_1. This means that, when we differentiate either U_1 or U_2 with respect to X_1, we need to use the chain rule to find the effect of a change in X_1 through X_2. We followed a similar procedure when we investigated convexity of isoquants in Chapter 5, Section 5.10.1. Using the quotient rule of differentiation, we find

$$\frac{d^2X_2}{dX_1^2} = -\frac{1}{U_2^2}\left[U_2\left(U_{11} + U_{12}\left(\frac{dX_2}{dX_1}\right)\right) - U_1\left(U_{21} + U_{22}\left(\frac{dX_2}{dX_1}\right)\right)\right] \quad (9\text{-}12)$$

Substituting in $dX_2/dX_1 = -U_1/U_2$ yields

$$\frac{d^2X_2}{dX_1^2} = -\frac{1}{U_2^2}\left[U_2\left(U_{11} - U_{12}\left(\frac{U_1}{U_2}\right)\right) - U_1\left(U_{21} - U_{22}\left(\frac{U_1}{U_2}\right)\right)\right] \quad (9\text{-}13)$$

Figure 9.2

Convexity and the Convex Indifference Curve

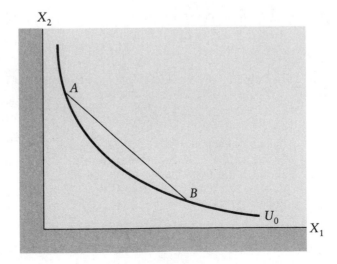

Multiplying out U_2 and U_1 within the brackets yields

$$\frac{d^2X_2}{dX_1^2} = -\frac{1}{U_2^2}\left(U_2U_{11} - U_{12}U_1 - U_1U_{21} + U_{22}\frac{U_1^2}{U_2}\right) \qquad \text{(9-14)}$$

Multiplying (within the brackets) and dividing (outside the brackets) by U_2 and remembering that U_{12} equals U_{21}, we have

$$\frac{d^2X_2}{dX_1^2} = -\frac{1}{U_2^3}(U_2^2U_{11} - 2U_1U_2U_{12} + U_1^2U_{22}) \qquad \text{(9-15)}$$

Because U_2 is assumed to be positive (see the nonsatiation postulate 3), the second derivative is positive if the expression in parentheses is negative. Therefore, indifference curves are convex (MRS diminishes) as long as

$$U_2^2U_{11} - 2U_1U_2U_{12} + U_1^2U_{22} < 0 \qquad \text{(9-16)}$$

If you compare (9-16) with equation (7-11), in Chapter 7, Section 7.2.1, and equation (8-99), Chapter 8, Section 8.7.2, you will see that strict convexity of indifference curves has the same implications for a utility function as the sufficient conditions for constrained utility maximization. Let's review what we know about the model of constrained utility maximization and explore the comparative statics of consumer theory.

9.4

CONSTRAINED UTILITY MAXIMIZATION REVIEWED

In the two-good case, our problem is to maximize

$$U = U(X_1, X_2) \qquad \text{(9-17)}$$

subject to the constraint that

$$M = P_1X_1 + P_2X_2 \qquad \text{(9-18)}$$

The Lagrangian function is

$$\mathcal{L} = U(X_1, X_2) + \mu[M - P_1X_1 - P_2X_2] \qquad \text{(9-19)}$$

The choice variables of the model are X_1, X_2, and μ, and the parameters are M, P_1, and P_2. Recall the first-order conditions for constrained utility maximization from Chapter 7, Section 7.2.2.

$$\mathcal{L}_1 = U_1 - \mu P_1 = 0 \qquad \text{(7-22)}$$
$$\mathcal{L}_2 = U_2 - \mu P_2 = 0 \qquad \text{(7-23)}$$
$$\mathcal{L}_\mu = M - P_1X_1 - P_2X_2 = 0 \qquad \text{(7-24)}$$

We showed in Chapter 8 that the second-order conditions are expressed in terms of the determinant of the bordered Hessian matrix as

$$|H_B| = \begin{vmatrix} U_{11} & U_{12} & -P_1 \\ U_{21} & U_{22} & -P_2 \\ -P_1 & -P_2 & 0 \end{vmatrix} > 0 \tag{8-98}$$

In Chapter 7 we saw that the first-order conditions of this model imply that utility is maximized subject to the budget constraint at that combination of goods and services at which the budget constraint is just tangent to an indifference curve. This was pictured graphically in Figure 7.1, which we reproduce here for your convenience. We have suggested a number of times that the second-order conditions imply that the indifference curves are strictly convex to the origin.

We have reviewed this model in order to explain consumer behavior. To do this we would like to generate some comparative statics results; that is, we want to investigate how the equilibrium values of the choice variables are affected by changes in the parameters. In the next section we will follow the same procedures we have used throughout the text in order to obtain comparative statics results. We recognize that implicit in the equilibrium conditions are optimum values of the choice variables expressed as functions of the parameters of the model. We assume that the equilibrium conditions are true and substitute those optimum values back into the equilibrium conditions. Then we differentiate the resulting identities with respect to some parameter of interest and solve for the partial derivatives of the optimum values of the choice variables with respect to the parameter.

Figure 7.1

Equilibrium of Constrained Utility Maximization

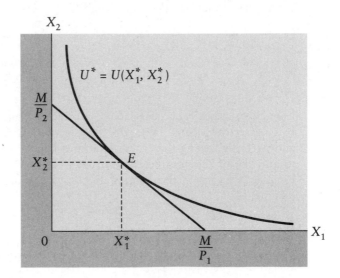

9.5

THE COMPARATIVE STATICS OF CONSTRAINED UTILITY MAXIMIZATION

The first-order conditions for maximization represent a consumer equilibrium; they imply optimal values of the two goods (and the Lagrange multiplier) for given values of the parameters. That is, implicit in the first-order conditions are the following functional relationships, in which the asterisks denote maximizing values of the two goods X_1 and X_2 and the Lagrange multiplier μ.[1]

$$X_1^* = X_1^*(P_1, P_2, M) \tag{9-20}$$

$$X_2^* = X_2^*(P_1, P_2, M) \tag{9-21}$$

$$\mu^* = \mu^*(P_1, P_2, M) \tag{9-22}$$

Recognize that these relationships represent equilibrium consumer behavior. The first one, in which the quantity consumed of good 1 is expressed as a function of its own price, the price of good 2, and money income, represents this individual's demand function for good 1. Similarly, the second represents this individual's demand function for good 2. This is useful information. Our simple, two-good model tells us that the important parameters explaining consumer demand are own price, other prices, and income. If we were attempting to estimate consumer demand using econometric techniques, we would know to include own price, other prices, and income as explanatory variables in our specification of a regression model. If we knew the exact functional form of the utility function, we could solve for X_1^*, X_2^*, and μ^* explicitly and differentiate with respect to P_1, P_2, and M to obtain our comparative statics results. Because we do not know the utility function in more detail, we must find our comparative statics results by a more indirect method.

We assume the equilibrium conditions hold by substituting these equilibrium values, equations (9-20) through (9-22), back into the first-order conditions, equations (7-22) through (7-24), creating the identities

$$U_1(X_1^*, X_2^*) - \mu^* P_1 \equiv 0 \tag{9-23}$$

$$U_2(X_1^*, X_2^*) - \mu^* P_2 \equiv 0 \tag{9-24}$$

$$M - P_1 X_1^* - P_2 X_2^* \equiv 0 \tag{9-25}$$

Remember that any choice variable marked with an asterisk is an equilibrium value of that choice variable; that is, it is a function of the parameters P_1, P_2, and M. This means that these identities can be differentiated with respect to any one of the parameters in order to obtain comparative statics results. First, let's examine the comparative statics analysis of changes in money income, M.

---

[1]As we noted in Chapter 6, footnote 3, the SOC of optimization models also satisfy the conditions of the implicit function theorem, enabling us to express the optimal values of the choice variables as functions of the parameters.

9.5.1 Comparative Statics Analysis of a Change in Money Income

In order to examine the effects of a change in money income on consumer behavior, we differentiate the three identities, (9-23) through (9-25), with respect to M, money income. Note that, wherever X_1^*, X_2^*, or μ^* appears in the identities, we must use the chain rule when differentiating because the equilibrium values of the choice variables are functions of the parameters. Of course, whenever M appears directly in the identities, it must also be differentiated,

$$U_{11}\frac{\partial X_1^*}{\partial M} + U_{12}\frac{\partial X_2^*}{\partial M} - P_1\frac{\partial \mu^*}{\partial M} \equiv 0 \tag{9-26}$$

$$U_{21}\frac{\partial X_1^*}{\partial M} + U_{22}\frac{\partial X_2^*}{\partial M} - P_2\frac{\partial \mu^*}{\partial M} \equiv 0 \tag{9-27}$$

$$-P_1\frac{\partial X_1^*}{\partial M} - P_2\frac{\partial X_2^*}{\partial M} + 0\frac{\partial \mu^*}{\partial M} \equiv -1 \tag{9-28}$$

We have three equations, *linear in three unknowns.* The unknowns are $\partial X_1^*/\partial M$, $\partial X_2^*/\partial M$, and $\partial\mu^*/\partial M$. We can express this system of linear equations in matrix form as

$$\begin{bmatrix} U_{11} & U_{12} & -P_1 \\ U_{21} & U_{22} & -P_2 \\ -P_1 & -P_2 & 0 \end{bmatrix} \begin{bmatrix} \dfrac{\partial X_1^*}{\partial M} \\ \dfrac{\partial X_2^*}{\partial M} \\ \dfrac{\partial \mu^*}{\partial M} \end{bmatrix} = \begin{bmatrix} 0 \\ 0 \\ -1 \end{bmatrix} \tag{9-29}$$

You should recognize the matrix of coefficients in this system as the bordered Hessian matrix of second partial derivatives of the Lagrangian function. In fact, *no matter what parameter we choose to differentiate the identities with respect to, we obtain a system of linear equations in which the matrix of coefficients is the bordered Hessian matrix.* We can use Cramer's rule to solve for any particular element of the vector of unknowns,

$$\frac{\partial X_1^*}{\partial M} = \frac{\begin{vmatrix} 0 & U_{12} & -P_1 \\ 0 & U_{22} & -P_2 \\ -1 & -P_2 & 0 \end{vmatrix}}{\begin{vmatrix} U_{11} & U_{12} & -P_1 \\ U_{21} & U_{22} & -P_2 \\ -P_1 & -P_2 & 0 \end{vmatrix}};\quad \frac{\partial X_2^*}{\partial M} = \frac{\begin{vmatrix} U_{11} & 0 & -P_1 \\ U_{21} & 0 & -P_2 \\ -P_1 & -1 & 0 \end{vmatrix}}{\begin{vmatrix} U_{11} & U_{12} & -P_1 \\ U_{21} & U_{22} & -P_2 \\ -P_1 & -P_2 & 0 \end{vmatrix}};$$

$$\frac{\partial \mu^*}{\partial M} = \frac{\begin{vmatrix} U_{11} & U_{12} & 0 \\ U_{21} & U_{22} & 0 \\ -P_1 & -P_2 & -1 \end{vmatrix}}{\begin{vmatrix} U_{11} & U_{12} & -P_1 \\ U_{21} & U_{22} & -P_2 \\ -P_1 & -P_2 & 0 \end{vmatrix}} \qquad (9\text{-}30)$$

In each of these expressions, the denominator is the determinant of the bordered Hessian matrix, $|H_B|$. Our second-order conditions for constrained utility maximization tell us that that determinant must be positive. Unfortunately, the second-order conditions do not allow us to determine the sign of any of the numerators. None of the determinants in the numerators is a border-preserving principal minor. We expand the numerator in the expression for $\partial X_1^*/\partial M$ to illustrate.

$$\frac{\partial X_1^*}{\partial M} = \frac{\begin{vmatrix} 0 & U_{12} & -P_1 \\ 0 & U_{22} & -P_2 \\ -1 & -P_2 & 0 \end{vmatrix}}{\begin{vmatrix} U_{11} & U_{12} & -P_1 \\ U_{21} & U_{22} & -P_2 \\ -P_1 & -P_2 & 0 \end{vmatrix}} = \frac{-1 \begin{vmatrix} U_{12} & -P_1 \\ U_{22} & -P_2 \end{vmatrix}}{|H_B|} = \frac{P_2 U_{12} - P_1 U_{22}}{|H_B|} \qquad (9\text{-}31)$$

Although we might be comfortable assuming that U_{22} is negative because of diminishing marginal utility in good 2, we cannot know the sign of U_{12}. If U_{12} is positive, the goods are said to be cooperative in consumption, and we could argue that $\partial X_1^*/\partial M$ is positive. If, however, U_{12} is negative, the goods are said to be competitive in consumption, and $\partial X_1^*/\partial M$ could be negative.

normal goods: goods for which consumption levels increase with increases in money income and decrease with decreases in money income, *ceteris paribus*.

inferior goods: goods for which consumption levels decrease with increases in money income and increase with decreases in money income, *ceteris paribus*.

To understand this result, think about what is meant by the partial derivative $\partial X_1^*/\partial M$. It measures the instantaneous rate of change of the equilibrium level of X_1 with respect to a change in money income, holding P_1 and P_2 constant. Normally, we would expect it to be positive; that is, we expect equilibrium consumption levels to increase with increases in money income and to decrease with decreases in money income. In fact, we call goods for which $\partial X_1^*/\partial M$ is positive **normal goods**. On the other hand, our comparative statics result suggests that this partial derivative might be negative. Consumption might decrease with an increase in income and increase with a decrease in income. As you already know, we call these goods **inferior goods**, and our comparative statics results are consistent with the possibility that inferior goods may exist. The effects of changes in M on

X_2^* are symmetrical with what we have found for X_1^* and we leave it to you to find the exact expression for $\partial X_2^*/\partial M$.

The comparative statics results for changes in the parameter M are pictured graphically in Figure 9.3. Panel (a) illustrates the situation in which money income changes and both goods are normal. A shift in the budget constraint to the northeast results in increases in the consumption of both goods. Panel (b) illustrates the situation in which money income changes and good 1 is inferior. An increase in money income results in an increase in X_2 but a decrease in X_1.[2]

Figure 9.3

(*a*) **Both Goods Normal**
(*b*) **Good 1 Is Inferior**

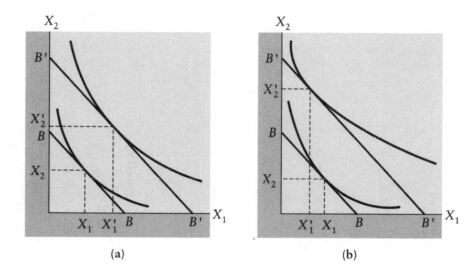

(a)

(b)

We stated that we could not determine a sign for $\partial\mu^*/\partial M$ because the determinant in the numerator is not a border-preserving principal minor. You may already have noticed that the numerator *is*, in fact, a principal minor but it does not preserve the border. Evaluating the determinant gives us the following result.

$$\frac{\partial\mu^*}{\partial M} = \frac{-[U_{11}U_{22} - U_{12}^2]}{|H_B|} \tag{9-32}$$

We cannot say what the sign of this partial derivative is. What does this mean?

Recall Chapter 7, Section 7.2.3. There, we found that the equilibrium value of the Lagrange multiplier, μ^*, could be interpreted as measuring the effect of relaxing the constraint, M, on the indirect objective function, $U^*(X_1^*, X_2^*)$. We interpreted μ^* as the marginal utility of money income at the optimum. The partial derivative $\partial\mu^*/\partial M$ measures the effect of income on the

---

[2]In a two-good model it is impossible for both goods to be inferior. In order to demonstrate this to yourself, try to picture the situation graphically. An increase in M implies a parallel shift of the budget constraint away from the origin. How could the equilibrium quantities of both goods decrease? In models with more than two goods it is impossible for *all* the goods to be inferior.

marginal utility of income. The fact that we cannot determine the sign of this partial derivative means that, without further assumptions regarding the nature of the utility function, we are unable to argue for the proposition of declining marginal utility of money income. Modern, ordinal utility theory does not require the assumption of declining marginal utility.

NUMERICAL EXAMPLE

Suppose a consumer maximizes the utility function $U = U(X_1, X_2) = X_1X_2$, subject to the budget constraint $M = P_1X_1 + P_2X_2$. The Lagrangian objective function is

$$\mathscr{L} = X_1X_2 + \mu[M - (P_1X_1 + P_2X_2)] \tag{9-33}$$

and the FOC are

$$\mathscr{L}_1 = X_2 - \mu P_1 = 0 \tag{9-34}$$

$$\mathscr{L}_2 = X_1 - \mu P_2 = 0 \tag{9-35}$$

$$\mathscr{L}_\mu = M - (P_1X_1 + P_2X_2) = 0 \tag{9-36}$$

The bordered Hessian matrix of second partial derivatives of (9-33) and its determinant are

$$H_B = \begin{bmatrix} 0 & 1 & -P_1 \\ 1 & 0 & -P_2 \\ -P_1 & -P_2 & 0 \end{bmatrix}; \quad |H_B| = 2P_1P_2 > 0 \tag{9-37}$$

You might remember this problem as the example we used in Chapter 7, Section 7.2.3. There, we solved the FOC directly for the demand functions, $X_1^* = M/(2P_1)$ and $X_2^* = M/(2P_2)$, as well as the Lagrange multiplier, $\mu^* = M/(2P_1P_2)$. These could be differentiated directly with respect to M in order to obtain the comparative statics of changes in money income. Instead, we find the partial derivatives of the equilibrium values of the choice variables with respect to M by setting up the matrix equation

$$\begin{bmatrix} 0 & 1 & -P_1 \\ 1 & 0 & -P_2 \\ -P_1 & -P_2 & 0 \end{bmatrix} \begin{bmatrix} \dfrac{\partial X_1^*}{\partial M} \\ \dfrac{\partial X_2^*}{\partial M} \\ \dfrac{\partial \mu^*}{\partial M} \end{bmatrix} = \begin{bmatrix} 0 \\ 0 \\ -1 \end{bmatrix} \tag{9-38}$$

We use Cramer's rule to solve for the three unknowns,

$$\frac{\partial X_1^*}{\partial M} = \frac{\begin{bmatrix} 0 & 1 & -P_1 \\ 0 & 0 & -P_2 \\ -1 & -P_2 & 0 \end{bmatrix}}{|H_B|} = \frac{1}{2P_1}; \qquad \frac{\partial X_2^*}{\partial M} = \frac{\begin{bmatrix} 0 & 0 & -P_1 \\ 1 & 0 & -P_2 \\ -P_1 & -1 & 0 \end{bmatrix}}{|H_B|} = \frac{1}{2P_2}$$

(9-39)

$$\frac{\partial \mu^*}{\partial M} = \frac{\begin{bmatrix} 0 & 1 & 0 \\ 1 & 0 & 0 \\ -P_1 & -P_2 & -1 \end{bmatrix}}{|H_B|} = \frac{1}{2P_1 P_2}$$

As you can see, we could have obtained the same results by differentiating the demand functions and the Lagrange multiplier with respect to M. Note that both goods are normal in this example, because the partial derivatives with respect to M are both positive.

EXERCISES
Section 9.5.1
Comparative Statics
Analysis of a
Change in Money
Income

Find the Lagrangian objective function, the first- and second-order conditions, and the comparative statics results for changes in money income for the following constrained utility maximization problems.

1. $U = U(X_1, X_2) = X_1^\alpha X_2^\beta$, $M = P_1 X_1 + P_2 X_2$

2. $U = U(Z(X_1, X_2)) = 100Z^{-2}$, where $Z = 0.5X_1^{-0.5} + 0.5X_2^{-0.5}$, $M = P_1 X_1 + P_2 X_2$

3. $U = U(X_1, X_2, X_3) = X_1 X_2 X_3$, $M = P_1 X_1 + P_2 X_2 + P_3 X_3$

4. $U = \alpha \ln X_1 + (1 - \alpha) \ln X_2$, $M = P_1 X_1 + P_2 X_2$

9.5.2 Comparative Statics Analysis of a Change in Price

Let's find the comparative statics results of a change in a price, holding the other price and money income constant. To do so, we differentiate the identities (9-23) through (9-25) with respect to a price, P_1, obtaining

$$U_{11} \frac{\partial X_1^*}{\partial P_1} + U_{12} \frac{\partial X_2^*}{\partial P_1} - P_1 \frac{\partial \mu^*}{\partial P_1} \equiv \mu^* \qquad (9\text{-}40)$$

$$U_{21} \frac{\partial X_1^*}{\partial P_1} + U_{22} \frac{\partial X_2^*}{\partial P_1} - P_2 \frac{\partial \mu^*}{\partial P_1} \equiv 0 \qquad (9\text{-}41)$$

$$-P_1 \frac{\partial X_1^*}{\partial P_1} - P_2 \frac{\partial X_2^*}{\partial P_1} + 0 \frac{\partial \mu^*}{\partial P_1} \equiv X_1^* \qquad (9\text{-}42)$$

Here μ^* and X_1^* appear on the right-hand sides of the first and third equations because the parameter P_1 appears multiplicatively in the first and third first-order conditions, equations (9-23) and (9-25). We must use the product rule when we differentiate the terms in which the parameter appears, and we bring the "extra" term resulting from the application of the product rule over to the right-hand side. Recognizing what we have done here is the key to using matrix algebra to solve for comparative statics results for any optimization model with respect to any parameter.

In general, you can always generate the matrix form of the system of equations that generates comparative statics results for any particular parameter by premultiplying the vector of unknown partial derivatives by the Hessian matrix of second partials of the objective function. The trick is to state the vector of constants on the right-hand side correctly. To do this, imagine differentiating the first-order conditions with respect to some parameter. If the parameter does not appear directly in a particular first-order condition, the term on the right-hand side will be 0. If the parameter does appear, as P_1 does in equations (9-23) and (9-25), there will be a term left over when you differentiate with respect to that parameter. Because P_1 is multiplied by $-\mu^*$ in equation (9-23), we must use the product rule to differentiate that term, obtaining $-P_1(\partial \mu^*/\partial P_1) - \mu^*$. Because $-\mu^*$ is not a coefficient of one of our unknowns, we bring it over to the right-hand side when we express our system of linear equations in matrix form. Similarly, we must use the product rule when differentiating the term $-P_1 X_1^*$ in equation (9-25), leaving $-X_1^*$ as a term that can be brought over to the right-hand side. According to this reasoning, we arrive at the following matrix equation.

$$\begin{bmatrix} U_{11} & U_{12} & -P_1 \\ U_{21} & U_{22} & -P_2 \\ -P_1 & -P_2 & 0 \end{bmatrix} \begin{bmatrix} \dfrac{\partial X_1^*}{\partial P_1} \\[2mm] \dfrac{\partial X_2^*}{\partial P_1} \\[2mm] \dfrac{\partial \mu^*}{\partial P_1} \end{bmatrix} = \begin{bmatrix} \mu^* \\ 0 \\ X_1^* \end{bmatrix} \qquad (9\text{-}43)$$

We can use Cramer's rule to solve for any of the unknowns.

$$\frac{\partial X_1^*}{\partial P_1} = \frac{\begin{vmatrix} \mu^* & U_{12} & -P_1 \\ 0 & U_{22} & -P_2 \\ X_1^* & -P_2 & 0 \end{vmatrix}}{\begin{vmatrix} U_{11} & U_{12} & -P_1 \\ U_{21} & U_{22} & -P_2 \\ -P_1 & -P_2 & 0 \end{vmatrix}}; \qquad \frac{\partial X_2^*}{\partial P_1} = \frac{\begin{vmatrix} U_{11} & \mu^* & -P_1 \\ U_{21} & 0 & -P_2 \\ -P_1 & X_1^* & 0 \end{vmatrix}}{\begin{vmatrix} U_{11} & U_{12} & -P_1 \\ U_{21} & U_{22} & -P_2 \\ -P_1 & -P_2 & 0 \end{vmatrix}};$$

$$\frac{\partial \mu^*}{\partial P_1} = \frac{\begin{vmatrix} U_{11} & U_{12} & \mu^* \\ U_{21} & U_{22} & 0 \\ -P_1 & -P_2 & X_1^* \end{vmatrix}}{\begin{vmatrix} U_{11} & U_{12} & -P_1 \\ U_{21} & U_{22} & -P_2 \\ -P_1 & -P_2 & 0 \end{vmatrix}} \tag{9-44}$$

Let's examine the result for $\partial X_1^*/\partial P_1$ more closely. Expand the determinant in the numerator by the first column, obtaining

$$\frac{\partial X_1^*}{\partial P_1} = \frac{\begin{vmatrix} \mu^* & U_{12} & -P_1 \\ 0 & U_{22} & -P_2 \\ X_1^* & -P_2 & 0 \end{vmatrix}}{\begin{vmatrix} U_{11} & U_{12} & -P_1 \\ U_{21} & U_{22} & -P_2 \\ -P_1 & -P_2 & 0 \end{vmatrix}} = \mu^* \frac{\begin{vmatrix} U_{22} & -P_2 \\ -P_2 & 0 \end{vmatrix}}{|H_B|} + X_1^* \frac{\begin{vmatrix} U_{12} & -P_1 \\ U_{22} & -P_2 \end{vmatrix}}{|H_B|} \tag{9-45}$$

Evaluating the two second-order determinants in the numerators gives us

$$\frac{\partial X_1^*}{\partial P_1} = -\mu^* \frac{P_2^2}{|H_B|} + X_1^* \frac{-P_2 U_{12} + P_1 U_{22}}{|H_B|} \tag{9-46}$$

What does this result mean? The partial derivative we have evaluated signifies the effect on the equilibrium consumer choice of X_1 of a change in its price. That is, it represents the slope of the demand curve for good 1. Because it is a partial derivative, we are holding constant the other parameters, P_2 and M. The law of demand says that, *ceteris paribus*, price and quantity demanded are negatively related. That should mean that we expect a negative sign for this partial derivative. Our algebraic result, however, does not permit us to determine the sign of $\partial X_1^*/\partial P_1$. We can determine that the first term is unambiguously negative. The second-order conditions tell us that $|H_B|$ is positive, and P_2^2 is certainly positive, as is the marginal utility of money income, μ^*. However, the second term in this expression cannot be given a sign. In fact, you might have recognized part of this second term as $-\partial X_1^*/\partial M$ from equation (9-31). We could rewrite our comparative static result as

$$\frac{\partial X_1^*}{\partial P_1} = -\mu^* \frac{P_2^2}{|H_B|} - X_1^* \frac{\partial X_1^*}{\partial M} \tag{9-47}$$

Slutsky equation: the expression for $\partial X_1^*/\partial P_1$ in which the income and substitution effects are separated out.

substitution effect: effect on the consumption of a good due only to changes in the price ratio, holding real income (or utility) constant, when the price of a good changes.

income effect: effect on the consumption of a good due only to changes in real income (or utility), holding the price ratio and money income constant, when the price of a good changes.

In equation (9-47), known as the *Slutsky equation*, there are two components of the effect of a change in P_1 on X_1^*. The first is always negative and is equal to $-\mu^*(P_2^2/|H_B|)$. This is the *substitution effect of a change in price*. The second component is equal to $-X_1^*(\partial X_1^*/\partial M)$ and can be negative if $\partial X_1^*/\partial M > 0$, as it is for a normal good, or positive if $\partial X_1^*/\partial M < 0$, as it is for an inferior good. This is the *income effect of a change in price*. The substitution effect isolates the effects due to changes in the price ratio, holding real income (or utility) constant. The income effect isolates the effects due to changes in real income (or level of utility) and holds the price ratio constant. A change in price, holding *money income* constant, leads to both of these effects, $\partial X_1^*/\partial P_1$. This is the total effect on a consumer's demand for a good of a change in its price. The comparative statics of a decrease in P_1 holding M constant is illustrated in Figure 9.4.

When P_1 decreases, the budget constraint changes from BB to BB'. The total effect of the change in price is the change in equilibrium from L to N. It is this total effect that is captured by the comparative statics results of changes in P_1^*, i.e., the Slutsky equation. In order to visualize the substitution and income effects, a hypothetical budget constraint, HH, is constructed with the same slope as BB', but tangent to the original indifference curve, U_0, at point M. The substitution effect is represented by the change from L to M, because the price ratio, pictured by the slope of HH, has changed compared to BB, but real income, pictured by the indifference curve, has remained constant at U_0. The income effect is represented by the change from M to N, because the price ratio is constant between HH and BB', but the level of utility (representing real income) has increased from U_0 to U_1. In Figure 9.4 it is assumed that both goods are normal.

Figure 9.4

Income and Substitution Effects of a Change in P_1

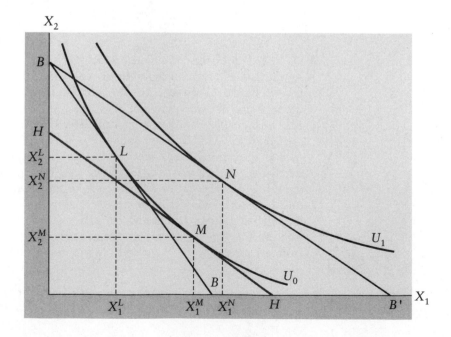

NUMERICAL EXAMPLE

We use the same numerical example to illustrate the comparative statics of a change in price that we used earlier in Section 9.5.1. Our consumer maximizes the utility function $U = U(X_1, X_2) = X_1 X_2$, subject to the budget constraint $M = P_1 X_1 + P_2 X_2$. The Lagrangian objective function, the first- and second-order conditions, and the consumer demand functions are provided in equations (9-33) through (9-37). Recall that we can solve the FOC for X_1^*, X_2^*, and μ^*, obtaining $X_1^* = M/(2P_1)$, $X_2^* = M/(2P_2)$, and $\mu^* = M/(2P_1 P_2)$. We can differentiate these expressions directly with respect to P_1 in order to obtain the comparative statics of changes in the price of good 1. Doing so gives us

$$\frac{\partial X_1^*}{\partial P_1} = \frac{-M}{2P_1^2} < 0; \qquad \frac{\partial X_2^*}{\partial P_1} = 0; \qquad \frac{\partial \mu^*}{\partial P_1} = -\frac{-M}{2P_1^2 P_2} < 0 \qquad (9\text{-}48)$$

We see that the demand for good 1 and the marginal utility of money income are negatively related to changes in P_1 and that demand for good 2 is unaffected by changes in P_1.

We are unable to distinguish the substitution and income effects of a change in P_1 from equations (9-48), because they provide the total effect of a change in P_1. In order to decompose the total effect into its substitution and income effect components, we must find the comparative statics results of changes in P_1 by setting up the matrix equation

$$\begin{bmatrix} 0 & 1 & -P_1 \\ 1 & 0 & -P_2 \\ -P_1 & -P_2 & 0 \end{bmatrix} \begin{bmatrix} \dfrac{\partial X_1^*}{\partial P_1} \\[2ex] \dfrac{\partial X_2^*}{\partial P_1} \\[2ex] \dfrac{\partial \mu^*}{\partial P_1} \end{bmatrix} = \begin{bmatrix} \mu^* \\[2ex] 0 \\[2ex] X_1^* \end{bmatrix} \qquad (9\text{-}49)$$

We use Cramer's rule to solve for the three unknowns,

$$\frac{\partial X_1^*}{\partial P_1} = \frac{\begin{vmatrix} \mu^* & 1 & -P_1 \\ 0 & 0 & -P_2 \\ X_1^* & -P_2 & 0 \end{vmatrix}}{|H_B|} = -\frac{\mu^* P_2}{2P_1} - \frac{X_1^*}{2P_1};$$

$$\frac{\partial X_2^*}{\partial P_1} = \frac{\begin{vmatrix} 0 & \mu^* & -P_1 \\ 1 & 0 & -P_2 \\ -P_1 & X_1^* & 0 \end{vmatrix}}{|H_B|} = \frac{-\mu^*}{2} - \frac{X_1^*}{2P_1}$$

$$\frac{\partial \mu^*}{\partial P_1} = \frac{\begin{vmatrix} 0 & 1 & \mu^* \\ 1 & 0 & 0 \\ -P_1 & -P_2 & X_1^* \end{vmatrix}}{|H_B|} = \frac{\mu^*}{2P_1} - \frac{X_1^*}{2P_1 P_2} \qquad (9\text{-}50)$$

From the expression for $\partial X_1^*/\partial P_1$ we can identify the substitution effect as $-\mu^* P_2/(2P_1)$ and the income effect as $-X_1^*/2P_1$. As you can see, the substitution effect is negative, as expected. Because both goods are normal in this example, the income effect is also negative. Note that, if you substitute the expressions for μ^* and X_1^* into the equations in (9-50), you obtain the same comparative statics results as in (9-48).

How do we know that $-\mu^*(P_2^2/|H_B|)$ is the algebraic representation of the substitution effect? We have only asserted that this is the case, not demonstrated it. In order to demonstrate mathematically that this expression shows the effect of changing price while holding utility constant, we need a model that holds utility constant. Developing such a model provides us with an excellent example of duality in economic modeling.

EXERCISES
Section 9.5.2
Comparative Statics
Analysis of a
Change in Price

Find all of the comparative statics results for changes in P_1 for the following constrained utility maximization problems. Identify the substitution and income effects on X_1 of the change in its own price.

1. $U = U(X_1, X_2) = X_1^\alpha X_2^\beta,\ M = P_1 X_1 + P_2 X_2$

2. $U = U(Z(X_1, X_2)) = 100Z^{-2}$, where $Z = 0.5X_1^{-0.5} + 0.5X_2^{-0.5}$, $M = P_1 X_1 + P_2 X_2$

3. $U = U(X_1, X_2, X_3) = X_1 X_2 X_3,\ M = P_1 X_1 + P_2 X_2 + P_3 X_3$

4. $U = \alpha \ln X_1 + (1 - \alpha) \ln X_2,\ M = P_1 X_1 + P_2 X_2$

9.6

THE DUAL OF CONSTRAINED UTILITY MAXIMIZATION: CONSTRAINED EXPENDITURE MINIMIZATION

primal: the original constrained optimization problem, to which a dual may be found.

dual: another way to describe the optimum of a constrained optimization problem, in which the objective and the constraints reverse roles, along with the sense of optimization.

All *primal* optimization models have *dual* counterparts. Dual models recognize that the same question can be approached from different directions. The way in which the goal of an optimization model is expressed determines what the parameters of the model are. Constrained utility maximization is an intuitively appealing approach. Consumers are modeled as being saddled with a limited opportunity set (the budget constraint) and are assumed to want to maximize utility within the confines of that opportunity set. The parameters of the model $(M, P_1,$ and $P_2)$ determine the opportunity set.

Suppose we take a less intuitive approach to modeling consumer choice. We can argue that the consumer's goal is *to minimize the expenditures necessary to achieve some specified level of utility.* This is the dual counterpart of the problem of constrained utility maximization. The dual of a constrained optimization model reverses the roles of objective and constraint. The objective of the expenditure minimization model (restricting ourselves to the two-good case) is to minimize expenditures, $M = P_1X_1 + P_2X_2$, subject to $U_0 = U(X_1, X_2)$, in which U_0 represents some specified level of utility. In order to write the Lagrangian objective function of this constrained optimization model, we specify the constraint so that its right-hand side is equal to zero, multiply it by the Lagrange multiplier, and add the product to the objective. We obtain

$$\mathscr{L} = P_1X_1 + P_2X_2 + \lambda(U_0 - U(X_1 \; X_2)) \tag{9-51}$$

The choice variables are $X_1, X_2,$ and λ and the parameters are $U_0, P_1,$ and P_2. We use λ to denote our Lagrange multiplier in this model in order to distinguish it from μ, the Lagrange multiplier of the primal, constrained utility maximization model. The first-order conditions for minimization are

$$\mathscr{L}_1 = P_1 - \lambda U_1 = 0 \tag{9-52}$$

$$\mathscr{L}_2 = P_2 - \lambda U_2 = 0 \tag{9-53}$$

$$\mathscr{L}_\lambda = U_0 - U(X_1, X_2) = 0 \tag{9-54}$$

These first-order conditions define an implicit functional relationship between the equilibrium values of the choice variables and the parameters,[3]

$$X_1^{**} = X_1^{**}(P_1, P_2, U_0) \tag{9-55}$$

$$X_2^{**} = X_2^{**}(P_1, P_2, U_0) \tag{9-56}$$

$$\lambda^{**} = \lambda^{**}(P_1, P_2, U_0) \tag{9-57}$$

The equilibrium values of the choice variables can be substituted back into the FOC in order to create the identities

$$P_1 - \lambda^{**}U_1(X_1^{**}, X_2^{**}) \equiv 0 \tag{9-58}$$

$$P_2 - \lambda^{**}U_2(X_1^{**}, X_2^{**}) \equiv 0 \tag{9-59}$$

$$\mathscr{L}_\lambda = U_0 - U(X_1^{**}, X_2^{**}) \equiv 0 \tag{9-60}$$

We will differentiate the identities with respect to the parameters later in the chapter to generate comparative statics results for the constrained expenditure minimization model. First, let's examine the second-order conditions.

---

[5]Ordinal utility is distinguished from **cardinal utility**, which requires that differences in utility actually be measurable according to some scale of units.

The bordered Hessian matrix of second partial derivatives is

$$E_B = \begin{bmatrix} -\lambda U_{11} & -\lambda U_{12} & -U_1 \\ -\lambda U_{21} & -\lambda U_{22} & -U_2 \\ -U_1 & -U_2 & 0 \end{bmatrix} \tag{9-61}$$

We denote the bordered Hessian of the expenditure minimization model by E_B to distinguish it from H_B, the bordered Hessian from the primal. We will directly compare the determinants of these two bordered Hessians. Our rule for the second-order conditions of a constrained minimization problem says that the determinant of the bordered Hessian matrix must be negative, as are all border-preserving principal minors of dimension 3 or greater. In this case the rule means that $|E_B| < 0$.

We have stated above that the constrained expenditure minimization model is simply an alternative approach to consumer choice. We introduce it in order to make the level of utility a parameter in the model because we want to isolate the substitution effect of a price change. The model ought to generate the same equilibrium conditions as its primal, constrained utility maximization. Looking at the first-order conditions, we see that

$$\frac{P_1}{P_2} = \frac{U_1}{U_2} \quad \text{and} \quad \lambda = \frac{P_1}{U_1} = \frac{P_2}{U_2} \tag{9-62}$$

The first relationship implies that equilibrium is where the expenditure line, or budget constraint, is tangent to an indifference curve. This is the same as the description of equilibrium we obtained from constrained utility maximization. The second relationship implies that the Lagrange multiplier, λ^{**}, from the expenditure minimization model is the inverse of μ^*, the Lagrange multiplier from the utility maximization model. Equations (9-23) and (9-24) imply that μ^* equals U_1/P_1 and U_2/P_2.

In the primal model, the level of expenditures (income) is a parameter and we find the quantities of goods that maximize utility. In the dual model, the level of utility is a parameter and we find the quantities of goods that minimize expenditures. No matter how we approach the problem of choice, equilibrium is at the point of tangency between an indifference curve and the budget constraint. The equilibria of the two models are equivalent if the given level of utility in the dual is the optimum level in the primal or if the given level of money income in the primal equals the optimum level of expenditures in the dual.

We now turn to the second-order conditions. It is easy to show that the second-order conditions of the constrained expenditure minimization model also imply convex indifference curves, as do the second-order conditions of the utility maximization model. Simply expand the determinant of the bordered Hessian matrix. We leave that to you as Supplemental Problem 1 at the end of the chapter. In what follows, we want to show you the exact relationship between $|E_B|$ and $|H_B|$, where H_B is the bordered Hessian of the constrained utility maximization model in which money income is a parameter.

Starting with $|E_B|$, factor out $-\lambda$ from all three rows (remember property 2 of determinants in Chapter 8, Section 8.5.2).

$$|E_B| = \begin{vmatrix} -\lambda U_{11} & -\lambda U_{12} & -U_1 \\ -\lambda U_{21} & -\lambda U_{22} & -U_2 \\ -U_1 & -U_2 & 0 \end{vmatrix} = -\lambda^3 \begin{vmatrix} U_{11} & U_{12} & \dfrac{U_1}{\lambda} \\ U_{21} & U_{22} & \dfrac{U_2}{\lambda} \\ \dfrac{U_1}{\lambda} & \dfrac{U_2}{\lambda} & 0 \end{vmatrix} \qquad (9\text{-}63)$$

Recognize from the first-order conditions that $U_1 = P_1/\lambda$ and $U_2 = P_2/\lambda$ and factor out $-1/\lambda^2$ from the third column and the third row,

$$|E_B| = -\lambda^3 \begin{vmatrix} U_{11} & U_{12} & \dfrac{P_1}{\lambda^2} \\ U_{21} & U_{22} & \dfrac{P_2}{\lambda^2} \\ \dfrac{P_1}{\lambda^2} & \dfrac{P_2}{\lambda^2} & 0 \end{vmatrix} = -\dfrac{1}{\lambda} \begin{vmatrix} U_{11} & U_{12} & -P_1 \\ U_{21} & U_{22} & -P_2 \\ -P_1 & -P_2 & 0 \end{vmatrix} = -\dfrac{1}{\lambda}|H_B|$$

$$(9\text{-}64)$$

Clearly, if $|H_B|$ is positive, then $|E_B|$ is negative, since $\lambda > 0$. This means that, if the SOC of constrained utility maximization are satisfied, then so are the SOC of its dual, constrained expenditure minimization.

We have already shown that λ^{**} equals $1/\mu^*$. What is the economic interpretation of λ^{**}? We stated in Chapter 7, Section 7.2.3 that, in general, the Lagrange multiplier measures the effect on the optimal value of the objective function of relaxing the constraint, or the partial derivative of the indirect objective function with respect to the constraint. In the primal model μ^* measures the effect on maximum utility (the objective) of increased money income (the constraint). In the dual model λ^{**} measures the effect on minimum expenditures (the objective) of increased utility (the constraint), or

$$\lambda^{**} = \frac{\partial M^{**}}{\partial U^0} \quad \text{and} \quad \mu^* = \frac{\partial U^*}{\partial M} \Leftrightarrow \lambda^{**} = \frac{1}{\mu^*} \qquad (9\text{-}65)$$

That is, λ^{**} is the marginal cost of utility. This is consistent with our finding that λ^{**} equals $1/\mu^*$.

We can demonstrate the meaning of λ^{**} mathematically by substituting the equilibrium values, X_1^{**} and X_2^{**}, into the expenditure function to create the **indirect expenditure function**,

indirect expenditure function: the indirect objective function from the constrained expenditure minimization model.

$$M^{**} = P_1 X_1^{**} + P_2 X_2^{**} = M^{**}(P_1, P_2, U_0) \qquad (9\text{-}66)$$

and differentiating it with respect to U_0. Remember that X_1^{**} and X_2^{**} are functions of the parameters P_1, P_2, and U_0.

$$\frac{\partial M^{**}}{\partial U_0} = P_1 \frac{\partial X_1^{**}}{\partial U_0} + P_2 \frac{\partial X_2^{**}}{\partial U_0} \tag{9-67}$$

Recall from the first-order identities [equations (9-58) and (9-59)] that $P_1 = \lambda^{**} U_1$ and $P_2 = \lambda^{**} U_2$. Substituting and factoring out λ^{**}, we obtain

$$\frac{\partial M^{**}}{\partial U_0} = \lambda^{**} U_1 \frac{\partial X_1^{**}}{\partial U_0} + \lambda^{**} U_2 \frac{\partial X_2^{**}}{\partial U_0} = \lambda^{**} \left(U_1 \frac{\partial X_1^{**}}{\partial U_0} + U_2 \frac{X_2^{**}}{\partial U_0} \right) \tag{9-68}$$

The expression inside the parentheses can be evaluated by differentiating the third first-order identity, equation (9-60), by U_0,

$$1 - U_1 \frac{\partial X_1^{**}}{\partial U_0} - U_2 \frac{\partial X_2^{**}}{\partial U_0} \equiv 0 \Leftrightarrow 1 \equiv U_1 \frac{\partial X_1^{**}}{\partial U_0} + U_2 \frac{\partial X_2^{**}}{\partial U_0} \tag{9-69}$$

Substituting this result back into our expression for $\partial M^{**}/\partial U_0$ gives us the result we are seeking, that

$$\frac{\partial M^{**}}{\partial U_0} = \lambda^{**} \tag{9-70}$$

Because M^{**} represents the minimum level of expenditures necessary to attain a certain level of utility, λ^{**} equals the instantaneous rate at which expenditures must be increased per unit increase in utility. What we have demonstrated is another application of the envelope theorem (see Chapter 7, Section 7.4). The partial derivative of the indirect objective function with respect to a parameter equals the partial derivative of the Lagrangian objective function with respect to the same parameter, when both functions are evaluated at the optimum.

NUMERICAL EXAMPLE

We will continue to use the same utility function, $U = U(X_1, X_2) = X_1 X_2$ that we used in the previous numerical examples so that you can see the relationship between the dual and primal problems. In the dual, the consumer is assumed to minimize expenditures, $M = P_1 X_1 + P_2 X_2$ subject to the utility constraint, $U_0 = X_1 X_2$. The Lagrangian objective function is

$$\mathcal{L} = P_1 X_1 + P_2 X_2 + \lambda(U_0 - X_1 X_2) \tag{9-71}$$

and the FOC are

$$\mathcal{L}_1 = P_1 - \lambda X_2 = 0 \tag{9-72}$$

$$\mathcal{L}_2 = P_2 - \lambda X_1 = 0 \tag{9-73}$$

$$\mathcal{L}_\lambda = U_0 - X_1 X_2 = 0 \tag{9-74}$$

Equations (9-72) through (9-74) can be solved for the equilibrium values of the choice variables. We find that

$$X_1^{**} = \left(\frac{U_0 P_2}{P_1}\right)^{1/2} \tag{9-75}$$

$$X_2^{**} = \left(\frac{U_0 P_1}{P_2}\right)^{1/2} \tag{9-76}$$

$$\lambda^{**} = \left(\frac{P_1 P_2}{U_0}\right)^{1/2} \tag{9-77}$$

We stated earlier that the primal and dual models are equivalent if the given level of utility in the dual is the optimum level in the primal. Therefore, if we set $U_0 = U^*(X_1^*, X_2^*)$, we should find that $X_1^{**} = X_1^*$ and $X_2^{**} = X_2^*$. We should also find that $\lambda^{**} = 1/\mu^*$.

We found U^* in equation (7-37), Chapter 7, Section 7.2.3, which we reproduce for you here

$$U^* = X_1^* X_2^* = \frac{M^2}{4P_1 P_2} \tag{7-37}$$

If we substitute (7-37) for U_0 in equations (9-75) through (9-77), we find that, as expected,

$$X_1^{**} = X_1^* = \frac{M}{2P_1} \tag{9-78}$$

$$X_2^{**} = X_2^* = \frac{M}{2P_2} \tag{9-79}$$

$$\lambda^{**} = 1/\mu^* = \frac{2P_1 P_2}{M} \tag{9-80}$$

Next, we turn to the second-order conditions of the dual model. The bordered Hessian matrix of second partial derivatives of (9-71) and its determinant are

$$E_B = \begin{bmatrix} 0 & -\lambda & -X_2 \\ -\lambda & 0 & -X_1 \\ -X_2 & -X_1 & 0 \end{bmatrix}; \quad |E_B| = -2\lambda X_1 X_2 < 0 \tag{9-81}$$

From (9-72) and (9-73) we know that, at the optimum, $X_1^{**} = P_2/\lambda^{**}$ and $X_2^{**} = P_1/\lambda^{**}$. Substituting these into (9-81), we see that $|E_B| = -(1/\lambda^{**})(2P_1 P_2)$. Comparing this result with the second-order conditions of the primal problem, found in equation (9-37), we see that $|E_B| = -(1/\lambda^{**})|H_B|$, as implied by equation (9-64).

9.6.1   Comparative Statics of Expenditure Minimization: A Change in Price

Our motive for introducing the expenditure minimization model was to demonstrate mathematically the substitution effect of a price change. We stated that a model which included utility as a parameter would enable us to hold utility constant when we examine the effects of a change in price. Therefore, we want to explore the comparative statics of a price change. To do so, we differentiate the identities formed from the FOC, equations (9-58) through (9-60), with respect to P_1. The resulting system of equations can be expressed in matrix form as

$$
\begin{bmatrix}
-\lambda^{**}U_{11} & -\lambda^{**}U_{12} & -U_1 \\
-\lambda^{**}U_{21} & -\lambda^{**}U_{22} & -U_2 \\
-U_1 & -U_2 & 0
\end{bmatrix}
\begin{bmatrix}
\dfrac{\partial X_1^{**}}{\partial P_1} \\[2mm]
\dfrac{\partial X_2^{**}}{\partial P_1} \\[2mm]
\dfrac{\partial \lambda^{**}}{\partial P_1}
\end{bmatrix}
\equiv
\begin{bmatrix}
-1 \\
0 \\
0
\end{bmatrix}
\tag{9-82}
$$

We use Cramer's rule to solve for $\partial X_1^{**}/\partial P_1$, which is negative because $|E_B| < 0$.

$$
\frac{\partial X_1^{**}}{\partial P_1} = \frac{\begin{vmatrix} -1 & -\lambda^{**}U_{12} & -U_1 \\ 0 & -\lambda^{**}U_{22} & -U_2 \\ 0 & -U_2 & 0 \end{vmatrix}}{|E_B|} = \frac{U_2^2}{|E_B|} < 0
\tag{9-83}
$$

From equation (9-59) we know that $U_2 = P_2/\lambda^{**}$. We also know that $|E_B| = -(1/\lambda^{**})|H_B|$. When we substitute these expressions, we find

$$
\frac{\partial X_1^{**}}{\partial P_1} = -\frac{P_2^2}{\lambda^{**}|H_B|}
\tag{9-84}
$$

Because $1/\lambda^{**} = \mu^*$, we can write

$$
\frac{\partial X_1^{**}}{\partial P_1} = -\frac{\mu^* P_2^2}{|H_B|}
\tag{9-85}
$$

The term $-\mu^*(P_2^2/|H_B|)$ is precisely what we identified as the substitution effect in the Slutsky equation, equation (9-47), when we found comparative statics results using the constrained utility maximization model. It is the partial derivative of X_1^{**} with respect to P_1 holding utility and P_2 constant. Note that there is no income effect here. The expenditure minimization model permits expenditures to change when price changes, rotating the budget constraint about a parametric (fixed) indifference curve. See Figure 9.5 for a graphical illustration of $\partial X_1^{**}/\partial P_1$. When P_1 increases in the constrained

Figure 9.5

Effect of a Price Change, Holding Utility Constant

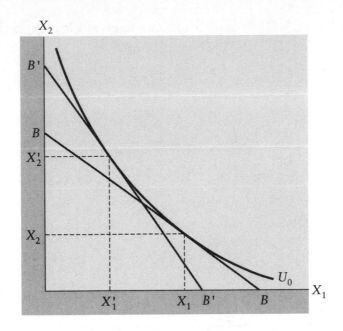

expenditure minimization model, the level of expenditures increases just enough so that the consumer can attain the same indifference curve. That is, the consumer's money income must be compensated to make up for the rise in P_1.

compensated demand: the demand function that results when a consumer's money income is compensated for the income effect of price changes.

When economists speak of *compensated demand*, they are speaking of the demand function $X_1^{**} = X_1^{**}(P_1, P_2, U_0)$. It refers to a situation in which a consumer's money income is compensated for the income effect of price changes. Unlike demand functions in which money income is held constant, the slope of a compensated demand curve is *necessarily* negative. We know this from equation (9-72), whose result can be generalized to include many goods and services in the utility function. Although it is difficult, if not impossible, to measure compensated demand in practice, it is a popular concept for a theorist because it provides an unambiguously downward-sloping demand curve.[4]

NUMERICAL EXAMPLE

Let's consider the comparative statics of the expenditure minimization model we examined in the previous numerical example. To do so, we differentiate the identities formed by substituting X_1^{**}, X_2^{**}, and λ^{**} into the FOC, equations

---

[4]One way to approximate compensated demand in practice is to construct a constrained utility maximization model holding the purchasing power of a consumer's income constant, rather than money income. When a price changes in such a model, money income adjusts to permit the consumer to buy some original combination of goods and services. We ask you to examine the comparative statics of such a model in self-help problem 8 at the end of the chapter.

(9-72) through (9-74), with respect to P_1. The resulting system of equations can be expressed in matrix form as

$$
\begin{bmatrix}
0 & -\lambda^{**} & -X_2^{**} \\
-\lambda^{**} & 0 & -X_1^{**} \\
-X_2^{**} & -X_1^{**} & 0
\end{bmatrix}
\begin{bmatrix}
\dfrac{\partial X_1^{**}}{\partial P_1} \\[2ex]
\dfrac{\partial X_2^{**}}{\partial P_1} \\[2ex]
\dfrac{\partial \lambda^{**}}{\partial P_1}
\end{bmatrix}
\equiv
\begin{bmatrix}
-1 \\
0 \\
0
\end{bmatrix}
\tag{9-86}
$$

We use Cramer's rule to solve for $\partial X_1^{**}/\partial P_1$,

$$
\frac{\partial X_1^{**}}{\partial P_1} = \frac{
\begin{vmatrix}
-1 & -\lambda^{**} & -X_2^{**} \\
0 & 0 & -X_1^{**} \\
0 & -X_1^{**} & 0
\end{vmatrix}
}{|E_B|} = -\frac{1}{2}\frac{X_1^{**}}{\lambda^{**}X_2^{**}} < 0
\tag{9-87}
$$

Remember that $X_1^{**} = P_2/\lambda^{**}$, $X_2^{**} = P_1/\lambda^{**}$, and $\mu^* = 1/\lambda^{**}$, and it is easy to see that $\partial X_1^{**}/\partial P_1 = -\mu^* P_2/(2P_1)$. This is the expression we found for the substitution effect in the primal model with this utility function, equation (9-50) in Section 9.5.2.

EXERCISES
Section 9.6.1
Comparative Statics
of Expenditure
Minimization: A
Change in Price

For the following constrained expenditure minimization problems, find the Lagrangian objective function and the first- and second-order conditions. Find the partial derivative of X_1^{**} with respect to P_1. Show that the partial derivative from this exercise equals the substitution effect you found in the previous set of exercises.

1. $M = P_1 X_1 + P_2 X_2$, $U_0 = U(X_1, X_2) = X_1^\alpha X_2^\beta$

2. $M = P_1 X_1 + P_2 X_2$, $U_0 = U(Z(X_1, X_2)) = 100Z^{-2}$, if
   $Z = 0.5X_1^{-0.5} + 0.5X_2^{-0.5}$

3. $M = P_1 X_1 + P_2 X_2 + P_3 X_3$, $U_0 = U(X_1, X_2, X_3) = X_1 X_2 X_3$

4. $M = P_1 X_1 + P_2 X_2$, $U_0 = \alpha \ln X_1 + (1 - \alpha) \ln X_2$

9.6.2 The Slutsky Equation and the Envelope Theorem

We have demonstrated both analytically and in the numerical examples the relationship of the utility maximization model (the primal) and the expenditure minimization model (the dual). The equilibria of the two models are equivalent if the given level of utility in the dual is the optimum level in the primal or if the given level of money income in the primal equals the optimum level of expenditures in the dual. We can use this equivalence along with the envelope theorem to derive the Slutsky equation in a more intuitive and economical fashion.

Consider the equilibrium values of X_1 in the two models. Utility maximization gives us $X_1^* = X_1^*(P_1, P_2, M)$, and expenditure minimization gives us $X_1^{**} = X_1^{**}(P_1, P_2, U_0)$. They are equivalent if the value of the parameter M in the primal is equal to the optimum value of expenditures $M^{**}(P_1, P_2, U_0)$ in the dual. Therefore, we can write

$$X_1^{**}(P_1, P_2, U_0) \equiv X_1^*(P_1, P_2, M^{**}(P_1, P_2, U_0)) \qquad (9\text{-}88)$$

where the identity sign indicates the equivalence of the two expressions. We differentiate (9-88) with respect to P_1. Remembering to use the chain rule when we differentiate the right-hand side, we obtain

$$\frac{\partial X_1^{**}}{\partial P_1} \equiv \frac{\partial X_1^*}{\partial P_1} + \frac{\partial X_1^*}{\partial M^{**}} \frac{\partial M^{**}}{\partial P_1} \qquad (9\text{-}89)$$

We can use the envelope theorem to find an expression for $\partial M^{**}/\partial P_1$. The envelope theorem tells us that the partial derivative of the indirect objective function with respect to a parameter equals the partial derivative of the Lagrangian objective function with respect to the same parameter, when both functions are evaluated at the optimum. Because M^{**} is the indirect expenditure function from the dual problem, $\partial M^{**}/\partial P_1$ equals the partial derivative of $\mathcal{L} = P_1 X_1 + P_2 X_2 + \lambda(U_0 - U(X_1, X_2))$ with respect to P_1, evaluated at the optimum. Therefore, $\partial M^{**}/\partial P_1 = X_1^{**}$. We substitute this result into (9-89), recognizing that we have made X_1^{**} equivalent to X_1^*,

$$\frac{\partial X_1^{**}}{\partial P_1} \equiv \frac{\partial X_1^*}{\partial P_1} + X_1^* \frac{\partial X_1^*}{\partial M^{**}} \qquad (9\text{-}90)$$

Subtracting $X_1^*(\partial X_1^*/\partial M)$ from both sides and rearranging gives us

$$\frac{\partial X_1^*}{\partial P_1} \equiv \frac{\partial X_1^{**}}{\partial P_1} - X_1^* \frac{\partial X_1^*}{\partial M^{**}} \qquad (9\text{-}91)$$

If you substitute (9-85) into (9-91) and recognize that M has been made identical to M^{**}, you see that (9-91) is the same as (9-47), the Slutsky equation,

$$\frac{\partial X_1^*}{\partial P_1} = -\mu^* \frac{P_2^2}{|H_B|} - X_1^* \frac{\partial X_1^*}{\partial M} \qquad (9\text{-}47)$$

Here, you see that an understanding of the relationship between the primal and dual consumer models, along with the envelope theorem, enables you to derive an important theoretical result rather easily.

9.7

MONOTONIC TRANSFORMATIONS OF THE UTILITY FUNCTION, OR ORDINAL UTILITY

The concept of ordinal utility means that only the rank ordering of consumption bundles is important.[5] Given a map of indifference curves, any system of labeling levels of utility which preserves the preference rankings is as good as any other. We can demonstrate that our model of constrained utility maximization is consistent with the concept of ordinal utility by showing that our equilibrium conditions are unaffected by transformations of the utility function that preserve rank orderings. Such a transformation is called a ***monotonic transformation***. Remember from Chapter 2, Section 2.3, that a function is monotonic if its value either increases or decreases consistently as its argument increases. A monotonic transformation is similar in that the value of the transformed function increases (decreases) consistently as the value of the original function increases (decreases).

> **monotonic transformation:** given a function $U = U(X_1, X_2)$, a transformation $V = V(U(X_1, X_2))$ is monotonic if and only if $V'(U(X_1, X_2)) > 0$.

Given a utility function $U = U(X_1, X_2)$, a transformation $V = V(U(X_1, X_2))$ is monotonic if and only if $dV/dU \equiv V'(U(X_1, X_2)) > 0$. In other words, any new consumption bundle that increases $U(X_1, X_2)$ also increases $V(U(X_1, X_2))$, and any new consumption bundle that decreases $U(X_1, X_2)$ also decreases $V(U(X_1, X_2))$. Let's see how our model is affected by a monotonic transformation of the utility function. We want to maximize $V(U(X_1, X_2))$ subject to $M - P_1 X_1 - P_2 X_2 = 0$. The Lagrangian objective function is

$$\mathcal{L} = V(U(X_1, X_2)) + \mu[M - P_1 X_1 - P_2 X_2] \tag{9-92}$$

The first-order conditions are

$$\mathcal{L}_1 = V'U_1 - \mu P_1 = 0 \tag{9-93}$$

$$\mathcal{L}_2 = V'U_2 - \mu P_2 = 0 \tag{9-94}$$

$$\mathcal{L}_\mu = M - P_1 X_1 - P_2 X_2 = 0 \tag{9-95}$$

Only (9-93) and (9-94) are affected by the transformation of the utility function. We used them to show that the equilibrium values of X_1 and X_2 are where the budget constraint is tangent to an indifference curve. If we divide one by the other we find that

$$\frac{V'U_1}{V'U_2} = \frac{P_1}{P_2} \quad \text{or} \quad \frac{U_1}{U_2} = \frac{P_1}{P_2} \tag{9-96}$$

Equation (9-96) implies that the first-order conditions of the transformed model imply exactly the same equilibrium that is implied by the first-order conditions of the original model.

> **cardinal utility:** a concept of utility according to which the individual assigns meaningful amounts of utility to consumption bundles.

---

[5]Ordinal utility is distinguished from ***cardinal utility***, which requires that differences in utility actually be measurable according to some scale of units.

The determinant of the bordered Hessian matrix of the transformed model (denoted by a superscript T) is

$$|H_B^T| = \begin{vmatrix} V'U_{11} + V''U_1^2 & V'U_{12} + V''U_1U_2 & -P_1 \\ V'U_{21} + V''U_2U_1 & V'U_{22} + V''U_2^2 & -P_2 \\ -P_1 & -P_2 & 0 \end{vmatrix} > 0 \quad (9\text{-}97)$$

Expanding this determinant by the third column, we find that

$$|H_B^T| = -P_1^2(V'U_{22} + V''U_2^2) + 2P_1P_2(V'U_{12} + V''U_1U_2)$$
$$- P_2^2(V'U_{11} + V''U_1^2) > 0 \quad (9\text{-}98)$$

Recognize from the first-order conditions that $U_1 = \mu P_1/V'$ and $U_2 = \mu P_2/V'$ and substitute.

$$|H_B^T| = -P_1^2 V'U_{22} + 2P_1P_2 V'U_{12} - P_2^2 V'U_{11}$$
$$= V'(-P_1^2 U_{22} + 2P_1P_2 U_{12} - P_2^2 U_{11}) = V'|H_B| > 0 \quad (9\text{-}99)$$

We have shown that the determinant of the bordered Hessian from the model with the transformed utility function, $|H_B^T|$, equals the determinant of the bordered Hessian from the original model, $|H_B|$, multiplied by V'. Because V' is positive by assumption of a monotonic transformation, $|H_B^T|$ will always have the same sign as $|H_B|$. This result can be generalized to argue that the second-order conditions of any n-dimensional model with a monotonically transformed utility function are identical to those of the same model without the transformation.[6] This completes the argument that our model of constrained utility maximization is unaffected by a monotonic transformation of the utility function. In other words, any utility function which preserves the rank ordering of consumption bundles has the same implications as any other. Utility is an ordinal concept.

9.8

SUMMARY

In this chapter, we use the mathematical techniques developed in earlier chapters to explore consumer behavior. First, we review the meaning of utility and the mathematics of indifference curves. Then we examine the model of constrained utility maximization, deriving and interpreting the comparative statics of the model in the process. Although we discover that none of the partial derivatives of choice variables with respect to parameters can be confidently signed, the mathematical results are consistent with what we intuitively know about consumer behavior. Because we know so little about

---

[6]See Silberberg, Eugene, *The Structure of Economics: A Mathematical Analysis*, 2nd editor (New York: McGraw-Hill Book Company, 1990), pp. 311–312.

consumer tastes and preferences, goods can be inferior or normal and cooperative or competitive in consumption. We cannot even establish the law of demand unambiguously. However, we gain insight into the demand function; we find the *ceteris paribus* conditions and we separate out substitution and income effects of a price change.

Examining substitution and income effects gives us the opportunity to introduce the concept of a dual model. The dual of constrained utility maximization is constrained expenditure minimization. Dual models have the same equilibrium conditions as their primals; the first- and second-order conditions of both models have the same implications. The parameters of the models differ, however, and so do the comparative statics. We introduce the concept in order to hold utility constant when relative price changes because we want to identify the substitution effect. To perform comparative statics is to find partial derivatives of the choice variables with respect to one parameter, holding constant the other parameters. Utility is a parameter in the expenditure minimization model, so it is held constant when the partial derivative of consumption with respect to price is found. This partial derivative represents the slope of the compensated demand curve.

Finally, we show that the constrained utility maximization model is consistent with an ordinal conception of utility. We demonstrate that the implications of the model were unchanged by a monotonic transformation of the utility function. That is, we can relabel the utility associated with any consumption bundle as long as we maintain rank orderings of those bundles. When we make such a transformation, the equilibrium conditions of the utility maximization are unaffected.

◆ REFERENCES

Hicks, J. R., *Value and Capital* (Oxford: Clarendon Press, 1939), Chapters 1, 2, and 3 and their mathematical appendices.

Samuelson, Paul A., *Foundations of Economic Analysis* (New York: Atheneum, 1965), Chapters 5, 6, and 7.

Silberberg, Eugene, *The Structure of Economics*, 2nd edition (New York: McGraw-Hill Book Company, 1990), Chapters 10 and 11.

◆ ANSWERS TO END-OF-SECTION EXERCISES

Section 9.5.1 Comparative Statics Analysis of Changes in Money Income

1. The Lagrangian is $\mathscr{L} = X_1^\alpha X_2^\beta + \mu(M - P_1X_1 - P_2X_2)$. The first-order necessary conditions are

$$\mathscr{L}_1 = \alpha X_1^{\alpha-1} X_2^\beta - \mu P_1 = 0$$
$$\mathscr{L}_2 = \beta X_1^\alpha X_2^{\beta-1} - \mu P_2 = 0$$
$$\mathscr{L}_\mu = M - P_1X_1 - P_2X_2 = 0$$

The second-order sufficient condition is

$$|H_B| = \begin{vmatrix} \alpha(\alpha-1)(X_1^*)^{\alpha-2}(X_2^*)^{\beta} & \alpha\beta(X_1^*)^{\alpha-1}(X_2^*)^{\beta-1} & -P_1 \\ \alpha\beta(X_1^*)^{\alpha-1}(X_2^*)^{\beta-1} & \beta(\beta-1)(X_1^*)^{\alpha}(X_2^*)^{\beta-2} & -P_2 \\ -P_1 & -P_2 & 0 \end{vmatrix}$$

$$= P_1 P_2 \left(\frac{\alpha}{\alpha+\beta}\frac{M}{P_1}\right)^{\alpha-1}\left(\frac{\beta}{\alpha+\beta}\frac{M}{P_2}\right)^{\beta-1} > 0$$

where $X_1^* = \alpha M/[P_1(\alpha+\beta)]$ and $X_2^* = \beta M/[P_2(\alpha+\beta)]$. The comparative statics results for a change in income, M, are

$$\frac{\partial X_1^*}{\partial M} = \frac{\alpha}{P_1(\alpha+\beta)}$$

$$\frac{\partial X_2^*}{\partial M} = \frac{\beta}{P_2(\alpha+\beta)}$$

$$\frac{\partial \mu^*}{\partial M} = \frac{(\alpha+\beta-1)\mu^*}{M}$$

where $\mu^* = (\alpha/P_1)^{\alpha}(\beta/P_2)^{\beta}(M/(\alpha+\beta))^{\alpha+\beta-1}$.

2. The Lagrangian is $\mathscr{L} = 100(0.5X_1^{-0.5} + 0.5X_2^{-0.5})^{-2} + \mu(M - P_1X_1 - P_2X_2)$. The first-order necessary conditions are

$$\mathscr{L}_1 = 50X_1^{-1.5}(0.5X_1^{-0.5} + 0.5X_2^{-0.5})^{-3} - \mu P_1 = 0$$

$$\mathscr{L}_2 = 50X_2^{-1.5}(0.5X_1^{-0.5} + 0.5X_2^{-0.5})^{-3} - \mu P_2 = 0$$

$$\mathscr{L}_\mu - M - P_1X_1 - P_2X_2 = 0$$

The second-order sufficient condition is

$$|H_B| - \begin{vmatrix} -75(X_1^*)^{-2.5}Z^{*-3} + 37.5(X_1^*)^{-3}Z^{*-4} & 37.5(X_1^*X_2^*)^{-1.5}Z^{*-4} & -P_1 \\ 37.5(X_1^*X_2^*)^{-1.5}Z^{*-4} & -75(X_2^*)^{-1.5}Z^{*-3} + 37.5(X_2^*)^{-3}Z^{*-4} & -P_2 \\ -P_1 & -P_2 & 0 \end{vmatrix} > 0$$

where $Z^* = 0.5X_1^{*-0.5} + 0.5X_2^{*-0.5}$, $X_1^* = M/(P_1[1 + (P_2/P_1)^{1/3}])$, $X_2^* = M/(P_2[1 + (P_1/P_2)^{1/3}])$, and $\mu^* = [50P_1^{1/2}(1 + (P_2/P_1)^{1/3})^{3/2}]/(M^{3/2}Z^{*3})$.

The comparative statics results for a change in income, M, are

$$\frac{\partial X_1^*}{\partial M} = \frac{1}{P_1[1 + (P_2/P_1)^{1/3}]}$$

$$\frac{\partial X_2^*}{\partial M} = \frac{1}{P_2[1 + (P_1/P_2)^{1/3}]}$$

$$\frac{\partial \mu^*}{\partial M} = 0$$

3. The Lagrangian is $\mathscr{L} = X_1X_2X_3 + \mu(M - P_1X_1 - P_2X_2 - P_3X_3)$. The first-order necessary conditions are

$$\mathscr{L}_1 = X_2X_3 - \mu P_1 = 0$$

$$\mathscr{L}_2 = X_1X_3 - \mu P_2 = 0$$

$$\mathscr{L}_3 = X_1X_2 - \mu P_3 = 0$$

$$\mathscr{L}_\mu = M - P_1X_1 - P_2X_2 - P_3X_3 = 0$$

The second-order sufficient conditions are

$$|H_{11}| = \begin{vmatrix} 0 & \dfrac{M}{3P_1} & -P_2 \\[2mm] \dfrac{M}{3P_1} & 0 & -P_3 \\[2mm] -P_2 & -P_3 & 0 \end{vmatrix} = \frac{3}{2}\frac{MP_2P_3}{P_1} > 0$$

and

$$|H_B| = \begin{vmatrix} 0 & \dfrac{M}{3P_3} & \dfrac{M}{3P_2} & -P_1 \\[2mm] \dfrac{M}{3P_3} & 0 & \dfrac{M}{3P_1} & -P_2 \\[2mm] \dfrac{M}{3P_2} & \dfrac{M}{3P_1} & 0 & -P_3 \\[2mm] -P_1 & -P_2 & -P_3 & 0 \end{vmatrix} = -\frac{1}{3}M^2 < 0$$

The comparative statics results for a change in income, M, are

$$\frac{\partial X_1^*}{\partial M} = \frac{1}{3P_1}$$

$$\frac{\partial X_2^*}{\partial M} = \frac{1}{3P_2}$$

$$\frac{\partial X_3^*}{\partial M} = \frac{1}{3P_3}$$

$$\frac{\partial \mu^*}{\partial M} = \frac{2M}{9P_1P_2P_3}$$

4. The Lagrangian is $\mathcal{L} = \alpha \ln X_1 + (1-\alpha)\ln X_2 + \mu(M - P_1X_1 - P_2X_2)$. The first-order necessary conditions are

$$\mathcal{L}_1 = \frac{\alpha}{X_1} - \mu P_1 = 0$$

$$\mathcal{L}_2 = \frac{(1-\alpha)}{X_2} - \mu P_2 = 0$$

$$\mathcal{L}_\mu = M - P_1X_1 - P_2X_2 = 0$$

The second-order sufficient condition is

$$|H_B| = \begin{vmatrix} -\dfrac{P_1^2}{\alpha M^2} & 0 & -P_2 \\[3mm] 0 & -\dfrac{P_2^2}{(1-\alpha)M^2} & -P_2 \\[3mm] -P_1 & -P_2 & -P_3 \end{vmatrix} = \frac{(P_1P_2)^2}{\alpha M^2} + \frac{(P_1P_2)^2}{(1-\alpha)M^2} > 0$$

The comparative statics results for a change in income, M, are

$$\frac{\partial X_1^*}{\partial M} = \frac{\alpha}{P_1}$$

$$\frac{\partial X_2^*}{\partial M} = \frac{(1-\alpha)}{P_2}$$

$$\frac{\partial \mu^*}{\partial M} = \frac{-1}{M^2}$$

Section 9.5.2 Comparative Statics Analysis of a Change in Price

1. $\partial X_1^*/\partial P_1 = -\alpha M/P_1^2$; $\partial X_2^*/\partial P_1 = 0$; $\partial \mu^*/\partial P_1 = -\alpha \mu^*/P_1$. The substitution effect is $-(\alpha + \beta)/(\alpha\beta P_1^2 M)$. The income effect is $-M(\alpha/[P_1(\alpha + \beta)])^2$

2. $$\frac{\partial X_1^*}{\partial P_1} = -\left[1 + \left(\frac{2}{3}\right)\left(\frac{P_2}{P_1}\right)^{1/3}\right]\frac{M}{P_1^2}\left[1 + \left(\frac{P_2}{P_1}\right)^{1/3}\right]^2$$

$$\frac{\partial X_2^*}{\partial P_1} = \left(\frac{P_2}{P_1}\right)^{2/3}\frac{M}{3P_2^2}\left[1 + \left(\frac{P_2}{P_1}\right)^{1/3}\right]^2$$

$$\frac{\partial \mu^*}{\partial P_1} = -\frac{\mu^*}{P_1[1 + (P_2/P_1)^{1/3}]}$$

   The substitution effect is $-P_2^2\mu^*/|H_B|$. The income effect is $-M/(P_1[1 + (P_2/P_1)^{2/3}])$.

3. $\partial X_1^*/\partial P_1 = -3M/P_1^2$; $\partial X_2^*/\partial P_1 = \partial X_3^*/\partial P_1 = 0$; $\partial \mu^*/\partial P_1 = M^2/(9P_1^2 P_2 P_3)$
   The substitution effect is $-2M/(9P_1^2)$. The income effect is $-M/(9P_1^2)$

4. $\partial X_1^*/\partial P_1 = -\alpha M/P_1^2$; $\partial X_2^*/\partial P_1 = 0$; $\partial \mu^*/\partial P_1 = 0$
   The substitution effect is $-M/(P_1^2\alpha(1 - \alpha))$. The income effect is $-\alpha^2/(MP_1^2)$

Section 9.6 The Dual of Constrained Utility Maximization

1. The Lagrangian is $\mathcal{L} = P_1 X_1 + P_2 X_2 + \lambda(U_0 - X_1^\alpha X_2^\beta)$
   The first-order necessary conditions are

$$\mathcal{L}_1 = P_1 - \lambda\alpha X_1^{\alpha-1}X_2^\beta = 0$$

$$\mathcal{L}_2 = P_2 - \lambda\beta X_1^\alpha X_2^{\beta-1} = 0$$

$$\mathcal{L}_\lambda = U_0 - X_1^\alpha X_2^\beta = 0$$

The second-order sufficient condition is

$$|E_B| = \begin{vmatrix} -\lambda^{**}\alpha(\alpha-1)X_1^{**\alpha--}X_2^{**\beta} & -\lambda^{**}\alpha\beta X_1^{**2-1}X_2^{**\beta-1} & -\alpha X_1^{**\alpha-1}X_2^{**\beta} \\ -\lambda^{**}\alpha\beta X_1^{**\alpha-2}X_2^{**\beta-1} & -\lambda^{**}\beta(\beta-1)X_1^{**\alpha}X_2^{**\beta-2} & -\beta X_1^{**\alpha}X_2^{**\beta-1} \\ -\alpha X_1^{**\alpha-1}X_2^{**\beta} & -\beta X_1^{**\alpha}X_2^{**\beta-1} & 0 \end{vmatrix}$$

$$= -\frac{\alpha\beta(\alpha+\beta)U_0^3}{X_1^{**2}X_2^{**2}} < 0$$

where $X_1^{**} = U_0^{1/(\alpha+\beta)}((\alpha P_2)/(\beta P_1))^{\beta/(\alpha+\beta)}$, $X_2^{**} = U_0^{1/(\alpha+\beta)}((\beta P_1)/(\alpha P_2))^{\alpha/(\alpha+\beta)}$, and $\lambda^{**} = U_0^{1-(\alpha+\beta)}(P_2/\beta)^{\beta/(\alpha+\beta)}(P_1/\alpha)^{\alpha/(\alpha+\beta)}$.
$\partial X_1^{**}/\partial P_1 = -[\beta/((\alpha+b)P_1)][U_0^{1/(\alpha+\beta)}((\alpha P_2)/(\beta P_1))^{\beta/\alpha+\beta}]$. To verify that this equals the substitution effect found in the previous exercise, substitute the indirect utility function from the primal problem and simplify.

2. The Lagrangian is $\mathscr{L} = P_1 X_1 + P_2 X_2 + \lambda[U_0 - 100(0.5X_1^{-0.5} + 0.5X_2^{-0.5})^{-2}]$

The FOC are

$$\mathscr{L}_1 = P_1 - 50\lambda X_1^{-1.5}(0.5X_1^{-0.5} + 0.5X_2^{-0.5})^{-3} = 0$$
$$\mathscr{L}_2 = P_2 - 50\lambda X_2^{-1.5}(0.5X_1^{-0.5} + 0.5X_2^{-0.5})^{-3} = 0$$
$$\mathscr{L}_\lambda = U_0 - 100(0.5X_1^{-0.5} + 0.5X_2^{-0.5})^{-2} = 0$$

The second-order sufficient condition is

$$|E_B| = (12.5)^3 Z^{**-3} \begin{vmatrix} 6\lambda^{**}X_1^{**-2.5} - 3\lambda^{**}X_1^{**-3}Z^{**-1} & \lambda^{**}(X_1^{**}X_2^{**})^{-1.5}Z^{**-1} & -4X_1^{**-1.5} \\ \lambda^{**}(X_1^{**}X_2^{**})^{-1.5}Z^{**-1} & 6\lambda^{**}X_2^{**-2.5} - 3\lambda^{**}X_2^{**-3}Z^{**-1} & -4X_2^{**-1.5} \\ -4X_1^{**-1.5} & -4X_2^{**-1.5} & 0 \end{vmatrix} < 0$$

where $Z^{**} = 0.5X_1^{**-0.5} + 0.5X_2^{**-0.5}$, $X_1^{**} = U_0/(400(1 + P_1/P_2)^{2/3})$,
$X_2^{**} = U_0/(400(1 + P_2/P_1)2/3)$, and $\lambda^{**} = P_1/(50X_1^{**-1.5}Z^{**-3})$.
$$\partial X_1^{**}/\partial P_1 = -(2U_0/(1200P_2))(1 + P_1/P_2)^{-5/2}$$

3. The Lagrangian objective function is

$$\mathscr{L} = P_1 X_1 + P_2 X_2 + P_3 X_3 - \lambda(U_0 - X_1 X_2 X_3)$$

The FOC are
$$\mathscr{L}_1 = P_1 - \lambda X_2 X_3 = 0$$
$$\mathscr{L}_2 = P_2 - \lambda X_1 X_3 = 0$$
$$\mathscr{L}_3 = P_3 - \lambda X_1 X_2 = 0$$
$$\mathscr{L}_\lambda = U_0 - X_1 X_2 X_3 = 0$$

The second-order sufficient conditions are

$$|E_{11}| = \begin{vmatrix} 0 & -\lambda^{**}X_1^{**} & -X_1^{**}X_3^{**} \\ -\lambda^{**}X_1^{**} & 0 & -X_1^{**}X_2^{**} \\ -X_1^{**}X_3^{**} & X_1^{**}X_2^{**} & 0 \end{vmatrix} = -\frac{2U_0 P_2 P_3}{P_1} < 0$$

and

$$|E_B| = \begin{vmatrix} 0 & -\lambda^{**}X_3^{**} & -\lambda^{**}X_2^{**} & -X_2^{**}X_3^{**} \\ -\lambda^{**}X_3^{**} & 0 & -\lambda^{**}X_1^{**} & -X_1^{**}X_3^{**} \\ -\lambda^{**}X_2^{**} & -\lambda^{**}X_1^{**} & 0 & -X_1^{**}X_2^{**} \\ -X_2^{**}X_3^{**} & -X_1^{**}X_3^{**} & -X_1^{**}X_2^{**} & 0 \end{vmatrix}$$

$$= -3(U_0 P_1 P_2 P_3)^{3/2} < 0$$
$$\partial X_1^{**}/\partial P_1 = -(2/3)[(U_0 P_2 P_3)/P_1^5]^{1/3}.$$

4. The Lagrangian is $\mathscr{L} = P_1 X_1 + P_2 X_2 + \lambda[U_0 - \alpha \ln X_1 - (1 - \alpha) \ln X_2]$
   The FOC are $\mathscr{L}_1 = P_1 - \lambda\alpha/X_1 = 0$
$$\mathscr{L}_2 = P_2 - \lambda(1 - \alpha)/X_2 = 0$$
$$\mathscr{L}_\lambda = U_0 - \alpha \ln X_1 - (1 - \alpha) \ln X_2 = 0$$

The second-order sufficient condition is

$$
|E_B| = \begin{vmatrix} \dfrac{\lambda^{**}\alpha}{X_1^{**2}} & 0 & -\dfrac{\alpha}{X_1^{**}} \\[2ex] 0 & \dfrac{\lambda^{**}(1-\alpha)}{X_2^{**2}} & -\dfrac{(1-\alpha)}{X_2^{**}} \\[2ex] -\dfrac{\alpha}{X_1^{**}} & -\dfrac{(1-\alpha)}{X_2^{**}} & 0 \end{vmatrix} = -\dfrac{\lambda\alpha(1-\alpha)}{X_1^{**2}X_2^{**2}} < 0
$$

$$\partial X_1^{**}/\partial P_1 = -[(1-\alpha)^2/(\lambda^{**}\alpha)]X_1^{**2}.$$

◆ SELF-HELP PROBLEMS

Answers to these problems are given at the end of the text.

To answer questions 1 through 6, suppose the utility function of a consumer is of the form $U = X_1^\alpha X_2^{1-\alpha}$. She faces a budget constraint of the form $M = P_1 X_1 + P_2 X_2$.

1. Find the first-order and second-order conditions for utility maximization, and solve them for the demand functions X_1^*, X_2^*. Find the indirect utility function for this problem.

2. What are the effects on the demand functions of multiplying M, P_1, and P_2 by a constant factor k? Explain your result.

3. Find comparative statics results for changes in P_1 and M. Identify the income and substitution effects of a change in P_1. Explain whether you believe X_1 and X_2 to be normal or inferior goods.

4. Find expressions for the price elasticity of demand for good 1, the cross-price elasticity of demand for good 1 with respect to changes in P_2, and the income elasticity for good 1. Find the sum of the three elasticities and explain the meaning of the sum in words.

5. Find expressions for this consumer's shares of total income spent on each good, $S_1 = P_1 X_1^{**}/M$ and $S_2 = P_2 X_2^*/M$. Explain the meaning of your result.

6. Set up the dual of the constrained utility maximization problem above. Show that your identification of the substitution effect in question 3 was accurate. Compare the indirect expenditure function of the dual to the indirect utility function from the primal.

7. Answer question 1 again, this time assuming that the utility function is $U = (X_1^\alpha X_2^{1-\alpha})^2$. What principle of utility theory is illustrated by this transformation of the utility function?

8. This problem asks you to find the slope of a compensated demand curve, where purchasing power of the consumer is held constant instead of money income, as suggested in footnote 4. Purchasing power is considered to be the ability to purchase some given market basket of goods, (X_1^0, X_2^0). Find the objective function, the first- and second-order conditions, and $\partial X_1^*/\partial P_1$ if the consumer

maximizes utility, $U(X_1, X_2)$, subject to the constraint that $P_1 X_1^0 + P_2 X_2^0 = P_1 X_1 + P_2 X_2$. Picture the effects of the change in price graphically, assuming that the initial equilibrium is where $(X_1^*, X_2^*) = (X_1^0, X_2^0)$.

◆ SUPPLEMENTAL PROBLEMS

1. Show that the second-order conditions for constrained utility maximization (two-good model) imply convex indifference curves by expanding the determinant of the bordered Hessian matrix. Show the same thing for the constrained expenditure minimization model.

2. Consider a consumer with utility function $U = U(X_1, X_2)$ and budget constraint $M = P_1 X_1 + P_2 X_2$.

   a. Find $\partial X_2^* / \partial P_2$. Separate the expression into the substitution and income effects. Demonstrate mathematically that your identification of the income and substitution effects is correct.

   b. Find $\partial X_1^* / \partial P_2$. Can you determine the sign of this partial derivative? Why or why not? Interpret the meaning of this partial derivative for consumer behavior.

3. Contrast the expenditure minimization model of consumer behavior to the utility maximization model of consumer behavior. Compare first- and second-order conditions, Lagrange multipliers, and the interpretation of the demand functions derivable from each model.

4. A consumer chooses the quantities of two goods, X_1 and X_2, so as to maximize $U = (0.5 X_1^{-2} + 0.5 X_2^{-2})^{-0.5}$ subject to $M = P_1 X_1 + P_2 X_2$.

   a. Set up the Lagrangian objective function and find the first-order conditions for maximization.

   b. Find the bordered Hessian matrix for this constrained optimization problem and check the second-order conditions in terms of the border-preserving, principal minors of the determinant of the bordered Hessian.

   c. Find all comparative statics results for X_1^* and X_2^* with respect to changes in M and P_1. Write the Slutsky equation for this problem.

5. Set up the general, *n-good*, constrained utility maximization problem. This means the consumer has utility function $U = U(X_1, X_2, \ldots, X_n)$ subject to $M = P_1 X_1 + P_2 X_2 + \cdots + P_n X_n$. Find the Lagrangian objective function and the first- and second-order conditions. What is the effect of multiplying money income and all prices by a positive constant on the equilibrium of this problem? How are the consumer's demand functions X_i^*, $i = 1, 2, \ldots, n$, affected?

6. A consumer maximizes the utility, $U(N, F)$, she can gain by consuming quantities of a good in the present, N, and in the future, F. She earns an endowment of present and future quantities equal to (N_0, F_0). She can consume more than she earns in the present by borrowing from her future earnings at an interest rate of r on her borrowings, so that $N = N_0 + (F_0 - F)/(1 + r)$.

   a. Find the first- and second-order conditions for maximization.

   b. Find the comparative statics results for changes in the interest rate. Can you sign the partial derivatives? Explain why or why not, and provide a graphical illustration of the change in r.

7. Suppose a consumer maximizes the utility function $U = U(X_1, X_2) = X_1 X_2$, subject to the budget constraint $M = (P_1 + t)X_1 + P_2 X_2$, where t represents a per unit tax on consumption.

   a. Find the first- and second-order conditions.

   b. Find the comparative statics results for changes in t.

   c. Find the partial derivative of the indirect utility function with respect to t, and discuss the effects of the tax on consumer well-being.

8. Suppose a consumer maximizes the utility function $U = U(X_1, X_2) = X_1 X_2$, subject to the budget constraint $(1 - \tau)M = P_1 X_1 + P_2 X_2$, where τ represents a proportional tax on income and $0 < \tau < 1$.

   a. Find the first- and second-order conditions.
   b. Find the comparative statics results for changes in τ.

   c. Find the partial derivative of the indirect utility function with respect to τ, and discuss the effects of the tax on consumer well-being.

   d. Discuss your interpretation of the Lagrange multiplier for this problem.

9. An individual maximizes a utility function $U(M, R)$ in which M equals money income and R equals leisure time. Money income equals $wL + E$, where E represents some endowment of nonwage income, w equals the wage rate, and L equals time spent working. He has T hours available to him each week in which he can either earn money by working or consume leisure.

   a. Find the first- and second-order conditions. Express the SOC in determinantal form.

   b. Set up the matrix equation that permits you to find comparative statics results for changes in E, and use Cramer's rule to solve for the partial derivatives of the choice variables with respect to E. Interpret your results.

   c. Set up the matrix equation that permits you to find comparative statics results for changes in w, and use Cramer's rule to solve for the partial derivatives of the choice variables with respect to w. Interpret your results.

C H A P T E R   1 0

A Mathematical Treatment of Production

10.1

INTRODUCTION

cardinal: the property of being quantifiable in numerical units.

In this chapter we examine producer behavior in more detail than in the simple two-input, profit-maximization model that we considered in Chapter 6. One feature of producer models that bears further examination is the production function. Unlike the utility function we studied in Chapter 9, the production function can be considered to be *cardinal*; that is, we are comfortable measuring the output of a firm in quantifiable units. Because of this, we are able to discuss some specific properties of particular classes of functions. We look at the connection between returns to scale and production functions, and, in the process, we discuss the mathematical concepts of a homogeneous function and a homothetic function. We apply these concepts in Section 10.6 by looking in detail at the familiar Cobb–Douglas production function. Finally, we introduce the concept of elasticity of substitution in Section 10.7.

10.2

THE PRODUCTION FUNCTION REVISITED

In Chapter 9 we suggested that microeconomic theory treats the consumer as a mysterious machine that converts goods and services into something called utility, and we described the process with a utility function. Similarly, conventional microeconomic theory treats the firm as a "black box" that converts production inputs into outputs. This process is described by the production function, which, in its most general form, characterizes the maximum, technologically feasible rate per unit time of output of m products, $Y_1, Y_2, \ldots, Y_m$, as dependent on the employment rate of n inputs, $X_1, X_2, \ldots, X_n$. This generalized production function can be expressed in implicit form as

$$F(Y_1, Y_2, \ldots, Y_m; X_1, X_2, \ldots, X_n) = 0 \qquad (10\text{-}1)$$

The production function represents the current "state of the art" of known production techniques. This means that different combinations of inputs, representative of different techniques, can be used to produce output levels.

We will restrict our attention to production functions with one output, which can be expressed explicitly as

$$Y = f(X_1, X_2, \ldots, X_n) \qquad (10\text{-}2)$$

To begin with, we further restrict ourselves to production functions with only two inputs, X_1 and X_2. Graphically, we describe such a production function with an isoquant map, as in Figure 10.1. Recall from Chapter 3, Section 3.7.5, that we define an isoquant as a representation of combinations of two inputs which produce the same rate of output. Different points on an isoquant represent different techniques of combining inputs to produce output at a particular rate. For example, point M on the isoquant labeled Y_0 is representative of a technique that uses input 2 relatively intensively and saves on input 1, while point N is representative of a technique that uses input 1 relatively more intensively and saves on input 2. As one moves from point M to point N, input 1 is being substituted for input 2. The three isoquants pictured in Figure 10.1 are distinguished from one another by the rate of output that each one represents.

The ray extending out from the origin, which is labeled $X_2/X_1 = k$, describes the behavior of the production function as both inputs are increased proportionally. The input ratio X_2/X_1 is a constant, k, along the ray. We call the response of output to proportional increases in inputs ***returns to scale*** and examine it in more detail in Section 10.3. The horizontal line labeled $\overline{X}_2$ describes the behavior of the production function as one input, X_1, is

returns to scale: the response of output to proportional increases in inputs.

Figure 10.1

Isoquant Map

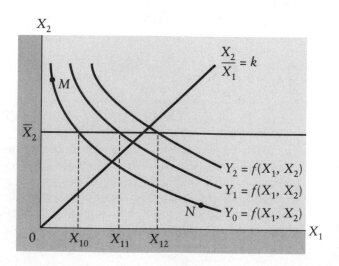

Figure 10.2

(*a*) Total Product; (*b*) Marginal and Average Products

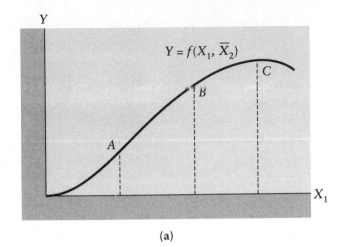

(a)

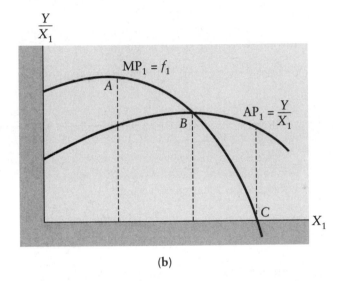

(b)

increased while the other input, X_2, is held constant. By observing how output changes as X_1 changes while X_2 is constant, we can determine the total, marginal, and average products of X_1.

We can graph (on a separate set of axes) the total product curve for increases in X_1 holding X_2 constant by plotting the quantities Y_0, Y_1, and so on against X_{10}, X_{11}, etc. A total product curve is pictured in Figure 10.2*a*. Figure 10.2*b* pictures the marginal and average products of X_1, which are measured in units of Y/X_1, as indicated by the label on the vertical axis. Points A, B, and C represent, respectively, an inflection point in the total product curve, the point where average product is at a maximum, and the point where total product is at a maximum. Note that what we are discussing here is short-run behavior of the firm, where short run is defined (as in Chapter 2) as a situation in which at least one input is held fixed.

Mathematically, the total product of X_1, TP_1, is

$$TP_1 = Y|_{X_2 = \overline{X_2}} = f(X_1, \overline{X_2}) \tag{10-3}$$

The marginal product of X_1, MP_1, is

$$MP_1 = \frac{\partial Y}{\partial X_1} = f_1 \tag{10-4}$$

Remember that $MP_1 = f_1$ equals the slope of the total product curve. The average product of input 1, AP_1 is

$$AP_1 = \frac{Y}{X_1} = \frac{f(X_1, \overline{X_2})}{X_1} \tag{10-5}$$

If the total product function reaches a maximum, it is where the derivative of total product with respect to X_1 is equal to zero.

$$TP_1' = MP_1 = f_1 = 0 \tag{10-6}$$

The second-order condition for maximization of total product is that the second derivative of TP is negative, or

$$TP_1'' = MP_1' = f_{11} < 0 \tag{10-7}$$

This condition corresponds, of course, to diminishing marginal returns to X_1, or downward-sloping marginal product. We see maximum total product pictured in Figure 10.2 at point C.

We can also determine where average product attains a maximum by taking the derivative of AP_1 with respect to X_1 and setting it equal to zero. Using the quotient rule, we find

$$AP_1' = \frac{\partial (f(X_1, \overline{X_2})/X_1)}{\partial X_1} = \frac{1}{X_1^2}(X_1 f_1 - f(X_1, \overline{X_2})) = 0 \tag{10-8}$$

Equation (10-8) can be simplified to

$$AP_1' = \frac{1}{X_1}\left(f_1 - \frac{f(X_1, \overline{X_2})}{X_1}\right) = \frac{1}{X_1}(MP_1 - AP_1) = 0 \tag{10-9}$$

This condition is satisfied when $MP_1 - AP_1 = 0$, or when marginal product equals average product. This is pictured at point B in Figure 10.2. The second-order condition for maximum average product is that the second derivative of AP_1 with respect to X_1 be negative. We must use the quotient rule again when finding AP_1''.

$$AP_1'' = \frac{1}{X_1^2}(X_1(MP_1' - AP_1') - (MP_1 - AP_1)) < 0 \tag{10-10}$$

Remembering from the first-order condition that $AP_1' = 0$ and $MP_1 - AP_1 = 0$ leaves us with

$$AP_1'' = \frac{MP_1'}{X_1} = \frac{f_{11}}{X_1} < 0 \tag{10-11}$$

Stage I: the range of a two-input production function in which the marginal product of one of the inputs is negative.

Stage II: the range of a two-input production function in which the marginal products of both inputs are positive.

Stage III: the range of a two-input production function in which the marginal product of the other input is negative.

The condition required by (10-11) also corresponds to diminishing marginal returns to X_1, or downward-sloping marginal product. The region between points B and C is called *Stage II* of the production function. *Stage I* is the region between the origin and point B, and *Stage III* is the region to the right of point C, where MP_1 is negative. Firms that maximize profits always operate in Stage II. The fact that AP_1 is rising to the left of point B is an indication that the fixed input, X_2, is being underutilized, so firms would not choose to operate in Stage I. The fact that MP_1 is negative to the right of point C indicates that the firm could increase output by reducing X_1, so firms would not choose to operate in Stage III. We examine this issue mathematically in Section 10.5, where we examine homogeneous functions and Euler's theorem.

Point A in Figure 10.2 is a point of inflection in the total product curve. At this point, the slope of total product reaches its maximum. This is where marginal product reaches its maximum, or where the second derivative of total product with respect to X_1 equals zero.

Looking back at Figure 10.1, the isoquant map, reminds us of the mathematical description of the isoquant we discuss in Chapter 5, Sections 5.8.1 and 5.10.1. Consider the isoquant described as $Y_0 = f(X_1, X_2)$. Rewriting this expression as

$$Y_0 - f(X_1, X_2) = 0 \qquad (10\text{-}12)$$

gives us the equation of the isoquant in implicit form. If we were given a specific production function we could solve explicitly for X_2 in terms of X_1, as we do in Section 10.6. Even without the explicit form of the production function, we can find the slope of the isoquant by taking the total differential of equation (10-12), remembering that the differential of a constant equals zero.

$$d[Y_0 - f(X_1, X_2)] = -f_1 \, dX_1 - f_2 \, dX_2 = 0 \qquad (10\text{-}13)$$

Solving for dX_2/dX_1 gives us the familiar expression for the slope of the isoquant

$$\frac{dX_2}{dX_1} = -\frac{f_1}{f_2} = -\frac{MP_1}{MP_2} \qquad (10\text{-}14)$$

Recall that, by setting output equal to a specific value, Y_0, we create a functional relationship between X_2 and X_1.[1] That functional relationship must be taken into account when we differentiate again to examine the behavior of the slope of the isoquant. We show in Chapter 5, equation (5-74), that the derivative of the slope of the isoquant equals

$$\left.\frac{d^2X_2}{dX_1^2}\right|_{dY=0} = -\frac{1}{f_2^3}[f_2^2 f_{11} - 2f_1 f_2 f_{12} + f_1^2 f_{22}] > 0 \qquad (5\text{-}74)$$

---

[1] It is purely a matter of choice whether we consider X_2 a function of X_1 or vice versa. We choose to treat X_2 as the dependent variable in this relationship because we have placed X_1 on the horizontal axis of the isoquant graph, with X_2 on the vertical axis, where the dependent variable typically belongs. As long as isoquants are monotonic in the relevant ranges, the inverse function exists, which means we could express X_1 as a function of X_2 if we wanted to.

Figure 10.3

Isoquant Map with Ridge Lines

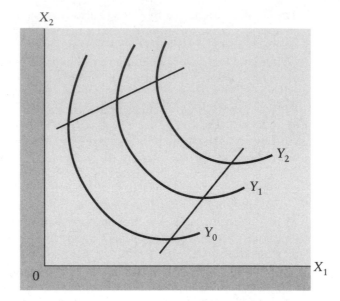

and that, if this expression is positive, the isoquant is strictly convex.

Can the isoquants ever become upward sloping? Looking at equation (10-14), we see that the slope of the isoquant can be positive if one of the inputs has a negative marginal product. This is pictured in Figure 10.2, where X_1 has a negative marginal product at employment levels beyond point C. At point C, MP_1 equals zero, so the slope of the isoquant must also equal zero and the isoquant is horizontal at that point. Beyond that point, the isoquant curves upward with a positive slope. If X_2 has a marginal product equal to zero, equation (10-14) is undefined, but we can see that it approaches $-\infty$ as MP_2 approaches 0. That is, the isoquant becomes vertical when MP_2 equals zero. Beyond that point, when MP_2 is negative, the isoquant becomes positively sloped. Isoquants that behave in this manner are pictured in Figure 10.3.

ridge lines: lines in an isoquant diagram joining the points where the isoquants begin to bend in, i.e., become vertical or horizontal rather than downward sloping.

If we join the points where the isoquants begin to bend in, we form curves called *ridge lines*. Inside the ridge lines, both marginal products are positive, and we are in Stage II of the production function, where the firm can maximize profits. Outside the ridge lines, one or both marginal products are negative and the firm cannot maximize profits.

NUMERICAL EXAMPLE

Suppose output, Y, is produced according to the production function

$$Y = f(X_1, X_2) = 10X_1^{1/4}X_2^{3/4} \qquad (10\text{-}15)$$

We take the partial derivatives of (10-15) in order to find the marginal products of the inputs.

$$MP_1 = f_1 = 2.5X_1^{-3/4}X_2^{3/4} \qquad (10\text{-}16)$$
$$MP_2 = f_2 = 7.5X_1^{1/4}X_2^{-1/4} \qquad (10\text{-}17)$$

Both marginal products are positive for positive values of X_1 and X_2. The second partials give us the slopes of the marginal product curves,

$$f_{11} = -1.875X_1^{-7/4}X_2^{3/4} \tag{10-18}$$

$$f_{22} = -1.875X_1^{1/4}X_2^{-5/4} \tag{10-19}$$

Both are negative, indicating downward-sloping marginal products. We can find the average product of X_1 by dividing (10-15) by X_1,

$$\mathrm{AP}_1 = \frac{Y}{X_1} = 10X_1^{-3/4}X_2^{3/4} \tag{10-20}$$

When you compare (10-20) and (10-16), you can see that, for this production function, average product exceeds marginal product for all strictly positive values of the inputs. Therefore, a firm with this production function will always operate in Stage II of production.

We can find the equation of an isoquant by fixing output at some level, say $Y_0 - 100$, and solving equation (10-15) for X_2 in terms of X_1.

$$X_2 = 10^{4/3}X_1^{-1/3} \tag{10-21}$$

The slope of the isoquant equals the derivative of (10-21) with respect to X_1, or

$$\frac{dX_2}{dX_1} = -7.18X_1^{-4/3} \tag{10-22}$$

Because (10-22) is negative, we see that the isoquant is downward sloping. We verify that it is convex by differentiating (10-22) with respect to X_1 again, obtaining

$$\frac{d^2X_2}{dX_1^2} = 9.57X_1^{-7/3} \tag{10-23}$$

Because (10-23) is positive, we conclude that the $Y_0 = 100$ isoquant is strictly convex.

We will return to the importance of downward-sloping, convex isoquants when we look at the cost curves of the firm in Chapter 11. We will also consider short- and long-run behavior of the firm in the context of the cost of production. Before we discuss these issues, we must return to Figure 10.1 and discuss the behavior of the production function along the ray labeled $X_2/X_1 = k$.

For the following production functions, (a) find the marginal products of the inputs; (b) find the slope of the marginal products and state whether or not there are diminishing marginal returns; (c) find the equation of the $Y_0 = 50$ isoquant; and (d) find the slope of the isoquant and determine whether or not it is convex.

1. $Y = f(X_1, X_2) = 20X_1^{1/3}X_2^{1/2}$ **4.** $Y = f(X_1, X_2) = 25(X_1 + X_2)$

2. $Y = f(X_1, X_2) = X_1^3 X_2^{0.3}$

5. $Y = f(X_1, X_2) = 10X_1^{0.5}X_2^{0.5}\left(\dfrac{X_2}{X_1}\right)^2$

3. $Y = f(X_1, X_2) = 100X_1^{0.4}X_2^{0.6}$

10.3

HOMOGENEOUS PRODUCTION FUNCTIONS AND RETURNS TO SCALE

homogeneous function: a function

$$Y = f(X_1, X_2, \ldots, X_n)$$

is homogeneous of degree r if

$$t^r Y \equiv t^r f(X_1, X_2, \ldots, X_n)$$
$$\equiv f(tX_1, tX_2, \ldots, tX_n)$$

constant returns to scale (CRS): output increasing proportionally to increases in the inputs.

decreasing returns to scale (DRS): output increasing less than proportionally to the increases in inputs.

increasing returns to scale (IRS): output increasing more than proportionally to the increases in inputs.

degree of homogeneity: the exponent r in the definition of a homogeneous function.

Given only the general form of the production function, $Y = f(X_1, X_2)$, there is nothing we can say about how output responds to proportional increases in the inputs. However, there is a special class of functions, called **homogeneous functions**, for which we can determine the effect of proportionally increasing all the independent variables. We turn to this class of functions next. To increase all inputs in a production function proportionally is to increase the scale of production. We want to examine how output responds to changes in scale. If output increases equiproportionately to the increases in the inputs, we consider the production function to exhibit **constant returns to scale (CRS)**. If output increases less than proportionally to the increases in inputs, we consider the production function to exhibit **decreasing returns to scale (DRS)**. If output increases more than proportionally to the increases in inputs, we consider the production function to exhibit **increasing returns to scale (IRS)**. Mathematically, we can describe returns to scale in terms of homogeneous functions. A homogeneous function of degree r is one whose value increases by a positive constant raised to the power $r \geq 0$ when all independent variables are increased by that constant. Mathematically, this means, for a production function with one output, Y, and n inputs X_i, $i = 1, 2, \ldots, n$,

$$t^r Y \equiv t^r f(X_1, X_2, \ldots, X_n) \equiv f(tX_1, tX_2, \ldots, tX_n) \qquad (10\text{-}24)$$

for any value of $t > 0$. Equation (10-24) is the mathematical definition of a homogeneous function, in which t represents the common factor by which all independent variables are multiplied so that they increase proportionally and r represents the **degree of homogeneity**. While t can take any positive value, the value of r determines whether the production function exhibits CRS, DRS, or IRS.

Suppose $r = 1$. Then equation (10-24) becomes

$$tY \equiv tf(X_1, X_2, \ldots, X_n) \equiv f(tX_1, tX_2, \ldots, tX_n) \qquad (10\text{-}25)$$

This describes CRS. When all the inputs are multiplied by some constant t, output is also multiplied by the same constant. If the firm were to double its scale, output would be doubled. A function which has a degree of homogeneity equal to one is called *linearly homogeneous*. An example of a linearly homogeneous function is

linearly homogeneous: homogeneous of degree one.

$$Y = f(X_1, X_2, X_3) = aX_1 + bX_2 + cX_3 \qquad (10\text{-}26)$$

We demonstrate that this is a homogeneous function by multiplying each independent variable by the factor t.

$$f(tX_1, tX_2, tX_3) = atX_1 + btX_2 + ctX_3 \qquad (10\text{-}27)$$

Factoring out t gives us the result that this is a linearly homogeneous function

$$f(tX_1, tX_2, tX_3) = t(aX_1 + bX_2 + cX_3) = t^1 Y \qquad (10\text{-}28)$$

If $r < 1$, the function is said to be homogeneous of degree less than one. A production function which is homogeneous of degree less than one exhibits DRS. Substituting $r < 1$ into equation (10-24) shows us that multiplying all the inputs by some factor t multiplies output by t^r, which is less than t if r is less than one. An example of a function which is homogeneous of degree less than one is

$$Y = f(X_1, X_2, X_3) = AX_1^{0.2}X_2^{0.3}X_3^{0.4} \qquad (10\text{-}29)$$

Again, we demonstrate that this is a homogeneous function by multiplying each independent variable by the factor t.

$$f(tX_1, tX_2, tX_3) = A(tX_1)^{0.2}(tX_2)^{0.3}(tX_3)^{0.4} = At^{0.2}X_1^{0.2}t^{0.3}X_2^{0.3}t^{0.4}X_3^{0.4} \quad (10\text{-}30)$$

Rearranging and adding the exponents in order to multiply together the t's gives us

$$f(tX_1, tX_2, tX_3) = t^{0.2 + 0.3 + 0.4}AX_1^{0.2}X_2^{0.3}X_3^{0.4} = t^{0.9}AX_1^{0.2}X_2^{0.3}X_3^{0.4} = t^{0.9}Y$$
$$(10\text{-}31)$$

We find that this production function is homogeneous of degree $r = 0.9$. Doubling all inputs increases output by a factor of $2^{0.9}$, which is less than 2.

Similarly, if $r > 1$, the function is said to be homogeneous of degree greater than one. A production function with this property exhibits IRS. Multiplying all the inputs by some factor t multiplies output by t^r, which is greater than t if r is greater than one. An example of a function which is homogeneous of degree greater than one is

$$Y = f(X_1, X_2) = X_1 X_2 \qquad (10\text{-}32)$$

Again, we demonstrate that this is a homogeneous function by multiplying each independent variable by the factor t.

$$f(tX_1, tX_2) = tX_1 tX_2 = t^2 X_1 X_2 = t^2 Y \qquad (10\text{-}33)$$

As you can see, this function is homogeneous of degree two. Double all inputs and output is quadrupled.

Recall that we introduced this discussion of homogeneous functions by describing the behavior of the production function along the ray labeled $X_2/X_1 = k$ in Figure 10.1. Along any straight ray out of the origin, two graphed variables (inputs in the example of a production function) are maintaining the same proportion to one another; that is, they are being multiplied by some common factor. The property of homogeneity describes how the dependent variable (output in the example of a production function) responds. This means that homogeneity has implications for the placement of isoquants along rays emanating from the origin.

To understand this point, consider the three different production functions $W = f(X_1, X_2) = 10X_1^{0.4}X_2^{0.3}$, $Y = g(X_1, X_2) = 7.58X_1^{0.6}X_2^{0.4}$,   and $Z = h(X_1, X_2) = 5X_1^{0.8}X_2^{0.6}$. Verify yourself that W exhibits DRS, Y exhibits CRS, and Z exhibits IRS. At the input combination $(X_1, X_2) = (2, 4)$, $W = Y = Z = 20$. This is pictured in Figure 10.4 as the isoquant labeled 20. In order to achieve 40 units of output, the CRS function, $Y = g(X_1, X_2)$, requires double the inputs, $(X_1, X_2) = (4, 8)$. However, in order to achieve 40 units of output, the DRS function, $W = f(X_1, X_2)$, requires more than double the inputs, $(X_1, X_2) = (5.4, 10.8)$, whereas the IRS production function, $Z = h(X_1, X_2)$, requires less than double the inputs, $(X_1, X_2) = (3.3, 6.6)$. We turn to the implications of homogeneity for the *shape* of production isoquants next.

Figure 10.4

Returns to Scale Illustrated in an Isoquant Map

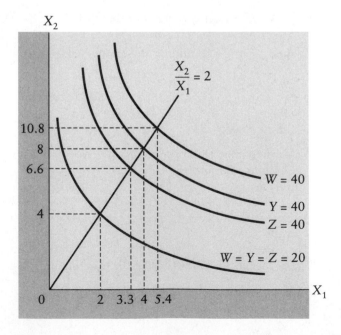

10.4

THE ISOQUANTS OF HOMOGENEOUS PRODUCTION FUNCTIONS

To explore the isoquants of a homogeneous production function, we need to take its total differential. We know that homogeneity means

$$t^r Y \equiv f(tX_1, tX_2, \ldots, tX_n) \tag{10-34}$$

The total differential of this identity is

$$t^r \, dY \equiv \frac{\partial f}{\partial tX_1} \frac{dtX_1}{dX_1} dX_1 + \frac{\partial f}{\partial tX_2} \frac{dtX_2}{dX_2} dX_2 + \cdots + \frac{\partial f}{\partial tX_n} \frac{dtX_n}{dX_n} dX_n \tag{10-35}$$

Recognize that

$$\frac{dtX_i}{dX_i} = t, \qquad i = 1, 2, \ldots, n \tag{10-36}$$

Substitute (10-36) into (10-35) and factor out the t.

$$t^r \, dY \equiv t \left(\frac{\partial f}{\partial tX_1} dX_1 + \frac{\partial f}{\partial tX_2} dX_2 + \cdots + \frac{\partial f}{\partial tX_n} dX_n \right) \tag{10-37}$$

Dividing both sides by t gives us

$$t^{r-1} \, dY \equiv \frac{\partial f}{\partial tX_1} dX_1 + \frac{\partial f}{\partial tX_2} dX_2 + \cdots + \frac{\partial f}{\partial tX_n} dX_n \tag{10-38}$$

Equation (10-38) is useful for two reasons. First, it implies something important about the first-order total differential of a homogeneous function. When all the independent variables are multiplied by a constant factor, t, the total differential is multiplied by t^{r-1}! This means that the total differential of a homogeneous function is also homogeneous, but the degree of homogeneity is reduced by one. This is true not only of the total differential but also of all the partial derivatives. This is easily seen by holding all but one input constant, that is, by setting all $dX_i = 0$, $i \neq j$. Doing so shows us that

$$t^{r-1} \frac{dY}{dX_j} \bigg|_{dX_i = 0, i \neq j} \equiv t^{r-1} f_j \equiv \frac{\partial f}{\partial tX_j} \tag{10-39}$$

A second important implication of equation (10-38) concerns the slopes of isoquants for any positive value of t. To investigate the slope of an isoquant of a homogeneous production function, set $dY = 0$ in equation (10-38). This gives us

$$0 = \frac{\partial f}{\partial tX_1} dX_1 + \frac{\partial f}{\partial tX_2} dX_2 + \cdots + \frac{\partial f}{\partial tX_n} dX_n \tag{10-40}$$

In order to examine the slope of the isoquant for the two inputs X_j and X_k, we hold all other inputs constant. That is, $dX_i = 0, i \neq j, k$. This permits us to write

$$0 = \frac{\partial f}{\partial tX_j} dX_j + \frac{\partial f}{\partial tX_k} dX_k \tag{10-41}$$

The slope of the isoquant for inputs X_j and X_k equals

$$\frac{dX_j}{dX_k} = - \frac{\partial f/\partial tX_k}{\partial f/\partial tX_j} = - \frac{t^{r-1}f_k}{t^{r-1}f_j} = - \frac{f_k}{f_j} \tag{10-42}$$

Notice that we made use of the result derived in equation (10-39) that first-order partial derivatives of a function that is homogeneous of degree r are homogeneous of degree $r - 1$.

homothetic functions: the class of functions for which the slopes of the level curves are the same along any straight ray emanating from the origin.

This equation tells us that multiplying the inputs by a factor of t does not affect the slope of the isoquant. In other words, the slopes of the isoquants are the same along a straight ray emanating from the origin. Yet another way to describe this property is to say that isoquants are radial blowups of one another. The slope of the isoquant and its negative, the marginal rate of technical substitution, are functions of the input proportions, not the levels of the inputs. This is a property of a class of functions called *homothetic functions*. Whereas all homogeneous functions are homothetic, not all homothetic functions are homogeneous.

The class of homothetic functions includes not only all homogeneous functions but also all monotonic transformations of homogeneous functions. Monotonic transformations of homogeneous functions all have the property that the slopes of isoquants are the same along a straight ray emanating from the origin, but they are not necessarily homogeneous. As you know from Chapter 9, Section 9.7, a monotonic transformation preserves the ranking of level curves but not the value associated with them. It is easy to imagine a monotonic transformation of a homogeneous function which does not preserve homogeneity. For example, we found that the function $Y = f(X_1, X_2) = X_1 X_2$ is homogeneous of degree 2. However, you may verify that its logarithmic transformation, $Z = \ln Y = \ln(X_1 X_2)$, is not homogeneous by multiplying both inputs by $t > 0$ and observing the value that the function achieves.

Linearly homogeneous production functions are particularly favored for theoretical and empirical analysis. One reason is that the notion of constant returns to scale has considerable intuitive appeal. It is hard to imagine that production would not double if all the inputs that contribute to production were doubled. Recognize that this means that nothing is fixed—not even the intangible inputs such as entrepreneurial talent, or location, or managerial style. If a production process could be duplicated in every detail, it seems intuitively sensible that output would double.

For empirical purposes, the assumption that a production function is homogeneous of degree 1 is easily incorporated into the way the inputs are measured. Suppose that the function $Y = f(X_1, X_2, \ldots, X_n)$ is linearly homogeneous. The definition of homogeneity allows us to write

$$tY \equiv f(tX_1, tX_2, \ldots, tX_n) \tag{10-43}$$

This identity holds for all values of t. If we let $t = 1/X_1$ we obtain

$$\frac{Y}{X_1} = f\left(1, \frac{X_2}{X_1}, \ldots, \frac{X_n}{X_1}\right) \qquad (10\text{-}44)$$

The dependent variable, Y/X_1, is the average product of input 1. This result tells us that, if a production function is linearly homogeneous, we can express the average product of an input as a function of the ratios of all the other inputs to it. We demonstrated this property with the input X_1, but we could have chosen any of the inputs to express average product as a function of input ratios.

There are times when this result is very useful to the econometrician or empirical economist who is attempting to measure production. Often one finds that data are reported only as average productivity or input ratios. The assumption of linear homogeneity permits the production function to be estimated with such limited data. At other times, one has sufficient data but wishes to use *a priori* theoretical information that a production function exhibits CRS to improve an estimate of a production function. One easy way to incorporate CRS into an estimate of a production function is to measure average productivity as a function of input ratios, as above.

NUMERICAL EXAMPLE

Suppose, as in our previous numerical example, that output, Y, is produced according to the production function

$$Y = f(X_1, X_2) = 10X_1^{0.25}X_2^{0.75} \qquad (10\text{-}15)$$

We check for homogeneity by multiplying both inputs by a factor t,

$$10(tX_1)^{0.25}(tX_2)^{0.75} = t^1 Y \qquad (10\text{-}45)$$

finding that the function is homogeneous of degree $r = 1$. The total differential of (10-15) is

$$dY = f_1\, dX_1 + f_2\, dX_2 = 2.5\left(\frac{X_2}{X_1}\right)^{0.75} dX_1 + 7.5\left(\frac{X_1}{X_2}\right)^{0.25} dX_2 \quad (10\text{-}46)$$

The total differential is homogeneous of degree $r - 1 = 1 - 1 = 0$. You should verify this by multiplying X_1 and X_2 by t. Because the inputs appear in equation (10-46) as ratios to one another, the factor t cancels, and the differential is unaffected by proportional increases in the inputs.

The slope of the isoquants of this production function equals the negative of the ratio of the marginal products, or

$$-\frac{f_1}{f_2} = -\frac{1}{3}\frac{X_2}{X_1} \qquad (10\text{-}47)$$

As you can see from (10-47), the slope of the isoquant is a function of the ratio of inputs. It is unaffected when both inputs are multiplied by the same factor.

We can use this production function to demonstrate that we can express the average product of an input as a function of the ratios of all the other inputs to it. We divide (10-15) by X_1 to obtain an expression for the average product of input 1

$$\frac{Y}{X_1} = \frac{10X_1^{0.25}X_2^{0.75}}{X_1} = 10\left(\frac{X_2}{X_1}\right)^{0.75} \tag{10-48}$$

From (10-48) we see that the average product of input 1 is a function of the ratio of input 2 to input 1.

EXERCISES
Section 10.4
The Isoquants of
Homogeneous
Production
Functions

For the following production functions, (a) determine whether or not the function is homogeneous and, if so, to what degree it is homogeneous. (b) If the function is homogeneous, show that the total differential of the function is also homogeneous, but of a degree less by one. (c) If the function is homogeneous, show that the slope of an isoquant can be expressed as a function of the input proportions. (d) If the function is linearly homogeneous, show that the average product of input 2 can be expressed as a function of X_1/X_2.

1. $Y = f(X_1, X_2) = 20X_1^{1/3}X_2^{1/2}$ 3. $Y = f(X_1, X_2) = 100X_1^{0.4}X_2^{0.6}$

2. $Y = f(X_1, X_2) = X_1^3 X_2^{0.3}$ 4. $Y = f(X_1, X_2) = 25(X_1 + X_2)$

10.5

EULER'S THEOREM

Euler's theorem: a theorem describing the relationship between the dependent variable of a homogeneous function and its first derivatives.

An important mathematical theorem, known as *Euler's theorem*, will enable us to investigate further the relationship between input productivity and input ratios. Euler's theorem describes a relationship between the dependent variable of a homogeneous function and its first-order partial derivatives.

Euler's theorem states that, if the function $Y = f(X_1, X_2, \ldots, X_n)$ is homogeneous of degree r, then

$$rY \equiv f_1 X_1 + f_2 X_2 + \cdots + f_n X_n \tag{10-49}$$

That is, the sum of the products of the partial derivatives and their corresponding independent variables is identically equal to the product of the dependent variable and the degree of homogeneity. To derive Euler's theorem, differentiate equation (10-24), the definition of homogeneity, with respect to t.

$$rt^{r-1}Y \equiv \frac{\partial f}{\partial tX_1}\frac{dtX_1}{dt} + \frac{\partial f}{\partial tX_2}\frac{dtX_2}{dt} + \cdots + \frac{\partial f}{\partial tX_n}\frac{dtX_n}{dt} \tag{10-50}$$

Recognize that

$$\frac{dtX_i}{dt} = X_i, \qquad i = 1, 2, \ldots, n \tag{10-51}$$

and substitute.

$$rt^{r-1}Y \equiv \frac{\partial f}{\partial tX_1} X_1 + \frac{\partial f}{\partial tX_2} X_2 + \cdots + \frac{\partial f}{\partial tX_n} X_n \tag{10-52}$$

This identity holds for all positive values of t. If we set $t = 1$, we derive Euler's theorem

$$rY \equiv \frac{\partial f}{\partial X_1} X_1 + \frac{\partial f}{\partial X_2} X_2 + \cdots + \frac{\partial f}{\partial X_n} X_n = \sum_{i=1}^{n} f_i X_i \tag{10-53}$$

Consider a production function with two inputs, X_1 and X_2, which is homogeneous of degree 1. Euler's theorem states that, in this case,

$$rY \equiv Y \equiv f_1 X_1 + f_2 X_2 \tag{10-54}$$

Dividing through both sides by X_1 gives us

$$\frac{Y}{X_1} = f_1 + f_2 \frac{X_2}{X_1} \tag{10-55}$$

Recognizing that Y/X_1 is the average product of X_1, AP_1, and that f_1 and f_2 are the marginal products of X_1 and X_2, MP_1 and MP_2, respectively, leaves us with

$$AP_1 = MP_1 + MP_2 \frac{X_2}{X_1} \Rightarrow AP_1 - MP_1 = MP_2 \frac{X_2}{X_1} \tag{10-56}$$

This result is particularly interesting in light of what we already know about the relationship between marginal and average products. Recall Figure 10.2, in which we picture the relationship between marginal product and average product in a two-input production function. We show that average product reaches its maximum when it is equal to marginal product, and we suggest that profit-maximizing firms will operate in Stage II of production, where average product is downward sloping and marginal product is positive. Equation (10-56) tells us that in Stage I, where $MP_1 > AP_1$, MP_2 must be negative. In Stage II, where $MP_1 < AP_1$, MP_2 must be positive. At point B, where AP_1 reaches its maximum, $MP_1 = AP_1$ and MP_2 must equal zero. In other words, for a linearly homogeneous production function with two inputs, Stage II is where both marginal products are positive. In Stage I MP_2 is negative, and in Stage III MP_1 is negative.

Another interesting theoretical application of Euler's theorem is to the problem of equating aggregate demand and aggregate supply. Consider a linearly homogeneous production function in n inputs, $Y = f(X_1, X_2, \ldots, X_n)$. According to Euler's theorem,

$$Y = f_1 X_1 + f_2 X_2 + \cdots + f_n X_n \tag{10-57}$$

If we multiply both sides by output price, P, we obtain

$$PY = Pf_1 X_1 + Pf_2 X_2 + \cdots + Pf_n X_n \tag{10-58}$$

Remembering from Chapter 6, Section 6.3.3, that, under conditions of perfect competition in both input and output markets, $Pf_i = \text{VMP}_i = w_i$ gives us

$$PY = w_1 X_1 + w_2 X_2 + \cdots + w_n X_n \tag{10-59}$$

Say's law: the proposition of classical economics that supply creates its own demand, or that income sufficient to purchase output is guaranteed.

Equation (10-59) suggests that the value of output, PY, equals the total payments to all the inputs. This means that the production process generates income sufficient to purchase its output under conditions of perfect competition and CRS production functions. This is a mathematical statement of *Say's law*, that "supply creates its own demand."

NUMERICAL EXAMPLE

We continue to use the same production function as in our previous numerical examples, which we know is homogeneous of degree one.

$$Y = f(X_1, X_2) = 10X_1^{0.25}X_2^{0.75} \tag{10-15}$$

We verify Euler's theorem in this case by summing the products of the inputs times their marginal products.

$$f_1 X_1 + f_2 X_2 = 2.5X_1^{-0.75}X_2^{0.75}X_1 + 7.5X_1^{0.25}X_2^{-0.25}X_2 \tag{10-60}$$

We multiply out each term in (10-60) and factor in order to obtain our result, that

$$f_1 X_1 + f_2 X_2 = 2.5X_1^{0.25}X_2^{0.75} + 7.5X_1^{0.25}X_2^{0.75} = 10X_1^{0.25}X_2^{0.75} = Y \tag{10-61}$$

If we divide both sides of (10-61) by X_1, we can find the average product of input 1,

$$2.5X_1^{-0.75}X_2^{0.75} + 7.5X_1^{0.25}X_2^{-0.25}\left(\frac{X_2}{X_1}\right) = f_1 + f_2\left(\frac{X_2}{X_1}\right) = Y/X_1 \tag{10-62}$$

Euler's theorem has many useful applications, and not only in production theory. Before we turn to the theory of production cost in the next chapter, let's use the Cobb–Douglas production function as a concrete example to illustrate what we know about production in general.

EXERCISES
Section 10.5
Euler's Theorem

For the following production functions, (a) if the function is homogeneous, verify Euler's theorem; if it is not homogeneous, show that Euler's theorem does not hold. (b) If the function is homogeneous, use Euler's theorem to find an expression for the average product of input 2 in terms of the marginal products of both inputs and the ratio of input 1 to input 2.

1. $Y = f(X_1, X_2) = 20X_1^{1/3}X_2^{1/2}$
4. $Y = f(X_1, X_2) = 25(X_1 + X_2)$

2. $Y = f(X_1, X_2) = X_1^3 X_2^{0.3}$

3. $Y = f(X_1, X_2) = 100X_1^{0.4}X_2^{0.6}$
5. $Y = f(X_1, X_2) = 10X_1^{0.5}X_2^{0.5}\left(\dfrac{X_2}{X_1}\right)^2$

10.6

THE COBB–DOUGLAS PRODUCTION FUNCTION

You may recall that we have discussed the Cobb–Douglas (C–D) production function in several sections of this text. We see it in Chapter 2, Section 2.5; Chapter 3, Section 3.7.4; as well as exercises 7 through 10 of Chapter 5. Its general form for the two-input case is

$$Y = f(X_1, X_2) = AX_1^\alpha X_2^\beta, \qquad 0 < \alpha, \beta < 1, A > 0 \qquad \text{(10-63)}$$

The partial derivatives of the production function give us the marginal products of the inputs.

$$\text{MP}_1 = f_1 = \alpha AX_1^{\alpha-1}X_2^\beta = \alpha\frac{Y}{X_1} \qquad \text{(10-64)}$$

$$\text{MP}_2 = f_2 = \beta AX_1^\alpha X_2^{\beta-1} = \beta\frac{Y}{X_2} \qquad \text{(10-65)}$$

Examination of equations (10-64) and (10-65) reveals that the marginal product of an input can be expressed as a constant fraction of its average product. As long as the exponents, α and β, are restricted to values between zero and one, marginal product is positive but less than average product. This suggests that a firm with a C–D production function is always in Stage II of production, with decreasing average product and positive marginal product. A graph of the average product and marginal product of input 1 is presented in Figure 10.5.

We examine the behavior of the marginal products further by taking the second-order partial derivatives of the production function.

$$\frac{\partial\text{MP}_1}{\partial X_1} = f_{11} = \alpha(\alpha-1)AX_1^{\alpha-2}X_2^\beta = \alpha(\alpha-1)\frac{Y}{X_1^2} \qquad \text{(10-66)}$$

$$\frac{\partial\text{MP}_2}{\partial X_2} = f_{22} = \beta(\beta-1)AX_1^\alpha X_2^{\beta-2} = \beta(\beta-1)\frac{Y}{X_2^2} \qquad \text{(10-67)}$$

Figure 10.5

Average and Marginal
Products of the C–D
Production Function

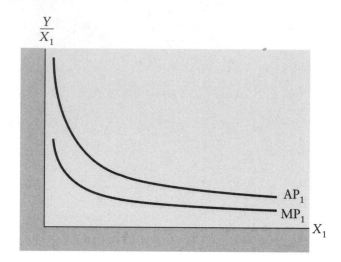

Both inputs exhibit decreasing marginal product, because both α and β are less than one. The cross-partial derivative tells us how changes in one input affect the marginal product of the other.

$$\frac{\partial \mathrm{MP}_1}{\partial X_2} = \frac{\partial \mathrm{MP}_2}{\partial X_1} = f_{12} = f_{21} = \alpha\beta A X_1^{\alpha-1} X_2^{\beta-1} = \frac{\alpha\beta Y}{X_1 X_2} \qquad (10\text{-}68)$$

Because both α and β are positive, the cross-partial derivative is positive. This means that, for the C–D production function, increases in one input increase the marginal product of the other, or they are cooperative in production.

Is the C–D a homogeneous function? To answer this question, multiply all inputs by some positive factor t.

$$f(tX_1, tX_2) = A(tX_1)^\alpha (tX_2)^\beta \qquad (10\text{-}69)$$

Carry out the exponentiation over t and rearrange the expression.

$$f(tX_1, tX_2) = t^\alpha t^\beta A X_1^\alpha X_2^\beta = t^{\alpha+\beta} Y \qquad (10\text{-}70)$$

We see that the C–D is homogeneous to degree $\alpha + \beta$. If $\alpha + \beta = 1$, it is a linearly homogeneous production function, exhibiting CRS.[2] If $\alpha + \beta < 1$ it exhibits DRS, and if $\alpha + \beta > 1$ it exhibits IRS.

When we are given a specific production function, such as the C–D, we are able to find the equation of an isoquant explicitly. In order to do this, we set output equal to some level, Y_0, and solve for one input in terms of the other. Following this procedure with the C–D production function gives us

$$Y_0 = f(X_1, X_2) = A X_1^\alpha X_2^\beta \qquad (10\text{-}71)$$

---

[2]If we express the C–D function as $Y = A X_1^\alpha X_2^{1-\alpha}$ we guarantee that the exponents sum to one. Therefore, the C–D production function expressed in this way is automatically homogeneous of degree 1 and exhibits CRS.

Dividing both sides by AX_1^α and solving for X_2^β gives us

$$X_2^\beta = Y_0 A^{-1} X_1^{-\alpha} \tag{10-72}$$

If we raise both sides to the power $1/\beta$, we solve for X_2 in terms of X_1.

$$X_2 = Y_0^{1/\beta} A^{-1/\beta} X_1^{-\alpha/\beta} \tag{10-73}$$

Equation (10-73) represents the equation of the Y_0 isoquant.

We can find the slope of the isoquant by differentiating X_2 with respect to X_1, holding $Y = Y_0$.

$$\left.\frac{dX_2}{dX_1}\right|_{Y=Y_0} = -\frac{\alpha}{\beta} Y_0^{1/\beta} A^{-1/\beta} X_1^{-(\alpha/\beta)-1} \tag{10-74}$$

Substituting in $Y_0 = AX_1^\alpha X_2^\beta$ and rearranging gives us

$$\left.\frac{dX_2}{dX_1}\right|_{Y=Y_0} = -\frac{\alpha}{\beta} (AX_1^\alpha X_2^\beta)^{1/\beta} A^{-1/\beta} X_1^{-(\alpha/\beta)-1} = -\frac{\alpha}{\beta}\frac{X_2}{X_1} \tag{10-75}$$

There are two points worth mentioning about equation (10-75). First, it is precisely the result you would obtain by recalling that the slope of the isoquant equals $-f_1/f_2$. Second, it is evident that the slope of the isoquant, which equals $-\text{MRTS}$, is a function of the input ratio, X_2/X_1. Remember that this is a characteristic which we associated with homogeneous functions, the property of homotheticity.

We can determine if the isoquants of the C–D production function are convex to the origin by differentiating the expression for the slope of the isoquant with respect to X_1 again. Remember that, if the slope of the isoquant increases (becomes less negative) as X_1 increases, then the isoquant is convex and the derivative of the slope of the isoquant with respect to X_1 is positive. Recall also that we must treat X_2 as a function of X_1 when we differentiate, because we are dealing with an isoquant. We use the quotient rule.

$$\frac{d\left(\left.\frac{dX_2}{dX_1}\right|_{Y=Y_0}\right)}{dX_1} = -\frac{\alpha}{\beta}\frac{1}{X_1^2}\left(X_1\frac{dX_2}{dX_1} - X_2\right) = -\frac{\alpha}{\beta X_1^2}\left(-X_1\frac{\alpha}{\beta}\frac{X_2}{X_1} - X_2\right) \tag{10-76}$$

Canceling and factoring X_2 within the parentheses leaves us with

$$\frac{d\left(\left.\frac{dX_2}{dX_1}\right|_{Y=Y_0}\right)}{dX_1} = \frac{\alpha X_2}{\beta X_1^2}\left(\frac{\alpha}{\beta} + 1\right) > 0 \tag{10-77}$$

Equation (10-77) is positive as long as α and β are both positive, as required by the C–D function.

In Section 10.4 we found that, for a linearly homogeneous production function, the average product of an input can be expressed as a function of input ratios, as in equation (10-44), which we reproduce here

$$\frac{Y}{X_1} = f\left(1, \frac{X_2}{X_1}, \ldots, \frac{X_n}{X_1}\right) \tag{10-44}$$

Does this relationship hold for the C–D production function? If we divide both inputs in equation (10-63) by X_1, we obtain

$$f\left(1, \frac{X_2}{X_1}\right) = A\left(\frac{X_1}{X_1}\right)^\alpha \left(\frac{X_2}{X_1}\right)^\beta \tag{10-78}$$

Rearranging the expression gives us

$$f\left(1, \frac{X_2}{X_1}\right) = A X_1^\alpha X_2^\beta X_1^{-(\alpha + \beta)} = \frac{Y}{X_1^{\alpha + \beta}} \tag{10-79}$$

If $\alpha + \beta = 1$, as required by linear homogeneity, then we can express the average product of X_1 as a function of X_2/X_1,

$$AP_1 = \frac{Y}{X_1} = A\left(\frac{X_2}{X_1}\right)^\beta \tag{10-80}$$

It should be fairly clear by now why the C–D production function is popular with economists. It has many features that are consistent with what we believe is true about production, including positive but diminishing marginal product and convex isoquants. In addition, it is homogeneous and flexible enough to exhibit IRS, CRS, and DRS. It has another feature that makes it especially useful for econometric work. The C–D is a nonlinear function which is linear in its logarithmic form. To see this, take the logarithm of both sides of $Y = A X_1^\alpha X_2^\beta$.

$$\ln Y = \ln A + \alpha \ln X_1 + \beta \ln X_2 \tag{10-81}$$

Linear functions are more readily estimated by econometric methods than nonlinear forms. The C–D function can be specified as a linear equation simply by measuring output and inputs in logarithmic form. By taking the total differential of the log-linear form of the C–D we can discover a useful interpretation of the coefficients α and β.

$$d(\ln Y) = \alpha d(\ln X_1) + \beta d(\ln X_2) \tag{10-82}$$

Recognize that, for any positive variable Z, $d(\ln Z) = (1/Z)\, dZ$, and substitute.

$$\frac{1}{Y} dY = \frac{\alpha}{X_1} dX_1 + \frac{\beta}{X_2} dX_2 \tag{10-83}$$

If we let $dX_2 = 0$ we can solve for α in terms of the partial derivative of Y with respect to X_1.

$$\alpha = \frac{\partial Y}{\partial X_1}\frac{X_1}{Y} \qquad (10\text{-}84)$$

partial output elasticity: the ratio of the percentage change in output to the percentage change in an input, *ceteris paribus.*

A review of Chapter 3, Section 3.7.3, will remind you that (10-84) looks like an elasticity expression. In fact, it is called the *partial output elasticity* of X_1. It measures the ratio of the percentage change in output to the percentage change in an input. You should show that β is the partial output elasticity of X_2 by using the same procedure we used with α.

EXERCISES
Section 10.6
The Cobb-Douglas
Production Function

Answer these questions using the following three-variable, Cobb–Douglas production function.

$$Y = AX_1^\alpha X_2^\beta X_3^\gamma, \qquad 0 < \alpha, \beta, \gamma < 1; A > 0$$

1. Express the marginal product of each input as a constant fraction of its average product.

2. Show that each input exhibits decreasing marginal product, and demonstrate that each input is cooperative in production with each other input.

3. Verify that this is a homogeneous production function, and determine the degree of homogeneity.

4. Find the equation of the Y_0 isoquant for inputs 2 and 3, holding input 1 constant at X_{10}, and demonstrate that its slope is a function of the ratio of inputs 2 and 3 and that it is convex.

5. Show that the average product of input 1 can be expressed as a function of X_2/X_1 and X_3/X_1.

6. Show that this production function is linear in its logarithmic form.

10.7

ELASTICITY OF SUBSTITUTION

elasticity of substitution: measure of the degree of substitutability of two inputs at different points on an isoquant.

Another important measure which can be used to describe production functions is the *elasticity of substitution*, which measures the degree of substitutability of two inputs at different points on an isoquant. We measure substitutability by the slope of the slope of the isoquant, and we identify different points on an isoquant by the ratio of the inputs. Remember that the slope of an isoquant equals $-f_1/f_2 = -\text{MRTS}$. We define the elasticity of substitution as

$$\text{Elasticity of substitution} \equiv \sigma \equiv \frac{d\left(\dfrac{X_2}{X_1}\right)\dfrac{f_1}{f_2}}{d\left(\dfrac{f_1}{f_2}\right)\dfrac{X_2}{X_1}} \qquad (10\text{-}85)$$

The slope of the isoquant measures the rate at which one input can be substituted for another, holding output constant. In general, we expect it to be more difficult to substitute input 1 for input 2 as we move down the isoquant. This is why isoquants are convex: we expect it to take more of input 1 to substitute for a unit of input 2 as the ratio of X_2 to X_1 becomes smaller. If this were not the case, the slope of the isoquant would not change as the input ratio changed, and the elasticity of substitution would approach infinity. This situation describes perfectly substitutable inputs and linear, not strictly convex isoquants and is pictured in Figure 10.6*a*. Conversely, the more rapidly the slope of the isoquant changes as we increase X_1 and decrease X_2, the more sharply curved is the isoquant and the smaller the elasticity of substitution. In the extreme case, no substitution is possible between inputs, and the isoquant is a right angle, as pictured in Figure 10.6*b*.

As expressed in equation (10-85), the elasticity of substitution is difficult to calculate. We can derive an expression by remembering that, along an isoquant, X_2 is a function of X_1, and therefore

$$\frac{d\left(\dfrac{X_2}{X_1}\right)}{d\left(\dfrac{f_1}{f_2}\right)} = \frac{\dfrac{d(X_2/X_1)}{dX_1}}{\dfrac{d(f_1/f_2)}{dX_1}} \qquad (10\text{-}86)$$

We use the quotient rule to evaluate the numerator, and we use the fact that $f_1/f_2 = -dX_2/dX_1$ to evaluate the denominator. Recall that we have already evaluated the latter in equation (5-74), repeated for you in Section 10.2. Therefore, we can write (10-86) as

$$\frac{d\left(\dfrac{X_2}{X_1}\right)}{d\left(\dfrac{f_1}{f_2}\right)} = \frac{\dfrac{d(X_2/X_1)}{dX_1}}{\dfrac{d(f_1/f_2)}{dX_1}} = \frac{-\dfrac{X_1(f_1/f_2) + X_2}{X_1^2}}{\dfrac{f_2^2 f_{11} - 2f_1 f_2 f_{12} + f_1^2 f_{22}}{f_2^3}} \qquad (10\text{-}87)$$

Figure 10.6

(*a*) Isoquant of Perfectly Substitutable Inputs; (*b*) Isoquant of Nonsubstitutable Inputs

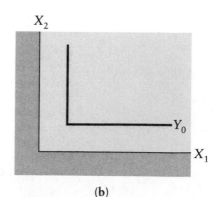

(a)   (b)

We can rewrite the numerator of (10-87) as $-(f_1X_1 + f_2X_2)/(f_2X_1^2)$. Therefore,

$$\frac{d\left(\dfrac{X_2}{X_1}\right)}{d\left(\dfrac{f_1}{f_2}\right)} = -\frac{f_2^3(f_1X_1 + f_2X_2)}{f_2X_1^2(f_2^2f_{11} - 2f_1f_2f_{12} + f_1^2f_{22})} \tag{10-88}$$

Substituting (10-88) into (10-85) gives us an expression that can be used to calculate the elasticity of substitution for any production function,

$$\sigma = \frac{d\left(\dfrac{X_2}{X_1}\right)}{d\left(\dfrac{f_1}{f_2}\right)}\frac{\dfrac{f_1}{f_2}}{\dfrac{X_2}{X_1}} = -\frac{f_1f_2(f_1X_1 + f_2X_2)}{X_1X_2(f_2^2f_{11} - 2f_1f_2f_{12} + f_1^2f_{22})} \tag{10-89}$$

Equation (10-89) is still a complicated expression. Calculating the elasticity of substitution is considerably easier for homothetic production functions. Remember that, as we showed in equation (10-42), homothetic production functions have the property that the slope of the isoquant is a function of the input ratio. For the monotonically downward-sloping portions of isoquants, the inverse function, for which the input ratio is a function of the slope of the isoquant, exists. Therefore, for homothetic (and, therefore, homogeneous) production functions, we can write

$$\frac{X_2}{X_1} = g\left(\frac{f_1}{f_2}\right) \tag{10-90}$$

If we simply differentiate this function and multiply it by $(f_1/f_2)(X_2/X_1)$, we obtain an expression for the elasticity of substitution.

Consider, for example, the C–D production function. We found in equation (10-75) that, if $Y = AX_1^\alpha X_2^\beta$, the slope of an isoquant equals $-(\alpha/\beta)(X_2/X_1)$. Therefore,

$$\frac{f_1}{f_2} = \frac{\alpha}{\beta}\frac{X_2}{X_1} \Leftrightarrow \frac{X_2}{X_1} = \frac{\beta}{\alpha}\frac{f_1}{f_2} \tag{10-91}$$

To obtain the elasticity of substitution, we find the derivative of X_2/X_1 with respect to f_1/f_2 and multiply by $(f_1/f_2)/(X_2/X_1)$

$$\sigma = \frac{d\left(\dfrac{X_2}{X_1}\right)}{d\left(\dfrac{f_1}{f_2}\right)}\frac{\dfrac{f_1}{f_2}}{\dfrac{X_2}{X_1}} = \frac{\beta}{\alpha}\left(\frac{\dfrac{\alpha X_2}{\beta X_1}}{\dfrac{X_2}{X_1}}\right) = 1 \tag{10-92}$$

We see from (10-92) that the C–D production function has an elasticity of substitution that is always equal to 1, no matter what the values of α and β.

constant-elasticity-of-substitution (CES) production function: class of functions that have a constant elasticity of substitution, which can take any value between zero and infinity.

The Cobb–Douglas is an example of a *constant-elasticity-of-substitution (CES) production function*. As the name indicates, all CES functions have a constant elasticity of substitution, which can take any value between zero and infinity. The CES function can be expressed as

$$Y = A(\alpha X_1^{-\rho} + (1 - \alpha)X_2^{-\rho})^{-1/\rho}, \qquad A > 0, 0 < \alpha < 1, -1 < \rho \neq 0$$

$$(10\text{-}93)$$

We leave it as an exercise for you to demonstrate that the CES is linearly homogeneous. Because it is homogeneous, we are able to express the slope of an isoquant as a function of the input ratio. To do so, we find the marginal products of the inputs as

$$f_1 = \frac{\alpha}{A^\rho} \left(\frac{Y}{X_1} \right)^{1+\rho} \tag{10-94}$$

$$f_2 = \frac{1 - \alpha}{A^\rho} \left(\frac{Y}{X_2} \right)^{1+\rho} \tag{10-95}$$

Dividing (10-94) by (10-95) gives us the negative of the slope of an isoquant expressed as a function of the input ratio and its inverse function,

$$\frac{f_1}{f_2} = \frac{\alpha}{1 - \alpha} \left(\frac{X_2}{X_1} \right)^{1+\rho} \Leftrightarrow \frac{X_2}{X_1} = \left(\frac{1 - \alpha}{\alpha} \frac{f_1}{f_2} \right)^{1/(1+\rho)} \tag{10-96}$$

We find the elasticity of substitution by taking the derivative of X_2/X_1 with respect to f_1/f_2 and multiplying by $(f_1/f_2)/(X_2/X_1)$

$$\sigma = \frac{d\left(\dfrac{X_2}{X_1} \right)}{d\left(\dfrac{f_1}{f_2} \right)} \frac{\dfrac{f_1}{f_2}}{\dfrac{X_2}{X_1}} = \left[\frac{1}{1 + \rho} \left(\frac{1 - \alpha}{\alpha} \right)^{1/(1+\rho)} \left(\frac{f_1}{f_2} \right)^{1/(1+\rho) - 1} \right]$$

$$\times \left(\frac{\dfrac{f_1}{f_2}}{\left(\dfrac{1 - \alpha}{\alpha} \right)^{1/(1+\rho)} \left(\dfrac{f_1}{f_2} \right)^{1/(1+\rho)}} \right) = \frac{1}{1 + \rho} \tag{10-97}$$

The elasticity of substitution of a CES production function equals $1/(1 + \rho)$. As $\rho \Rightarrow -1$, $\sigma \Rightarrow \infty$, and as $\rho \Rightarrow \infty$, $\sigma \Rightarrow 0$.

10.8

SUMMARY

In this chapter we examine some of the mathematical treatment of the theory of the firm. Neoclassical microeconomic theory examines production as though it is a black box that converts inputs into output, that is, as a production function. We examine production functions from a graphical and a mathematical point of view and explain the mathematics of total, average, and marginal products. We discuss a special class of functions, called homogeneous functions, which are especially apt for describing the concept of returns to scale. Euler's theorem applies to homogeneous functions and can be used to derive Say's law concerning the relationship between value of output and payments to inputs. We illustrate the general concepts regarding production functions with a detailed examination of the Cobb–Douglas production function, which we discovered to be homogeneous and to have positive but downward-sloping marginal products and convex isoquants. Finally, we introduce the concept of elasticity of substitution and demonstrate how to calculate it for homothetic functions using both the Cobb–Douglas and the CES production functions.

We use the Cobb–Douglas production function as a particular example to illustrate what we discuss for production functions in general. If firms were nothing more than black boxes that convert inputs into output, our theory of the behavior of the firm would simply be an analysis of production functions along the lines we have introduced. However, firms are profit-maximizing market agents. They must choose the rates of output to produce and the combinations of inputs to employ. In making both of these decisions, a firm cannot be maximizing profits unless it is minimizing cost. We see what cost minimization implies about the behavior of the firm in Chapter 11.

◆ REFERENCES

Arrow, K. J., Chenery, H. B., Minhas, B. S., and Solow, R. M., "Capital-Labor Substitution and Economic Efficiency," *Review of Economics and Statistics*, August 1961, pp. 225–250.

Binger, Brian R. and Hoffman, Elizabeth, *Microeconomics with Calculus* (Glenview, IL: Scott, Foresman and Company, 1985), Chapter 10.

Douglas, Paul H. and Cobb, C. W., "A Theory of Production," *American Economic Review 16*, 1928, pp. 139–165.

Samuelson, Paul A., *Foundations of Economic Analysis* (New York: Atheneum, 1965), Chapter 4.

Shephard, Ronald W., *Theory of Cost and Production Functions* (Princeton, NJ: Princeton University Press, 1970), Chapters 1, 2, and 3.

Varian, Hal R., *Microeconomic Analysis*, 3rd edition (New York: W. W. Norton and Company, 1992), Chapters 1, 2, and 3.

◆ ANSWERS TO END-OF-SECTION EXERCISES

Section 10.2 The Production Function Revisited

1. **a.** $MP_1 = f_1 = (20/3)X_1^{-2/3}X_2^{1/2}$; $MP_2 = f_2 = 10X_1^{1/3}X_2^{-1/2}$
    b. Slope of MP_1 equals $f_{11} = -(40/9)X_1^{-5/3}X_2^{1/2} > 0$; yes.
    Slope of MP_2 equals $f_{22} = -5X_1^{1/3}X_2^{-3/2} < 0$; yes.
    c. $X_2 = (25/4)X_1^{-2/3}$; **d.** $dX_2/dX_1 = -(25/4)X_1^{-5/3}$;
    $d^2X_2/dX_1^2 = (125/18)X_1^{-8/3} > 0$. It is convex.

2. **a.** $MP_1 = f_1 = 3X_1^2X_2^{0.3}$; $MP_2 = f_2 = 0.3X_1^3X_2^{-0.7}$

    b. Slope of MP_1 equals $f_{11} = 6X_1X_2^{0.3} > 0$; no.
        Slope of MP_2 equals $f_{22} = -0.21X_1^3X_2^{-1.7} < 0$; yes.

    c. $X_2 = 11825.76X_1^{-6.67}$; **d.** $dX_2/dX_1 = -78,877.83X_1^{-7.67}$;
        $d^2X_2/dX_1^2 = 604,992.98X_1^{-8.67} > 0$. It is convex.

3. **a.** $MP_1 = f_1 = 40X_1^{-0.6}X_2^{0.6}$; $MP_2 = f_2 = 60X_1^{0.4}X_2^{-0.4}$

    b. Slope of MP_1 equals $f_{11} = -24X_1^{-1.6}X_2^{0.6} < 0$; yes.
        Slope of MP_2 equals $f_{22} = -24X_1^{0.4}X_2^{-1.4} < 0$; yes.

    c. $X_2 = 1.45X_1^{-2/3}$; **d.** $dX_2/dX_1 = -0.97X_1^{-5/3}$;
        $d^2X_2/dX_1^2 = 1.62X_1^{-8/3} > 0$. It is convex.

4. **a.** $MP_1 = f_1 = 25$; $MP_2 = f_2 = 25$

    b. Slope of MP_1 equals $f_{11} = 0$; no.
        Slope of MP_2 equals $f_{22} = 0$; no.

    c. $X_2 = 2 - X_1$; **d.** $dX_2/dX_1 = -1$;
        $d^2X_2/dX_1^2 = 0$. It is not strictly covex.

5. **a.** $MP_1 = f_1 = -15X_1^{-5/2}X_2^{5/2}$; $MP_2 = f_2 = 25X_1^{-3/2}X_2^{3/2}$

    b. Slope of MP_1 equals $f_{11} = 37.5X_1^{-7/2}X_2^{5/2} > 0$; no.
        Slope of MP_2 equals $f_{22} = 37.5X_1^{-3/2}X_2^{1/2} > 0$; no.

    c. $X_2 = 1.9X_1^{3/5}$; **d.** $dX_2/dX_1 = 1.14X_1^{-2/5}$;
        $d^2X_2/dX_1^2 = -0.46X_1^{-7/5} < 0$. It is not convex.

Section 10.4 The Isoquants of Homogeneous Production Functions

1. **a.** Homogeneous to degree $r = 5/6$.

    b. $df(X_1, X_2) = (20/3)X_1^{-2/3}X_2^{1/2}dX_1 + 10X_1^{1/3}X_2^{-1/2}dX_2$. Homogeneous to degree $r = -1/6$

    c. Slope of isoquant equals $-f_1/f_2 = -(2/3)(X_2/X_1)$

    d. Not linearly homogeneous

2. **a.** Homogeneous to degree $r = 3.3$.

    b. $df(X_1, X_2) = 3X_1^2X_2^{0.3}dX_1 + 0.3X_1^3X_2^{-0.7}dX_2$. Homogeneous to degree $r = 2.3$

    c. Slope of isoquant equals $-f_1/f_2 = -10(X_2/X_1)$

    d. Not linearly homogeneous

3. **a.** Homogeneous to degree $r = 1$.

    b. $df(X_1, X_2) = 40X_1^{-0.6}X_2^{0.6}dX_1 + 60X_1^{0.4}X_2^{-0.4}dX_2$. Homogeneous to degree $r = 0$

    c. Slope of isoquant equals $-f_1/f_2 = -(2/3)(X_2/X_1)$

    d. $AP_2 = 100(X_1/X_2)^{0.4}$

4. **a.** Homogeneous to degree $r = 1$

    b. $df(X_1, X_2) = 25(dX_1 + dX_2)$. Homogeneous to degree $r = 0$

    c. Slope of isoquant equals $-f_1/f_2 = -1$

    d. $AP_2 = 25(X_1/X_2) + 25$

5. **a.** Homogeneous to degree $r = 1$.

    b. $df(X_1, X_2) = -15X_1^{-5/2}X_2^{5/2}dX_1 + 25X_1^{-3/2}X_2^{3/2}dX_2$. Homogeneous to degree $r = 0$

c. Slope of isoquant equals $-f_1/f_2 = -(3/5)(X_2/X_1)$
d. $AP_2 = 10(X_1/X_2)^{-3/2}$

Section 10.5 Euler's Theorem

1. a. $rY = (5/6)Y = (20/3)X_1^{-2/3}X_2^{1/2}X_1 + 10X_1^{1/3}X_2^{-1/2}X_2$
   b. $AP_2 = (6/5)[MP_1(X_1/X_2) + MP_2]$

2. a. $rY = 3.3Y = 3X_1^2 X_2^{0.3}X_1 + 0.3X_1^3 X_2^{-0.7}X_2$
   b. $AP_2 = 0.303[MP_1(X_1/X_2) + MP_2]$

3. a. $rY = Y = 40X_1^{-0.6}X_2^{0.6}X_1 + 60X_1^{0.4}X_2^{-0.4}X_2$
   b. $AP_2 = [MP_1(X_1/X_2) + MP_2]$

4. a. $rY = Y = 25(X_1 + X_2)$
   b. $AP_2 = [MP_1(X_1/X_2) + MP_2]$
5. a. $rY = Y = -15X_2^{-5/2}X_2^{5/2}X_1 + 25X_1^{-3/2}X_2^{3/2}X_2$
   b. $AP_2 = [MP_1(X_1/X_2) + MP_2]$

Section 10.6 The Cobb–Douglas Production Function

1. $MP_1 = \alpha Y/X_1 = \alpha AP_1$; $MP_2 = \beta Y/X_1 = \beta AP_1$; $MP_3 = \gamma Y/X_1 = \gamma AP_1$

2. $\partial MP_1/\partial X_1 = \alpha(\alpha - 1)Y/X_1^2 < 0$; $\partial MP_1/\partial X_2 = \alpha\beta Y/X_1 X_2 > 0$;
   $\partial MP_1/\partial X_3 = \alpha\gamma Y/X_1 X_3 > 0$
   $\partial MP_2/\partial X_2 = \beta(\beta - 1)Y/X_2^2 < 0$; $\partial MP_2/\partial X_1 = \alpha\beta Y/X_1 X_2 > 0$;
   $\partial MP_2/\partial X_3 = \beta\gamma Y/X_2 X_3 > 0$
   $\partial MP_3/\partial X_3 = \gamma(\gamma - 1)Y/X_2^3 < 0$; $\partial MP_3/\partial X_1 = \alpha\gamma Y/X_1 X_3 > 0$;
   $\partial MP_3/\partial X_2 = \beta\gamma Y/X_2 X_3 > 0$

3. It is homogeneous of degree $r = \alpha + \beta + \gamma$.

4. Equation of isoquant: $X_3 = (Y_0/A)^{1/\gamma}X_{10}^{-\alpha/\gamma}X_2^{-\beta/\gamma}$
   Slope of isoquant: $dX_3/dX_2 = -(\beta/\gamma)(X_3/X_2)$
   It is convex because $d^2X_3/dX_2^2 = (\beta/\gamma)(X_3/X_2^2) > 0$.

5. $AP_1 = (1/(\alpha + \beta + \gamma))[MP_1 + MP_2(X_2/X_1) + MP_3(X_3/X_1)]$.
   If $\alpha + \beta + \gamma = 1$, then $AP_1 = A(X_2/X_1)^\beta(X_3/X_1)^\gamma$

6. $\ln Y = \ln A + \alpha \ln X_1 + \beta \ln X_2 + \gamma \ln X_3$

◆ SELF-HELP PROBLEMS

Answers to these problems are given at the end of the text.

Use the following production functions to answer questions 1 through 5

a. $Y = 5X_1 + 3X_2$
b. $Y = 5X_1 + 10X_2 - 2(X_1 X_2)^{.5}$
c. $Y = X_1^{.25}X_2^{.5}$
d. $Y = (0.25X_1^{-2} + 0.75X_2^{-2})^{-1/2}$
e. $Y = (X_1 + 2)^2(X_2 + 5)$

1. Find the marginal products of both inputs for each production function. Determine whether or not the marginal products are positive and whether or not the marginal product curves are downward sloping.

2. For each production function, let $X_2 = 100$, and find equations for total product, average product, and marginal product of X_1. Graph the total, average, and marginal product curves.

3. For each production function, find an equation for the $Y = 10$ isoquant, and find the slope of the isoquant. Graph the isoquant. Are the isoquants convex to the origin?

4. Test each production function for homogeneity. If homogeneous, determine the degree of homogeneity, determine whether it exhibits constant, increasing, or decreasing returns to scale, and verify that Euler's theorem holds.

5. For each homogeneous function, show that the slope of the isoquant can be expressed as a function of the ratio of the inputs. This demonstrates that the homogeneous functions are also homothetic. Find the elasticity of substitution for each of the functions.

◆ SUPPLEMENTAL PROBLEMS

1. a. State and prove Euler's theorem.

   b. Use Euler's theorem to demonstrate that, for any linearly homogeneous production function with two inputs, capital and labor, the average product of labor is at a maximum when the marginal product of capital equals zero and vice versa.

   c. Describe the relationship between the average product of labor and the marginal product of capital if the production function is homogeneous of degree greater than one.

   d. Describe the relationship between the average product of labor and the marginal product of capital if the production function is homogeneous of degree less than one.

2. It is an interesting and useful fact that the demand functions derived from constrained utility maximization problems are all homogeneous. This problem asks you to demonstrate this fact. Suppose the utility function of a consumer is of the form $U = X_1^\alpha X_2^{1-\alpha}$. She faces a budget constraint of the form $M = P_1 X_1 + P_2 X_2$. Find the demand functions $X_1^*(M, P_1, P_2)$ and $X_2^*(M, P_1, P_2)$.

   a. Show that the demand functions are homogeneous and determine the degree of homogeneity.

   b. Now suppose that her utility function is of the general form $U = U(X_1, X_2)$. Show that the demand functions are homogeneous and determine the degree of homogeneity.

Use the following production functions to answer questions 3 through 7.

   a. $Y = X_1^\alpha X_2^{1-\alpha}$

   b $Y = X_1^\alpha X_2^{1-\alpha} + X_1$

   c. $Y = A[\alpha X_1^{-\rho} + (1 - \alpha)X_2^{-\rho}]^{-1/\rho}$

3. Find the marginal products of both inputs for each production function. Determine whether or not the marginal products are positive and whether or not the marginal product curves are downward sloping.

4. For each production function, let $X_2 = 100$, and find equations for total product, average product, and marginal product of X_1. Graph the total, average, and marginal product curves.

5. For each production function, find an equation for the $Y = 10$ isoquant, and find the slope of the isoquant. Graph the Isoquant. Are the isoquants convex to the origin?

6. Test each production function for homogeneity. If homogeneous, determine the degree of homogeneity, determine whether it exhibits constant, increasing, or decreasing returns to scale, and verify that Euler's theorem holds.

7. For each homogeneous function, show that the slope of the isoquant can be expressed as a function of the ratio of the inputs. This demonstrates that the homogeneous functions are also homothetic. Find the elasticity of substitution for each of the functions.

Answer questions 8 through 12 using the following two functions, which were estimated for industrial production in the USSR. The first was estimated for the period 1950–1969, the second for 1965–1984.[3]

   a. 1950–1969 $Y = 0.8(0.64K^{-1.5} + 0.36L^{-1.5})^{-.67}$

   b. 1965–1984 $\dfrac{Y}{L} = 0.06\left(\dfrac{K}{L}\right)^{.52}$

where Y, K, and L, represent output, capital inputs, and labor inputs, respectively.

8. What types of production function are these representative of?

9. Are the production functions homogeneous? If so, of what degree?

10. Compare the marginal products of capital and labor for the two periods.

11. Find expressions for the partial output elasticities of capital and labor in the two periods.

12. Compare the elasticities of substitution between the two periods. Discuss the economic meaning of the results.

---

[3]The first production function was estimated by Martin Weitzman, "Soviet Postwar Growth and Capital-Labor Substitution," *American Economic Review* 60, no. 4 (September 1970), pp. 676–692. The second was estimated by Peter Toumanoff, "Economic Reform and Industrial Performance in the Soviet Union: 1950–1984," *Comparative Economic Studies* 29, no. 4 (Winter 1987), pp. 128–149.

C H A P T E R   11

The Mathematics of Cost Minimization

11.1

INTRODUCTION

Producers do not deal only with technical problems of production. They must concern themselves with the cost of production as well. In order to maximize profit, firms must produce their output at minimum cost. We use a constrained optimization model to examine the producer problem of cost minimization in Section 11.2. You will find that the mathematics of cost minimization is very similar to the consumer model of constrained expenditure minimization, which was the dual of the model of constrained utility maximization. This model is extended to handle the economic concepts of short run and long run. We revisit our model of profit maximization in order to examine the important relationship between profit maximization and cost minimization. The examination of this relationship depends heavily on the envelope theorem. We turn now to the model of constrained cost minimization.

11.2

CONSTRAINED COST MINIMIZATION

In Chapter 4, Section 4.4, we discussed profit maximization models in which both revenue and cost were expressed as functions of output. The standard cost curves of the firm, explained in Chapter 3, Section 3.7.1 and illustrated graphically in Figure 3.10, are functional relationships between various costs and rate of output. However, whenever we discuss firms' input decisions, costs are always modeled as the sum of the products of input prices and employment levels, or

$$C = \sum_{i=1}^{n} w_i X_i \qquad (11\text{-}1)$$

Output does not appear in this formulation. How can we speak of cost as a function of output?

To answer this, we recognize that the firm does not simply choose any input level, but rather is constrained in its choices by its desire to achieve some objective, for example, maximum profits. A necessary (but not sufficient) condition for profit maximization is that a firm minimize the cost of producing any level of output it might choose. The parameters the firm faces in such a minimization task are the level of output and the prices of the inputs. If we view cost as the sum of products of input prices, w_i, and *optimum* employment levels, X_i, and recognize that *optimum* employment levels depend on output level, Y, and input prices, then we can write cost as

$$C^* = \sum_{i=1}^{n} w_i X_i^*(Y, w_i) \qquad (11\text{-}2)$$

This cost function, C^*, is a function of output. This is the cost function we have in mind when we draw total, average, and marginal cost curves as functions of output rate.

We generate C^* through a constrained optimization model very similar to the expenditure-minimization model of consumer behavior we examined in Chapter 9, Section 9.6. The firm's objective is to minimize cost subject to an output constraint. In the case in which there are only two inputs, the firm wishes to minimize

$$w_1 X_1 + w_2 X_2 \qquad (11\text{-}3)$$

subject to

$$Y_0 = f(X_1, X_2) \qquad (11\text{-}4)$$

In order to write the Lagrangian objective function of this constrained optimization model we respecify the constraint so that the right-hand side is equal to zero, multiply the result by the Lagrange multiplier, and add the product to the objective. We obtain

$$\mathcal{L} = w_1 X_1 + w_2 X_2 + \lambda(Y_0 - f(X_1, X_2)) \qquad (11\text{-}5)$$

The choice variables are X_1, X_2, and λ and the parameters are Y_0, w_1, and w_2. We use λ to denote our Lagrange multiplier in this model. The first-order conditions for minimization are

$$\mathcal{L}_1 = w_1 - \lambda f_1 = 0 \qquad (11\text{-}6)$$

$$\mathcal{L}_2 = w_2 - \lambda f_2 = 0 \qquad (11\text{-}7)$$

$$\mathcal{L}_\lambda = Y_0 - f(X_1, X_2) = 0 \qquad (11\text{-}8)$$

The bordered Hessian matrix of second partial derivatives is

$$H_B = \begin{bmatrix} -\lambda f_{11} & -\lambda f_{12} & -f_1 \\ -\lambda f_{21} & -\lambda f_{22} & -f_2 \\ f_1 & f_2 & 0 \end{bmatrix} \tag{11-9}$$

Our rule for the second-order conditions of a constrained minimization problem, which you may review in Chapter 8, Section 8.7.2, states, for this case, that the determinant of the bordered Hessian matrix must be negative, as are all border-preserving principal minors of dimension 3 or greater. In this case it means that $|H_B| < 0$. We leave it to you to evaluate the determinant of the bordered Hessian. When you do so, you discover that the SOC of the cost-minimization model require that the isoquants of the production function be convex to the origin.

The first-order conditions can be interpreted as meaning that the equilibrium values of X_1 and X_2 are at a point of tangency between an isocost line and the isoquant defined by equation (11-8). Equations (11-6) and (11-7) can be solved to show that

$$\frac{w_1}{w_2} = \frac{f_1}{f_2} \tag{11-10}$$

or that the ratio of input prices equals the ratio of marginal products at the minimum cost combination of inputs. In Chapter 5, Section 5.10.2, we show that the slope of an isocost line is the negative of the ratio of input prices. We also know that the slope of an isoquant is the negative of the ratio of marginal products. Where the slopes of the isocost and isoquant are equal, there is a point of tangency. This equilibrium is pictured in Figure 11.1.

Figure 11.1

Minimum-Cost Combination of Two Inputs to Produce Y_0

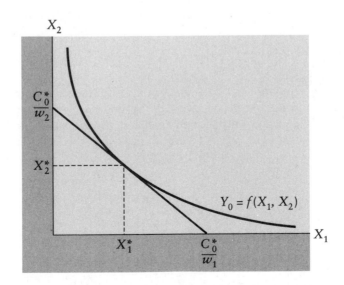

Another implication of the FOC is that

$$\lambda = \frac{w_1}{f_1} = \frac{w_2}{f_2} \tag{11-11}$$

We are accustomed to interpreting the Lagrange multiplier as the effect on the objective of relaxing the constraining parameter. In this case, the objective is the cost of production and the constraining parameter is the rate of output. Therefore, we interpret λ as the effect that increasing the rate of output has on cost, or the marginal cost of production. This can be demonstrated with the help of the envelope theorem, which, as you recall from Chapter 7, Section 7.4, states that the partial derivative of the indirect objective function with respect to a parameter equals the partial derivative of the original objective function with respect to the same parameter, evaluated at the optimum. In our case, the indirect objective function is the cost function with the equilibrium values of the choice variables, X_1^* and X_2^*, substituted in. This is

$$C^* = w_1 X_1^*(Y_0, w_1, w_2) + w_2 X_2^*(Y_0, w_1, w_2) \tag{11-12}$$

According to the envelope theorem,

$$\frac{\partial C^*}{\partial Y_0} = \frac{\partial \mathscr{L}}{\partial Y_0} = \lambda^* \tag{11-13}$$

Recognize that equation (11-12), the indirect cost function, is the functional relationship between total cost and output that we discuss at the beginning of this section.

In order to perform comparative statics analysis with this model, we recognize that the FOC implicitly contain functional relationships between the equilibrium values of the three choice variables and the parameters, or

$$X_1^* = X_1^*(Y_0, w_1, w_2) \tag{11-14}$$

$$X_2^* = X_2^*(Y_0, w_1, w_2) \tag{11-15}$$

$$\lambda^* = \lambda^*(Y_0, w_1, w_2) \tag{11-16}$$

Equations (11-14) and (11-15) are the cost-minimizing input choices for the firm, for given levels of output and given input prices. They represent constant-output input demand functions. We substitute these equilibrium values of X_1^*, X_2^*, and λ^* back into the FOC, creating the identities

$$w_1 - \lambda^* f_1(X_1^*, X_2^*) \equiv 0 \tag{11-17}$$

$$w_2 - \lambda^* f_2(X_1^*, X_2^*) \equiv 0 \tag{11-18}$$

$$Y_0 - f(X_1^*, X_2^*) \equiv 0 \tag{11-19}$$

These identities can be differentiated with respect to any of the parameters.

For example, if we differentiate with respect to w_1, we generate the matrix equation

$$
\begin{bmatrix}
-\lambda^* f_{11} & -\lambda^* f_{12} & -f_1 \\
-\lambda^* f_{21} & -\lambda^* f_{22} & -f_2 \\
-f_1 & -f_2 & 0
\end{bmatrix}
\begin{bmatrix}
\dfrac{\partial X_1^*}{\partial w_1} \\[2mm]
\dfrac{\partial X_2^*}{\partial w_1} \\[2mm]
\dfrac{\partial \lambda^*}{\partial w_1}
\end{bmatrix}
\equiv
\begin{bmatrix}
-1 \\ 0 \\ 0
\end{bmatrix}
\qquad (11\text{-}20)
$$

We use Cramer's rule to solve for $\partial X_1^*/\partial w_1$, $\partial X_2^*/\partial w_1$, and $\partial \lambda^*/\partial w_1$.

$$
\frac{\partial X_1^*}{\partial w_1} = \frac{\begin{vmatrix} -1 & -\lambda^* f_{12} & -f_1 \\ 0 & -\lambda^* f_{22} & -f_2 \\ 0 & -f_2 & 0 \end{vmatrix}}{|H_B|} = -\frac{|H_{11}|}{|H_B|} = \frac{f_2^2}{|H_B|} < 0 \qquad (11\text{-}21)
$$

$$
\frac{\partial X_2^*}{\partial w_1} = \frac{\begin{vmatrix} -\lambda^* f_{11} & -1 & -f_1 \\ -\lambda^* f_{21} & 0 & -f_2 \\ -f_1 & 0 & 0 \end{vmatrix}}{|H_B|} = -\frac{|H_{12}|}{|H_B|} = -\frac{f_1 f_2}{|H_B|} > 0 \qquad (11\text{-}22)
$$

$$
\frac{\partial \lambda^*}{\partial w_1} = \frac{\begin{vmatrix} -\lambda^* f_{11} & -\lambda^* f_{12} & -1 \\ -\lambda^* f_{21} & -\lambda^* f_{22} & 0 \\ -f_1 & -f_2 & 0 \end{vmatrix}}{|H_B|} = -\frac{|H_{13}|}{|H_B|} = -\lambda^* \frac{(f_{21} f_2 - f_1 f_{22})}{|H_B|} \qquad (11\text{-}23)
$$

We find that $\partial X_1^*/\partial w_1 < 0$; that is, an increase in its own price decreases the cost-minimizing employment of input 1. On the other hand, an increase in the price of input 1 increases the cost-minimizing employment of input 2, because $\partial X_2^*/\partial w_1 > 0$. Finally, we find that we cannot determine how an increase in the price of input 1 affects marginal cost, because we cannot determine a sign for $\partial \lambda^*/\partial w_1$. These are all interesting results. The first two are easily explained by examining the effects of a change in w_1 graphically, as in Figure 11.2.

When w_1 increases, the effect is to make the isocost line steeper, changing C^* to $C^{*\prime}$. The new isocost line is tangent to the Y_0 isoquant to the left of the original point of tangency, decreasing X_1^* to $X_1^{*\prime}$ and increasing X_2^* to $X_2^{*\prime}$. Be sure to recognize that our ability to determine a sign for $\partial X_2^*/\partial w_1$ is strictly a result of the fact that our model has only two inputs. The only way to maintain output while decreasing X_1 is to increase X_2. In a model with

Figure 11.2

The Effect of Increasing
w_1 on X_1^* and X_2^*

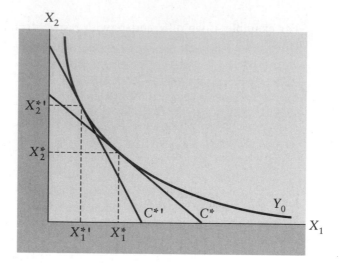

more than two inputs we are not, in general, able to determine a sign for
$\partial X_i^*/\partial w_j$, $i \neq j$.

The third comparative statics result, that we cannot determine a sign for
$\partial\lambda^*/\partial w_1$, is not as easy to visualize. It means that we do not know the effect
of a change in an input price on the marginal cost of production. Intuitively,
one would think that this partial derivative would be positive—that an
increase in an input price would increase marginal cost. Certainly, increasing
an input price increases the total cost of production, but our model does not
permit us to conclude that it increases marginal cost. In fact, there are
circumstances in which marginal cost is decreased by an increase in an input
price, but we must look at some other comparative statics results in order to
understand those circumstances.

Suppose we look at the comparative statics of a change in Y_0, the output
level. Differentiating the identities (11-17), (11-18), and (11-19) with respect
to Y_0 generates the matrix equation

$$\begin{bmatrix} -\lambda^* f_{11} & -\lambda^* f_{12} & -f_1 \\ -\lambda^* f_{21} & -\lambda^* f_{22} & -f_2 \\ -f_1 & -f_2 & 0 \end{bmatrix} \begin{bmatrix} \dfrac{\partial X_1^*}{\partial Y_0} \\[2ex] \dfrac{\partial X_2^*}{\partial Y_0} \\[2ex] \dfrac{\partial \lambda^*}{\partial Y_0} \end{bmatrix} \equiv \begin{bmatrix} 0 \\ 0 \\ -1 \end{bmatrix} \qquad \textbf{(11-24)}$$

We use Cramer's rule to solve for $\partial X_1^*/\partial Y_0$, $\partial X_2^*/\partial Y_0$, and $\partial \lambda^*/\partial Y_0$.

$$\frac{\partial X_1^*}{\partial Y_0} = \frac{\begin{vmatrix} 0 & -\lambda^* f_{12} & -f_1 \\ 0 & -\lambda^* f_{22} & -f_2 \\ -1 & -f_2 & 0 \end{vmatrix}}{|H_B|} = -\frac{|H_{31}|}{|H_B|} = -\lambda^* \frac{(f_2 f_{12} - f_1 f_{22})}{|H_B|} \qquad \textbf{(11-25)}$$

$$\frac{\partial X_2^*}{\partial Y_0} = \frac{\begin{vmatrix} -\lambda^* f_{11} & 0 & -f_1 \\ -\lambda^* f_{21} & 0 & -f_2 \\ -f_1 & -1 & 0 \end{vmatrix}}{|H_B|} = \frac{|H_{32}|}{|H_B|} = \lambda^* \frac{(f_2 f_{11} - f_1 f_{21})}{|H_B|} \tag{11-26}$$

$$\frac{\partial \lambda^*}{\partial Y_0} = \frac{\begin{vmatrix} -\lambda^* f_{11} & -\lambda^* f_{12} & 0 \\ -\lambda^* f_{21} & -\lambda^* f_{22} & 0 \\ -f_1 & -f_2 & -1 \end{vmatrix}}{|H_B|} = -\frac{|H_{33}|}{|H_B|} = -\lambda^{*2} \frac{(f_{11} f_{22} - f_{12}^2)}{|H_B|} \tag{11-27}$$

The effect of a change in Y_0 on the equilibrium of the cost-minimization problem is pictured in Figure 11.3.

Even though none of the comparative statics results can be signed, they are all interesting. Compare the result for $\partial X_1^*/\partial Y_0$, equation (11-25), with the result previously obtained for $\partial \lambda^*/\partial w_1$, equation (11-23). They are identical, because the minor $|H_{13}|$ of the determinant of the bordered Hessian equals the minor $|H_{31}|$. The reason the minors equal one another is that the bordered Hessian matrix is symmetric. This means that the effect of increasing output on the minimum-cost choice of X_1 is the same as the effect of an increase in the price of X_1 on marginal cost. We normally expect both of them to be positive as shown in Figure 11.3, but there is the possibility of an **inferior input**, just as we found a good could be inferior in consumer models. For an

inferior input: an input that a firm uses less of as output increases.

Figure 11.3

The Effect of Increasing Y_0 on X_1^* and X_2^*

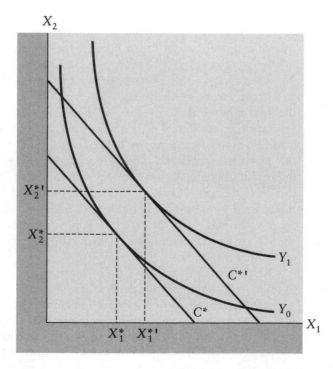

input to be inferior, a firm would use less of it as output increases. Our result
tells us that, if the price of an inferior input rises, marginal cost decreases.
If a firm uses more of an input as output increases, it is considered to be a
normal input.

We can also obtain this result—that the effect of increasing output on the
minimum-cost choice of X_1 is the same as the effect of an increase in the price
of X_1 on marginal cost—via the envelope theorem. The partial derivative of
the indirect cost function with respect to some parameter equals the partial
derivative of the Lagrange objective function with respect to the same
parameter, evaluated at the optimum. We differentiate twice, first with respect
to w_1 and second with respect to Y_0. Recognize that Young's theorem
allows us to reverse the order in which we differentiate. Thus we obtain the
result that $\partial X_1^*/\partial Y_0 = \partial \lambda^*/\partial w_1$,

$$\frac{\partial^2 C^*}{\partial w_1\, \partial Y_0} = \frac{\partial^2 \mathscr{L}}{\partial w_1\, \partial Y_0} = \frac{\partial X_1^*}{\partial Y_0} = \frac{\partial \lambda^*}{\partial w_1} = \frac{\partial^2 \mathscr{L}}{\partial Y_0\, \partial w_1} = \frac{\partial^2 C^*}{\partial Y_0\, \partial w_1} \quad \text{(11-28)}$$

We can perform a similar exercise by using the envelope theorem to differentiate the indirect cost function twice more, this time with respect to w_1 and
w_2. In this instance, we find

$$\frac{\partial^2 C^*}{\partial w_1\, \partial w_2} = \frac{\partial^2 \mathscr{L}}{\partial w_1\, \partial w_2} = \frac{\partial X_1^*}{\partial w_2} = \frac{\partial X_2^*}{\partial w_1} = \frac{\partial^2 \mathscr{L}}{\partial w_2\, \partial w_1} = \frac{\partial^2 C^*}{\partial w_2\, \partial w_1} \quad \text{(11-29)}$$

That is, the effect on X_1 of a change in w_2 is the same as the effect on X_2 of
a change in w_1. We leave it to you to verify this result by examining the
comparative statics of a change in w_2.

Look carefully at the comparative statics result for $\partial \lambda^*/\partial Y_0$, Equation
(11-27). It can be interpreted as the slope of the marginal cost curve. We
cannot determine a sign for it because the principal minor in the numerator
of the expression, $|H_{33}|$, is not a *border-preserving* principal minor. If we
knew that $(f_{11}f_{22} - f_{12}^2)$ was positive, we could determine that the marginal
cost curve was upward sloping. However, that is not required by the SOC of
the cost-minimization model. We have seen $(f_{11}f_{22} - f_{12}^2)$ before. It is a
second-order condition of the two-input perfectly competitive profit-maximization model from Chapter 6, Section 6.3.3. There we saw that the SOC of
the profit-maximization model require $(f_{11}f_{22} - f_{12}^2)$ to be positive. Two
important inferences can be drawn from this. First, as we noted in Chapter 6,
the second-order condition from the profit-maximization model can be
interpreted as meaning that the marginal cost curve must slope upward.
Second, the SOC from the profit-maximization model are more stringent than
the SOC from cost minimization; the former require upward-sloping marginal
cost, the latter do not.

Remember that, while a firm must minimize cost at each level of output
in order to maximize profit, the converse is not true. A firm can minimize cost
without maximizing profit. All that is required by cost-minimizing behavior is
that the least-cost combination of inputs be chosen whatever the level of
output. Profit maximization requires a particular level of output (where
marginal cost equals marginal revenue) *in addition to* least-cost combinations

of inputs. This relationship between the profit-maximization and cost-minimization models of firm behavior bears further examination in the next section.

NUMERICAL EXAMPLE

Suppose a firm, facing a production function of $Y = X_1^{1/2} X_2^{1/2}$ and input prices w_1 and w_2, wishes to minimize the cost of producing a rate of output equal to Y_0. The Lagrangian objective function is $\mathscr{L} = w_1 X_1 + w_2 X_2 + \lambda(Y_0 - X_1^{1/2} X_2^{1/2})$. The FOC are

$$\mathscr{L}_1 = w_1 - \tfrac{1}{2}\lambda X_1^{-1/2} X_2^{1/2} = 0 \tag{11-30}$$

$$\mathscr{L}_2 = w_2 - \tfrac{1}{2}\lambda X_1^{1/2} X_2^{-1/2} = 0 \tag{11-31}$$

$$\mathscr{L}_\lambda = Y_0 - X_1^{1/2} X_2^{1/2} = 0 \tag{11-32}$$

These three equations can be solved for the three unknowns, X_1^*, X_2^*, and λ^*. We obtain $X_1^* = (w_2/w_1)^{1/2} Y_0$, $X_2^* = (w_1/w_2)^{1/2} Y_0$, and $\lambda^* = 2(w_1 w_2)^{1/2}$. The SOC requires that the determinant of the bordered Hessian matrix of second-order partial derivatives of the Lagrangian be negative,

$$|H_B| = \begin{vmatrix} \tfrac{1}{4}\lambda^* X_1^{*-3/2} X_2^{*1/2} & -\tfrac{1}{4}\lambda^* X_1^{*-1/2} X_2^{*-1/2} & -\tfrac{1}{2}X_1^{*-1/2} X_2^{*1/2} \\ -\tfrac{1}{4}\lambda^* X_1^{*-1/2} X_2^{*-1/2} & \tfrac{1}{4}\lambda^* X_1^{*1/2} X_2^{*-3/2} & -\tfrac{1}{2}X_1^{*1/2} X_2^{*-1/2} \\ -\tfrac{1}{2}X_1^{*-1/2} X_2^{*1/2} & -\tfrac{1}{2}X_1^{*1/2} X_2^{*-1/2} & 0 \end{vmatrix}$$

$$= -\frac{1}{2}\frac{(w_1 w_2)^{1/2}}{Y_0} < 0 \tag{11-33}$$

We can find the comparative statics results either by substituting X_1^*, X_2^*, and λ^* back into equations (11-30), (11-31), and (11-32) to create the identities that can be differentiated with respect to the parameters, or by differentiating $X_1^* = (w_2/w_1)^{1/2} Y_0$, $X_2^* = (w_1/w_2)^{1/2} Y_0$, and $\lambda^* = 2(w_1/w_2)^{1/2}$ directly. Taking the latter course of action and differentiating with respect to w_1 gives us

$$\frac{\partial X_1^*}{\partial w_1} = -\frac{1}{2}\left(\frac{w_2}{w_1^3}\right)^{1/2} Y_0 < 0 \tag{11-34}$$

$$\frac{\partial X_2^*}{\partial w_1} = \frac{1}{2} Y_0 \left(\frac{1}{w_1 w_2}\right)^{1/2} > 0 \tag{11-35}$$

$$\frac{\partial \lambda^*}{\partial w_1} = \left(\frac{w_2}{w_1}\right)^{1/2} > 0 \tag{11-36}$$

We see from equations (11-34) through (11-36) that, as expected, X_1^* is negatively related to w_1; that X_2^* is positively related to w_1; and that marginal cost, λ^*, increases with increases in w_1. This last result indicates that input 1 must be a normal input.

We verify that λ^* represents marginal cost by finding the indirect cost function and differentiating it with respect to Y_0. The indirect cost function is

$$C^* = w_1 X_1^* + w_2 X_2^* = w_1 \left(\frac{w_2}{w_1}\right)^{1/2} Y_0 + w_2 \left(\frac{w_1}{w_2}\right)^{1/2} Y_0 \qquad \textbf{(11-37)}$$

Equation (11-37) can be simplified to

$$C^* = 2(w_2 w_1)^{1/2} Y_0 \qquad \textbf{(11-38)}$$

The derivative of (11-38) with respect to Y_0 equals $\partial C^*/\partial Y_0 = 2(w_2 w_1)^{1/2} = \lambda^*$.

We can also differentiate X_1^*, X_2^*, and λ^* with respect to Y_0. Doing so gives us

$$\frac{\partial X_1^*}{\partial Y_0} = \left(\frac{w_2}{w_1}\right)^{1/2} > 0 \qquad \textbf{(11-39)}$$

$$\frac{\partial X_2^*}{\partial Y_0} = \left(\frac{w_1}{w_2}\right)^{1/2} > 0 \qquad \textbf{(11-40)}$$

$$\frac{\partial \lambda^*}{\partial Y_0} = 0 \qquad \textbf{(11-41)}$$

We see from (11-39) and (11-40) that both inputs are normal; that is, the firm chooses to increase employment of both when output increases. We see from (11-41) that the slope of the marginal cost curve is zero; that is, the marginal cost curve for this firm is horizontal.

EXERCISES
Section 11.2
Constrained Cost
Minimization

Consider a firm with the production function $Y = \ln(X_1 X_2)$ to answer the following questions.

1. Find the Lagrangian objective function and the first- and second-order conditions if the firm wishes to minimize cost subject to producing Y_0 units of output. Assume the input prices are w_1 and w_2.

2. Solve the first-order conditions for optimal values of the inputs and marginal cost, and find the indirect cost function. Verify that the derivative of the indirect cost-function with respect to Y_0 equals the Lagrange multiplier.

3. Find and interpret the comparative statics results for changes in w_2.

4. Find and interpret the comparative statics results for changes in Y_0

11.3

MARGINAL COST AND HOMOGENEOUS PRODUCTION FUNCTIONS

The last result of our numerical example, that the marginal cost curve is horizontal, is an interesting one. The production function for this firm, $Y = X_1^{1/2}X_2^{1/2}$, is a linear homogeneous Cobb–Douglas function. Intuitively, it makes sense that a linear homogeneous production function should yield a horizontal marginal cost curve. The cost of production, $w_1X_1 + w_2X_2$, is linearly homogeneous in the inputs, so if output is also linearly homogenous in the inputs, then proportional increases in the inputs increase both output and cost proportionately. This means that the change in cost will always maintain the same proportion to the change in output, no matter what the output level, so marginal cost is constant. By similar reasoning, production functions which are homogeneous of degree less than one yield upward-sloping marginal cost curves, and production functions which are homogeneous of degree greater than one yield downward-sloping marginal cost.

This relationship between the slope of the marginal cost curve and homogeneous production functions can be derived mathematically. To do so, recall equation (11-12), the indirect cost function, which we reproduce here.

$$C^* = w_1 X_1^*(Y_0, w_1, w_2) + w_2 X_2^*(Y_0, w_1, w_2) \qquad \textbf{(11-12)}$$

From (11-6) and (11-7) we know that $w_1 = \lambda f_1$ and $w_2 = \lambda f_2$. Substituting these expressions into (11-12) gives us

$$C^* = \lambda^* f_1 X_1^*(Y_0, w_1, w_2) + \lambda^* f_2 X_2^*(Y_0, w_1, w_2) \qquad \textbf{(11-42)}$$

Factoring λ^* allows us to write

$$C^* = \lambda^*(f_1 X_1^* + f_2 X_2^*) \qquad \textbf{(11-43)}$$

If the production function is homogeneous of degree r, Euler's theorem requires that $rY_0 = f_1 X_1^* + f_2 X_2^*$. We substitute this into (11-43) in order to obtain

$$C^* = \lambda^* r Y_0 \qquad \textbf{(11-44)}$$

We can differentiate (11-44) with respect to Y_0 to get an expression for marginal cost. Remember to use the product rule when differentiating. We obtain

$$\frac{\partial C^*}{\partial Y_0} = \lambda^* = rY_0 \frac{\partial \lambda^*}{\partial Y_0} + r\lambda^* \qquad \textbf{(11-45)}$$

Solving for $\partial \lambda^*/\partial Y_0$ gives us an expression for the slope of the marginal cost curve,

$$\frac{\partial \lambda^*}{\partial Y_0} = \frac{\lambda^*(1 - r)}{rY_0} \qquad \textbf{(11-46)}$$

Equation (11-46) relates the slope of the marginal cost curve to r, the degree of homogeneity of the production function. If $r < 1$, the production function exhibits decreasing returns to scale and the slope of the marginal cost curve is positive. If $r = 1$, the production function exhibits constant returns to scale and the slope of the marginal cost curve equals zero. If $r > 1$, the production function exhibits increasing returns to scale and the slope of the marginal cost curve is negative.

**EXERCISES
Section 11.3
Marginal Cost and
Homogeneous
Production
Functions**

For each of the following production functions, find (a) the degree of homogeneity and (b) the slope of the marginal cost curve.

1. $Y = f(X_1, X_2, X_3) = aX_1 + bX_2 + cX_3$

2. $Y = f(X_1, X_2, X_3) = AX_1^{0.2}X_2^{0.3}X_3^{0.4}$

3. $Y = f(X_1, X_2) = X_1 X_2$

4. $Y = f(X_1, X_2) = A(\alpha X_1^{-\rho} + (1 - \alpha)X_2^{-\rho})^{-1/\rho}$

11.4

PROFIT MAXIMIZATION AND COST MINIMIZATION COMPARED

For simplicity and clarity, we compare the cases in which there are only two inputs. Table 11.1 provides a side-by-side comparison of the first- and second-order conditions of the two models.

Table 11.1 Profit Maximization and Cost Minimization Compared

Profit Maximization	Cost Minimization
Maximize	Minimize
$\pi = Pf(X_1, X_2) - w_1X_1 - w_2X_2$	$\mathscr{L} = w_1X_1 + w_2X_2 + \lambda(Y_0 - f(X_1, X_2))$
FOC: $Pf_1 - w_1 = 0$	FOC: $w_1 - \lambda f_1 = 0$
$Pf_2 - w_2 = 0$	$w_2 - \lambda f_2 = 0$
These imply	$Y_0 - f(X_1, X_2) = 0$
$P = w_1/f_1 = w_2/f_2$ and $f_1/f_2 = w_1/w_2$	These imply
SOC:	$\lambda = w_1/f_1 = w_2/f_2$ and $f_1/f_2 = w_1/w_2$
$\begin{vmatrix} Pf_{11} & Pf_{12} \\ Pf_{21} & Pf_{22} \end{vmatrix} > 0;\ Pf_{11}, Pf_{22} < 0$	SOC:
	$\begin{vmatrix} -\lambda f_{11} & -\lambda f_{12} & -f_1 \\ -\lambda f_{21} & -\lambda f_{22} & -f_2 \\ -f_1 & -f_2 & 0 \end{vmatrix} < 0$
These imply strictly convex isoquants, downward-sloping marginal products and upward-sloping marginal cost.	This implies only strictly convex isoquants.

Compare the FOC of the two models. Both models imply that equilibrium occurs at a point of tangency between an isoquant and an isocost line. Although that is all that is required by the FOC of cost minimization, profit maximization requires in addition that $P = w_1/f_1 = w_2/f_2$. This is a more stringent requirement than we see in the case of cost minimization because the output price, P, is a parameter; it is determined outside the model. The Lagrange multiplier, λ, is endogenous in the cost-minimization model. The FOC of cost minimization do not constrain w_1/f_1 and w_2/f_2 to a particular value, determined externally. They only identify w_1/f_1 and w_2/f_2 as expressions for λ^*, or marginal cost. Profit maximization requires that the firm choose input levels (and output) such that price equals marginal cost. Cost minimization is consistent with any level of output.

As we mentioned in Section 11.2, the second-order conditions of the profit-maximization model, which require upward-sloping marginal cost, are also more demanding than those of cost minimization. A production function must be concave in order to satisfy the SOC for unconstrained profit maximization, while a production function that satisfies the SOC for constrained cost minimization is considered to be **quasi-concave**. A function which is concave is also quasi-concave, but the reverse is not true. Quasi-concavity does not imply concavity.[1]

quasi-concave: the property that the level curves of an increasing (decreasing) function are convex (concave).

Recognize both the differences and the similarities of the two models. They share the same choice variables, and input prices are parameters in both. Output price is a parameter in the profit-maximization model, while output level is a parameter in cost minimization. In the profit-maximization model output is endogenous, determined by the optimal levels of the inputs. This means that the profit-maximizing choices of input levels are functions of w_1, w_2, and P, and the cost-minimizing choices of input levels are functions of w_1, w_2, and Y_0. The input levels are the same only if the output level at which costs are minimized is equal to Y^π, the profit-maximizing level. This last observation can be stated mathematically as

$$X_1^\pi(w_1, w_2, P) \equiv X_1^C(w_1, w_2, Y^\pi(w_1, w_2, P)) \qquad (11\text{-}47)$$

Instead of using superscript asterisks to denote equilibrium values of X_1, we distinguish between profit-maximizing and cost-minimizing levels by using superscript π to denote the former and C to denote the latter. The equality between X_1^π and X_1^C is an identity because, by replacing the parameter Y_0 by Y^π, we define X_1^C to be identical to X_1^π. We ensure that costs are minimized at the profit-maximizing level of output.

The reason for stating this identity is that it can be used to compare the comparative statics of the profit-maximization model with the comparative statics of cost minimization. Specifically, we can differentiate the identity with respect to w_1 in order to compare the slopes of the factor demands derivable from each model. Note that we must account for both the direct effect of w_1

---

[1]This is demonstrated in the two-input case in Silberberg, Eugene, *The Structure of Economics*, 2nd edition (New York: McGraw-Hill Book Company, 1990), pp. 109–112. Don't be confused by the terminology; a *concave* (or *quasi-concave*) production function has isoquants which are *convex*.

on X_1^C and the indirect effect through Y^π when differentiating.

$$\frac{\partial X_1^\pi}{\partial w_1} \equiv \frac{\partial X_1^C}{\partial w_1} + \frac{\partial X_1^C}{\partial Y^\pi}\frac{\partial Y^\pi}{\partial w_1} \qquad (11\text{-}48)$$

What do you expect the relationship between these two types of factor demand functions to be? The profit-maximization model requires the firm to respond to a change in input price in two ways: (1) by adjusting the cost-minimizing combinations of inputs for each level of output and (2) by adjusting the level of output so that profit is maximized. The first adjustment is represented in equation (11-48) by $\partial X_1^C/\partial w_1$ and the second adjustment by $(\partial X_1^C/\partial Y^\pi)(\partial Y^\pi/\partial w_1)$. The cost-minimization model requires the firm to respond to a change in input price holding output constant. Because the cost-minimization model constrains the ways the firm is able to respond more than the profit-maximization model, we expect $\partial X_1^\pi/\partial w_1$ to be numerically larger in absolute value than $\partial X_1^C/\partial w_1$. Because factor demand curves are negatively sloped, this means that $\partial X_1^\pi/\partial w_1 < \partial X_1^C/\partial w_1$. This can be shown mathematically with the help of the envelope theorem.

Recall the indirect profit function, which you saw first in Chapter 7, Section 7.4, and which we reproduce here. Note that we have replaced K^* and L^* with X_1^π and X_2^π, and w and r with w_1 and w_2, so that we conform to the notation in this chapter.

$$\pi^\pi = Pf(X_1^\pi(P, w_1, w_2), X_2^\pi(P, w_1, w_2)) - w_1 X_1^\pi(P, w_1, w_2) - w_2 X_2^\pi(P, w_1, w_2)$$
$$(7\text{-}75)$$

Differentiate (7-75) twice, first with respect to P and then with respect to w_1. The envelope theorem along with Young's theorem tell us that

$$\frac{\partial^2 \pi^\pi}{\partial P\,\partial w_1} = \frac{\partial^2 \pi}{\partial P\,\partial w_1} = \frac{\partial Y^\pi}{\partial w_1} = -\frac{\partial X_1^\pi}{\partial P} = \frac{\partial^2 \pi}{\partial w_1\,\partial P} = \frac{\partial^2 \pi^\pi}{\partial w_1\,\partial P} \qquad (11\text{-}49)$$

Equation (11-49) means that the effect on profit-maximizing output of a change in input price is equal to the effect on input level of a change in output price, but in the opposite direction. Normally, we expect $\partial Y^\pi/\partial w_1$ to be negative, but in the case of an inferior input both it and $-\partial X_1^\pi/\partial P$ are positive. Substitute (11-49) into (11-48). We obtain

$$\frac{\partial X_1^\pi}{\partial w_1} \equiv \frac{\partial X_1^C}{\partial w_1} - \frac{\partial X_1^C}{\partial Y^\pi}\frac{\partial X_1^\pi}{\partial P} \qquad (11\text{-}50)$$

We can find another expression for $\partial X_1^\pi/\partial P$ by differentiating the identity (11-47) with respect to P. We use the chain rule in the differentiation.

$$\frac{\partial X_1^\pi}{\partial P} \equiv \frac{\partial X_1^C}{\partial Y^\pi}\frac{\partial Y^\pi}{\partial P} \qquad (11\text{-}51)$$

Substituting (11-51) into (11-50) gives us

$$\frac{\partial X_1^\pi}{\partial w_1} \equiv \frac{\partial X_1^C}{\partial w_1} - \left(\frac{\partial X_1^C}{\partial Y^\pi}\right)^2 \frac{\partial Y^\pi}{\partial P} \tag{11-52}$$

We know the squared expression in parentheses is positive. What is the sign of $\partial Y^\pi/\partial P$? We know that Y^π is the profit-maximizing output level. It is the firm's production function with the profit-maximizing levels of X_1 and X_2 substituted in, or $Y^\pi(w_1, w_2, P) = f(X_1^\pi(w_1, w_2, P), \; X_2^\pi(w_1, w_2, P))$. This function represents the firm's supply function; that is, it tells us the output levels the firm is willing and able to supply as a function of input prices and output price. The partial derivative $\partial Y^\pi/\partial P$ is the slope of the profit-maximizing firm's supply, and it is positive for the perfectly competitive firm. Therefore,

$$\frac{\partial X_1^\pi}{\partial w_1} \equiv \frac{\partial X_1^C}{\partial w_1} - \left(\frac{\partial X_1^C}{\partial Y^\pi}\right)^2 \frac{\partial Y^\pi}{\partial P} < \frac{\partial X_1^C}{\partial w_1} \tag{11-53}$$

We have shown that the profit-maximization model implies a bigger response by the firm to a change in an input price than the cost-minimization model, as expected. This is shown graphically in Figure 11.4, which illustrates $\partial X_1^\pi/\partial w_1$ and $\partial X_1^C/\partial w_1$ as well as the factor demand curves associated with each model.

Figure 11.4

The Effect of Increasing w_1 on X_1^π and X_1^C
(*a*) **Isoquant diagram**
(*b*) **Input demand curves**

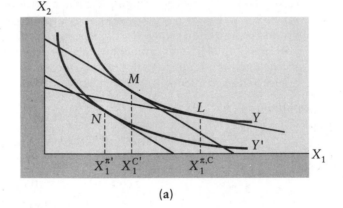

(a)

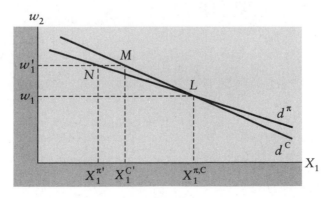

(b)

The initial equilibrium is at point L in both graphs. Cost minimization requires that output remain constant at Y_0 when w_1 increases, so point M, where $X_1 = X_1^{C'}$, represents the new equilibrium for that model. If the input is normal, we expect profit-maximizing output to decrease when w_1 increases, so point N, where $X_1 = X_1^{\pi'}$ represents the new equilibrium for the profit-maximization model. In the diagram of input demand curves, notice that, even though we found $\partial X_1^{\pi}/\partial w_1$ to be more negative than $\partial X_1^{C}/\partial w_1$, the input demand curve associated with the profit-maximization model, d^{π}, is flatter than the input demand curve associated with cost minimization, d^c. The explanation for this is one you have seen before; remember that we put w_1, the independent variable, on the vertical axis and X_1, the dependent variable, on the horizontal axis.

In all of the foregoing analysis of a firm's costs of production we have assumed that the firm can vary all of its inputs when parameters change. That is, we have assumed long-run equilibrium. We know the short run as a situation in which one or more inputs are held constant, with at least one variable input. Short-run costs are easily treated within the framework we use to analyze the long run. We discuss the treatment of short-run costs and compare them to the long run in the next section.

NUMERICAL EXAMPLE

At the end of Section 6.4 in Chapter 6, we presented a numerical example of a profit-maximizing price-taker firm with two inputs. Its production function is $Y = 10X_1^{1/4}X_2^{1/4}$, where capital, X_1, has a price of w_1 and labor, X_2, has a price of w_2. The firm sells its output at a price of P. Here we compare the profit-maximization model to cost minimization, using this specific production function. Note that optimum values associated with profit maximization are denoted with a superscript π and optimum values associated with cost minimization are denoted with a superscript C.

Profit Maximization

Max $\pi = P(10X_1^{1/4}X_2^{1/4}) - w_1X_1 - w_2X_2$

FOC: $(10/4)PX_1^{-3/4}X_2^{1/4} - w_1 = 0$

$(10/4)PX_1^{1/4}X_2^{-3/4} - w_2 = 0$

SOC:
$$\begin{vmatrix} -P\dfrac{3Y^{\pi}}{16X_1^{\pi2}} & \dfrac{PY^{\pi}}{16X_1^{\pi}X_2^{\pi}} \\[3mm] \dfrac{PY^{\pi}}{16X_1^{\pi}X_2^{\pi}} & -P\dfrac{3Y^{\pi}}{16X_2^{\pi2}} \end{vmatrix}$$

$$= \frac{1}{32}\left(\frac{PY^{\pi}}{X_1^{\pi}X_2^{\pi}}\right)^2 > 0$$

$$-P\frac{3Y^{\pi}}{16X_1^{\pi2}} < 0, \qquad -P\frac{3Y^{\pi}}{16X_2^{\pi2}} < 0$$

Cost Minimization

Min $\mathscr{L} = w_1X_1 + w_2X_2 + \lambda(Y_0 - 10X_1^{1/4}X_2^{1/4})$

FOC: $w_1 - \lambda(10/4)X_1^{-3/4}X_2^{1/4} = 0$

$w_2 - \lambda(10/4)X_1^{1/4}X_2^{-3/4} = 0$

$Y_0 - 10X_1^{1/4}X_2^{1/4} = 0$

SOC:
$$\begin{vmatrix} \dfrac{\lambda^C 3Y_0}{16X_1^{C2}} & -\dfrac{\lambda^C Y_0}{16X_1^C X_2^C} & -\dfrac{Y_0}{4X_1^C} \\[3mm] -\dfrac{\lambda^C Y_0}{16X_1^C X_2^C} & \dfrac{\lambda^C 3Y_0}{16X_2^{C2}} & -\dfrac{Y_0}{4X_2^C} \\[3mm] -\dfrac{Y_0}{4X_1^C} & -\dfrac{Y_0}{4X_2^C} & 0 \end{vmatrix}$$

$$= \frac{-\lambda^C Y_0^3}{32X_1^{C2}X_2^{C2}} > 0$$

The FOC can be solved for equilibrium values of the choice variables in terms of the parameters P, w_2, and w_1, as well as the supply function $Y^\pi = f(X_1^\pi, X_2^\pi)$,

$$X_1^\pi = 6.25 P^2 w_1^{-3/2} w_2^{-1/2} \qquad (11\text{-}54)$$

$$X_2^\pi = 6.25 P^2 w_1^{-1/2} w_2^{-3/2} \qquad (11\text{-}55)$$

$$Y^\pi = (25P)(w_1 w_2)^{-1/2} \qquad (11\text{-}56)$$

The FOC can be solved for equilibrium values of the choice variables in terms of the parameters Y_0, w_2, and w_1

$$X_1^C = (Y_0/10)^2 (w_2/w_1)^{1/2} \qquad (11\text{-}57)$$

$$X_2^C = (Y_0/10)^2 (w_1/w_2)^{1/2} \qquad (11\text{-}58)$$

$$\lambda^C = (Y_0/25)(w_1 w_2)^{1/2} \qquad (11\text{-}59)$$

We can use these examples to illustrate the propositions we derived regarding the comparison of profit-maximization and cost-minimization models. First, we suggested that, if we evaluate X_1^C at $Y_0 = Y^\pi$, it is identically equal to X_1^π. Substituting (11-56) for Y_0 in (11-57) gives us this result, that

$$X_1^C = \left(\frac{25P(w_1 w_2)^{-1/2}}{10} \right)^2 \left(\frac{w_2}{w_1} \right)^{1/2} = 6.25 P^2 w_1^{-3/2} w_2^{-1/2} = X_1^\pi \qquad (11\text{-}60)$$

Second, we showed in equation (11-54) that the profit-maximization model implies a bigger response by the firm to a change in an input price than the cost-minimization model, or $\partial X_1^\pi / \partial w_1 < \partial X_1^C / \partial w_1$. We can illustrate this proposition by differentiating (11-54) and (11-57) directly with respect to w_1. We obtain

$$\frac{\partial X_1^\pi}{\partial w_1} = -9.375 P^2 w_1^{-5/2} w_2^{-1/2}, \qquad \frac{\partial X_1^C}{\partial w_1} = -\frac{1}{2} \left(\frac{Y_0}{10} \right)^2 w_1^{-3/2} w_2^{1/2} \qquad (11\text{-}61)$$

We evaluate X_1^C at $Y_0 = Y^\pi$ by substituting (11-56) for Y_0 in (11-61), obtaining

$$\frac{\partial X_1^C}{\partial w_1} = -3.125 P^2 w_1^{-5/2} w_2^{-1/2} \qquad (11\text{-}62)$$

Therefore, we have demonstrated that $\partial X_1^\pi / \partial w_1 < \partial X_1^C / \partial w_1$.

You may have noticed in the numerical example an interesting relationship between the profit-maximizing firm's supply function, $Y^\pi(w_1, w_2, P)$, and the cost-minimizing firm's marginal cost function, $\lambda^C(w_1, w_2, Y_0)$. If you let λ^C equal P and Y_0 equal Y^π, you see that the marginal cost function, equation (11-59), is the inverse of the supply function, (11-56). This is an illustration of the idea that the supply function of the price-taker firm is its marginal cost curve, keeping in mind that supply describes quantity as a function of price, whereas marginal cost is a function of quantity.

EXERCISES
Section 11.4
Profit Maximization
and Cost
Minimization
Compared

Consider a firm with the production function $Y = X_1^{0.3}X_2^{0.6}$ to answer the following questions.

1. Compare the first- and second-order conditions of profit-maximization to the first- and second-order conditions of cost minimization.

2. Solve the first-order conditions for optimal values of the inputs, the profit-maximization supply function, and marginal cost.

3. Show that, when you evaluate X_1^C at $Y_0 = Y^\pi$, $X_1^C = X_1^\pi$.

4. Show that, when you evaluate X_1^C at $Y_0 = Y^\pi$, $\partial X_1^\pi/\partial w_1 < \partial X_1^C/\partial w_1$.

11.5

SHORT-RUN COSTS

We do not use the two-input model discussed above to investigate short-run costs. The reason is that, if we hold one input constant and model the firm as though it minimizes cost subject to an output constraint, we have trivialized the firm's choice. Fixing output and one input in a two-input cost-minimization model determines the other input level. Remember the discussion of constrained optimization in Chapter 7, Section 7.2. There we suggest that to obtain nontrivial results the number of constraints must be less than the number of choice variables. This is not the case with two inputs and two constraints; therefore, we use a three-input production function to analyze short-run costs.

As we imply above, holding an input fixed is adding a constraint to the cost-minimization model. We could accomplish this simply by substituting some fixed level of an input into the production function, or we could use the Lagrangian technique with two constraints. Let's use the Lagrangian technique to give you some experience with multiple constraints. The objective of the firm is to minimize

$$w_1 X_1 + w_2 X_2 + w_3 X_3 \tag{11-63}$$

subject to

$$Y_0 = f(X_1, X_2, X_3) \tag{11-64}$$

and

$$X_{30} = X_3 \tag{11-65}$$

To incorporate two constraints we need two Lagrange multipliers, λ and ξ. We write both constraints so that their right-hand sides are equal to zero, multiply each by its Lagrange multiplier, and add the products to the objective. We obtain

$$\mathcal{L} = w_1 X_1 + w_2 X_2 + w_3 X_3 + \lambda(Y_0 - f(X_1, X_2, X_3)) + \xi(X_{30} - X_3) \tag{11-66}$$

The choice variables are X_1, X_2, X_3, λ, and ξ, and the parameters are Y_0, w_1, w_2, w_3, and X_{30}.

The FOC of this constrained minimization problem are

$$\mathcal{L}_1 = w_1 - \lambda f_1 = 0 \tag{11-67}$$

$$\mathcal{L}_2 = w_2 - \lambda f_2 = 0 \tag{11-68}$$

$$\mathcal{L}_3 = w_3 - \lambda f_3 - \xi = 0 \tag{11-69}$$

$$\mathcal{L}_\lambda = Y_0 - f(X_1, X_2, X_3) = 0 \tag{11-70}$$

$$\mathcal{L}_\xi = X_{30} - X_3 = 0 \tag{11-71}$$

The bordered Hessian matrix of second partial derivatives is

$$
H_B = \begin{bmatrix}
-\lambda f_{11} & -\lambda f_{12} & -\lambda f_{13} & -f_1 & 0 \\
-\lambda f_{21} & -\lambda f_{22} & -\lambda f_{23} & -f_2 & 0 \\
-\lambda f_{31} & -\lambda f_{32} & -\lambda f_{33} & -f_3 & -1 \\
-f_1 & -f_2 & -f_3 & 0 & 0 \\
0 & 0 & -1 & 0 & 0
\end{bmatrix} \tag{11-72}
$$

The border of this bordered Hessian consists of the last two rows and the last two columns, because those are the second-order partials involving the Lagrange multipliers. Recall from Chapter 8, Section 8.7.2, that the rule for SOC of a constrained minimization states that all border-preserving principal minors of dimension m have the same sign as $(-1)^r$, where r is the number of constraints, and $m \geq 1 + 2r$. In this case $r = 2$, so we need not examine border-preserving principal minors of dimension less than 5, and our SOC requires that $|H_B| > 0$. When we expand $|H_B|$, first by the last column and then by the last row, we see that the SOC of this short-run three-input model are identical to the SOC of the long-run, two-input model. That is, the isoquants for the two variable inputs must be convex to the origin.

$$
|H_B| = \begin{vmatrix}
-\lambda f_{11} & -\lambda f_{12} & -\lambda f_{13} & -f_1 & 0 \\
-\lambda f_{21} & -\lambda f_{22} & -\lambda f_{23} & -f_2 & 0 \\
-\lambda f_{31} & -\lambda f_{32} & -\lambda f_{33} & -f_3 & -1 \\
-f_1 & -f_2 & -f_3 & 0 & 0 \\
0 & 0 & -1 & 0 & 0
\end{vmatrix} = -1 \begin{vmatrix}
-\lambda f_{11} & -\lambda f_{21} & -f_1 \\
-\lambda f_{21} & -\lambda f_{22} & -f_2 \\
-f_1 & -f_2 & 0
\end{vmatrix} > 0 \tag{11-73}
$$

The FOC of the short-run three-input model also remind us of the FOC of the long-run two-input model because the first two equations imply a point of tangency between the isoquant for inputs X_1 and X_2 and an isocost line. The Lagrange multipliers have the usual interpretation—the effect on the objective of relaxing the constraint. That is, λ is the short-run marginal cost and ξ is the effect on short-run cost of increasing the fixed factor, X_3. Taken together, the FOC make up five equations with five unknowns. They can be solved for equilibrium values of the choice variables in terms of the parameters. Therefore, we can write

$$X_1^S = X_1^S(Y_0, w_1, w_2, w_3, X_{30}) \tag{11-74}$$

$$X_2^S = X_2^S(Y_0, w_1, w_2, w_3, X_{30}) \tag{11-75}$$

$$X_3^S = X_{30} \tag{11-76}$$

$$\lambda^S = \lambda^S(Y_0, w_1, w_2, w_3, X_{30}) \tag{11-77}$$

$$\xi^S = \xi^S(Y_0, w_1, w_2, w_3, X_{30}) \tag{11-78}$$

Note that we use the superscript S instead of the more usual asterisk to denote short-run equilibrium values of the choice variables. This eases comparison with long-run equilibrium values.

In order to perform comparative statics analysis, we substitute these equilibrium values of the choice variables back into the FOC, creating identities that can be differentiated with respect to some parameter. For example, differentiating with respect to w_1 generates the matrix equation

$$
\begin{bmatrix}
-\lambda f_{11} & -\lambda f_{12} & -\lambda f_{13} & -f_1 & 0 \\
-\lambda f_{21} & -\lambda f_{22} & -\lambda f_{23} & -f_2 & 0 \\
-\lambda f_{31} & -\lambda f_{32} & -\lambda f_{33} & -f_3 & -1 \\
-f_1 & -f_2 & -f_3 & 0 & 0 \\
0 & 0 & -1 & 0 & 0
\end{bmatrix}
\begin{bmatrix}
\dfrac{\partial X_1^S}{\partial w_1} \\[2mm]
\dfrac{\partial X_2^S}{\partial w_1} \\[2mm]
\dfrac{\partial X_3^S}{\partial w_1} \\[2mm]
\dfrac{\partial \lambda^S}{\partial w_1} \\[2mm]
\dfrac{\partial \xi^S}{\partial w_1}
\end{bmatrix}
\equiv
\begin{bmatrix}
-1 \\
0 \\
0 \\
0 \\
0
\end{bmatrix}
\tag{11-79}
$$

Cramer's rule can be used to solve for any of the partial derivatives in the vector of unknowns. Solving for $\partial X_1^S / \partial w_1$, we find

$$
\frac{\partial X_1^S}{\partial w_1} = \frac{
\begin{vmatrix}
-1 & -\lambda f_{12} & -\lambda f_{13} & -f_1 & 0 \\
0 & -\lambda f_{22} & -\lambda f_{23} & -f_2 & 0 \\
0 & -\lambda f_{32} & -\lambda f_{33} & -f_3 & -1 \\
0 & -f_2 & -f_3 & 0 & 0 \\
0 & 0 & -1 & 0 & 0
\end{vmatrix}
}{|H_B|} = -\frac{f_2^2}{|H_B|} < 0 \tag{11-80}
$$

You may remember this as the expression we found in the long-run two-input model, equation (11-21). This result, combined with what we know about the FOC and SOC, tells us that, mathematically speaking, two variable inputs behave the same way, whether they belong to a short-run three-input model or a long-run two-input model.

How do we expect the fixed input, X_3^S, to respond to changes in a parameter? Since it is fixed, we do not expect it to respond at all. That is, we expect the partial derivatives of X_3^S with respect to any parameter to equal zero. When we solve the preceding matrix equation for $\partial X_3^S/\partial w_1$ we find

$$\frac{\partial X_3^S}{\partial w_1} = \frac{\begin{vmatrix} -\lambda f_{11} & -\lambda f_{12} & -1 & -f_1 & 0 \\ -\lambda f_{21} & -\lambda f_{22} & 0 & -f_2 & 0 \\ -\lambda f_{31} & -\lambda f_{32} & 0 & -f_3 & -1 \\ -f_1 & -f_2 & 0 & 0 & 0 \\ 0 & 0 & 0 & 0 & 0 \end{vmatrix}}{|H_B|} = 0 \qquad (11\text{-}81)$$

Note that the last row of the determinant in the numerator is all zeros. Obviously, when the determinant is expanded by that row, it equals zero. You may verify for yourself that you obtain a similar result when you differentiate X_3^S with respect to any other parameter.

What happens when we investigate the effects of changes in w_3, the price of the fixed input? This will affect only fixed cost in the short-run total cost function. We show in Chapter 3, Section 3.7, that marginal cost equals the slope of variable cost and that fixed cost does not affect it. We do not expect changes in fixed cost to have any effect on the equilibrium of the short-run cost-minimization model.[2] Differentiating the first-order identities with respect to w_3 generates the matrix equation

$$\begin{bmatrix} -\lambda f_{11} & -\lambda f_{12} & -\lambda f_{13} & -f_1 & 0 \\ -\lambda f_{21} & -\lambda f_{22} & -\lambda f_{23} & -f_2 & 0 \\ -\lambda f_{31} & -\lambda f_{32} & -\lambda f_{33} & -f_3 & -1 \\ -f_1 & -f_2 & -f_3 & 0 & 0 \\ 0 & 0 & -1 & 0 & 0 \end{bmatrix} \begin{bmatrix} \dfrac{\partial X_1^S}{\partial w_3} \\[2mm] \dfrac{\partial X_2^S}{\partial w_3} \\[2mm] \dfrac{\partial X_3^S}{\partial w_3} \\[2mm] \dfrac{\partial \lambda^S}{\partial w_3} \\[2mm] \dfrac{\partial \xi^S}{\partial w_3} \end{bmatrix} \equiv \begin{bmatrix} 0 \\ 0 \\ -1 \\ 0 \\ 0 \end{bmatrix} \qquad (11\text{-}82)$$

_____

[2]As the saying goes, "sunk costs are sunk." A change in fixed costs will change short-run total cost, but, by definition, in the short-run the firm can do nothing about it. It can have no effect on short-run behavior.

Look at the column vector of constants on the right-hand side. It is identical to the last column of the bordered Hessian matrix. When we use Cramer's rule to solve for any of the unknown partial derivatives, we insert the column vector of constants into the corresponding column of $|H_B|$ to form the determinant in the numerator, and divide it by $|H_B|$. If we insert the vector of constants into any of the first four columns, we create a determinant with two identical columns. Those columns are linearly dependent, and the value of the determinant is zero. This tells us that none of the equilibrium values of the inputs is affected by a change in the price of the fixed input, nor is the value of short-run marginal cost. If we insert the column vector of constants into the last column of $|H_B|$, the resulting determinant is $|H_B|$. This tells us that $\partial \xi^S / \partial w_3$ is equal to one. Remember that we interpret ξ^S as the effect on short-run total cost of an increase in the fixed input. These results confirm our belief that a change in the price of a fixed factor does affect the fixed input's effect on short-run total cost, but it does not affect a firm's short-run behavior.

The indirect cost function of the short-run model is short-run total cost. We find the indirect short-run cost function by replacing the input levels with their equilibrium values in the expression for cost.

$$C^S = w_1 X_1^S(Y_0, w_1, w_2, w_3, X_{30}) + w_2 X_2^S(Y_0, w_1, w_2, w_3, X_{30}) \quad \text{(11-83)}$$
$$+ w_3 X_3^S(Y_0, w_1, w_2, w_3, X_{30})$$

The envelope theorem tells us that the partial derivatives of the indirect short-run cost function with respect to any of its parameters are equal to the partial derivatives of the Lagrangian objective function with respect to the same parameters, evaluated at the optimum. We combine this result with Young's theorem to find the same relationships among comparative statics results that we were able to find in the two-input long-run cost-minimization model. We find that the response of a variable input to a change in output is the same as the response of short-run marginal cost to a change in the price of the variable input by differentiating (11-83) with respect to w_1 and Y_0.

$$\frac{\partial^2 C^S}{\partial w_1 \, \partial Y_0} = \frac{\partial^2 \mathcal{L}}{\partial w_1 \, \partial Y_0} = \frac{\partial X_1^S}{\partial Y_0} = \frac{\partial \lambda^S}{\partial w_1} = \frac{\partial^2 \mathcal{L}}{\partial Y_0 \, \partial w_1} = \frac{\partial^2 C^S}{\partial Y_0 \, \partial w_1} \quad \text{(11-84)}$$

We can also find that input price effects on the variable inputs are reciprocal by differentiating (11-83) with respect to w_1 and w_2; that is, a change in w_2 affects X_1^S in the same way as a change in w_1 affects X_2^S, or

$$\frac{\partial^2 C^S}{\partial w_1 \, \partial w_2} = \frac{\partial^2 \mathcal{L}}{\partial w_1 \, \partial w_2} = \frac{\partial X_1^S}{\partial w_2} = \frac{\partial X_2^S}{\partial w_1} = \frac{\partial^2 \mathcal{L}}{\partial w_2 \, \partial w_1} = \frac{\partial^2 C^S}{\partial w_2 \, \partial w_1} \quad \text{(11-85)}$$

NUMERICAL EXAMPLE

Suppose a firm wishes to minimize the costs of producing Y_0 units of output, given three inputs, X_1, X_2, and X_3, with prices w_1, w_2, and w_3, respectively. It produces according to the production function $Y = X_1 X_2 X_3$. For the short run, the firm chooses to hold input 3 fixed at a level of X_{30}. We wish to find the short-run input demand functions, the short-run marginal cost function, and the comparative statics results. Our Lagrangian and FOC are

$$\mathcal{L} = w_1 X_1 + w_2 X_2 + w_3 X_3 + \lambda(Y_0 - X_1 X_2 X_3) + \xi(X_{30} - X_3) \quad (11\text{-}86)$$

$$\text{FOC:} \quad \mathcal{L}_1 = w_1 - \lambda X_2 X_3 = 0 \quad (11\text{-}87)$$

$$\mathcal{L}_2 = w_2 - \lambda X_1 X_3 = 0 \quad (11\text{-}88)$$

$$\mathcal{L}_3 = w_3 - \lambda X_1 X_2 - \xi = 0 \quad (11\text{-}89)$$

$$\mathcal{L}_\lambda = Y_0 - X_1 X_2 X_3 = 0 \quad (11\text{-}90)$$

$$\mathcal{L}_\xi = X_{30} - X_3 = 0 \quad (11\text{-}91)$$

The second-order condition requires that the determinant of the bordered Hessian be positive, or

$$|H_B| = \begin{vmatrix} 0 & -\lambda^S X_{30} & -\lambda^S X_2^S & -X_2^S X_{30} & 0 \\ -\lambda^S X_{30} & 0 & -\lambda^S X_1^S & -X_1^S X_{30} & 0 \\ -\lambda^S X_2^S & -\lambda^S X_1^S & 0 & -X_1^S X_2^S & -1 \\ -X_2^S X_{30} & -X_1^S X_{30} & -X_1^S X_2^S & 0 & 0 \\ 0 & 0 & -1 & 0 & 0 \end{vmatrix} \quad (11\text{-}92)$$

$$= 2(Y_0 w_1 w_2)^{1/2} X_{30}^{3/2} > 0$$

Solving (11-86) through (11-91) for equilibrium values of the choice variables, we find that

$$X_1^S = \left(\frac{w_2}{w_1}\right)^{1/2} \left(\frac{Y_0}{X_{30}}\right)^{1/2} \quad (11\text{-}93)$$

$$X_2^S = \left(\frac{w_1}{w_2}\right)^{1/2} \left(\frac{Y_0}{X_{30}}\right)^{1/2} \quad (11\text{-}94)$$

$$X_3^S = X_{30} \quad (11\text{-}95)$$

$$\lambda^S = \left(\frac{w_1 w_2}{Y_0 X_{30}}\right)^{1/2} \quad (11\text{-}96)$$

$$\xi^S = w_3 - (w_1 w_2)^{1/2} \left(\frac{Y_0}{X_{30}^2}\right)^{1/2} \quad (11\text{-}97)$$

Notice from equations (11-93), (11-94), and (11-96) that w_3 does not appear in the input demand functions or in the short-run marginal cost functions. Therefore, as we expect, changes in w_3 will have no effect on either input demand or marginal cost. On the other hand, the partial derivative of ξ^S with respect to w_3 equals 1, also as we expect. We also find that $\partial X_1^S/\partial w_1 = -(1/2)w_2^{1/2}w_1^{-3/2}(Y_0/X_{30})^{1/2}$ and $\partial X_2^S/\partial w_2 = -(1/2)w_1^{1/2}w_2^{-3/2}(Y_0/X_{30})^{1/2}$. Both are negative, implying downward-sloping input demand curves. Changes in the price of one input have reciprocal effects on the equilibrium of the other input, as we find when we differentiate X_1^S with respect to w_2 and X_2^S with respect to w_1. We see that $\partial X_1^S/\partial w_2 = (1/2)(w_2 w_1)^{-1/2}(Y_0/X_{30})^{1/2} = \partial X_2^S/\partial w_1$. Finally, we find that the slope of the short-run marginal cost curve equals $\partial \lambda^S / \partial Y_0 = -(1/2)((w_1 w_2)/(Y_0^3 X_{30}))^{1/2}$. Note that this production function gives us a negatively sloped short-run marginal cost curve. This is a production function that does not satisfy the SOC for profit maximization, which require upward-sloping marginal cost, although it does satisfy the SOC for cost minimization.

11.6

COMPARING SHORT-RUN AND LONG-RUN COSTS

How does our short-run model of cost minimization compare to our long-run model? We show in the previous section that, mathematically speaking, two variable inputs generate the same results whether they belong to a two-input long-run model or a three-input short-run model. A more reasonable comparison of long run and short run, however, comes from contrasting short- and long-run models which have the same number of inputs. Therefore, let's compare the short-run three-input model to a long-run three-input model.

In the long-run model, the firm is free to choose cost-minimizing combinations of three inputs, X_1, X_2, and X_3 subject to an output constraint. The parameters of the model are the three input prices w_1, w_2, and w_3 and the level of output, Y_0. The equilibrium conditions of the model describe the optimal values of X_1^L, X_2^L, X_3^L, and λ^L as functions of the parameters, or

$$X_1^L = X_1^L(Y_0, w_1, w_2, w_3) \tag{11-98}$$

$$X_2^L = X_2^L(Y_0, w_1, w_2, w_3) \tag{11-99}$$

$$X_3^L = X_2^L(Y_0, w_1, w_2, w_3) \tag{11-100}$$

$$\lambda^L = \lambda^L(Y_0, w_1, w_2, w_3) \tag{11-101}$$

Note that we use the superscript L to indicate equilibrium long-run values of the choice variables. The indirect long-run cost function is the sum of the products of the input prices times the equilibrium input levels, or

$$C^L = w_1 X_1^L(Y_0, w_1, w_2, w_3) + w_2 X_2^L(Y_0, w_1, w_2, w_3) \tag{11-102}$$
$$+ w_3 X_3^L(Y_0, w_1, w_2, w_3)$$

Long-run average cost equals C^L / Y_0, and the Lagrange multiplier, λ^L, represents the long-run marginal cost. The relationships among long-run and short-run values of total cost, average cost, and marginal cost are graphed in Figure 11.5.

Compare the indirect long-run cost function and the equilibrium values of the long-run choice variables to the indirect short-run cost function and the equilibrium of the short-run choice variables. Long-run total cost is a function of output and input prices. Short-run total cost is a function of output, input prices, and the level of the fixed input, X_{30}. In general, long-run total cost will

Figure 11.5

Long-run and Short-run
Total, Average, and
Marginal Cost Curves
(*a*) Long- and Short-run
Total Costs (*b*) Long
and Short-run Average
and Marginal Costs

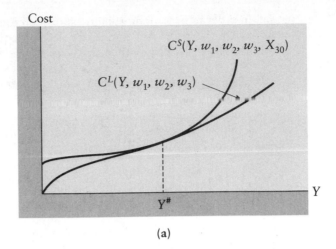

(a)

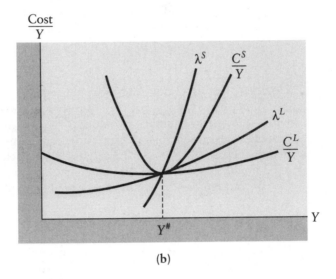

(b)

be less than or equal to short-run total cost because it is determined by the cost-minimizing values of the inputs. In the short-run model, the level of X_3 is fixed, and as long as it is fixed at some level other than the cost-minimizing level, short-run total cost must be greater than long-run total cost. Only in the situation in which the short-run fixed level of X_3 exactly coincides with the long-run cost-minimizing level can short-run total cost equal long-run total cost. This can hold for only one level of output, because when output changes, the long-run cost-minimizing level of X_3 changes, while the short-run level remains fixed. Therefore, in our graph of long-run and short-run cost curves in Figure 11.5, short-run total and average costs are equal to long-run total and average costs at only one output level, $Y^\#$. At all other output levels, the short-run total and average costs are higher.

How does short-run marginal cost compare to long-run marginal cost? In Figure 11.5, we draw the marginal cost curves so that the short-run marginal cost is steeper than the long-run marginal cost curve, and they are equal at the output level $Y^\#$. In order to demonstrate these relationships between long- and short-run marginal costs, let's examine the situation in which the costs are equal. In order to make long-run and short-run total costs identical, we must require that the short-run parameter X_{30} be equal to the long-run cost-minimizing level, X_3^L. In mathematical terms, we write

$$C^L(Y_0, w_1, w_2, w_3) \equiv C^S(Y_0, w_1, w_2, w_3, X_3^L(Y_0, w_1, w_2, w_3)) \quad (11\text{-}103)$$

Because we have defined the two cost functions to be equal, the equality is an identity. If we differentiate the identity with respect to Y_0, we find an expression for long-run marginal cost.

$$\text{LRMC} = \lambda^L = \frac{\partial C^L}{\partial Y_0} \equiv \frac{\partial C^S}{\partial Y_0} + \frac{\partial C^S}{\partial X_3} \frac{\partial X_3^L}{\partial Y_0} \equiv \lambda^S + \xi^S \frac{\partial X_3^L}{\partial Y_0} \quad (11\text{-}104)$$

Note that we substituted the facts that $\lambda^S = \partial C^S / \partial Y_0$ and $\xi^S = \partial C^S / \partial X_3$ in equation (11-104). Doing so gives us a general expression for the relationship between long-run and short-run marginal costs.[3] From equation (11-69) of the FOC of the short-run model, we know that

$$\xi^S = w_3 - \lambda f_3 \quad (11\text{-}105)$$

However, we also know that long-run equilibrium requires $w_3 - \lambda f_3 = 0$. Therefore, when the level of the input that is fixed in the short-run coincides with its long-run equilibrium value, $\xi^S = w_3 - \lambda f_3 = 0$. Substituting $\xi^S = 0$ into (11-104) tells us that $\lambda^L = \lambda^S$. Stated in words, this means that short-run marginal cost equals long-run marginal cost when the short-run level of the fixed input is exactly equal to its long-run cost-minimizing level.

We can rephrase this into another mathematical identity, obtaining

$$\lambda^L(Y_0, w_1, w_2, w_3) \equiv \lambda^S(Y_0, w_1, w_2, w_3, X_3^L(Y_0, w_1, w_2, w_3)) \quad (11\text{-}106)$$

Differentiating this identity with respect to Y_0, which is really the same as taking the second-order derivative of Equation (11-103) with respect to Y_0, gives us an expression for the slope of the long-run marginal cost curve.

$$\frac{\partial \text{LRMC}}{\partial Y_0} = \frac{\partial \lambda^L}{\partial Y_0} = \frac{\partial \lambda^S}{\partial Y_0} + \frac{\partial \lambda^S}{\partial X_3} \frac{\partial X_3^L}{\partial Y_0} \quad (11\text{-}107)$$

Equation (11-107) tells us that the slope of the long-run marginal cost curve equals the slope of the short-run marginal cost curve plus a term which accounts for changes in the fixed factor when output changes. We can discover the sign of this last term with the help of the envelope theorem. Recall that in Section 11.2 we demonstrated with comparative statics analysis and with the use of the envelope theorem that the effect of a change in output on the equilibrium value of an input equals the effect on marginal cost of a change

---

[3]Recognize that the FOC of the three-input long-run model require that $w_3 - \lambda f_3 = 0$ and $\xi^S = 0$ in long-run equilibrium. In fact, $\xi^S > 0$ when $X_{30} < X_3^L$ and $\xi^S < 0$ when $X_{30} > X_2^L$. This suggests that short-run marginal cost is less than long-run marginal cost when the fixed factor is fixed at a lower than optimal level and that short-run marginal cost is greater than long-run marginal cost when the fixed factor is fixed at a greater than optimal level.

in the price of the input. The same result holds for X_3 in the three-input model. Therefore, we can write

$$\frac{\partial X_3^L}{\partial Y_0} = \frac{\partial \lambda^L}{\partial w_3} \tag{11-108}$$

We can find another expression for $\partial \lambda^L / \partial w_3$ by differentiating (11-106) with respect to w_3, obtaining

$$\frac{\partial X_3^L}{\partial Y_0} = \frac{\partial \lambda^L}{\partial w_3} = \frac{\partial \lambda^S}{\partial X_3} \frac{\partial X_3^L}{\partial w_3} \tag{11-109}$$

Substituting (11-109) into (11-107) yields

$$\frac{\partial \text{LRMC}}{\partial Y_0} = \frac{\partial \lambda^L}{\partial Y_0} = \frac{\partial \lambda^S}{\partial Y_0} + \left(\frac{\partial \lambda^S}{\partial X_3}\right)^2 \frac{\partial X_3^L}{\partial w_3} \tag{11-110}$$

Because the squared term is unambiguously positive and the partial derivative $\partial X_3^L / \partial w_3$ is negative (it is the slope of the factor demand curve), this result tells us that the slope of the short-run marginal cost curve is greater than the slope of the long-run marginal cost curve. This is how we draw the marginal cost curves in Figure 11.5.

NUMERICAL EXAMPLE

Let's compare the long-run cost-minimization model for the firm with the production function $Y = X_1 X_2 X_3$ to the short-run model of the same firm that we examined in the numerical example of Section 11.5. Our long-run Lagrangian and FOC are

$$\mathcal{L} = w_1 X_1 + w_2 X_2 + w_3 X_3 + \lambda(Y_0 - X_1 X_2 X_3) \tag{11-111}$$

$$\text{FOC:} \quad \mathcal{L}_1 = w_1 - \lambda X_2 X_3 = 0 \tag{11-112}$$

$$\mathcal{L}_2 = w_2 - \lambda X_1 X_3 = 0 \tag{11-113}$$

$$\mathcal{L}_3 = w_3 - \lambda X_1 X_2 = 0 \tag{11-114}$$

$$\mathcal{L}_\lambda = Y_0 - X_1 X_2 X_3 = 0 \tag{11-115}$$

The second-order conditions require that the naturally ordered principal minors of dimension greater than or equal to 3 of the determinant of the bordered Hessian be negative, or

$$|H_B| = \begin{vmatrix} 0 & -\lambda^L X_3^L & -\lambda^L X_2^L & -X_2^L X_3^L \\ -\lambda^L X_3^L & 0 & -\lambda^L X_1^L & -X_1^L X_3^L \\ -\lambda^L X_2^L & -\lambda^L X_1^L & 0 & -X_1^L X_2^L \\ -X_2^L X_3^L & -X_1^L X_3^L & -X_1^L X_2^L & 0 \end{vmatrix} < 0 \tag{11-116}$$

and

$$|H_{11}| = \begin{vmatrix} 0 & -\lambda^L X_1^L & -X_1^L X_3^L \\ -\lambda^L X_1^L & 0 & -X_1^L X_2^L \\ -X_1^L X_3^L & -X_1^L X_2^L & 0 \end{vmatrix} < 0 \qquad (11\text{-}117)$$

Solving (11-112) through (11-115) for equilibrium values of the choice variables, we find that

$$X_1^L = \left(\frac{w_2 w_3 Y_0}{w_1^2} \right)^{1/3} \qquad (11\text{-}118)$$

$$X_2^L = \left(\frac{w_1 w_3 Y_0}{w_2^2} \right)^{1/3} \qquad (11\text{-}119)$$

$$X_3^L = \left(\frac{w_1 w_2 Y_0}{w_3^2} \right)^{1/3} \qquad (11\text{-}120)$$

$$\lambda^L = \left(\frac{w_1 w_2 w_3}{Y_0^2} \right)^{1/3} \qquad (11\text{-}121)$$

We determined that short-run marginal cost equals long-run marginal cost when the short-run level of the fixed input is exactly equal to its long-run cost-minimizing level. In equation (11-96), we found that short-run marginal cost equals $\lambda^S = ((w_1 w_2)/(Y_0 X_{30}))^{1/2}$. Substituting (11-120), the long-run level of X_3, for X_{30}, we obtain the expected result, that

$$\lambda^S = \left(\frac{w_1 w_2}{Y_0 \left(\frac{w_1 w_2 Y_0}{w_3^2} \right)^{1/3}} \right)^{1/2} = \left(\frac{w_1 w_2 w_3}{Y_0^2} \right)^{1/3} = \lambda^L \qquad (11\text{-}122)$$

An important result of our comparison of short- and long-run costs is contained in equation (11-110)—that the slope of the short-run marginal cost curve is greater than the slope of the long-run marginal cost curve. In the previous numerical example, we found the slope of the short-run marginal cost curve to equal $\partial \lambda^S / \partial Y_0 = -(1/2)((w_1 w_2)/(Y_0^3 X_{30}))^{1/2}$. We differentiate (11-121) with respect to Y_0 to find the slope of the long-run marginal cost curve, obtaining $\partial \lambda^L / \partial Y_0 = -(2/3)((w_1 w_2 w_3)/Y_0^5)^{1/3}$. We can compare these two expressions by substituting (11-120), the long-run level of X_{30}, into $\partial \lambda^S / \partial Y_0$. We find

$$\frac{\partial \lambda^S}{\partial Y_0} = -\frac{1}{2} \left(\frac{w_1 w_2}{Y_0^3 \left(\frac{w_1 w_2 Y_0}{w_3^2} \right)^{1/3}} \right)^{1/2} = -\frac{1}{2} \left(\frac{w_1 w_2 w_3}{Y_0^5} \right)^{1/3}$$

$$> \frac{\partial \lambda^L}{\partial Y_0} = -\frac{2}{3} \left(\frac{w_1 w_2 w_3}{Y_0^5} \right)^{1/3} \qquad (11\text{-}123)$$

In this example, both marginal cost curves are downward sloping, but the slope of the long-run marginal cost curve is less than the slope of the short-run marginal cost curve; that is, it is more steeply downward sloping.

EXERCISES
Section 11.6
Comparing Short-Run and Long-Run Costs

Consider a firm with the production function $Y = X_1^{0.2} X_2^{0.3} X_3^{0.4}$ to answer the following questions.

1. Find the Lagrangian objective function and the first- and second-order conditions of the long-run cost-minimization model. Solve the first-order conditions for optimal values of the inputs and marginal cost.

2. Find the Lagrangian objective function and first- and second-order conditions of the short-run cost-minimization model if X_1 is held fixed at $X_1 = X_{10}$. Solve the first-order conditions for optimal values of the inputs and short-run marginal cost.

3. Show that, if X_{10} is equal to its long-run equilibrium value, short-run marginal cost equals long-run marginal cost.

4. Compare the slope of the short-run marginal cost curve to the slope of the long-run marginal cost curve, if X_{10} is equal to its long-run equilibrium value.

11.7

SUMMARY

In this chapter we show that the concept of cost as a function of output requires that we have some model of how a firm chooses combinations of inputs to produce output levels. The model we use for this purpose is constrained cost minimization. We explore the two-input model of constrained cost minimization in detail, discovering that the input demand curves are downward sloping, that the Lagrange multiplier can be interpreted as marginal cost, and that whether an input is inferior or normal determines the effect that a change in the input's price has on marginal cost.

The cost-minimization model, which implies that the cost curves and the firm's input choices are functions of input prices and the level of output, is compared directly with the model of profit maximization, which implies that the firm's input choices are functions of input prices and output price. We show that, while the profit-maximization model requires that costs be minimized, the cost-minimization model does not necessarily imply that profits are maximized. That is, a firm cannot maximize profits without minimizing costs but it can minimize costs without maximizing profit.

Throughout the chapter, we see a close relationship between a firm's production function and its cost function. This relationship is seen very explicitly in Section 11.3, which relates the degree of homogeneity of homogeneous production functions to the slope of the long-run marginal cost curve. Linear homogeneous production functions, representing constant returns to scale, yield horizontal marginal cost curves. Production functions that are homogeneous of degree greater than one, representing increasing returns to scale, yield downward-sloping marginal cost curves, whereas production functions that are homogeneous of degree less than one, representing decreasing returns to scale, yield upward-sloping marginal cost curves.

Finally, we show how short-run costs can be analyzed by using a three-input model with two constraints. The results of the short-run model are compared with those of a three-input long-run model, demonstrating that, in general, short-run total and average costs are greater than or equal to long-run total and average costs and the slope of the short-run marginal cost curve is greater than the slope of the long-run marginal cost curve.

◆ REFERENCES

Binger, Brian R. and Hoffman, Elizabeth, *Microeconomics with Calculus* (Glenview, IL: Scott, Foresman and Company, 1985), Chapters 11 and 12.

Shephard, Ronald W., *Theory of Cost and Production Functions* (Princeton, NJ: Princeton University Press, 1970), Chapters 4, 5, 6, and 7.

Silberberg, Eugene, *The Structure of Economics*, 2nd edition (New York: McGraw-Hill Book Company, 1990), Chapters 8 and 9.

Varian, Hal R., *Microeconomic Analysis*, 3rd edition (New York: W. W. Norton and Company, 1992), Chapters 3, 4, and 5.

◆ ANSWERS TO END-OF-SECTION EXERCISES

Section 11.2 Constrained Cost Minimization

1. $\mathcal{L} = w_1 X_1 + w_2 X_2 + \lambda(Y_0 - \ln(X_2 X_2))$

   FOC: $\mathcal{L}_1 = w_1 - \dfrac{\lambda}{X_1} = 0$

   $\mathcal{L}_2 = w_2 - \dfrac{\lambda}{X_2} = 0$

   $\mathcal{L}_\lambda = Y_0 - \ln(X_1 X_2) = 0$

   SOC: $\begin{vmatrix} \dfrac{\lambda^*}{X_1^{*2}} & 0 & -\dfrac{1}{X_1^*} \\[2mm] 0 & \dfrac{\lambda^*}{X_2^{*2}} & -\dfrac{1}{X_2^{*2}} \\[2mm] -\dfrac{1}{X_1^{*2}} & -\dfrac{1}{X_2^{*2}} & 0 \end{vmatrix} = -2(w_1 w_2)^{1/2} < 0$

2. $X_1^* - e^{Y_0/2}(w_2/w_1)^{1/2}, \quad X_2^* = e^{Y_0/2}(w_1/w_2)^{1/2}, \quad \lambda^* = e^{Y_0/2}(w_1 w_2)^{1/2},$
   $C^* = 2e^{Y_0/2}(w_1 w_2)^{1/2} \Rightarrow \partial C^*/\partial Y_0 = e^{Y_0/2}(w_1 w_2)^{1/2} = \lambda^*$

3. $\partial X_1^*/\partial w_2 = (1/2)e^{Y_0/2}(w_2 w_1)^{-1/2}, \quad \partial X_2^*/\partial w_2 = -(1/2)e^{Y_0/2}(w_1/w_2^3)^{1/2},$
   $\partial \lambda^*/\partial w_2 = (1/2)e^{Y_0/2}(w_1/w_2)^{1/2}.$

An increase in the price of input 2 causes the firm to substitute input 1 for input 2, holding output constant. Marginal cost increases.

4. $\partial X_1^*/\partial Y_0 = (1/2)e^{Y_0/2}(w_2/w_1)^{1/2}, \qquad \partial X_2^*/\partial Y_0 = (1/2)e^{Y_0/2}(w_1/w_2)^{1/2},$
$\partial\lambda^*/\partial Y_0 = (1/2)e^{Y_0/2}(w_1w_2)^{1/2}.$

An increase in output requires increases in both inputs. Marginal cost is upward sloping. Note that $\partial X_2^*/\partial Y_0 = \partial\lambda^*/\partial w_2$ as implied by the envelope theorem.

Section 11.3 Marginal Cost and Homogeneous Production Functions

1. a. $r = 1$
   b. Slope MC $= 0$

2. a. $r = 0.9$
   b. Slope MC $=$ MC$/(9Y_0)$

3. a. $r = 2$
   b. Slope MC $= -$MC$/(2Y_0)$

4. a. $r = 1$
   b. Slope MC $= 0$

Section 11.4 Profit Maximization and Cost Minimization Compared

1.

Profit Maximization

Max $\pi = P(X_1^{0.3}X_2^{0.6}) - w_1X_1 - w_2X_2$

FOC: $0.3PX_1^{-0.7}X_2^{0.6} - w_1 = 0$
$0.6PX_1^{0.3}X_2^{-0.4} - w_2 = 0$

SOC:
$$\begin{vmatrix} -\dfrac{.21PY^{\pi}}{X_1^{\pi 2}} & \dfrac{.18PY^{\pi}}{X_1^{\pi}X_2^{\pi}} \\[3mm] \dfrac{.18PY^{\pi}}{X_1^{\pi}X_2^{\pi}} & -\dfrac{.24PY^{\pi}}{X_2^{\pi 2}} \end{vmatrix}$$
$$= .018\left(\dfrac{PY^{\pi}}{X_1^{\pi}X_2^{\pi}}\right)^2 > 0$$
$$-\dfrac{.21PY^{\pi}}{X_1^{\pi 2}} < 0, \qquad -\dfrac{.24PY^{\pi}}{X_2^{\pi 2}} < 0$$

Cost Minimization

Min $\mathcal{L} = w_1X_1 + w_2X_2 + \lambda(Y_0 - X_1^{0.3}X_2^{0.6})$

FOC: $w_1 - \lambda 0.3X_1^{-0.7}X_2^{0.6} = 0$
$w_2 - \lambda 0.6X_1^{0.3}X_2^{-0.4} = 0$
$Y_0 - X_1^{0.3}X_2^{0.6} = 0$

SOC:
$$\begin{vmatrix} \dfrac{.21\lambda^C Y_0}{X_1^{C2}} & -\dfrac{.18\lambda^C Y_0}{X_1^C X_2^C} & -\dfrac{.3Y_0}{X_1^C} \\[3mm] -\dfrac{.18\lambda^C Y_0}{X_1^C X_2^C} & \dfrac{.24\lambda^C Y_0}{X_2^{C2}} & -\dfrac{.6Y_0}{X_2^C} \\[3mm] -\dfrac{.3Y_0}{X_1^C} & -\dfrac{.6Y_0}{X_2^C} & 0 \end{vmatrix}$$
< 0

The determinant of the bordered Hessian is
$-.162\lambda^C Y_0^3/(X_1^C X_2^C)^2 < 0$

2. $X_1^{\pi} = 0.00038P^{10}w_1^{-4}w_2^{-6}, \quad X_1^C = Y_0^{10/9}(w_2/2w_1)^{2/3}$
   $X_2^{\pi} = 0.00075P^{10}w_1^{-3}w_2^{-7}, \quad X_2^C = Y_0^{10/9}(2w_1/w_2)^{1/3}$
   $Y^{\pi} = 0.00126P^9w_1^{-3}w_2^{-6}, \quad \lambda^C = 2.1Y_0^{1/9}w_1^{1/3}w_2^{2/3}$

3. At $Y_0 = Y^{\pi}$, $X_1^C = (0.00126P^9w_1^{-3}w_2^{-6})^{10/9}w_1^{-2/3}w_2^{2/3}$
   $= 0.00038P^{10}w_1^{-4}w_2^{-6} = X_1^{\pi}$

4. $\partial X_1^C/\partial w_1 = -(2/3)2^{-2/3}Y_0^{10/9}w_2^{2/3}w_1^{-5/3}$, evaluated at $Y_0 = Y^{\pi}$, it equals
   $-(2/3)0.00038P^{10}w_1^{-5}w_2^{-6}$, which is greater than
   $\partial X_1^C/\partial w_1 = -(4)0.00038P^{10}w_1^{-5}w_2^{-6}$

Section 11.6 Comparing Short-Run and Long-Run Costs

1. $\mathcal{L} = w_1 X_1 + w_2 X_2 + w_3 X_3 + \lambda(Y_0 - X_1^{0.2} X_2^{0.3} X_3^{0.4})$

   FOC: $w_1 - 0.2\lambda Y_0/X_1 = 0$

   $w_2 - 0.3\lambda Y_0/X_2 = 0$

   $w_3 - 0.4\lambda Y_0/X_3 = 0$

   $Y_0 - X_1^{0.2} X_2^{0.3} X_3^{0.4} = 0$

   $X_1^L = 0.642 Y_0^{10/9} w_1^{-7/9} w_2^{1/3} w_3^{4/9},$ $X_2^L = 0.963 Y_0^{10/9} w_1^{2/9} w_2^{-2/3} w_3^{4/9}$

   $X_3^L = 1.28 Y_0^{10/9} w_1^{2/9} w_2^{1/3} w_3^{-5/9},$ $\lambda^L = 3.21 Y_0^{1/9} w_1^{2/9} w_2^{1/3} w_3^{4/9}$

   SOC:
   $$
   \begin{vmatrix}
   .16\dfrac{\lambda^L Y_0}{X_1^{L2}} & -.06\dfrac{\lambda^L Y_0}{X_1^L X_2^L} & -.08\dfrac{\lambda^L Y_0}{X_1^L X_3^L} & -.2\dfrac{Y_0}{X_1^L} \\[2ex]
   -.06\dfrac{\lambda^L Y_0}{X_1^L X_2^L} & .21\dfrac{\lambda^L Y_0}{X_2^{L2}} & -.12\dfrac{\lambda^L Y_0}{X_2^L X_3^L} & -.3\dfrac{Y_0}{X_2^L} \\[2ex]
   -.08\dfrac{\lambda^L Y_0}{X_1^L X_3^L} & -.12\dfrac{\lambda^L Y_0}{X_2^L X_3^L} & .24\dfrac{\lambda^L Y_0}{X_3^{L2}} & -.4\dfrac{Y_0}{X_3^L} \\[2ex]
   -.2\dfrac{Y_0}{X_1^L} & -.3\dfrac{Y_0}{X_2^L} & -.4\dfrac{Y_0}{X_3^L} & 0
   \end{vmatrix} < 0
   $$

2. $\mathcal{L} = w_1 X_1 + w_2 X_2 + w_3 X_3 + \lambda(Y_0 - X_1^{0.2} X_2^{0.3} X_3^{0.4}) + \xi(X_{10} - X_1)$

   FOC: $w_1 - 0.2\lambda Y_0/X_1 = 0$

   $w_2 - 0.3\lambda Y_0/X_2 = 0$

   $w_3 - 0.4\lambda Y_0/X_3 = 0$

   $Y_0 - X_1^{0.2} X_2^{0.3} X_3^{0.4} = 0$

   $X_{10} - X_1 = 0$

   SOC:
   $$
   \begin{vmatrix}
   .16\dfrac{\lambda^S Y_0}{X_1^{S2}} & -.06\dfrac{\lambda^S Y_0}{X_1^S X_2^S} & -.08\dfrac{\lambda^S Y_0}{X_1^S X_3^S} & -.2\dfrac{Y_0}{X_1^S} & -1 \\[2ex]
   -.06\dfrac{\lambda^S Y_0}{X_1^S X_2^S} & .21\dfrac{\lambda^S Y_0}{X_2^{S2}} & -.12\dfrac{\lambda^S Y_0}{X_2^S X_3^S} & -.3\dfrac{Y_0}{X_2^S} & 0 \\[2ex]
   -.08\dfrac{\lambda^S Y_0}{X_1^S X_3^S} & -.12\dfrac{\lambda^S Y_0}{X_2^S X_3^S} & .24\dfrac{\lambda^S Y_0}{X_3^{S2}} & -.4\dfrac{Y_0}{X_3^S} & 0 \\[2ex]
   -.2\dfrac{Y_0}{X_1^S} & -.3\dfrac{Y_0}{X_2^S} & -.4\dfrac{Y_0}{X_3^S} & 0 & 0 \\[2ex]
   -1 & 0 & 0 & 0 & 0
   \end{vmatrix} > 0
   $$

   $X_1^S = X_{10}$ $X_2^S = 0.848 Y_0^{10/7} X_{10}^{-2/7} w_2^{-4/7} w_3^{4/7}$

   $X_3^S = 1.13 Y_0^{10/7} X_{10}^{-2/7} w_2^{3/7} w_3^{-3/7},$ $\lambda^S = 2.83 Y_0^{3/7} X_{10}^{-2/7} w_2^{3/7} w_3^{4/7}$

   $\zeta^S = w_1 - 0.566 Y_0^{10/7} X_{10}^{-9/7} w_2^{3/7} w_3^{4/7}$

3. At $X_{10} = X_1^L$, $\lambda^S = 2.83 Y_0^{3/7}(0.642 Y_0^{10/9} w_1^{-7/9} w_2^{1/3} w_3^{4/9})^{-2/7} w_2^{3/7} w_3^{4/7}$

   $= 3.21 Y_0^{1/9} w_1^{2/9} w_2^{1/3} w_3^{4/9} = \lambda^L$

4. $\partial\lambda^S/\partial Y_0 = (27/7) Y_0^{3/7}(\partial\lambda^L/\partial Y_0)$

◆ SELF-HELP PROBLEMS

Answers to these problems are given at the end of the text.

Consider a firm with the production function $Y = X_1^{1/3}X_2^{1/3} + X_3^{2/3}$ to answer questions 1 through 9.

1. Find the first- and second-order conditions of the long-run cost-minimization model. Solve the first-order conditions for optimal values of the inputs and marginal cost.

2. Verify that this production function is homogeneous. Use the degree of homogeneity to find the slope of the long-run marginal cost curve.

3. Find the first- and second-order conditions for profit maximization. Solve the first-order conditions for optimal values of the inputs.

4. Find the profit-maximizing supply function and compare its slope to the slope of the long-run marginal cost.

5. Show that, when you evaluate X_1^C at $Y_0 = Y^\pi$, $X_1^C = X_1^\pi$.

6. Show that $\partial X_1^\pi/\partial w_1 < \partial X_1^C/\partial w_1$.

7. Find the first- and second-order conditions of the short-run cost-minimization model, if X_3 is held fixed at $X_3 = X_{30}$. Solve the first-order conditions for optimal values of the inputs and short-run marginal cost.

8. Show that, if X_{30} is equal to its long-run equilibrium value, short-run marginal cost equals long-run marginal cost.

9. Compare the slope of the short-run marginal cost curve to the slope of the long-run marginal cost curve, if X_{30} is equal to its long-run equilibrium value.

◆ SUPPLEMENTAL PROBLEMS

Use the following production function to answer questions 1 through 7: $Y_0 = AX_1^\alpha X_2^\beta$. Note that this is the Cobb–Douglas production function.

1. Find the first-order conditions for cost minimization and solve them for X_1^C, X_2^C, and λ^C, where λ is the Lagrange multiplier.

2. Show that the second-order conditions for cost minimization require the isoquants to be convex to the origin.

3. Find expressions for $\partial X_1^C/\partial Y_0$ and $\partial \lambda^C/\partial w_1$. Show that they are equal for this production function.

4. Under what circumstances is $\partial \lambda^C/\partial Y_0 > 0$? In other words, what is required for the marginal cost curve to be upward sloping? Show that the requirements for upward-sloping marginal cost also satisfy the second-order conditions for profit maximization.

5. Find the profit-maximizing supply function and compare its slope to the slope of the long-run marginal cost.

6. Show that, when you evaluate X_1^C at the profit-maximizing level of output, $X_1^C = X_1^\pi$.

7. Show that $\partial X_1^{\pi}/\partial w_1 < \partial X_1^{C}/\partial w_1$.

8. Consider the following two long-run cost-minimization models: the two-input case, in which the firm minimizes $C = w_1 X_1 + w_2 X_2$ subject to $Y_0 = f(X_1, X_2)$; and the three-input case, in which the firm minimizes $C = w_1 X_1 + w_2 X_2 + w_3 X_3$ subject to $Y_0 = f(X_1, X_2, X_3)$. Show that, although you can determine the sign $\partial X_1/\partial w_2$ in the two-input model, you cannot determine the sign in the three-input model, and explain why this is the case.

9. Consider the following cost-minimization problem: minimize $C = w_1 X_1 + w_2 X_2$ subject to $Y_0 = A X_1^{\alpha} X_2^{1-\alpha}$

   a. Find an expression for the slope of the long-run marginal cost curve.

   b. Hold X_2 fixed at a level equal to X_{20}. Find an expression for the slope of the short-run marginal cost curve.

   c. Show that the slope of the short-run marginal cost curve is greater than the slope of the long-run marginal cost curve.

   d. Explain why a firm with this production function cannot be modeled as a profit-maximizing price-taker in the long run, but it can be so modeled in the short run.

For questions 10 through 12, suppose a firm minimizes costs subject to $Y_0 = f(X_1, X_2)$. The firm faces input prices w_1 and w_2.

10. Determine how total cost, marginal cost, and average cost are affected by a per unit tax, t, on input 1. *Hint*: The cost to the firm of using input 1 becomes $(w_1 + t)X_1$.

11. Determine how total cost, marginal cost, and average cost are affected by a per unit tax, τ, on output 1. *Hint*: the firm's costs are increased by an amount equal to τY_0.

12. Determine how total cost, marginal cost, and average cost are affected by a lump-sum tax, θ. *Hint*: the firm's costs are increased by an amount equal to θ.

Models of Aggregate Economic Activity

12.1

INTRODUCTION

partial equilibrium: an analytical methodology that focuses on individual behavior by treating variables not *directly* affected by the individual as exogenous.

In Chapters 9, 10, and 11, we looked at the behavior of individual consumers and producers from a mathematical point of view. Because of the focus on the individual, we used a *partial equilibrium* framework combined with optimization models. This is appropriate because individual consumers and producers make choices, and we want to examine those choices in an isolated analytical framework. In this chapter, we examine the aggregate effects of individual production and consumption choices. Individual decisions, made in the context of government and central bank policy, combine to determine aggregate production and income. Our approach cannot be partial equilibrium; aggregate income is determined simultaneously by the actions of households and firms. Optimization models aren't appropriate, because the aggregate economy is not a rational actor that makes choices according to some objective. Instead, we use a *general equilibrium* model, which considers the aggregate effects of simultaneous actions of households and firms.

general equilibrium: an analytical methodology that incorporates more economic variables as endogenous in order to explain the effects of many simultaneous actions.

Partial equilibrium models and general equilibrium models have different assumptions and are useful for different purposes. Because partial equilibrium models focus on the individual firm, household, or market, it is reasonable to assume that variables, such as income or production, which depend on other economic agents are exogenously determined. This assumption is reasonable if the economic agent being modeled is relatively insignificant compared to the aggregate; the individual actions will have an imperceptible effect on the variable. If the assumption is, in fact, realistic, partial equilibrium models explain behavior well.

Because general equilibrium models focus on the combined effects of many individual economic agents, it is not reasonable to assume that variables

361

that are assumed to be constant in partial models are unaffected by aggregate actions. Therefore, our models must treat such variables as endogenous; that is, they are determined by the model. The more endogenous variables, the more relationships must be simultaneously determined and the more complex the model. Therefore, the trade-off we face with more generality is more complexity. Although the aggregate models we examine in this chapter are relatively simple, we present them in an order which allows you to see how complexity increases as more variables are incorporated as endogenous variables.

The biggest differences you will notice between the analysis in this chapter and that in the three previous chapters are that the models we use are not optimization models, and that we perform comparative statics analysis using total differentiation rather than partial differentiation. As we saw when we examined national income determination models in Chapter 1, Section 1.4.2, and Chapter 5, Section 5.4, equilibrium at the aggregate level is achieved when the consumption and production plans of households and firms are simultaneously satisfied. Therefore, simultaneous equation models are used to describe aggregate behavior. Because we must take account of the effects of policy changes on the behavior of households and firms simultaneously, partial derivatives which hold one or the other constant are not appropriate.

In this chapter we make the model of national income determination we described in Chapter 5 considerably more sophisticated. We add the rate of interest as an endogenous variable and a money market as an equilibrating mechanism between the supply of money and households' demand for cash. We use the model to perform comparative statics analysis of the effects of government spending, tax policy, and monetary policy on national income and the rate of interest.

12.2

EXTENDED MODEL OF INCOME DETERMINATION: INCLUDING THE RATE OF INTEREST IN THE PRODUCT MARKET

Recall the simple model of income determination we examined in Chapter 1, Section 1.4.2, and Chapter 5, Section 5.4. In this section we extend that model, which can be considered a product market model because of its focus on consumption and real income, to include a new endogenous variable, the rate of interest. This can be done in either of two ways. One way is through household behavior, by respecifying the consumption function so that, in addition to disposable income, it includes the rate of interest as an independent variable. This requires us to define the dependent variable broadly to include consumption of both nondurable and durable goods, because it is the latter type of spending that is responsive to the rate of interest. Most durable goods are big-ticket items, such as refrigerators or automobiles, that are usually purchased on credit. One would expect that, as the rate of interest on consumer loans rises, consumers reduce their demand for durable goods.

The second approach to incorporating the rate of interest in the product market is through the investment decisions of firms. Thus far we have treated investment as an exogenous variable, whose value is determined outside the model. We can specify investment as a negative function of the rate of interest. The rationale for this is that the rate of interest represents the opportunity cost of investable funds, regardless of whether these are a firm's own funds or are to be borrowed. As this cost increases, the number of investment projects that are profitable on the margin declines and total investment expenditures diminish.

We use this second approach to introduce the rate of interest into the model by making investment a function of interest rate. Therefore, we specify the investment function as

$$I = I(r), \qquad \frac{dI}{dr} \equiv I' < 0 \tag{12-1}$$

The fact that $I' < 0$ simply captures the negative relationship between investment and the rate of interest. The remainder of the model is unchanged from the model in Chapter 5; that is, consumption spending is a function of disposable income,

$$C = C(Y_d), \qquad 0 < \frac{dC}{dY_d} \equiv C' < 1 \tag{12-2}$$

where

$$Y_d = Y - T \tag{12-3}$$

and

$$T = T(Y), \qquad 0 < \frac{dT}{dY} \equiv T' < 1 \tag{12-4}$$

We specify that $0 < C' < 1$ in order to build in the assumption that households consume some positive fraction of increases in their disposable income. We specify that $0 < T' < 1$ because we assume that the marginal income tax rate is positive but less than 100%. Government spending, G, is exogenous in our product market model. As in Chapters 1 and 5, the equilibrium condition is that income must equal planned expenditures,[1]

$$Y = C + I + G = C(Y_d) + I(r) + G \tag{12-5}$$

or

$$Y = C(Y - T(Y)) + I(r) + G \tag{12-6}$$

Our extended model of the product market is quite simple and very general. Because we have made no assumptions regarding the specific func-

---

[1]Note that this model pertains to be a closed economy. If we were to incorporate the foreign sector, we would add exports minus imports, or net exports, to the flow of expenditures. You are asked to do this in self-help problem 4 and supplemental problem 8 at the end of the chapter.

tional forms of the consumption and investment functions, we have not incorporated any parameters into the model. This means that we are unable to solve the model for the equilibrium value of income explicitly. Even if we had assumed that both the consumption and investment functions were linear and had assigned numerical values to the parameters and exogenous variables, still we would not be able to solve for the value of income. This is because, in addition to income, the extended model includes another unknown variable, the rate of interest. If we did know the value of the interest rate, we would be able to determine the corresponding value of income that would bring the product market into equilibrium.

What can we make of the product market equilibrium condition, equation (12-6), if the rate of interest is to be treated as an endogenous variable? We can interpret it as the locus of all possible combinations of income and interest rate that equate income and planned expenditures. This is referred to as the IS equation and is one of the two main ingredients of the model of joint determination of equilibrium income and rate of interest which we examine in Section 12.4 of this chapter.[2]

What is the relationship between income and interest that is implied by IS? In order to determine the effect of a change in the rate of interest on equilibrium level of income, totally differentiate the equilibrium condition, equation (12-6),

$$dY = C'(1 - T')\, dY + I'\, dr + dG \qquad (12\text{-}7)$$

Hold government spending constant by setting $dG = 0$ and solve for dY/dr,

$$\frac{dY}{dr} = \frac{I'}{1 - C'(1 - T')} < 0 \qquad (12\text{-}8)$$

The expression in (12-8) is negative. Remember that we assumed that $I' < 0$, so the numerator is negative. The denominator is positive because we assumed that both C' and T' are positive fractions, making the term $C'(1 - T')$ a positive fraction. Equation (12-8) indicates that at higher interest rates the equilibrium level of income is lower and vice versa. This happens because higher interest rates depress investment spending, which, through the multiplier process, results in lower levels of income, provided government expenditures are held constant. The graph of this relationship between the equilibrium level of income and interest rate in the product market is the *IS curve*. Equation (12-8) represents the inverse of the slope of the IS curve as it is graphed in Figure 12.1, with r along the vertical axis and Y along the horizontal. In other words, the slope of IS is

IS curve: the graph of the relationship between equilibrium levels of income for different interest rates in the product market.

$$\frac{dr}{dY} = \frac{1 - C'(1 - T')}{I'} < 0 \qquad (12\text{-}9)$$

[2]In the label IS, the letter *I* stands for investment and *S* for saving. The label is an abbreviation for the fact that, at product market equilibrium, planned injections, of which *I* is a component, must equal planned leakages, which include *S*.

Figure 12.1

**Product Market
Equilibrium: The IS
Curve**

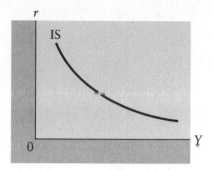

Even though we cannot solve the extended model of the product market for the equilibrium level of income, we can still perform comparative statics analysis in this model. Our version of the IS equation involves only one exogenous variable, government expenditures, G. This means that we can find an expression for the effect of a change in G on the equilibrium level of income, the familiar government spending multiplier. Hold the rate of interest constant by setting $dr = 0$ in equation (12-7) and then solve for dY/dG,

$$\frac{dY}{dG} = \frac{1}{1 - C'(1 - T')} \qquad (12\text{-}10)$$

Equation (12-10) is similar to the expenditures multiplier we found in Chapter 5, Section 5.4. We find that changes in government spending change equilibrium income in the same direction by a factor of $1/(1 - C'(1 - T'))$, holding the rate of interest constant.

What is the implication of the fact that dY/dG is positive for the IS curve? Since G is exogenous in the model, it acts as a shift variable for the IS curve. The fact that dY/dG is positive means that an increase in G will shift IS to the right and a decrease in G will shift IS to the left. In Section 12.4 we use this fact to examine the effect of government spending on both income and the rate of interest. It is important to note that with r on the vertical axis and Y on the horizontal axis, IS shifts *horizontally* in response to a change in government expenditures, because the rate of interest is assumed to remain constant as G changes. In other words, the horizontal intercept of IS shifts along the income axis by an amount equal to the spending multiplier times the change in G. This is shown in Figure 12.2.

Every point on the IS curve represents an equilibrium in the product market. What particular product market equilibrium might be achieved by the economy? An equilibrium at a high interest rate and low income, or an equilibrium at a low interest rate and high income? By itself the IS curve is not sufficient to answer this question, because it represents one equation in two unknowns, r and Y. What we need is another relation between equilibrium values of income and interest rate so that, together with IS, we would have a system of two equations in two unknowns. You may have guessed correctly that such a relation is to be found in the money market.

Figure 12.2

Shifting the IS Curve When G Increases

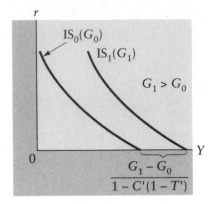

EXERCISES
Section 12.2
Extended Model of Income Determination

1. Consider the following extended model of the product market. Note that, unlike the standard model developed in this section, in this model the consumption function includes the rate of interest, r, as an argument in addition to disposable income.

$$C = C(Y_d, r) \qquad\qquad 0 < C_{Y_d} < 1, \; C_r < 0$$
$$Y_d = Y - T, \qquad T = T(Y), \qquad 0 < dT/dY \equiv T' < 1$$
$$Y = C + I + G, \qquad I = I(r), \qquad I' < 0$$

   a. Find the total differential of the IS equation.

   b. Find the slope of IS and determine its sign.

2. Consider the following linear model of the product market.

$$C = 125 + 0.75Y_d - 1000r, \qquad Y_d = Y - T$$
$$T = 100 + 0.2Y, \qquad\qquad I = 385 - 3000r$$
$$G = 125 \qquad\qquad\qquad Y = C + I + G$$

   a. Find the IS equation and determine its slope.

   b. Assume $r = 0.12$. What is the equilibrium level of income?

12.3

MONEY MARKET EQUILIBRIUM

In the previous section we examined the determination of equilibrium income while treating the rate of interest as given. In this section we have two objectives. First, we analyze the determination of an equilibrium interest rate taking income as given. Second, we use the interest rate model to derive the money market counterpart of the IS curve, the *LM curve*. In Section 12.4 we use the LM and IS curves to develop a model of joint determination of equilibrium levels of income and interest rate.

LM curve: the graph of the relationship between equilibrium rate of interest for different income levels in the money market.

Treating income as given, the equilibrium rate of interest is determined by the interaction between the demand for and the supply of money. According to the Keynesian theory of liquidity preference, demand by households for real cash balances is a positive function of real income and a negative function of the rate of interest. That is, households are willing to hold larger cash balances the higher their incomes and smaller cash balances the higher the interest rate, *ceteris paribus*. Letting M^d represent the quantity of nominal money balances demanded and P the general price level, the demand for real cash balances is

$$\frac{M^d}{P} = L(r, Y), \qquad \frac{\partial L}{\partial r} \equiv L_r < 0, \qquad \frac{\partial L}{\partial Y} \equiv L_Y > 0 \qquad (12\text{-}11)$$

liquidity: the ability to transform an asset into general purchasing power without losing its value.

We use L to describe the demand for real cash balances because consumers use cash because of its *liquidity,* the ability to transform an asset into general purchasing power without losing its value. The reason that $L_r < 0$ is that the rate of interest represents the opportunity cost of holding idle, but liquid, cash balances, which earn no or low interest. When the market rate of interest exceeds the level households expect, liquidity becomes relatively more expensive than expected. Holding cash diverts funds from unexpectedly higher income-earning assets such as bonds. In response, households rearrange their asset portfolios by reducing their cash holdings while increasing their holdings of bonds. On the other hand, when interest rates are lower than households expect them to be, liquidity becomes relatively less expensive than expected. Then households rearrange their portfolios by increasing cash holdings and decreasing their holdings of bonds, the income from which is unexpectedly low.

The positive sign on the partial derivative of money demand with respect to real income, L_Y, can be explained as follows. All else the same, an increase in real income gives individuals more purchasing power, inducing them to increase their consumption expenditures. But in order to carry out the higher volume of transactions, they will need more cash balances. Thus demand for money varies directly with real income.

Note that the money demand function involves three variables: quantity of real money balances, real income, and the rate of interest. Measuring the rate of interest on the vertical axis and real money balances on the horizontal axis, we graph money demand by holding income constant. This makes income a shift variable for the money demand. An increase in real income causes money demand to shift to the right at all interest rate levels, and a reduction in income results in a leftward shift in the money demand function. Figure 12.3 shows two money demand curves corresponding to two different levels of income, Y_0 and Y_1, respectively.

We assume nominal money supply, M^s, to be an exogenous policy variable over which a monetary authority (e.g., the Federal Reserve) can exercise control. This allows us to express real money supply as M^s/P, where the general price level, P, is assumed to be constant. Equilibrium in the money market occurs if the demand for money meets the supply, $M^d/P = M^s/P$, or

$$L(r, Y) = \frac{M}{P} \qquad (12\text{-}12)$$

Note that M, on the right-hand side of (12-12), does not carry a d or an s superscript. This is because, at equilibrium, quantity demanded equals quan-

Figure 12.3

Changes in Income and Money Demand

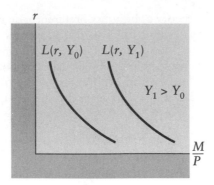

tity supplied. Figure 12.4 depicts an equilibrium of the money market with r^* denoting equilibrium rate of interest.

In drawing Figure 12.4 we fixed the position of the money demand curve by assuming an income level of Y_0. On the other hand, we drew the real money supply line based on a nominal money stock of M_0 and a price level of P_0. Let us examine the effect of a change in each of these variables on the equilibrium rate of interest. First, suppose the level of income increases to Y_1 while nominal money stock and the price level remain unchanged. This shifts the money demand curve to the right along the unchanged money supply line, and the equilibrium interest rate increases. We can establish this mathematically by taking the total differential of the equilibrium condition, equation (12-12). Note that we use the quotient rule in this differentiation.

$$\frac{P\, dM - M\, dP}{P^2} = L_Y\, dY + L_r\, dr \tag{12-13}$$

Setting $dP = dM = 0$ and solving for dr/dY gives us

$$\frac{dr}{dY} = \frac{-L_Y}{L_r} > 0 \tag{12-14}$$

which is positive, because $L_Y > 0$ and $L_r < 0$. An intuitive explanation for this result is that, when real income increases, consumers' transactions demand for

Figure 12.4

Money Market Equilibrium

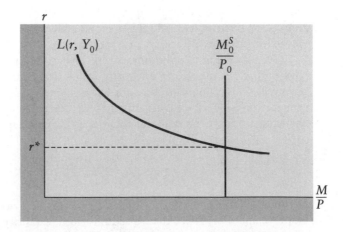

Figure 12.5

The Effect of Changes in Income on Interest Rates

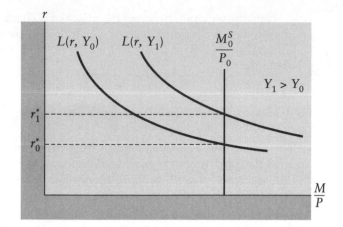

cash balances also increases. The resulting excess demand for money puts upward pressure on the rate of interest until a new equilibrium is established at the old quantity but at a higher equilibrium interest rate. This result is shown in Figure 12.5.

We can examine the effect of a change in nominal money supply on the equilibrium rate of interest by setting $dY = dP = 0$ in equation (12-13) and solving for dr/dM,

$$\frac{dr}{dM} = \frac{1}{PL_r} < 0 \tag{12-15}$$

Equation (12-15) takes a negative value because we have assumed that $L_r < 0$. According to this result, with the price level and real income constant, an increase in the supply of money results in a lower interest rate, while a decrease results in a higher equilibrium interest rate. Given an unexpected increase in the money supply, households find themselves with more cash balances than they expect to hold. They substitute income-earning assets, such as bonds, for money. The increased demand for bonds increases their price, which reduces their yield, which is represented by the rate of interest. Figure 12.6 illustrates this result.

Figure 12.6

The Effect of Changes in Nominal Money Supply on Interest Rates

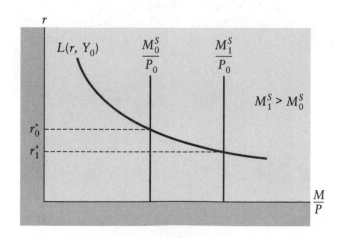

Finally, we can determine the effect of a change in price on equilibrium interest rate by holding income and nominal money supply constant. We accomplish this by setting $dM = dY = 0$ and solving (12-13) for dr/dP, obtaining

$$\frac{dr}{dP} = \frac{-M}{P^2 L_r} > 0 \qquad (12\text{-}16)$$

This expression is positive because both the numerator and the denominator are negative. Thus as the price level increases, the equilibrium level of interest rate increases as well, holding everything else constant. The effect on the equilibrium level of r of an increase in the price level is the opposite of the effect of an increase in the nominal money supply because higher prices have the effect of reducing the real money stock. Therefore, households respond to higher prices in the same way they would to a reduced nominal money supply.

We are now ready to develop the money market counterpart of the IS curve. The money market equilibrium condition, equation (12-12), defines an implicit functional relation between the equilibrium interest rate and levels of real income. For a given price level, equation (12-12) shows all possible combinations of real income, Y, and interest rate, r, that bring about equilibrium in the money market. It is known as the *LM equation*, as a reminder that it is obtained by setting the demand for cash balances, L, equal to the supply of money, M.

What is the slope of the LM curve? Equation (12-14), derived earlier, is an expression for the effect of a change in income on equilibrium interest rate while holding nominal money supply and the price level constant. For your convenience we reproduce that expression here:

$$\frac{dr}{dY} = \frac{-L_Y}{L_r} > 0 \qquad (12\text{-}14)$$

Equation (12-14) represents the slope of LM, graphed with r on the vertical axis and Y on the horizontal as illustrated in Figure 12.7.

The LM curve is positively sloped, as indicated by the sign of (12-14) and as shown in Figure 12.7. The LM curve can also be derived graphically from Figure 12.5, which shows an upward shift in money demand caused by an increase in income. If we were to determine the corresponding equilibrium

Figure 12.7

Money Market Equilibrium: The LM Curve

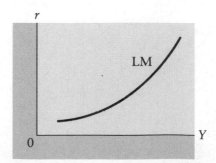

rate of interest for several different income levels, we would have a set of ordered pairs whose graph is the LM curve.

The LM equation, (12-12), contains two exogenous variables, the price level and the nominal money supply, which represent the shift variables associated with LM. That is, holding income and nominal money supply constant, an increase in P reduces real money supply and shifts LM up, and a decrease in P results in a downward shift in LM. This is a result we derived in equation (12-16). An increase in nominal money supply, M, causes LM to shift down, whereas a reduction in M results in an upward shift in LM, as we see from equation (12-15). Remember that changes in real income do not shift the LM curve; they are represented by movements along the curve. We can use these results to analyze the effects of monetary policy on real income and interest rate in the next section.

EXERCISES
Section 12.3
Money Market
Equilibrium

1. Consider the following model of the money market. Note that, unlike the standard model developed in this section, the supply of money is endogenous as it is an increasing function of the rate of interest.

$$\frac{M^d}{P} = L(r, Y), \qquad L_r < 0, \ L_Y > 0$$

$$\frac{M^s}{P} = m(r), \qquad m' > 0$$

$$\frac{M^d}{P} = \frac{M^s}{P}$$

   a. Find the total differential of the LM equation.
   b. Find an expression for the slope of LM and determine its sign.

2. Consider the following linear model of the money market.

$$\frac{M^d}{P} = Y - 2000r, \qquad \frac{M^s}{P} = 200$$

$$P = 1, \qquad \frac{M^d}{P} = \frac{M^s}{P}$$

   a. Find the LM equation and determine its slope.
   b. Assume $Y = 500$. What is the equilibrium rate of interest?

12.4

GENERAL EQUILIBRIUM IN THE PRODUCT AND MONEY MARKETS

The product and money market models we examined in the previous two sections are considered partial equilibrium models because each is concerned with equilibrium in one market while ignoring possible interactions with the other market. In the product market model of Section 12.2 we took the rate of interest as given and studied the determination of an equilibrium income. Then in the money market model of Section 12.3 we did the opposite, taking the level of income as given and analyzing the determination of an equilibrium rate of interest. In this section we merge these two models into a more general equilibrium model that allows us to analyze the simultaneous determination of equilibrium levels of income and interest rate. This model can then be used for comparative statics analysis of stabilization policies.

Product market equilibrium is summarized by the IS equation, derived earlier as equation (12-6),

$$\text{IS:} \qquad Y = C(Y - T(Y)) + I(r) + G \qquad\qquad \textbf{(12-6)}$$

and money market equilibrium is captured by the LM equation, (12-12),

$$\text{LM:} \qquad L(r, Y) = \frac{M}{P} \qquad\qquad \textbf{(12-12)}$$

These define a system of two simultaneous equations in two unknowns, income, Y, and interest rate, r, which is known as the *IS-LM model*.[3] The IS-LM model can be illustrated graphically by placing both the IS and the LM curves on the same set of axes, as in Figure 12.8. The intersection of the curves represents the values of r and Y that simultaneously satisfy equilibria in both the product market (IS) and the money market (LM).

Figure 12.8

The IS-LM Model

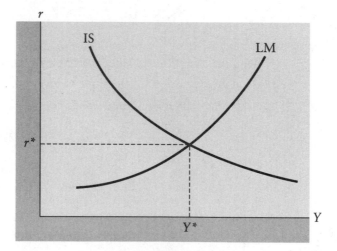

Mathematically, we want to solve the simultaneous equations in order to determine equilibrium values of Y and r. These can be used to find equilibrium values of the other endogenous variables of the model, income taxes, T, disposable income, $Y - T$, consumption, C, investment, I, and money demand, L. The model contains three exogenous (shift) variables: government expenditures, G, which shifts IS; nominal money supply, M, which shifts LM;

---

[3]The IS-LM model was first developed by the British economist John Hicks after John Maynard Keynes had published *The General Theory of Employment, Interest, and Money*. It was subsequently refined by the American economist Alvin Hansen and others.

and the price level, P, which is also a shift variable for LM. In the analysis that follows, we assume that P is constant.

In its present form the model is too general to be solved explicitly for the equilibrium values of income and interest rate. This is because the IS and LM curves are implicit functions in Y and r. However, we can perform comparative statics analysis of the effect of changes in the exogenous variables by assuming that the equilibrium condition is satisfied and totally differentiating it. Below we derive expressions for the effect of changes in G and M on the equilibrium levels of income and interest rate.

Because we are concerned with changes in variables, we need total differentials of the IS and LM functions. We found these in the previous two sections in equations (12-7) and (12-13) when we performed comparative statics analysis in the partial equilibrium models of the product and money markets. These are reproduced here:

$$dY = C'(1 - T')\, dY + I'\, dr + dG \qquad (12\text{-}7)$$

$$\frac{P\, dM - M\, dP}{P^2} = L_Y\, dY + L_r\, dr \qquad (12\text{-}13)$$

Equations (12-7) and (12-13) define a system of two simultaneous equations in two unknowns, dY and dr. Because both equations are linear in dY and dr, they can be expressed as a matrix equation,

$$\begin{bmatrix} 1 - C'(1 - T') & -I' \\ L_Y & L_r \end{bmatrix} \begin{bmatrix} dY \\ dr \end{bmatrix} = \begin{bmatrix} dG \\ \left(\dfrac{1}{P}\right) dM - \left(\dfrac{M}{P^2}\right) dP \end{bmatrix} \qquad (12\text{-}17)$$

Recall from Chapter 8, Section 8.4.1, that this system has a unique solution if and only if the determinant of the matrix of coefficients is not zero; that is, the coefficient matrix is nonsingular. The determinant of the coefficient matrix is

$$|D| \equiv [1 - C'(1 - T')]L_r + L_Y I' \qquad (12\text{-}18)$$

stabilization policy: macroeconomic policy designed to respond to undesirable changes in the level of real income or output. It includes fiscal and monetary policies.

fiscal policy: changes in government expenditures or income tax rates by policy makers such as the President or Congress.

monetary policy: changes in the money supply by monetary authorities such as a central bank or the Federal Reserve.

The term $L_Y I'$ is clearly negative (remember that L_Y is positive and I' is negative). You should recognize the term $[1 - C'(1 - T')]$; it is the numerator of equation (12-9), the slope of IS. We know the term is positive, because the IS curve is downward sloping and its denominator is negative. This, together with the fact that L_r and $L_Y I'$ are both negative, makes $|D|$ negative, assuring us that this matrix equation has a unique solution. This condition, that $|D|$ is negative, ensures that an equilibrium with positive levels of income and interest rate exists.

Policy makers use what is known as *stabilization policy*, which includes fiscal and monetary policies, in response to undesirable changes in the level of real income or output. *Fiscal policy* refers to changes in government expenditures or income tax rates by policy makers such as the President or Congress, and *monetary policy* refers to changes in the money supply by monetary authorities such as a central bank or the Federal Reserve. We can use equation (12-17) to analyze the effects of both forms of stabilization policy on equilibrium income and interest rates.

12.4.1   Output and Interest Rate Effects of Fiscal Policy

We can use Cramer's rule to solve equation (12-17) for the effect of government expenditures, G, on the equilibrium level of income, Y, and rate of interest, r. In order to solve for dY, we replace the first column of the coefficient matrix with the right-hand side column vector of differentials of exogenous variables,

$$dY = \frac{\begin{vmatrix} dG & -I' \\ \left(\dfrac{1}{P}\right) dM - \left(\dfrac{M}{P^2}\right) dP & L_r \end{vmatrix}}{|D|} \tag{12-19}$$

The denominator, $|D|$, is the determinant of the coefficient matrix from equation (12-17). Expanding the 2×2 determinant in the numerator yields

$$dY = \frac{L_r \, dG + I'\left[\left(\dfrac{1}{P}\right) dM - \left(\dfrac{M}{P^2}\right) dP\right]}{|D|} \tag{12-20}$$

We want to find dY/dG, which measures the effect of a change in government expenditures on national income and can be considered the spending multiplier. We set $dM = dP = 0$ and divide equation (12-20) by dG, yielding

$$\frac{dY}{dG} = \frac{L_r}{|D|} > 0 \tag{12-21}$$

The numerator of (12-21) is negative by assumption, and the denominator is negative as we see from equation (12-18). Therefore, $dY/dG > 0$, indicating that an increase (decrease) in government spending increases (decreases) the equilibrium level of income, holding real money supply constant.

We see that there is a positive relationship between government spending and equilibrium income. This is the same result as we found in equation (12-10) when we examined the product market alone, without accounting for the effects of the money market. Although the results are similar qualitatively (i.e., the derivatives have the same sign), they are different quantitatively. We can compare the two results if we divide the numerator and the denominator of equation (12-21) by L_r, obtaining

$$\frac{dY}{dG} = \frac{1}{1 - C'(1 - T') + I'(L_Y/L_r)} \quad \text{with the money market} \tag{12-22}$$

We reproduce (12-10) for comparison

$$\frac{dY}{dG} = \frac{1}{1 - C'(1 - T')} \quad \text{without the money market} \tag{12-10}$$

Except for the last term in the denominator of equation (12-22), these equations are identical. The term $I'(L_Y/L_r)$ in the denominator of (12-22) is positive, because I' and L_r are negative by assumption and L_Y is positive by assumption. Therefore, the multiplier which takes account of the interaction between the product and money markets is smaller than the multiplier from the product market alone. In other words, adding the money market to the model of product market makes government spending a less effective tool of stabilization policy.

What is the intuitive reason for this result? The answer is found in the way the money market responds to a change in government expenditures. With the rate of interest at an initial equilibrium level, an increase in government expenditures increases income by the full multiplier effect, $1/[1 - C'(1 - T')]$. The higher income leads to increased demand for transactional balances, shifting the money demand curve up. Assuming that the monetary authority does not accommodate the fiscal expansion so that money supply is unchanged, there will be excess demand for money, forcing the rate of interest up. Higher interest rates depress investment, partially offsetting the initial rise in income.

This feedback from the money market is known as the **crowding-out effect**; by increasing the rate of interest, government expenditures crowd out interest-sensitive private expenditures. Figure 12.9 shows the relationship between the old and new spending multipliers and highlights the crowding-out effect.

The term $I'(L_Y/L_r)$ in the denominator of equation (12-22), known as the **monetary feedback term**, captures the crowding-out effect. It shows that the extent of crowding out depends on the absolute value of the slope of the LM curve, L_Y/L_r, and the interest responsiveness of investment demand, I'. The steeper the LM curve, the larger the crowding-out effect. In the limiting case of a vertical LM curve, the monetary feedback term will approach infinity and the spending multiplier will approach zero, indicating complete crowding out; government spending would be totally ineffective in stimulating output. Complete crowding out is pictured in Figure 12.10.

Let's examine the effect of government spending on the equilibrium rate of interest, dr/dG. This can be done in the same way as we found dY/dG. Here we outline the process and urge you to follow it to see if you can arrive at the result given below. First, use Cramer's rule to solve the matrix equation

crowding-out effect: government expenditures having the effect of reducing interest-sensitive private expenditures by increasing the rate of interest.

monetary feedback term: the term in the IS-LM model that shows the extent of crowding out.

Figure 12.9

The Crowding-out Effect of Fiscal Expansion

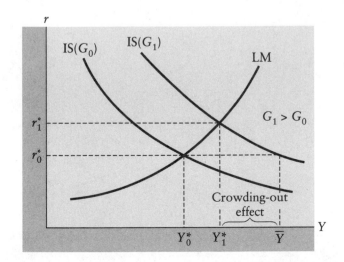

Figure 12.10

Interest Insensitive Money Demand and Complete Crowding-out

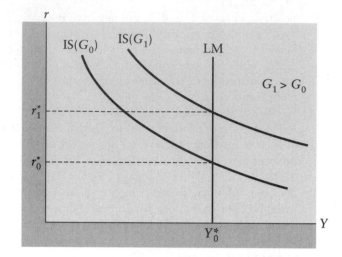

(12-17) for dr by replacing the second column of the coefficient matrix with the right-hand side column vector of differentials of exogenous variables. Next, expand the resulting 2×2 determinant in the numerator of the expression for dr. You should obtain

$$dr = \frac{(1 - C'(1 - T'))\left[\left(\frac{1}{P}\right) dM - \left(\frac{M}{P^2}\right) dP\right] - L_Y\, dG}{|D|} \qquad (12\text{-}23)$$

Next, set $dM = dP = 0$ and solve for dr/dG. Your solution should be

$$\frac{dr}{dG} = \frac{-L_Y}{|D|} > 0 \qquad (12\text{-}24)$$

We know that (12-24) is positive, because L_Y is positive by assumption and $|D|$ is negative, as we established in (12-18). Thus an increase in government expenditures leads to an increase in the rate of interest. The effects of increased

Figure 12.11

The Effect of Fiscal Policy on Income and Interest Rates

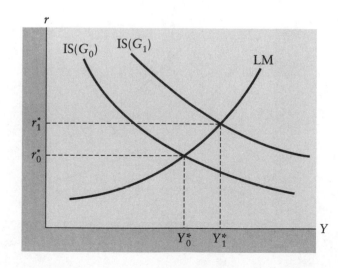

government expenditures on equilibrium level of output and rate of interest are shown in Figure 12.11.

Consider the following model of the joint equilibrium of the product and money markets:

$$C = C(Y_d, r), \qquad\qquad\qquad 0 < C_{Yd} < 1, \quad C_r < 0$$

$$Y_d = Y - T, \qquad T = T(Y), \qquad 0 < \frac{dT}{dY} \equiv T' < 1$$

$$Y = C + I + G, \qquad I = I(r), \qquad I' < 0$$

$$\frac{M^d}{P} = \frac{M^s}{P}, \qquad \frac{M^d}{P} = L(r, Y), \qquad L_r < 0; \quad L_Y > 0$$

1. Totally differentiate the IS and LM equations and express the total differentials of Y and r as a matrix equation. Use the matrix equation to determine whether it has a unique solution. Use Cramer's rule to solve for dY and dr, and use the results to find expressions for the government spending multipliers, dY/dG and dr/dG.

2. Determine the effect on dY/dG and dr/dG if
   a. $I' = 0$
   b. $L_r = 0$
   c. $L_r \to \infty$ as $r \to 0$

12.4.2 Effects of Tax Policies

In our IS-LM model government expenditures, G, and money supply, M, are exogenous policy variables. Another fiscal policy instrument available to policy makers is taxation. Because of the general form of the tax function in our model, the income tax rate, $T' \equiv dT(Y)/dY$, is endogenous. This means that in order to perform comparative statics analysis of the effect of changes in the income tax rate we must use a more specific form of the tax function. The simplest form to use is a linear tax function, $T = \tau Y$, where the income tax rate, $T' = \tau$, is a positive fraction. With this more specific tax function the IS equation becomes

$$Y = C(Y - \tau Y) + I(r) + G \qquad\qquad (12\text{-}25)$$

The total differential of equation (12-25) is

$$dY = C'[(1 - \tau)\, dY - Y\, d\tau] + I'\, dr + dG \qquad\qquad (12\text{-}26)$$

Note that in taking the total differential of the consumption function we used the product rule when differentiating the term τY.

The effect of specifying a linear tax function is to provide us with a parameter, τ, which we can use to derive comparative statics results for changes in tax policy. We can now derive expressions for the effect of changes in the income tax rate on the equilibrium level of income and rate of interest. The procedure is the same as the one we used in the case of government expenditures. The total differential of the modified IS equation, (12-26), and that of LM, equation (12-12), define a system of two simultaneous linear equations in two unknowns, dY and dr, and total differentials of three exogenous policy variables, dG, dM, and $d\tau$. This is expressed in matrix form as

$$
\begin{bmatrix} 1 - C'(1 - \tau) & -I' \\ L_Y & L_r \end{bmatrix} \begin{bmatrix} dY \\ dr \end{bmatrix} = \begin{bmatrix} -C'Y\,d\tau + dG \\ \left(\dfrac{1}{P}\right) dM - \left(\dfrac{M}{P^2}\right) dP \end{bmatrix} \tag{12-27}
$$

As before, the determinant of the coefficient matrix, $|D|$ is negative, so the existence of a unique, positive solution is assured. Therefore, we can use Cramer's rule to solve this system for dY,

$$
dY = \frac{L_r(-C'Y\,d\tau + dG) + I'\left[\left(\dfrac{1}{P}\right) dM - \left(\dfrac{M}{P^2}\right) dP\right]}{|D|} \tag{12-28}
$$

Hold the other exogenous variables constant by setting $dG = dM = dP = 0$. Solve for $dY/d\tau$ by dividing both sides by $d\tau$, and divide the numerator and denominator by L_r, yielding

$$
\frac{dY}{d\tau} = \frac{-C'Y}{1 - C'(1 - \tau) + I'(L_Y/L_r)} \tag{12-29}
$$

The income tax rate multiplier is negative because the numerator is negative (remember $C'Y > 0$) and the denominator is positive (we have divided $|D|$, which is negative, by L_r, which is also negative). This means that, *ceteris paribus*, an increase in the income tax rate results in a lower level of equilibrium income. This follows from the fact that, for a given level of pretax income, an increase in the income tax rate causes an initial reduction in disposable income which, in turn, lowers consumption spending. Then, through the usual multiplier process, reduced consumption brings about a cumulative decline in the equilibrium level of real income. The initial reduction in disposable income is captured by the term $-C'Y$ in the numerator of the income tax rate multiplier, and the subsequent cumulative decline is captured by the usual spending multiplier, $1/[1 - C'(1 - \tau) + I'(L_Y/L_r)]$.[4]

The effect of a change in the income tax rate on the equilibrium rate of

---

[4]Notice an interesting aspect of the income tax rate multiplier; it depends on the level of income, implying that, *ceteris paribus*, tax policies are more potent at higher levels of income.

interest can also be found. Use Cramer's rule to solve the matrix equation (12-27) for dr,

$$dr = \frac{[1 - C'(1 - \tau)]\left[\left(\dfrac{1}{P}\right)dM - \left(\dfrac{M}{P^2}\right)dP\right] + (C'Y\,d\tau - dG)L_Y}{|D|} \quad (12\text{-}30)$$

Set $dG = dM = dP = 0$ to hold all other exogenous variables constant, solve for $dr/d\tau$, and divide the numerator and denominator by L_r,

$$\frac{dr}{d\tau} = \frac{(L_Y/L_r)C'Y}{1 - C'(1 - \tau) + I'(L_Y/L_r)} \quad (12\text{-}31)$$

This expression for $dr/d\tau$ is negative because the numerator is negative while the denominator is positive. Therefore, an increase (decrease) in the tax rate decreases (increases) the equilibrium rate of interest, *ceteris paribus*.

We can use the graphical representation of the IS-LM model to study the effect of tax policies. Being a product market parameter, the tax rate, τ, can affect only the IS curve.[5] Changes in the tax rate affect both the intercept and slope of the IS curve. Look at the expression for the total differential of IS, equation (12-26), and you see that $d\tau$ enters with a negative sign; an increase in the tax rate shifts the IS curve to the left and a decrease in the tax rate shifts IS to the right, as pictured in Figure 12.12.

Figure 12.12

The Effects of Tax Cuts on Income and Interest Rates

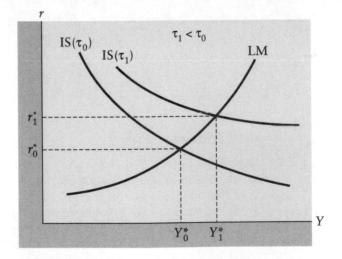

We need to find an expression for the slope of the IS curve, dr/dY, in order to see how it is affected by changes in τ. We find it by solving the total differential of the IS curve, equation (12-26), for dr/dY, obtaining

$$\frac{dr}{dY} = \frac{1 - C'(1 - \tau)}{I'} \quad (12\text{-}32)$$

---

[5]We ask you to examine a model in which the tax rate affects both IS and LM in supplemental problem 5 at the end of the chapter.

The slope is negative, as expected, because the numerator is positive and the denominator is negative. As you can see in (12-32), an increase in τ increases the numerator, making the slope of IS more steeply negative.

Therefore, an increase in tax rates affects IS by shifting it to the left and increasing the steepness of its negative slope. A decrease in τ affects IS by shifting it to the right and making its negative slope flatter. With LM unaffected, an increase (decrease) in the tax rate results in a decrease (increase) in both equilibrium income and interest rate. Figure 12.12 illustrates that, at the lower tax rate, the IS curve, $IS(\tau_1)$, is shifted to the right and is flatter, resulting in a higher equilibrium income and interest rate.

EXERCISES
Section 12.4.2
Effects of Tax
Policies

Consider the following IS-LM model, in which investment function includes disposable income as an argument in addition to the rate of interest.

$$C = C(Y_d, r), \qquad\qquad\qquad 0 < C_{Yd} < 1, \quad C_r < 0$$
$$Y_d = Y - T, \qquad T = \tau Y, \qquad 0 < \tau < 1$$
$$Y = C + I + G, \qquad I = I(r, Y_d), \quad I_r < 0, \qquad I_{Yd} > 0$$
$$\frac{M^d}{P} = \frac{M^s}{P} \qquad \frac{M^d}{P} = L(r, Y), \quad L_r < 0, \qquad L_Y > 0$$

1. Totally differentiate the IS and LM equations and express the total differentials of Y and r as a matrix equation. Determine whether it has a unique solution and, if so, use Cramer's rule to solve for dY and dr, and use the results to find expressions for the tax rate multipliers, $dY/d\tau$ and $dr/d\tau$.

2. Determine the effect on $dY/d\tau$ and $dr/d\tau$ if
   a. $I' = 0$
   b. $L_r = 0$
   c. $L_r \to \infty$ as $r \to 0$

12.4.3   Effects of Monetary Policy

Monetary policy is the other important component of stabilization policy. Changes in nominal money supply affect the level of output through their impact on the rate of interest, which, in turn, affects interest-sensitive spending (investment, in the model we are working with). We can derive comparative statics results for monetary policy by using the same procedure we used to analyze the output and interest rate effects of fiscal policy.

To find the effects of changes in the nominal money supply on output, solve the expression for dY, equation (12-20), for dY/dM, setting $dG = dP = 0$. Following this procedure, we find

$$\frac{dY}{dM} = \frac{I'/P}{|D|} = \frac{I'}{PD} \tag{12-33}$$

where, as in Section 12.4.1, $|D| = [1 - C'(1 - T')]L_r + L_Y I'$, which is negative. The money multiplier is positive because both the numerator and denominator of (12-33) are negative; increasing the supply of money increases equilibrium income and decreasing money supply reduces income.

As we suggested, this result stems from the fact that with the price level assumed constant, monetary expansion leads to lower interest rates and thus stimulates investment spending. This first-round effect is captured in equation (12-33) by the numerator, which measures the interest sensitivity of investment demand. Following this initial effect, income increases in response to increased investment through the usual multiplier process.

We use the IS-LM model to picture the effects of monetary policy on real income and interest rates. Changes in the nominal money supply affect LM; increases shift LM down, decreases shift LM up. [6] Figure 12.13 illustrates this, showing that an increase in M increases Y, as suggested by equation (12-33). The graph also shows that the equilibrium interest rate decreases with an increase in M. We derive this result mathematically next.

We said that the effect of monetary policy on output is transmitted through the rate of interest. We can determine the effect of changes in money supply on the rate of interest using the same method we have used to derive all of our comparative statics results. Equation (12-23) provides us with an expression for dr, which we reproduce here.

$$dr = \frac{(1 - C'(1 - T'))\left[\left(\frac{1}{P}\right)dM - \left(\frac{M}{P^2}\right)dP\right] - L_Y\,dG}{|D|} \quad (12\text{-}23)$$

Set $dG = dP = 0$ and solve for dr/dM, obtaining

$$\frac{dr}{dM} = \frac{1 - C'(1 - T')}{P|D|} < 0 \quad (12\text{-}34)$$

Equation (12-34) is negative because the numerator is positive and the denominator is negative. An increase (decrease) in the nominal supply of money reduces (increases) the rate of interest, provided government expenditures, tax rates, and the price level are held constant.

Figure 12.13

The Effect of Monetary Expansion on Income and Interest Rates

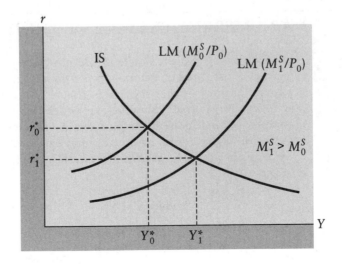

[6]In supplemental problem 6, we give you a model in which changes in nominal money supply shift not only LM but also IS.

Use the following model to answer these exercises.

$$C = C(Y_d), \qquad\qquad\qquad\qquad 0 < \frac{dC}{dY_d} \equiv C' < 1$$

$$Y_d = Y - T, \qquad T = T(Y), \qquad 0 < \frac{dT}{dY} \equiv T' < 1$$

$$Y = C + I + G, \qquad I = I(r), \qquad I' < 0,$$

$$\frac{M^d}{P} = L(r, Y), \qquad\qquad\qquad L_r < 0, L_Y > 0$$

$$\frac{M^d}{P} = \frac{M^s}{P}, \qquad \frac{M^s}{P} = \frac{M}{P} + m(r), \qquad m' > 0$$

1. Totally differentiate the IS and LM equations and express the total differentials of Y and r as a matrix equation. Determine whether it has a unique solution and, if so, use Cramer's rule to solve for dY and dr. Use the results to find expressions for the money supply multipliers, dY/dM and dr/dM.

2. Determine the effect on dY/dM and dr/dM if
   a. $I' = 0$
   b. $L_r = 0$
   c. $L_r \to \infty$ as $r \to 0$

12.5

A NUMERICAL EXAMPLE OF THE IS-LM MODEL

In this section we use a simple IS-LM model to perform comparative statics analysis of fiscal and monetary policies. We assume linear functional forms for all relationships so that the model can be solved for specific values of the endogenous variables. However, in order to facilitate comparative statics analysis, we first present the model in a parametric form and then provide numerical values for its parameters and exogenous variables.

Consider the following model of a hypothetical economy.

Product Market   **Money Market**

$$C = C_0 + cY_d \qquad\qquad \frac{M^d}{P} = L_0 + mY - \beta r$$

$$Y_d = Y - T \qquad\qquad \frac{M^s}{P} = \frac{M_0}{P_0}$$

$$T = T_0 + \tau Y \qquad \frac{M^s}{P} = \frac{M^d}{P}$$

$$I = I_0 - \alpha r$$
$$G = G_0$$
$$Y = C + I + G$$

In this model the subscript 0 represents exogenous variables. That is, C_0 represents autonomous consumption, I_0 autonomous investment, and L_0 autonomous demand for real cash balances. Similarly, G_0, M_0, and P_0 are given levels of government spending, nominal money stock, and prices, respectively. The variable T_0 represents autonomous taxes, independent of income, which can be interpreted as lump-sum taxes. In order to make this example numerical, let $C_0 = 50$, $T_0 = 10$, $I_0 = 368$, $G_0 = 30$, $c = 0.80$, $\tau = 0.25$, $\alpha = 3600$, $L_0 = 600$, $m = 2$, $\beta = 2000$, $M_0 = 800$, and $P_0 = 1$.

In order to determine equilibrium income and interest rate we must solve the IS and LM equations simultaneously. The IS equation is derived from the product market equilibrium condition, $Y = C + I + G$,

$$Y = 50 + 0.80(Y - 10 - 0.25Y) + 368 - 3600r + 30 \qquad \text{(12-35)}$$

Solving this for Y as a function of r yields the IS equation,

$$Y = 1100 - 9000r \qquad \text{(12-36)}$$

The LM equation is derived from the money market equilbrium condition, $M^d/P = M^s/P$,

$$600 + 2Y - 2000r = 800 \qquad \text{(12-37)}$$

Rearranging terms so that Y is expressed as a function of r gives us the LM equation,

$$Y = 100 + 1000r \qquad \text{(12-38)}$$

Equations (12-36) and (12-38) represent a system of two linear equations in two unknowns. Given the way the equations are expressed, the easiest way to solve the system is by the method of elimination. Since both equations have the same left-hand sides, it follows that their right-hand sides must be equal,

$$Y = 1100 - 9000r = 100 + 1000r = Y \qquad \text{(12-39)}$$

It is easy to verify that the solution to this is $r^* = 0.1$. Substitute this in either the IS or LM equation and solve for equilibrium income, Y^*,

$$Y^* = 1100 - 9000(0.1) = 100 + 100(0.1) = 200 \qquad \text{(12-40)}$$

Thus at an interest rate of 10% and an income level of 200, the product and money markets are simultaneously in equilibrium. This equilibrium is shown in Figure 12.14.

Figure 12.14

IS: $Y = 1100 - 9000r$;
LM: $Y = 100 + 1000r$

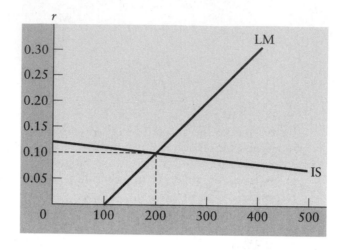

In order to find comparative statics derivatives of Y and r with respect to G, M, and τ, we must first incorporate them into the IS and LM equations. This can be done by replacing numerical values of the policy variables in equations (12-35) and (12-37) with the symbols that denote them,

$$Y = 50 + 0.80(Y - 10 - \tau Y) + 368 - 3600r + G_0 \quad (12\text{-}41)$$

$$600 + 2Y - 2000r = M_0 \quad (12\text{-}42)$$

The total differentials of (12-41) and (12-42) are

$$dY = 0.80(dY - \tau\,dY - Y\,d\tau) - 3600\,dr + dG_0 \quad (12\text{-}43)$$

$$2\,dY - 2000\,dr = dM_0 \quad (12\text{-}44)$$

Equations (12-43) and (12-44) represent two equations in two unknowns, dY and dr, that can be expressed in matrix form,

$$\begin{bmatrix} 0.8(1 - \tau) & 3600 \\ 2 & 2000 \end{bmatrix} \begin{bmatrix} dY \\ dr \end{bmatrix} = \begin{bmatrix} -0.8Y\,d\tau + dG_0 \\ dM_0 \end{bmatrix} \quad (12\text{-}45)$$

Substituting 0.25 for τ results in

$$\begin{bmatrix} 0.4 & 3600 \\ 2 & -2000 \end{bmatrix} \begin{bmatrix} dY \\ dr \end{bmatrix} = \begin{bmatrix} -0.8Y\,d\tau + dG_0 \\ dM_0 \end{bmatrix} \quad (12\text{-}46)$$

We test for existence of a unique solution by checking to see if the coefficient matrix is nonsingular. It is, because its determinant equals $0.4(-2000) - 2(3600) = -8000$.

In order to derive comparative statics results with respect to Y we use Cramer's rule to solve (12-46) for dY, obtaining

$$dY = \frac{-2000(-0.8Y\,d\tau + dG_0) - 3600\,dM_0}{-8000} \tag{12-47}$$

Find the expenditures multiplier by setting $d\tau = dM_0 = 0$ and solving for dY/dG_0,

$$\frac{dY}{dG_0} = \frac{-2000}{-8000} = 0.25 \tag{12-48}$$

Find the tax multiplier by setting $dG_0 = dM_0 = 0$ and solving for $dY/d\tau$,

$$\frac{dY}{d\tau} = \frac{-2000(-0.8Y)}{-8000} = -0.2Y \tag{12-49}$$

Substituting the equilibrium level of income, $Y^* = 200$, for Y we find that $dY/d\tau = -40$. This means that, starting with an equilibrium income of 200, an increase of one percentage point in the proportional income tax rate will bring about a reduction of 40 units in national income.

The money multiplier can be found by setting $dG_0 = d\tau = 0$ and solving for dY/dM_0,

$$\frac{dY}{dM_0} = \frac{-3600}{-8000} = 0.45 \tag{12-50}$$

At equilibrium, an increase of one unit in the supply of money results in an increase of 0.45 units in national income.

In order to find comparative statics results with respect to r, we use Cramer's rule to solve (12-46) for dr, obtaining

$$dr = \frac{0.4\,dM_0 - 2(-0.8Y\,d\tau + dG_0)}{-8000} \tag{12-51}$$

Find the effect of government spending by setting $d\tau = dM_0 = 0$ and solving for dr/dG_0

$$\frac{dr}{dG_0} = \frac{-2}{-8000} = 0.00025 \tag{12-52}$$

An increase of one unit in government spending from an initial income of 200 results in an increase of 0.025 percentage points in the rate of interest.

To find the effect of tax rate changes on r, set $dG_0 = dM_0 = 0$ and solve for $dr/d\tau$,

$$\frac{dr}{d\tau} = \frac{1.6Y}{-8000} = -0.0002Y \tag{12-53}$$

Evaluated at the equilibrium level of income of 200, this equals -0.04, suggesting that a one percentage point increase in the tax rate results in a 0.04 of a percentage point decrease in the interest rate.

Finally, we can find the effect on the interest rate of changes in the nominal money supply by setting $dG_0 = d\tau = 0$,

$$\frac{dr}{dM_0} = \frac{-0.4}{8000} = -0.00005 \tag{12-54}$$

A one-unit increase in the money supply decreases the equilibrium rate of interest by 0.005 percentage points.

EXERCISES
Section 12.5
A Numerical
Example of the
IS-LM Model

Use the following linear IS-LM model to answer these exercises.

$$C = 250 + 0.75Y_d - 1000r, \qquad T = 100 + \tau Y, \tau = 0.2$$
$$I = 160 - 3000r, \qquad\qquad G = 225$$
$$Y_d = Y - T$$

$$Y = C + I + G, \qquad\qquad \frac{M^d}{P} = Y - 2000r$$

$$\frac{M^s}{P} = 200, \qquad\qquad P = 1$$

$$\frac{M^d}{P} = \frac{M^s}{P}$$

1. Determine the equilibrium values of income and interest rate. Draw a graph of your solution.

2. Determine the equilibrium values of consumption, investment, taxes, and money demand.

3. Find the government spending multipliers, dY/dG and dr/dG.

4. Find the tax rate multipliers, $dY/d\tau$ and $dr/d\tau$.

5. Find the money supply multipliers, dY/dM and dr/dM.

12.6

SUMMARY

Chapter 12 shows you how to use some of the mathematical techniques covered in earlier chapters to analyze aggregate economic activity. First, we analyzed the product market, in which firms' production and investment decisions are meshed with households' consumption and savings decisions. For any given rate of interest, equilibrium in the product market occurs at that level of income which equals planned expenditures. The lower the interest rate, the higher the equilibrium level of income, because lower interest rates spur higher planned expenditures in the form of investment. The negative relationship between the rate of interest and the equilibrium level of income in the product market is summarized graphically by the downward-sloping IS curve.

Next, we analyzed the money market, in which the supply of money is meshed with households' demand for liquidity, represented by real cash balances. For any given level of income, equilibrium in the money market occurs at the interest rate at which the demand for real money equals the supply of money by the monetary authority. The higher the level of income, the higher the equilibrium interest rate, because households demand more liquidity when their income is greater. The positive relationship between income and the equilibrium interest rate is summarized graphically by the upward-sloping LM curve.

Finally, we combined the product and money markets by realizing that equilibrium could be achieved in each at an income and interest rate that satisfied simultaneously both. Graphically, this is the point at which the IS curve intersects the LM curve. Mathematically, we set the IS equation equal to the LM equation. Taking the total differential, we found a system of simultaneous equations which were linear in the differentials of income and interest rate. We used this system of linear equations to perform comparative statics analysis of the effects on interest rates and real income of changes in exogenous variables such as government spending, taxes, and the money supply.

◆ REFERENCES

Hansen, Alvin H., *A Guide to Keynes* (New York: McGraw-Hill Book Company, 1953).

Hicks, John R., "Mr. Keynes and the 'Classics'; a Suggested Interpretation," *Econometrica*, Vol. 5 (April 1937), pp. 147–159.

Keynes, John M., *The General Theory of Employment, Interest, and Money* (New York: Harcourt, Brace, and World, 1964).

◆ ANSWERS TO END-OF-SECTION EXERCISES

Section 12.2 Extended Model of Income Determination

1. **a.** $dY = dG/[1 - C_{Yd}(1 - T')] + ((C_r + I')/[1 - C_{Yd}(1 - T')])\, dr$
   b. $dr/dY = [1 - C_{Yd}(1 - T')]/(C_r + I') < 0$

2. **a.** $Y = 1400 - 10{,}000r$; $dr/dY = -1/10{,}000$; **b.** $Y^* = 200$

Section 12.3 Money Market Equilibrium

1. **a.** $dY = ((m' - L_r)/L_Y)dr$; **b.** $dr/dY = L_Y/(m' - L_r) > 0$

2. **a.** $Y = 200 + 2000r$; $dr/dY = 1/2000$; **b.** $r^* = 0.15$

Section 12.4.1 Output and Interest Rate Effects of Fiscal Policy

1. $dY/dG = 1/([1 - C_{Yd}(1 - T')] + (C_r + I')L_Y/L_r) > 0$
   $dr/dG = -(L_Y/L_r)/([1 - C_{Yd}(1 - T')] + (C_r + I')L_Y/L_r) > 0$

2. a. $dY/dG = 1/[1 - C_{Yd}(1 - T')]$; $dr/dG = -(L_Y/L_r)/[1 - C_{Yd}(1 - T')]$
   b. $dY/dG = 0$; $dr/dG = -(L_Y/L_r)/(I' + C_r)$
   c. $dY/dG = 1/[1 - C_{Yd}(1 - T')]$; $dr/dG = 0$

Section 12.4.2 Effects of Tax Policies

1. $dY/d\tau = -(C_{Yd} + I_{Yd})Y/([(1 - C_{Yd} + I_{Yd})(1 - \tau)] + (C_r + I_r)L_Y/L_r) < 0$
   $dr/d\tau = (L_Y/L_r)(C_{Yd} + I_{Yd})Y/([(1 - C_{Yd} + I_{Yd})(1 - \tau)] + (C_r + I_r)L_Y/L_r) < 0$

2. a. $dY/d\tau = -(C_{Yd} + I_{Yd})Y/[(1 - C_{Yd} + I_{Yd})(1 - \tau)]$
   $dr/d\tau = (L_Y/L_r)(C_{Yd} + I_{Yd})Y/[(1 - C_{Yd} + I_{Yd})(1 - \tau)]$
   b. $dY/d\tau = 0$
   $dr/d\tau = (C_{Yd} + I_{Yd})Y/C_r + I_r$
   c. $dY/d\tau = -(C_{Yd} + I_{Yd})Y/[(1 - C_{Yd} + I_{Yd})(1 - \tau)]$
   $dr/d\tau = 0$

Section 12.4.3 Effects of Monetary Policy

1. $dY/dM = (I'/(Pm' + L_r))/([1 - C_{Yd}(1 - T')] + I'L_Y)/(m' + L_r) > 0$
   $dr/dM = [1 - C_{Yd}(1 - T')]/[P(m' + L_r)[1 - C_{Yd}(1 - T')]$
   $+ (I'L_Y))/(m' + L_r)] < 0$

2. a. $dY/dM = 0$; $dr/dM = I'/(P[1 - C_{Yd}(1 - T')]m' + I'L_Y)$
   b. $dY/dM = I'/(Pm'[1 - C_{Yd}(1 - T')] + I'L_Y) > 0$; $dr/dM = 1/(Pm') < 0$
   c. $dY/dM = 0$; $dr/dM = 0$

Section 12.5 A Numerical Example of the IS-LM Model

1. $Y^* = 400$; $r^* = 0.10$

2. $C^* = 215$; $I^* = 60$; $T^* = 180$; $M^{d*}/P = 200$

3. $dY/dG = 0.42$; $dY/dr = -0.00021$

4. $dY/d\tau = -125$; $dr/d\tau = -0.0625$

5. $dY/dM = 0.83$; $dr/dM = -0.00008$

◆ SELF-HELP PROBLEMS

Answers to these problems are given at the end of the text.

1. Consider the following model of a hypothetical economy:

$$C = 120 + 0.8Y_d, \qquad T = 10 + 0.5Y, \qquad I = 200 - 300r, \qquad G = 138$$
$$M^d/P = 0.4Y - 200r, \qquad M^s/P = 250$$

   a. Find the equations for the IS and LM curves. Find the equilibrium level of real income, Y, and the rate of interest, r. Draw a graph of your solution.

   b. Suppose the government wants to increase its expenditures so as to increase the equilibrium level of income by 25. Find the required increase in G. Find the equilibrium rate of interest after this increase in G. Draw the graph showing these changes.

c. Suppose instead of increasing G, the government decides to increase income by 25 by giving a one-time tax rebate. Find the required rebate and the effect on the interest rate.

d. Suppose instead of fiscal policy, the Federal Reserve is asked to use monetary policy to increase real income by 25. Find the required increase in nominal money supply. Determine the effect on the rate of interest.

2. Repeat all parts of Exercise 1 using the following model:
$$C = 100 + 0.4Y_d, \qquad T = 250 + 0.5Y, \qquad I = 58, \quad G = 50$$
$$M^d/P = 0.3Y - 100r, \qquad M^s/P = 30$$

3. Repeat all parts of Exercise 1 using the following model:
$$C = 20 + 0.6Y_d, \qquad T = 50 + 0.5Y, \qquad I = 40 - 140r, \qquad G = 40$$
$$M^d/P = 0.4Y, \qquad M^s/P = 20$$

4. Consider the following model of a hypothetical economy:
$$C = 25 + 0.8Y_d, \qquad T = 100 + 0.25Y, \qquad I = 250 - 300r, \qquad G = 80$$
$$X = 110 - 0.1Y - 0.5e, \qquad e = 10 + 400r$$
$$M^d/P = 0.75Y - 375r, \qquad M^s/P = 450$$

where X is net exports (exports minus imports) and e is the exchange rate.

a. Find equilibrium levels of Y and r.

b. Starting from the equilibrium in part a, suppose government expenditures are increased by 50. Find the new equilibrium level of GNP and interest rate.

c. Find the crowding out of *private spending* caused by the increase in government expenditures in part b. How much of this is due to crowding out of domestic spending, i.e., the reduction in investment demand caused by increased interest rates? How much is due to crowding out of net exports?

◆ SUPPLEMENTAL PROBLEMS

In these problems you are asked to modify a certain aspect of the standard IS-LM model and use the modified model to analyze a particular issue. This requires that you conduct comparative statics analysis of the issue under study using the standard and modified models. This should involve deriving the relevant multiplier(s), drawing pictures of your solution, and providing concise explanations of your findings. For your convenience the equations of the standard IS-LM model are reproduced below,

$$C = C(Y_d), \qquad 0 < \frac{dC}{dY_d} \equiv C' < 1 \tag{E1}$$

$$Y_d = Y - T \tag{E2}$$

$$T = T(Y), \qquad 0 < \frac{dT}{dY} \equiv T' < 1 \tag{E3}$$

$$I = I(r), \qquad I' < 0 \tag{E4}$$

$$Y = C + I + G \tag{E5}$$

$$\frac{M^d}{P} = L(r, Y), \qquad L_r < 0, L_Y > 0 \tag{E6}$$

$$\frac{M^d}{P} = \frac{M^s}{P} \tag{E7}$$

where government expenditures, G, nominal money supply, M^s, and the general price level, P, are assumed to be exogenous.

1. The tax function given by equation (E3) represents income taxes. Suppose in addition to income taxes, households and firms also pay lump-sum taxes which are independent of income. A tax function incorporating both types of taxes would be

$$T = T_0 + T(Y), \qquad 0 < T' < 1 \tag{E9}$$

   where T_0 represents lump-sum taxes. Replace equation (E3) with (E9) and use the resulting model to drive the following multipliers:

$$dY/dG, \qquad dY/dM^s, \qquad dY/dT_0$$

2. Consider investment demand function (E4). Modify this so that, in addition to the rate of interest, output is included as determinant of investment spending. Assume $\partial I/\partial Y > 0$.

   a. What are the implications of this for the existence of a unique, positive, solution of the modified model?

   b. What are the implications of this modification for the effectiveness of fiscal and monetary policies? That is, does this modification make the fiscal and/ or monetary policy multipliers greater or smaller?

3. Modify the consumption function, equation (E1), so that it contains only the rate of interest as a determinant. Does this modification make monetary policy more or less effective? What about fiscal policy?

4. Modify the tax function, equation (E3), by replacing income with consumption spending, equation (E1), as the tax base. What are the implications of this modification for fiscal policy? For monetary policy?

5. In the standard IS-LM model, the money demand function in equation (E7) is specified as a positive function of income and a negative function of interest rate. Recall from our earlier discussion that income enters money demand as a proxy for transactions demand for money. The justification is that, in order to satisfy their consumption spending, individuals hold part of their income in the form of money. But this suggests that the transactions demand for money depends on consumption expenditures or disposable income but not on pretax income.

   a. Following this line of argument, modify the money demand function in equation (E7) by replacing pretax income, Y, with the consumption function, equation (E1). What are the implications of this for tax policies?

   b. This time modify the money demand function in (E7) so that disposable income, equation (E2), is used to replace Y. What are the implications of this for tax policies?

   c. Finally, modify equation (E7) so that, in addition to before-tax income, taxes, equation (E3), are included as a separate scale variable. What are the implications of this for tax policies?

6. Modify the consumption function, equation (E1), so that in addition to disposable income, it also contains real wealth as defined below.

a. Define real wealth as real money supply. Does this modification make monetary policy more or less effective? What about fiscal policy?

b. There are two types of bonds, variable price, fixed coupon and fixed price, variable coupon. In the former case, the price of the bond is inversely related to the rate of interest, $(P_b = 1/r)$. In the latter case, the nominal price of the bond is fixed (i.e., it is independent of the rate of interest) and may be set equal to unity. Define real wealth as the real value of fixed price, variable coupon government bonds, (B_0/P), where B_0 is the quantity of government bonds and P is the general price level. Does this modification make bond-financed fiscal policy more or less effective? By bond-financed fiscal policy, we mean that the Treasury sells government bonds (B) to the public and uses the proceeds to finance its expenditures (G).

7. Determine, both mathematically and graphically, the effect on interest rate of fiscal expansion accompanied by an accommodating monetary policy (i.e., $dG = dM^s$). Explain your finding.

8. The standard model pertains to a closed economy. Incorporate the foreign sector into this model by using the following specification of net exports (exports minus imports):

$$X = X(Y, e), \qquad \frac{\partial X}{\partial Y} < 0, \frac{\partial X}{\partial e} < 0 \qquad \text{(E10)}$$

where e denotes the change rate, which is assumed to be fully flexible and given by

$$e = e(r), \qquad e' > 0 \qquad \text{(E11)}$$

The rest of the model is unchanged.

a. In terms of size of the multiplier for output, does this modification make fiscal policy more or less effective? How about monetary policy?

b. Determine the effect of an increase in money supply and government spending on net exports, X.

C H A P T E R   1 3

Linear Modeling: Input–Output Analysis and Linear Programming

13.1

INTRODUCTION

This text focuses on mathematical techniques that are especially useful for neoclassical economic modeling: differential calculus and matrix algebra. These techniques are applied to models of consumer behavior in Chapter 9, producer behavior in Chapters 10 and 11, and aggregate, macroeconomic behavior in Chapter 12. A special focus is on performing comparative statics analysis at the margin, because we examine marginal responses to marginal changes in conditions. The models we have examined require little specific information about exact functional forms except that they are smooth and continuous, i.e., differentiable. This chapter, however, examines two modeling techniques in which specifically linear functional forms are used. It presents two useful applications of the techniques of matrix algebra that were covered in Chapter 8: *input–output analysis* and *linear programming*.

Both of these applications require that we know more about specific functional forms than we typically do. Input–output analysis requires that we assume linear, or fixed-coefficient, production functions for all products in the system; linear programming requires that both the objective function and the constraints are linear functions. Both applications illustrate the disadvantage and advantage of making specific assumptions regarding functional forms. The disadvantage is that the models are less generally applicable than models that make less specific assumptions. We cannot use input–output analysis or linear programming to examine situations in which we are not comfortable assuming linear functional forms. The advantage is that the models can be much more detailed and provide information about much more behavior than

input–output analysis: a description of the allocation of resources in a multisectoral economic system.

linear programming: a mathematical technique for optimizing linear objective functions, subject to linear constraints.

models that do not make specific assumptions regarding functional forms. When used appropriately, both input–output analysis and linear programming are powerful tools of applied economic analysis. We turn now to input–output analysis, pioneered by the 1973 Nobel laureate Wassily Leontief.

13.2

INPUT–OUTPUT ANALYSIS

Input–output analysis is a way of describing the allocation of resources in a multisectoral economy. It focuses attention on the flows of outputs and inputs among the various sectors of the system. It is frequently used as an aid in regional or national economic planning, because it is capable of revealing the impacts of decisions or shocks in all sectors, fully accounting for their interrelated and balanced nature.

transactions table: a description of the intersectoral flows of an input–output model in tabular form.

The *transactions table* describes intersectoral flows in tabular form. Suppose an economic system or region has a total of n production sectors. The output of a given sector is used by intermediate demanders (the production sectors use each other's output in their production activities) and by final demanders (typically households, the government, and other regions or nations that trade with the given system). We present a transactions table of such an economy in Table 13.1. In this table, X_i is the gross output of the ith sector, X_{ij} represents the amount of the ith sector's output used by the jth sector to produce its output, and Y_i is the final demanders' use of the ith sector's output. The use of primary inputs such as labor, L, and land, T, is described in the bottom two rows of the table. In those rows L_i represents the use of labor in the production of the ith product, Y_L is the use of labor by final demanders, T_i is the use of land in the production of other goods, and Y_T is the final demand for land.

Table 13.1 Transactions Table

Output	Input X_1	X_2	$\cdots$	X_i	$\cdots$	X_n	Y
X_1	X_{11}	X_{12}	$\cdots$	X_{1i}	$\cdots$	X_{1n}	Y_1
X_2	X_{21}	X_{22}	$\cdots$	X_{2i}	$\cdots$	X_{2n}	Y_2
$\cdots$	$\cdots$	$\cdots$	I	$\cdots$	$\cdots$	$\cdots$	II
X_i	X_{i1}	X_{i2}	$\cdots$	X_{ii}	$\cdots$	X_{in}	Y_i
$\vdots$	$\vdots$	$\vdots$	$\vdots$	$\vdots$	$\vdots$	$\vdots$	$\vdots$
X_n	X_{n1}	X_{n2}	$\cdots$	X_{ni}	$\cdots$	X_{nn}	Y_n
L	L_1	L_2	$\cdots$	L_i	$\cdots$	L_n	Y_L
T	T_1	T_2	III	T_i	$\cdots$	T_n	Y_T

↑
IV

The rows of the table describe the deliveries of the total amount of a product or primary input to all uses, both intermediate and final. For example, suppose sector 1 represents steel. Then the first row tells us that, out of a gross output of X_1 tons of steel, an amount X_{11} is used in the production of steel itself, an amount X_{12} must be delivered to sector 2, X_{1i} tons are delivered to sector i, X_{1n} to sector n, and Y_1 tons are consumed by final end users of steel.

The columns of the table describe the input requirements to produce the gross output totals. Thus, producing the X_1 tons of steel requires X_{11} tons of steel, along with X_{21} units of output from sector 2 (coal, perhaps), X_{i1} from sector i, X_{n1} from sector n, L_1 hours of labor, and T_1 acres of land. An entry of 0 in one of the cells of the table indicates that none of the product represented by the row is required by the product represented by the column, so none is delivered.

The table is divided into four quadrants. Quadrant I describes all the intermediate flows among sectors required to maintain production. The focus of this quadrant is the interdependent nature of production; each sector's production depends on the production of the other sectors. Quadrant II describes the final consumption of produced goods and services in the economy. Quadrant III describes the employment of factors of production by producers, and quadrant IV describes the employment of production factors by the end users themselves. An example of the latter is the use of land for recreational purposes or the employment of a domestic servant.

In order to appreciate the interdependent nature of production, imagine that we are policy makers and we want to increase the amount of steel available for export. This requires an increase in Y_1, which necessitates either that we increase the gross output of steel, X_1, or that we decrease deliveries of steel to intermediate users, X_{1i}. Either option requires adjustments in the other production sectors that are interdependent with steel. To increase the output of steel, all the sectors that deliver to steel must increase their deliveries. If we choose to decrease the steel sector's intermediate deliveries, then each of its intermediate users will have to decrease output. In either case, consequences occur that reverberate through the system. Changes by the sectors that are interdependent with steel will set off another wave of effects, to which another round of adjustments must be made. We need a technique for balancing the outputs and inputs in the interrelated production sectors. Matrix algebra provides such a technique.

The transactions table can be described mathematically as a set of equations that must be satisfied simultaneously for the gross output of each sector to balance the intermediate and final demand for its product. We can describe the allocation of the output of the ith sector by

$$X_i = X_{i1} + X_{i2} + X_{i3} + \cdots + X_{ij} + \cdots + X_{in} + Y_i \qquad \textbf{(13-1)}$$

If you permit each term in equation (13-1) to represent a cell in the transactions table, then the equation represents row i of the table. There are n equations similar to equation (13-1), one for each production sector in the economic system and, therefore, one equation for each row in quadrants I and II of the table.[1]

Consider the variable that represents intermediate use, X_{ij}. The jth sector produces some gross output, X_j, itself. It uses many intermediate inputs to produce that output, including what it requires from the ith sector, X_{ij}. Let's define a new number, $a_{ij} \equiv X_{ij}/X_j$. This new number, called a *direct technical coefficient*, can be interpreted as the amount of input i used per unit output of product j. If we assume a linear production function, we assume that the direct technical coefficient is a fixed input requirement for every unit of output by sector j. By definition, we can say

direct technical coefficient: the amount of an input used per unit output of product.

$$X_{ij} \equiv a_{ij}X_j \qquad (13\text{-}2)$$

Substituting (13-2) into (13-1) gives us

$$X_i = a_{i1}X_1 + a_{i2}X_2 + a_{i3}X_3 + \cdots + a_{ij}X_j + \cdots + a_{in}X_n + Y_i = \sum_{j=1}^{n} a_{ij}X_j + Y_i \qquad (13\text{-}3)$$

Equation (13-3) balances the supply of the ith sector with the demands for product i. A similar equation can be written for each of the n production sectors of the economy.

$$X_1 = a_{11}X_1 + a_{12}X_2 + a_{13}X_3 + \cdots + a_{1j}X_j + \cdots + a_{1n}X_n + Y_1 = \sum_{j=1}^{n} a_{1j}X_j + Y_1$$

$$X_2 = a_{21}X_1 + a_{22}X_2 + a_{23}X_3 + \cdots + a_{2j}X_j + \cdots + a_{2n}X_n + Y_2 = \sum_{j=1}^{n} a_{2j}X_j + Y_2$$

$$\vdots \qquad \vdots \qquad \vdots \qquad \vdots \qquad \vdots \qquad \vdots \qquad \vdots \qquad \vdots$$

$$X_i = a_{i1}X_1 + a_{i2}X_2 + a_{i3}X_3 + \cdots + a_{ij}X_j + \cdots + a_{in}X_n + Y_i = \sum_{j=1}^{n} a_{ij}X_j + Y_i$$

$$\vdots \qquad \vdots \qquad \vdots \qquad \vdots \qquad \vdots \qquad \vdots \qquad \vdots \qquad \vdots$$

$$X_n = a_{n1}X_1 + a_{n2}X_2 + a_{n3}X_3 + \cdots + a_{nj}X_j + \cdots + a_{nn}X_n + Y_n = \sum_{j=1}^{n} a_{nj}X_n + Y_n \qquad (13\text{-}4)$$

---

[1]Note that we do not incorporate quadrants III and IV in our system of equations. If we were to include them in a manner consistent with our treatment of the production sectors, we would have to treat them as outputs, "produced" by the consumption of final goods and services. Doing so would "close" the system, making one row or column a linear combination of the other rows or columns. In that situation, we could not find a unique, nontrivial solution for our system of equations. For our input–output model to be usable, we focus only on the production interdependences and final demand segments of the transactions table and let the policy makers worry about whether the system is sufficiently endowed with primary inputs to make production feasible.

You should be able to recognize this as a system of n linear equations in n unknowns. It can be represented in matrix form as

$$
\begin{bmatrix} X_1 \\ X_2 \\ \vdots \\ X_n \end{bmatrix} = \begin{bmatrix} a_{11} & a_{12} & a_{13} & \cdots & a_{1n} \\ a_{21} & a_{22} & a_{23} & \cdots & a_{2n} \\ \vdots & \vdots & \vdots & \vdots & \vdots \\ a_{n1} & a_{n2} & a_{n3} & \cdots & a_{nn} \end{bmatrix} \begin{bmatrix} X_1 \\ X_2 \\ \vdots \\ X_n \end{bmatrix} + \begin{bmatrix} Y_1 \\ Y_2 \\ \vdots \\ Y_n \end{bmatrix} \qquad (13\text{-}5)
$$

$$
(n \times 1) \qquad\qquad (n \times n) \qquad\qquad (n \times 1) \quad (n \times 1)
$$

It can be written more simply as

$$
X = AX + Y \qquad (13\text{-}6)
$$

where X is the column vector of gross outputs, A is the square matrix of direct technical coefficients, and Y is the column vector of final demand. As you can see, the matrices in equation (13-5) are conformable for multiplication and addition.

We can solve equation (13-6) for the vector of final demand, Y, by subtracting AX from both sides. We obtain

$$
X - AX = [I_n - A]X = Y \qquad (13\text{-}7)
$$

where I_n is the identity matrix of order n. If the vector of gross outputs is known, then (13-7) can be used to solve for the quantities of each product that will be available for final consumption. Alternatively, we can solve equation (13-6) for the vector of gross outputs, X, by premultiplying both sides by $[I_n - A]^{-1}$ (assuming that $I_n - A$ is nonsingular, so that the inverse exists). Doing so gives us

$$
X = [I_n - A]^{-1}Y \qquad (13\text{-}8)
$$

If the vector of final demand targets is known, (13-8) can be used to solve for the vector of gross outputs necessary to achieve those targets.

The matrix $[I_n - A]^{-1}$ solves the balancing problem faced by policy-makers wishing to increase the exports of steel. They have only to specify the final demand targets they wish to achieve, and equation (13-8) solves for the gross outputs of all sectors, fully accounting for the interdependences among the production sectors. For this reason, $[I_n - A]^{-1}$ is called the matrix of *full coefficients*, which takes into account the direct and indirect technical requirements.

full coefficients: coefficients that take into account the direct and indirect technical requirements in an input–output system.

The input–output model makes economic sense only if all of the elements in the vector of gross outputs, X, are greater than zero and if all of the elements in the vector of final demand, Y, are greater than or equal to zero, with at least one element strictly positive. After all, if the gross output of a sector were equal to or less than zero, it would not be a producing sector at all. If some element of Y were negative, the system would not be self-sustaining; it would require injections to the sector in question from outside. If all the elements in Y were equal to zero, then, according to equation (13-8), all the elements in

Hawkins–Simon condition: condition that ensures strictly positive values for gross output and nonnegative values for final consumption in an input–output model.

X would also be zero. We can be assured that $X_i > 0$ and $Y_i \geq 0$, $i = 1, 2, \ldots, n$, and that at least one element of Y is greater than zero, if all of the principal minors of the matrix $[I_n - A]$, including the determinant of the matrix itself, are strictly greater than zero. This condition is known as the *Hawkins–Simon condition*, after the economists who first demonstrated it.

13.3

NUMERICAL EXAMPLE OF INPUT–OUTPUT ANALYSIS[2]

Suppose we are responsible for economic planning for an economic region with four production sectors: steel, coal, electricity, and agriculture. We have two primary inputs, labor and land. We keep an updated transactions table, which is shown in Table 13.2. In this table, the first column represents the vector of gross outputs for the four production sectors and the total amount of labor and land used as the primary inputs. We find the elements in the first column by summing up the other entries in each row, the intermediate use and the final demand. Reading the row for the coal sector, for example, tells us that coal delivers 5 units of output to the steel sector, 4 units to electricity, and 3 units to agriculture. Coal consumes 1 unit in its own production process and 2 more units are consumed by final demanders, for a total of 15 units of total output. Reading the column for the coal sector tells us that, in order to produce the 15 units of gross output, the sector needs 2 units of inputs from steel, 1 unit from coal, 3 units from electricity, nothing from agriculture, 5 units of labor, and 3 units of land. Note that the output of the agricultural sector is not used as an input by steel, coal, or electricity, but it is used as an input in its own production.

Table 13.2 Numerical Example of Transactions Table

Gross Output	Sector	Steel	Coal	Elec.	Agric.	Final Demand
11	Steel	2	2	3	3	1
15	Coal	5	1	4	3	2
14	Elec.	4	3	2	1	4
7	Agric.	0	0	0	2	5
15	Labor	5	5	2	2	1
13	Land	1	3	2	5	2

---

[2]Most spreadsheet software programs available commercially for a personal computer can do matrix computations, including matrix inversion, very easily. You might want to follow this numerical example using a computer spreadsheet.

Working with quadrants I and II, the rows corresponding to the four production sectors, which are shaded in Table 13.2, we find the matrix of direct technical coefficients by dividing each column entry by the gross output of the product represented by the column. Therefore, we divide the steel column by 11, the coal column by 15, the electricity column by 14, and the agriculture column by 7. We find that A, the matrix of direct technical coefficients, equals

$$A = \begin{bmatrix} 0.1818 & 0.1333 & 0.2143 & 0.4286 \\ 0.4545 & 0.0667 & 0.2857 & 0.4286 \\ 0.3636 & 0.2000 & 0.1429 & 0.1429 \\ 0 & 0 & 0 & 0.2857 \end{bmatrix} \tag{13-9}$$

We can express the first four rows (quadrants I and II) of the transactions table as

$$\begin{bmatrix} 11 \\ 15 \\ 14 \\ 7 \end{bmatrix} = \begin{bmatrix} 0.1818 & 0.1333 & 0.2143 & 0.4286 \\ 0.4545 & 0.0667 & 0.2857 & 0.4286 \\ 0.3636 & 0.2000 & 0.1429 & 0.1429 \\ 0 & 0 & 0 & 0.2857 \end{bmatrix} \begin{bmatrix} 11 \\ 15 \\ 14 \\ 7 \end{bmatrix} + \begin{bmatrix} 1 \\ 2 \\ 4 \\ 5 \end{bmatrix} \tag{13-10}$$

$$X \quad = \qquad\qquad\qquad A \qquad\qquad\qquad\qquad X \quad + \quad Y$$

In order to solve this equation for Y, as in equation (13-7), we need to subtract A from the fourth-order identity matrix I_4.

$$I_4 - A = \begin{bmatrix} 1 & 0 & 0 & 0 \\ 0 & 1 & 0 & 0 \\ 0 & 0 & 1 & 0 \\ 0 & 0 & 0 & 1 \end{bmatrix} - \begin{bmatrix} 0.1818 & 0.1333 & 0.2143 & 0.4286 \\ 0.4545 & 0.0667 & 0.2857 & 0.4286 \\ 0.3636 & 0.2000 & 0.1429 & 0.1429 \\ 0 & 0 & 0 & 0.2857 \end{bmatrix} \tag{13-11}$$

which equals

$$I_4 - A = \begin{bmatrix} 0.8181 & -0.1333 & -0.2143 & -0.4286 \\ -0.4545 & 0.9333 & -0.2857 & -0.4286 \\ -0.3636 & -0.2000 & 0.8571 & -0.1429 \\ 0 & 0 & 0 & 0.7143 \end{bmatrix} \tag{13-12}$$

We evaluate the naturally ordered principal minors of $|I_4 - A|$ in order to determine whether the Hawkins–Simon condition is met.[3]

$$\begin{vmatrix} 0.8181 & -0.1333 & -0.2143 & -0.4286 \\ -0.4545 & 0.9333 & -0.2857 & -0.4286 \\ -0.3636 & -0.2000 & 0.8571 & -0.1429 \\ 0 & 0 & 0 & 0.7143 \end{vmatrix} = 0.321 > 0$$

$$\begin{vmatrix} 0.8181 & -0.1333 & -0.2143 \\ -0.4545 & 0.9333 & -0.2857 \\ -0.3636 & -0.2000 & 0.8571 \end{vmatrix} = 0.450 > 0$$

$$\begin{vmatrix} 0.8181 & -0.1333 \\ -0.4545 & 0.9333 \end{vmatrix} = 0.703 > 0, \quad |0.8181| = 0.818 > 0 \quad (13\text{-}13)$$

From (13-13) we see that the Hawkins–Simon condition is met, because the principal minors of $|I_4 - A|$ are all positive. Thus, we expect the elements of the final demand vector to be nonnegative with at least one element strictly positive. The vector of final demand, Y, equals

$$Y = [I_4 - A]X$$

$$= \begin{bmatrix} 0.8181 & -0.1333 & -0.2143 & -0.4286 \\ -0.4545 & 0.9333 & -0.2857 & -0.4286 \\ -0.3636 & -0.2000 & 0.8571 & -0.1429 \\ 0 & 0 & 0 & 0.7143 \end{bmatrix} \begin{bmatrix} 11 \\ 15 \\ 14 \\ 7 \end{bmatrix}$$

$$= \begin{bmatrix} 1 \\ 2 \\ 4 \\ 5 \end{bmatrix} \quad (13\text{-}14)$$

You should carry out the matrix multiplication on the right-hand side of this equation to verify that it is correct.[4]

In order to solve this equation for X, as in equation (13-8), we must find

---

[3] Recall from Chapter 8 that all of the principal minors of dimension k have the same sign as a naturally ordered principal minor of dimension k.

[4] Do not be concerned by small rounding errors.

the multiplicative inverse of $[I_4 - A]$. You might want to review matrix inversion, in Chapter 8, Section 8.6.1, to check the following result.

$$[I_4 - A]^{-1} = \begin{bmatrix} 1.6516 & 0.3494 & 0.5294 & 1.3064 \\ 1.0972 & 1.3859 & 0.7363 & 1.6372 \\ 0.9567 & 0.4716 & 1.5630 & 1.1696 \\ 0 & 0 & 0 & 1.4000 \end{bmatrix} \qquad (13\text{-}15)$$

Therefore, the vector of gross output, X, equals

$$X = [I_4 - A]^{-1}Y = \begin{bmatrix} 1.6516 & 0.3494 & 0.5294 & 1.3064 \\ 1.0972 & 1.3859 & 0.7363 & 1.6372 \\ 0.9567 & 0.4716 & 1.5630 & 1.1696 \\ 0 & 0 & 0 & 1.4000 \end{bmatrix} \begin{bmatrix} 1 \\ 2 \\ 4 \\ 5 \end{bmatrix}$$

$$= \begin{bmatrix} 11 \\ 15 \\ 14 \\ 7 \end{bmatrix} \qquad (13\text{-}16)$$

Again, you should verify the accuracy of this result by carrying out the matrix multiplication.

All that we have accomplished so far, in equations (13-14) and (13-16), is to illustrate that the system is balanced. That is, the gross output of each sector does satisfy the intermediate and final demands. How can we use this input–output model to help us to do our economic planning? Suppose that we want to increase steel exports by 2 units. Doing so would increase the steel entry in the final demand vector from 1 to 3. We can use equation (13-16) to determine the full effects of the change on the gross output of every sector. We simply premultiply the new vector of final demand, $\hat{Y}$, by $[I_4 - A]^{-1}$ to find the new vector of gross outputs, $\hat{X}$. Therefore, we find

$$\hat{X} = [I_4 - A]^{-1}\hat{Y} = \begin{bmatrix} 1.6516 & 0.3494 & 0.5294 & 1.3064 \\ 1.0972 & 1.3859 & 0.7363 & 1.6372 \\ 0.9567 & 0.4716 & 1.5630 & 1.1696 \\ 0 & 0 & 0 & 1.4000 \end{bmatrix} \begin{bmatrix} 3 \\ 2 \\ 4 \\ 5 \end{bmatrix}$$

$$= \begin{bmatrix} 14.303 \\ 17.194 \\ 15.913 \\ 7 \end{bmatrix} \qquad (13\text{-}17)$$

We see that, in order to increase the exports of steel by 2 units while maintaining all other amounts available for final demand, we must increase the gross output of steel from 11 to 14.303, of coal from 15 to 17.194, and of electricity from 14 to 15.913. No increase is required in the gross output of agriculture. This is not surprising because agricultural products do not serve as inputs to any of the other production sectors, so when their output rises to accommodate an increase in the final demand for steel, agriculture is unaffected.

In order to see the new intersectoral flows required by the new final demand vector, we must reconstruct the transactions table using the new gross output amounts. Recall that we found the matrix of direct technical coefficients, A, by dividing the entries of each column of quadrant I of the transactions table by the gross output of the product represented by the column. We can find quadrants I and II of the transactions table for the new final demand vector by multiplying each column of A by the new gross output of the product represented by the column. Therefore, we multiply the elements of the first column of A by 14.303 to obtain the entries in the steel column of the new transactions table; we multiply the elements of the second column of A by 17.194 to generate the entries in the coal column, and so on. This procedure gives us new entries for quadrants I and II of the transactions table, which we reproduce in Table 13.3.

Is our economic system capable of raising its output levels to the amounts necessary to export 2 additional units of steel? The preceding analysis shows us how to balance gross output with intermediate and final demands, but it does not tell us whether the increased output levels are feasible. To determine the feasibility of the change, we must know whether we have sufficient primary inputs to sustain the higher gross output amounts. Consider the bottom two rows, quadrants III and IV, of the transactions table in Table 13.2. We can find direct technical coefficients for labor and land by dividing the column entries by the gross output of the product represented by the column. Let's call the resulting 2×4 matrix of direct technical coefficients for the primary inputs $A^{\#}$.

$$A^{\#} = \begin{bmatrix} 0.4545 & 0.3333 & 0.1429 & 0.2857 \\ 0.0909 & 0.2000 & 0.1429 & 0.7143 \end{bmatrix} \tag{13-18}$$

We can construct the bottom two rows of the new transactions table by multiplying the columns of $A^{\#}$ by the corresponding gross output amounts.

Table 13.3 Intersectoral Transactions Necessary to Achieve Revised Final Demand

Gross Output	Sector	Steel	Coal	Elec.	Agric.	Final Demand
14.303	Steel	2.600	2.293	3.410	3	3
17.194	Coal	6.501	1.146	4.547	3	2
15.913	Elec.	5.201	3.439	2.273	1	4
7	Agric.	0	0	0	2	5

Table 13.4 Revised Transactions Table for New Final Demand Vector

Gross Output	Sector	Steel	Coal	Elec.	Agric.	Final Demand
14.303	Steel	2.600	2.293	3.410	3	3
17.194	Coal	6.501	1.146	4.547	3	2
15.913	Elec.	5.201	3.439	2.273	1	4
7	Agric.	0	0	0	2	5
17.506	Labor	6.501	5.731	2.273	2	1
14.012	Land	1.300	3.439	2.273	5	2

Doing so gives us a completely new transactions table, consistent with the new final demand vector $\hat{Y}$. We find the total amounts of labor and land necessary to produce the new output levels by summing the intermediate use and final demand entries of each row. The completely new transactions table is presented in Table 13.4.

If we are able to summon 17.506 units of labor and 14.012 units of land from our primary input suppliers, the new plan is feasible. The input–output analysis does not tell us how to obtain the greater supply of primary inputs. Unless we offer primary input suppliers a claim on the increased final demand, it may be impossible to increase the available primary inputs.

The tables and equations of input–output analysis represent nothing more than a description of a balance between gross output and total demand for all sectors of an economic system. They take into account intersectoral flows— the fact that sector *j* depends on the outputs of itself and the other sectors to produce its output. The balanced resource allocation that results from the input–output model does not represent an optimum, either in the sense that the final demand vector maximizes some individual or social utility function or in the sense that the outputs are produced at minimum cost. No objective function is optimized to arrive at the balance. Also, no mechanism is implied by the system of equations that brings about the balance. There are no prices that bring about an equilibrium between supply and demand, as there are in a market model. Because there is no equilibrating mechanism, we cannot consider this a *behavioral* model, in the sense that optimization and market models represent models of social behavior. Input–output models can only be considered as *descriptive* of balanced resource allocation.

We mention this distinction between descriptive and behavioral models because it affects the uses to which we can appropriately put input–output analysis. We cannot use it to predict the responses of economic agents to changes in conditions. Rather, we can use it to describe balanced outcomes under different assumptions about gross output, final demand, or production functions. Whether or not and how those outcomes are achieved are other questions, and ones that input–output analysis does not address. Our next topic, linear programming, does address optimization in the context of linear functional forms and so can be used to find equilibria of the sort needed in behavioral models.

Suppose you are in charge of economic planning for a region characterized by three production sectors; grain production, automobiles, and electrical power. Last year, the grain sector consumed 3 units of its gross output in its own production process and delivered 5 units to automobiles and 10 units to final consumers. The automobile sector delivered 4 units to grain, 2 units to electrical power, and 6 units to final consumers, and it used 2 units in its own production. Electrical power used 3 units of electricity in its own production, and it delivered 20 units to automobiles, 5 units to grain, and 8 units to final consumers. Your region has one primary input, labor, which supplied 15 units to grain, 10 units to automobiles, and 5 units to electrical power. In addition, 4 units of labor were employed by final consumers.

1. Set up the transactions table for this economic region.

2. Express quadrants I and II of your transactions table as a matrix equation, with a vector of gross output, X, a matrix of direct technical coefficients, A, and a vector of final demand, Y.

3. Solve your matrix equation for Y, and then solve it for X.

4. Describe the impact of a 3-unit decrease in the gross output of the grain sector on all sectors of your region. Construct the transactions table for the new situation.

5. Describe the impact of an increase in the final demand for automobiles of 2 units (assume the original transactions table from question 1 to begin with). Construct the transactions table for the new situation.

13.4

LINEAR PROGRAMMING

Linear programming (LP) describes the mathematics of constrained optimization in situations in which both the objective function and the constraints are linear functions. This is not the case with the constrained optimization models we have already examined in Chapters 7, 9, and 11. A common feature of those constrained optimization models and their applications is that either the objective or the constraint is not linear. For example, in the model of constrained utility maximization, the utility function, $U(X_1, X_2)$, that is to be maximized is nonlinear. If it were linear, then the second partial derivatives U_{11}, U_{22}, and U_{12} would all be equal to zero, and the indifference curves would be straight lines. The budget constraint, $M = P_1 X_1 + P_2 X_2$, on the other hand, is linear in both the choice variables and the parameters. Similarly, whereas the objective of the model of constrained cost minimization, $TC = wL + rK$, is linear, the constraint, $Q = f(L, K)$, is not. Linear programming models represent a class of constrained optimization models in which both the objective function and the constraints are linear. We introduce this type of model with two simple examples.

13.4.1   Output Choice Subject to Two Resource Constraints

A firm produces two products, X_1 and X_2, using inputs of labor, L, and capital, K. The firm's production function is linear, so the direct technical coefficients associated with labor and capital, denoted by $a_{Lj}^{\#}$ and $a_{Kj}^{\#}$, $j = 1, 2$, are fixed. Recall from our discussion of input–output models in Section 13.3 that these coefficients represent the input requirement per unit of output, that is, $a_{Lj}^{\#} \equiv L_j/X_j$ and $a_{Kj}^{\#} \equiv K_j/X_j$, where $j = 1, 2$ in this example.

Assume that the direct technical coefficients for labor and capital in the production of X_1 are $a_{L1}^{\#} = 12$ and $a_{K1}^{\#} = 6$, whereas for the production of X_2 these coefficients equal $a_{L2}^{\#} = 6$ and $a_{K2}^{\#} = 10$. Because $a_{Lj}^{\#} \equiv L_j/X_j$ and $a_{Kj}^{\#} \equiv K_j/X_j$, we can find capital-labor ratios for the two products by dividing $a_{Kj}^{\#}$ by $a_{Lj}^{\#}$. We find that the capital-labor ratio for product 1 equals $K_1/L_1 = a_{K1}^{\#}/a_{L1}^{\#} = 1/2$ and the capital-labor ratio for product 2 equals $K_2/L_2 = a_{K2}^{\#}/a_{L2}^{\#} = 5/3$. Because the production of good 2 uses capital relatively more intensively than does production of good 1, we consider good 2 to be more *capital intensive*. The production of good 1 uses labor relatively more intensively than does production of good 2, so we consider good 1 to be more *labor intensive*.

Given the firm's linear technology, the total labor requirement for the production of the two goods is $a_{L1}^{\#}X_1 + a_{L2}^{\#}X_2 = 12X_1 + 6X_2$. Likewise, the total amount of capital needed for the production of X_1 and X_2 equals $a_{K1}^{\#}X_1 + a_{K2}^{\#}X_2 = 6X_1 + 10X_2$. The firm has up to $L^0 = 78$ workers available to it and its stock of capital is $K^0 = 60$. In the current planning period, the firm cannot increase the quantities of these two inputs. This inability imposes the following resource constraints on the firm.

capital intensive: a property of production according to which a product uses relatively more capital per unit of another input than some other product requires.

labor intensive: a property of production according to which a product uses relatively more labor per unit of another input than some other product requires.

$$a_{L1}^{\#}X_1 + a_{L2}^{\#}X_2 \leq L^0 \tag{13-19}$$

$$a_{K1}^{\#}X_1 + a_{K2}^{\#}X_2 \leq K^0 \tag{13-20}$$

or

$$12X_1 + 6X_2 \leq 78 \tag{13-21}$$

$$6X_1 + 10X_2 \leq 60 \tag{13-22}$$

The left-hand side of each of these inequalities represents total input requirement and the right-hand side is total input availability. The inequalities state the feasibility requirement that there must be at least enough labor and capital available to produce amounts of the two products equal to X_1 and X_2.

Assume that the firm is a price-taker and sells its two products for \$10 and \$8, respectively. The firm's objective is to produce the rate of output of products 1 and 2 that maximizes total revenue, R, subject to the resource availability constraints it faces. Mathematically, we state the problem as

Maximize	$R(X_1, X_2) = 10X_1 + 8X_2$	**(13-23)**
Subject to:		
labor constraint	$12X_1 + 6X_2 \leq 78$	**(13-24)**
capital constraint	$6X_1 + 10X_2 \leq 60$	**(13-25)**
nonnegativity constraints	$X_1 \geq 0, X_2 \geq 0$	**(13-26)**

Note that the last constraint rules out negative amounts of the two products.

Notice the differences between this LP model and the typical classical constrained optimization model that we have solved using the Lagrange and substitution methods. First, as already noted, in the LP model both the objective function and the constraints are linear functions of the choice variables and parameters. In classical constrained optimization models either the objective function or the constraint(s) was nonlinear. Second, the constraints can hold with an equality sign or an inequality sign. In the classical constrained optimization models that we studied in earlier chapters all constraints are equality constraints. Finally, here the requirement that the choice variables must not be negative is made explicitly. Other than these, the nature of the present LP problem is essentially the same as that of the general framework we discussed in Chapter 7. In particular, for a pair of values of X_1 and X_2 to be optimum, it must satisfy the two input constraints and the nonnegativity constraints (i.e., it must be a feasible solution), and it must yield a value for the objective function that is no less than that generated by any other feasible solution.

How is such a model solved? Several approaches are available for this purpose. One of the most popular computational algorithms for solving LP problems is based on the *simplex* method. Much of the existing computer software for solving LP models utilizes this method. For LP problems that involve no more than three choice variables, such as the present example, the graphical method is usually used. In addition to its simplicity, the graphical approach has the advantage that it highlights the nature of the solution and how it varies with changes in the parameters of the model. We illustrate the graphical approach to solving LP models by solving the preceding numerical example.

The first step in the graphical approach is to find the *set of feasible solutions*. This is determined by finding the intersection of the constraints in the first quadrant of a graph in which X_1 and X_2 are measured along the axes. We specify the first quadrant because there X_1 and X_2 are necessarily greater than or equal to zero and the nonnegativity constraint is automatically satisfied. We illustrate the *feasible set* using our numerical example of a hypothetical firm in Figure 13.1. We temporarily treat the input constraints as equalities and plot the resulting straight lines in the first quadrant. Together with the axes, each of these lines defines a triangle, which we have labeled *ABO* and *CDO* for the labor and capital constraints, respectively.

The labor inequality constraint is satisfied everywhere within and on the boundaries of the triangle *ABO*. Similarly, the capital inequality constraint is satisfied inside and on the boundaries of the triangle *CDO*. In other words, each inequality constraint is represented by the points on and below the corresponding equality constraint; points above a given constraint are infeasible. The feasible set, where both input constraints are simultaneously satisfied, is the intersection of the triangles *ABO* and *CDO*, or the area *CZBO*.

Any pair of values of X_1 and X_2 that lies within the area *CZBO* or on its boundaries is a feasible solution, but not all such points maximize the objective function; a feasible point is only a candidate for being an optimum value. In order to determine the optimum solution, in addition to the set of feasible solutions, we need to take into account the objective function,

Figure 13.1

**Feasible Set with Labor
and Capital Constraints**

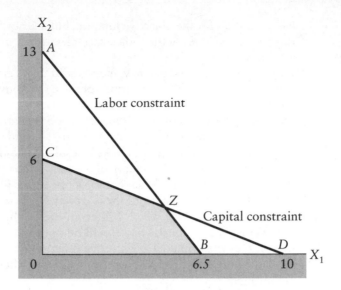

isorevenue line: graph of
the combinations of
products for which total
revenue to the firm is
constant.

$R = P_1X_1 + P_2X_2 = 10X_1 + 8X_2$. If we assign a fixed value to R, say R_0, we can express X_2 as a function of X_1, or $X_2 = R_0/P_2$ $(P_1/P_2)X_1$. You see that this is a straight line with a slope of $-P_1/P_2$ which is equal to $-5/4$ in this example. We can draw a family of such lines by varying the value of R so that lines representing higher total revenues would lie farther from the origin. These lines are similar to isocost lines and can be called *isorevenue lines*, lines along which total revenue is constant. Three isorevenue lines, R_1 through R_3, corresponding to total revenues of 54, 74, and 94, are drawn in Figure 13.2, in which we have also copied the feasible solutions set, $CZBO$, from the previous picture.

Looking at Figure 13.2, we observe that point Z satisfies the two conditions for optimality: it is a feasible solution, and no other feasible solution yields a value for the objective function greater than that which corresponds to isorevenue line R_2. Points on isorevenue line R_1 that lie in the feasible set represent feasible solutions but are associated with smaller values for the objective function. Points that belong to isorevenue line R_3 represent

Figure 13.2

**Feasible Set and
Isorevenue Lines**

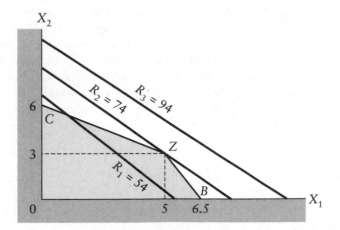

greater values for the objective function but are not feasible. We conclude that the optimum values of the choice variables are $X_1^* = 5$ and $X_2^* = 3$ generating a total revenue of 74.

You should notice a few facts about Figure 13.2 and the solution it represents. The optimum solution (point Z) will not be affected if we change the slope of the objective function (the price ratio) so that it rotates about point Z, without becoming steeper than ZB or flatter than CZ. For example, suppose the price of good 1 increases to 12, which makes the slope of the isorevenue lines equal to $-3/2$. As a result, while the isorevenue lines rotate clockwise, the optimal amounts of X_1 and X_2 remain the same, at point Z. What if P_1 increases to 16 so that the slope of the objective function becomes -2? In that case, the slope of the isorevenue line will coincide with the slope of the labor constraint. There will be multiple solutions, and all values of X_1 and X_2 between points Z and B will be optimum. Similarly, if P_1 is reduced to 6 so that the slope of the objective function is $-3/5$, which coincides with the slope of the capital constraint, then all values between points C and Z will be optimum.

interior solution: an optimum solution to a linear programming problem that includes only positive (nonzero) values of all choice variables.

corner solution: an optimal solution to a linear programming problem that includes zero values for some of the choice variables.

When optimum solutions include nonzero, positive values of the choice variables, we call the solution an *interior solution*. On the other hand, if the optimal solution includes zero values for some of the choice variables, they are referred to as *corner solutions*. For example, in the present case for price ratios less than $3/5$ the optimum solution will be at point C, where $X_1^* = 0$ and $X_2^* = 6$, with total revenue being 30. But if the price ratio is greater than 2 the solution will be at point B, where $X_2^* = 0$, $X_1^* = 6.5$, and total revenue is 65.

These experiments of shifting and rotating the objective function highlight an important feature of LP solutions. Optimal points are found, in general, on the boundary of the feasible set. A solution is unique if it occurs at one of the kinks or corners of this set; otherwise there are multiple solutions.

A final point concerning the solution of LP problems has to do with the sign of the constraints. In the preceding example both input constraints were specified as less-than-or-equal, $\leq$, relations. Obviously, this will not always be the case. In certain applications all of the constraints may be greater-than-or-equal, $\geq$, constraints, and in others a combination of less-than-or-equal, greater-than-or-equal, and equal constraints may be called for. When all constraints are less-than-or-equal, as in the preceding example, the set of feasible solutions will be bounded, which means that the solution values of the choice variables are finite. However, if the constraints are of the greater-than-or-equal form, the feasible solution set may be unbounded, which means that the solution values could be infinite. An unbounded feasible set coupled with maximization as the sense of optimization results in no finite solution. In order to obtain finite solutions in cases in which the set of feasible solutions is unbounded, the sense of optimization must be minimization. We illustrate a minimization problem using LP in Section 13.5. In the next section we extend the problem we have just analyzed by adding a third resource constraint.

13.4.2   Output Choice Subject to Three Resource Constraints

The preceding example was intentionally simple, involving only two choice variables and two constraints. Let us add a new constraint and see how the solution is affected. Consider the same firm as before, but assume that in addition to inputs of labor and capital, it uses materials, M, to produce its two products. Continue with the assumption of linear technology with fixed direct technical coefficients. Suppose that in the production of X_1 these coefficients equal $a^{\#}_{L1} = 12$, $a^{\#}_{K1} = 6$, and $a^{\#}_{M1} = 4$ for labor, capital, and materials, respectively. For the production of X_2 these coefficients are $a^{\#}_{L2} = 6$, $a^{\#}_{K2} = 10$, and $a^{\#}_{M2} = 1$. As before, the firm has a labor force of $L^0 = 78$ and a capital stock of $K^0 = 60$. It also has an inventory of $M^0 = 24$ units of materials. Assuming that the firm is unable to increase the quantities of these inputs in the current period, we have the following three resource constraints, which state the feasibility requirement that for each input use must not exceed availability:

labor constraint	$12X_1 + 6X_2 \le 78$	(13-27)
capital constraint	$6X_1 + 10X_2 \le 60$	(13-28)
materials constraint	$4X_1 + X_2 \le 24$	(13-29)

The firm's two products sell for 10 and 8 per unit, respectively. The objective is to choose the levels of output of goods 1 and 2 that maximize total revenue, $R = P_1X_1 + P_2X_2$, subject to the foregoing resource constraints as well as nonnegativity constraints on output levels. Note that the only difference between this example and that of Section 13.4.1 is the addition of the material constraint.

Recall that the first step in solving this problem using the graphical method is to determine the feasible solution set. To do this we must plot the input constraints assuming, momentarily, that they hold with equality signs. The intersection of the three constraints together with the X_1 and X_2 axes defines the feasible set. In Figure 13.3 this is shown by the shaded area $ABCDO$.

Based on our discussion in Section 13.4.1, we know that the optimum solution will have to be on the boundary of the feasible solution set.

Figure 13.3

Feasible Set with Three Constraints

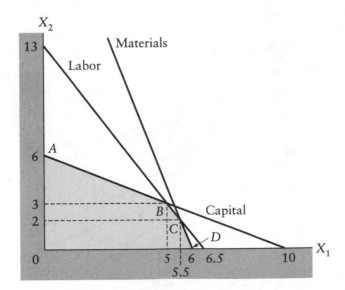

Moreover, if the solution is unique, it will be at one of the kinks or corners of the set, point A, B, C, or D. Exactly which of these is the solution depends on the slope of the isorevenue functions, i.e., the relative price ratio. With $P_1 = 10$ and $P_2 = 8$, the negative of the price ratio equals $-5/4$, and point B is the solution, where $X_1^* = 5$, $X_2^* = 3$, and $R^* = 74$. But this is the same solution as in the earlier example with only two input constraints. At point B capital and labor represent **binding constraints**, but the materials constraint is not binding, because point B lies inside the boundary of the materials constraint. However, if P_1/P_2 is changed to a level greater than 2, which is the negative of the slope of the labor constraint, but less than 4 (the negative of the slope of the materials constraint), then point C will be the optimum solution, where $X_1^* = 5.5$ and $X_2^* = 2$. In this situation the capital constraint is not binding. If $P_1/P_2 = 4$, there will be multiple solutions on the line segment CD, and if the price ratio increases above 4, there will be a corner solution at D where $X_1^* = 6$ and $X_2^* = 0$. We leave it to you to determine other optimal solutions that would result from other ranges of values for the price ratio. In the next section we demonstrate the effects on the optimal solution of changing one of the resource constraints in order to illustrate the comparative statics of LP problems.

binding constraint: an inequality constraint in an optimization problem which is just satisfied, i.e., satisfied as an equality constraint.

13.4.3   Linear Programming and Comparative Statics Analysis

We can use this example of revenue maximization with three input constraints to illustrate comparative statics analysis in linear programming models. In order to perform comparative statics analysis, we see how the optimal solution is affected by a change in a parameter or an exogenous variable. We have seen that, at the original output price ratio of $P_1/P_2 = 5/4$, the optimal solution is at $X_1^* = 5$, $X_2^* = 3$, and $R^* = 74$. Now suppose we relax one of the constraints by increasing the available quantity of capital to 74 units. This gives us a new capital constraint, parallel to the original but farther from the origin. The new feasible set is illustrated in Figure 13.4 as $A'B'CDO$. As you

Figure 13.3

Feasible Set with Three Constraints

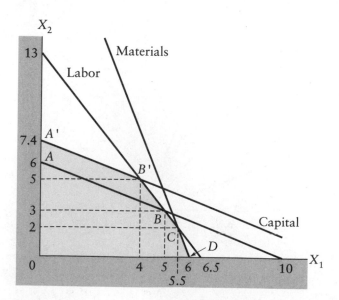

can see by the graph, the intersection of the labor constraint with the new capital constraint is at B'. At the price ratio of $P_1/P_2 = 5/4$ this is also the solution that maximizes revenue, so we can write the optimal solution as $X_1^{*\prime} = 4$, $X_2^{*\prime} = 5$, and $R^{*\prime} = 80$. The reason that the optimal solution is again at the intersection of the capital and labor constraints is that the slopes of the isorevenue curves as well as the constraints are unchanged by the increase in availability of capital.

We see that an increase in the available quantity of capital increases the output of X_2, the capital-intensive product, while it decreases the output of X_1, the labor-intensive product. This result has been generalized and is known as the *Rybczynski theorem*. It states that the effect of an increase in the endowment of some resource is to increase the output of the resource-intensive industry and to decrease the output of the industry that is intensive in the use of the other resource.[5] Recognize that an increase in the endowment of materials would have no effect on output or revenue in this problem. At the given price ratios and production functions, the materials constraint is nonbinding; the firm already has more materials than it can use.

Rybczynski theorem: a theorem describing the effect on output of an increase in the endowment of some resource.

**EXERCISES
Section 13.4.3
Linear Programming
and Comparative
Statics Analysis**

1. Maximize each of the following objective functions
   a. $3X_1 + X_2$ b. $2X_1 + X_2$ c. $1.5X_1 + X_2$
   d. $0.5X_1 + X_2$ e. $X_1 + X_2$

   subject to the constraints

   $$X_1 + X_2 \leq 10 \quad \text{and} \quad 4X_1 + 2X_2 = 32$$

2. A manufacturing firm produces two different products. The plant capacity constrains output of product 1 to a maximum of 50 units per production day and that of product 2 to 70 units per production day. It takes 4.8 minutes to manufacture a unit of product 1 and 8 minutes to produce a unit of product 2. A production day is 8 hours long. Profit per unit of each of the two products is $1. The firm's problem is to choose the rates of production of its two products so as to maximize profits subject to the feasibility constraints it faces.

   a. Set up an LP model for this firm's problem.

   b. Using the graphical method, find the optimum rates of production of the two products per day.

   c. Repeat part b assuming that the capacity constraint on the output of good 1 is 70 units per day.

   d. Repeat part b assuming that the capacity constraint on the output of good 1 is 70 units per day and that there are 10 hours in a production day.

---

[5]The Rybczynski theorem has been demonstrated not only for the case of linear production functions but also for all linearly homogeneous production functions.

13.5

THE GENERAL LINEAR PROGRAMMING PROBLEM

The preceding examples represent two particular applications of the general linear programming problem, which can be stated as a linear optimization model with n choice variables and m constraints. The problem is to optimize (either maximize or minimize) the objection function

$$c_1 X_1 + c_2 X_2 + \cdots + c_n X_n = \sum_{j=1}^{n} c_j X_j \qquad (13\text{-}30)$$

subject to the constraints

$$a_{11} X_1 + a_{12} X_2 + \cdots + a_{1n} X_n = \sum_{j=1}^{n} a_{1j} X_j \le b_1$$

$$a_{21} X_1 + a_{22} X_2 + \cdots + a_{2n} X_n = \sum_{j=1}^{n} a_{2j} X_j \le b_2 \qquad (13\text{-}31)$$

$$\vdots \qquad \vdots \qquad \qquad \vdots \qquad \vdots \qquad \vdots$$

$$a_{m1} X_1 + a_{m2} X_2 + \cdots + a_{mn} X_n = \sum_{j=1}^{n} a_{mj} X_j \le b_m$$

$$X_j \ge 0, \qquad j = 1, 2, \ldots, n \qquad (13\text{-}32)$$

Using matrix notation, the general LP problem can be written more compactly,

$$\text{Maximize (minimize)} \qquad cX \qquad (13\text{-}33)$$

$$\text{subject to:} \qquad AX \le b \qquad (13\text{-}34)$$

$$X \ge 0 \qquad (13\text{-}35)$$

where $c = (c_1, c_2, \ldots, c_n)$ is a $1 \times n$ row vector of constants, $X = (X_1, X_2, \ldots, X_n)$ is an $n \times 1$ column vector of choice variables, $b = (b_1, b_2, \ldots, b_m)$ is an $m \times 1$ column vector of constants, and

$$A = \begin{bmatrix} a_{11} & a_{12} & \cdots & a_{1n} \\ a_{21} & a_{22} & \cdots & a_{2n} \\ \vdots & \vdots & \vdots & \vdots \\ a_{m1} & a_{m2} & \cdots & a_{mn} \end{bmatrix} \qquad (13\text{-}36)$$

is an $m \times n$ matrix of coefficients. For ease of exposition we have expressed all of the constraints except the nonnegativity constraints on X as less-than-or-equal, $\le$, constraints. As mentioned earlier, in many applications some of these constraints may be greater-than-or-equal, $\ge$, constraints and others may hold with strict equality signs.

13.5.1   The Dual of an LP Model

In Chapter 9 we suggested that all primal constrained optimization models have dual counterparts. This is true for LP constrained optimization as well. Associated with every LP problem is a dual LP problem. The dual problem may provide both computational and analytical advantages. Computationally, sometimes it is easier to solve the dual problem than the primal. Analytically, by complementing the primal problem, the dual problem can provide valuable insight into the nature of the primal and thus add to the usefulness of linear programming.

In order to understand the relationship between a primal and its dual problem, consider the general LP problem as presented in the previous section in equations (13-33) through (13-35). As in Chapter 9, Section 9.6, we find the dual by reversing the sense of optimization as well as the roles of the constraints and the objective function. In this case, the corresponding dual problem is

$$\text{Minimize (maximize)} \quad b'Y \qquad \text{(13-37)}$$

$$\text{subject to:} \quad A'Y \geq c' \qquad \text{(13-38)}$$

$$Y \geq 0 \qquad \text{(13-39)}$$

where Y is a $1 \times m$ vector of choice variables, A' is the $n \times m$ transpose of the coefficient matrix of the primal problem, and b' and c' are the transposes of the corresponding vectors of constants from the primal problem.

Comparing the primal and dual shows the following relations between the two problems.

1. The sense of optimization is reversed in going from the primal problem to the dual; if the primal problem is a maximization problem, the dual will be a minimization problem and vice versa.
2. The sense of inequality in the constraints of the primal problem is opposite that in the dual; less-than-or-equal, $\leq$, constraints in the primal will correspond to greater-than-or-equal, $\geq$, constraints in the dual and vice versa.
3. If you transpose the vector of the coefficients of the objective function of the primal problem, you will have the vector of the right-hand side constants of the constraints of the dual problem.
4. The transpose of the vector of the right-hand side constants of the primal problem is the vector of the coefficients of the objective function of the dual problem.
5. In both the primal and dual problems the choice variables are subject to nonnegativity constraints.

We have discussed the relationship between the primal and dual problems but have not offered an interpretation for the choice variables of the dual problem. Each dual variable measures the change in the optimum value of the primal objective function brought about by relaxing the primal constraint associated with that dual variable. You might recognize this interpretation if you recall from Chapter 7, Section 7.2.3, the interpretation of the Lagrange multiplier of the general constrained optimization problem. Even though we do not use the Lagrangian technique to solve the primal LP problem, the solution to the dual problem provides us with the optimum value of the Lagrange multiplier. This is very important because, as you recall, in many economic applications the Lagrange multiplier has a very useful economic interpretation. In the following we see an example of this.

Suppose we want to find the dual of the primal problem in Section 13.4.2. Using the five rules governing the relationship between the primal and dual problems, we can specify the dual problem as

$$\text{Minimize} \quad 78Y_1 + 60Y_2 + 24Y_3 \qquad (13\text{-}40)$$

$$\text{subject to:} \quad 12Y_1 + 6Y_2 + 4Y_3 \geq 10 \qquad (13\text{-}41)$$

$$6Y_1 + 10Y_2 + Y_3 \geq 8 \qquad (13\text{-}42)$$

$$Y_1 \geq 0, \qquad Y_2 \geq 0, \qquad Y_3 \geq 0 \qquad (13\text{-}43)$$

According to our interpretation of the dual variables, Y_1, Y_2, and Y_3 represent the effect on revenue of relaxing the labor, capital, and materials constraints, respectively. That is, they measure the marginal valuation, in dollar units, of labor, capital, and materials, respectively. Therefore, $78Y_1$ is the total dollar value, or cost, of labor; $60Y_2$ is the cost of capital; and $24Y_3$ is the cost of materials to the firm. The dual problem asks the firm to minimize the total cost of inputs, subject to the constraints that the price of good 1 is less than or equal to the unit cost of producing it, that the price of good 2 is less than or equal to the unit cost of producing it, and that the marginal valuations of labor, capital, and materials are nonnegative. The constraints can be interpreted to mean that the value of output cannot exceed the value of the inputs used to produce it.

The solutions to the primal and dual problems are related to one another in several ways. For example, the value of the primal objective function evaluated at the optimum, cX^*, equals the value of the dual objective function at the optimum, $b'Y^*$, where X^* and Y^* are the primal and dual solutions, respectively. This means that the minimimum total cost of production, obtained from the dual problem, equals the maximum total revenue, obtained from the primal. Another relationship between the two sets of solution values is known as ***complementary slackness***. It states that, at the optimum, the product of each dual variable times the corresponding primal constraint, as well as the product of a primal variable times the corresponding dual constraint, equals zero, or

complementary slackness: the principle that, at the optimum, the product of each dual variable times the corresponding primal constraint equals zero.

$$(AX^* - b)Y^* = X^*(c' - A'Y^*) = 0 \qquad (13\text{-}44)$$

An interesting implication of the fact that $(AX^* - b)Y^* = 0$ is that, if a primal constraint is not binding (i.e., $AX^* - b \neq 0$), its corresponding dual variable will be zero. On the other hand, if the optimum value of a dual variable is not zero, it must be that the corresponding primal constraint is binding.

Let's use the graphical method to solve our numerical example of the dual problem. Figure 13.5 presents the solution with the optimum at point Q, where $Y_1^* = 0.62$ and $Y_2^* = 0.43$.

The principle of complementary slackness tells us that, because materials are a nonbinding constraint in the primal problem, $Y_3^* = 0$. This allows us to

Figure 13.5

Cost Minimization with
Two Binding
Constraints: the Dual to
Figure 13.3

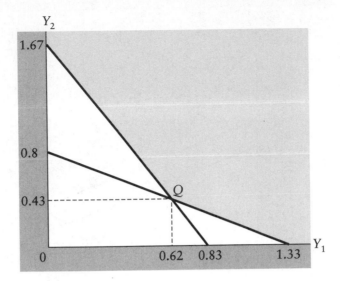

omit the Y_3 axis in Figure 13.5 and show the solution in only two dimensions. As expected, the solution is on the boundary of the feasible set at the intersection of the two constraints. Note that because the constraints on the sum of Y_1 and Y_2 are greater-than-or-equal constraints, the feasible set, the shaded area, is unbounded. However, the optimum values of Y_1 and Y_2 are finite because the optimization is a minimization.

What do these solution values measure? Remember that the dual variables can be interpreted as Lagrange multipliers; they represent the partial derivative of the primal objective function with respect to the right-hand side of the constraints of the primal problem. In the present example the primal objective function is total revenue or price times quantity and the first primal constraint is the labor input constraint. Thus $Y_1^* = 0.6$ measures the change in total revenue per unit change in labor input, holding output price and capital input constant. But this is the same as output price times marginal physical product or the value of the marginal product of labor. Similarly, $Y_2^* = 0.43$ reflects the value of the marginal product of capital. The fact that they are both positive means that both the capital and labor constraints are binding in the primal. The fact that $Y_3^* = 0$ means that there is no value to the firm of increasing a nonbinding resource constraint. Under competitive conditions in input markets these solution values would equal input prices.

13.5.2 Comparative Statics Analysis of the Dual LP Problem

When we performed comparative statics analysis of the primal problem, we relaxed the capital constraint and observed that the optimal quantity of the capital-intensive good increased, while the optimal quantity of the labor-intensive good decreased. In order to perform comparative statics analysis of the dual, we relax one of the price constraints. Suppose the price of good 2 increases to 10. Because the slope of neither the objective function nor the constraints has changed, Y_3^* is still equal to 0, and the optimal solution continues to be at the intersection of the two constraints in the $Y_1 - Y_2$ plane. The constraint associated with good 2 shifts out from the origin as shown in

Figure 13.6

An Increase in the Price of Good 2

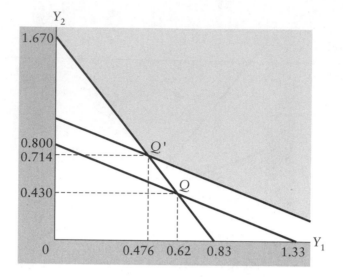

Figure 13.6, changing the intersection with the other constraint to Q'. The optimal value of Y_2^* increases to 0.714, while the optimal value of Y_1^* decreases to 0.476.

These results bear an interesting similarity to the comparative statics results we found for the primal. There, we illustrated the Rybczynski theorem, showing that an increase in a resource endowment increases the output of the resource-intensive product and decreases the output of the product that is intensive in the other resource. Here, we see that an increase in the price of a product, good 2, increases the value of the marginal product, Y_2, of the resource which that product uses more intensively, while it decreases the value of the marginal product, Y_1, of the other resource. This result illustrates the *Stolper–Samuelson theorem*. The Stolper–Samuelson theorem is the dual counterpart to the Rybczynski theorem.

Stolper–Samuelson theorem: a theorem describing the effects of an increase in the price of a product on the value of the marginal product of the resources.

EXERCISES
Section 13.5.2
Comparative Statics
Analysis of the Dual
LP Problem

A small country uses inputs of capital and labor to produce two goods for export to foreign countries. The production technologies are linear with fixed input requirement coefficients. To produce one unit of good 1 requires 1 unit of capital and 1 unit of labor. To produce one unit of good 2 requires 1 unit of capital and 2 units of labor. The export sector can summon up to 4 units of capital and 6 units of labor. The country is a price-taker in the world market for the two products, where the price of good 1 is $3 per units and that of good 2 is $4 per unit.

1. Set up the primal LP problem for maximizing this country's total revenue from exporting the two products subject to resource availability and nonnegativity constraints. Determine the factor intensities of the two goods produced in this country.

2. Use the graphical method to find the optimum quantities of goods 1 and 2.

3. Suppose the quantity of labor available to the export sector increases from 6 to 7. Show that the resulting optimum solution satisfies the Rybczynski theorem.

4. Set up the dual LP problem corresponding to the primal problem in part b. What is the economic interpretation of the dual variables?

5. Using the graphical method, solve the dual problem.

6. Show that the value of the primal objective function evaluated at its optimum equals the value of the dual objective function evaluated at its optimum. Explain this result.

7. Suppose the price of good 2 increases to $5 per unit. Find the new optimum values of the dual variables and use them to demonstrate the Stolper–Samuelson theorem. Also explain how this result is related to the Rybczynski theorem you illustrated in question 3.

13.6

LINEAR PROGRAMMING AND INPUT–OUTPUT ANALYSIS

When we introduced linear programming, we claimed that it differs from input–output analysis in the sense that it optimizes some objective function, whereas input–output models are strictly descriptive. In our numerical example of economic planning using input–output analysis, the planner could only check the feasibility of potential allocations of resources by looking at the availability of primary inputs. Linear programming is a technique that permits us to impose an objective function on an input–output system and impose primary input constraints to ensure feasibility.

Recall the input–output model of Section 13.2, represented by equation (13-6),

$$X = AX + Y \qquad (13\text{-}6)$$

where X is the $n \times 1$ column vector of gross sectoral outputs, A is the $n \times n$ matrix of direct technical coefficients, and Y is the $n \times 1$ column vector of final demand. Also recall the transactions table in Table 13.1 and note that quadrants III and IV represent employment of primary inputs. For simplicity, assume the only primary input is labor, L, which we assume is used in production but is not used by final demanders. Let us denote by $a^{\#}$ the $1 \times n$ vector of direct sectoral technical coefficients associated with labor. Then we have

$$L = a^{\#}X \qquad (13\text{-}45)$$

Denote total final demand (a weighted sum of the individual elements of final demand) by ψ and assume that sectoral final demands, Y_i, are proportional to total final demand, $Y_i = \beta_i \psi$. Suppose the "planner's" objective is to maximize total final demand subject to the feasibility requirements. The LP set up for this problem is

$$\text{Maximize} \quad \psi \tag{13-46}$$

$$\text{subject to:} \quad (A - I_n)X + \beta\psi \leq 0 \tag{13-47}$$

$$a^{\#}X \leq L^0 \tag{13-48}$$

Here the choice variables are X and ψ, the vector of the coefficients of the objective function is $c = (0, 1)$, and the vector of the right-hand side constants of the constraints is $b = (0, L^0)$. If we denote the dual variables by P_1 and P_2, we can state the dual to this problem

$$\text{Minimize} \quad 0(P_1) + L(P_2) = L(P_2) \tag{13-49}$$

$$\text{subject to:} \quad P_1(A - I_n) + P_2 L \geq 0 \tag{13-50}$$

$$P_1 \beta \geq 1 \tag{13-51}$$

Because the dual variables represent prices, the dual objective function is total factor cost. The left-hand side of (13-50) represents the negative of sectoral average profits. To see this, write out the first element of the vector representing this constraint

$$P_1(a_{11} - 1) + P_2 a_{21} + \cdots + P_n a_{n1} = P_1 a_{11} + P_2 a_{21} + \cdots + P_n a_{n1} - P_1$$

$$= AC_1 - AR_1 = -A\pi_1 \tag{13-52}$$

where π_1 is total profit of sector 1. The left-hand side of the second constraint measures cost of aggregate final demand.

Using the relationships between the primal and dual problems and their solutions, we can characterize the optimal plan as having the following properties:

1. $\psi^* = P_2^* L^0$; at the optimum, total expenditures on final goods equal total income of the primary factor.
2. The complementary slackness principle implies that if $X > 0$ then $P_1(A - I_n) + P_2 L^0 = 0$; sectors that produce a positive rate of output will earn zero profits, i.e., $P = AC$.
3. The complementary slackness principle also yields the result that if $P_1(A - I_n) > P_2 L^0$, then $X = 0$; in sectors where profits are negative (i.e., $P < AC$) nothing is produced.

13.7

SUMMARY

This chapter introduces two mathematical techniques for using linear functional forms in some economic applications. Input–output analysis enables us to describe in great detail all of the transactions, intermediate and final, that take place in an economic system composed of production sectors, primary inputs, and final demanders. It requires that all production functions be linear, with fixed input coefficients. We see that the input–output model enables us to determine gross outputs of all the production sectors, as well as all the intermediate, intersectoral transactions, if we know what final demand targets we wish to achieve. If we know what gross output levels we are capable of attaining, the input–output model enables us to determine what amounts of products are available for final demand. Although the input–output model does not explain how economic agents behave and has no choice mechanism built into it, it can be used to determine whether sufficient primary inputs exist to make a given plan feasible.

Linear programming provides a technique for incorporating a choice mechanism in a model with exclusively linear functional forms in the objective function as well as the constraints. It is a model that optimizes a function, and it can therefore be used to describe how economic agents choose among alternatives. When graphed, linear constraints describe a feasible set of alternatives which is kinked wherever two constraint functions are equal to one another. These kinks, along with the corners where the constraints intersect the axes, represent candidates for the best among the alternatives contained in the feasible set. Linear programming requires that we use the objective function to find the optimal solution or solutions among the kinks and corners defined by the constraints.

Any time an objective function is maximized subject to binding constraint functions, the resulting optimum could be described as a minimization of the constraint functions, subject to the objective function achieving some level. This feature of optimization models is duality, and we show that any linear programming problem can be described in terms of a primal problem and a dual, which reverses the sense of optimization and the roles of the objective function and the constraints. As we found in Chapter 9 when we examined the dual to constrained utility maximization, the principle of duality provides us with insights into the nature of optimization, as well as useful economic interpretations.

◆ REFERENCES

Dorfman, Robert, Samuelson, Paul A., and Solow, Robert M., *Linear Programming and Economic Analysis* (New York: McGraw-Hill Book Company, 1958).

Hawkins, David, and Simon, Herbert A., "Note: Some Conditions of Macroeconomic Stability," *Econometrica*, July–October 1949, pp. 245–248.

Leontief, Wassily, *Input–Output Economics*, 2nd edition (New York: Oxford University Press, 1986).

Rybczynski, T. M., "Factor Endowment and Relative Commodity Prices," *Economica*, November 1955, pp. 336–341.

Stolper, W. F., and Samuelson, P. A., "Protection and Real Wages," *Review of Economic Studies*, 1941, pp. 58–73.

◆ ANSWERS TO END-OF-SECTION EXERCISES

Section 13.3 Numerical Example of Input–Output Analysis

1.

Gross Output	Sector	Grain	Auto	Elec.	Final Demand
18	Grain	3	5	0	10
14	Auto.	4	2	2	6
36	Elec.	5	20	3	8
34	Labor	15	10	5	4

2.

$$X = AX + Y \Rightarrow \begin{bmatrix} 18 \\ 14 \\ 36 \end{bmatrix} = \begin{bmatrix} 0.167 & 0.357 & 0 \\ 0.222 & 0.143 & 0.056 \\ 0.278 & 1.429 & 0.083 \end{bmatrix} \begin{bmatrix} 18 \\ 14 \\ 36 \end{bmatrix} + \begin{bmatrix} 10 \\ 6 \\ 8 \end{bmatrix}$$

3.

$$Y = [I - A]X \Rightarrow \begin{bmatrix} 10 \\ 6 \\ 8 \end{bmatrix} = \begin{bmatrix} 0.833 & -0.357 & 0 \\ -0.222 & 0.857 & -0.056 \\ -0.278 & -1.429 & 0.917 \end{bmatrix} \begin{bmatrix} 18 \\ 14 \\ 36 \end{bmatrix}$$

$$X = [I - A]^{-1}Y \Rightarrow \begin{bmatrix} 18 \\ 14 \\ 36 \end{bmatrix} = \begin{bmatrix} 1.38 & 0.641 & 0.039 \\ 0.429 & 1.497 & 0.091 \\ 1.089 & 2.527 & 1.244 \end{bmatrix} \begin{bmatrix} 10 \\ 6 \\ 8 \end{bmatrix}$$

4.

Gross Output	Sector	Grain	Auto	Elec.	Final Demand
15	Grain	2.5	5	0	7.5
14	Auto.	3.3	2	2	6.7
36	Elec.	4.167	20	3	8.83
31.5	Labor	12.5	10	5	4

5.

Gross Output	Sector	Grain	Auto	Elec.	Final Demand
19.28	Grain	3.21	6.07	0	10
17	Auto.	4.29	2.43	2.28	8
41.05	Elec.	5.36	24.28	3.42	8
37.9	Labor	16.07	12.14	5.70	4

Section 13.4.3 Linear Programming and Comparative Statics Analysis

1. **a.** $X_1^* = 8$, $X_2^* = 0$

   b. Multiple solutions along the boundary of the feasible set below the kink (where $6 \leq X_1 \leq 8$ and $0 \leq X_2 \leq 4$)

   c. $X_1^* = 6$, $X_2^* = 4$

   d. Multiple solutions along the boundary of the feasible set above the kink (where $0 \leq X_1 \leq 6$ and $4 \leq X_2 \leq 10$).

   e. $X_1^* = 0$, $X_2^* = 10$

2. **a.** $X_1^* = 50$, $X_2^* = 30$, **b.** $X_1^* = 70$, $X_2^* = 18$,   **c.** $X_1^* = 70$, $X_2^* = 34$

Section 13.5.2 Comparative Statics Analysis of the Dual LP Problem

1. Maximize $3X_1 + 4X_2$ subject to $X_1 + X_2 \leq 4$; $X_1 + 2X_2 \leq 6$; $X_1 \geq 0$, $X_2 \geq 0$

   Product 1 is capital intensive relative to product 2, and product 2 is labor intensive relative to product 1.

2. $X_1^* = X_2^* = 2$

3. $X_1^{**} = 1$, $X_2^{**} = 3$

4. Minimize $4Y_1 + 6Y_2$ subject to $Y_1 + Y_2 \geq 3$; $Y_1 + 2Y_2 \leq 4$; $Y_1 \geq 0$, $Y_2 \geq 0$

5. $Y_1^* = 2$, $Y_2^* = 1$

6. $14 = 3(2) + 4(2) = 3X_1^* + 4X_2^* = 4Y_1^* + 6Y_2^* = 4(2) + 6(1) = 14$

7. The new solution values for the dual variables are $Y_1^{**} = 1$, $Y_2^{**} = 2$. Therefore, the value of the marginal product of labor increased and that of capital decreased following the increase in the price of the labor-intensive good. This is precisely what the Stolper–Samuelson theorem predicts.

◆ **SELF-HELP PROBLEMS**

Answers to these problems are given at the end of the text.

1. Maximize $1.5X + 4.25Y$ subject to $X + Y \leq 3$, $4X + Y \leq 6$, $3.5X + 2Y \leq 7$, $X \geq 0$, and $Y \geq 0$.

2. A dietician suggests that Jim should obtain a minimum of 60 units of vitamin C and 56 units of vitamin E per day by drinking enough orange juice, milk, or both. The dietician points out that a typical serving of orange juice contains 6 units of vitamin C and 1 unit of vitamin E. One serving of milk, on the other hand, contains 2 units of vitamin C and 8 units of vitamin E. Jim finds out that the price of orange juice is $1.50 per serving and the price of milk is $0.75 per serving.

   a. How many servings of orange juice, X_1, and milk, X_2, should Jim buy to minimize the cost of achieving his minimum daily vitamin requirements?

   b. Solve the dual problem associated with this LP problem and explain what the dual variables measure.

   c. Show that the value of the primal objective function, evaluated at the optimum, equals the value of the dual objective function at the optimum.

3. A firm manufactures two products, X_1 and X_2, using two different machines, M_1 and M_2. It takes 30 minutes of operation of M_1 and 20 minutes of M_2 to produce a unit of X_1. Similarly, each unit of X_2 requires 15 minutes of operation of M_1 and 30 minutes of M_2. The market price of X_1 is $200 per unit and that of X_2 is $240 per unit. The firm operates 40 hours a week and wants to produce that rate of output of X_1 and X_2 that maximizes total revenue.

   a. Determine the optimum quantities of X_1 and X_2.

   b. Solve the dual problem associated with this LP problem and explain what the dual variables measure.

   c. Show that the value of the primal objective function evaluated at the optimum equals the value of the dual objective function at the optimum

   d. Express and interpret the complementary slackness principle as it applies to the primal and dual of this LP problem.

4. Show that the dual of a dual is the primal.

◆ SUPPLEMENTAL PROBLEMS

Use the following transactions table to answer questions 1 through 4.

Gross Output	Sector	Steel	Coal	Elec.	Agric.	Final Demand
23	Steel	1	3	5	4	10
11	Coal	2	1	4	2	2
16	Elec.	5	1	2	5	3
5	Agric.	0	0	0	1	4
15	Labor	3	5	2	3	2

1. a. State in words all of the information contained in the transactions table.

   b. Explain the distinctions among quadrants I, II, III, and IV.

2. a. Find A, the matrix of direct technical coefficients; X, the vector of gross outputs; and Y, the vector of final demand.

   b. Express quadrants I and II of the transactions table as a matrix equation. Solve the matrix equation for Y and then for X.

   c. Find $I - A$ and $[I - A]^{-1}$.

   d. Perform the matrix multiplications in your equations from part b to demonstrate that your equations for X and Y are correct.

3. Suppose a very cold winter increases the final demand for coal to 3 units.

   a. Find the new vector of gross output necessary to increase output of coal to accommodate the increase in final demand.

   b. How much labor will be needed to accommodate the changes you find in part a?

   c. Write the new transactions table for the changes you find in parts a and b, and describe in words the changes in resource allocation which are needed.

4. Working with the original situation, i.e., before question 3, suppose that a strike by steel workers decreases gross steel output by 2 units.

a. Find the new vector of final demand that can be achieved.

b. Write the new transactions table for the situation as it is changed by the strike.

5. Consider the following primal LP problem,

$$\text{Maximize} \quad X_1 + 2X_2$$
$$\text{subject to:} \quad X_1 + 2X_2 \leq 4$$
$$X_1 - X_2 \geq 0$$
$$X_1 \geq 0, \quad X_2 \geq 0$$

a. Determine the solution values of the choice variables.

b. Solve the dual problem associated with this LP problem.

c. Apply the complementary slackness principle to this problem.

6. Consider an input–output model with two production sectors and one primary factor. Suppose the planner's goal is to maximize total factor income. Using the relationships between the primal and dual LP problems, characterize the resulting optimal plan. *Do not* use the matrix representation of the problem.

C H A P T E R   14

Efficiency and Exchange

14.1

INTRODUCTION

The models of producer and consumer behavior presented in previous chapters focused on the choices made by an individual firm or household in isolation from other firms or households. Decisions of other economic agents impinge only indirectly on these models, through their effects on market prices of inputs or outputs. In this chapter we present a production model and a consumption model in which two individual economic agents interact directly with one another. In the production model, given amounts of inputs are allocated between two firms; in the consumption model, given amounts of goods are allocated between two consumers.

Achieving an allocation of inputs between two firms or an allocation of goods between two consumers implies that some transactions or exchanges take place. For example, to increase the output of computers, inputs must somehow be transferred from the production of other goods, whose output declines. The models in this chapter are motivated by the concept of *Pareto efficiency*, which describes a state in which it is not possible to make one individual better off without making another worse off.[1] A *Pareto-improving* action is one that improves at least one individual's situation without worsening any other's. A *Pareto-optimal* state is one in which all Pareto-improving actions have been taken. After considering the implications of Pareto efficiency for production and for consumption, we combine the two models into a description of resource allocation in a two-good, two-input, two-consumer economic system.

Pareto efficiency: a state in which it is not possible to make one person better off without making another person worse off.

Pareto-improving: describes an action that makes at least one individual better off without harming another.

Pareto-optimal: describes Pareto efficiency, a state in which no further Pareto-improving actions are possible.

---

[1]Named in honor of the Italian welfare economist Vilfredo Pareto.

425

14.2

PARETO-OPTIMAL PRODUCTION IN A TWO-FIRM, TWO-INPUT MODEL

As in Chapter 10, we treat firms as production functions, converting inputs into output. One firm produces the good X at a rate per unit time described by the production function $X = f^X(K_X, L_X)$, in which K_X and L_X represent rates of employment of capital and labor in the production of X, respectively. Similarly, another firm produces the good Y at a rate equal to $Y = f^Y(K_Y, L_Y)$, in which K_Y and L_Y represent rates of employment of capital and labor in the production of Y, respectively. The total amount of capital available to be allocated between the two firms equals K_T and the total amount of labor to be allocated between them equals L_T.

For the purposes of this model, let's assume that more production is better than less. Therefore, a Pareto-optimal state is one in which no more of one good can be produced without decreasing the production of the other good. Mathematically, this proposition can be stated as a constrained optimization problem in which the production of one good, $Y = f^Y(K_Y, L_Y)$, is maximized subject to a constrained level of production of the other good, $X = X_0 = f^X(K_X, L_X)$, as well as constraints imposed by the fixed availability of capital and labor, $K_T = K_X + K_Y$ and $L_T = L_X + L_Y$. Note that the choice of which good's output to maximize and which to constrain is purely arbitrary; we could as easily have chosen to maximize X subject to a constrained level of Y and the same resource constraints.

We write our Lagrangian objective function as

$$\mathcal{L} = f^Y(K_Y, L_Y) + \theta[X_0 - f^X(K_X, L_X)] + \kappa(K_T - K_X - K_Y) + \lambda(L_T - L_X - L_Y)$$

$$(14\text{-}1)$$

in which θ, κ, and λ represent the Lagrange multipliers. In this model, the choice variables are K_Y, L_Y, K_X, L_X and the Lagrange multipliers. The parameters are X_0, K_T, and L_T.

14.2.1   Equilibrium Conditions for Efficiency in Production

To find the first-order conditions for maximization, we differentiate (14-1) with respect to the choice variables and set the partial derivatives equal to zero,

$$\mathcal{L}_{KY} = f_K^Y - \kappa = 0 \qquad (14\text{-}2)$$

$$\mathcal{L}_{LY} = f_L^Y - \lambda = 0 \qquad (14\text{-}3)$$

$$\mathcal{L}_{KX} = -\theta f_K^X - \kappa = 0 \qquad (14\text{-}4)$$

$$\mathcal{L}_{LX} = -\theta f_L^X - \lambda = 0 \qquad (14\text{-}5)$$

$$\mathcal{L}_{\theta} = X_0 - f(K_X, L_X) = 0 \qquad (14\text{-}6)$$

$$\mathcal{L}_{\kappa} = K_T - K_X - K_Y = 0 \qquad (14\text{-}7)$$

$$\mathcal{L}_{\lambda} = L_T - L_X - L_Y = 0 \qquad (14\text{-}8)$$

Note that we have expressed the partial derivatives of Y with respect to K_Y and L_Y as f_K^Y and f_L^Y in order to avoid unnecessary notational clutter, and we have expressed the partial derivatives of X correspondingly. Note also that $\mathscr{L}_{KY}$ is the first-order partial derivative of $\mathscr{L}$ with respect to K_Y, not a second-order partial derivative, and similarly for the partials of the Lagrangian with respect to the other inputs.

We differentiate equations (14-2) through (14-8) with respect to each choice variable in turn to find the bordered Hessian matrix of second partial derivatives, H_B.

$$
H_B = \begin{vmatrix}
f_{KK}^Y & f_{KL}^Y & 0 & 0 & 0 & -1 & 0 \\
f_{LK}^Y & f_{LL}^Y & 0 & 0 & 0 & 0 & -1 \\
0 & 0 & -\theta f_{KK}^X & -\theta f_{KL}^X & -f_K^X & -1 & 0 \\
0 & 0 & -\theta f_{LK}^X & -\theta f_{LL}^X & -f_L^X & 0 & -1 \\
0 & 0 & -f_K^X & -f_L^X & 0 & 0 & 0 \\
-1 & 0 & -1 & 0 & 0 & 0 & 0 \\
0 & -1 & 0 & -1 & 0 & 0 & 0
\end{vmatrix} \qquad (14\text{-}9)
$$

The bordered Hessian has seven rows and columns, of which the last three comprise the border, because our optimization model has three constraints. Therefore, the second-order condition for maximization requires that the determinant of the bordered Hessian, $|H_B|$, have the same sign as $-1^{7\text{-}3}$, that is, $|H_B| > 0$.

The first-order conditions can be manipulated to provide us with some insights regarding the constrained maximization of Y. We add κ to both sides of (14-2) and (14-4) and λ to both sides of (14-3) and (14-4), giving us

$$
f_K^Y = \kappa = -\theta f_K^X \qquad (14\text{-}10)
$$

$$
f_L^Y = \lambda = -\theta f_L^X \qquad (14\text{-}11)
$$

If we divide (14-10) by (14-11) we find that, at the constrained optimum,

$$
\frac{f_K^Y}{f_L^Y} = \frac{\kappa}{\lambda} = \frac{f_K^X}{f_L^X} \qquad (14\text{-}12)
$$

You should recognize the ratios of marginal products in (14-12) as the marginal rates of technical substitution of labor for capital in the production of Y and X, respectively. They are, of course, equal to the negative of the slopes of the isoquants of the Y and X production functions.

This result tells us that the output of Y is maximized, subject to the constraints that $X_0 = f(K_X, L_X)$, $K_T = K_X + K_Y$, and $L_T = L_X + L_Y$, at a point where $\mathrm{MRTS}_{L,K}^Y = \mathrm{MRTS}_{L,K}^X$. That point is where the slope of the optimum Y isoquant equals the slope of the X_0 isoquant. The equality of marginal rates of technical substitution can be considered a mathematical criterion for Pareto-optimal production. The logic of this criterion is easily seen by imagining that the marginal rates of technical substitution are not equal. Suppose, for example, that $\mathrm{MRTS}_{L,K}^X$, the rate at which labor can be substituted for capital in producing X, is 1/2. That is, 1 unit of labor can be substituted for 2 units of capital without affecting the level of X. If $MRTS^Y_{L,K} = 1$, an exchange by the producer of good Y of 1 unit of labor for 2 units of capital will result in the same level of X but a greater level of Y.

Pareto-optimal resource allocation in production is pictured in Figure 14.1, which is an example of a diagram known as an ***Edgeworth–Bowley box diagram***, named after the economists credited with devising it. The box represents all possible allocations of two inputs, K and L, between two outputs, Y and X. The diagram is created by rotating an isoquant map of the production of X by 180° and superimposing it on an isoquant map of the production of Y.

Therefore, the Y origin is in the usual place, the southwest corner of the diagram, whereas the X origin is in the northeast corner. The isoquants of both Y and X are convex, given the orientation of their respective origins. The dimensions of the box are L_T in the horizontal direction and K_T in the vertical direction. A point on the axes or in the interior of the box represents a particular allocation of capital and labor between X and Y that uses all the capital and labor available. For example, the Y origin represents an allocation in which $Y = 0$ and all the available capital and labor are employed in the production of X, whereas the X origin represents an allocation in which $X = 0$ and all the available capital and labor are employed in the production of Y. Moving from left to right in a horizontal direction allocates more labor to the production of Y and less to the production of X, whereas moving from right to left shifts labor from Y to X. Similarly, moving up in the vertical direction allocates more capital to the production of Y and less to X, whereas moving down shifts capital from Y to X.

Although the Edgeworth–Bowley box is, conceptually speaking, entirely filled with Y and X isoquants, we have shown only two: the constrained level

Edgeworth–Bowley box diagram: a graphical representation of resource allocation.

Figure 14.1

Edgeworth–Bowley Box Describing Pareto-Optimal Production

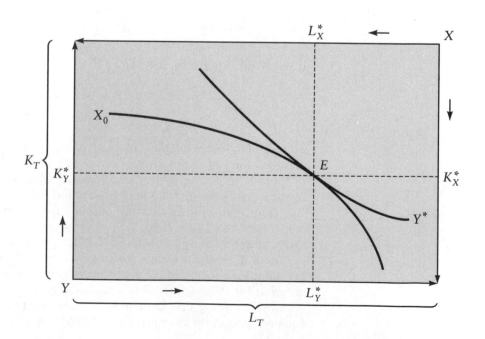

of $X = X_0$ and the maximum achievable level of $Y = Y^*$. The Y^* isoquant is just tangent to the X_0 isoquant, so their slopes are equal and $\text{MRTS}_{L,K}^Y = \text{MRTS}_{L,K}^X$. Any reallocation of inputs toward the Y origin results in lower output of Y, and any reallocation toward the X origin results in lower output of X. Therefore, point E in Figure 14.1 represents a Pareto-optimal allocation of K_T and L_T between Y and X.

The Edgeworth–Bowley box diagram as pictured in Figure 14.1 is also consistent with the second-order conditions for maximization, which require that the determinant of the bordered Hessian matrix be positive. Although it is a somewhat tedious exercise, we find that it can be quite character-building to evaluate $|H_B|$. Try it, making certain that you choose rows or columns that have the most 1's and 0's in them and that you are careful with the signs of the cofactors. You might find it useful to review Chapter 8, Section 8.5.1 on evaluating determinants. If you recognize from equations (14-2) through (14-5) that

$$\theta = \frac{-f_K^Y}{f_K^X} = \frac{-f_L^Y}{f_L^X} \tag{14-13}$$

you should obtain the following result when you evaluate the determinant:

$$|H_B| = \theta[f_K^{X2}f_{LL}^X - 2f_K^X f_L^X f_{KL}^X + f_L^{X2}f_{KK}^X] \tag{14-14}$$

$$- \left(\frac{1}{\theta}\right)^2 [f_K^{Y2}f_{LL}^Y - 2f_K^Y f_L^Y f_{KL}^Y + f_L^{Y2}f_{KK}^Y] > 0$$

The expressions inside the brackets of each term of (14-14) are familiar to you. You saw in Chapter 5, equation (5-74), that they determine the convexity of the isoquants. If the expressions inside the brackets are negative, the isoquants are convex. We know from equation (14-13) that θ is negative as long as the inputs have positive marginal products. Therefore, the bordered Hessian is assured to be positive and the second-order condition satisfied as long as both the Y and X isoquants are convex, as we pictured them in Figure 14.1.

The first-order conditions, equations (14-2) through (14-8), describe implicitly the functional relationships between the optimum values of the choice variables and the parameters of the model. Therefore, we write

$$K_Y^* = K_Y^*(X_0, K_T, L_T) \tag{14-15}$$

$$L_Y^* = L_Y^*(X_0, K_T, L_T) \tag{14-16}$$

$$K_X^* = K_X^*(X_0, K_T, L_T) \tag{14-17}$$

$$L_X^* = L_X^*(X_0, K_T, L_T) \tag{14-18}$$

$$\theta^* = \theta^*(X_0, K_T, L_T) \tag{14-19}$$

$$\kappa^* = \kappa^*(X_0, K_T, L_T) \tag{14-20}$$

$$\lambda^* = \lambda^*(X_0, K_T, L_T) \tag{14-21}$$

Equations (14-15) through (14-18) signify that the Y-maximizing allocations of capital and labor depend on the constrained level of X and the total quantities of capital and labor that are available. These relationships are evident in Figure 14.1, the Edgeworth–Bowley box. If X were constrained at an isoquant other than X_0, the point of tangency with a Y isoquant would be at a different place in the box, implying a different allocation of capital and labor between the two goods. If either K_T or L_T were changed, the dimensions of the box and the X origin would be affected, along with the point of tangency between the X_0 isoquant and Y's isoquant. We examine the comparative statics analysis of the production model after looking at the economic interpretation of the Lagrange multipliers in the next section.

EXERCISES
Section 14.2.1
Equilibrium
Conditions for
Efficiency in
Production

Use the following information for problems 1 through 3. The output of X is determined by the production function $X = 50K_X^{0.5}L_X^{0.5}$ and the output of Y is determined by the production function $Y = 100K_Y^{0.25}L_Y^{0.25}$. The total amount of capital available, K_T, is allocated to the production of X in the amount K_X and to the production of Y in the amount K_Y. The total amount of labor available, L_T, is allocated to the production of X in the amount L_X and to the production of Y in the amount L_Y.

1. Find the Langrangian objective function, the choice variables, and the parameters if the goal is to maximize the production of Y, holding X constant at $X = X_0$.

2. Find the first-order conditions for optimization.

3. Solve the first-order conditions for optimal values of K_X^*, L_X^*, K_Y^*, and L_Y^*, if $X_0 = 50$, $K_T = 16$, and $L_T = 4$. Find the optimal value of Y^*.

14.2.2 Interpretation of the Lagrange Multipliers

Before turning to the comparative statics analysis, let's interpret the economic meaning of the optimum levels of the Lagrange multipliers, θ^*, κ^*, and λ^*. As is usually the case, they have interesting economic interpretations. We can use the envelope theorem to demonstrate that the Lagrange multipliers represent derivatives of the indirect objective function,

$$Y^* = f^Y(K_Y^*(X_0, K_T, L_T), L_Y^*(X_0, K_T, L_T)) \tag{14-22}$$

with respect to the parameters. In this model, the indirect objective function is the maximum levels of production of Y, for given levels of the other good, X, and capital and labor. If we vary X, holding capital and labor constant, the resulting levels of Y^* represent the ***production possibilities frontier (PPF)***, or the maximum combinations of goods that can be produced with a given technology and endowment of inputs. The PPF, sometimes called the transformation curve, is pictured in Figure 14.2.

production possibilities frontier (PPF): the maximum combinations of goods that can be produced with a given technology and endowment of inputs.

The envelope theorem assures us that the derivative of Y^* with respect to X_0 equals the derivative of the Lagrangian objective function with respect to X_0, evaluated at the optimum, or $\partial Y^*/\partial X_0 = \partial \mathscr{L}/\partial X_0 = \theta^*$. Combining this result with (14-13) tells us that

$$\frac{\partial Y^*}{\partial X_0} = \frac{\partial \mathscr{L}}{\partial X_0} = \theta^* = \frac{-f_K^Y}{f_K^X} = \frac{-f_L^Y}{f_L^X} \tag{14-23}$$

Figure 14.2

The Production Possibilities Frontier

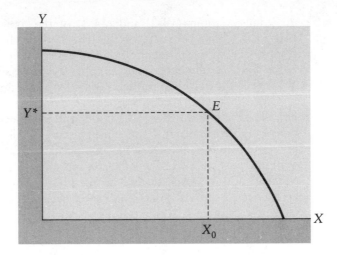

Therefore, the Lagrange multiplier, θ^*, equals the instantaneous rate of change of Y^* with respect to changes in the level of X, holding endowments of capital and labor constant. This is the slope of the PPF, which is downward sloping if the marginal products of the inputs are positive.

The ***marginal rate of transformation (MRT)*** between Y and X is defined as the negative of the slope of the PPF, or

marginal rate of transformation (MRT): the negative of the slope of the production possibilities frontier, or the rate at which a reallocation of a given endowment of inputs can transform one output into another.

$$\text{MRT}_{X,Y} = -\theta^* = \frac{f_K^Y}{f_K^X} = \frac{f_L^Y}{f_L^X} \tag{14-24}$$

The ratio of marginal products, f_K^Y/f_K^X, shows the rate at which Y decreases per unit increase in X as capital is transferred from Y to X. Similarly, f_L^Y/f_L^X shows the rate at which Y decreases per unit increase in X as labor is transferred from Y to X. At the optimum, the $\text{MRT}_{X,Y}$ is the same regardless of which input is transferred. The marginal rate of transformation can also be considered the marginal cost of X, expressed in terms of units of Y sacrificed.

Recognize that we could have set up the model with X the variable we maximized and Y the constrained variable. If you do so, you will find that $\text{MRT}_{X,Y} = 1/\text{MRT}_{Y,X}$ and that the marginal cost of Y expressed in terms of X sacrificed is the inverse of the marginal cost of X expressed in terms of Y. We ask you to demonstrate this in supplemental problem 1 at the end of the chapter.

We can also use the envelope theorem to interpret the optimum levels of the other Lagrange multipliers, κ^* and λ^*. By differentiating (14-22) with respect to K_T and L_T, respectively, we find

$$\frac{\partial Y^*}{\partial K_T} = \frac{\partial \mathcal{L}}{\partial K_T} = \kappa^* \quad \text{and} \quad \frac{\partial Y^*}{\partial L_T} = \frac{\partial \mathcal{L}}{\partial L_T} = \lambda^* \tag{14-25}$$

These results tell us that κ^* and λ^* represent the effects on the maximum level of Y of changes in the total amounts of capital and labor available, respectively. That is, κ^* is the marginal benefit of increasing K_T measured in terms of Y, and λ^* is the marginal benefit of increasing L_T, also measured in terms of

Y. From equations (14-2) and (14-3) of the first-order conditions we see that $\kappa^* = f_K^Y$ and $\lambda^* = f_L^Y$, or the marginal products of capital and labor, respectively, in the production of *Y*. This result makes sense, because, with *X* fixed at X_0, any increase in capital and labor is applied toward increasing *Y*. Because the marginal products are positive, so are κ^* and λ^*.

We think of the market prices as measuring the marginal benefits of outputs or inputs to their purchasers and the marginal costs of outputs or inputs to their suppliers. These three Lagrange multipliers, θ^*, κ^*, and λ^*, can all be interpreted as measuring marginal benefits or marginal costs. The marginal cost of *X* equals $-\theta^*$; the marginal benefits of capital and labor equal κ^* and λ^*, respectively. For this reason, Lagrange multipliers that can be so interpreted are sometimes called **shadow prices** to indicate that they have an economic interpretation like a price but are not actually prices in the commercial sense of the word.

shadow price: a mathematically constructed variable that, within its model, has the characteristics of a market price; that is, it measures either marginal benefits or marginal costs.

14.2.3 Comparative Statics Analysis of the Production Model

The model of efficiency in production that we have presented in this chapter is, like the input-output model in Chapter 13, descriptive rather than predictive. The equilibrium of the model shows the conditions under which two firms, each producing a different good with two scarce inputs, achieve maximum production of one good for a given level of production of the other. The model does not provide a mechanism that motivates the firms to achieve such a Pareto-optimal equilibrium, nor does it take account of any resources that might be required to carry out the transactions or exchanges within or between the firms that might cause equilibrium to be reached. The model simply describes the allocation of scarce inputs that maximizes *Y* for a given amount of *X*.

For this reason, the comparative statics results of the model are not testable predictions of producer behavior, in the way that comparative statics results from profit-maximization models are. Instead, we look at the comparative statics analysis to gain more insight into our notion of Pareto efficiency. For example, in Figure 14.2 we draw a production possibilities frontier that is downward sloping and concave, following the standard practice of textbooks of economic theory. Identifying θ^* as the slope of the PPF tells us that it is downward sloping, but nothing in the mathematics of the previous two sections indicates that it is concave. However, if we examine the comparative statics result for $\partial\theta^*/\partial X_0$, we can investigate the behavior of the slope as X_0 changes. Other interesting insights are gleaned by examining the effects of changes in input availabilities on their respective shadow prices.

To examine the effects of changes in X_0, we differentiate with respect to X_0 the identities formed by substituting equilibrium values of the choice variables, equations (14-15) through (14-21), into the first-order conditions, equations (14-2) through (14-8). Doing so gives us the matrix equation,

$$
\begin{bmatrix}
f^Y_{KK} & f^Y_{KL} & 0 & 0 & 0 & -1 & 0 \\
f^Y_{LK} & f^Y_{LL} & 0 & 0 & 0 & 0 & -1 \\
0 & 0 & -\theta^* f^X_{KK} & -\theta^* f^X_{KL} & -f^X_K & -1 & 0 \\
0 & 0 & -\theta^* f^X_{LK} & -\theta^* f^X_{LL} & -f^X_L & 0 & -1 \\
0 & 0 & -f^X_K & -f^X_L & 0 & 0 & 0 \\
-1 & 0 & -1 & 0 & 0 & 0 & 0 \\
0 & -1 & 0 & -1 & 0 & 0 & 0
\end{bmatrix}
\begin{bmatrix}
\dfrac{\partial K^*_Y}{\partial X_0} \\[1.5ex]
\dfrac{\partial L^*_Y}{\partial X_0} \\[1.5ex]
\dfrac{\partial K^*_X}{\partial X_0} \\[1.5ex]
\dfrac{\partial L^*_X}{\partial X_0} \\[1.5ex]
\dfrac{\partial \theta^*}{\partial X_0} \\[1.5ex]
\dfrac{\partial \kappa^*}{\partial X_0} \\[1.5ex]
\dfrac{\partial \lambda^*}{\partial X_0}
\end{bmatrix}
\equiv
\begin{bmatrix}
0 \\ 0 \\ 0 \\ 0 \\ -1 \\ 0 \\ 0
\end{bmatrix}
$$

$$(14\text{-}26)$$

We show changes in X_0 graphically in Figure 14.3a, where an Edgeworth–Bowley box diagram with three X isoquants, three Y isoquants, and three points of tangency, D, E, and F, is pictured.

As we move from point F to point D, away from the X origin and toward the Y origin, X increases and Y decreases. This occurs because capital and labor are reallocated from the production of Y to the production of X. Although we have drawn these reallocations in such a way that $K^F_X < K^E_X < K^D_X$ and $L^F_X < L^E_X < L^D_X$, it is not necessarily the case that both inputs must increase with increases in X_0. Recall from Chapter 11, Section 11.2, the possibility of an inferior input over some production ranges. Even though both inputs cannot be inferior over the same output range, we are unable to determine an unambiguous sign for $\partial K^*_X/\partial X_0$, $\partial L^*_X/\partial X_0$, $\partial K^*_Y/\partial X_0$, or $\partial L^*_Y/\partial X_0$ simply by solving (14-26) for these partial derivatives.

We are able to learn something about $\partial K^*_X/\partial X_0$, $\partial L^*_X/\partial X_0$, $\partial K^*_Y/\partial X_0$, and $\partial L^*_Y/\partial X_0$ by looking at the identities

$$K_T - K^*_X - K^*_Y \equiv 0 \qquad (14\text{-}27)$$

$$L_T - L^*_X - L^*_Y \equiv 0 \qquad (14\text{-}28)$$

created by substituting K^*_X, L^*_X, K^*_Y, and L^*_Y into the first-order conditions, equations (14-7) and (14-8). We differentiate (14-27) and (14-28) with respect to X_0 to obtain

$$\frac{-\partial K^*_X}{\partial X_0} - \frac{\partial K^*_Y}{\partial X_0} \equiv 0 \Leftrightarrow \frac{\partial K^*_X}{\partial X_0} \equiv \frac{-\partial K^*_Y}{\partial X_0} \qquad (14\text{-}29)$$

$$\frac{-\partial L^*_X}{\partial X_0} - \frac{\partial L^*_Y}{\partial X_0} \equiv 0 \Leftrightarrow \frac{\partial L^*_X}{\partial X_0} \equiv \frac{-\partial L^*_Y}{\partial X_0} \qquad (14\text{-}30)$$

Figure 14.3

(*a*) Efficient Allocation in Production; (*b*) Production Possibilities Frontier

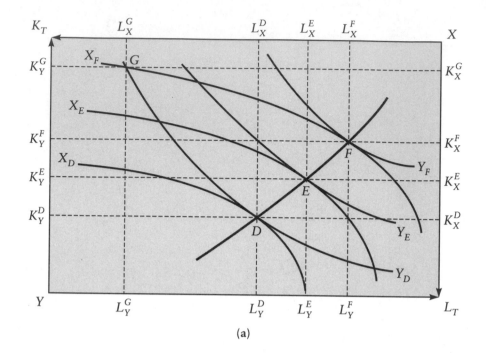

(a)

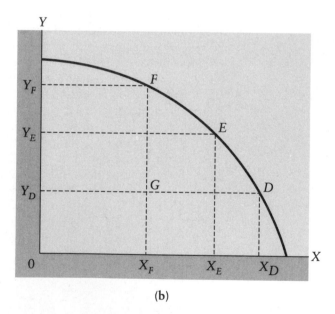

(b)

The identities (14-29) and (14-30) are intuitively obvious when you realize that, because of the capital and labor constraints, any change in capital or labor going to the production of X can only come from an equal but opposite change in capital or labor employed in the production of Y.

Figure 14.3*b* shows the production possibilities frontier that corresponds to the Edgeworth–Bowley box in panel *a*. It shows that, as we move from points F to E to D, X increases and Y decreases. At all three points, the Y and X isoquants are tangent, $MRTS_{L,K}^{Y} = MRTS_{L,K}^{X}$, and the Pareto criterion for efficiency in production is satisfied. At each point, capital and labor are allocated so that a maximum of Y is produced, given the level of X. In Figure 14.3*b* each of these points is on the frontier itself. At point G in the Edgeworth–Bowley box, however, there is no point of tangency, $\mathrm{MRTS}^Y_{L,K} \neq \mathrm{MRTS}^X_{L,K}$, and reallocating capital and labor between Y and X can result in more Y for the same amount of X, X_F. In fact, an exchange or transaction between the firms that sends an amount of labor equal to $L^G_X - L^F_X$ from the production of X to the production of Y and an amount of capital equal to $K^G_Y - K^F_Y$ from the production of Y to the production of X places the firms at point F in both panels. The line segment DEF is called the **locus of efficient exchange**, or the **contract curve**, because it represents allocations of inputs where all Pareto-improving exchanges or contracts have been accomplished.[2] Every point on the contract curve, which extends to the origins, corresponds to a point on the PPF. Points not on the contract curve, like G, lie inside the PPF.

We already showed in equation (14-23) that the slope of the PPF is negative, $\partial Y^*/\partial X_0 = \theta^* < 0$; however, we have not yet shown how the slope of the PPF changes as X changes. We can do so by examining the comparative statics result, $\partial^2 Y^*/\partial X_0^2 = \partial\theta^*/\partial X_0$. If $\partial\theta^*/\partial X_0 < 0$, the slope of the PPF becomes more steeply negative as X increases, and the PPF is strictly concave. We find $\partial\theta^*/\partial X_0$ by applying Cramer's rule to equation (14-26), obtaining

$$\frac{\partial\theta^*}{\partial X_0} = \frac{\begin{vmatrix} f^Y_{KK} & f^Y_{KL} & 0 & 0 & 0 & -1 & 0 \\ f^Y_{LK} & f^Y_{LL} & 0 & 0 & 0 & 0 & -1 \\ 0 & 0 & -\theta^* f^X_{KK} & -\theta^* f^X_{KL} & 0 & -1 & 0 \\ 0 & 0 & -\theta^* f^X_{LK} & -\theta^* f^X_{LL} & 0 & 0 & -1 \\ 0 & 0 & -f^X_K & -f^X_L & -1 & 0 & 0 \\ -1 & 0 & -1 & 0 & 0 & 0 & 0 \\ 0 & -1 & 0 & -1 & 0 & 0 & 0 \end{vmatrix}}{|H_B|} = \frac{-|H_{55}|}{|H_B|} \quad \textbf{(14-31)}$$

where $|H_{55}|$ is the principal minor associated with the element at the intersection of the fifth row and column.

The second-order conditions assure us that the denominator of (14-31) is positive, but they give us no guidance as to the sign of the numerator. Therefore, we must evaluate the determinant in the numerator. We find

$$-|H_{55}|$$
$$= -\theta^{*2}\underbrace{(f^X_{KK}f^X_{LL} - f^{X2}_{LK})}_{A} - \underbrace{(f^Y_{KK}f^Y_{LL} - f^{Y2}_{LK})}_{B} + \theta^*\underbrace{(f^X_{LL}f^Y_{KK} - 2f^X_{LK}f^Y_{LK} + f^X_{KK}f^Y_{LL})}_{C}$$
$$= -\theta^{*2} \qquad A \qquad - \qquad B \qquad + \theta^* \qquad C$$

$$\textbf{(14-32)}$$

---

[2]Stay mindful of the qualifications we made earlier regarding the predictive capability of the model. The model does not provide a mechanism that motivates the firms to achieve Pareto-optimal equilibria, nor does it take account of any resources that might be required to carry out the transactions or exchanges within or between the firms that might cause equilibrium to be reached.

---

locus of efficient exchange: line joining points of tangency in an Edgeworth–Bowley box diagram. Also known as contract curve.

contract curve: same as locus of efficient exchange.

In Chapter 6, equations (6-6) through (6-8), we found conditions sufficient for a function with two variables to be strictly concave or convex. Our production functions, $f^X(K_X, L_X)$ and $f^Y(K_Y, L_Y)$, are strictly concave if

$$f^X_{KK}, f^X_{LL}, f^Y_{KK}, f^Y_{LL} < 0 \qquad (14\text{-}33)$$

and

$$(f^X_{KK} f^X_{LL} - f^{X2}_{LK}), (f^Y_{KK} f^Y_{LL} - f^{Y2}_{LK}) > 0$$

Therefore, if these conditions hold, the two production functions are strictly concave, A and B in (14-32) are positive, and $-\theta^{*2} A - B < 0$.

To find the sign of C in (14-32), we multiply and divide by $f^X_{LL} f^Y_{KK}$ and add and subtract $(f^X_{LK} f^Y_{LK})^2$ from the expression inside the parentheses.[3] The result of these manipulations is

$$\theta^* C = \frac{\theta^*}{f^X_{LL} f^Y_{KK}} [(f^X_{LL} f^Y_{KK})^2 - 2f^X_{LK} f^Y_{LK} f^X_{LL} f^Y_{KK} + (f^X_{LK} f^Y_{LK})^2 \qquad (14\text{-}34)$$
$$+ (f^X_{KK} f^Y_{LL} f^Y_{KK} f^X_{LL} - (f^X_{LK} f^Y_{LK})^2)]$$

which can be written

$$\theta^* C = \frac{\theta^*}{f^X_{LL} f^Y_{KK}} [(f^X_{LL} f^Y_{KK} - f^X_{LK} f^Y_{LK})^2 + (f^X_{KK} f^Y_{LL} f^Y_{KK} f^X_{LL} - f^X_{LK} f^Y_{LK})^2] \qquad (14\text{-}35)$$

We know that the squared term, $(f^X_{LL} f^Y_{KK} - f^X_{LK} f^Y_{LK})^2$, is positive and that $\theta^* < 0$. If (14-33) is satisfied, the production functions are strictly concave, $f^X_{LL} f^Y_{KK} > 0$ and $(f^X_{KK} f^Y_{KK} f^Y_{LL} f^X_{LL} - (f^X_{LK} f^Y_{LK})^2) > 0$, and equations (14-35), (14-34), (14-32), and (14-31) are all negative, as is $\partial\theta^*/\partial X_0$. Under these conditions, the PPF is strictly concave.[4] You might remember from Chapter 11, equation (11-27), that these are the same conditions that give us upward-sloping marginal cost curves for X and Y, given parametric input prices. We obtain the same result here, considering our interpretation of the MRT, $-\theta^*$, as the marginal cost of X, expressed in terms of units of Y sacrificed. If $\partial\theta^*/\partial X_0 < 0$, then $\partial[-\theta^*]/\partial X_0 = -\partial\theta^*/\partial X_0 > 0$.

In the previous section we interpreted κ^* and λ^* as shadow prices, measuring the marginal benefits of capital and labor, respectively. We can discover how changes in the input endowments affect their shadow prices by examining the comparative statics results $\partial\kappa^*/\partial K_T$ and $\partial\lambda^*/\partial L_T$. To find $\partial\kappa^*/\partial K_T$, we differentiate with respect to K_T the identities formed by substituting equilibrium values of the choice variables, equations (14-15) through

---

[3]These manipulations are representative of the algebraic procedure known as completing the square.

[4]Note that these are sufficient, not necessary conditions for concavity. It is possible for linear homogeneous production functions, which are not concave, to generate a concave PPF if they require different factor intensities.

(14-21), into the first-order conditions, equations (14-2) through (14-8). Doing so gives us the matrix identity

$$
\begin{bmatrix}
f^Y_{KK} & f^Y_{KL} & 0 & 0 & 0 & -1 & 0 \\
f^Y_{LK} & f^Y_{LL} & 0 & 0 & 0 & 0 & -1 \\
0 & 0 & -\theta^* f^X_{KK} & -\theta^* f^X_{KL} & -f^X_K & -1 & 0 \\
0 & 0 & -\theta^* f^X_{LK} & -\theta^* f^X_{LL} & -f^X_L & 0 & -1 \\
0 & 0 & -f^X_K & -f^X_L & 0 & 0 & 0 \\
-1 & 0 & -1 & 0 & 0 & 0 & 0 \\
0 & -1 & 0 & -1 & 0 & 0 & 0
\end{bmatrix}
\begin{bmatrix}
\dfrac{\partial K^*_Y}{\partial K_T} \\[6pt]
\dfrac{\partial L^*_Y}{\partial K_T} \\[6pt]
\dfrac{\partial K^*_X}{\partial K_T} \\[6pt]
\dfrac{\partial L^*_X}{\partial K_T} \\[6pt]
\dfrac{\partial \theta^*}{\partial K_T} \\[6pt]
\dfrac{\partial \kappa^*}{\partial K_T} \\[6pt]
\dfrac{\partial \lambda^*}{\partial K_T}
\end{bmatrix}
\equiv
\begin{bmatrix}
0 \\ 0 \\ 0 \\ 0 \\ 0 \\ -1 \\ 0
\end{bmatrix}
\tag{14-36}
$$

We use Cramer's rule to solve for $\partial \kappa^*/\partial K_T$, obtaining

$$
\frac{\partial \kappa^*}{\partial K_T} = \frac{
\begin{vmatrix}
f^Y_{KK} & f^Y_{KL} & 0 & 0 & 0 & 0 & 0 \\
f^Y_{LK} & f^Y_{LL} & 0 & 0 & 0 & 0 & -1 \\
0 & 0 & -\theta^* f^X_{KK} & -\theta^* f^X_{KL} & -f^X_K & 0 & 0 \\
0 & 0 & -\theta^* f^X_{LK} & -\theta^* f^X_{LL} & -f^X_L & 0 & -1 \\
0 & 0 & -f^X_K & -f^X_L & 0 & 0 & 0 \\
-1 & 0 & -1 & 0 & 0 & -1 & 0 \\
0 & -1 & 0 & -1 & 0 & 0 & 0
\end{vmatrix}
}{|H_B|}
\tag{14-37}
$$

Evaluating the determinant in the numerator gives us

$$
\frac{\partial \kappa^*}{\partial K_T} = \frac{-\theta^* f^Y_{KK}(f^{X2}_K f^X_{LL} - 2f^X_K f^X_L f^X_{KL} + f^{X2}_L f^X_{KK}) - f^{X2}_K(f^Y_{LL} f^Y_{KK} - f^{Y2}_{KL})}{|H_B|}
\tag{14-38}
$$

We know that $\theta^* < 0$ and that $|H_B| > 0$. We also know from Chapter 5, equation (5-74), that if f^X has strictly convex isoquants, then $f^{X2}_K f^X_{LL} - 2f^X_K f^X_L f^X_{KL} + f^{X2}_L f^X_{KK} < 0$. If $f^Y_{KK} < 0$ and $(f^Y_{KK} f^Y_{LL} - f^{Y2}_{LK}) > 0$, then f^Y is strictly concave and $\partial \kappa^*/\partial K_T < 0$.

This result tells us that, if f^X has strictly convex isoquants, the conditions sufficient for f^Y to be a strictly concave production function also guarantee that an increase in the endowment of capital decreases its shadow price. To interpret the result, remember that the same conditions imply upward-sloping marginal cost and diminishing marginal productivity to its inputs. Under these circumstances, increasing K_T results in diminishing increments in Y. We measure the marginal benefits of K_T in terms of increased production of Y, so those marginal benefits decrease with increases in K_T. This is an example of the economic proposition that an increase in the availability of a resource results in a decrease in its price, and a decrease in its availability increases its price. We leave it to you as an exercise to demonstrate similar results for $\partial \lambda^* / \partial L_T$.

The equilibrium and comparative statics of the two-firm, two-input model describe Pareto-optimal production in an abstract and mathematical manner. Any allocation of inputs that utilizes the total amounts available and results in equal marginal rates of technical substitution in the production of the two outputs is efficient, according to the model. The reason for the abstractness of the analysis is in the nature of the model: what it incorporates and what it omits. By treating the firm as a production function, it incorporates the fact that firms combine inputs and produce output, but it omits any notion that firms are social organizations with complex and mutable processes that accomplish resource allocation. By treating inputs as limited collections of indistinguishable units with positive marginal products, it incorporates the fact that inputs are scarce and contribute positively to production, but it omits a recognition of their diversity. As we have mentioned previously, abstractness brings with it the benefit of generality at the cost of detail.

EXERCISES
Section 14.2.3
Comparative Statics
Analysis of the
Production Model

Use the following information for problems 1 through 4. The output of X is determined by the production function $X = 50K_X^{0.5}L_X^{0.5}$ and the output of Y is determined by the production function $Y = 100K_Y^{0.25}L_Y^{0.25}$. The total amount of capital available, K_T, is allocated to the production of X in the amount K_X and to the production of Y in the amount K_Y. The total amount of labor available, L_T, is allocated to the production of X in the amount L_X and to the production of Y in the amount L_Y. Note that this is the same problem as in the exercises at the end of Section 14.2.1.

1. Solve the first-order conditions for optimal values of the Lagrange multipliers in terms of the parameters, and provide economic interpretations of the Lagrange multipliers.

2. Evaluate the partial derivative of $\mathrm{MRT}_{X,Y}$ with respect to X_0 at $K_T = 16$, $L_T = 4$, and $X_0 = 50$. Interpret the economic meaning of your result.

3. Evaluate the partial derivative of the shadow price of capital with respect to K_T at $K_T = 16$, $L_T = 4$, and $X_0 = 50$. Interpret the economic meaning of your result.

4. Evaluate the partial derivative of the shadow price of labor with respect to L_T at $K_T = 16$, $L_T = 4$, and $X_0 = 50$. Interpret the economic meaning of your result.

14.3

PARETO-OPTIMAL CONSUMPTION IN A TWO-CONSUMER, TWO-GOOD MODEL

Our two-consumer, two-good model of Pareto-optimal consumption is very similar to the production model, both in its level of abstractness and in its mathematics. You will see that the two models are identical as far as the mathematics go. Just replace the inputs and production functions of the production model with the goods and utility functions of the consumption model, and they are the same. We take advantage of the similarities, and of the fact that you have seen the math before, to make our presentation more concise. An important difference in the analyses is our unwillingness to consider strict concavity as a likely characteristic of utility functions. In fact, we try to stay within the bounds defined by the four behavioral postulates of consumer behavior discussed in Chapter 9.

The consumption model is sometimes called a model of pure exchange because it assumes fixed quantities of two goods, X_T and Y_T, that must be allocated, or exchanged, between two consumers. Where the goods come from is irrelevant for the purposes of this model; we will assume that they represent a point on the production possibilities frontier pictured in the last section. The two consumers, A and B, are represented by their utility functions, $U^A = U^A(X_A, Y_A)$ and $U^B = U^B(X_B, Y_B)$. The variables X_A, Y_A, X_B, and Y_B represent the amounts of X and Y allocated to A and B, respectively. Pareto-improving allocations or exchanges in this context are those that increase one consumer's utility without decreasing the other's. Therefore, we model Pareto-optimal consumption by maximizing one consumer's utility, $U^A(X_A, Y_A)$, subject to a given level of utility for the other consumer, $U_0^B = U^B(X_B, Y_B)$, and the fixed availability of goods, $X_T = X_A + X_B$ and $Y_T = Y_A + Y_B$.

14.3.1 Equilibrium Conditions of the Two-Good, Two-Consumer Model

Our Lagrangian objective function is

$$\mathcal{L} = U^A(X_A, Y_A) + \phi[U_0^B - U^B(X_B, Y_B)] + \chi(X_T - X_A - X_B) \quad \textbf{(14-39)}$$
$$+ \psi(Y_T - Y_A - Y_B)$$

The choice variables of this model are the amounts of goods allocated to each consumer, X_A, X_B, Y_A, and Y_B, as well as the Lagrange multipliers, ϕ, χ, and ψ. The parameters are the constrained level of B's utility, U_0^B, as well as the fixed levels of available goods, X_T and Y_T. As with the production model, it is a purely arbitrary decision whose utility to maximize and whose to constrain, so we ask you to carry out the analysis by maximizing B's utility subject to a constrained level of utility for A in supplemental problem 2.

We find the first-order conditions for optimization by differentiating

(14-39) with respect to the choice variables and setting the partial derivatives equal to zero,

$$\mathscr{L}_{XA} = U_X^A - \chi = 0 \tag{14-40}$$

$$\mathscr{L}_{YA} = U_Y^A - \psi = 0 \tag{14-41}$$

$$\mathscr{L}_{XB} = -\phi U_X^B - \chi = 0 \tag{14-42}$$

$$\mathscr{L}_{YB} = -\phi U_Y^B - \psi = 0 \tag{14-43}$$

$$\mathscr{L}_\phi = U_0^B - U^B(X_B, Y_B) = 0 \tag{14-44}$$

$$\mathscr{L}_\chi = X_T - X_A - X_B = 0 \tag{14-45}$$

$$\mathscr{L}_\psi = Y_T - Y_A - Y_B = 0 \tag{14-46}$$

We have expressed the partial derivatives of U^A with respect to X_A and Y_A as U_X^A and U_Y^A to avoid unnecessary notational clutter, and we have expressed the partial derivatives of U^B correspondingly. Note also that $\mathscr{L}_{XA}$ is the first-order partial derivative of $\mathscr{L}$ with respect to X_A, not a second-order partial derivative, and similarly for the partials of the Lagrangian with respect to the other goods.

The bordered Hessian matrix of second partial derivatives is

$$H_B = \begin{bmatrix} U_{XX}^A & U_{XY}^A & 0 & 0 & 0 & -1 & 0 \\ U_{XY}^A & U_{YY}^A & 0 & 0 & 0 & 0 & -1 \\ 0 & 0 & -\phi U_{XX}^B & -\phi U_{XY}^B & -U_X^B & -1 & 0 \\ 0 & 0 & -\phi U_{YX}^B & -\phi U_{YY}^B & -U_Y^B & 0 & -1 \\ 0 & 0 & -U_X^B & -U_Y^B & 0 & 0 & 0 \\ -1 & 0 & -1 & 0 & 0 & 0 & 0 \\ 0 & -1 & 0 & -1 & 0 & 0 & 0 \end{bmatrix} \tag{14-47}$$

As in the production model, we have a 7×7 bordered Hessian matrix with three constraints. Therefore, the second-order conditions require that its determinant, $|H_B|$, have the same sign as $(-1)^{7-3}$, which is greater than zero.

A visual comparison of equations (14-40) through (14-47) with the equilibrium conditions of the production model, equations (14-2) through (14-9), reveals the similarity between the consumption and production models. For this reason, we leave it to you to show that the second-order condition is satisfied if both utility functions have strictly convex indifference curves in supplemental problem 3. Strictly convex indifference curves are assured by the convexity postulate of consumer behavior in Chapter 9, Section 9.2. We turn instead to interpreting the first-order conditions as a criterion for Pareto-optimal allocation of goods between consumers.

14.3.2 Pareto-Optimal Allocation of Goods Among Consumers

From (14-40) through (14-43) we find that

$$\frac{U_X^A}{U_Y^A} = \frac{\chi}{\psi} = \frac{U_X^B}{U_Y^B} \tag{14-48}$$

As you already know from Chapters 3, 5, and 9, the ratio of marginal utilities is equal to the consumer's marginal rate of substitution between the two goods, which is the negative of the slope of the indifference curve. Therefore, (14-48) implies that A's maximum utility, given a fixed level of utility for B as well as fixed amounts of the two goods, is achieved at an allocation of goods where $MRS_{X,Y}^A = MRS_{X,Y}^B$. This equality of marginal rates of substitution is a mathematical criterion for Pareto-optimal consumption. It means that, if the marginal rates of substitution are not equal for two consumers, one of them can be made better off without any sacrifice by the other by reallocating the goods between them.

As in the production model, this equilibrium can be pictured as a point of tangency in an Edgeworth–Bowley box diagram, as we show in Figure 14.4. The origin of A's indifference map is in the usual location, in the southwest corner of the box, and B's is in the northeast corner. The maximum obtainable level of utility for A, holding B's utility constant at U_0^B, is at point E on indifference curve U^{A*}, where the indifference curves are tangent and $MRS_{X,Y}^A = MRS_{X,Y}^B$. At point E the total amounts of goods available are allocated between the two consumers, in amounts X_A^*, X_B^*, Y_A^*, and Y_B^*. These

Figure 14.4

Edgeworth–Bowley Box Diagram Describing Pareto-Optimal Consumption

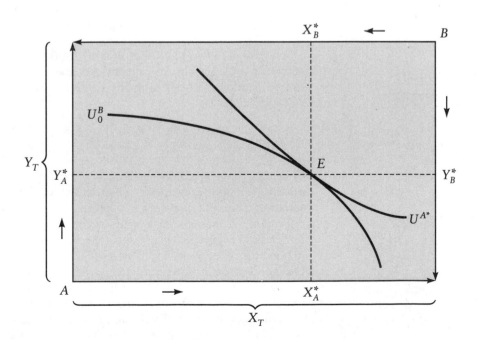

equilibrium values, along with the equilibrium values of the Lagrange multipliers, ϕ^*, χ^*, and ψ^*, can be expressed as functions of the parameters, or

$$X_A^* = X_A^*(U_0^B, X_T, Y_T) \tag{14-49}$$

$$X_B^* = X_B^*(U_0^B, X_T, Y_T) \tag{14-50}$$

$$Y_A^* = Y_A^*(U_0^B, X_T, Y_T) \tag{14-51}$$

$$Y_B^* = Y_B^*(U_0^B, X_T, Y_T) \tag{14-52}$$

$$\phi^* = \phi^*(U_0^B, X_T, Y_T) \tag{14-53}$$

$$\chi^* = \chi^*(U_0^B, X_T, Y_T) \tag{14-54}$$

$$\psi^* = \psi^*(U_0^B, X_T, Y_T) \tag{14-55}$$

We use the envelope theorem to interpret the Lagrange multipliers. In this model, the indirect objective function is the maximum achievable level of A's utility, or

$$U^{A*} = U^{A*}(X_A^*(U_0^B, X_T, Y_T), Y_A^*(U_0^B, X_T, Y_T)) \tag{14-56}$$

According to the envelope theorem, the partial derivative of (14-56) with respect to a parameter is equal to the partial of (14-39) with respect to the same parameter, evaluated at the optimum. We find that

$$\frac{\partial U^{A*}}{\partial U_0^B} = \frac{\partial \mathcal{L}}{\partial U_0^B} = \phi^* \tag{14-57}$$

$$\frac{\partial U^{A*}}{\partial X_T} = \frac{\partial \mathcal{L}}{\partial X_T} = \chi^* \tag{14-58}$$

$$\frac{\partial U^{A*}}{\partial Y_T} = \frac{\partial \mathcal{L}}{\partial Y_T} = \psi^* \tag{14-59}$$

Equation (14-57) indicates that ϕ^* measures the effect on A's maximum utility of a change in the constrained level of B's utility. From equations (14-40) through (14-43) of the first-order conditions we see that

$$\phi^* = -\frac{U_X^A}{U_X^B} = -\frac{U_Y^A}{U_Y^B} \tag{14-60}$$

This expression is negative as long as the marginal utilities of both goods are positive for both consumers, which is assumed to be the case by the non-satiation postulate discussed in Chapter 9, Section 9.2. It means that, at the optimum, an increase in B's utility results in a decrease in A's; i.e., no reallocations of goods are possible that make one consumer better off without making the other worse off. Therefore, the equilibrium of the two-consumer, two-good model describes a Pareto-optimal allocation of goods.

Equations (14-58) and (14-59) indicate that χ^* and ψ^* measure the effects on A's maximum utility of changes in the available amounts of the two goods, X_T and Y_T, respectively. From equations (14-40) and (14-41) of the first-order conditions we see that χ^* and ψ^* equal the marginal utilities of X and Y to A

and are therefore positive. Given that B's utility is held fixed at $U^B = U_0^B$, increases in X_T or Y_T result in increases in A's utility.

As in the production model, the Lagrange multipliers represent marginal benefits or costs, or shadow prices, in this model of efficiency in consumption. The multipliers χ^* and ψ^* represent the marginal benefits of increases in X_T and Y_T, measured in terms of A's utility. The negative of ϕ^* represents the marginal rate at which A sacrifices utility when B's utility increases, or the marginal cost of increases in B's utility measured in terms of losses in A's utility.

We do not perform the comparative statics analysis of the consumption model the way we did with the production model. The reason is that, as with the production model, our ability to sign comparative statics results in this model depends on our making assumptions about the specifics of the utility functions, such as strict concavity. Such assumptions make some sense in the context of production functions, which are required to be strictly concave by the second-order conditions of the price-taker profit-maximization models. They make less sense in the context of utility functions, which are not required to be concave by the second-order conditions of the utility maximization model. Utility functions are governed only by the four behavioral postulates discussed in Chapter 9. Therefore, we conclude our discussion of the two-consumer, two-good model by examining the trade-off between A's and B's utility graphically.

Figure 14.5a pictures an Edgeworth–Bowley box diagram with three points of tangency, F, G, and H. Note that the dimensions of the box are determined by the point M on a production possibilities frontier. The point was chosen arbitrarily; another point such as L or N could have been chosen. The three points of tangency represent maximum achievable utilities for A given three different constrained levels of B's utility, U_F^B, U_G^B, and U_H^B. Point J does not represent an optimal allocation of goods; an exchange in which A traded Y in return for X from B could increase A's utility, holding B's utility constant. Only points of tangency between A's and B's indifference curves satisfy the mathematical criterion for Pareto-optimal resource allocation, $\text{MRS}_{X,Y}^A = \text{MRS}_{X,Y}^B$. As in the production model, such points lie on the locus of efficient exchange, or contract curve, which is pictured as line segment FGH in the diagram.

Moving from H to G to F on the contract curve, U^A decreases as U^B increases. This means that each of these points represents a Pareto-optimal allocation of the two goods between the two consumers. They can be plotted in a graph that is the consumer model equivalent of the PPF, the **utilities possibilities frontier (UPF)**, which is pictured in Figure 14.5b. We have labeled the utilities possibilities frontier UPF$_M$ in the figure because it is associated with point M on the PPF. From equation (14-57) we know that the slope of the UPF equals ϕ^*, which we know is negative from (14-60). We do not know if the UPF is concave, convex, neither, or some combination of the three, however, because we are not willing to make assumptions about the utility functions beyond the four postulates about consumer behavior from Chapter 9. For that reason, we include both convex and concave portions in the UPF pictured in Figure 14.5b.

Every point on the contract curve in the Edgeworth–Bowley box diagram and on the UPF satisfies the efficiency criterion that $\text{MRS}_{X,Y}^A = \text{MRS}_{X,Y}^B$. Given the assumptions of our model, they describe Pareto-optimal allocation of

utilities possibilities frontier (UPF): the maximum combinations of utilities that can be generated by given quantities of goods.

Figure 14.5

(*a*) Efficient Allocation in Consumption; (*b*) Utilities Possibilities Frontier

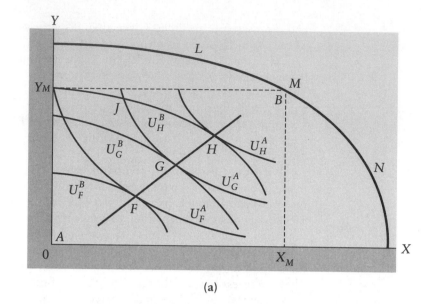

(a)

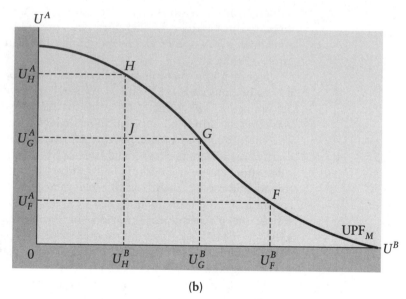

(b)

goods between the consumers. Among these assumptions are the concepts that one individual's utility is independent of the utility of others, that production is independent of consumption, and that the processes that carry out exchanges or reallocations require no resources. Although the model is simplified by these assumptions, its abstractness seriously limits the usefulness of the notion of Pareto efficiency.

We have examined pure production in the absence of consumption in Section 14.2 and pure exchange in the absence of production in Section 14.3. The next step is to bring production and exchange together in a more general model of resource allocation, to which we turn next.

EXERCISES
Section 14.3.2
Pareto-Optimal
Allocation of Goods
Among Consumers

Use the following information for problems 1 through 3. Consumer A's utility is determined by the utility function $U^A = (X_A Y_A)^\alpha$ and B's utility is determined by the utility function $U^B = (X_B Y_B)^\beta$. The total amount of good X available, X_T, is allocated to A in the amount X_A and to B in the amount X_B. The total amount of good Y available, Y_T, is allocated to A in the amount Y_A and to B in the amount Y_B.

1. Find the Lagrangian objective function, the choice variables, and the parameters if the goal is to maximize the utility of A, holding B's utility constant at $U^B = U_0^B$.

2. Find the first-order conditions for optimization.

3. Solve the first-order conditions for optimal values of X_B^*, Y_B^*, X_A^*, and Y_A^*. Also find the slope of the UPF and determine whether it is greater or less than zero.

14.4

RESOURCE ALLOCATION IN A TWO-INPUT, TWO-GOOD, TWO-CONSUMER MODEL

We stated in the previous section that the choice of point M on the PPF in Figure 14.5a was purely arbitrary. After all, the quantities of goods available to the consumers are parameters in this model, determined exogenously. Had we chosen point L, we would have drawn a different Edgeworth–Bowley box and generated a different contract curve and a different UPF. Similarly, had we chosen point M on the PPF, we would have generated yet another UPF. In fact, every point on the PPF pictured in Figure 14.5 has a particular UPF associated with it. These can all be graphed on a set of axes with U^A on one axis and U^B on the other. We have drawn such a graph, called a ***grand utilities possibilities frontier (GUPF)***, in Figure 14.6. We have shown only three UPFs, associated with points L, M, and N from Figure 14.5a, in Figure 14.6.

grand utilities possibilities frontier: collection of all utilities possibilities frontiers associated with a production possibilities frontier.

Figure 14.6

Grand Utilities Possibilities Frontier

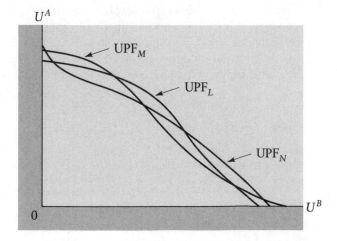

In one sense, the GUPF accomplishes our objective of combining our production and consumption models into a single model of allocative efficiency. Every point on the GUPF is associated with a point on a PPF, so we are assured of efficiency in production. At the same time, every point on the GUPF is associated with a point on a UPF, so we are assured of efficiency in consumption. However, examining the GUPF adds no insight into the mathematics of Pareto efficiency beyond what we already know from the production and consumption models. We can gain some more insight from a model that maximizes a *social welfare function (SWF)*, subject to constrained input endowments and given production and utility functions.

social welfare function (SWF): a function that converts the utilities of individuals into a value for the general well-being of society.

A social welfare function has as its dependent variable the general well-being, or welfare, of society and as its independent variables the utilities of the individual members of society. Therefore, we can write

$$W = W(U^A, U^B) \tag{14-61}$$

to represent the social welfare function in our simple, two-consumer system. Be aware that the existence and use of a social welfare function are controversial issues in economic theory. In fact, Kenneth Arrow, the 1972 Nobel Laureate in Economics, proves that, given the standard behavioral assumptions regarding utility, a consistent social welfare function cannot be generated by collective means, either through market mechanisms or through voting schemes. That is, the existence of a social welfare function is possible only if it is imposed on society, or if it represents a dictator's will.[5]

Warnings aside, what insight can be gained by examining a model that maximizes social welfare, subject to constraints on the availability of inputs and goods? To find out, we set up the constrained optimization problem:

Maximize $\quad W = W(U^A, U^B)$

subject to: $\quad K_T = K_X + K_Y$

$\qquad\qquad L_T = L_X + L_Y$

$\qquad\qquad X_A + X_B = f^X(K_X, L_X)$

$\qquad\qquad Y_A + Y_B = f^Y(K_Y, L_Y)$

Our notation in this model follows that used in Sections 14.2 and 14.3. Therefore, our constraints simply state that the capital and labor used to produce X and Y must sum up to the total amounts of capital and labor available and that the total amounts of X and Y consumed by A and B sum up to the total amounts producible by the production functions using the available inputs. Our Lagrangian objective function is

$$\mathcal{L} = W(U^A, U^B) + \Omega_1(K_T - K_X - K_Y) + \Omega_2(L_T - L_X - L_Y) \tag{14-62}$$
$$+ \Omega_3(X_A + X_B - f^X(K_X, L_X)) + \Omega_4(Y_A + Y_B - f^Y(K_Y, L_Y))$$

---

[5] A seminal article in the modern development of the social welfare function is Bergson, Abram, "A Reformulation of Certain Aspects of Welfare Economics," *Quarterly Journal of Economics*, 52 (1938): pp. 310–334. For Arrow's possibility theorem, see Arrow, Kenneth, "A Difficulty in the Concept of Social Welfare," *The Journal of Political Economy*, 58 (1950): pp. 328–346. Both articles are reprinted in Arrow, K., and Scitovsky, T., eds., *A.E.A. Readings in Welfare Economics*, Vol. 12, Homewood, IL: Richard D. Irwin, 1969.

This problem has 12 choice variables: $K_X, L_X, K_Y, L_Y, X_A, Y_A, X_B, Y_B$ and the Lagrange multipliers, Ω_1 through Ω_4. The first-order conditions require that the partial derivatives of $\mathscr{L}$ with respect to each of the choice variables be equal to zero,

$$\mathscr{L}_{KX} = -\Omega_1 - \Omega_3 f_K^X = 0 \tag{14-63}$$

$$\mathscr{L}_{LX} = -\Omega_2 - \Omega_3 f_L^X = 0 \tag{14-64}$$

$$\mathscr{L}_{KY} = -\Omega_1 - \Omega_4 f_K^Y = 0 \tag{14-65}$$

$$\mathscr{L}_{LY} = -\Omega_2 - \Omega_4 f_L^Y = 0 \tag{14-66}$$

$$\mathscr{L}_{XA} = W_{UA} U_X^A + \Omega_3 = 0 \tag{14-67}$$

$$\mathscr{L}_{YA} = W_{UA} \dot{U}_Y^A + \Omega_4 = 0 \tag{14-68}$$

$$\mathscr{L}_{XB} = W_{UB} U_X^B + \Omega_3 = 0 \tag{14-69}$$

$$\mathscr{L}_{YB} = W_{UB} U_Y^B + \Omega_4 = 0 \tag{14-70}$$

$$\mathscr{L}_{\Omega1} = K_T - K_X - K_Y = 0 \tag{14-71}$$

$$\mathscr{L}_{\Omega2} = L_T - L_X - L_Y = 0 \tag{14-72}$$

$$\mathscr{L}_{\Omega3} = X_A + X_B - f^X(K_X, L_X) = 0 \tag{14-73}$$

$$\mathscr{L}_{\Omega4} = Y_A + Y_B - f^Y(K_Y, L_Y) = 0 \tag{14-74}$$

The bordered Hessian matrix of second partial derivatives is a 12×12 matrix. Because the problem has four constraints, the second-order conditions require that the border-preserving principal minors of the determinant of the bordered Hessian of dimension n, $n = 9, 10, 11,$ and 12, have the same sign as $(-1)^{n-4}$. This means that the determinant of the bordered Hessian itself must be positive and that its naturally ordered border-preserving principal minors of dimension 11, 10, and 9 alternate in sign, the 11×11 minor being negative. For the sake of the environment, we do not pursue the implications of the SOC further, but we will assume that they are satisfied.

From equations (14-63) through (14-66) it is easy to show that

$$\frac{\Omega_1}{\Omega_2} = \frac{f_K^X}{f_L^X} = \frac{f_K^Y}{f_L^Y} = \text{MRTS}_{L,K}^X = \text{MRTS}_{L,K}^Y \tag{14-75}$$

You should recognize (14-75) as the criterion for Pareto-optimal allocation of inputs in production, because the ratios of the marginal products of capital and labor in the production of X and Y are equal to the respective marginal rates of technical substitution. Similarly, from equations (14-67) through (14-70) it follows that

$$\frac{\Omega_3}{\Omega_4} = \frac{U_X^A}{U_Y^A} = \frac{U_X^B}{U_Y^B} = \text{MRS}_{X,Y}^A = \text{MRS}_{X,Y}^B \tag{14-76}$$

Equation (14-76) is a restatement of the criterion for Pareto-optimal allocation of goods in consumption, because the ratios of marginal utilities for consumers A and B are equal to their respective marginal rates of substitution.

Thus far, the general model that combines production and consumption only duplicates what we already knew from the individual production and consumption models. We can gain additional insight into Pareto-optimal resource allocation by noting that equations (14-63) through (14-66) also imply that

$$\frac{\Omega_3}{\Omega_4} = \frac{f_L^Y}{f_L^X} = \frac{f_K^Y}{f_K^X} \qquad (14\text{-}77)$$

From equation (14-24) we know that $f_L^Y/f_L^X = f_K^Y/f_K^X = \text{MRT}_{X,Y}$. Therefore, combining (14-77) and (14-76) allows us to conclude that, at the optimum,

$$\text{MRT}_{X,Y} = \text{MRS}_{X,Y} \qquad (14\text{-}78)$$

This last mathematical criterion for Pareto-optimal resource allocation joins production with consumption by requiring that the marginal rate of transformation in production equal the marginal rate of substitution in consumption.

Like the other criteria, this criterion also makes intuitive sense. The marginal rate of transformation is the rate at which the productive capacity *is capable* of trading off one good for another by reallocating inputs. The marginal rate of substitution is the rate at which the consumers are just willing to trade one good for the other. If the two rates are different, it means that the amount consumers are required to sacrifice for one of the goods is less than they are willing to sacrifice. At least one consumer could be made better off and no one worse off if more of that good and less of the other were produced, until the marginal rate of transformation equals the marginal rate of substitution. Therefore, Pareto-optimal resource allocation is not achieved unless MRT = MRS. Remember that this notion of optimality does not take into account all the aspects of resource allocation that are omitted from these simple production and consumption models, such as the costs of carrying out transactions and exchanges.

14.5

PARETO-OPTIMAL RESOURCE ALLOCATION AND THE MARKET SYSTEM

Much has been made of the fact that, under conditions of perfect competition in input and output markets, a system of market prices results in Pareto-optimal resource allocation. The equilibrium conditions of our models of utility-maximizing consumer behavior in Chapters 7 and 9 and profit-maximizing producer behavior in Chapters 4, 6, and 11 satisfy the mathematical criteria for Pareto-optimal resource allocation. In Chapters 7 and 9 we saw that an individual chooses to consume where her marginal rate of substitution equals the ratio of prices. If consumers A and B face the same prices, P_X and P_Y, we can write

$$\frac{P_X}{P_Y} = \frac{U_X^A}{U_Y^A} = \frac{U_X^B}{U_Y^B} = \text{MRS}_{X,Y}^A = \text{MRS}_{X,Y}^B \qquad (14\text{-}79)$$

In Chapters 6 and 11 we saw that individual firms choose input combinations such that the marginal rate of technical substitution between two inputs equals the ratio of input prices. If the firms producing X and Y face the same input prices, r and w, we can write

$$\frac{r}{w} = \frac{f_K^X}{f_L^X} = \frac{f_K^Y}{f_L^Y} = \text{MRTS}_{L,K}^X = \text{MRTS}_{L,K}^Y \tag{14-80}$$

Finally, in Chapter 4 we saw that individual firms produce a quantity such that the price of the output equals marginal cost expressed in dollars per unit. Recall that the marginal rate of transformation represents the marginal cost of X expressed in terms of Y and its inverse represents the marginal cost of Y expressed in terms of X. Therefore, we can write

$$\frac{P_X}{P_Y} = \frac{\text{MC}_X}{\text{MC}_Y} = \text{MRT}_{X,Y} = \text{MRS}_{X,Y}^A = \text{MRS}_{X,Y}^B \tag{14-81}$$

We have shown that the equilibrium conditions of our models of perfectly competitive profit-maximizing firm behavior and utility-maximizing consumer behavior are consistent with the mathematical criteria for Pareto-optimal resource allocation. If the assumptions underlying these models were satisfied, we could conclude that perfect competition results in Pareto-optimal resource allocation. However, remember from Chapter 1 that models of economic behavior are designed to abstract sufficiently from reality to generate substantive hypotheses. In the process, we *assume* that the equilibrium conditions are satisfied in order to perform comparative statics analysis. The equilibrium conditions are part of what Milton Friedman called the language of a model, the purpose of which is to organize the reasoning process. To argue that the competitive market results in Pareto-optimal resource allocation because the language of our consumer and producer models is consistent with the language of our model of efficiency and exchange is a misuse of the methodology of economic reasoning.

14.6

SUMMARY

The primary purpose of this chapter is to show you how individual models of producer and consumer behavior can be brought together to describe resource allocation in a model with more than one consumer and producer. In the process, we introduced the notion of Pareto-improving actions to give a motivating principle, or objective function, for our models. The equilibria of both the producer model, which describes the allocation of scarce inputs between two firms, and the consumer model, which describes the allocation of scarce goods between two consumers, can be pictured graphically by Edgeworth–Bowley box diagrams. Points on the contract curves within the Edgeworth–Bowley boxes can be pictured as possibilities frontiers, the PPF in the case of production and the UPF in the case of consumption.

The Lagrange multipliers of our models measure the marginal benefits or costs of increases in the available levels of inputs or outputs, so we interpret them as shadow prices. Because our models are descriptive and not behavioral, comparative statics results do not predict behavior. However, in the case of the production model, they give us additional insight into the concept of Pareto-optimal resource allocation. We see that strictly concave production functions yield a strictly concave PPF and imply rising marginal cost. Similarly, strictly concave production functions imply that an increased endowment, or supply, of an input results in a decrease in its shadow price.

We combine the production and consumption models by recognizing that the endowments of goods in the consumption model come from the PPF of the production model. Therefore, each point on the PPF is associated with a UPF, the collection of which can be graphed to form a GUPF. Every point on every UPF satisfies the mathematical criteria for Pareto-optimal resource allocation in production and consumption. We introduce the problematic concept of a social welfare function in order to advance further in distinguishing among the equally Pareto-optimal points on the GUPF.

This chapter has brought together elements from many prior chapters. These include the discussions of profit-maximizing and cost-minimizing firm behavior, utility-maximizing consumer behavior, competitive markets, the mathematics of optimization, the envelope theorem, the techniques of matrix algebra, and the methodology of economic reasoning. For this reason, we believe it serves as a good synthesizing and concluding chapter for the text. The concepts and techniques that you have mastered up to this point can serve you in many applications and investigations not discussed in this text. Our hope is that the mix of theory and application we have provided has developed in you a measure of both competence in and appreciation for the power of a mathematical approach to economic analysis that will serve you well in further studies as well as in practical applications.

◆ REFERENCES

Arrow, K., and Scitovsky, T., eds., *A.E.A. Readings in Welfare Economics*, Vol. 12 (Homewood, IL: Richard D. Irwin, 1969).

Binger, B., and Hoffman, E., *Microeconomics with Calculus* (Glenview, IL: Scott, Foresman and Company, 1988), Chapters 7 and 14.

Graaff, J. de V., *Theoretical Welfare Economics* (Cambridge: Cambridge University Press, 1967).

Quirk, J., and Saposnik, R., *Introduction to General Equilibrium Theory and Welfare Economics* (New York: McGraw-Hill Book Company, 1968).

◆ ANSWERS TO END-OF-SECTION EXERCISES

Section 14.2.1 Equilibrium Conditions for Efficiency in Production

1.
$$\mathcal{L} = 100K_Y^{0.25}L_Y^{0.25} + \theta[X_0 - 50K_X^{0.5}L_X^{0.5}]$$
$$+ \kappa(K_T - K_X - K_Y) + \lambda(L_T - L_X - L_Y)$$

Choice variables: K_X, L_X, K_Y, L_Y, θ, κ, and λ.
Parameters: X_0, K_T, and L_T.

2. $\mathcal{L}_{KY} = 25K_Y^{-0.75}L_Y^{0.25} - \kappa = 0$ $\qquad$ $\mathcal{L}_{LY} = 25K_Y^{0.25}L_Y^{-0.75} - \lambda = 0$

$\mathcal{L}_{KX} = -25\theta K_X^{-0.5}L_X^{0.5} - \kappa = 0$ $\qquad$ $\mathcal{L}_{LX} = -25\theta K_X^{0.5}L_X^{-0.5} - \lambda = 0$

$\mathcal{L}_\theta = X_0 - 50K_X^{0.5}L_X^{0.5} = 0$ $\qquad$ $\mathcal{L}_\kappa = K_T - K_X - K_Y = 0$

$\mathcal{L}_\lambda = L_T - L_X - L_Y = 0$

3. $K_X^* = 4$; $K_Y^* = 12$; $L_X^* = 1$; $L_Y^* = 3$; $Y^* = 245$

Section 14.2.3 Comparative Statics Analysis of the Production Model

1. $\theta^* = -[K_T - (X_0/50)(K_T/L_T)^{0.5}]^{-0.75}[L_T - (X_0/50)(L_T/K_T)^{0.5}]^{0.25}(K_T/L_T)^{0.5}$

θ^* is the slope of the PPF and the negative of the $\mathrm{MRT}_{X,Y}$, the rate at which X can be increased by decreasing Y, given the production functions and the fixed quantitites of capital and labor. The $\mathrm{MRT}_{X,Y}$ represents the marginal cost of increasing X.

$\kappa^* = 25[K_T - (X_0/50)(K_T/L_T)^{0.5}]^{-0.75}[L_T - (X_0/50)(L_T/K_T)^{0.5}]^{0.25}$.

κ^* is the shadow price of capital. It represents the increased benefits, measured as increases in Y, of increasing the fixed quantity of capital.

$\lambda^* = 25[K_T - (X_0/50)(K_T/L_T)^{0.5}]^{0.25}[L_T - (X_0/50)(L_T/K_T)^{0.5}]^{-0.75}$.

λ^* is the shadow price of labor. It represents the increased benefits, measured as increases in Y, of increasing the fixed quantity of labor.

2. $\partial\theta^*/\partial X_0 = -0.158$. Because it is negative, we know that the production possibilities frontier is strictly concave and that the marginal cost of X increases as X increases.

3. $\partial\theta^*/\partial K_T = -3.38$. Because it is negative, we know that the marginal benefits or the shadow price of K decrease if the endowment of K increases.

4. $\partial\kappa^*/\partial L_T = -3.38$. Because it is negative, we know that the marginal benefits or the shadow price of L decrease if the endowment of L increases.

14.3.2 Pareto-Optimal Allocation of Goods Among Consumers

1. $\mathcal{L} = (X_A Y_A)^\alpha + \phi[U_0^B - (X_B Y_B)^\beta] + \chi(X_T - X_A - X_B) + \psi(Y_T - Y_A - Y_B)$.
Choice variables: X_A, Y_A, X_B, Y_B, ϕ, χ, and ψ.
Parameters: U_0^B, X_T, and Y_T.

2. $\mathcal{L}_{XA} = \alpha X_A^{\alpha-1}Y_A^\alpha - \chi = 0$ $\qquad$ $\mathcal{L}_{YA} = \alpha X_A^\alpha Y_A^{\alpha-1} - \psi = 0$

$\mathcal{L}_{XB} = -\beta\phi X_B^{\beta-1}Y_B^\beta - \chi = 0$ $\qquad$ $\mathcal{L}_{YB} = -\beta\phi X_B^\beta Y_B^{\beta-1} - \psi = 0$

$\mathcal{L}_\phi = U_0^B - (X_B Y_B)^\beta = 0$ $\qquad$ $\mathcal{L}_\chi = X_T - X_B - X_A = 0$

$\mathcal{L}_\psi = Y_T - Y_B - Y_A = 0$

3. $X_A^* = X_T - [(U_0^B)^{1/\alpha}(X_T/Y_T)]^{1/2}$ $\qquad$ $Y_A^* = Y_T - [(U_0^B)^{1/\alpha}(L_T/K_T)]^{1/2}$

$X_B^* = [U_0^{B1/\alpha}(X_T/Y_T)]^{1/2}$ $\qquad\qquad$ $Y_B^* = [U_0^{B1/\alpha}(L_T/K_T)]^{1/2}$

$\phi^* = -(\alpha/\beta)(X_A^{*\alpha}Y_A^{*(\alpha-1)})/(X_B^{*\beta}Y_B^{*(\beta-1)}) < 0$

The slope of the UPF is equal to ϕ^*. It is negative because the marginal utilities of both consumers are positive for both goods.

◆ SELF-HELP PROBLEMS

Answers to these problems are given at the end of the text.

For questions 1 through 5 consider the following resource allocation problem. Robinson Crusoe (RC) is stranded by himself on a desert island, with only his own labor as an input and the know-how to produce two goods, food and shelter, from which he derives utility.

1. Set up this resource allocation problem as a constrained optimization. What are the Lagrangian objective function, the choice variables, and parameters of your model?

2. What are the first- and second-order conditions for maximization?

3. Demonstrate that the second-order conditions are satisfied if the production functions are strictly concave and if RC's indifference curves are convex.

4. Provide economic interpretations of the Lagrange multipliers in your problem.

5. Suppose the invigorating sea air permits RC to sleep less, increasing the availability of his labor. Find and interpret comparative statics results for the effects of an increase in labor on all choice variables and Lagrange multipliers in your problem.

6. Now suppose that every week RC is capable of producing food according to the function $F = 10L - L^2/2$ and shelter according to the function $S = 10 + 2L$, where F and S represent food and shelter and L represents labor. His utility function is $U = FS$ and the total amount of labor available every week is 100 hours.

   a. Find the objective function and the first- and second-order conditions.

   b. Solve the first-order conditions for the optimal values of the choice variables and determine whether the second-order conditions are satisfied.

   c. Find RC's shadow price for labor and how an increase in labor affects it.

   d. Find the equation of RC's production possibilities frontier with F^* expressed as a function of S and determine whether or not it is concave.

◆ SUPPLEMENTAL PROBLEMS

1. a. Find the Lagrangian objective function and the first- and second-order conditions of a model of production in which the objective is to maximize $X = f^X(K_X, L_X)$, subject to a constrained level of production of Y, $Y_0 = f^Y(K_Y, L_Y)$, as well as constraints imposed by the fixed availability of capital and labor, $K_T = K_X + K_Y$ and $L_T = L_X + L_Y$.

   b. Find expressions for the Lagrange multipliers and provide economic interpretations. Show that $MRT_{X,Y} = 1/MRT_{Y,X}$ by comparing your results with the results from equation (14-23) in Section 14.2.

   c. Show that, if $f^X(K_X, L_X)$ is strictly concave, an increase in an input's endowment decreases its shadow prices.

2. a. Find the Lagrangian objective function and the first- and second-order conditions of a model of consumption in which the objective is to maximize $U^B = U^B(X_B, Y_B)$, subject to a constrained level of utility of A, $U_0^A =$

$U^A(X_A, Y_A)$, as well as constraints imposed by the fixed availability of two goods, $X_T = X_A + X_B$ and $Y_T = Y_A + Y_B$.

    b. Find expressions for the Lagrange multipliers and provide economic interpretations.

3. Show that the second-order conditions of the model presented in problem 2 are satisfied if both utility functions have convex indifference curves

For questions 4 through 8 consider the following resource allocation problem. Robinson Crusoe (RC) is stranded by himself on a desert island, with his own labor as an input, a fixed amount of capital equipment he was able to salvage from the shipwreck, and the know-how to produce two goods, food and shelter, from which he derives utility.

4. Set up this resource allocation problem as a constrained optimization. What are the Lagrangian objective function, the choice variables, and parameters of your model?

5. What are the first- and second-order conditions for maximization?

6. Demonstrate that the second-order conditions are satisfied if the production functions are strictly concave and if RC's indifference curves are convex.

7. Provide economic interpretations of the Lagrange multipliers in your problem.

8. Suppose RC saves a young cannibal, named Friday. The addition of Friday to RC's economy augments the amount of available labor and it adds another consumer. Answer problems 4 through 7 for this new, augmented system.

Answers to Self-Help Problems

Chapter 1

1.a. $Y^* = 3400$, $C^* = 2775$

1.b. $Y^* = 3600$, $C^* = 2925$

2. $Q_d = a - bP + cY + dP_T$,
$Q_s = eP - fw - gE$

Effect on Q^* per unit change in $Y = ce/(e + b)$
Effect on Q^* per unit change in $P_T = de/(e + b)$
Effect on Q^* per unit change in $w = -bf/(e + b)$
Effect on Q^* per unit change in $E = -bg/(e + b)$

Effect on P^* per unit change in $Y = c/(e + b)$
Effect on P^* per unit change in $P_T = d/(e + b)$
Effect on P^* per unit change in $w = f/(e + b)$
Effect on P^* per unit change in $E = g/(e + b)$

In this model twidgets and widgets are substitutes since an increase in P_T leads to an increase in quantity of widgets demanded.

3.a. $Q^* = (\alpha b - a\beta)/(b - \beta) - [b\beta/(b - \beta)]t$,
$P^* = (\alpha - a)/(b - \beta) - [\beta/(b - \beta)]t$

3.b. Effect on Q^* per unit change in
$t = -b\beta/(b - \beta) < 0$ since $b < 0$ and $\beta > 0$.
Effect on P^* per unit change in
$t = -\beta/(b - \beta) > 0$ since $b < 0$ and $\beta > 0$. The tax is shifted to consumers partially because
$-\beta/(b - \beta) < 1$

3.c. Effect on Q^* per unit change in
$t = -b\beta/(b - \beta) < 0$ since $b < 0$ and $\beta > 0$.
Effect on P^* per unit change in
$t = -b/(b - \beta) < 0$ since $b < 0$ and $\beta > 0$.

Chapter 2

1.a. This is an exponential function. Its domain is the set of all real numbers and its range is the set of positive real numbers.

1.b. This is a logarithmic function. Its domain is the set of positive real numbers and its range is the set of all real numbers.

1.c. This is a function. Its domain is the set of all real numbers and its range is the set of nonnegative real numbers.

1.d. This is a constant function. Its domain is the set of all real numbers. Its range is the number c.

2.a. $AR = 50 - 0.5Q$, $TR = 50Q - 0.5Q^2$
TR is at a maximum at $Q = 50$.

2.b. $TC = 20Q$

2.c. $\pi(Q) = 30Q - 0.5Q^2$
π crosses the horizontal axis at $Q = 60$ and is at a maximum at $Q = 30$.

3.a. $Q_d = a - bP$, $AC = c$

3.b. $AR = a/b - (1/b)Q$, $TR = (a/b)Q - (1/b)Q^2$
TR is at a maximum at $Q = a/2$.

3.c. $TC = cQ$

3.d. $\pi(Q) = [(a/b) - c]Q - (1/b)Q^2$
π crosses the horizontal axis at $Q = a + cb$ and reaches a maximum at $Q = (a - cb)/2$.

4.a. $e^Q = e^\alpha Y^\tau P^{-\beta}$

4.b. $Q = e^{(\alpha + \tau Y - \beta P)}$

Chapter 3

1. This question can be answered either way. Better yet, recognize that behavior that is discontinuous or nonsmooth when viewed from one perspective seems continuous and smooth when viewed from another. For example, when a consumer buys an automobile, she appears to suddenly change from owning $0 worth of automobile to owning $10,000, clearly discontinuous behavior. However, if we consider the good in question to be "transportation services," then her purchase may seem more continuous. The new automobile may vary only incrementally from other forms of transportation such as public transportation, or taxi, in terms of dollars per mile of transportation. Furthermore, when we aggregate individual behavior to describe, for example, market demand, many apparently discontinuous decisions seem smooth and continuous when combined. A 100% change in demand by an individual translates to only a 1% change for the aggregated demand of 100 individuals.

2. Let our original polynomial equal

$$Y = a_0 + a_1X + a_2X^2 + a_3X^3 + \cdots + a_nX^n$$

The derivative equals

$$\frac{dY}{dX} = a_1 + 2a_2X + 3a_3X^2 + 4a_4X^3 + \cdots + na_nX^{n-1}$$

The derivative is clearly a polynomial of degree $n - 1$.

3.a. Let

$$Y = \frac{f(X)}{g(X)} = [f(X)]z(g(X))$$

where

$$z(g(X)) = g(X)^{-1}$$

According to the product rule,

$$\frac{dY}{dX} = f'z + z'f = \frac{f'}{g(X)} + z'f(X)$$

We apply the chain rule and the power function rule to find that

$$z' = -g(X)^{-2}g'(X)$$

Substitute z' into dY/dX to obtain

$$\frac{dY}{dX} = \frac{f'}{g(X)} - \frac{[g'(X)f(X)]}{[g(X)^2]}$$

If we multiply and divide the first term by $g(X)$, we have derived the quotient rule, or

$$\frac{dY}{dX} = \frac{[g(X)f'(X) - g'(X)f(X)]}{[g(X)^2]}$$

b. See Rule 9: Logarithmic Function Rule in Section 3.4

4.a. MR $= 20 - 10Q - 3Q^2$
      MC $= 14 - 10Q + 3Q^2$

4.b. $Q^* = 1$, $P^* = 14$

4.c. $\varepsilon = -2$

4.d. This firm operates under imperfect competition because it faces a downward-sloping demand function, AR$' = -5 - 2Q < 0$ for $Q > 0$.

5.a. $\ln Q = 0.5 \ln K + 0.5 \ln L = 1.61 + 0.5 \ln L$

5.b. See the top panel of Figure 3.56 in the chapter

5.c. $MP_L = 2.5/L^{0.5}$

5.d. $MP_L' = -1.25/L^{1.5} < 0$.

Chapter 4

1.

Price taker in both markets	Price searcher in both markets
FOC: $\pi' = PQ' - w$ $= 0$	$\pi' = P'Q'Q + PQ'$ $- Lw' - w = 0$
MRP $= w$	MRP $=$ MFC
SOC: $\pi'' = PQ'' < 0$	$\pi'' = P''Q'^2Q + P'Q''Q$ $+ 2P'Q'^2 + Q''P$ $- w''L - 2w' < 0$
MRP$' < 0$	MRP$' <$ MFC$'$

2.a.
Revenue function:	TR $= PQ(L)$
Cost function:	TC $= w(L)L$
Profit function:	$\pi = PQ(L) - w(L)L$
Choice variable:	L
Parameter:	P

2.b. FOC: $d\pi(L)/dL = P(dQ/dL) - w(L)$
                $- L(dw/dL)$
                $= 0$
       SOC: $d^2\pi(L)/dL^2 = P(d^2Q/dL^2) - dw/dL$
                $- L(d^2w/dL^2) - dw/dL$
                < 0

2.c. $dL^*/dP = (-dQ/dL)/[P(d^2Q/dL^2)$
       $- dw/dL - L(d^2w/dL^2) - dw/dL] > 0$

2.d. $dL^*/dP = (-dQ/dL)/[P(d^2Q/dL^2)] > 0$ is larger than the expression in part c.

3.a. $w = 26$

3.b. $w = 18$

4.a. MC $= 9Q^2 - 15Q + 2$

4.b. $Q = 15/18$

5.a. FOC: $d\,\mathrm{TR}/dL = (d\,\mathrm{TR}/dQ)(dQ/dL)$
                $= \mathrm{MRP}_L = 0$
       SOC: $d^2\mathrm{TR}/dL^2 = (d^2\mathrm{TR}/dQ^2)(dQ/dL)^2$
                $+ (d^2Q/dL^2)(d\,\mathrm{TR}/dQ)$
                $= \mathrm{MRP}' < 0$

5.b. FOC: $dQ/dL = \mathrm{MP}_L = 0$
       SOC: $d^2Q/dL^2 = \mathrm{MP}_L' < 0$

5.c. If the firm is a price-taker, then P = MR, and the FOC and SOC of the two models imply the same thing.

Chapter 5

1. $dY/dG = 1/[1 - C'(1 - T')] > 0$

2. $dY/dI = 1/[1 - C'(1 - T') - T']$

3. $dY/dI = 1/[1 - C'(1 - T') - G']$

4. $dY/dG = 1/[1 - C'/(1 + C'T')]$

5. $\partial Q_d^*/\partial Y > 0$ if the good is normal. $\partial Q_d^*/\partial Y < 0$ if the good is inferior.
   $\partial Q_d^*/\partial P_c < 0$, $\partial Q_d^*/\partial P_s > 0$, $\partial Q_s^*/\partial w < 0$,
   $\partial Q_s^*/\partial r < 0$

6. Equilibrium condition: $Q_d = Q_s$
   Endogenous variables: Q_d, Q_s, and P
   Exogenous variables: Y, P_c, P_s, w, and r
   Reduced-form $\quad P^* = P^*(Y, P_c, P_s, w, r)$,
   equations: $\quad Q^* = Q^*(Y, P_c, P_s, w, r)$

7. $\partial P^*/\partial Y = -D_Y/(D_{P^*} - S_{P^*})$, sign ?
   $\partial Q^*/\partial Y = S_{P^*}(\partial P^*/\partial Y)$, sign ?
   $\partial P^*/\partial P_c = -D_{Pc}/(D_{P^*} - S_{P^*}) < 0$,
   $\partial Q^*/\partial P_c = S_{P^*}(\partial P^*/\partial P_C) < 0$
   $\partial P^*/\partial P_s = -D_{Ps}/(D_{P^*} - S_{P^*}) > 0$,
   $\partial Q^*/\partial P_s = S_{P^*}(\partial P^*/\partial P_S) > 0$
   $\partial P^*/\partial w = S_w/(D_{P^*} - S_{P^*}) > 0$,
   $\partial Q^*/\partial w = S_{P^*}(\partial P^*/\partial w) < 0$
   $\partial P^*/\partial r = S_r/(D_{P^*} - S_{P^*}) > 0$,
   $\partial Q^*/\partial r = S_{P^*}(\partial P^*/\partial r) < 0$

Chapter 6

1.a. FOC: $\quad \partial Y/\partial X_1 = 3X_1^2 - a = 0$
$\quad \partial Y/\partial X_2 = -2X_2 = 0$
Critical points: $\quad X_1 = \pm\sqrt{(a/3)}$, $X_2 = 0$
SOC: $\quad f_{11} = \partial^2 Y/\partial X_1^2 = 6X_1$
$\quad f_{22} = \partial^2 Y/\partial X_2^2 = -2$
$\quad f_{12} = 0$
$\quad f_{11}f_{22} - f_{12}^2 = -12X_1$
The point $X_1 = -\sqrt{(a/3)}$ and $X_2 = 0$ is a maximum.
The point $X_1 = \sqrt{(a/3)}$ and $X_2 = 0$ is neither a maximum nor a minimum.

1.b. FOC: $\quad \partial Y/\partial X_1 = -X_1^{-2} + X_2 = 0$
$\quad \partial Y/\partial X_2 = -X_2^{-2} + X_1 = 0$
Critical point: $X_1^* = X_2^* = 1$
SOC: $\quad f_{11} = \partial^2 Y/\partial X_1^2 = -2/X_1^3$
$\quad f_{22} = \partial^2 Y/\partial X_2^2 = -2/X_2^3$
$\quad f_{12} = 1$
$\quad f_{11}f_{22} - f_{12}^2 = 4/(X_1^3 X_2^3) - 1$
The point $X_2^* = X_2^* = 1$ is a maximum.

2.a. FOC: $\quad \partial\pi/\partial Q_1 = 6 - 6(Q_1 + Q_2) = 0$
$\quad \partial\pi/\partial Q_2 = 12 - 24Q_2^2$
$\quad\quad\quad - 6(Q_1 + Q_2) = 0$
Critical point: $\quad Q_1^* = 0.5$ and
$\quad\quad Q_2^* = 0.5$
SOC: $\quad\quad f_{11} = -6$
$\quad\quad f_{22} = -48Q_2 - 6$
$\quad\quad f_{12} = -6$
$\quad\quad f_{11}f_{22} - f_{12}^2 = 288Q_2 > 0$
The point $Q_1^* = 0.5$ and
$Q_2^* = 0.5$.
$P_1^* = 20$, $P_2^* = 10$

2.b. $\varepsilon_1 = -1.43$; $\varepsilon_2 = -2.5$

3. $Q_1^* = 8$, $Q_2^* = 7.67$
$P_1^* = 39.33$, $P_2^* = 46.66$
$\pi^* = 488.33$

4. $Q_1^* = 2$, $Q_2^* = 4$

5.a. $K^* = 4$, $L^* = 1$

5.b. $\text{VMP}_L = \text{PMP}_L = 40(0.5L^{-0.5}) = 20 = w$
$\text{VMP}_K = \text{PMP}_K = 40(0.5K^{-0.5}) = 10 = r$

6. $\partial L^*/\partial w = f_{KK}/P(f_{LL}f_{KK} - f_{KL}^2) < 0$
$\partial K^*/\partial w = -f_{KL}/P(f_{LL}f_{KK} - f_{KL}^2)$, sign ?

Chapter 7

1.a. FOC: $\quad dU/dX_1 = 2.5X_1^{-0.5}(20 - 2X_1)^{0.5}$
$\quad\quad - 5X_1^{0.5}(20 - 2X_1)^{-0.5} = 0$
SOC: $\quad d^2U/dX_1^2 = -(5/4)X_1^{-1.5}(20 - 2X_1)^{0.5}$
$\quad\quad - (5/2)X_1^{-0.5}(20 - 2X_1)^{-0.5}$
$\quad\quad - 5X_1^{0.5}(20 - 2X_1)^{-1.5}$
$\quad\quad - (5/2)X_1^{-0.5}(20 - 2X_1)^{-0.5}$
$\quad\quad < 0$
Solution values: $\quad X_1^* = 5$, $X_2^* = 10$

1.b. FOC: $\quad dU/dX_1 = 1200X_1 - (90/25)X_1^2 = 0$
SOC: $\quad d^2U/dX_1^2 = 1200 - (36/5)X_1 < 0$
Solution values: $\quad X_1^* = 333.33$, $X_2^* = 6.67$

1.c. FOC: $\quad dE/dX_1 = 10 - 250/X_1^2 = 0$
SOC: $\quad d^2E/dX_1^2 = 500/X_1^3 > 0$
Solution values: $\quad X_1^* = 5$, $X_2^* = 10$

1.d. FOC: $\quad dU/dL = 0.25L^{-0.75}(240 - 10L)^{0.25}$
$\quad\quad - 2.5L^{0.25}(240 - 10L)^{-0.75}$
$\quad\quad = 0$

SOC: d^2U/dL^2
$$= -(3/16)L^{-1.75}(240 - 10L)^{0.25}$$
$$- (5/8)L^{-0.75}(240 - 10L)^{-0.75}$$
$$- (5/8)L^{-0.75}(240 - 10L)^{-0.75}$$
$$- 18.75L^{-0.75}(240 - L)^{-1.75}$$
$$< 0$$

Solution values: $L^* = 12, M^* = 120$

1.e. FOC: $dU/dL = 52,920,000L^2$
$$- 840,000L^3 + 3125L^4$$
$$= 0$$

SOC: $d^2U/dL^2 = 105,840,000L$
$$- 2,520,000L^2$$
$$+ 12,500L^3 < 0$$

Solution values: $L^* = 100.8, M^* = 1,680$

2.a. FOC: $\mathcal{L}_1 = 2.5X_1^{-0.5}X_2^{0.5} - 10\mu = 0$
$\mathcal{L}_2 = 2.5X_1^{0.5}X_2^{-0.5} - 5\mu = 0$
$\mathcal{L}_\mu = 100 - 10X_1 - 5X_2 = 0$

Solution values: $X_1^* = 5; X_2^* = 10; \mu^* = \sqrt{2}/4$

2.b. FOC: $\mathcal{L}_1 = 60X_1X_2 - \mu = 0$
$\mathcal{L}_2 = 30X_1^2 - 25\mu = 0$
$\mathcal{L}_\mu = 500 - X_1 - 25X_2 = 0$

Solution values: $X_1^* = 333.33; X_2^* = 6.67;$
$\mu^* = 133,398.67$

2.c. FOC: $\mathcal{L}_1 = 10 - \mu X_2 = 0$
$\mathcal{L}_2 = 5 - \mu X_1 = 0$
$\mathcal{L}_\mu = 50 - X_1X_2 = 0$

Solution values: $X_1^* = 5; X_2^* = 10; \mu^* = 1$

2.d. FOC: $\mathcal{L}_M = 0.25M^{-0.75}L^{0.25} - \mu/10 = 0$
$\mathcal{L}_L = 0.25M^{0.25}L^{-0.75} - \mu = 0$
$\mathcal{L}_\mu = 24 - M/10 - L = 0$

Solution values: $L^* = 12; M^* = 120; \mu^* = 0.128$

2.e. FOC: $\mathcal{L}_M = 2ML^3 - \mu/25 = 0$
$\mathcal{L}_L = 3M^2L^2 - \mu = 0$
$\mathcal{L}_\mu = 168 - M/25 - L = 0$

Solution values: $L^* = 100.8; M^* = 1680;$
$\mu^* = 86,032,000,000$

3.a. $U^* = (\sqrt{2}/4)M$
$dU^*/dM = \sqrt{2}/4 = \mu^*$

3.b. $U^* = (120/675)M^3$
$dU^*/dM = 133,333.33 = \mu^*$

3.c. $E^* = (20/\sqrt{2})U_0^{1/2}$
$dE^*/dU_0 = 1 = \mu^*$

3.d. $U^* = (5/2)^{0.25}T^{-0.25}$
$dU^*/dT = 0.128 = \mu^*$

3.e. $U^* = (2700/125)^{0.25}T^5$
$dU^*/dT = 86,032,000,000 = \mu^*$

4. Lagrangian objective function:
$$\mathcal{L} = U(X_1, X_2) + \mu(M - P_1X_1 - P_2X_2)$$

Choice variables: X_1 and X_2
Parameters: $M, P_1,$ and P_2
FOC: $\mathcal{L}_1 = U_1 - \mu P_1 = 0$
$\mathcal{L}_2 = U_2 - \mu P_2 = 0$
$\mathcal{L}_\mu = M - P_1X_1 - P_2X_2 = 0$
μ^* can be interpreted as marginal utility of money income.

5. Lagrangian objective function:
$$\mathcal{L} = P_1X_1 + P_2X_2 + \mu[U_0 - U(X_1, X_2)]$$

Choice variables: X_1 and X_2
Parameters: $U_0, P_1,$ and P_2
FOC: $\mathcal{L}_1 = P_1 - \mu U_1 = 0$
$\mathcal{L}_2 = P_2 - \mu U_2 = 0$
$\mathcal{L}_\mu = U_0 - U(X_1, X_2) = 0$
μ^* can be interpreted as marginal cost of utility.

6. Lagrangian objective function:
$$\mathcal{L} = U(M, R) + \mu[T - (M - E)/w - R]$$

Choice variables: M and R
Parameters: $T, w,$ and E
FOC: $\mathcal{L}_M = U_M - \mu/w = 0$
$\mathcal{L}_R = U_R - \mu = 0$
$\mathcal{L}_\mu = T - (M - E)/w - R = 0$
μ^* can be interpreted as marginal cost of time.

Chapter 8

1.a. Objective function:
$$\pi(X_1, X_2) = PAX_1^\alpha X_2^\beta - w_1X_1 - w_2X_2$$

FOC: $\pi_1 = \alpha PAX_1^{\alpha-1}X_2^\beta - w_1 = 0$
$\pi_2 = \beta PAX_1^\alpha X_2^{\beta-1} - w_2 = 0$

$$\begin{bmatrix} \pi_{11} & \pi_{12} \\ \pi_{21} & \pi_{22} \end{bmatrix}$$

$$= \begin{bmatrix} \alpha(\alpha-1)PAX_1^{\alpha-2}X_2^\beta & \alpha\beta PAX_1^{\alpha-1}X_2^{\beta-1} \\ \alpha\beta X_1^{\alpha-1}X_2^{\beta-1} & \beta(\beta-1)PAX_1^\alpha X_2^{\beta-2} \end{bmatrix}$$

1.b. $|H_{11}| = \alpha(\alpha-1)PAX_1^{\alpha-2}X_2^\beta < 0$
$|H_B| = \alpha(\alpha-1)\beta(\beta-1)P^2A^2X_1^{2\alpha-2}X_2^{2\beta-2}$
$- \alpha^2\beta^2P^2A^2X_1^{2\alpha-2}X_2^{2\beta-2} > 0$

1.c

$$\begin{bmatrix} \pi_{11} & \pi_{12} \\ \pi_{21} & \pi_{22} \end{bmatrix} \begin{bmatrix} \dfrac{\partial X_1^*}{\partial w_1} \\ \dfrac{\partial X_2^*}{\partial w_1} \end{bmatrix} = \begin{bmatrix} 1 \\ 0 \end{bmatrix}$$

1.d. $\dfrac{\partial X_1^*}{\partial w_1} =$

$$\frac{\beta(\beta - 1)PAX_1^{\alpha}X_2^{\beta-2}}{\alpha(\alpha - 1)\beta(\beta - 1)P^2A^2X_1^{2\alpha-2}X_2^{2\beta-2} - \alpha^2\beta^2P^2A^2X_1^{2\alpha-2}X_2^{2\beta-2}}$$

This measures the slope of the firm's demand curve for input 1.

$\dfrac{\partial X_2^*}{\partial w_1} =$

$$\frac{-\alpha\beta PAX_1^{\alpha-1}X_2^{\beta-1}}{\alpha(\alpha - 1)\beta(\beta - 1)P^2A^2X_1^{2\alpha-2}X_2^{2\beta-2} - \alpha^2\beta^2P^2A^2X_1^{2\alpha-2}X_2^{2\beta-2}}$$

This measures the effect of a change in the price of input 1 on the firm's demand for input 2.

2.a. Lagrangian objective function:

$$\mathcal{L} = U(X_1, X_2, X_3) + \mu(M - P_1X_1 - P_2X_2 - P_3X_3)$$

FOC:
$$\mathcal{L}_1 = U_1 - \mu P_1 = 0$$
$$\mathcal{L}_2 = U_2 - \mu P_2 = 0$$
$$\mathcal{L}_3 = U_3 - \mu P_3 = 0$$
$$\mathcal{L}_\mu = M - P_1X_1 - P_2X_2 - P_3X_3 = 0$$

2.b. Bordered Hessian matrix:

$$H_B = \begin{bmatrix} U_{11} & U_{12} & U_{13} & -P_1 \\ U_{21} & U_{22} & U_{23} & -P_2 \\ U_{31} & U_{32} & U_{33} & -P_3 \\ -P_1 & -P_2 & -P_3 & 0 \end{bmatrix}$$

SOC: $|H_B| < 0$

$$|H_{11}| = \begin{vmatrix} U_{22} & U_{23} & -P_2 \\ U_{32} & U_{33} & -P_3 \\ -P_2 & -P_3 & 0 \end{vmatrix} > 0$$

3.a. Lagrangian function:

$$\mathcal{L} = 10(0.5X_1^{-2} + 0.5X_2^{-2})^{-0.5}$$
$$+ \mu(810 - 48X_1 - 6X_2)$$

FOC: $\mathcal{L}_1 = 5X_1^{-3}(0.5X_1^{-2} + 0.5X_2^{-2})^{-1.5} - 48\mu$
$= 0$
$\mathcal{L}_2 = 5X_2^{-3}(0.5X_1^{-2} + 0.5X_2^{-2})^{-1.5} - 6\mu$
$= 0$
$\mathcal{L}_\mu = 810 - 48X_1 - 6X_2 = 0$

3.b. Solution values: $X_1^* = 13.5$, $\quad X_2^* = 27$

3.c.

$$\begin{bmatrix} -0.450 & 0.225 & -48 \\ 0.225 & -0.112 & -3 \\ -48 & -6 & 0 \end{bmatrix}$$

SOC: $\quad |H_B| = 403.85 > 0$

4.

$$\begin{bmatrix} 1 & 1 & 1 & -1 & 0 & 0 \\ -1 & 0 & 0 & 0 & 0 & 0.8 \\ 0 & 0 & 0 & 1 & -1 & -1 \\ 0 & 0 & 0 & 0.25 & -1 & 0 \\ 0 & -1 & 0 & 0.2 & 0 & 0 \\ 0 & 0 & 1 & 0 & 0 & 0 \end{bmatrix} \begin{bmatrix} C \\ I \\ G \\ Y \\ T \\ Y_d \end{bmatrix} = \begin{bmatrix} 0 \\ -108 \\ 0 \\ -10 \\ -100 \\ 400 \end{bmatrix}$$

4.b. Determinant of the coefficients matrix = 0.2

4.c. Solution values: $Y^* = 3000$; $C^* = 1900$; $Yd^* = 2240$; $T^* = 760$; $I^* = 700$

4.d. Inverse matrix:

$$\begin{bmatrix} -3 & -4 & -3.2 & 3.2 & -3 & 3 \\ -1 & -1 & -0.8 & 0.8 & -2 & 1 \\ 0 & 0 & 0 & 0 & 0 & 1 \\ -5 & -5 & -4 & 4 & -5 & 5 \\ -1.25 & -1.25 & -1 & 0 & -1.25 & 1.25 \\ -3.75 & -3.75 & -4 & 4 & -3.75 & 3.75 \end{bmatrix}$$

5. Determinant of the coefficients matrix = 8

5.b. Inverse matrix:

$$\begin{bmatrix} 0.125 & -0.125 & 0.626 \\ -0.125 & 0.125 & 0.375 \\ -0.625 & -0.375 & 0.875 \end{bmatrix}$$

Solution values: $X^* = Y^* = Z^* = 0$

5.c. Solution values: $X^* = Y^* = Z^* = 0$

5.d. The solution to any system of linear homogeneous equations with a nonsingular coefficients matrix is a vector whose elements are all zeros.

Chapter 9

1. FOC:
$$\mathcal{L}_1 = \alpha X_1^{\alpha-1}X_2^{1-\alpha} - \mu P_1 = 0$$
$$\mathcal{L}_2 = (1 - \alpha)X_1^{\alpha}X_2^{-\alpha} - \mu P_2 = 0$$
$$\mathcal{L}_\mu = M - P_1X_1 - P_2X_2 = 0$$

SOC:

$$|H_B| =$$

$$\begin{vmatrix} \alpha(\alpha - 1)X_1^{\alpha-2}X_2^{1-\alpha} & \alpha(1-\alpha)X_1^{\alpha-1}X_2^{-\alpha} & -P_1 \\ \alpha(1-\alpha)X_1^{\alpha-1}X_2^{-\alpha} & -\alpha(1-\alpha)X_1^{\alpha}X_2^{-\alpha-1} & -P_2 \\ -P_1 & -P_2 & 0 \end{vmatrix}$$

$$= \alpha(\alpha-1)(P_1X_1^{\alpha-1}X_2^{-\alpha} + X_1^{\alpha}X_2^{-\alpha-1}$$
$$- P_2^2X_1^{\alpha-2}X_2^{1-\alpha} + P_1P_2$$

Demand functions: $X_1^* = \alpha M/P_1$,
$X_2^* = (1-\alpha)M/P_2$
Indirect utility function:
$U^* = (\alpha/P_1)^{\alpha}[(1-\alpha)/P_2]^{1-\alpha}M$

2. Multiplying P_1, P_2, and M by a constant factor, k, leaves X_1^* and X_2^* unchanged.

3. $\partial X_1^*/\partial M = [\alpha(1-\alpha)P_2X_1^{\alpha-1}X_2^{-\alpha}$
    $\qquad + [\alpha(1-\alpha)P_1X_1^{\alpha}X_2^{-\alpha-1}]/|H_B|$
    $\quad = (1-\alpha)/P_2$
    $\partial X_2^*/\partial M = [-\alpha(\alpha-1)P_2X_1^{\alpha-2}X_2^{1-\alpha}$
    $\qquad + \alpha(1-\alpha)P_1X_1^{\alpha-1}X_2^{-\alpha}]/|H_B|$
    $\quad = \alpha/P_1$
    $\partial X_1^*/\partial P_1 = \underbrace{-\mu^* P_2^2/|H_B|}_{\text{sub effect}} - \underbrace{X_1^*(\partial X_1^*/\partial M)/|H_B|}_{\text{income effect}}$
    $\quad = \underbrace{-(\alpha M)/P_1^2}_{\text{total effect}}$

    $\partial X_2^*/\partial P_1 = -\mu^* P_1 P_2/|H_B| - X_1^*(\partial X_2^*/\partial M) = 0.$
    X_1 and X_2 are normal goods, since $\partial X_1^*/\partial M$ and $\partial X_2^*/\partial M$ are positive.

4. $\varepsilon_{11} = -\alpha M/P_1X_1^*$; $\varepsilon_{12} = 0$; $\varepsilon_{1M} = \alpha M/P_1X_1^*$;
    $\varepsilon_{11} + \varepsilon_{12} + \varepsilon_{1M} = 0.$

5. $S_1 = \alpha$; $S_2 = 1 - \alpha$

6. Lagrangian objective function:
    $$\mathcal{L} = P_1X_1 + P_2X_2 + \lambda(U_0 - X_1^{\alpha}X_2^{1-\alpha})$$
    $$\frac{\partial X_1^{**}}{\partial P_1} = \frac{(1-\alpha)^2 X_1^{2\alpha}X_2^{-2\alpha}}{|E_B|} = -\frac{\mu^* P_2^2}{|H_B|}$$

    Substituting
    $$|E_B| = -\frac{|H_B|}{\lambda^{**}}$$
    and
    $$\frac{1}{\lambda^{**}} = \mu^*$$

    in the above expression, you will get
    $$\frac{\partial X_1^{**}}{\partial P_1} = -\frac{M^* P_2^2}{|H_B|}$$

which is the substitution effect in question 3.
Indirect expenditure function:

$$M^{**} = \left[\frac{(1-\alpha)^{\alpha-1}}{\alpha^{\alpha-1}} + \frac{(1-\alpha)^{\alpha}}{\alpha^{\alpha}}\right]\frac{P_1^{\alpha}}{P_2^{\alpha-1}}U_0$$

This is a function of P_1, P_2, and U_0, whereas the indirect utility function (see the answer to problem 1) is a function of P_1, P_2, and M. If the indirect expenditure function, M^{**}, is substituted in the indirect utility function, U^*, the result will be the same as that of substituting the indirect utility function in the indirect expenditure function, that is,

$$U^*(P_1, P_2, M^{**}) = M^{**}(P_1, P_2, U^*)$$

7. FOC: $\mathcal{L}_1 = 2\alpha X_1^{2\alpha-1}X_2^{2-2\alpha} - \mu P_1 = 0$
    $\qquad \mathcal{L}_2 = 2(1-\alpha)X_1^{2\alpha}X_1^{1-2\alpha} - \mu P_2 = 0$
    $\qquad \mathcal{L}_\mu = M - P_1X_1 - P_2X_2 = 0$

    SOC:

$$\begin{vmatrix} 2\alpha(2\alpha-1)X_1^{2\alpha-2}X_2^{2-2\alpha} & 4\alpha(1-\alpha)X_1^{2\alpha-1}X_1^{1-2\alpha} & -P_1 \\ 4\alpha(1-2\alpha)X_1^{2\alpha-1}X_2^{1-2\alpha} & \alpha(1-2\alpha)X_1^{2\alpha}X_2^{-2\alpha} & -P_2 \\ -P_1 & -P_2 & 0 \end{vmatrix}$$

> 0

Demand functions: $X_1^* = \alpha M/P_1$;
$X_2^* = (1-\alpha)M/P_2$
Indirect utility function:
$U^* = (\alpha/P_1)^{2\alpha}[(1-\alpha)/P_2]^{2-2\alpha}M^2$
Utility is an ordinal concept.

8. Lagrangian objective function:

$$\mathcal{L} = U(X_1, X_2) + \mu(P_1X_1^0 + P_2X_2^0 - P_1X_1 - P_2X_2)$$

FOC: $\mathcal{L}_1 = U_1 - \mu P_1 = 0$
$\qquad \mathcal{L}_2 = U_2 - \mu P_2 = 0$
$\qquad \mathcal{L}_\mu = P_1X_1^0 + P_2X_2^0 - P_1X_1 - P_2X_2 = 0$

SOC:

$$|H_B| = \begin{vmatrix} U_{11} & U_{12} & -P_1 \\ U_{21} & U_{22} & -P_2 \\ -P_1 & -P_2 & 0 \end{vmatrix} > 0$$

If $X_1^* = X_1^0$, then
$$\frac{\partial X_1^*}{\partial P_1} = -\frac{\mu^* P_2^2}{|H_B|} + \frac{P_1(X_1^* - X_1^0)(U_{22} - U_{12})}{|H_B|}$$
$$= -\frac{\mu^* P_2^2}{|H_B|} < 0$$

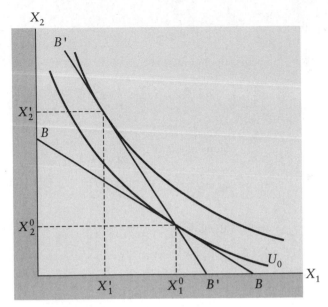

Chapter 10

1.a. $\partial Y/\partial X_1 = 5 > 0$
$\partial^2 Y/\partial X_1^2 = 0$, MP_1 horizontal
$\partial Y/\partial X_2 = 3 > 0$
$\partial^2 Y/\partial X_2^2 = 0$, MP_2 horizontal

1.b. $\partial Y/\partial X_1 = 5 - X_1^{-0.5}X_2^{0.5} > 0 \Leftrightarrow (X_2/X_1)^{0.5} < 5$
$\partial^2 Y/\partial X_1^2 = 0.5X_1^{-1.5}X_2^{0.5} > 0$, MP_1 upward sloping
$\partial Y/\partial X_2 = 10 - X_1^{0.5}X_2^{-0.5} > 0 \Leftrightarrow (X_1/X_2)^{0.5} < 10$
$\partial^2 Y/\partial X_2^2 = 0.5X_1^{0.5}X_2^{-1.5} > 0$, MP_2 upward sloping

1.c. $\partial Y/\partial X_1 = 0.25X_1^{-0.75}X_2^{0.5} > 0$
$\partial^2 Y/\partial X_1^2 = -0.1875X_1^{-1.75}X_2^{0.5} < 0$,
MP_1 downward sloping
$\partial Y/\partial X_2 = 0.5X_1^{0.25}X_2^{-0.5} > 0$
$\partial^2 Y/\partial X_2^2 = -0.25X_1^{0.25}X_2^{-1.5} < 0$, MP_2 downward sloping

1.d. $\partial Y/\partial X_1 = 0.25X_1^{-3}(0.25X_1^{-2} + 0.75X_2^{-2})^{-1.5} > 0$
$\partial^2 Y/\partial X_1^2 = -0.75X_1^{-4}[(0.25X_1 - 2 + 0.75X_2^{-2})^{-1.5}$
$\quad + 0.1875X_1^{-6}(0.25X_1$
$\quad - 2 + 0.75X_2^{-2})]^{-2.5} < 0$
MP_1 downward sloping
$\partial Y/\partial X_2 = 0.75X_2^{-3}(0.25X_1 - 2 + 0.75X_2^{-2})^{-1.5} > 0$
$\partial^2 Y/\partial X_2^2 = -2.25X_2^{-4}[(0.25X_1 - 2 + 0.75X_2^{-2})^{-1.5}$
$\quad + 1.6875X_2^{-6}(0.25X_1 - 2$
$\quad + 0.27X_2^{-2})]^{-2.5} < 0$
MP_2 downward sloping

1.e. $\partial Y/\partial X_1 = 2(X_1 + 2)(X_2 + 5) > 0$
$\partial^2 Y/\partial X_1^2 = 2(X_2 + 5) > 0$, MP_1 upward sloping
$\partial Y/\partial X_2 = (X_1 + 2)^2 > 0$
$\partial^2 Y/\partial X_2^2 = 0$, MP_2 horizontal

2.a. $TP_1 = 5X_1 + 300$
$MP_1 = 5$
$AP_1 = 5 + (300/X_1)$

2.b. $TP_1 = 5X_1^{0.5}(X_1^{0.5} - 4) + 1000$
$MP_1 = 5 - (10/\sqrt{X_1})$
$AP_1 = 5 + (1000/X_1) - 20X_1^{-0.5}$

2.c. $TP_1 = 10X_1^{0.25}$
$MP_1 = 2.5X_1^{-0.75}$
$AP_1 = 10X_1^{-0.75}$

2.d. $TP_1 = (0.25X_1^{-2} + 0.000075)^{-0.5}$
$MP_1 = 0.25X_1^{-3}(0.25X_1^{-2} + 0.000075)^{-1.5}$
$AP_1 = X_1^{-1}(0.25X_1^{-2} + 0.000075)^{-0.5}$

2.e. $TP_1 = 105(X_1 + 2)^2$
$MP_1 = 210(X_1 + 2)$
$AP_1 = [105(X_1 + 2)^2]/X_1$

3.a. $X_2 = -5X_1/3 + 10/3$
$dX_2/dX_1 = -5/3$
$d^2X_2/dX_1^2 = 0$
Linear isoquant, not strictly convex

3.h. $X_2 = 1 - 0.5X_1 + 0.2X_1^{0.5}X_2^{0.5}$
$dX_2/dX_1 = 0.5 + 0.1X_1^{-0.5}X_2^{0.5}$
$d^2X_2/dX_1^2 = -0.05X_1^{-1.5}X_2^{0.5} < 0$
Isoquant not convex

3.c. $X_2 = 100X_1^{-0.5}$
$dX_2/dX_1 = -50X_1^{-1.5}$
$d^2X_2/dX_1^2 = 75X_1^{-2.5} > 0$
Convex isoquant

3.d. $X_2 = 8.66X_1(X_1^2 - 25)^{-1/2}$
$dX_2/dX_1 = 8.66(X_1^2 - 25)^{-1/2}$
$\quad \times [1 - X_1^2(X_1^2 - 25)^{-1}]$
Downward sloping for $X_1 > 5$
$d^2X_2/dX_1^2 = 25.98X_1(X_1^2 - 25)^{-3/2}$
$\quad \times [X_1^2(X_1^2 - 25)^{-1}]$
Convex for $X_1 > 5$.

3.e. $X_2 = 10(X_1 + 2)^{-2} - 5$
$dX_2/dX_1 = -20(X_1 + 2)^{-3}$
$d^2X_2/dX_1^2 = 60(X_1 + 2)^{-4} > 0$
Convex isoquant

4.a. Homogeneous of degree 1, CRS

4.b. Homogeneous of degree 1, CRS

4.c. Homogeneous of degree 0.75, DRS

4.d. Homogeneous of degree 1, CRS

4.e. Not homogeneous

5.a. $dX_2/dX_1 = -(5/3)(X_2/X_1)^0$
$\sigma = \infty$

5.b. $dX_2/dX_1 = [-10 - (X_2/X_1)^{0.5}]/[5 - (X_2/X_1)^{0.5}]$
$\sigma = -[(10 - (X_2/X_1)^{-1/2})$
$\quad \times (5 - (X_2/X_1)^{1/2}]/[5/((X_2/X_1)^{1/2}$
$\quad + (1/2)(X_2/X_1)^{-1/2}) + 1]$

5.c. $dX_2/dX_1 = -(1/2)(X_2/X_1)$
$\sigma = 1$

5.d. $dX_2/dX_1 = -(1/3)(X_2/X_1)^3$
$\sigma = 1/3$

5.e. Function not homogeneous

Chapter 11

1. FOC: $\mathcal{L}_1 = w_1 - (\lambda/3)X_1^{-2/3}X_2^{1/3} = 0$
$\mathcal{L}_2 = w_2 - (\lambda/3)X_1^{1/3}X_2^{-2/3} = 0$
$\mathcal{L}_3 = w_3 - (2\lambda/3)X_3^{-1/3} = 0$
$\mathcal{L}_\lambda = Y_0 - X_1^{1/3}X_2^{1/3} - X_3^{2/3} = 0$

SOC:

$$\begin{vmatrix} (2\lambda/9)X_1^{-5/3}X_2^{1/3} & -(\lambda/9)X_1^{-2/3}X_2^{-2/3} & 0 & -(1/3)X_1^{-2/3}X_2^{1/3} \\ -(\lambda/9)X_1^{-2/3}X_2^{-2/3} & (2\lambda/9)X_1^{1/3}X_2^{-5/3} & 0 & -(1/3)X_1^{1/3}X_2^{-2/3} \\ 0 & 0 & (2\lambda/9)X_3^{-4/3} & -(2/3)X_3^{-1/3} \\ -(1/3)X_1^{-2/3}X_2^{1/3} & -(1/3)X_1^{1/3}X_2^{-2/3} & -(2/3)X_3^{-1/3} & 0 \end{vmatrix} < 0$$

$$X_1^c = \left(\frac{w_2}{w_1}\right)\left(\frac{Y_0}{(w_2/w_1)^{1/3} + 4w_1^{2/3}w_2^{4/3}w_3^{-2}}\right)^{3/2}$$

$$X_2^c = \left(\frac{Y_0}{(w_2/w_1)^{1/3} + 4w_1^{2/3}w_2^{4/3}w_3^{-2}}\right)^{3/2}$$

$$X_3^c = \left(\frac{8w_1w_2^2}{w_3^3}\right)\left(\frac{Y_0}{(w_2/w_1)^{1/3} + 4w_1^{2/3}w_2^{4/3}w_3^{-2}}\right)^{3/2}$$

$MC = \lambda^C$

$$= 3w_1^{1/3}w_2^{2/3}\left(\frac{Y_0}{(w_2/w_1)^{1/3} + 4w_1^{2/3}w_2^{4/3}w_3^{-2}}\right)^{1/2}$$

2. The function is homogeneous of degree 2/3.
Slope of LRMC

$$= \frac{\partial \lambda^*}{\partial Y_0} = \frac{1}{2}\frac{\lambda^*}{Y_0}$$

$$= \frac{3w_1^{1/3}w_2^{2/3}}{2Y_0}\left(\frac{Y_0}{(w_2/w_1)^{1/3} + 4w_1^{2/3}w_2^{4/3}w_3^{-2}}\right)^{1/2}$$

3. FOC: $\pi_1 = (P/3)X_1^{-2/3}X_2^{1/3} - w_1 = 0$
$\pi_2 = (P/3)X_1^{1/3}X_2^{-2/3} - w_2 = 0$
$\pi_3 = (2P/3)X_3^{-1/3} - w_3 = 0$

SOC:
$-(2P/9)X_1^{-5/3}X_2^{1/3} < 0, \quad -(2P/9)X_1^{1/3}X_2^{-5/3} < 0,$
$-(2P/9)X_3^{-4/3} < 0$

$$\begin{vmatrix} -(2P/9)X_1^{-5/3}X_2^{1/3} & (P/9)X_1^{-2/3}X_2^{-2/3} & 0 \\ (P/9)X_1^{-2/3}X_2^{-2/3} & -(2P/9)X_1^{1/3}X_2^{-5/3} & 0 \\ 0 & 0 & -(2P/9)X_3^{-4/3} \end{vmatrix} < 0$$

$$X_1^\pi = \frac{P^3}{27w_1^2w_2}, \quad X_2^\pi = \frac{P^3}{27w_1w_2^2}, \quad X_3^\pi = \frac{8P^3}{27w_3^3}$$

4.
$$Y^\pi = \left(\frac{1}{9w_1w_2} + \frac{4}{9w_3^2}\right)P^2$$

Slope of supply function

$$= \frac{\partial Y^\pi}{\partial P} = \left(\frac{2}{9w_1w_2} + \frac{8}{9w_3^2}\right)P$$

Slope of LRMC $= \dfrac{\partial \lambda^*}{\partial Y_0} = \dfrac{1}{2}\dfrac{\lambda^*}{Y_0}$

Substituting in $\lambda^* = P$ and $Y^\pi = Y_0$,

Slope of LRMC $= \dfrac{1}{\left(\dfrac{2}{9w_1w_2} + \dfrac{8}{9w_3^2}\right)P}$

$$= \frac{1}{\text{slope of supply function}}$$

5. Start with the expression for X_1^c you found in problem 1. In it, substitute for Y_0 the expression you found for Y^π in problem 4. Through simplifications and factorizations, the result will reduce to the expression for X^π you found in problem 3.

6. Recall equation (11-51),

$$\frac{\partial X_1^\pi}{\partial w_1} = \frac{\partial X_1^c}{\partial w_1} - \left(\frac{\partial X_1^c}{\partial Y^\pi}\right)^2\frac{\partial Y^\pi}{\partial P}$$

The squared term is clearly positive. According to the result in problem 4, the term $\partial Y^\pi/P$ is also positive. Thus the product on the right-hand side of the above equation is positive. It follows that

$$\frac{\partial X_1^\pi}{\partial w_1} < \frac{\partial X_1^C}{\partial w_1}$$

7. FOC: $\mathcal{L}_1 = w_1 - (\lambda/3)X_1^{-2/3}X_2^{1/3} = 0$
$\mathcal{L}_2 = w_2 - (\lambda/3)X_1^{1/3}X_2^{-1/3} = 0$
$\mathcal{L}_3 = w_3 - (2\lambda/3)X_3^{-1/3} - \zeta = 0$
$\mathcal{L}_\lambda = Y_0 - X_1^{1/3}X_2^{1/3} - X_3^{2/3} = 0$
$\mathcal{L}_\zeta = X_{30} - X_3 = 0$

SOC:

$$\begin{vmatrix} (2\lambda/9)X_1^{-5/3}X_2^{1/3} & -(\lambda/9)X_1^{-2/3}X_2^{-2/3} & 0 & -(1/3)X_1^{-2/3}X_2^{1/3} & 0 \\ -(\lambda/9)X_1^{-2/3}X_2^{-2/3} & (2\lambda/9)X_1^{1/3}X_2^{-5/3} & 0 & -(1/3)X_1^{1/3}X_2^{-2/3} & 0 \\ 0 & 0 & (2\lambda/9)X_3^{-4/3} & -(2/3)X_3^{-1/3} & -1 \\ -(1/3)X_1^{-2/3}X_2^{1/3} & -(1/3)X_1^{1/3}X_2^{-2/3} & -(2/3)X_3^{\times 1/3} & 0 & 0 \\ 0 & 0 & -1 & 0 & 0 \end{vmatrix} > 0$$

$$X_1^S = \left(\frac{w_2}{w_1}\right)^{1/2} (Y_0 - X_{30})^3,$$

$$X_2^S = \left(\frac{w_1}{w_2}\right)^{3/2} (Y_0 - X_{30})^3,$$

$$X_3^S = X_{30}$$

$$\text{SRMC} = \lambda^S = 3w_1\left(\frac{w_2}{w_1}\right)^{5/6} (Y_0 - X_{30})^{1/2}$$

8. Start with the expression for short-run marginal cost (λ^S) you found in problem 7. In it, substitute for X_{30} the expression you found for X_3^c in problem 1. Through simplifications and factorizations, the result will reduce to the expression for long-run marginal cost (λ^C) that you found in problem 1.

9. From equation (11-110) we see that

$$\frac{\partial \text{LRMC}}{\partial Y_0} = \frac{\partial \lambda^L}{\partial Y_0} = \frac{\partial \lambda^S}{\partial Y_0} + \left(\frac{\partial \lambda^S}{\partial X_3}\right)^2 \frac{\partial X_3^L}{\partial w_3}$$

The squared term is unambiguously positive. From self-help problem 1 we can find

$$\frac{\partial X_3^L}{\partial w_3} = -3\frac{X_3^L}{w_3} - 12\left(\frac{w_1^{2/3} w_2^{4/3}}{w_3^3}\right)$$

$$\times \left(\frac{Y_0}{(w_2/w_1)^{1/3} + 4w_1^{2/3} w_2^{4/3} w_3^{-2}}\right)^{1/2}$$

Since this expression is negative, $\partial \lambda^L / \partial Y_0 < \partial Y_0 / \partial Y_0$.

Chapter 12

1.a. IS: $r = 1.5 - 0.002Y$
LM: $r = -1.25 + 0.002Y$
$Y^* = 687.5, r^* = .125$

1.b. $\Delta G = 30, r^* = 0.175$

1.c. $\Delta T_0 = -37.5, r^* = 0.175$

1.d. $\Delta M = 20, r^* = 0.075$

2.a. IS: $Y = 135$
LM: $r = -0.3 + 0.03Y$
$Y^* = 135, r^* = 0.105$

2.b. $\Delta G = 20, r^* = .18$

2.c. $\Delta T_0 = -50;   r^* = 0.18$

2.d. Because investment is not responsive to the rate of interest (IS is vertical), changes in money supply have no effect on the level of equilibrium income.

3.a. IS: $r = 0.5 - 0.005Y$
LM: $Y = 50$
$Y^* = 50;   r^* = 0.25$

3.b. Because money demand is not responsive to the rate of interest (LM is vertical), changes in government spending have no effect on the level of equilibrium income; there is complete crowding out.

3.c. Because money demand is not responsive to the rate of interest (LM is vertical), changes in taxes have no effect on the level of equilibrium income; there is complete crowding out.

3.d. $\Delta M = 30;   r^* = 0.125$

4.a. $Y^* = 653.33;   r^* = 0.107$

4.b. $Y^* = 686.67;   r^* = 0.173$

4.c. Total crowding out of private spending $= -33.30$
ΔI^* due to $\Delta r^* = -300\Delta r^* = -19.98$
ΔX^* due to $\Delta r^* = -200\Delta r^* = -13.32$

Chapter 13

1. $X^* = 1.11,   Y^* = 1.56$

2.a. $X_1^* = 8,   X_2^* = 6$

2.b. $Y_1^* = 0.24 =$ marginal cost of vitamin C
$Y_2^* = 0.03 =$ marginal cost of vitamin E

2.c. Value of primal objective function at the optimum $= 16.5 =$ value of dual objective function at the optimum.

3.a. $X_1^* = 60;   X_2^* = 40$

3.b. $Y_1^* = 120 =$ value of marginal product of M_1
$Y_2^* = 420 =$ value of marginal product of M_2

3.c. Value of primal objective function at the optimum $= 21,600 =$ value of dual objective function at the optimum.

3.d. $[(1/2)X_1^* + (1/4)X_2^* - 40]Y_1^* = 0$. This implies that the first constraint of the primal problem is binding because Y_1^* is different from zero.
$[(1/3)X_1^* + (1/2)X_2^* - 40]Y_2^* = 0$. This implies that the second constraint of the primal problem is binding because Y_1^* is different from zero.
$[(1/2)Y_1^* + (1/3)Y_2^* - 200]X_1^* = 0$. This implies that the first constraint of the dual problem is binding because X_1^* is different from zero.
$[(1/4)Y_1^* + (1/2)Y_2^* - 240]X_2^* = 0$. This implies that the second constraint of the primal problem is binding because X_2^* is different from zero.

4. Start with the general LP problem: Maximize (minimize) cX subject to $AX \le b$ and $X \ge 0$. The corresponding dual problem is: Minimize (maximize) $b'Y$ subject to $A'Y \ge c'$ and $Y \ge 0$. Now treat the dual problem as a primal and specify its dual: Maximize (minimize) $(c')'X$

subject to $(A')'X \leq (b')'$ and $X \geq 0$. But this is the original model because the transpose of a transposed matrix (vector) equals the original matrix (vector).

Chapter 14

1. $\mathcal{L} = U(F(L_F), S(L_S)) + \Omega(L_T - L_F - L_S)$; choice variables: L_S, L_F, Ω; parameter: L_T.

2. FOC:
$$\mathcal{L}_{LF} = U_F F' - \Omega = 0$$
$$\mathcal{L}_{LS} = U_S S' - \Omega = 0$$
$$\mathcal{L}_{\Omega} = L_T - L_F - L_S = 0$$

SOC:

$$|H_B| = \begin{vmatrix} U_{FF}F'^2 + U_F F'' & U_{FS}F'S' & -1 \\ U_{SF}S'F' & U_{SS}S'^2 + U_S S'' & -1 \\ -1 & -1 & 0 \end{vmatrix} > 0$$

3. $|H_B| = -U_{SS}S'^2 + 2U_{FS}F'S' - U_{FF}F'^2$
$- U_S S'' - U_F F'' > 0$
$= (F'S'/\Omega)^2 \underbrace{(-U_F^2 U_{SS} + 2U_{FS}U_F U_S - U_S^2 U_{FF})}_{\substack{> 0 \text{ because of convex} \\ \text{indifference curves}}}$
$\underbrace{- (U_S S'' + U_F F'')}_{\substack{< 0 \text{ because of concave} \\ \text{production functions}}} > 0$

4. Ω^* represents the marginal utility of labor or the shadow price of labor to RC.

5.

$$\frac{\partial L_S^*}{\partial L_T} = \frac{\begin{vmatrix} 0 & U_{FS}F'S' & -1 \\ 0 & U_{SS}S'^2 + U_S S'' & -1 \\ -1 & -1 & 0 \end{vmatrix}}{|H_B|}$$

This partial derivative measures the effect of increasing the supply of available labor on the amount of labor devoted to producing shelter. Its sign is indeterminate.

$$\frac{\partial L_F^*}{\partial L_T} = \frac{\begin{vmatrix} U_{FF}F'^2 + U_F F'' & 0 & -1 \\ U_{SF}S'F' & 0 & -1 \\ -1 & -1 & 0 \end{vmatrix}}{|H_B|}$$

This partial derivative measures the effect of increasing the supply of available labor on the amount of labor devoted to producing food. Its sign is indeterminate.

$$\frac{\partial \Omega^*}{\partial L_T} = \frac{\begin{vmatrix} U_{FF}F'^2 + U_F F'' & U_{FS}F'S' & 0 \\ U_{SF}S'F' & U_{SS}S'^2 + U_S S'' & 0 \\ -1 & -1 & -1 \end{vmatrix}}{|H_B|}$$

This partial derivative measures the effect of increasing the supply of available labor on the shadow price of labor. Its sign is indeterminate. However, if we are willing to assume diminishing marginal utility for both food and shelter in addition to concave production functions, its sign is negative.

6.a. $\mathcal{L} = (10L_F - L_F^2/2)(10 + 2L_S) + \Omega(100 + L_F + L_S)$
FOC:
$$\mathcal{L}_{LF} = (10 + 2L_S)(10 - L_F) - \Omega = 0$$
$$\mathcal{L}_{LS} = 20L_F - L_F^2 - \Omega = 0$$
$$\mathcal{L}_{\Omega} = 100 - L_F - L_S = 0$$
SOC: $50 - 4L_F + 2L_S > 0$

6.b. $L_F^* = 9.48$; $L_S^* = 90.52$; $\Omega^* = 99.728$.
SOC: $50 - 4L_F + 2L_S = 193 > 0$.

6.c. Shadow price equals $\Omega^* = 99.728$. If labor increases to $L_T = 101$, the shadow price increases to $\Omega^* = 99.733$. Note: This utility function does not exhibit diminishing marginal utility.

6.d. In order to answer this part, F must be maximized subject to a given amount of S and a fixed amount of labor. See Section 14.2. You find that

$$F^* = 10\left(L_T - \frac{S_0}{2} + 5\right) - \frac{1}{2}\left(L_T - \frac{S_0}{2} + 5\right)^2$$

The slope of the PPF equals

$$\frac{\partial F^*}{\partial S_0} = -2.5 + \frac{L_T}{2} - \frac{S_0}{4}$$

The PPF is concave because

$$\frac{\partial^2 F^*}{\partial S_0^2} = \frac{-1}{4} < 0$$

adjoint: the transpose of a matrix obtained from an original matrix A by replacing its elements a_{ij} with their corresponding cofactors $|C_{ij}|$. Denoted by adj(A).

alien cofactor: the cofactor of some other element.

arc elasticity: a unitless measure of the discrete response of a dependent variable to a discrete change in an independent variable. Mathematically, if $Y = f(X)$, then the arc elasticity between the points (X_1, Y_1) and (X_2, Y_2) is

$$\left(\frac{Y_2 - Y_1}{X_2 - X_1} \right) \left(\frac{X_1 + X_2}{Y_1 + Y_2} \right)$$

argument: if the function is $Y = f(X)$, then its arguments are the particular quantities taken by X, the independent variable.

associative property: the arithmetic property by which the result of the operation is unaffected by the groupings of the components in the operation. For example, multiplication has the associative property $a(bc) = (ab)c$.

autonomous consumption: the component of consumption that is exogenous. That is, consumption determined by forces entirely external to the model.

autonomous investment: the component of investment that is exogenous. That is, investment determined by forces entirely external to the model.

average revenue: total revenue, PQ, divided by quantity, Q. It equals price, P. The graph of average revenue is the inverse of the demand curve.

bordered Hessian matrix: the Hessian matrix for a constrained optimization, in which the second partials with respect to the Lagrange multiplier make up the borders.

border-preserving principal minor: a principal minor not associated with an element that belongs to the border of a bordered Hessian.

budget constraint: the combinations of goods and services that a consumer can purchase with a given money income and prices. Mathematically, it is defined as

$$M = \sum_{i=1}^{n} P_i X_i$$

where M equals money income, P_i equals the price of the ith good or service, and X_i equals the quantity of the ith good or service purchased.

capital-intensive: a property of production that a product uses relatively more capital per unit of another input than some other product requires.

cardinal: the property of being quantifiable in numerical units.

cardinal utility: a concept of utility according to which the individual assigns meaningful amounts of utility to consumption bundles.

choice variables: variables that represent the choices individual economic actors make in their efforts to optimize.

Cobb-Douglas production function: a general class of production functions that take the form $Y = AX_1^\alpha X_2^\beta$, where Y represents rate of output, X_1 and X_2 represent inputs, and A, α, and β are positive parameters.

cofactor: a minor that has a sign equal to $(-1)^{i+j}$ associated with it.

column vector: a matrix with one column.

commutative property: the arithmetic property that the result of the operation is unaffected by the order in which the components appear in the operation. For example, addition is commutative: $a + b = b + a$.

comparative statics: a methodology by which behavior is explained as changes in equilibrium positions.

compensated demand: the demand function that results when a consumer's money income is compensated for the income effect of price changes.

competitive factors of production: factors of production which compete to perform similar tasks. When more of a competitive factor is employed, marginal product of the other factor is decreased. Mathematically, two factors are competitive when their cross-partial derivatives of the production function are negative.

complementary slackness: the principle that, at the optimum, the product of each dual variable times the corresponding primal constraint, as well as the product of a primal variable times the corresponding dual constraint, equals zero.

composite function: a function whose argument is itself a function. It is the function of a function.

conformable: of the appropriate dimension for some matrix operation. For multiplication, the number of columns in the lead matrix must equal the number of rows in the lag matrix. For addition or subtraction, the dimensions of the matrices must be the same.

constant function: a polynomial of degree zero.

constant-elasticity-of-substitution (CES) production function: class of functions that have a constant elasticity of substitution, which can take any value between zero and infinity. Mathematically, the general form of the CES function is

$$Y = A(\alpha X_1^{-\rho} + (1 - \alpha)X_2^{-\rho})^{-1/\rho},$$
$$A > 0, 0 < \alpha < 1, -1 < \rho \neq 0$$

constant returns to scale (CRS): when output increases proportionally to increases in the inputs. A homogeneous production function exhibits CRS when the degree of homogeneity equals one.

constrained optimization: behavioral models in which the choice variables of the objective function are constrained by some other functional relationship.

continuous: a function is continuous at a point if the value of the function and its limit exist at that point and are equal to one another. Mathematically, a function is continuous at a point c if

1. $\lim_{x \to c} f(x)$ exists

2. $f(c)$ exists and

3. $\lim_{x \to c} f(x) = f(c)$

contour curve: the graph of the relationship between two independent variables when the dependent variable is held constant at some level. Also called a level curve.

contract curve: line joining points of tangency in an Edgeworth-Bowley box diagram. Also known as the locus of efficient exchange.

cooperative factors of production: factors of production which perform complementary tasks. When more of a cooperative factor is employed, marginal product of the other factor is increased. Mathematically, two factors are cooperative when their cross-partial derivatives of the production function are positive.

corner solution: an optimal solution to an LP problem that includes zero values for some of the choice variables.

Cramer's rule: a method of solving for individual elements of the vector X in the matrix equation $AX = C$, where A is an $n \times n$ matrix of coefficients, X is an $n \times 1$ vector of unknowns, and C is an $n \times 1$ vector of constant terms.

critical point: the point at which a function is neither increasing nor decreasing. For a function with one independent variable, where the first derivative equals zero. Also known as stationary point.

cross-partial derivative: a higher-order partial derivative for which you first differentiate with respect to one independent variable and subsequently differentiate with respect to some other independent variable. Mathematically, if $Y = f(X_1, X_2)$, the cross-partial derivative is denoted by

$$\frac{\partial^2 Y}{\partial X_1 \partial X_2} \equiv f_{12}$$

Also known simply as a cross-partial.

crowding-out effect: when government expenditures have the effect of reducing interest-sensitive private expenditures by increasing the rate of interest.

cubic function: a polynomial of degree three.

decreasing returns to scale (DRS): when output increases less than proportionally to the increases in inputs. A homogeneous production function exhibits DRS when the degree of homogeneity is less than one.

degree of homogeneity: see homogeneous function.

degree of polynomial: the highest power in a polynomial.

dependent variable: the variable which is described uniquely by a functional relationship.

derivative: If $Y = f(X)$, then the derivative of Y with respect to X equals

$$f'(X) \equiv \frac{dY}{dX} \equiv \lim_{\Delta X \to 0} \frac{\Delta Y}{\Delta X}$$

It represents the instantaneous rate of change of a dependent variable with respect to a change in an independent variable, or the slope of the line tangent to a function at a point.

determinant: a number associated with a square matrix.

diagonal elements: those elements of a matrix whose row and column indices are the same, i.e., $a_{11}, a_{22}, \ldots, a_{nn}$.

difference quotient: a ratio of finite changes, e.g., $\Delta Y / \Delta X$.

differentiable: a function is differentiable if it is both smooth and continuous.

differential: an infinitesimal change in a variable, denoted by the symbol d in front of the variable. Mathematically, if $Y = f(X)$ then the differential of Y equals

$$dY \equiv \frac{dY}{dX} dX \equiv f'(X) \, dX$$

differentiation: the act of determining the derivative of a function.

dimension: the number of rows and columns of a matrix. The first number mentioned in the dimension of a matrix refers to the number of rows and the second number indicates the number of columns of the matrix. If only one number is mentioned, the matrix is a vector.

diminishing marginal returns to a variable input: the incremental output from additional units of a variable input decreases as more of the variable input is added, holding other inputs constant.

direct objective function: the function to be optimized in an optimization model, in which the choice variables appear as independent variables and the parameters appear as constants. In an unconstrained optimization model, it is simply the objective function. If the Lagrangian method is used in a constrained optimization model, it is the Lagrangian objective function.

direct technical coefficient: the amount of an input used per unit output of product. It represents a fixed coefficient in a production function of an input–output system.

discontinuous: a function is discontinuous at a point if one or more of the following is not satisfied at that point.

1. $\lim_{x \to c} f(x)$ exists

2. $f(c)$ exists and

3. $\lim_{x \to c} f(x) = f(c)$

distributive property: the arithmetic property by which one operation can be distributed over another operation, leaving the result unchanged. For example, the distributive property of multiplication over addition means that $a(b + c) = ab + ac$.

domain: the set of permissible arguments of a function.

dual: another way of describing the optimum of a constrained optimization problem, in which the objective and the constraints reverse roles, along with the sense of optimization. See primal.

econometrics: The branch of economics that uses statistical methods to estimate the unknown parameters of theoretical relationships, test hypotheses about these parameters, and use the estimates to make quantitative predictions.

Edgeworth-Bowley box diagram: a graphical representation of resource allocation.

elastic demand: a situation in which the price elasticity of demand, ε_{QP}, is less than -1; that is, quantity demanded changes by a larger percentage than the change in price.

elasticity: a unitless measure of the response of a dependent variable to a change in an independent variable. It can be interpreted as the percentage change in the dependent variable per percent change in the independent variable.

elasticity of substitution: A measure of the degree of substitutability of two inputs at different points on an isoquant. Mathematically, if $Y = f(X_1, X_2)$, then the elasticity of substitution equals

$$\sigma = \frac{d\left(\dfrac{X_2}{X_1}\right) \dfrac{f_1}{f_2}}{d\left(\dfrac{f_1}{f_2}\right) \dfrac{X_2}{X_1}}$$

elements (set): the name for the entities which comprise a set.

elements (matrix): placeholders in a matrix. Each element is associated with a row and a column in a matrix.

endogenous variables: those variables which are explained by a simultaneous equations model.

envelope theorem: a theorem in optimization theory which states that the partial derivative of the indirect objective function with respect to a parameter equals the partial derivative of the direct objective function with respect to the same parameter, evaluated at the optimum.

equilibrium: The logically deduced values of choice variables or endogenous variables for a given set of parameters and exogenous variables.

equilibrium condition: The behavioral rule that determines the equilibrium of a model.

Euler's theorem: if the function

$$Y = f(X_1, X_2, \ldots, X_n)$$

is homogeneous of degree r, then

$$rY = f_1 X_1 + f_2 X_2 + \cdots + f_n X_n$$

That is, the sum of the products of the partial derivatives and their corresponding independent variables equals the product of the dependent variable and the degree of homogeneity.

evaluation of a determinant: see expansion of a determinant.

exogenous variables: those variables which represent information that is external to a simultaneous equations model, used to explain the endogenous variables.

expansion of a determinant: the process of computing the number that is the determinant. Also called evaluating the determinant.

expenditures multiplier: the factor by which a change in an exogenous spending variable changes equilibrium national income.

explicit function: a function in which the dependent variable is isolated on one side of the equation, as in $Y = f(X)$.

exponential function: a function whose independent variable appears as the exponent of a parameter.

feasible set: see set of feasible solutions.

first-order condition for optimization: condition which must necessarily hold for a function to have a critical point. Also called necessary condition.

first-order partial derivative: see partial derivative.

fiscal policy: changes in government expenditures or income tax rates by policy makers, such as the President or Congress, in response to undesirable changes in the level of real income or output.

full coefficients: coefficients which take into account the direct and indirect technical requirements in an input–output system. The matrix of full coefficients equals $[I_n - A]^{-1}$, if A is the matrix of direct technical coefficients.

function: a set of ordered pairs $\{(X_i, Y_j)\}$, $i = 1, 2, \ldots, n$ and $j = 1, 2, \ldots, m$, with the property that any X value determines a unique Y value.

Denoted by $Y = f(X)$ and expressed "Y is a function of X" or "Y depends on X."

general equilibrium: an analytical methodology that incorporates more economic variables as endogenous in order to explain the aggregate effects of simultaneous actions by many individual agents.

global maximum or minimum: a point that is the maximum or minimum value relative to every other point in the entire range of the function.

grand utilities possibilities frontier (GUPF): collection of all utilities possibilities frontiers associated with a production possibilities frontier.

Hawkins-Simon condition: condition that ensures strictly positive values for gross output, $X_i > 0$, and nonnegative values for final consumption, $Y_i \geq 0$, $i = 1, 2, \ldots, n$, in the input–output model $X = AX + Y$. It requires that the principal minors of the matrix $[I_n - A]$ are all strictly greater than zero.

Hessian matrix: the matrix of second-order partial derivatives of an objective function.

higher-order partial derivative: the partial derivative of a partial derivative. For example, the function $Y = f(X_1, X_2)$ has two first-order partial derivatives, f_1 and f_2. Each of the first-order partials can be differentiated with respect to X_1 and X_2, generating four second-order partial derivatives, f_{11}, f_{12}, f_{21}, and f_{22}. The second-order partials can be differentiated, yielding third-order partials, and so on. Higher-order partial derivatives can be taken as long as the functions are differentiable.

higher-order total differentials: the total differential of a total differential. Suppose $Y = f(X_1, X_2, \ldots, X_n)$. The first-order total differential (dY) is the total differential of the primitive function. The second-order total differential $(d^2 Y)$ is the total differential of dY; the third-order total differential $(d^3 Y)$ is the total differential of $d^2 Y$, and so on.

homogeneous function: a function

$$Y = f(X_1, X_2, \ldots, X_n)$$

is homogeneous of degree r if and only if

$$t^r Y \equiv t^r f(X_1, X_2, \ldots, X_n) \equiv f(tX_1, tX_2, \ldots, tX_n)$$

homothetic functions: the class of functions for which the slopes of the level curves are the same along a straight ray emanating out of the origin. That is, the level curves of the function are radial blowups of one another.

hypothesis: a conditional proposition of how one variable affects another.

identity: an equation that is true for all values of the variables. It is signified by the symbol $\equiv$.

identity matrix: an $n \times n$ matrix with ones as elements on its principal diagonal and zeros elsewhere. It plays a role similar to the number one in scalar algebra, so that the product of any matrix and the identity matrix of conformable dimensions equals the original matrix.

implicit function: a function in which the dependent variable is not isolated on one side of the equation, but rather some expression containing the function is expressed as equal to zero, as in $F(Y, X) = 0$.

implicit function theorem: given the relationship $F(X, Y) = 0$, if F_X and F_Y are continuous at a point and $F_Y \neq 0$ at that point, then the implicitly defined function $Y = f(X)$ exists in the neighborhood of that point. Furthermore, the function $f(X)$ is continuous and so is its derivative, dY/dX.

income effect: measures the effect on the consumption of the good due only to changes in real income (or utility), holding the price ratio and money income constant, when the price of a good changes.

increasing returns to scale (IRS): when output increases more than proportionally to the increases in inputs. A homogeneous production function exhibits IRS when the degree of homogeneity is greater than one.

independent variable: the variable (or variables) which provides the information that uniquely determines the dependent variable.

index: the subscripts which indicate the row and column of an element in a matrix. For element a_{ij}, i is the index of the element's row and j is the index of the element's column.

indifference curve: a graphical representation of the consumption rates of two goods that achieve a given rate of utility. If utility equals

$$U = U(X, Y)$$

then the indifference curve associated with the utility level U_0 is the implicitly defined function between Y and X

$$F(X, Y) \equiv U_0 - U(X, Y) = 0$$

indirect expenditure function: the indirect objective function from the constrained expenditure minimization model. Mathematically, it equals $M^{**} = P_1 X_1^{**}(P_1, P_2, U_0) + P_2 X_2^{**}(P_1, P_2, U_0)$ for a two-good model.

indirect objective function: a function created by substituting the optimum values of the choice variables, which are themselves functions of the parameters, into the original objective of an optimization model.

indirect utility function: the optimum level of utility obtainable in a model of constrained utility maximization. That is, it is the utility function we obtain when we replace the unconstrained and unoptimized levels of goods and services with their constrained and optimized levels.

inelastic demand: a situation in which the price elasticity of demand, ε_{QP}, is between 0 and -1; that is, quantity demanded changes by a smaller percentage than the change in price.

inferior goods: goods for which consumption levels decrease with increases in money income and increase with decreases in money income, *ceteris paribus*. Mathematically, good 1 is considered inferior if $\partial X_1^*/\partial M < 0$.

inferior input: an input that a firm uses less of as output increases.

input–output analysis: a description of the allocation of resources in a multisectoral economic system which includes production sectors that depend on one another's output, primary inputs that are not produced, and a final demand sector. All production is characterized by linear, fixed-coefficient production functions.

interior solution: an optimum solution to a linear programming problem which includes only positive (nonzero) values of all choice variables.

inverse function: a monotonic function has an inverse function, in which the dependent and independent variables reverse roles. The value of the original function is the argument of the inverse and the argument of the original is the value of the inverse.

IS curve: a graph representing all combinations of income and interest rate at which the product market is in equilibrium. Mathematically, the graph of the IS equation,

$$Y = C(Y - T(Y)) + I(r) + G$$

with r on the vertical axis and Y on the horizontal.

isocost line: a graph of the combinations of two inputs that cost the same.

isorevenue line: graph of the combinations of products for which total revenue to the firm is constant.

isoquant: a graphical representation of the rates of usage of two inputs that achieve a given rate of output. If output equals

$$Q = f(K, L)$$

then the isoquant associated with the output level Q_0 is the implicitly defined function between K and L

$$F(K, L) \equiv Q_0 - f(K, L) = 0$$

labor-intensive: a property of production that a product uses relatively more labor per unit of another input than some other product requires.

lag matrix: the second matrix in the product of two matrices.

Lagrange method of constrained optimization: a method of constrained optimization in which the constraint is incorporated into the objective function in such a way that the first-order conditions themselves ensure that the constraint is satisfied.

Lagrange multiplier: a contrived variable used in the Lagrange method of constrained optimization. See Lagrangian objective function.

Lagrangian objective function: a constraint-augmented objective function, in which the Lagrange multiplier is multiplied by the constraint function (written so that it equals zero) and added to the objective function.

Laplace method: a method of expanding a determinant by which the result equals the sum of the products of the elements of a row or column by their cofactors.

law of diminishing marginal returns: the empirical observation that, as more of an input (in production) or a good or service (in consumption) is utilized, the smaller is the increment to output (in production) or satisfaction (in consumption), holding all other inputs or goods and services constant.

lead matrix: the first matrix in the product of two matrices.

level curve: the graph of the relationship between two independent variables when the dependent variable is held constant at some level. Also called a contour curve.

limit: the value of a function as the argument approaches some value.

linear function: a polynomial of degree one.

linearly homogeneous: homogeneous of degree one.

linearly independent: the property according to which it is impossible to express any one equation in a linear system as some linear combination of the other equations.

linear programming: a mathematical technique for optimizing linear objective functions, subject to linear constraints.

liquidity: the ability to transform an asset into general purchasing power without losing its value.

LM curve: a graph representing all combinations of income and interest rate at which the money market is in equilibrium. Mathematically, the graph of the LM equation,

$$L(r, Y) = M/P$$

with r on the vertical axis and Y measured on the horizontal.

local maximum or minimum: a point that is a maximum or minimum value relative to its immediate neighbors.

locus of efficient exchange: line joining points of tangency in an Edgeworth-Bowley box diagram. Also known as contract curve.

logarithmic function: the inverse of an exponential function. The dependent variable is expressed as the logarithm of the independent variable.

long-run: a situation in which nothing is arbitrarily held constant.

marginal factor cost (MFC): the incremental change in total cost due to an incremental change in the employment of some input.

marginal product: the rate of change of output per unit change in the quantity of one input, holding all other inputs constant. The derivative of the production function with respect to one input, holding the quantities of all other inputs constant.

marginal rate of substitution (MRS): the rate at which one good can be substituted for another, holding utility constant. The slope of an indifference curve multiplied by -1.

marginal rate of technical substitution (MRTS): the rate at which one input can be substituted for another, holding output constant. The slope of an isoquant multiplied by -1.

marginal rate of transformation (MRT): the slope of the production possibilities frontier, or the rate at which a given endowment of inputs can transform one output into another.

marginal revenue (MR): the incremental revenue for an increase in quantity. Mathematically, the derivative of total revenue with respect to quantity.

marginal revenue product (MRP): the incremental change in revenue due to an incremental change in the employment of some input. Mathematically, MRP equals marginal revenue multiplied by marginal product of the input.

marginal utility: the rate of change of utility for a change in the quantity of one good, holding all other goods constant. The derivative of the utility function with respect to one good, holding the quantities of all other goods constant.

marginal utility of money income: the rate of change of utility with respect to money income, *ceteris paribus*. Mathematically, it is the partial derivative of the indirect utility function with respect to money income.

mathematical optimization: the mathematical technique of finding the maximum or minimum value of some objective function.

matrix: a systematic arrangement of elements in rows and columns.

matrix inversion: the process of finding the inverse of a matrix.

methodology: a system by which analysis is conducted.

minor: the subdeterminant associated with an element a_{ij} of some determinant, $|A|$, obtained by deleting the ith row and jth column of $|A|$. The minor associated with the element a_{ij} of $|A|$ is denoted $|A_{ij}|$.

model: an abstract representation of reality.

monetary feedback term: the term $I'(L_Y/L_r)$ in the denominator of the multiplier associated with the IS-LM model, equation (12-22). It shows that the extent of crowding out depends on the absolute value of the slope of the LM curve, L_Y/L_r, and the interest responsiveness of investment demand, I'.

monetary policy: changes in the money supply by monetary authorities such as a central bank or the Federal Reserve in response to undesirable changes in the level of real income or output.

monopoly: a market in which there is a single seller of a commodity or input, modeled as a price-searcher.

monopsony: a market in which there is a single buyer of a commodity or input, which is modeled as a price-searcher.

monotonic function: a function whose values either increase or decrease consistently as its argument increase. Graphically, it is either consistently upward sloping or consistently downward sloping.

monotonic transformation: given a function $U = U(X_1, X_2)$, a transformation $V = V(U(X_1, X_2))$ is monotonic if and only if $dV/dU \equiv V'(U(X_1, X_2)) > 0$.

multiplicative inverse matrix: a matrix which, when multiplied by another matrix, yields a product equal to the identity matrix.

naturally ordered principal minors: principal minors of ascending order k that start with the upper left diagonal element and include k contiguous rows and columns. Alternatively, they may start with the lower right diagonal element.

necessary condition for optimization: condition which must necessarily hold for a function to have a critical point. Mathematically, for functions with one independent variable, the first derivative of the function equals zero. Also known as the first-order condition.

nonpolynomial functions: functions that cannot be expressed as a polynomial or rational function. Include exponential, logarithmic, and trigonometric functions. Also known as nonalgebraic or transcendental functions.

nonsingular matrix: a matrix in which all the rows (columns) are linearly independent.

normal good: good for which consumption levels increase with increases in money income and decrease with decreases in money income, *ceteris paribus*. Mathematically, good 1 is considered normal if $\partial X_1^*/\partial M > 0$.

normal input: an input that a firm uses more of as output increases.

nth-order derivative test: a general test by which one may determine whether a critical point is a maximum, a minimum, or a point of inflection. It involves taking successively higher-order derivatives of the objective function until a nonzero derivative is reached.

objective function: the mathematical function whose dependent variable is to be optimized, that is, maximized or minimized.

optimization models: models in which an economic actor makes choices which bring her closer to whatever her goal is than any other alternative.

order: the dimension of a square matrix.

ordered pair: a pair of elements (X_i, Y_j) such that the first element is from one set $\{X\}$ and the second element is from another set $\{Y\}$. A set of ordered pairs expresses a relation.

ordinal utility: a concept of utility according to which the individual is capable only of ordering consumption bundles by rank.

parabola: the graph of a second-degree polynomial. It is a U-shaped or an inverted U-shaped curve.

parameters: necessary information considered as "given" to a model. Parameters can be interpreted to include the exogenous variables.

Pareto-efficient: describes an action which makes at least one individual better off without harming another.

Pareto-optimal: describes a state in which no further Pareto-efficient actions are possible.

partial derivative: if $Y = f(X_1, X_2, \ldots, X_n)$ a first-order partial derivative represents the instantaneous rate of change of Y with respect to one of the independent variables, holding all the others constant. Mathematically, it is defined as

$$\frac{\partial Y}{\partial X_i} \equiv f_i \equiv \lim_{\Delta X_i \to 0} \frac{\Delta Y}{\Delta X_i}\bigg|_{\text{holding all } X_j \neq X_i \text{ constant}},$$

$$i = 1, 2, \ldots, n$$

partial differentiation: the process of finding partial derivatives.

partial equilibrium: an analytical methodology that focuses on individual behavior by treating variables not directly affected by the individual as exogenous.

partial output elasticity: the ratio of the percentage change in output to the percentage change in an input. Mathematically, if $Y = f(X_1, X_2)$ is a production function, then the output elasticity of X_1 is

$$\varepsilon_{Y1} = \frac{\partial Y}{\partial X_1} \frac{X_1}{Y}$$

perfect competition: a market in which there are sufficient numbers of buyers and sellers so that no single buyer or seller can influence price. The buyers and sellers are modeled as price-takers.

point elasticity: a unitless measure of the instantaneous response of a dependent variable to an infinitesimal change in an independent variable. Mathematically, if $Y = f(X)$, then point elasticity is

$$\frac{dY}{dX} \frac{X}{Y}$$

point of inflection: a point on the graph of a primitive function where its slope changes from increasing to decreasing, or vice versa. The second-order derivative equals zero at an inflection point.

polynomial function: a function that has the following general form:

$$\begin{aligned} Y = f(X) &= a_0 X^0 + a_1 X^1 + a_2 X^2 + \cdots + a_n X^n \\ &= a_0 + a_1 X + a_2 X^2 + \cdots + a_n X^n \\ &= \sum_{i=0}^{n} a_i X^i \end{aligned}$$

there the coefficients $a_0, a_1, \ldots, a_n$ are all real numbers.

premultiply: to find the product of two matrices such that the lead matrix is placed before the lag matrix.

price discrimination: the practice of selling the same product at different prices, unjustified by different costs.

price elasticity of demand: the responsiveness of quantity demanded to changes in price. Mathematically,

$$\varepsilon_{QP} = \frac{dQ}{dP} \frac{P}{Q}$$

price-searcher: a firm whose output or input decisions have an effect on output or input price. Price is treated as a function of quantity in price-searcher models.

price-taker: a firm whose output or input decisions have no effect on output or input price. Price is treated as a parameter in price-taker models.

primal: the original constrained optimization problem, to which a dual may be found. See dual.

primitive function: the original function from which first-, second-, and higher-order derivatives may be taken.

principal diagonal: the elements in a square matrix which lie in the same-numbered row as column. That is, if A is an $n \times n$ square matrix, the principal diagonal is made up of all the elements $a_{ii}, i = 1, 2, \ldots, n$.

principal minors: the minors associated with the diagonal elements.

production possibilities frontier (PPF): the maximum combinations of goods that can be produced with a given technology and endowment of inputs.

quadratic formula: a formula for solving a quadratic equation. If $aX^2 + bX + c = 0$, then

$$X = \frac{-b \pm \sqrt{b^2 - 4ac}}{2a}$$

quadratic function: a polynomial of degree two. When equal to zero, a quadratic function becomes a quadratic equation.

quasi-concave: the property that the level curves of an increasing (decreasing) function are convex (concave).

range: the set of possible values of a function.

rational function: a function which is the ratio of two polynomials.

rectangular hyperbola: the graph of functions which have the form $Y = k/X$, where k is a constant.

reduced-form equation: an equation in which an endogenous variable is expressed as a function solely of exogenous variables and parameters.

relation: an association between one entity and another, or a set of ordered pairs.

returns to scale: the response of output to proportional increases in inputs.

ridge lines: lines in an isoquant diagram which join the points where the isoquants begin to bend in; i.e., they become vertical or horizontal rather than downward sloping.

row vector: a matrix with one row.

Rybczynski theorem: given linear homogeneous production functions, two industries, and two binding resource constraints, the effect of an increase in the endowment of some resource is to increase the output of the resource-intensive industry and to decrease the output of the industry that is intensive in the use of the other resource.

saddle point: a point on a surface which is flat in every direction but is neither a local minimum nor a maximum because it increases in one direction but decreases in another.

Say's law: the proposition of classical economics that supply creates its own demand, or that income sufficient to purchase output is guaranteed.

scalar: a number, as opposed to a matrix.

scalar multiplication: the operation of multiplying a matrix by a number.

second-order condition: condition which, given the necessary condition, is sufficient to guarantee the existence of a maximum or a minimum. Also called sufficient condition.

second-order derivative: the derivative of the derivative of a function.

second-order partial derivatives: the partial derivative of a first-order partial derivative.

second-order total differential: see higher-order total differential.

second partial: an abbreviated name for second-order partial derivative.

set: any definable collection of entities.

set of feasible solutions: combinations of choice variables which can be attained, given constraints of an LP problem. It is bounded by the axes and the linear constraint functions, treated as equalities. Also known as the feasible set.

shadow price: a mathematically constructed variable that, within its model, has the characteristics of a market price; that is, it measures either marginal benefits or marginal costs.

short-run: a situation in which some variable is arbitrarily held constant.

simplex: a computational algorithm used for solving LP problems.

singular matrix: a matrix in which one row (column) can be expressed as a linear combination of the other rows (columns).

Slutsky equation: the expression for $\partial X_1^*/\partial P_1$ which separates out the income and substitution effects. Mathematically,

$$\frac{\partial X_1^*}{\partial P_1} = -\mu^* \frac{P_2^2}{|H|} - X_1^* \frac{\partial X_1^*}{\partial M}$$

smooth: a function is smooth if it does not have sharp corners. Mathematically, a function $Y = f(X)$ is smooth at a point $X = b$ if the following limit exists

$$\lim_{\Delta X \to 0} \frac{\Delta Y}{\Delta X}$$

social welfare function (SWF): a function that converts the utilities of individuals into a value for the general well-being of society.

square matrix: a matrix with the same number of rows as columns.

stabilization policy: macroeconomic policy designed to respond to undesirable changes in the level of real income or output. It includes fiscal and monetary policies.

Stage I: the range of a two-input production function in which the marginal product of one of the inputs is negative. Stage III is the range in which the marginal product of the other input is negative.

Stage II: the range of a two-input production function in which the marginal products of both inputs are positive.

Stage III: see Stage I.

stationary point: a point at which a function is neither increasing nor decreasing, where the first derivative equals zero. Also known as critical point.

Stolper-Samuelson theorem: given the same conditions as for the Rybczynski theorem, an increase in the price of a product increases the value of the marginal product of the resource which that product uses more intensively, while it decreases the value of the marginal product of the other resource.

strictly concave function: a function whose graph looks like a concave curve to a viewer looking up from the horizontal axis. The function $Y = f(X)$ is strictly concave if $f''(X) < 0$.

strictly convex function: a function whose graph looks like a convex curve to a viewer looking up from the horizontal axis. The function $Y = f(X)$ is strictly convex if $f''(X) > 0$.

substitution effect: measures the effect on the consumption of the good due only to changes in the price ratio, holding real income (or utility) constant, when the price of a good changes.

sufficient condition for optimization: condition which, given the necessary condition, is sufficient to guarantee the existence of a maximum or a minimum.

symmetric: the property that the graph of a function on one side of a straight line is the mirror image of the graph on the other side.

theory: a coherent set of propositions, assumptions, and hypotheses that explain a general class of phenomena.

total differential: the differential of a function with more than one independent variable. Mathematically, if $Y = f(X_1, X_2, \ldots, X_n)$, the total differential equals

$$dY = f_1 \, dX_1 + f_2 \, dX_2 + \cdots + f_n \, dX_n$$

total differentiation: the process of finding the total differential.

transactions table: a description of the intersectoral flows of an input–output model in tabular form.

transpose: a matrix that is obtained by interchanging the rows and columns of another matrix. If A is a matrix, its transpose is denoted A'.

utilities possibilities frontier (UPF): the maximum combinations of utilities that can be generated by given quantities of goods.

value of a function: if the function is $Y = f(X)$, then its values are the quantities taken by Y, the dependent variable.

value of marginal product (VMP): the same thing as marginal revenue product when a firm is a price-taker in the output market. Mathematically, VMP equals output price multiplied by the marginal product of the input.

variable: mathematical symbol representing something that can vary in its value.

vector: a matrix with only one row or one column.

Young's theorem: the mathematical theorem that cross-partial derivatives are invariant to the order of differentiation, provided that the primitive function is twice differentiable. For example, if $Y = f(X_1, X_2, \ldots, X_n)$, then Young's theorem requires that $f_{ij} = f_{ji}$, $i \neq j$, $i, j = 1, 2, \ldots, n$.

INDEX